FIRST PRINCIPLES, SECOND THOUGHTS: Aboriginal Peoples, Constitutional Reform and Canadian Statecraft

FIRST PRINCIPLES, SECOND THOUGHTS: Aboriginal Peoples, Constitutional Reform and Canadian Statecraft

Bryan Schwartz

The Institute for Research on Public Policy
L'Institut de recherches politiques

Printed in Canada

Legal Deposit Fourth Quarter
Bibliothèque nationale du Québec

Canadian Cataloguing in Publication Data

Schwartz, Bryan, date
First principles, second thoughts : aboriginal peoples, constitutional reform and Canadian statecraft

Bibliography: p.
ISBN 0-88645-045-4

1. Canada – Native races. 2. Indians of North America – Canada – Legal status, laws, etc. 3. Inuits – Canada – Legal status, laws, etc. 4. Métis – Legal status, laws, etc. I. Institute for Research on Public Policy II. Title.

E92.S442 1986 323.1'197'071 C86-090335-4

The Institute for Research on Public Policy/
L'Institut de recherches politiques
2149 Mackay Street
Montreal, Quebec H3G 2J2

Contents

Foreword

The Constitution Act, 1982 give recognition to the aboriginal and treaty rights of Canada's aboriginal peoples and made provision for a process of defining their further constitutional rights.

In doing this, the Government of Canada and of the provinces did not resolve the debate on aboriginal government but rather intensified it.

As we move closer to the spring of 1987, when a scheduled First Minister's Conference is expected to conclude the current phase of this debate, at least officially, it is extremely timely for the Institute to publish this study by Dr. Bryan Schwartz.

Schwartz examines the evolution of the formal negotiations which have taken place since 1982, provides an analysis of the policy and legal implications of the significant proposals that have come forward and advances a set of proposals for reform of his own. This analysis is carried out within a general framework developed by Schwartz to consider "the constitutional and political management of history-based groupist claims". In other words, Schwartz provides us not only with a compelling analysis of aboriginal constitutional reform but also a framework which can be applied to other similar "groupist" claims in Canadian society.

The questions surrounding aboriginal government in Canada represent a major political issue. The reviewers who examined Mr. Schwartz' manuscript on behalf of the Institute described it respectively as "a meticulous work of scholarship . . .

brilliant, original, creative . . . "; one whose "strength lies in its comprehensiveness, its inventiveness, its practicality, its thoughtfulness and its readability"; and "clearly the most comprehensive in this field". Thus, both the topic and the way in which it has been treated by Dr. Schwartz recommend this work for the interested reader.

The Institute is pleased to be able to make this definitive monograph, an outgrowth of a Yale dissertation, available to the policy community and the people of Canada.

Rod Dobell
President

December 1986

Avant-propos

La loi constitutionnelle de 1982 confirme les droits existants, ancestraux ou issus de traités, des peuples autochtones du Canada, et prévoit la détermination et la définition de leurs droits constitutionnels.

En faisant cela, le gouvernement du Canada et les gouvernements provinciaux n'ont pas mis fin au débat sur le gouvernement des autochtones mais l'ont plutôt intensifié.

Comme nous nous rapprochons du printemps 1987, époque prévue pour la Conférence des premiers ministres devant mettre un terme à la phase actuelle des discussions, au moins officiellement, la publication de l'étude du Dr. Bryan Schwartz par l'Institut tombe extrêmement à propos.

M. Schwartz examine l'évolution des négociations officielles depuis 1982, analyse les implications politiques et légales des principales propositions qui en ont résulté, et avance ses propres suggestions de réforme. Il effectue cette étude à partir d'un système de références plus général qu'il a mis au point pour examiner "le traitement constitutionnel et politique des revendications de groupements qui s'appuient sur une prétention historique." Ainsi, l'auteur met à notre disposition, non seulement une analyse convaincante de la réforme constitutionelle à l'égard des autochtones, mais également une méthode de travail applicable à des revendications similaires émanant d'autres groupes de la société canadienne.

Les questions qui se rattachent au gouvernement des autochtones au Canada représentent une importance politique majeure. Les lecteurs chargés par l'Institut d'examiner le manuscrit de M. Schwartz l'ont respectivement décrit comme "un travail d'érudition . . . brillant, original, stimulant", dont "la force tient dans son étendue, dans son inventivité, dans son caractère pratique et réfléchi et dans sa lisibilité", et comme étant "certainement le plus complet dans sa spécialité." C'est ainsi que ce travail se recommande à l'attention du lecteur intéressé, à la fois par le sujet qu'il traite et par la façon dont il est traité.

L'Institut est heureux de pouvoir mettre à la disposition de la communauté politique et du public canadien cette monographie exemplaire tirée d'une thèse de Yale.

Rod Dobell
Président

Décembre 1986

Acknowledgements

For the past five years, I have had the privilege of acting as legal advisor to the Attorney General of Manitoba on constitutional reform with respect to the aboriginal peoples of Canada. In this capacity, I have witnessed or participated in practically all of the intergovernmental meetings described and analyzed in this study. My understanding of the process is owed in large part to the many kind and thoughtful people from many different camps who have shared their knowledge and perceptions with me. Some of these people have gone out of their way to provide documentation, recollections or explanations that have assisted with the preparation of this work. I owe a special debt to Jim Wastasecoot, of the Native Affairs Secretariat of the Government of Manitoba, for his political insight and archival assistance; and to Jeff Richstone, of the Inuit Committee on National Issues, who often was able to relate to me not only the official story, but the real story and surreal story.

Versions of this manuscript benefitted from the scrutiny of David Brown, Butch Nepon, Kent Paterson and David Phillips of the University of Manitoba; Rosalie Daly Todd of the Institute for Research on Public Policy; and Sheldon Schwartz, who works on the financing of heavy oil upgrader projects. Sue Frenette skillfully carried out the word processing of the many versions of this manuscript. Trying to cope with the small details—of typography, punctuation, citations, etc.—can leave an author apostrophic, commatose or thoroughly bracketed off; and I wish to express my special thanks for the patient assistance I received with many of the most painstaking tasks.

Denis Marshall and John Davis at the Faculty of Law Library have been so helpful that I have once again decided, as a small gesture of appreciation, that they can have their collection of books back. For a while.

The Institute for Research on Public Policy has provided support and encouragement for this project for several years, and has been a gracious and co-operative publisher. Among the members of the Institute who have been closely involved: Rod Dobell, Louis Vagianos, Parker Staples, and Ruby Day.

This study is a revised and expanded (especially with respect to Part One) version of a thesis submitted in partial fulfillment of the requirements of the J.S.D. Degree at Yale Law School. The completion of the project was greatly facilitated by the intellectual guidance and personal encouragement of the late Professor Robert Cover. He was a man who practised, but did not preach; a scholar, and a mensch.

Note: The opinions of this book are those of the author, and not necessarily those of any government agency.

The Author

Bryan Schwartz holds the law degrees of LL.B. (Queen's, 1978), LL.M. (Yale, 1979) and J.S.D. (Yale, 1986) and is a member of the bars of Ontario and Manitoba. He articled at the federal Department of Justice in Ottawa in 1979-80, working primarily in the Constitutional and International Law section. During the height of the struggle over the Patriation of the Canadian Constitution in 1981, he served in the constitutional law branch of the Attorney General of Saskatchewan. For the past five years, he has been a member of the Faculty of Law, University of Manitoba, and has acted as legal advisor to the Attorney-General of Manitoba on constitutional reform with respect to aboriginal peoples. Dr. Schwartz has published in a variety of areas, including constitutional law, public international law, private international law, administrative law and legal philosophy.

Overview

The Context

First Principles, Second Thoughts attempts to present a comprehensive analysis of the politics, policy, and law of constitutional reform with respect to the aboriginal peoples of Canada since the patriation of the Canadian Constitution. A last-minute reinsertion in the massive constitutional reform package of 1982 was Part II, which read:

> s.35 (1) The existing aboriginal and treaty rights of the aboriginal peoples of Canada are hereby recognized and affirmed.
>
> (2) In this Act "aboriginal peoples of Canada" include the Indian, Inuit and Métis people of Canada.

There was so much uncertainty about the meaning of s.35 that First Ministers agreed to adding s.37 to the package, which guaranteed that First Ministers would meet in 1983 to try to clarify matters. They met in March '83 and produced two substantive amendments to the constitution. They also agreed to meet again another three times. The March '84 and April '85 meetings did not achieve final breakthrough, but many crucial issues have been canvassed, and the shape of the final "deal" is already in sight. The final conference, scheduled for 1987, may well produce fundamental constitutional reform.

The deliberations of the First Ministers have been fuelled by developments on other fronts. The *Penner Report* (by a Parliamentary sub-committee) has recommended radical, and ultimately constitutional, reform in the system of Indian self-government. The Inuit and Dene of the Northwest Territories have called for division of the Northwest Territories into new units that suit their political aspirations. Canadian courts have delivered judgments that have substantially altered the legal background of the debate.

This study attempts to provide a thorough account of the evolution of the negotiations and an in-depth analysis of the policy and legal implications of all of the significant proposals that have been made. It tries not only to explain and evaluate the positions of the parties, but also to advance its own proposals for reform. While every effort has been made to maintain scholarly standards of precision and objectivity, the study has been written with a view to being understandable and enjoyable for non-specialist readers. *First Principles, Second Thoughts* hopefully will be of interest to experts in public policy, constitutional law, federal-provincial relations, and native affairs; but it may also have value for non-specialists who are interested in public affairs and contemporary public affairs issues.

The Strategy of Statecraft

First Principles, Second Thoughts formulates a general strategy of statecraft that should be useful in resolving many other dilemmas of Canadian public life. The debate over the position of the aboriginal peoples of Canada belongs to a larger family of Canadian dilemmas. All of them involve claims by a segment of a community in Canada to special treatment based on the particular history of that community. The study calls these claims "history-based groupist." There is a competing view of Canada, which sees it as a community of equal individuals whose rights are more or less independent of historical development. The study calls this view "liberal individualist."

Some examples of divisive issues in recent Canadian life involve history-based groupist claims:

- French-language rights in Manitoba
- Catholic-school rights in Ontario
- minority-language educational rights throughout Canada
- affirmative action for traditionally disadvantaged groups in the federal public sector.

Part One of *First Principles, Second Thoughts* advances a general approach to the constitutional and political management of history-based groupist claims. This "strategy of statecraft" is illustrated in the context of two issues that have provoked great controversy in my home province of Manitoba – French-language rights in the government and French-language rights in the schools. The strategy provided the basis for the approach the study takes to the whole gamut of aboriginal rights issues that are discussed in the twenty-four subsequent chapters of *First Principles, Second Thoughts*. Thus, it is hoped, the study contributes not only a coherent approach to aboriginal peoples' issues, but also a method of dealing with a broader range of important public policy issues in Canada.

The Basic Approach of First Principles, Second Thoughts

The basic approach attempts to bring about principled accommodation between competing views. It argues, on philosophical and practical grounds, that it is better to view Canada as a political community of equal individuals, rather than as an agglomeration of historical communities. The way to find practical solutions, however, is not to expect parties to agree on underlying philosophy. Nor is it to give up on any principled approach and try *ad hoc* compromises. Here is what *is* proposed:

> The approach to Canadian constitutionalism that is recommended here is that we should work towards constitutional arrangements that advance the ideals of individualism, but which satisfy, or do as little affront as possible to, those whose constitutional programs are grounded in history-based groupism. When the positive law of the constitution allows Canadian statesmen a choice, and no reconciliation between conflicting philosophies can be expressed in practical arrangements, then liberal individualism ought to prevail. Often, however, it will be discovered that the arrangement advocated on the basis of history-based groupism can be justified on the basis of liberal individualism. If so, there is obviously a basis for practical progress. Having elucidated their alternate philosophical justifications for a proposed arrangement, various actors can work out a legal formula that specifies what arrangement they have agreed upon, but which is sufficiently neutral in its phraseology that no party finds it objectionable. In some cases the arrangement proposed by the adherents of history-based groupism may be inconsistent with

liberal individualism; the best practical course of a constitutional statesman is then to try to explore whether an alternate arrangement can be found which satisfies the basic goals of those who made the proposal, but which is consistent with liberal individualism.

It should be emphasized that the proposed strategy contemplates arrangements that are indeterminate only at the level of ultimate philosophical justification. The concrete, on-the-ground arrangements should be specified with as much precision as would ordinarily be prudent. (In drafting constitutions, it is usually necessary and desirable to leave some flexibility. The factual and political complexities of a problem may make it impracticable to go beyond a certain level of precision as constitutional texts are difficult to amend, and some room should be left for interpretations to vary as circumstances change.) To recall a trope I used at the Queen's conference on Aboriginal Peoples and Constitutional Reform (February 1985), there is a Gershwin song that goes 'you like potato (long *a*), I like potato (short *a*), let's call the whole thing off.' At the level of pronunciation, two parties may fundamentally disagree. The workable solution may be to have both parties agree on the purchase or consumption of one edible tuber (of the family *solanum tuberosum*). The physical dimensions of the vegetable might be described with considerable precision. No ambiguity at the level of practical operations is entailed by the failure to agree, at a different level, on English pronunciation. In drafting constitutional texts, considerable precision may be possible at the level of practical operations while the ultimate philosophical justification for it remains unsettled. It must be admitted that there will be hard cases in which the application of a constitutional text to a practical situation can only be settled by reference to its ultimate justification. My general strategy applies to interpretation no less than it does to the creation of norms. The interpreter should attempt, as far as possible, to adopt an interpretation that advances the ideals of liberal individualism but which does not offend those of a groupist philosophical persuasion. If no such interpretation is possible, and if the text so

> permits, a liberal interpretation should be chosen in preference to a history-based groupist one. The losers in such a case would be free to condemn the particular interpretation as mistaken and to continue to value the norm generally useful and theoretically sound.
>
> The general approach just sketched will be embodied in the discussion in this study of a score of issues concerning constitutional reform with respect to the aboriginal peoples of Canada. [Chapter I]

The application of the strategy to each new problem requires thorough research and analysis of its particular nature and then the propounding of creative solutions. Sometimes a persuasive, but previously unconsidered, liberal justification might be developed for a proposal by adepts of groupism. Very often an original proposal must be made for a new process, institution or legal norm.

The Need for the Strategy

Part One of *First Principles, Second Thoughts* attempts to highlight the importance to Canadian statecraft of the tension between history-based groupism and liberal individualism. The expression of that tension in the new *Canadian Charter of Rights* is carefully explicated. The importance of the tension in the academic theory and political practice of Prime Minister Trudeau is explored; it is shown how the stance he developed on French-Canadian nationalism carried over into his views on aboriginal rights. The strategy suggested in the thesis for dealing with these kinds of conflicts will be applicable to a broad variety of problems, some of them of the highest importance to the future of Canadian law and society.

The Philosophical Basis for the Strategy

The philosophical basis for the strategy is explained and defended in non-technical language. It is argued that the liberal individualist approach is more subtle, more egalitarian, easier to apply, and less socially-divisive than is the historically-based groupist stance.

The Strategy is Illustrated in Non-aboriginal Contexts

Once the strategy of statecraft is explained, its operation is illustrated by applying it to the problems of French-language rights in Manitoba. A problem that ripped apart the social fabric of the province for two years is analyzed and a solution proposed on the basis of the basic strategy. It is proposed that we develop a forward-looking, universalist approach to justifying the protection and advancement of the French-language community in Manitoba, rather than trying to justify special privileges on the basis of history.

The problem of s.23 of the new *Charter* is explored. The Ontario Court of Appeal has suggested that it guarantees traditional French-language communities political control over their own separate school boards. The study takes issue with that position. It proposes that s.23, properly understood, can be satisfied by a school system in which the children of the traditional French-language community attend the same school as French immersion children, and the political management of the board is similarly integrated and shared.

The Strategy Applied to Aboriginal Peoples Issues

The analysis of the problems of aboriginal peoples of Canada is throughout guided by the theory of statecraft proposed, defended, and illustrated in Part One. The connection between the general theory and the analysis of particular problems is frequently not made express. But the link informs the thesis throughout and provides it with a second unifying theme. The discussion of particulars is not only linked by the fact that they are interrelated problems that have been discussed in the course of a single stream of constitutional discussion; it is also linked by way of a clear prescription for the management of minority-rights problems in this country.

Some examples:

Statements of Principle (Chapter IV)
An analysis is provided of the problems drafters arrive at when attempting to facilitate progress through to non-binding agreements on "principle." What appear to be innocuous, "motherhood" statements are almost always offensive to the philosophy of at least one party. The strategy of *First Principles, Second Thoughts* suggests that we not expect nor insist that parties agree on the fundamental philosophical and political assumptions behind practical arrangements. We should agree on practical arrangements that are acceptable to parties of differing philosophies and cast those arrangements in the most neutral way possible. Ambiguity about the nature of the arrangements is not recommended. Deliberate agnosticism about competing normative theories is strongly urged.

Consultation on Constitutional Amendments (Chapters V, VI)
The history-based groupism theory of Canadian confederation would make it plausible for a constituent group in Canada to claim a veto over constitutional amendments affecting it. From the liberal individualist standpoint the study adopts, it is not acceptable for the political judgment of an overwhelming number of Canadians to be frustrated by a small dissident group. The strategy does urge, however, that we try as hard as possible to achieve practical accommodations that do not violate liberal first principles. Thus it is suggested that it would be entirely acceptable to make consultations with aboriginal groups a prerequisite to constitutional amendments affecting them. Not only is the problem of principle overcome, but so are a host of probably insoluble technical problems that would arise if it were necessary to determine the mechanisms whereby a veto would be voiced.

Treaty Making (Chapters VIII, XXI)
It is necessary to find a way of formulating a process for devolving powers on aboriginal governments that does not offend aboriginal peoples at the level of principle. It is contended that the treaty making process is ideally suited for this goal:

> Whether or not self-government agreements are constitutionalized, it does seem highly desirable that they be an essential aspect of establishing a new type of political order for aboriginal communities. They will help to ensure that the superior understanding of aboriginal communities of their own circumstances and aspirations will be adequately reflected in the legal order that emerges. The agreement making process will also help to overcome some of the disputes over symbolism that would otherwise stall progress for many groups. One of the longest debates in the history of the Canadian Parliament was over the replacement of the Red Ensign flag by the Maple Leaf. Whether an aboriginal group is characterized as a protected independent state, a domestic dependent nation, a band, or a municipality may not actually make a bit of difference in the distribution of power over it—but it may be a matter charged with significance for both the members of the community and the general Canadian public. The agreement making process is useful because it does not necessarily require either side to surrender their symbolism or accept the other's. An

aboriginal group can, if it wishes, regard an agreement as an international treaty between two sovereign states. No Canadian court will ever agree with it, but the group itself remains free to maintain its interpretation of the significance of the transaction. By contrast, if self-government is established by legislation alone, the exercise of authority by aboriginal governments may inescapably look like their acceptance of delegated authority from a superior power. There may be ways of drafting the legislation so as to some extent avoid this implication—for example, using the word "recognition" wherever possible, rather than "delegation"—but the process would not be as subject to diverse characterizations as would one that includes bilateral agreements. The agreement making mechanism might allow each party to say that the other has a bad theory—that works in practice. [Chapter XXI]

Creation of New Provinces, Regional Governments (Chapters I, IX, XVI)
The Inuit (Canadian "Eskimos") have traditionally sought self-government not on the basis of ethnic exclusivity but of political equality. They have sought the formation of regional governments in areas in which they form a majority. (Such an institution already exists in Northern Quebec, at the level of regional government. They are seeking a public territorial government in the Eastern Arctic.)

Chapter I provides an account of why the different aboriginal groups differ in their ideological orientation; why some are liberal, like the Inuit, while others are adamantly history-based and groupist. Chapter IX explains to the reader the Nunavut (territorial government) proposal. Chapter XVI recommends the regional government approach as a solution for the Métis. It is suggested that they avoid the practical, philosophical, and political problems of trying to obtain what are, in effect, reserves and instead concentrate on establishing regional governments in areas in which they are a majority. The regional government approach for the Métis illustrates perfectly the strategy of statecraft.

Fiscal Arrangements (Chapters XII to XV)
Whereas the issue of fiscal responsibility for the funding of aboriginal services and governments has been dodged by most governments, *First Principles, Second Thoughts* identifies it as

absolutely crucial to the development of aboriginal self-government. It discusses the entire issue and contrasts the history-based groupist approach that some Indian governments and some academics have urged; and, consistent with my general theory, condemns it on practical, political and philosophical grounds. The basic strategy demands that we see how the fiscal demands of aboriginals can be made consistent with liberal principles. Chapter XIV proposes that we look at the analogy of s.37 of the constitution, which creates a constitutional duty on the part of the federal government to make equalization payments to provincial governments. This historical, liberal, egalitarian provision of the constitution provides an excellent precedent for a constitutional provision on the funding of aboriginal communities.

The discussion of fiscal arrangements is not limited to "how much." I also discuss the extent to which the federal government should be able to attach strings to the money, in order to ensure that there are maintained liberal standards such as adequate education for all aboriginal children and universal access to health care.

Another approach to fiscal arrangements would be to consider whether existing constitutional guarantees imply a duty on the part of federal or provincial governments to provide adequate levels of fiscal support and service delivery for aboriginal communities. It is argued in Chapter XII that the "trust responsibility" of the federal government implied by s.91(24) of the *Constitution Act, 1867* is basically confined to protecting Indian land rights, rather than promoting the general welfare of Indian communities. The history-based groupist claim of a "trust responsibility" does not yield a forceful claim. In Chapter XIII, the liberal individualist approach is considered. Do the equality guarantees of the *Canadian Bill of Rights* or *Canadian Charter of Rights and Freedoms* guarantee members of Indian communities a level of support roughly equal to that provided to members of other Canadian communities? An argument is made that they do.

Aboriginal Self-Government and its Limits (Chapter X)
Chapter X agrees with the *Penner Report* that the powers of Indian governments should be substantially enhanced. Limited local or regional government is certainly consistent with liberal individualism. At present, Indian governments have far less power than the average municipality. In an ideal world, adequate and equal legal provisions would be made for individuals of any shared interest or identity—Indian, Métis,

Mennonite, whoever, who wished to join together, acquire land, and participate in a partly-autonomous community. Indian self-government will likely have some special characteristics flowing from treaty entitlements or aboriginal title and from the special constitutional relationship that exists between Indians and the federal government under s.91(24) of the *Constitution Act, 1867*. The strategy of statecraft does not recommend destroying history-based groupist rights that already exist. It does recommend, however, that, as far as possible, self-government arrangements for Indians ought to be consistent with the basic principles of liberal individualist theory. Allowing Indian communities complete political autonomy is thus not recommended.

The analysis of the *Penner Report* criticizes its failure to consider how the claims of Indian governments to autonomy must be limited by various liberal principles. Some comments are made on the way in which these limits should be introduced. Chapter X favours an early, frank and public discussion of the limits, rather than leaving them to be defined on an *ad hoc* and cryptic basis by federal officials negotiating self-government, by attaching strings to federal funding or by allowing federal officials unilateral powers to veto the actions of aboriginal governments.

Special Status for the Métis (Chapters XVI, XVII)
Chapter XVI analyzes, on policy grounds, whether it is necessary for the Métis to have the special status of "federal people." It concludes, on the basis of the basic strategy, that it is not. The strategy would allow almost all of the ambitions of the Métis to be realized without the granting to them of special legal and political status. Their ambitions to political autonomy can be realized through regional governments, the boundaries of which would be gerrymandered, if necessary, to ensure that there is a Métis majority. Federal funding to assist them with economic development can and should be provided, regardless of whether they have special status. On the other hand, the creation of special status would jeopardize existing gains of the Métis and subject them to even worse federal-provincial squabbling over who is responsible for what.

Chapters XVII discusses whether the legal history actually gives the Métis special status; in an analysis of the history, relying on primary sources, Chapter XVII concludes that they do not.

The Application of the Charter of Rights to Aboriginal Self-Government (Chapter XXV)
Chapter XXV tackles a number of very hard technical questions about whether the *Charter* would, without special effort on the part of constitutional drafters, apply to aboriginal governments. It goes on to discuss what ought to be done; the prescription is based on the basic strategy. The liberal rights contained in the *Charter* ought to apply to aboriginal governments. It would be contrary to liberal first principles to leave the citizens of aboriginal governments totally unprotected by the *Charter*. There are special reasons, tied up with the way aboriginal self-government is being developed, and the small policies that will be created, to worry about abuses of basic human rights. Aboriginal peoples are concerned, however, about excessive intrusions on their political autonomy. The basic strategy asks us to try to accommodate this concern. I suggest it can be. Judges should be inspired by s.25 of the *Charter* (on the interpretation of it proposed) to be careful when applying *Charter* guarantees that they give due regard to the special circumstances and political rights of aboriginal peoples.

The Legal Definition of Aboriginal Rights (Chapter XXIV)
The approach in Chapter XXIV to the definition of "aboriginal and treaty rights," defined in s.35 of the *Constitution Act, 1982*, proposes that we reject the history-based definition of their limits. (The courts so far have been taking a strictly history-based approach.) It recommends instead that we rewrite the sections so that courts could assess the justifiability of limits on the merits. In doing so, judges would be guided by the liberal-leaning, but accommodationist, strategy recommended in Part One.

Selective Reading and Particular Interests

First Principles, Second Thoughts has been prepared so that it can be read through from start to finish. The account of the constitutional process unfolds in chronological order, and the appreciation of any given chapter is enhanced by the political, legal and policy context provided by other chapters.

Some readers, however, may be interested only in certain special areas. This study lends itself to selective reading as well. Someone interested in, say, fiscal relationships can direct his or her attention primarily to Chapters XI to XV and, it is hoped, will find these chapters to be readily comprehensible and edifying in their own right.

Another reader might be interested mainly in the analysis of aboriginal rights issues, and not in the larger theoretical framework. Such a reader can skip Part One and plunge straight into the "action." (Conversely, someone interested only in the theoretical framework does not have to plough through the entire range of practical applications.)

The Synopsis at the end of this study may be of help to a reader in locating discussions of particular interest to him or her, and in providing some appreciation of the overall context.

The Style of First Principles, Second Thoughts

Every effort has been made to make this study accessible and enjoyable to the general reader. As far as possible, legal jargon has been avoided. An attempt has been made to define in plain and simple language the few technical terms that are employed or referred to. An effort has also been made to be succinct while maintaining breadth of coverage of the subject mater.

The Cut-Off Date for New Developments

This study is based on legal and political developments up to and including the April '85 First Ministers' Conference. Parts II and III were drafted prior to the end of 1984, in preparation for an academic conference. These chapters have been left fairly close to their original form. The advantages in doing so seemed to be that the grammar is simpler (e.g. "should" rather than "should have"); the reader may have a greater sense of the immediacy of the events described; and the opportunity is created to compare the study's predictions and prescriptions for the April '85 First Ministers' Conference.

Vue d'ensemble

Le contexte

First Principles, Second Thoughts (Principes et Réalités) essaie d'analyser les travaux préparatoires, l'esprit et la loi de la réforme constitutionnelle relativement aux peuples autochtones, depuis le rapatriement de la Constitution canadienne. L'article 35 de la deuxième partie, une addition de dernière minute, stipule:

> article 35 (1) Les droits existants – ancestraux ou issus de traités – des peuples autochtones du Canada sont reconnus et confirmés.
>
> (2) Dans la présente loi, "peuples autochtones du Canada" s'entend notamment des Indiens, des Inuit et des Métis du Canada.

Il y avait une telle incertitude sur le sens de l'article 35 que les premiers ministres ont ajouté l'article 37 à l'ensemble, pour garantir qu'ils se réuniraient de nouveau en 1983, afin d'essayer de clarifier la situation. Ils se sont rencontrés en mars 83 et cela a donné lieu à deux importants amendements à la constitution. Ils ont également convenu de se réunir à trois autres reprises. Les réunions de mars 84 et d'avril 85 n'ont pas abouti à une solution définitive, mais beaucoup de points délicats ont été soigneusement abordés et un règlement de la question est maintenant en vue. La dernière rencontre, prévue pour 1987, pourrait bien permettre une réforme constitutionnelle fondamentale.

Les délibérations des premiers ministres ont d'ailleurs été aidées par des changements sur d'autres fronts. Le *Rapport Penner* (par un sous-comité parlementaire) a recommandé une réforme radicale, avec des implications constitutionnelles, du système de gouvernement autonome des Indiens. Les Inuit et les Dene des Territoires du Nord-Ouest ont réclamé un redécoupage de ces territoires d'une manière à satisfaire leurs aspirations politiques. Les cours de justice canadiennes ont passé des jugements qui modifient considérablement le contexte légal du débat.

Cette étude veut être à la fois un compte rendu de l'évolution des négociations et une réflexion sérieuse sur les implications politiques et légales de toutes les propositions importantes qui ont été faites. Elle essaie non seulement d'expliquer et d'évaluer les positions respectives des parties en cause, mais aussi bien d'avancer des suggestions personnelles de réforme. L'étude, tout en maintenant les normes de précision et d'objectivité propres à un travail d'érudition, n'en a pas moins été rédigée de façon à être comprise et appréciée par les non-initiés. *First Principles, Second Thoughts* devrait intéresser ceux qui se spécialisent en sciences politiques, en droit constitutionnel et dans les études des affaires autochtones, et, également, être utile aux non-spécialistes qui suivent de près les affaires publiques et plus particulièrement les questions à l'ordre du jour.

La stratégie du savoir-faire politique

First Principles, Second Thoughts formule une stratégie du savoir-faire politique qui devrait pouvoir s'appliquer, d'une manière plus générale, à la conduite de la vie publique canadienne. Le débat sur les droits des peuples autochtones appartient à la grande famille des questions épineuses particulières au Canada. Toutes ont en commun les prétentions d'une communauté donnée à un statut privilégié, au nom de particularités historiques. L'étude les identifie comme des revendications communautaires historiques. Elles entrent en concurrence avec une autre conception du Canada, celle qui le voit comme une communauté d'individus dont les droits sont plus ou moins indépendants de l'évolution historique. Cette dernière conception est qualifiée d'individualisme libéral.

Parmi les sujets de discorde récents dans la vie canadienne, certains appartiennent à la catégorie des revendications communautaires historiques, par exemple:

- les droits du français au Manitoba
- les droits des écoles catholiques en Ontario
- les droits des groupes minoritaires à être éduqués dans leur langue maternelle
- l'action positive en faveur des groupes traditionnellement désavantagés dans le secteur public.

La première partie de *First Principles, Second Thoughts* propose une même approche dans le traitement constitutionnel et politique des revendications communautaires historiques. Cette "stratégie de politique générale" est expliquée à partir de deux affaires qui ont causé beaucoup de controverse dans ma province du Manitoba : la place de la langue française dans le gouvernement et les droits du français dans les écoles. Elle est ensuite appliquée à l'examen de l'ensemble des problèmes sur les droits des autochtones, lesquels font l'objet de vingt-quatre autres chapitres de *First Principles, Second Thoughts*. De telle sorte que cette méthode devrait non seulement permettre une étude cohérente des questions relatives aux droits des autochtones, mais aussi contribuer à une meilleure compréhension d'un plus grand nombre de problèmes d'importance dans la vie du Canada.

L'approche de base de First Principles, Second Thoughts

Cette approche tend à parvenir à un accord de principe entre des points de vue divergents. Elle se fonde sur l'idée philosophique et pratique qu'il est préférable de considérer le Canada comme une communauté politique d'individus égaux, plutôt que comme une agglomération de communautés historiques. Ce n'est toutefois pas en espérant voir les différents intéressés se mettre d'accord sur une politique commune qu'on aboutira à des solutions pratiques. Ce n'est pas non plus à partir d'une approche de principe, ni d'une tentative de compromis *ad hoc*. Voici ce qui est proposé:

> L'approche du constitutionnalisme canadien recommandée ici repose sur l'élaboration de solutions qui favorisent les idéaux de l'individualisme tout en demeurant compatibles, ou le moins possible en contradiction, avec les convictions de ceux dont les programmes constitutionnels sont fondés sur les droits communautaires historiques. Quand la loi proprement dite de la constitution permet un choix aux hommes d'Etat, et qu'il s'avère par ailleurs impossible de trouver un terrain d'entente entre deux philosophies

adverses, alors l'individualisme libéral devrait prévaloir. Souvent, cependant, on se rend compte que la solution demandée sur la base d'une revendication communautaire historique se justifie d'un point de vue libéral. Dans de tels cas, il y a évidemment un moyen pratique de progresser. Après clarification de leurs justifications philosophiques respectives, les différentes parties peuvent arriver à une formule légale qui spécifiera les points sur lesquels elles sont tombées d'accord, tout en restant suffisamment neutre dans les termes pour éviter de froisser les susceptibilités. D'autres fois, la solution proposée par les représentants du point de vue communautaire historique se révélera incompatible avec les principes de l'individualisme libéral; le rédacteur constitutionnel devra alors essayer de trouver une formule de rechange qui satisfasse à la fois les promoteurs de la première proposition et les principes de l'individualisme libéral.

Soulignons que la stratégie proposée n'admet le manque de précision qu'au niveau général de la justification philosophique. Les stipulations concrètes et particulières devraient être aussi précises que la prudence ordinaire le réclame. (En rédigeant une constitution, il est habituellement nécessaire et désirable de prévoir une marge de flexibilité. Les complexités politiques ou de fait d'un problème peuvent empêcher d'aller au-delà d'un certain degré de précision, étant donné que les textes constitutionnels sont difficiles à amender. Une latitude d'interprétation plus ou moins grande devrait donc être laissée, en prévision des circonstances futures.) Je rappellerai ici une citation que j'ai faite au congrès de Queen's sur les peuples autochtones et la réforme constitutionnelle (février 1985); il y a une chanson de Gershwin qui dit : "you like potato (long a), I like potato (short a), let's call the whole thing off" (tu aimes les pommes de terre, moi j'aime les patates, laissons tomber l'affaire). La solution, pour arriver à un accord, serait peut-être de recourir au terme botanique *solanum tuberosum*. L'aspect d'un tubercule peut être décrit avec précision. L'absence d'entente sur la façon dont un mot se prononce n'empêche pas l'absence d'ambiguïté à un niveau différent : celui des opérations pratiques. En

> préparant les textes constitutionnels, on peut parvenir à une grande précision au niveau de la pratique, tandis que la justification philosophique finale reste à définir. On doit cependant admettre qu'il y aura des cas difficiles qui ne pourront être réglés qu'en confrontant le texte constitutionnel avec sa justification finale. Ma stratégie générale ne s'applique pas moins à l'interprétation qu'à la création des normes. L'interprète de la loi devrait, dans la mesure du possible, tenter d'adopter une interprétation qui aille dans le sens de l'individualisme libéral, sans offenser ceux qui défendent le point de vue communautaire historique. Si cela s'avérait impossible, et dans le cas où le texte permettrait une interprétation libérale, celle-ci devrait prévaloir sur l'historique. Les perdants, dans une telle hypothèse, seraient libres de juger cette interprétation particulière fautive, et de continuer à estimer la norme habituellement utile et théoriquement juste.
>
> L'approche générale qui vient d'être ébauchée sera, dans cette étude, au coeur de la discussion d'une vingtaine de questions de réforme constitutionnelle en rapport avec les peuples autochtones du Canada. (Chapitre I)

L'application de la stratégie à chaque nouveau cas nécessite une recherche et une analyse sérieuse de sa nature particulière, et ensuite la présentation de solutions efficaces. Parfois, une justification libérale convaincante, jusqu'ici passée inaperçue, pourra être utilisée comme argument par les partisans des droits historiques. Une nouvelle action, institution ou norme, ne pourra très souvent se concrétiser sans la formulation d'une proposition originale.

L'utilité de la stratégie

La première partie de *First Principles, Second Thoughts* souligne l'importance, pour le savoir-faire politique canadien, de la tension qui existe entre les groupes communautaires historiques et l'individualisme libéral. L'expression de cette tension dans la nouvelle *Charte canadienne des droits* est soigneusement expliquée. L'étude examine également l'écart entre la théorie académique et la pratique politique du premier ministre Trudeau et montre comment l'attitude qu'il avait adoptée, vis-à-vis du nationalisme canadien-français, s'est retrouvée dans ses vues sur les droits des autochtones. La stratégie suggérée dans cet ouvrage, pour trouver une solution à ces sortes de conflits, est applicable à une grande variété de problèmes, dont certains sont de la plus haute importance pour l'avenir de la société et du système légal canadiens.

Le fondement philosophique de la stratégie

Ce fondement philosophique de la stratégie est expliqué et justifié dans une langue non-technique. La thèse, c'est que l'approche de l'individualisme libéral est plus nuancée, plus égalitaire, plus facile à mettre en oeuvre et moins susceptible de créer des dissensions que celle qui se fonde sur les droits historiques de groupes particuliers.

La stratégie appliquée à des contextes non-autochtones

Une fois expliquée, la stratégie du savoir-faire politique est mise à l'épreuve dans l'examen de la controverse sur le statut du français au Manitoba. Cette question, qui a déchiré la société de la province pendant deux années, est l'objet d'une analyse et d'une tentative de solution proposées à partir des principes de la stratégie de base. Ainsi, il est suggéré d'adopter une attitude d'avenir et universaliste pour justifier la protection et le progrès de la communauté de langue française du Manitoba, plutôt que d'essayer de légitimer des privilèges spéciaux en se fondant sur l'histoire.

Par ailleurs, le problème de l'article 23 de la nouvelle *charte* est examiné. La Cour d'appel de l'Ontario a laissé entendre que l'article 23 garantit le contrôle politique des communautés de langue française traditionnelles par priorité sur celui de leurs propres commissions scolaires séparées. L'étude conteste ce point de vue. D'après elle, l'article 23, proprement interprété, peut admettre un système scolaire dans lequel les enfants des communautés de langue française traditionnelles fréquentent la même école que ceux des programmes d'immersion en français, avec une direction de la commission scolaire également intégrée et partagée.

La stratégie appliquée aux questions des peuples autochtones

L'analyse des problèmes des peuples autochtones du Canada est, du début jusqu'à la fin, guidée par la théorie du savoir-faire politique proposée, défendue et illustrée dans la première partie. Le rapport entre la théorie générale et l'analyse des problèmes particuliers n'est habituellement pas souligné. Toutefois il structure la thèse entière et constitue un second thème unificateur. Les détails discutés ne sont pas seulement intégrés par le fait que ce sont des problèmes étroitement liés entre eux dans le contexte d'une discussion constitutionnelle, mais également parce qu'ils le sont encore par la ligne de conduite préconisée pour le traitement des problèmes des droits des minorités de ce pays.

Citons comme exemples :

Déclarations de principe (Chapitre IV)
Le chapitre détaille les difficultés auxquelles les rédacteurs se heurtent quand ils tentent de faciliter les choses par des accords de principe non contraignants. Des déclarations de principe apparemment inoffensives se révèlent presque toujours offensantes pour les convictions d'une des parties au moins. La stratégie de *First Principles, Second Thoughts* conseille de ne pas espérer, au-delà d'une entente sur des mesures pratiques, une réconciliation philosophique et politique, ni d'insister sur de telles exigences. On devrait se borner aux dispositions acceptables par les parties qui ont des convictions philosophiques différentes et rédiger l'accord de la manière la plus neutre possible. L'ambiguïté sur la nature des mesures est à déconseiller. Un agnosticisme délibéré à l'égard des systèmes normatifs concurrents est fortement recommandé.

Consultation sur les amendements constitutionnels
(Chapitres V, VI)
La théorie des communautés historiques de la Confédération canadienne rendrait plausible le droit de veto d'un groupe particulier, à propos d'amendements constitutionnels susceptibles de l'affecter. Du point de vue du libéralisme individuel, qui est celui adopté ici, il n'est pas acceptable de voir la volonté politique d'un nombre écrasant de Canadiens mise en échec par un petit groupe de dissidents. La stratégie exhorte cependant à entreprendre tout ce qui est possible pour parvenir à des arrangements pratiques qui ne violent pas les principes de base du libéralisme. Dans cette optique, il paraîtrait convenable de faire de la consultation avec les groupes autochtones une condition préalable à tout amendement constitutionnel pouvant les affecter. De cette manière, non seulement la question délicate du principe ne se poserait pas, mais aussi on éviterait une quantité énorme de problèmes techniques et procéduraux qui ne manqueraient pas de se présenter si le système du veto devait être envisagé.

L'élaboration des traités (Chapitres VIII, XXI)
Il faut trouver une formule pour la délégation de pouvoirs à des gouvernements autochtones qui n'offense pas les intéressés au niveau des principes. La procédure d'élaboration des traités préconisée ici paraît idéalement adaptée à cette fin:

> Que les accords d'autonomie soient constitutionnalisés ou non, il semble très souhaitable qu'ils jouent un rôle essentiel dans la mise en place d'un nouvel ordre politique parmi les communautés autochtones. Ne serait-ce que pour s'assurer que la connaissance fondamentale que ces communautés ont de leur situation soit adéquatement reflétée dans la structure légale en création. La procédure d'élaboration des accords servira également à surmonter certaines disputes d'ordre symbolique susceptibles de bloquer les progrès des négociations dans beaucoup de cas. On se rappellera que l'un des plus longs débats dans l'histoire du Parlement canadien a eu pour objet le remplacement du drapeau avec l'Union Jack par celui avec la feuille d'érable. Qu'un groupe autochtone soit considéré comme sous protectorat, ou bien comme une nation indépendante, une bande ou une municipalité, cela peut, dans la pratique, ne pas faire une grande différence; pourtant, sur le plan symbolique, cela peut avoir une grande importance, à la fois pour les membres de ce groupe et pour le public canadien en général. La procédure d'élaboration des accords est utile parce qu'elle ne requiert pas nécessairement l'abandon de son symbolisme par l'une des parties, ni son acceptation de celui de l'autre. Un groupe autochtone est en droit, s'il le désire, de considérer un tel accord comme un traité international entre deux états souverains. Aucune cour canadienne n'acceptera jamais ce point de vue, mais le groupe lui-même demeure libre de maintenir son interprétation de la nature de la transaction. En revanche, si l'autonomie n'est établie que par un acte législatif, l'exercice de l'autorité par les gouvernements autochtones sera automatiquement considéré comme l'acceptation d'une délégation d'autorité. Il existe peut-être, dans la manière de rédiger la loi, des moyens d'éviter en partie cet inconvénient – par exemple en employant reconnaissance au lieu de délégation, toutes les fois que cela est possible – mais le procédé paraîtra

toujours d'interprétation restreinte par rapport à celui qui se fonde sur des accords bilatéraux. Cette dernière procédure laisse en effet à chaque partie la possibilité de prétendre que la vision de l'autre est erronée, sans toutefois empêcher le fonctionnement des choses dans la pratique.

Création de nouvelles provinces et de gouvernements régionaux (Chapitres I, IX, XVI)

Les Inuit ont traditionnellement recherché l'autonomie sur une base non pas ethnique mais d'égalité politique. Ils essaient de former des gouvernements régionaux dans des régions où ils constituent une majorité. (Une telle institution existe déjà au Nord du Québec, au niveau du gouvernement régional. Leur but, c'est de constituer un gouvernement territorial recouvrant l'Arctique de l'Est.)

Le chapitre I fournit des renseignements sur la raison des différentes idéologies rencontrées parmi les groupes autochtones; pourquoi certains, comme les Inuit, sont libéraux, alors que d'autres demeurent irrévocablement attachés à la notion de groupe historique. Le chapitre VI explique la proposition de Nunavut (gouvernement territorial). Le chapitre XVI recommande cette approche comme solution pour les Métis. On leur conseille d'éviter les problèmes pratiques, philosophiques, et politiques attachés à leurs présentes revendications, c'est-à-dire les réserves, et d'essayer plutôt d'établir des gouvernements régionaux dans des endroits où ils se trouvent en majorité. L'approche du gouvernement régional, pour les Métis, est un bon exemple de stratégie du savoir-faire politique.

Aménagements fiscaux (Chapitres XII à XV)

Alors que, pour le financement des gouvernements et services autochtones, la question de la responsabilité fiscale avait été laissée de côté par la plupart des gouvernements, *First Principles, Second Thoughts* en a fait une condition sine qua non, pour le développement de l'autonomie des autochtones. L'ouvrage traite de la question dans son ensemble et met en contraste l'approche communautaire historique que certains gouvernements indiens et certains universitaires ont préconisée, pour la condamner, conformément à ma théorie générale, pour des raisons pratiques, politiques et philosophiques. La stratégie de base exige que nous examinions comment les réclamations fiscales des autochtones peuvent se concilier avec les principes libéraux. Le chapitre XIV suggère de se référer à l'exemple de l'article 37 de la Constitution, qui impose au gouvernement fédéral le devoir constitutionnel d'opérer des paiements compensatoires à l'égard des gouvernements provinciaux. Cette disposition historique, libérale et égalitaire de la Constitution offre un excellent précédent à une disposition constitutionnelle du même ordre pour le financement des communautés autochtones.

Cette discussion ne se limite pas à la question de savoir "combien". J'examine également dans quelle mesure les subventions devraient être conditionnelles pour assurer le maintien de certains standards libéraux, comme une éducation adéquate pour les enfants autochtones et le libre accès aux soins médicaux.

Une autre façon d'envisager les aménagements fiscaux serait d'examiner si les garanties constitutionnelles existantes entraînent l'obligation, de la part des gouvernements fédéral et provinciaux, d'assurer une assistance financière et des services adéquats aux communautés autochtones. Le chapitre XII soutient que la "responsabilité de protection" du gouvernement fédéral, d'après la *Loi constitutionnelle de 1867* (article 91(24)), est essentiellement conçue en vue de la protection des droits fonciers des Indiens, plutôt que pour le bien-être général des communautés indiennes. La prétention communautaire historique aux bénéfices de la "responsabilité de protection" ne représente pas une prétention contraignante. Le chapitre XIII traite de l'approche individualiste libérale. Est-ce que les garanties d'égalité de la *Loi canadienne des droits* ou de la *Charte canadienne des droits et libertés* garantissent aux membres des communautés indiennes un niveau d'assistance à peu près équivalent à celui fourni aux membres des autres communautés canadiennes? Il semble que oui.

L'autonomie autochtone et ses limites (Chapitre X)
Le chapitre X rejoint le *Rapport Penner* dans son opinion que les pouvoirs des gouvernements indiens devraient être substantiellement accrus. Un gouvernement local ou régional n'est certainement pas contraire à l'individualisme libéral. A l'heure actuelle, les gouvernements indiens ont moins de pouvoir qu'une municipalité ordinaire. Dans un monde idéal, la loi devrait fournir des dispositions adéquates pour tous les individus qui partagent les mêmes intérêts ou la même identité : Indiens, Métis, Mennonites, tous ceux qui acquièrent de la terre et font partie d'une communauté partiellement autonome. Du fait des traités ou de titres autochtones, ou encore du rapport constitutionnel spécial qui existe entre les Indiens et le gouvernement fédéral (article 91(24) de la *Loi constitutionnelle de 1867*), l'autonomie indienne aura vraisemblablement quelques

caractéristiques particulières. La stratégie du savoir-faire politique ne recommande pas la suppression des droits communautaires historiques existants. Elle conseille toutefois que, dans la mesure du possible, les accords avec les Indiens soient conformes aux principes de base du libéralisme individuel. Par conséquent l'octroi d'une autonomie complète à ces communautés ne peut être recommandé.

Le *Rapport Penner* est critiqué pour ne pas avoir remarqué que les revendications à l'autonomie des gouvernements indiens devaient être limitées par des principes libéraux divers. La manière dont ces limites devraient être définies fait l'objet de commentaires. Le chapitre X verrait un débat franc et rapide sur ces limites dans un avenir proche, plutôt que de laisser à des agents négociateurs fédéraux le soin de les définir sur une base circonstancielle et peu claire. Ceux-ci pourraient, en effet, mettre des conditions à l'octroi des subventions, ou s'arroger le droit de veto à l'égard des décisions des gouvernements autochtones.

Un statut spécial pour les Métis (Chapitres XVI, XVII)

Le chapitre XVI examine, sur des bases politiques, s'il est nécessaire pour les Métis d'avoir le statut spécial de "peuple fédéral", et conclut, dans l'optique de la stratégie de base, que cela ne l'est pas. La stratégie permettrait de donner satisfaction à la plupart des demandes des Métis, sans qu'il soit nécessaire de leur attribuer un statut politique et légal spécial. Leurs aspirations à l'autonomie politique peuvent en effet être réalisées dans des gouvernements régionaux dont les limites pourraient être arrangées, si cela était nécessaire, de façon à assurer une majorité métis. Les subventions fédérales d'aide économique devraient leur être acquises sans tenir compte du statut légal. La création d'un statut spécial remettrait en question les avantages dont jouissent actuellement les Métis et les entraînerait dans des querelles fédérales-provinciales encore pires, sur les problèmes de responsabilités respectives.

Le chapitre XVII étude la question de savoir si l'histoire légale donne réellement un statut spécial aux Métis; l'étude des sources historiques permet de conclure par la négative.

L'application de la Charte les droits à l'autonomie des autochtones (Chapitre XXV).

Le chapitre XXV étudie un certain nombre de problèmes techniques épineux quant à la question de savoir si la *Charte*, sans une intervention spéciale des rédacteurs constitutionnels, peut s'appliquer aux gouvernements autochtones. Il examine ensuite ce qui devrait être fait : la solution prescrite provient de la stratégie de base. Les droits libéraux contenus dans la *Charte* devraient s'appliquer aux gouvernements autochtones; il serait contraire aux principes de base du libéralisme de laisser les citoyens des gouvernements autochtones en dehors de la protection de la *Charte*. La manière dont les gouvernements autochtones s'organisent et les règlements trop particuliers qui vont être créés permettent de craindre pour les droits de la personne. D'un autre côté, les autochtones craignent des intrusions excessives dans leurs affaires. La stratégie de base demande que l'on tienne compte de cette inquiétude. Cela peut se faire. Les juges devraient s'inspirer de l'article 25 de la *Charte* (dans l'interprétation qui en a été proposée) pour s'assurer, quand ils traitent des garanties de la *Charte*, qu'ils donnent toute l'attention nécessaire aux circonstances particulières et aux droits politiques des peuples autochtones.

La définition légale des peuples autochtones (Chapitre XXIV)
Dans le chapitre XXIV, il est suggéré de rejeter la définition proprement historique des limites des droits existants, ancestraux ou issus de traités, des peuples autochtones, tels qu'ils ont été définis dans l'article 35 de la *Loi constitutionnelle de 1982*. (Les cours de justice, jusqu'ici, s'en sont tenu à un point de vue strictement historique.) Il est recommandé, au contraire, que l'on récrive le texte, de façon à permettre aux tribunaux d'estimer le bien-fondé de ces limites sur leurs mérites propres. Les juges se laisseraient ainsi guider par la stratégie à tendance libérale, mais souple, recommandée dans la première partie.

Lecture sélective et intérêt particulier

First Principles, Second Thoughts peut se lire du début jusqu'à la fin. La description du processus constitionnel suit l'ordre chronologique, et la compréhension de chaque chapitre est renforcée par le contexte politique, légal et réglementaire fourni par d'autres chapitres.

Certains lecteurs, cependant, peuvent ne vouloir étudier que certaines questions. L'ouvrage permet également une lecture sélective. Quelqu'un qui s'intéresse, disons, aux questions fiscales, pourra très bien porter son attention plus précisément sur les chapitres XI à XV, et trouver que ces chapitres sont compréhensibles et instructifs par eux-mêmes.

Un autre lecteur se révélera plus intéressé par les droits des peuples autochtones que par le contexte général. Un tel lecteur pourra sauter la première partie et entrer directement dans le vif du sujet. (Réciproquement, quelqu'un qui ne s'intéresse qu'à la partie théorique n'est pas obligé de lire tout le détail des applications pratiques.)

Le tableau synoptique, en fin de livre, peut aider le lecteur à localiser le passage qui l'intéresse plus particulièrement et à se faire une idée générale du contexte.

Le style de First Principles, Second Thoughts

Rien, n'a été négligé pour rendre cet ouvrage accessible et agréable au lecteur non spécialisé. Le jargon légal a été autant que possible évité. On a essayé d'expliquer en termes simples les expressions techniques qui ont dû être utilisées ou auxquelles il a été fait allusion. On s'est également efforcé d'être succint, tout en traitant entièrement le sujet à l'étude.

La date de départ pour une nouvelle évolution

Cette étude s'appuie sur l'évolution légale et politique d'une situation qui s'étend inclusivement jusqu'à la Conférence des premiers ministres d'avril 1985. Les parties II et III ont été rédigées avant la fin de 1984, en vue d'un congrés académique. Ces chapitres sont restés assez semblables à leur état originel. L'avantage de ce procédé, c'est de ne pas compliquer la grammaire du texte (par exemple "devrait" plutôt que "devrait avoir"); le lecteur peut avoir un plus grand sentiment du caractère immédiat des événements rapportés; par ailleurs, cela permet de comparer les prédictions de l'étude et les prescriptions pour la Conférence des premiers ministres de 1985.

Chapter I

Individuals, Groups and Canadian Statecraft

Two Strains of Canadian Constitutionalism

The debate over constitutional reform with respect to the aboriginal peoples of Canada embodies a basic tension in Canadian political and legal life. One vision of Canada is of a liberal individualist state. Every person is inherently equal in legal dignity with every other. No special personal or ethnic history is necessary to entitle a person to equal respect from the state. The individual is to be free from restrictions in defining and pursuing his or her own ends in life. A person may freely choose to associate with others to achieve a common goal. The group has no intrinsic claim to rights; the protection of the rights of groups is viewed as instrumental to protecting the individuals who comprise the group (see Garet 1982-83). The competing vision of Canada is of a "community of historical communities." The basic units of political philosophy are distinct groups – each one a different-coloured chip in the Canadian mosaic. These groups have rights against the Canadian state. The rights are not the same for every group. A group's rights depend in large part on its distinctive history. The group is entitled to exert considerable control over its own members; in cases of conflict between the rights of an individual member and the collectivity, the state may sustain the collectivity. One Canadian historian, Gerard Vano, went so far as to characterize Canada as a neo-feudal state. He argued that unlike both Britain and the United

States, Canada maintained the central position of parochial groups in its political and legal thought (Vano 1981).

The tension between liberal individualism and history-based groupism is embodied in the *Canadian Charter of Rights* of 1982. In many ways, this massive change to Canadian life seems to represent an adoption of American-style liberalism. Canada, which had never had an entrenched Bill of Rights at all, adopted a *Charter* which in some ways was more explicit and comprehensive in its expression of liberal individualistic rights than the American *Bill of Rights*.

The most revered article of the *Bill of Rights*, the First Amendment, provides that:

> Congress shall make no law respecting an establishment of religion, or prohibiting the free exercise thereof; or abridging the freedom or speech, or of the press; or the right of the people peaceably to assemble, and to petition the Government for a redress of grievances.

Some American constitutionalists contend that the First Amendment should be construed as protecting the political process, rather than free expression in general. They rely on statements of some of the framers of the bill and the historical context in which it was framed (see, for example, Bork 1971-72). They could also point to some of the wording of the amendment. The reference is to "Congress"; at the time it was originally enacted, the First Amendment did not apply to the states, who remained able to limit free speech for a variety of purposes – such as the suppression of obscenity, the regulation of commerce, and the enforcement of civil rights pertaining to slander and libel. Thus the original purpose of the amendment could be viewed as protection against the political tyranny of a central government, rather than affirmation of an individual's right to freedom in every possible realm of discourse. Furthermore, the reference to petitioning the government for redress could be viewed as indicating a predominantly democratic, rather than liberal, intent behind the First Amendment. In practice, the American courts have given special protection to political speech and, almost if not as much, protection to moral and literary expression; but they have extended protection of a lesser degree to commercial and recreational expression (*Valentine* v. *Christensen*, 316 U.S. 52 (1942) Cf. *Virginia Pharmacy Board* v. *Virginia Consumer Council*, 425 U.S. 748 (1976) and Gunther 1980, 1382). Section 2 of the *Canadian Charter of Rights and*

Freedoms seems clearly to extend to the whole range of free expression. It states:

> Everyone has the following fundamental freedoms:
> (a) freedom of conscience and religion;
> (b) freedom of thought, belief, opinion and expression, including freedom of the press and other media of communication;
> (c) freedom of peaceful assembly; and
> (d) freedom of association.

Section 7 of the *Charter* guarantees that:

> Everyone has the right to life, liberty and security of the person and the right not to be deprived thereof except in accordance with the principles of fundamental justice.

Section 7 is arguably more amenable than its American counterparts (the Fifth and Fourteenth Amendments) to the interpretation that an individual is protected from substantively (and not only procedurally) unfair impositions from the state. American Courts have used the "due process" clause to strike down legislation regarded as substantively invalid (in the early part of the 1900s social welfare legislation, see *Lochner* v. *New York*, 198 U.S. 45 (1905) and *Adair* v. *United States*, 208 U.S. 161 (1908); in the 1970s, restrictions on reproductive liberty, see *Roe* v. *Wade*, 410 U.S. 113 (1973)); but the phrase "due process" is obviously more process-oriented than is "principles of fundamental justice." (For a more extensive treatment see Schwartz, 1983.)

Section 15(1) of the Canadian *Charter* states that:

> Every individual is equal before and under the law and has the right to the equal protection and equal benefit of the law without discrimination and, in particular, without discrimination based on race, national or ethnic origin, colour, religion, sex, age or mental or physical disability.

The equivalent wording in the American Constitution is the Fourteenth Amendment's prohibition against any state's denying to "any person within its jurisdiction the equal protection of the laws." The reference to equal benefit of the law seems to make s.15(1) somewhat more expansive than its American counterpart.

It should be noted that rather than affirming race, ethnic origin, and religion as grounds for rights allocation in Canada, s.15(1) expressly identifies them as prohibited grounds of discrimination; and that the equality that is guaranteed is expressly said to be among *individuals*, rather than communities.

Section 1 makes all of the *Charter*'s guarantees subject to "such reasonable limits prescribed by law as can be demonstrably justified in a free and democratic society." The only values referred to in this crucial section are freedom and democracy; there is no reference to community-based norms. On careful scrutiny, however, the *Charter*—the only entrenched legal expression of liberal individualism in the Canadian constitution—makes some fundamental concessions to history-based group rights.

One of the most important concessions is made by s.29, which defers to denominational school rights affirmed elsewhere in the constitution. Section 93 of the *Constitution Act, 1867* guarantees denominational school rights existing at the time of Confederation (see *Roman Catholic Separate School Trustees* v. *The King*, [1928] A.C. 363; see also Leckow 1983.) The judicially enforceable rights that exist under this section depend entirely on the historical position of a religious denomination at the time a province joined the federation. Not all groups are treated equally. If there were no Jewish denominational school rights in Quebec in 1867, then none are to be found in s.93. The entitlements of any particular group have to be determined by reference to its particular historical position. One group might have a right to maintain its own schools, but be obliged to contribute to public schools; another might be entitled to exemption from public school taxation and to state assistance in collecting taxes from members of the group to operate its denominational schools. (By contrast, the anti-establishment part of the First Amendment greatly restricts American public authorities from subsidizing religious schools; see *Committee for Pub. Ed. and Rel. Lib.* v. *Regan*, 63 L.Ed. 2d 94 (1980).)

Section 29 of the *Charter* states: "Nothing in this *Charter* abrogates or derogates from any rights or privileges guaranteed by or under the Constitution of Canada in respect of denominational, separate or dissentient schools". Because of s.29 certain denominations in Canada will retain their special historically-based rights to state tolerance or support for their denominational school systems. The individual-based equality clause, s.15, cannot be construed as denying the special rights and privileges enjoyed by some, but not other, religious groups. There is a fascinating "flip side" to the inefficacy of s.15 in derogating from the special privileges of certain groups. It may be argued that s.15 entitles every religious or philosophical group in Canada to the *same* rights as the *most* privileged of denominations under pre-1982 constitutional law. If Roman Catholics have the right, for example, to channel their tax money to their denominational school system and to select their own separate school boards (see *Ottawa Separate Schools Trustees* v. *Ottawa Corporation*, 1917 A.C. 76), why not Jews or Jehovah's Witnesses? The consequences of following this reasoning in some provinces might be the dismantling of the public school system. Hundreds of groups would set up their own educational systems. The courts are unlikely to construe s.15, in combination with s.29, as leaving a provincial legislature powerless to prevent such a radical change in Canadian education. The courts' justification might be that s.15 refers to individual equality and has no application to inter-groupal equality; or that the historical intent of s.29 is simply to defend the constitutional status quo, not to create new rights in other groups—had such a radical change been contemplated, the framers would have been explicit. Thus the special privileges of certain religious groups are reaffirmed, rather than threatened, by the statement of liberal individualism in the Canadian constitution.

Section 25 of the *Constitution Act, 1982* shields the special, historically-based rights of the aboriginal peoples of Canada from the application of the *Charter*. The section states:

> 25. The guarantee in this *Charter* of certain rights and freedoms shall not be construed so as to abrogate or derogate from any aboriginal, treaty or other rights or freedoms that pertain to the aboriginal peoples of Canada including
>
> (a) any rights or freedoms that have been recognized by the Royal Proclamation of October 7, 1763; and
>
> (b) any rights or freedoms that now exist by way of land claims agreements or may be so acquired.

Section 25 was the only acknowledgement of the aboriginal peoples of Canada in the constitutional reform project as first conceived in 1980. It does not protect the rights of the aboriginal peoples of Canada from governmental interference in general. The thrust it does deflect is from the liberal individualistic human rights guarantees of the *Charter of Rights and Freedoms*. Absent section 25, the special regime established for Indians under the *Indian Act*, for example, might be challenged as a violation of the equality guarantee of s.15. One subsection of the *Indian Act*, s.95(b), (which makes it an offence for an Indian to be intoxicated off a reserve) was in fact struck down as repugnant to the equality guarantee of the (non-constitutional) *Canadian Bill of Rights* (*R*. v. *Drybones* (1970), 9 D.L.R. (3d) 473). The Supreme Court of Canada only added another element to a bitter and perplexing controversy when it declined to apply the same equality guarantee in the *Canadian Bill of Rights* to s.12(1)(b) of the *Indian Act*. That subsection revoked the Indian status of a woman who married a non-Indian man (*Attorney General of Canada* v. *Lavell* (1974), 38 D.L.R. (3d) 481). Aboriginal organizations were rightly unimpressed with s.25, and an intense lobbying effect on their part resulted in the enactment of Part II of the *Constitution Act, 1982*. Section 35 stated:

> (1) The existing aboriginal and treaty rights of the aboriginal peoples of Canada are hereby recognized and affirmed.
>
> (2) In this Act, "aboriginal peoples of Canada" includes Indian, Inuit and Métis peoples of Canada.

The reference to aboriginal rights, treaty rights, and any rights or freedoms under the Royal Proclamation of 1763 involves historically-based rights generally belonging to groups rather than individuals. Sections 25 and 35 again carve out from the liberal individualistic *Charter* an extensive area in which special rights and privileges are to be maintained for some groups, but not others, on the basis of their idiosyncratic places in the formation of Canada. If the right to self-government is among the aboriginal rights mentioned in sections 25 and 35 (political autonomy is an inherent right of Indian tribes under American constitutional law; *Cherokee Nation* v. *Georgia*, 30 U.S. (5 Pet.) 1 (1831) and *Worcester* v. *Georgia*, 31 U.. (6 Pet.) 515 (1832)) they will prove to be especially important exemptions from the liberal individualistic protection provided by the *Charter*. (Much more on this in Chapter XXV, which discusses whether the *Charter of Rights and Freedoms* should apply to aboriginal self-government.)

The rights that sections 25 and 29 protect from the rest of the *Charter* are predominantly constitutional rights. Aboriginal and treaty rights are recognized in s.35 of the *Constitution Act, 1982*; denominational school rights are entrenched by section 93 of the *Constitution Act, 1867* (and analogous sections in subsequent Constitution Acts which admitted later provinces). Another section that shields rights from the application of liberal individualistic sections of the *Charter* is section 15(2). These rights, however, are predominantly those under affirmative action programs created at the discretion of legislatures. (If the *Charter* applies – more on this in Chapter XXV – to the private sector, section 15(1) would be a prima facie threat to private sector affirmative action programs, and section 15(2) would parry the threat.) Some affirmative action programs, however, may be seen by their authors to be constitutionally mandated. A court, for example, might use its very broad remedial authority under s.24 of the *Charter* to order an affirmative action program to redress a violation of section 15(1). The important points to note in the context of this discussion are that section 15(2) protects affirmative action programs that benefit certain *groups* on the basis of their disadvantage, and that an assessment of which group warrants special treatment due to its "disadvantage" is likely to depend on an evaluation of its social and political history. Once again, there is express constitutional deference to history-based group rights. (For a further discussion of section 15(2), see Chapter XX.)

Section 27 of the *Charter* states:

> 27. This *Charter* shall be interpreted in a manner consistent with the preservation and enhancement of the multicultural heritage of Canadians.

It was in response to the appearance of representatives of Canadian ethnic organizations that the original federal package was amended to include section 27.

It is quite possible that section 27 will be construed in a liberal fashion. Liberal individualism supports the right of every individual to freely associate with any other to maintain and develop whatever cultural tradition they consider appropriate. The idea of liberal education is to expose children to as wide a range as possible of cultural materials in order that the child may choose which elements to incorporate into his or her own plan for the good life (Ackerman 1980, ch.5). It is also quite possible, however, that s.27 will be used to limit other liberal individualistic norms in the *Charter*. Government subsidies to various ethnic organizations are common at both the federal and provincial level. In some cases they might reflect a genuine governmental respect for cultural diversity; in other cases an attempt to buy votes in blocs. Section 27 might be used, for example, to defend governmental subsidies to organizations whose internal practices do not conform to *Charter* norms. A complaint about government support for some groups but not others (or support for groups but not individuals) might be rejected by the courts on the basis that rigid application of individualistic equality norms is bound to disrupt government attempts to nurture multiculturalism. The reference to "heritage" might give added protection to groups that are historically established in Canada, or that have long-standing cultural traditions, whereas groups that are formed to experiment with a new vision of the good life will not derive support from section 27. In sum, history-based groupist visions of Canada may derive considerable constitutional support from section 27.

Section 33 of the *Charter* provides: "(1) Parliament or the legislature of a province may expressly declare in an act of Parliament or of the legislature, as the case may be, that the Act or a provision thereof shall operate notwithstanding a provision included in section 2 or sections 7 to 15 of this *Charter*". Section 33 is not an express concession to a history-based groupist vision of Canada. It may be viewed as no more than an attempt to accommodate the tension between judicial and legislative understandings of what is appropriate in a free and democratic society. The legislature is not necessarily illiberal when it overrides the *Charter*; it may simply be overriding a court's interpretation of what is liberal (Slattery 1983; Cf. *Alliance Des Professeurs de Montreal* v. *A.G. Quebec* (1984), 5 D.L.R. (4th) 157). (Both the laissez-faire branch of the Supreme Court and the New Deal Congress were liberal; they simply had a family disagreement over which version of liberalism should prevail.)

Other dimensions of section 33, however, are history-based and groupist. First of all, section 33 preserves the ability of "provincial communities" to implement their distinct political philosophies at the expense of the liberal, individualist, *Charter*. Provincial boundaries are the consequence of distinct historical developments and not the application of liberal principles. Secondly, within a province, one particular ethnic group may be demographically dominant and therefore politically predominant. That group may then use its political authority, and section 33, to enhance the position of that distinct group. The province of Quebec is the example that is obviously behind the abstract formulation just presented. A government dedicated (at least in the long run) to separatism has ruled Quebec for two terms of office. It understands Quebec as the homeland of the

Quebecois people and believes it necessary to take special measures to preserve and enhance the position of that people – sometimes at the expense of minority groups in the province. Because of its rejection of the legitimacy of the patriation process in 1982 – the constitutional package came into force despite the dissent of the Quebec government on its merits – the government of Quebec has stamped *all* of its legislation as "notwithstanding the provisions of sections 2 and 7 to 15 of the *Constitution Act, 1982*" (*An Act Representing the Constitution Act,* 1982 (Bill 61); held to be a valid enactment under s.33 of the *Charter* by Deschenes C.J.S.C. in *Alliances Des Professeurs de Montreal* v. *A.G. Quebec* (1984), 5 D.L.R. (4th) 157). Some of this legislation is integral to the government's nationalistic program (see, for example, *The Charter of the French Language,* R.S.Q. 1977, c.C-11).

The "override" provided by s.33 is not available against certain guarantees in the *Charter*, including those on minority language rights. One of the latter is:

> 23. (1) Citizens of Canada
>
> (a) whose first language learned and still understood is that of the English or French linguistic minority population of the province in which they reside, or
>
> (b) who have received their primary school instruction in Canada in English or French and reside in a province where the language in which they received that instruction is the language of the English or French linguistic minority population of the province,
>
> have the right to have their children receive primary and secondary school instruction in the same language.
>
> (2) Citizens of Canada of whom any child has received or is receiving primary or secondary instruction in English or French in Canada, have the right to have all their children receive primary and secondary school instruction in the same language.

> (3) The right of citizens of Canada under subsections (1) and (2) to have their children receive primary and secondary school instruction in the language of the English or French linguistic minority population of a province
>
> (a) applies wherever in the province the number of children of citizens who have such a right is sufficient to warrant the provision to them out of public funds of minority language instruction; and
>
> (b) includes, where the number of those children so warrants, the right to have them receive that instruction in minority language educational facilities provided out of public funds.

Section 23 was held by the Supreme Court of Canada to render inoperative a section of the Quebec *Charter of the French Language* (Bill 101) that required all children newly-arrived to the province to attend French (rather than English) schools. The section even applied to children from other parts of Canada. The Supreme Court of Canada inferred from the wording of section 23 that it was expressly directed by its framers at affirming some parts, and disallowing other parts, of the Quebec Charter (*A.G. Quebec* v. *Quebec Assn. of Protestant School Bds.* (1984), 10 D.L.R. (4th) 321). The Court observed:

> By incorporating into the structure of s.23 of the *Charter* the unique set of criteria in s.73 of Bill 101, the framers of the Constitution identified the type of regime they wished to correct and on which they would base the remedy prescribed. The framers' objective appears simple, and may readily be inferred from the concrete method used by them: to adopt a general rule guaranteeing the Francophone and Anglophone minorities in Canada an important part of the rights which the Anglophone minority in Quebec has enjoyed with respect to the language of instruction before Bill 101 was adopted (10 D.L.R. (4th) 321, 335).

The Court found it unnecessary to consider the merits of counsel for Quebec's submission that s.73 of the Quebec Charter was a "reasonable limit, prescribed by law" that is "justified in a free and democratic society," and so authorized by s.1 of the *Canadian Charter of Rights and Freedoms*. First of all, reasoned the Court, the framers clearly intended to invalidate s.73, so they could not possibly have regarded it as a reasonable limitation on s.23 of the *Charter*. Furthermore, according to the Court, s.73 is such a substantial derogation from s.23 that it cannot be considered a mere limitation on s.23, but rather, in effect, an outright override of it. But the framers of the Constitution chose not to include s.23 in the list of rights that a legislature can unilaterally override. The second part of the Court's reasoning is, in my opinion, illogical. When a legislature uses its override power, it precludes a judicial interpretation of the legislation by the standards of the *Charter*; it must bear the political opprobrium that comes with labelling its legislation as notwithstanding the *Charter of Rights and Freedoms*; and the override ceases to take effect after five years unless expressly renewed (see s.33 *Charter of Rights and Freedoms*). By contrast, when a government appeals to the "reasonable limitations" clause, it submits to having an independent arbiter, the courts, measure the legislation against the *Charter*; no special manner and form of legislation is required, and the legislation can stand as long as it continues to be a demonstrably justified, reasonable limitation. The political and legal implications of the override process are fundamentally different from those involved in an appeal to the "reasonable limits" standard. The Supreme Court of Canada was not justified in equating the two merely because they would both result in a negation of a *Charter* guarantee. That the Court did resort to this specious equation may be indicative of the judges' anxiety to avoid the political flak and philosophical perplexity involved with a direct evaluation of the Quebec legislation by s.1 standards.

In the judgment of first instance in the case, however, Chief Justice Deschenes considered in some depth several of the philosophical and sociological implications. First, he carried out some basic legal analyses. He held that s.1 of the *Charter* did apply to s.23, but would only protect a limitation of the rights guaranteed under s.23 and not their "denial" ((1983), 140 D.L.R. (3d) 133). Section 1 refers to "reasonable limits"; how, asks Deschenes C.J.S.C., can the denial of a right be permissible where "the text permits only restrictions 'within reasonable limits'"? ((1983), 140 D.L.R. (3d) 33, 60). His rhetorical question is based on a false premise. Section 1 of the *Charter* refers to "reasonable limits ... as can be demonstrably justified," not restrictions that are within "reasonable limits." The phraseology that Deschenes C.J.S.C. mistakenly cites might imply that there are supposed to be boundaries to the extent to which a right can be limited. The language of the *Charter* does not contain such a nuance. The framers were well advised to have avoided it. It makes very little sense to suppose that there is never a set of social circumstances which requires the temporary elimination, as opposed to limitation, of a right. Furthermore, the distinction between "limitation" and "denial" is arbitrary. How does a court determine whether a section of the *Charter* contains five branches of one right or five different rights? If only one branch has been knocked off by the legislature, can it not be said that the right is only limited, but not denied? If the right is made completely unavailable to some people, but allowed to persist for others, is the right denied or merely limited? All legislative measures are open to revision by subsequent legislative action; measures that pass constitutional scrutiny may prove to be unacceptable when social circumstances change. Can a right be said to be denied, as opposed to merely limited, if the restriction lasts only one year? Or five? Or ten? The distinction between "limitations" and "denials" is an unnecessary and unworkable gloss on section 1.

In any event, the denial/limitation distinction is the jumping-off point for a philosophical discussion by Deschenes C.J.S.C. that is highly germane to the present discussion. Counsel for the government of Quebec argued that even if the court accepts the denial/limitation distinction, s.1 could apply because the s.23 rights belong to the English-language minority as a whole, and s.73 of the Quebec Charter only applied to some members of that minority. The constitutional position of the group was only limited by the total denial of rights to some of its members.

The text of s.23 points in both directions on whether it recognizes individual or collective rights, Deschenes C.J.S.C. finds. The reference to "minority language" and to "sufficient numbers" implies that s.23 involves collective rights; but the expressions "first language learned" or "language of instruction" favour the view that it is an individual right. There are some collective rights in the Canadian constitution, notes Deschenes C.J.S.C.: those referred to in s.25 of the *Charter* ("rights or freedoms that pertain to the aboriginal peoples of Canada") and the denominational school rights protected by s.93 of the *Constitution Act, 1867* (which refers to "any Class of persons" and "Separate Schools"). He concludes:

> A right may be granted to individuals as members of a group without becoming a collective right; thus, the individual exercise of his right militates strongly against it being described as collective. Linguistic minorities in the provinces do not constitute juridical entities; that goes without saying. But neither do they constitute entities with rights recognized by the *Charter* which may be enforced collectively. The *Charter* recognizes rights in individuals, citizens of Canada and members of a minority, with respect to the language of instruction; it is to these individuals that the door to the courts is opened in a case where their rights are violated. It seems clear that s.23 deals with individual rather than collective rights ((1983) 140 D.L.R. (3d) 33, 63).

Inasmuch as s.73 of the Quebec Charter denies entirely to an individual his right, it cannot be defended on the basis of the "reasonable limitations" clause of the *Charter*, concludes Deschenes C.J.S.C. But even if the rights guaranteed by s.23 are collective in nature, the result would be the same:

> It is not the minority as a group which may claim the benefit of these rights; it is not the minority as a group which may claim the right to sit in the classroom to receive instruction in its own language; it is each individual as a member of the minority who possesses this right and who may take advantage of this opportunity for learning. If this individual does not fulfil the additional conditions imposed by the Quebec clause, he comes up against a closed door and suffers a complete denial of his right.

The next part of the judgment is especially relevant to the theme of this discussion – the tension between individualist and collectivist theories of rights in the Canadian constitution. Deschenes C.J.S.C. writes:

> However – Quebec argues – a collective right implies that it was established in the interest of and for the benefit of the collectivity, and not for each of its members. The limitation on this collective right may well involve the loss of the right by certain members of the collectivity, but the right is not denied to the group as a whole; it is simply limited.

> The court is amazed, to use a euphemism, to hear this argument from a government which prides itself in maintaining in America the flame of French civilization with its promotion of spiritual values and its traditional respect for liberty.
>
> In fact, Quebec's argument is based on a totalitarian conception of society to which the court does not subscribe. Human beings are, to us, of paramount importance and nothing should be allowed to diminish the respect due to them. Other societies place the collectivity above the individual. They use the Kolkhoze steamroller and see merit only in the collective result even if some individuals are left by the wayside in the process.
>
> This concept of society has never taken root here – even if certain political initiatives seem at times to come dangerously close to it – and this court will not honour it with its approval. Every individual in Canada should enjoy his rights to the full when in Quebec, whether alone or as a member of a group; and if the group numbers 100 persons, the one hundredth has as much right to benefit from all the privileges of citizens as the other ninety-nine. The alleged restriction of a collective right which would deprive the one hundredth member of the group of the rights guaranteed by the *Charter* constitutes, for this one hundredth member, a real denial of his rights. He cannot simply be counted as an accidental loss in a collective operation: our concept of human beings does not accommodate such a theory.
>
> Whether the nature of the rights guaranteed to the minority by s.23 be individual or collective, it is always an individual citizen who suffers from the application of the Quebec clause, and for him, this clause involves a total denial of the rights which he may claim by virtue of the *Charter* ((1983) 140 D.L.R. (3d) 33, 64-65).

Deschenes C.J.S.C.'s panegyric to individualism is, unfortunately, misplaced in the context of s.23. In philosophical terms, s.23 must be viewed as much more consistent with the history-based groupist interpretation than the individualist strain in Canadian constitutionalism. The rights are guaranteed only to linguistic minorities in a province. An individual who doesn't fit into the group has no *Charter* language rights. An Italian who immigrates to Quebec has no right to send his children to an English language school in Quebec. Perhaps even more importantly, a francophone parent has no right to send his child to an English language school. The last point is of at least as much practical importance as the first. Many parents in Quebec would like their children to be fluent in both of Canada's languages. Bilingualism is preferable to unilingualism in the liberal scheme of education; a child who can speak the most widely-spoken language of his own political community, Canada, and the language spoken by people in more countries than any other has several liberal advantages. The child is better able to participate in the political debate in his state. More literature, more music, more theatre and film, more personal human contact will be open to the child; he will have a broader range of information and models on which to base his own decision of how to live. Section 23 is designed to ensure the survival of linguistic minorities; it does not directly protect liberal individualism on the linguistic front. (Of course, the continuing survival of linguistic minorities in the various provinces ensures that there will be a supply of minority language educators, and political supporters of the use of that language. Non-members of the minority may have improved opportunities to acquire and use the minority language as a result of the survival of the communities that speak it.)

It should be noted that s.23 protects the rights of parents, not children. It assumes, contrary to liberal principles, that the child must accept the linguistic choice of his parents, even if they differ from his own (compare with Ackerman, 1980, ch.5). Unlike some of the other sections of the *Charter* examined above, s.23 does not shield a historically-based group right from the liberal individualism of the *Charter*. Instead, s.23 adds to Canadian constitutional law a hitherto unknown right that is essentially groupist in nature.

The many concessions to history-based groupism in the Canadian constitution have been given insufficient attention by the academic commentators. For the most part, in the absence of much Canadian case law on the *Charter*, they have occupied themselves with discussing American, and occasionally European and international, cases on the counterparts of the liberal individualist sections of the *Charter*. The majority of Canadian legal academics do graduate work at American (usually Harvard) and English law schools, where the national constitutional traditions are much less corporatist than is

Canada's. As a result, Canadian legal academics may be less attentive than they should be to the distinctive features of their own constitution. The tension between group and individual rights in the *Charter* is, in fact, unusually explicit for a Canadian constitutional document. Generally speaking, Canadian constitutional texts are blueprints for the organization and jurisdiction of various governmental authorities. Canadian constitutional documents prior to the *Charter* generally did not recognize substantive right or values. They did not contain much in the way of ideological commitments.

The lead article in the November 1937 *Harvard Law Review* begins:

> The Canadian Constitution is an excellent medium for studying the problems of constitutional interpretation. The British North America Act, 1867 [now known as the *Constitution Act, 1867*] is a strictly business-like document. It contains no metaphysics, no political philosophy, and no party politics (Jennings 1937, 1).

Gerard Vano writes:

> Paradoxically, in fact, French Canadian ideological success in 1867 opened the way for subsequent political disasters. What could have saved the linguistically French from an "English" political counterstroke after 1867 would have involved enshrining in constitutional law, when the opportunity presented itself in 1867, certain "inalienable" and "self evident" principles such as the sanctity of different cultures, languages and religions. But that would have been a gesture too blatantly illiberal in fostering the legal creation of autonomous estates for the Imperial government which had to legislate the Canadian constitution.
>
> On the other hand, the parameters within which the British North America Act was framed by virtue of the Seventy Two Resolutions were certainly not liberal, lacking as they did, stress on private property and civil rights. The British North America Act did not precisely articulate either liberal or illiberal principles, either individualism or community interests, although the latter did not inhibit the reassertive ideology of French Canada and the Bleus

> with their unswerving stress on limited (ethnic) community interests (Vano 1981, 75).

The governmental blueprint of the *Constitution Act, 1867* is susceptible of a variety of different interpretations. The Canadian courts (and until 1949, the Judicial Committee of the British Privy Council) have always been required to produce authoritative decisions on whether a particular piece of legislation is within the legislative jurisdiction assigned to a level of government under section 91 (federal) or sections 92 and 93 (provincial) of the *British North America Act, 1867* (renamed the *Constitution Act, 1867*). Until recently, the courts have tended to write reasons for judgment that were technical rather than philosophical. The absence of an entrenched bill of rights meant that Canadian courts were not required to ponder the underlying meaning of Canadian constitutionalism to the extent that American courts were obliged to reflect on the deeper meanings of the U.S. Constitution. Over the years, political parties and governments expounded and implemented differing interpretations of the underlying basis of Canadian legal and political life. Canada was viewed variously as an essentially unified state with some limited concessions to provincial autonomy (see generally F. Scott 1977); as a compact among the founding peoples (see Black 1975, ch. 5); as the homeland of two founding peoples, the French and the English (Black 1975, ch. 6 and 7); and as a multicultural state. Once elected, a government had considerable freedom to implement its conception of Canada without running afoul of any constitutional limitation. Different political movements were able to interpret the structures established by the *British North America Act* as consistent with, or even the embodiment of, their own ideals. The most diverse question in Canadian history has been the position of the French-Canadians in Confederation. For a liberal, the province of Quebec is a province like the others; it happens to have a predominantly French population, but French-Canadians in Quebec have no special constitutional rights not shared by members of other ethnic groups. To a French-Canadian nationalist, the division of the province of Canada into the separate provinces of Ontario and Quebec reflected the special position of the French-Canadian people as a founding nation entitled to continued and substantial political autonomy. During the *Patriation Reference* ((1981) 125 D.L.R (3d) 1) a number of different conceptions of Canada were expressly advanced by counsel for various provincial governments. The Court dismissed some of the shakier ones, and then retreated behind an abysmally formalistic line of reasoning in order to uphold the federal government's legal claim. If any conception of Canada was embodied by the court's judgment it was, despite the Court's protestations to the contrary, that of Canada as a British colony (see Schwartz 1981 and Schwartz and Whyte 1982-83).

In mentioning the susceptibility of the *Constitution Act, 1867* to different ideological interpretations, I do not intend to cast negative aspersions on it. On the contrary, I recommend the *Constitution Act, 1867* as a model for dealing with aboriginal claims. The founding act of Canada was a sound framework for the social and political maturation of Canada. It enabled members of all sorts of different movements to participate in politics and government without surrendering their own philosophical commitments. In failing to state the political philosophy behind its enactment in 1867, the *Constitution Act* helped to ensure its continuing vitality as social circumstances and political ideas evolved over more than a century of Canadian history. We would be adept constitutional framers today if we were to achieve the same combination of philosophical modesty and practical efficiency in addressing the concerns of the aboriginal peoples of Canada.

History-Based Groupism Versus Liberal Individualism in the Context of Constitutional Reform with Respect to Aboriginal Peoples of Canada

The tension between individualism and history-based groupism has been, and will continue to be, a basic dimension of the debate over constitutional reform with respect to aboriginal peoples. In the course of demonstrating the contention just made, it will be useful to use the program and statements of Prime Minister Trudeau as a central theme. During his Prime Ministership the first modern Canadian cases on aboriginal title were litigated; major legislative reforms with respect to Indian peoples were proposed by the federal government; and the constitutional reform package came into force that included a recognition and affirmation of aboriginal and treaty rights. Pierre Trudeau came to the Prime Ministership as Canada's most trenchant academic proponent of a liberal individualist conception of the country, so his actions and comments about these developments are of special philosophical interest.

"My political action, or my theory – inasmuch as I can be said to have one – can be expressed very simply: create counterweights." So writes Pierre Trudeau, newly-chosen Prime Minister of Canada, in the foreword to a collection of essays entitled *Federalism and the French Canadians* (Trudeau 1968, xxiii). The pieces were written over the previous two decades and express a vehement opposition to the widely-held ideology of the intellectual left in Quebec: that the French-Canadian people of Quebec were entitled, under the principle of national self-determination, to separate from Canada and form an independent state; and that they ought to do so in order to preserve and enhance the French-Canadian culture and to produce a more progressive and energetic society in all areas. "Had French Canadians needed someone to preach collective pride to them, no doubt I would have been first on the soap-box," writes Trudeau (Trudeau 1968, xxiii). But in his view French-Canadian nationalism was a threat to liberty and social progress. First of all, argued Trudeau, the progressive left that supported separatism would find itself on the same side as, and dominated by, the separatist right. In the 1940s and 1950s the provincial government of Quebec, in Trudeau's view, was dominated by a nationalist government that was reactionary on labour and educational issues, pro-clerical and anti-secular, intolerant of religious minorities and repressive of civil liberties. (By the time the separatist Parti Québecois took power in 1976, the people of Quebec were far more liberal and secular than they had been twenty years earlier, and apart from the language issue, the government's program was essentially social democratic.)

Secondly, according to Trudeau:

> . . . the nationalists—even those of the left—are politically reactionary because, in attaching such importance to the idea of nation, they are surely led to a definition of the common good as a function of an ethnic group, rather than all the people, regardless of characteristics. That is why a nationalistic government is by nature intolerant, discriminatory, and, when all is said and done, totalitarian (Trudeau 1968, 169).

Trudeau's ideal state is essentially a liberal individualist one. By liberal I do not mean economically laissez-faire; both as an academic and as prime minister, Trudeau favoured governmental intervention in the economy to redistribute wealth and economic power to less prosperous segments of society. But Trudeau's vision was of a society in which every individual, regardless of ethnic origins, would be free to develop and express himself politically, socially, economically, culturally, scientifically. The state would not ally itself with the nationalistic passions of a majority and attempt to impose those passions on the minority. Cultural values would thrive or disappear according to their merits in the eyes of free individuals. Nationalism is a modern-day equivalent of primitive tribalism; it ought to, and will, be supplanted by more open, cosmopolite political ideologies. Writes Professor Trudeau:

> The nation is, in fact, the guardian of certain very positive qualities: a cultural heritage, common traditions, a community awareness, historical continuity, a set of mores; all of which, at this juncture in history, go to make a man what he is. Certainly these qualities are more private than public, more introverted than extroverted, more instinctive and primitive than intelligent and civilized, more self-centred and impulsive than generous and reasonable. They belong to a transitional period in world history (Trudeau 1968, 177).

A third argument for characterizing French-Canadian separatism as reactionary, according to Trudeau, is that it goes against an essential element of progress for any political unit, its willingness to subordinate some elements of sovereignty in order to achieve military, economic, and social co-operation with other political units. ". . . states will know no real peace and prosperity until they accept the submission of their relations with each other to a higher order. In truth, the very concept of sovereignty must be surmounted, and those who proclaim it for the nation of French Canada are not only reactionary, they are preposterous" (Trudeau 1968, 170).

In 1969, the second year of Trudeau's first term as prime minister, his minister of Indian affairs and northern development issued a white paper on Indian policy (Statement of the Government of Canada on Indian Policy, 1969). It strongly rejected history-based groupism in favour of a liberal individualist approach. It condemned the perpetration of special legal and constitutional status for Indian peoples.

> The policy rests upon the fundamental right of the Indian people to full and equal participation in the cultural, social, economic and political life of Canada.
>
> To argue against this right is to argue *for* discrimination, isolation and separation. No Canadian should be excluded from participation in community

> life, and none should expect to withdraw and still enjoy the benefits that flow to those who participate.
>
> The legal and administrative discrimination in the treatment of Indian people has not given them an equal chance of success. It has exposed them to discrimination in the broadest and worst sense of the term—a discrimination that has profoundly affected their confidence that success can be theirs. Discrimination breeds discrimination by example, and the separateness of the Indian people has affected the attitudes of other Canadians toward them (White Paper 1969, 8).

The special constitutional authority of the federal level of government over Indians (s.91(24) of the *Constitution Act, 1867*) would eventually be abolished, and the Department of Indian Affairs and Northern Development eliminated: "Services must come through the same channels and from the same government agencies for all Canadians" (White Paper 1969, 9). Indians would be granted full control over their lands; bands would be able to lease, mortgage and sell reserve land as they saw fit, without Crown involvement.

While the white paper proposed to move towards the elimination of special constitutional and legislative treatment for Indians, it did call for the recognition of "lawful obligations" to Indians, including those under treaty. According to the white paper, however, the importance of the latter tended to be exaggerated by Indians:

> The terms and effects of the treaties between the Indian people and the Government are widely misunderstood. A plain reading of the words used in the treaties reveals the limited and minimal promises which were included in them. As a result of the treaties, some Indians were given an initial cash payment and were promised land reserved for their exclusive use, annuities, protection of hunting, fishing and trapping privileges subject (in most cases) to regulation, a school or teachers in most instances, and, in one treaty only, a medicine chest. There were some other minor considerations such as the annual provision of twine and ammunition.

> The significance of the treaties in meeting the economic, educational, health and welfare needs of the Indian people has always been limited and will continue to decline. The services that have been provided go far beyond what could have been foreseen by those who signed the treaties (White Paper 1969, 11).

The white paper proposed that the federal government help to secure "positive recognition by everyone of the unique contribution of Indian culture to Canadian history." The secretary of state would assist groups and associations in "developing a greater appreciation of their cultural heritage" (White Paper 1969, 9). Provincial educational authorities would be encouraged to revise school curricula and course content "with a view to ensuring that they adequately reflect Indian culture and Indian contributions to Canadian development" (White Paper 1969, 9). The secretary of state in Canada (at least prior to the establishment of the Ministry of Multiculturalism) was usually responsible for national efforts at promoting Canadian cultural development, and the general thrust of the white paper in this regard seems to be that Indian culture should be promoted as part of the general liberal policy of respecting cultural diversity.

Prime Minister Trudeau's rejection of history-based groupism with respect to Indian policy is strongly evinced in this excerpt from a speech he delivered on 8 August 1969 a few months after the issuance of the white paper:

> . . . the time is now to decide whether the Indians will be a race apart in Canada or whether it will be Canadians of full status . . . a choice which is in our minds whether Canadians as a whole want to continue treating the Indian population as something outside, a group of Canadians with which we have treaties, a group of Canadians who have as the Indians, many of them claim, aboriginal rights or whether we will say well forget the past and begin today and this is a tremendously difficult choice because, if—well one of the things the Indian bands often refer to are their aboriginal rights and in our policy, the way we propose it, we say we won't recognize aboriginal rights. We will recognize treaty rights. We will recognize forms of contract which have been made with the Indian people by the Crown and we will try to bring justice in that

area and this will mean that perhaps the treaties shouldn't go on forever. It's inconceivable, I think, that in a given society one section of the society have a treaty with the other section of the society. We must be all equal under the laws and we must not sign treaties amongst ourselves and many of these treaties, indeed, would have less and less significance in the future anyhow but things that in the past were covered by the treaties like things like so much twine or so much gun powder and which haven't been paid this must be paid. But I don't think that we should encourage the Indians to feel that their treaties should last forever within Canada so that they be able to receive their twine or their gun powder. They should become Canadians as all other Canadians and if they are prosperous and wealthy they will be treated like the prosperous and wealthy and they will be paying taxes for the other Canadians who are not so prosperous and not so wealthy whether they be Indians or English Canadians or French or Maritimers and this is the only basis on which I see our society can develop as equals. But aboriginal rights, this really means saying, "We were here before you. You came and you took the land from us and perhaps you cheated us by giving us some worthless things in return for vast expanses of land and we want to re-open this question. We want you to preserve our aboriginal rights and to restore them to us." And our answer – it may not be the right one and may not be one which is accepted but it will be up to all of you people to make your minds up and to choose for or against it and to discuss with the Indians – our answer is "no."

If we think of restoring aboriginal rights to the Indians well what about the French who were defeated at the Plains of Abraham? Shouldn't we restore rights to them? And what about though the Acadians who were deported – shouldn't we compensate for this? And what about the other Canadians, the immigrants? What about the Japanese Canadians who were so badly treated at the end or during the last war? What can we do to redeem the past? I an only say as President Kennedy said when he was asked about what he would do to compensate for the injustice that the Negroes had received in American society. We will

> be just in our time. This is all we can do. We must be just today (reprinted in Cumming and Mickenberg 1972, 331).

The reaction of the Indian political organizations was overwhelmingly and vociferously negative. Indian leaders feared that the white paper policy was in substance equivalent to the disastrous "termination" policy of the American government in the 1950s (for a discussion of the "termination" policy see Canby 1981, 25); that it was directed at the assimilation of Indians, that it would lead to the break-up of the reserves as bits and pieces were sold off to outsiders (Weaver 1981, 177). Another objection was that provinces could not be relied upon to adequately substitute for the Department of Indian Affairs and Northern Development in the areas of service delivery vacated by the federal government (Weaver 1981, 176). A major objection at the level of process, rather than substance, was that the white paper had been formulated without adequate consultation with Indians (Weaver 1981, 176).

A year after the issuance of the white paper, the National Indian Brotherhood (NIB), forerunner of the Assembly of First Nations, adopted a "red paper" as its official response to the white paper. The document (formally titled *Citizens Plus*) was a position paper developed by the Indian Chiefs of Alberta. (The NIB amended the section on treaties to include aboriginal rights; Weaver 1981, 183). The red paper stated that: "Retaining the legal status of Indians is necessary [sic] if Indians are to be treated justly. Justice requires that the special history, rights and circumstances of Indian People be recognized" (Red Paper 1970, 4).

Fundamental importance is placed in the paper on the honouring of the treaties entered into with Alberta Indian bands. Where the white paper minimized the extent and continuing relevance of treaty obligations, the red paper interprets them as governmental assistance in all the vital areas of Indian development:

> The intent and spirit of the treaties must be our guide, not the precise letter of a foreign language. Treaties that run forever must have room for the changes in the conditions of life. The undertaking of the Government to provide teachers was a commitment to provide Indian children the educational opportunity equal to their white neighbors [sic]. The machinery and

> livestok [sic] symbolized economic development (Red Paper 1970, 8).
>
> We say that the Federal Government is bound by the British North America Act, Section 9k [sic], Head 24, to accept legislative responsibility for 'Indians and Indian Lands.' Moreover in exchange for the lands which the Indian people surrendered to the Crown the treaties ensure the following benefits:
>
> (a) To have and to hold certain lands called 'reserves' for the sole use and benefit of the Indian people forever and assistance in the social economic, and cultural development of the reserves.
>
> (b) The provision of health services to the Indian people on the reserve or off the reserve at the expense of the Federal government anywhere in Canada.
>
> (c) The provision of education of all types and levels to all Indian people at the expense of the Federal government.
>
> (d) The right of the Indian people to hunt, trap and fish for their livelihood free of governmental interference and regulation and subject only to the proviso that the exercise of this right must not interfere with the use and enjoyment of private property.
>
> These benefits are not 'handouts' because the Indian people paid for them by surrendering their lands. The Federal Government is bound to provide the actual services relating to education, welfare, health and economic development (Red Paper 1970, 6).

In the end, negative response by Indian organizations to the white paper caused Prime Minister Trudeau to announce that his government would not "force any solution" on Indian peoples. Trudeau reportedly told a meeting with Indian leaders:

> And I'm sure we were very naive in some of the statements we made in the paper. We had perhaps the prejudices of small 'l' liberals and white men at that

> who thought that equality meant the same law for everybody ... But we have learnt in the process that perhaps we were a bit too theoretical, we were a bit too abstract... (Weaver 1981, 185).

Prime Minister Trudeau was led to modify his denial of the existence of aboriginal title by the non-decision of the Supreme Court of Canada in the *Calder* case in 1973; 34 D.L.R. (3d) 145 (see Weaver 1981, 198). The Nishga Indians of British Columbia had brought an action for a declaration that their aboriginal title over their traditional land base had not been extinguished. Three of the seven judges of the Supreme Court who heard the case were prepared to grant the declaration. Hall J., their spokesman, referred to the claim as "not ... to title in *fee* but in the nature of an equitable title or interest ... a usufructuary right and a right to occupy the lands and to enjoy the fruits of the soil, the forest and of the rivers and streams which does not in any way deny the Crown's paramount title as it is recognized by the law of nations" (34 D.L.R. (3d), 145, 173-174). Three judges held against the Nishgas, on the ground that whatever aboriginal title they originally possessed had been extinguished by colonial ordinances and the *British Columbia Terms of Union*. Judson J., writing for the three, did not reject the possibility of a group's having aboriginal title; indeed, he offered the following definition:

> Although I think that it is clear that Indian title in British Columbia cannot owe its origin to the Proclamation of 1763, the fact is that when the settlers came, the Indians were there, organized in societies and occupying the lands as their forefathers had done for centuries. That is what Indian title means and it does not help one in the solution of this problem to call it a "personal or usufructuary right." What they are asserting in this action is that they had a right to continue to live on their lands as their forefathers had lived and that this right has never been lawfully extinguished. There can be no question that this right was "dependent on the goodwill of the Sovereign" (34 D.L.R. (3d) 145, 156).

The seventh and decisively nondeciding judge held on a technical point of procedure that the case was not properly before the courts. Ties in the Supreme Court of Canada are scored as an affirmation of the decision under appeal. The British Columbia

Court of Appeal had ruled against the Nishgas on the merits, so they ended up frustrated in their pursuit of a declaration.

The concept of "aboriginal title" acquired, however, a legal credibility it had not previously enjoyed in Canada. Precisely what it meant, however, was still far from understood. It is clear from the Canadian, English and American cases, however, that the concept is history-based and groupist. Aboriginal title is based on the historic use and occupation of a land area; the legal interest belongs to the aboriginal collectivity, not to any individual member. ("Admitting [an Indian tribe's] power to change their laws or usages, so far as to allow an individual to separate a portion of their lands from the common stock, and hold it in severalty, still it is a part of their territory, and is held under them, by a title dependent on their laws"; Chief Justice Marshall in the pre-eminent American case on Indian title, *Johnson and Graham's Lessee* v. *M'Intosh*, 8 Wheat 543, 593 (1823)). The American courts have found Indian tribes to be "domestic dependent nations" with an inherent right to self-government subject only to the overriding power of Congress (*Cherokee Nation* v. *The State of Georgia*, 30 U.S. 1 (1831), per Chief Justice Marshall; Canby 1981, 14, 65). The American *Bill of Rights* has been held to not apply to Indian tribes of its own force (*Talton* v. *Mayes*, 163 U.S. 376 (1896)); it applies in a modified form only because of the Congressional passage of the *Indian Civil Rights Act*, 1968. The appeal by Canadian Indians to aboriginal title or rights as a basis for Indian political autonomy is, like the proprietary claim, history-based and groupist. (It might be added here that reliance on treaties also tends to be consistent with history-based corporatism. The form of the treaties is generally a compact between representatives of the Crown and the chiefs of an Indian band. The post-Confederation treaties involve an exchange of the traditional land base of the group for a tract of reserve land that is assigned to the group. There are some benefits that are distributed on a per capita basis (e.g., annuities), but an individual Indian is only entitled to them as a member of the band.)

In the aftermath of *Calder*, the federal government entered into negotiations with a number of non-treaty aboriginal groups who asserted title over extensive areas. The process was dubbed "comprehensive land claims settlements" (Department of Indian Affairs and Northern Development [DIAND] 1981). (The federal government also established a process to discuss the redress of "specific claims" – allegations of federal violations of lawful obligations, including those under treaty, statute, and the federal trust responsibility with respect to Indian assets and so on;

DIAND 1982.) In exchange for the surrender of claims to aboriginal title, the federal government was prepared to offer packages of benefits that might include money, land, rights to participate in wildlife management, and legal structures to facilitate a group's management of its property or government of its affairs. The federal government argued that political negotiations were preferable to third-party arbitration or adjudication; that they permit more flexible arrangements to be made and offer aboriginal people more opportunity to participate in structuring them. While lengthy negotiations have taken place with aboriginal groups in the Yukon and Northwest Territories, the only comprehensive agreements thus far have been the James Bay and Northern Quebec Agreement of 1975 and the supplementary Northeastern Quebec Agreement of 1978 (DIAND 1981, 29). The agreements embodied no substantial departures from liberal principle. The Inuit accepted as a satisfactory form of self-government the establishment of a regional, non-ethnic government in their area in which they constituted a majority of the population. In addition, an Inuit-controlled corporation was established to manage certain lands and other assets that were assigned to the Inuit as part of the deal. The Cree and Naskapi bands were promised special self-government legislation of their own. Enacted into law in 1984, the *Cree-Naskapi (of Quebec) Act,* empowered band governments to exercise "local government" powers over lands vested in an Indian group under the Agreement. While the form of government was ethnically exclusive, the act provided for only limited government authority, required democratic and public decision-making procedures to be used, required by-laws to be published in English or French as well as an official language, and allowed judicial nullification of band decisions on grounds of illegality.

In 1980, Prime Minister Trudeau announced his plans for massive constitutional reform. He proposed that there be an entirely Canadian amending formula ("patriation of the constitution") and a charter of rights. There were no provisions, however, guaranteeing the special rights of the aboriginal peoples. He stated that he would have the request conveyed to Great Britain regardless of provincial opposition. Eight of the ten provinces objected to the substance of the proposal, and challenged in the courts the government's authority in law and "convention" (i.e. political custom) to proceed with the support of only two provinces (see Schwartz 1981; Schwartz and Whyte 1982-1983; Ackerman 1984). In order to bolster his political position and claim to legitimacy, Prime Minister Trudeau's government tried to satisfy as many special interest groups as possible with respect to the contents of the proposal. In response to complaints from aboriginal peoples, the federal government inserted s.25 into the *Charter of Rights*. Section 25 states that the *Charter* should be construed so as not to interfere with the rights of aboriginal peoples. Later on, in response to intense lobbying by aboriginal groups conducted in both Canada and Great Britain, the federal government put s.35 into the Constitution. Section 35 recognizes and affirms the aboriginal and treaty rights of the aboriginal peoples of Canada. In April 1981, the Supreme Court of Canada ruled that the federal government would be technically within its legal rights, but violative of constitutional convention, if it proceeded without a substantial measure of provincial support (*Reference Re Amendment of the Constitution of Canada* (1981), 125 D.L.R. (3d) 1). In November of 1982, the federal government and nine of the provinces (Quebec excluded) agreed upon a modified constitutional package. One of the concessions the federal government made was to delete s.35. Aboriginal groups responded with a highly energetic last-ditch lobbying effort. Just before the package was sent to Great Britain, the federal government and provinces agreed to re-insert s.35. The word "existing," however, was inserted before "aboriginal and treaty rights." As an acknowledgement of the vagueness of s.35, Canadian governments agreed that there would be a First Ministers' Conference in 1983 to discuss constitutional reform with respect to aboriginal peoples.

At his two post-patriation conferences on aboriginal rights, Prime Minister Trudeau generally confined his substantive comment to sympathetically identifying the main concerns of aboriginal peoples—recognition of title, self-government, cultural survival—and avoided potentially contentious statements of political philosophy. (The actual proposals of his government will be analyzed in detail in various chapters of this study.) Occasionally, however, the political philosophy of *Federalism and the French Canadians* and the white paper surfaced in some of his sharper counters to other participants. In the course of responding to Prime Minister Trudeau's request at the 1983 Conference for a precise definition of aboriginal title, Chief James Gosnell announced that the Indians had "ownership" of British Columbia, "lock, stock and barrel," from "subsurface rights" to "up in the air." The origin of this title was God's gift; through this bequest all of North America was Indian land—Columbus got "lost at sea" (1983 First Ministers' Conference [FMC] transcript, 115). Trudeau responded that God "also sent Columbus across, and at what point do you stop reading history?" (1983 FMC transcript, 127). He concluded: "I don't know any part of the world where history isn't constantly rewritten by migrations and immigrations and fights between countries ... are we going to sit down and bargain what your rights are and where your rights are, or are we just going to repeat historical claims?" (1983 FMC transcript, 128). In the course of a discussion about the application of the liberal norm of sexual equality to Indian bands, in particular, to the definition of their membership, an Indian chief suggested that there was a "collective right" of the overall membership to define "citizenship" (1983 FMC transcript, 263). Prime Minister Trudeau responded that he assumed that "we are all citizens of Canada" and that "whether within this country we can form into groups or tribes or clans or extended families ... is guaranteed by the constitution, the right of association ..." (1983 FMC transcript, 265).

At the 1984 conference, representatives of the Métis argued that "equality" among peoples required that the Métis, no less than the Indian and Inuit peoples, should be a subject of federal legislative jurisdiction. The Métis should not be "second class" aboriginal peoples, insisted Harry Daniels of the Native Council of Canada (NCC) (1984 FMC transcript, 154). Prime Minister Trudeau responded:

> I smiled when Mr. Daniels said that the Métis were second-class citizens. The reason he gave is that they came under provincial responsibility rather than federal responsibility, which means that there are a lot of Canadians who are second-class citizens because except those who live in the Territories, they all come under provincial responsibility as well as Federal (1984 FMC transcript, 161).

and later:

> provinces who argue [for federal responsibility for the Métis] will in effect say that hundreds of thousands of citizens of the provinces will suddenly become more directly under federal jurisdiction ... I say we don't object to an amendment which would take them over as it were, but it does have a lot of consequences in terms of maybe moving towards a more just but less equal society. There will be less second-class citizens

to use Mr. Daniels' expression. Only the whites will be second-class citizens (1984 FMC transcript, 174).

Prime Minister Trudeau's position was essentially that the federal government would be prepared to offer economic and other assistance to the Métis as it would to other "disadvantaged groups", but that he was dubious about extending a form of special political status to another group of Canadians.

The aboriginal organizations differ in their philosophical approach to constitutional reform. The Assembly of First Nations (AFN), the national organization of the status Indians, has tended to follow most closely the history-based groupist approach. They often appeal to the redress of historical injustice as the basis for accepting their reform proposals; they frequently characterize reform as the restoration or recognition of their historic rights, rather than the creative result of a political deal; they tend to favour arrangements that are ethnically exclusive, or which give special status or privileges on the basis of ethnic identity. The philosophical approach of any organization depends in part on the personal philosophies of its senior leaders, and these in turn are partly attributable to individual experience and the free movement of the intellect. Nonetheless, some background legal, historical and social circumstances explain in part the philosophical character of the AFN. The status Indians of today can look back on a period of history when their ancestors had sophisticated governmental structures and fairly well-defined territories which they militarily, politically and environmentally controlled. If an Indian group wishes to argue for a right as the restoration of an old one, there is often a rough historical basis for the claim. Indians may, with some justification, view the history of white-Indian relations as a story of dispossession by an invader. Many Indians have a strong sense of past injustice and of the need to redress it. That treaty Indians have a legal document of some antiquity as a crucial element of their legal and political status encourages them to emphasize past dealings as a basis for constitutional reform. The increasing recognition by the courts of aboriginal title, and the potentially extensive scope of that concept to include self-government, may lead non-treaty Indians to emphasize revitalized tradition as a basis for contemporary political arrangements. A stress on ethnicity as a basis for rights is not surprising from groups who had a distinct identity prior to European arrival, and who have had special constitutional (s.91(24) of the *Constitution Act, 1867*) and legislative status (the *Indian Act*) under Canadian law for more than a century.

The Inuit approach is generally the most liberal individualist of any aboriginal organization. The most ambitious goal of the Inuit is the achievement of a separate territorial government for the eastern Arctic. It would have, initially at least, a majority Inuit population, but would have a public government in which there would be equal rights for all. As mentioned earlier, the Inuit agreed to public regional government in the area of Northern Quebec in which they are a majority, whereas the Cree and Naskapi chose ethnically-based government over their exclusive land bases. While the Inuit mention from time to time that their presence in the Arctic has been instrumental in the assertion and maintenance of Canadian sovereignty in the area, their representatives rarely appeal to past injustice by white society or contributions by the Inuit to justify their present-day political program. ("The history of the relationship between governments and native peoples is a tragic one. We do not want to dwell on these past failings. We are here today because we look to the future. We are seeking to develop a new relationship with government; one based on trust and mutual respect"; John Amagoalik, co-chairman of the Inuit Committee on National Issues [ICNI], 1984 FMC transcript, 37). Inuit representatives do maintain that the Inuit have aboriginal land ownership and use rights which should be given detailed constitutional recognition and protection. Sometimes representatives of the ICNI refer to their firstness as a special ground for respecting their cultural autonomy; at the 1984 First Ministers' Conference, Mr. John Amagoalik cited as an analogy favourable to the protection of Inuit linguistic rights the statement of Opposition leader Brian Mulroney that French language rights should be respected in Manitoba because the francophones were a founding people of the province (1984 FMC transcript, 39). At the 1983 conference, however, Mr. Amagoalik stressed that the Inuit interest in maintaining their traditions was not special pleading:

> The right to cultural survival is a human right, and all these things, all these aboriginal rights that we are talking about, you know, shouldn't be seen as extraordinary rights or anything like that. They are there because we were here first, we had certain customs and traditions and the way we did things before the Europeans came, and we have the right to continue to practice and retain these things. It is a human right, it is not anything special that is given to us by anyone (1983 FMC transcript, 130).

The background conditions of Inuit political philosophy may now be compared with those of the Indians. The Inuit were never numerous in Canada, and to survive they had to spread out along the vast stretch of the Arctic sea-coast. They did not concentrate in small areas, and so never had to, nor did they, develop hierarchical political structures. Appeals to historical analogy are somewhat less helpful to the Inuit on self-government issues than they are to many Indian groups. The sense of historical injustice among the Inuit is generally somewhat different than among the Indian people of Canada. In some ways, the arrival by Europeans in the Arctic seriously harmed the Inuit; they encouraged the Inuit to switch from a subsistence economy to a fur-trading one, and when the fur market collapsed, there was, in many places, mass starvation. The Europeans also brought diseases, such as tuberculosis, to a people with little natural resistance to them. On the other hand, conditions in the high Arctic were extremely harsh prior to the arrival of the whites, and, in some cases, European technology and social welfare assistance improved the living conditions of the Inuit. For this reason, the Inuit do not always have the same feeling of resentment against white society and its state as do the Indians. Another factor which has caused the Inuit to be relatively less interested in redress of past wrongs is that whites came into contact with the Inuit considerably later than they did with the Indians. There has been less time during which the file of historical grievances could expand.

Perhaps the Inuit cultural values have a little bit to do with the negotiating approach of the ICNI: the human ideal of traditional Inuit culture was a laconic, even-tempered, practical person. "These qualities of the ideal Eskimo personality are often mentioned [by modern-day Inuit] in the context of the hardship and misfortune of earlier times, when discipline and good temper were of supreme importance" (Brody 1975, 140). Inuit negotiators at constitutional conferences tend to be succinct, precise, result-oriented; only rarely are there references to the devastating hardship the Inuit have undergone even in this century; practically never is there declamation of white behaviour, past or present.

The Métis National Council tends to advocate groupist solutions on some basic issues; it has proposed the creation of more ethnically-exclusive Métis land bases, and the establishment, with state participation, of an official Métis registry system. The registry proposal would make "community acceptance as well as self-identification" preconditions of Métis status. In a broad sense, the MNC asserts a historical foundation for its group claim; it cites the recognition of the Métis as an aboriginal people in s.35(2) of the *Constitution Act, 1982* and claims that special political rights should accrue to the Métis by virtue of their firstness. There is only limited emphasis, however, on historical practice and legal precedents as the foundations for present-day constitutional reform. The MNC tends to characterize the constitutional reform process as fundamentally political rather than legal.

The specifics of Métis history do not generally support groupist solutions to their contemporary problems. The Métis people were the result of a mixture of the intermarriage and association of people of many different ethnic groups, cultures, languages, and religions. Different Indian tribal groups were involved, and so were various European tribal groups – including English-speaking Protestants and French-speaking Roman Catholics. Many Métis made their living by assisting other groups in communication and trade with each other. While the Métis had certain group structures, such as that governing the buffalo hunt, they also participated in the public government of pre-Confederation Manitoba. They held land on an individual, rather than a collective, basis. While they sometimes claimed certain special hunting and trading rights by virtue of their Indian ancestry, the Métis were held by the British government and courts to be as equally subject to, and protected by, the law as every other British subject (see chapters XVI and XVII). It was consistent with Métis history and practice that Louis Riel sought and obtained provincial status for Manitoba in 1870. He did not demand ethnically based self-government for the Métis, nor did he seek areas of land that the Métis would hold on a collective and exclusive basis. The Métis were allotted individual land holdings by s.31 of the *Manitoba Act, 1870*, and again by the *Dominion Lands Act* of 1879. Apart from certain Métis who opted to "take treaty," the only ones who obtained a collective land base were the beneficiaries of the *Métis Betterment Act* of 1940. As a measure for the relief of poverty, rather than an acknowledgement of special political status, the Alberta government allotted extensive areas for the exclusive use of Métis.

The groupist approach of the Métis in the contemporary constitutional reform process reflects, to some extent, perception of Métis history as an unhappy experience to be avoided, rather than a precedent to be built on. Whereas the Métis were an overwhelming majority of the population of Manitoba when it was made a province in 1870, massive immigration from eastern Canada and, later on, Europe, eventually transformed the Métis into a small minority. The grants of land to individual Métis did not much assist them, according to some Métis, and maladministration on the part of the government, and exploitation by land speculators, resulted in the loss of these holdings.

The groupism of the Western Métis can be partly attributed to a desire on their part to affirm and strengthen their ethnic identity. The statement just made is not tautological. Some ethnic groups in Canada have maintained a strong sense of identity without having or seeking special political and legal status. The Métis, however, face serious challenges in maintaining their special identity. They were never a tightly homogenous group to begin with. The economic foundations of their collective identity—the buffalo hunt, trading, carting—disappeared. A distinct people for less than a century, they did not have a large store of history, literature or music to provide a focus for their identity (Frideres 1983, 271; Olmsted 1983). There did not develop a distinctive Métis language or dialect (although some scholars have claimed that there was, and still is, a distinctive Métis form of expression—which includes a "special accent" to which is added certain old French-Canadian expressions and some original words, probably borrowed from Indian (or Amerindian) tongues (Prefontaine 1980, 164)). The use of the term "Métis" to apply to anyone of mixed Indian and white ancestry, regardless of any descent from the distinct community centered on Red River in the 19th century, has helped to blur the boundaries of the Métis community. Over the years, many Métis left areas of Métis numerical predominance, intermarried, or chose to assimilate. The desire to assert an ethnic identity, to belong to a group, especially one with a "cause," is nowadays evident all over the world. The formidable obstacles to their asserting and maintaining a collective identity may strengthen the belief among the Métis that state assistance in the identification and maintenance of Métis identity is essential to its survival.

The Native Council of Canada was originally supposed to represent both Métis and non-status Indians. As an advocate for the latter, the organization has tended to adopt the history-based groupist approach of the status Indians. The approach is not surprising in view of the fact that a principal political goal of many non-status Indians is to gain or regain official Indian status, or to receive equal treatment with status Indians. As many non-status Indians are non-status because of the operation of the sexually discriminatory s.12(1)(b) of the *Indian Act*, however, the NCC has been a persistent and effective supporter of amendments to the constitution that would apply the liberal norm of sexual equality to the rights of aboriginal peoples, including rights to self-government.

The Philosophical and Constitutional Strategy of this Study

The remaining part of this introductory chapter will recommend a basic approach to Canadian constitutionalism in general and to constitutional reform with respect to the aboriginal peoples of Canada in particular. Part of my thesis is that liberal individualism is a more coherent, more egalitarian, more easily applicable and more widely acceptable political philosophy than history-based groupism. An equally essential part of the thesis is that, in devising legal and political arrangements, Canadian constitutional statements ought, as far as possible, to devise legal formulae and practical structures that advance the goals of liberal individualism but which satisfy, or do as little affront as possible to, those whose ideologies are history-based and groupist. Required are legal formulae that are precise and philosophically modest; and arrangements described by these formulae that are designed with imagination and sensitivity to be workable in practice, but susceptible to varying philosophical interpretations.

This subsection will provide an overview of the basic philosophical propositions that will be argued and the elements of the approach that is recommended. The remaining subsections of this Introduction will elaborate further.

The Political and Philosophical Advantages of Liberal Individualism

The starting point of the philosophical foundation is that the individual is the basic unit of human existence. There is an inherent crudeness in any political philosophy that makes the group a unit of ultimate importance. The insensitivity of the theory may be diminished, but cannot be solved, by a scheme that attributes to groups a level of importance that is equal to that of individuals. Group-based political philosophy is also inegalitarian. The variation among groups so greatly exceeds the variation among individuals that it is in principle, let alone practical application, impossible to determine what equal treatment would be. The "packages" that must be compared under individualism consist of one, and only one, entity who is, in liberal theory, free to determine his or her ends in life. Groups are composed of greater and lesser numbers of individuals; it is often arbitrary whether certain members belong or not; the memberships of different groups intersect; some groups are based on free association, others on custody and indoctrination. As a result, equal treatment of different groups is indefinable in theory, let alone practice. In Canada, the inegalitarianism is compounded by the fact that our groupism is largely based on assessments of the different roles of different groups in Canadian political and economic development. The allocation of rights is forever to be discriminatorily based on an irrevocable past.

Groupism is inherently antiliberal. Many important groups are ascriptive. People belong to them because they are born to members of the group and raised in its traditions. They are not capable, or at least not allowed, to choose whether to continue to belong until they reach adulthood. The group may impose highly illiberal values on persons who were never given a free choice whether to join. When the person comes of age, he or she may be too uneducated to function successfully outside the group, or too indoctrinated to leave. Even a person who freely joins may discover that leaving is expensive; the costs may include the wealth he brought to the group, and the increments to the group's possessions that he contributed during his membership. As a result, a person may not be in a fair position to escape tyrannical decisions of the majority by exiting.

The virtues of liberal individualism just identified are at the level of philosophical principle. Liberal individualism is also superior to history-based groupism at the level of practice. Its lack of reliance on history makes individualism easier to apply. Liberal individualism is more likely than history-based groupism to win and secure the cooperation of the people. History-based groupism creates resentment along those groups denied special privileges and breeds insularity and dependency among the groups advantaged by it. Liberal individualism grants no special favours to any group, and hence, fosters no continuing resentment. It encourages individuals to treat each other as equals and to learn and share from the best in each group.

A final advantage of liberal individualism that will be expounded here is that it provides a strong foundation for the tolerance of group activities, and even considerable grounds for their nurturance and support by the state. On the other hand, history-based groupism provides only minimal grounds for the protection of an individual *per se*, (his well-being may be instrumental to the protection of a group) and justifies the supression of an individual by his own group.

It is not adequate to be in favour of rights, regardless of their colour, charm, and flavour. In some situations, the choice of philosophy produces variant results; in others, the choice of philosophy produces opposite results. Even if the result is the same under either philosophy, the choice of justification may determine its political acceptability. An arrangement that is "objectively" identical may be cheerfully implemented by a government if it is called "municipal-style government for a reserve" but vehemently rejected if labelled "limited political sovereignty for a First Nation." The precedential effect and electoral appeal of an arrangement may very much depend on its philosophical characterization. Practitioners of constitutional politics and their academic critics ought therefore to be reflective about the philosophical foundations for their words and deeds. Sometimes the prescription, sometimes its palatability, depends on these foundations.

Thus far, the reader has been presented with an assertion that there are two contrasting political philosophies that are important to Canadian constitutional life in general; that the tension between them is a central aspect of the debate over constitutional reform with respect to aboriginal peoples; and that some fundamental philosophical and political considerations favour one view over the other.

The Strategy for Constitutional Reform

The discussion is starting to look Manichean. It seems like the theorist would divide constitutional operators into two camps and attribute to one side the superior philosophical virtue. Manichean yes, Canadian no. The Canadian way is to seek the accommodation of different interests and philosophies, rather than insist on a contest in which one line of thought must emerge triumphant. Some of the techniques that are typically used ought not to be. Parties can avoid the conflict that ensues from the assertion of competing philosophies by not articulating what their philosophy is, or worse still, by failing altogether to develop one. Reflection on first principles may lead a party to a framework for action that is superior to the set of principles and prejudices that underlies its feelings about particular issues. The failure of a constitutional actor to work out within its own mind a principled and systematic approach to Canadian constitutionalism is likely to make its interventions inconsistent, unpredictable and erratic. Its position on different issues is even more likely than usual to depend on its short-term interests, rather than an assessment of both its own long-range interests and those of Canada as a whole. The failure to articulate a philosophy that is actually held, in order to avoid confrontation, is sometimes an appropriate exercise of diplomacy, but often counterproductive. Much time and effort may be wasted in discussing solutions that a party finds objectionable at the level of principle. It is usually better that other parties know where a participant stands and attempt to alter its perceptions or accommodate them, rather than allow a prolonged lack of disagreement to stand in the way of ultimate progress.

Philosophical conflict is often not resolved, but merely postponed, by agreeing on verbal formulations that are so vague that they do not offend anyone's ideals. The state of affairs that is supposed to follow from the verbal formulation may be so indeterminate that when it comes time to put it into practice, everything from principle to detail must be debated anew.

The approach to Canadian constitutionalism that is recommended here is that we should work towards arrangements that advance the ideals of liberal individualism, but which satisfy, or do as little affront as possible to, those whose constitutional programs are grounded in history-based groupism. When the positive law of the constitution allows Canadian statesmen a choice, and no reconciliation between conflicting philosophies can be expressed in practical arrangements, then liberal individualism ought to prevail. Often, however, it will be discovered that the arrangement advocated on the basis of history-based groupism can be justified on the basis of liberal individualism. If so, there is obviously the basis for practical progress. Having elucidated their alternate philosophical justifications for a proposed arrangement, various actors can work out a legal formula that specifies what arrangement they have agreed upon, but which is sufficiently neutral in its phraseology that no party finds it objectionable. In some cases, the arrangement proposed by adherents of history-based groupism may be inconsistent with liberal individualism; the best practical course for a constitutional statesman is then to try to explore whether an alternate arrangement can be found which satisfies the basic goals of those who made the proposal, but which is consistent with liberal individualism.

It should be emphasized that the proposed strategy contemplates arrangements that are indeterminate only at the level of ultimate philosophical justification. The concrete, on-the-ground arrangements, should be specified with as much precision as would ordinarily be prudent. (In drafting constitutions, it is usually necessary and desirable to leave some flexibility. The factual and political complexities of a problem may make it impracticable to go beyond a certain level of precision, as constitutional texts are difficult to amend; and some room should be left for interpretations to vary as circumstances change.) To recall a trope I used at the Queen's conference on Aboriginal

Peoples and Constitutional Reform (February 1985), there is a Gershwin song that goes "you like potato (long *a*), I like potato (short *a*), let's call the whole thing off." At the level of pronunciation, two parties may fundamentally disagree. The workable solution may be to have both parties agree on the purchase or consumption of one edible tuber (of the family *solanum tuberosum*). The physical dimensions of the vegetable might be described with considerable precision. No ambiguity at the level of practical operations is entailed by the failure to agree, at a different level, on English pronunciation. In drafting constitutional texts, considerable precision may be possible at the level of practical operations while the ultimate philosophical justification for it remains unsettled. It must be admitted that there will be hard cases in which the application of a constitutional text to a practical situation can only be settled by reference to its ultimate justification. My general strategy applies to interpretation no less than it does to the creation of norms. The interpreter should attempt, as far as possible, to adopt an interpretation that advances the ideals of liberal individualism but which does not offend those of a groupist philosophical persuasion. If no such interpretation is possible, and if the text so permits, a liberal interpretation should be chosen in preference to a history-based groupist one. The losers in such a case would be free to condemn the particular interpretation as mistaken and to continue to value the norm generally useful and theoretically sound.

The general approach just sketched will be embodied in the discussion in this study of a score of issues concerning constitutional reform with respect to the aboriginal peoples of Canada.

The Advantages of Liberal Individualism

An unprovable axiom of my approach is that the only thing ultimately of moral concern is the conscious state of sentient beings. An entity that does not feel sensations and is never aware of thoughts is of no intrinsic moral importance. A painting may be valuable because it gives pleasure or stirs the contemplation of sentient beings; without their reaction, the object is of no significance to anyone, hence of no significance at all. A legal person is of no intrinsic importance either. It is important that what is done about it, or to it, has consequences for a human being, an entity that is alive and aware, and therefore of ultimate moral significance. A concept is of no intrinsic importance. Human dignity does not matter if there are no humans. Animal rights do not matter if there are no animals.

These concepts matter because how they are understood by certain sentient beings—human beings—affects how other sentient beings are treated.

It may be that some day some human will build a computer that can, for all practical purposes, simulate the behaviour of a human being. It would only be of ultimate moral significance if it had some states of consciousness. I should not consider it an ultimate reason against inflicting harm to it that it cried out in agony; I should consider it an ultimate reason against harming it that it felt pain.

There is a marvelous, incomprehensible, but natural organization to states of awareness. It seems that the states of awareness of a single human being are connected. Not necessarily by similarity in character. The baby of today may experience many moments of unreflective joy. The conscious old man he becomes eighty years later may be a bitter mix of brooded-over memories and physical pain. There may be no connection between the individual of today and the individual of tomorrow in moral character. The existentialist murderer of today may tomorrow be a genuinely repentant man of faith. There may be no connection of memory between the individual of today and the individual of tomorrow. A man today is injured in a car accident; he does not and cannot remember what happened the year before the crash. Yet the states of awareness of an individual throughout his life belong to the same distinct ontological order. They are infinitely more connected with each other than they are to the states of awareness of two different individuals. That you believe this is simple to establish. Imagine that you will be administered a drug that renders you an amnesiac; that you will be subjected to mind control techniques that affect your fundamental moral and philosophical beliefs. In many senses, you will be a "different person." Imagine that in this state you will be subjected to physical torture. Do you care about the last eventuality? Are you afraid? Why? Isn't the person a different person? Yes, but your intuition is that when the torture occurs, there will be a sensation of terrible pain, and that it will occur in the part of the universe that "you" feel. Many cultures and faiths have the intuition of the "soul" as a basic ontological constant despite physical, moral and intellectual change. The English language refers to the "individual," the that-which-cannot-be-divided-further. At the core of each of us human beings there is a "subjective realm," a set of states of awareness, that allows us to conceive of an individual as maintaining a unity through time despite all physiological, psychological, intellectual and environmental changes.

The interconnectedness at the primitive level just described is the basis for taking the individual as the unit of political philosophy. The interconnectedness at higher levels is a basic problem for political philosophy. Can we justifiably continue to imprison a person for a crime he committed twenty years ago? What if he has repented? What if he has forgotten? A just state cannot always attribute indefinite responsibility to an individual for the actions of his or her past. The individual is the only coherent basis for political philosophy. The individual is, nonetheless, a deeply problematic basis for political philosophy. What Churchill said (approximately) about democracy—that it makes no sense except that it is better than any other system—applies to individualism as a basis for political philosophy.

The group is an inherently crude basis for a political philosophy. To begin with, the boundaries of a group are almost always indefinite. The status of the offspring of marriages between an Indian and a non-Indian, for example, has been a recurring and vexing question for aboriginal policy in Canada. The sexually discriminatory system of the *Indian Act*—Indian men who marry non-Indian women maintain their status and pass it on to their children, but Indian women lose their status by marrying non-Indian men—was finally abolished in 1985. It was replaced by another problematic system, one which makes Indian status depend on the extent to which a person descends from non-registered Indians. Some people will have Indian status but be unable to transmit it to their children unless they marry a person with at least as much status Indian ancestry. In the 19th century, the intermarriage of white men and Indian women resulted in the emergence of a fairly distinct people in Western Canada, the Métis. The boundaries of the community that has descended from them is highly indeterminate. Is it enough to be of mixed ancestry to be a Métis? Or do you have to descend from a historic Métis? Do you have to identify yourself as a Métis? Do you have to be accepted by the Métis community as a Métis? Any political philosophy that makes group membership a fundamental element of the assignation of rights requires the state to officially classify individuals as belonging or not belonging to a group. But that initial determination is, in many cases, going to be highly arbitrary.

Once the group is defined, the state has to determine what its rights are. In doing so, the state must decide what the characteristics of the group are. Is the group in need of social welfare payments? That depends on whether the group is poor. Does the group need a special boost up the social and professional ladder? That depends on whether the group is historically disadvantaged (see s.15(2) of the *Canadian Charter of Rights and Freedoms*). But any description of the group is bound to misdescribe, and therefore do more than justice, or too little justice, to individuals that belong to the group. Sure, Indians as a group are less prosperous than non-Indians. But some Indians are wealthy, and many non-Indians are desperately poor. Some Indians have been discriminated against in the past, but some have had special political and career opportunities because of their Indian status. The inaccuracy and imprecision that comes from applying group generalizations to individuals is at the heart of the criticism of the worst forms of discrimination. People seem to be dangerously susceptible to applying stereotypes based on colour or ethnic origin to individuals, rather than treating individuals on their merit. When the stereotype is hateful and untrue to begin with, discrimination may be nothing short of heinous. When the stereotype is friendly or fairly accurate, the discrimination may be more benign; it must, nonetheless, result in the unfair denial of rights to some individuals, and very often the partial frustration of whatever social goal is supposed to be advanced by the attribution of rights to the group.

For the purpose of defining and implementing equality, the variety among individuals is always a formidable challenge. The state must determine what characteristics are, or should be, deemed as instinct in all individuals, and what characteristics should produce variations in the entitlements and responsibilities. For all the variety among human individuals, there is a core of shared identify at the most basic level; everyone is born, lives, dies; everyone consists of one, and just one, being whose experiences belong to the same realm of consciousness, one that is forever separate from everyone else's. Comparisons among a very large part of any population are facilitated by the common possession of certain attributes such as the abilities to speak a human language and have conscious purposes. Among individuals, even more so among certain types of individual persons, there is enough ontological similarity that a decent, largely rational, and somewhat successful attempt can be made by a state to define and implement the norm of political and legal equality.

When the equality norm is to be applied to groups, an order of complexity is added to the problem of comparison. First of all, the state must define the boundaries of the groups to be compared. It has already been contended that this task tends to be arbitrary. Once the contours of the group have been defined, it will often be discovered that they are intersected by the boundaries of a state or federal division of a state. Unlike individuals, groups can simultaneously inhabit two different jurisdictions at the same time. The state or federal division may find itself having to figure out how to treat equally a fragment of one group with the half of another with the entirety of another. Even comparing whole groups is conceptually, let alone practically, mind-twisting. The Yungolian and Eastern Eluvian groups both want funding for their school system. Does the state give them equal amounts of money? That wouldn't make much sense if there were twice as many Yungolians. Or maybe it would, if Yungolians were generally able to afford far better than Eluvians the costs of education for their children. In order to make the comparison, the state obviously begins to look at the individual characteristics of members of the groups. Even a determinedly groupist state would find itself incapable of groupwise comparisons unless it made a large number of inquires about individuals. The state will end up calculating where it ought to have started.

Groupist systems of justice must not only try to compare discrete groups, but also groups whose membership intersects. They must also figure out whether there can be such a thing as a group of one; whether there are individuals who do not, or choose not, to belong to any group; and if there are such individuals, how their situation is to be compared to that of the group.

As has been argued in the first part of this chapter, the groupist claims that have been constitutionally recognized, and the ones that are being currently pressed, are history-based. There is no need to press the abstract point about the *inherent* inequality of groupism in Canada because the historical element in our groupism guarantees inequality. Quite simply, every group in Canada has its distinct legal and constitutional history. The Indians of Canada, according to groupist thought, are supposed to have more rights than Ukrainians because Indians were here first. The French-Canadians, according to another line of groupist thought, have more rights than Japanese-Canadians because the French-Canadians were here first. Women, according to another line of groupist thought, are supposed to be the beneficiaries of "affirmative action" programs that discriminate against men, because women have been discriminated against in the past and have to "catch up."

It might be responded that differential treatment based on history is not necessarily unequal. Those whose philosophy is individualist would admit that past conduct and experience is relevant when determining an individual's rights and responsibilities. Cannot a state, which gives equal respect to all groups, take into account their special histories? Would it in fact be unjust not to do so?

There is a basic ontological difference between redressing and rewarding a group, as opposed to an individual, on account of the past. An individual usually has a sufficient identity with his past self such that it is fair to connect the two with a relation of responsibility or entitlement. The same relationship is generally far more tenuous when a group is involved. Contemporary "reverse discrimination" is sometimes justified on the basis of making up for past injustice to a group. But the individuals who will benefit from preferential treatment today may very well have never sustained injustice. There may have been individuals in a previous generation upon whom harm was inflicted or benefits denied, but they will not benefit from the program of today. Preferential treatment in a law firm may aid a young woman who has never been the subject of invidious sex-based discrimination, but it does little to recompense a legal secretary in the same firm whose legal ambitions were half-a-lifetime ago frustrated by the discriminatory policies of law schools.

To be sure, the effects on a group today of yesteryear's injustice may be strong and undeniable. If an Indian band was coerced a century ago into trading a large and rich expanse of traditional land for a small plot of scrub called a reserve, today's members of the band may well be subject to severe poverty. The sense of dispossession that was felt long ago may continue to be felt today. The argument that a group was "here first" may have not only an intense emotional appeal for those who make it, but some real substance. It is a commonplace of our English-speaking justice that vested rights are protected with far more vigour than uncrystallized expectations and speculative hopes. If the government changes the tax law that someone was going to use to save himself some money, there is likely to be grumbling but not outrage. If the government expropriates without compensation the property that someone bought with his tax break of last year, the cry of injustice is likely to be vehemently expressed and sympathetically heard. A conquered people who face the destruction of their political independence and cultural autonomy may feel far more oppressed than a group of immigrants that chose to enter an alien culture with some hope of tolerance but no guarantee of an exemption from social and state pressure to integrate. Had the initial dispossession not occurred, then the conquered people would have been able to pass their traditions on to succeeding generations intact. The chain of injustice may be perceived, perhaps with some justice, as continuing into the present.

When a specific legal or quasi-legal claim, based on a discrete incident, can be established by a group, then it may well be just and practical to satisfy it. When it is shown, for example, that a government appropriated without compensation part of a reserve a century ago, then, regardless of statutes of limitations and other procedural barriers, a settlement of that claim ought to be negotiated. Central to constitutional reform with respect to aboriginal peoples, and many other areas of Canadian constitutionalism, however, are history-based claims that go well beyond a once-and-for-all correction of a particular wrong. Instead, we hear a broad-ranging, long-term remedy proposed for a long chain of alleged injustice in the past. It is suggested, for example, that Canadian governments owe transfer payments to all Indian bands because Indians contributed the entire land base of Canada.

Of these ambitious claims, I would make the following contentions:

(i) their merits tend to be exaggerated by their advocates;

(ii) even more importantly, it is time-consuming, energy-wasting, and enmity-provoking to try to determine the merits of these questions. It is better instead to pursue practical progress today based on the principle of equal justice for all individuals.

To illustrate these contentions, consider the point that the Indians of Canada are forever owed transfer payments because they contributed the entire land base of Canada to Europeans. In reply, it could be observed, the Indian population of Canada was tiny when the Europeans arrived. There were large parts of Canada that were never occupied on any regular basis. (Some Indian groups actually arrived in Canada *after* the European settlers.) But suppose that the Indians were in every case first occupiers and users of all the land. Would it have been right for them not to share their surfeit of land with emigrants from an overpopulated Europe? If the question seems outrageously arrogant, consider whether it would be right today for North Americans to deny a share of their wealth to the impoverished people of the Third World. When the Europeans arrived in North America, there were Europeans back home starving to death or killing their infants because they could not manage to take care of them. In some cases, Europeans paid somewhat reasonable amounts for the acquisition of Indian lands, and these sums (many of which continue today in the form of annuities) must be taken into account in determining how much Indians are owed for their "contribution of a land base." It might also be considered that the use Indians can make of their remaining land has been substantially enhanced by the contribution of European technology or market demand. The oil and natural gas under some of the reserves in Alberta would not be worth much to a people still using stone-age technology; it is worth enviable amounts of money to the Indians who live over them today. The timber on some reserves is a highly valuable commodity today largely because of the demand for it by non-Indians.

Louis Riel offered the following explanation for Métis land entitlements in Manitoba:

> Well, on what principle can it be that the Canadian Government have [sic] given one-seventh to the half-breeds of Manitoba? I say it must be on this ground, civilization has the means of improving life that Indians or half-breeds have not. So when they come in our savage country, in our uncultivated land, they come and help us with their civilization, but we helped them with our lands, so the question comes: Your land, you cree or you half-breed, your land is worth to-day one-seventh of what it will be when the civilization will have opened it? Your country unopened is worth to you only one-seventh of what it will be when opened. I think it is a fair share to acknowledge the genius of civilization to such an extent as to give, when I have seven pair of socks, six, to keep one. (Flanagan 1983, 84).

There can be no doubt, on the other hand, that in many instances Europeans took Indian land without compensation; that they coerced Indians into one-sided treaties; that their overfishing or overhunting, or introduction of pollutants and poisons into the ecology, diminished the usability of lands to Indians. (These are ways in which Europeans damaged Indian proprietary interests; they do not even begin to list the social, cultural, physical and psychological harm the Europeans inflicted upon Indians.) So how do we balance the proprietary right of the original possessors of the land against the claim Europeans could have made to a share of the Earth's surface that reflected the needs of different populations? How do we calculate the benefits of European technology and market demand against the costs of European robbery, extortion, and destruction? The normative questions are highly contentious at the level of principle. Even if agreement could be reached at that level, the determination of the basic historical fact would be a hopelessly lengthy and expensive process. So would an array of non-facts—of speculations about "what might have been if something else hadn't happened or had happened differently". There is, perhaps, no need to say what would happen at the end of all these intellectual and moral contortions because the end would probably never be reached. In the meantime, which might be for all time, the practical business of improving the welfare and opportunities of Canadian aboriginal peoples might be furthered not one iota.

In addition to the imponderability on the level of principle and the unmanageability at the level of application, appeals to special history tend to be uninspiring on the level of political psychology. Proponents of special claims based on history may be too wrapped up in vindicating the past to do enough to improve the infinitely more important future. The audience for special claims based on special history is likely to find them unappealing, even offensive. Most people would rather be asked to contribute to a fund to build a new hospital than pay off a damage claim because they ran into the old hospital with their car. Most Canadians would respond better to a claim for fiscal transfers to aboriginal governments if they were characterized as a step towards the improvement of the the lives and opportunities of aboriginal peoples, rather than as the correction of a wrong done by Canadians in the past. People do not like to be reminded of the wrongs of their fathers or to feel that they have a debt to settle as opposed to a future to build. The inequality of appeals to special history adds nothing to their attractiveness. There is less sympathy for a group demanding special treatment than one seeking no more than equal justice. Later in this study, I recommend the liberal principle of equalization payments, already contained in s.36 of the *Constitution Act, 1982,* as a more solid and stable basis for fiscal transfers to aboriginal governments than compensation for real property received long ago.

History-based groupism either provides no philosophical basis to adjudicate disputes between a member of a group and the group as a whole or authorizes the tyranny of the group over one of its members. Under an individual scheme, the contest is between commensurable entities and values; on the one side, there is an individual who has the right to be free from domination of others, but who has an obligation to honour agreements he has freely entered into; on the other hand, there are individuals whose right of free association entitles them to establish and maintain a miniature society that suits their special vision of the past and future. There are those who believe in history-based groupism, but who also strongly support individual rights (see Garet 1982-83); on what basis do they decide contests between a group and an individual? Others may believe in the primacy of history-based group rights over individual rights; they are necessarily committed to the imposition of the values of the many on unwilling dissenters.

No elaborate attempt will be made in this Introduction to justify, as a general and philosophical basis, the liberal (as opposed to the individualist) aspect of the approach being recommended. (Later in this study, an analysis of the application of the *Charter of Rights* to Indian governments will study in some detail the merits and implications of a constitutional choice of individual freedom over collective control.) A few words are in order at this point, however, on the nature of the liberalism being prescribed. First of all, it is not laissez-faire liberalism but social welfare liberalism. A number of contemporary liberal theorists (Ackerman 1980; Rawls 1971) have offered visions of liberalism in which everyone is entitled not only to liberty and political dignity, but also to a fair share of the material resources of a society. The liberalism that is being recommended here would not only have the state allow every individual the freedom to define and pursue his own ends in life, but also have the state assist him with the education and material resources needed to do so.

Secondly, the liberalism that is recommended here would be appreciative and supportive of the value of groups in promoting liberal goals. State support for multiculturalism in Canada is too often based on objectionable philosophy and worse motives. The objectionable appeal to philosophy is that we Canadians (proud keepers of the mosaic law), in contrast to Americans (stirrers of the melting pot), respect the right of every group to preserve its culture and traditions. Even if we do, and ought to, why should some people be taxed to pay for other people's cultures and traditions? The motive for many contributions is quite likely that traditional groups seem to politicians to be a highly attractive unit in which to buy votes. Contribute some dollars to the Slubrian Dance Group, and a well-organized community will make sure that the generous contribution of the government is known and appreciated. In my view, state funding of multicultural activities is justifiable on the liberal basis that it maintains cultural models and knowledge that are assets to everyone in the community in their attempt to know and practice the good life. The government of Manitoba, for example, subsidizes the cultural activities of a variety of ethnic groups and provides bilingual schooling in various "heritage languages." The schooling aspect can be partly justified as respect for free liberal choice, but bilingual schooling is more expensive than unilingual education, and the subsidies are obviously an extra burden on the general taxpayer. Some of these measures may nonetheless be justifiable in liberal terms. Access to any second language and culture is an important part of a liberal education. It gives a student a basis on which to compare and criticize the values of the general culture and choose more wisely which ones to accept. It also brings a student into potential contact with a set of values that he or she may find worthy of emulation and into communication with a group of people whose association he or she may find valuable. The maintenance of traditional groups in Manitoba ensures that a valuable source of cultural material, and its practitioners, will be available to many people in Manitoba whose liberal education might otherwise be seriously diminished.

Social welfare liberals condemn as radically unjust that a child in a wealthy society should endure material impoverishment. Its theorists have less to say about a child who has only a single parent, no extended family, and no affiliation with a religious or cultural group. But is that child not relatively deprived of human instruction and encouragement? Senator Moynihan has long and ably maintained that the abandonment of families by men is a central cause of poverty in the United States. Should theorists not be at least as concerned about the human deprivation as the material deprivation? Social welfare theory seems to have much more to do with welfare payments than the society of other humans.

Obviously, there are some basic differences between the state allocation of material resources and its intervention with respect to human resources. Material resources have no inherent rights of their own, whereas individuals do; compelling someone to extend his love, friendship or collegiality to someone else would be a violation of his liberty. The state can, if necessary, use force to divide and parcel out material resources, whereas relational assistance that is extended because of state duress may be a simulacrum of what it would be if offered freely.

The theory of social welfare liberalism cannot be as tidy or precise in its application to human resources as it is when it speaks to material resources. But the production and distribution of human support might help to explain many of our laws and policies for which liberal theory tends to give no coherent explanation. Maybe we have tended to favour the traditional human family over other forms because it is likely to be the most reliable source of support for children. In the workplace, we tend to favour equal opportunity over the freedom of association of employers. One explanation is that workplace discrimination denies many individuals a fair opportunity for economic advancement. Workplace non-discrimination may be part of the economics of social welfare theory. Another explanation, however, may be our sense that it is inherently unfair for members of minority groups to have a drastically reduced opportunity to participate in the associations needed to achieve satisfaction in the performance of their vocations. Freedom of association is thus somewhat subordinated to a distributive justice of human association. A further explanation may be that we wish to change attitudes in general; to encourage the development of a society in which people do not because of traditional prejudices deny to themselves and others the benefits of human association. In other words, an attempt is made to enhance both the sharing and the "production" of human association. The political philosophy of liberal individualism does not necessarily view social life as a ruthless competition among individualists. While it denies that the group is a fundamental unit and denies that groups are intrinsically good, it affirms the value of the group as an instrument for the achievement of meaning by free individuals. The affirmation may extend to active state support and encouragement for groups. Liberal individualism is capable of giving a coherent account of the nature and function of groups and, when broadly understood, is capable of endorsing a great many of the claims that are made by adepts of history-based groupism.

The constitutional strategy recommended by this study is that Canadian statesmen should, as far as is legally possible and politically practicable, implement liberal individualism; but in doing so, they should seek legal formulae and arrangements that also satisfy, or disappoint as little as possible, proponents of history-based groupism. The strategy will be illustrated in this Introduction by a discussion of the bitter crisis over French-language rights in Manitoba that began in 1982; the rest of this study will then apply the approach to constitutional reform with respect to aboriginal peoples.

The Range of the Proposed Strategy

Some comments about the range of the application of the strategy. As the previous paragraph suggests, it is intended to have some prescriptive validity across the range of Canadian problems involving group demands, not only those concerning aboriginal peoples. The strategy is also supposed to provide some guidance for "non-constitutional" state activity, and not only that which is based on the creation, interpretation or implementation of entrenched constitutional norms. A principled basis for responding to group demands is of severely limited value if it is confined to the latter. Ordinary legislation can be of the same order of practical and educational importance as constitutional texts. The *Indian Act* has at least as much to say about the day-to-day lives of Indians on reserves, and on Indian and non-Indian attitudes about the just place of Indians in Canadian society, as do all the constitution acts from 1867 to the present.

As is suggested by the preceding discussion of minority-language educational rights, the strategy is intended to be useful with respect to the whole range of Canadian problems involving history-based groupist demands, and not merely those concerning the claims of aboriginal peoples. These kinds of problems are among the most difficult and diverse in Canada today; they include minority-language rights, affirmative action for traditionally disadvantaged groups, denominational school rights, and multicultural policy. In the next section, the operation of the strategy will be illustrated in connection with the fierce political dispute in Manitoba over French-language rights in governmental operations.

The strategy should be useful not only to judges who must interpret (potentially-groupist) sections of the constitution, but to governmental and legislative officials charged with the same task. Constitutional theorists tend to confine their attention to suggesting to courts how they should go about reviewing the actions of other branches of government. Even in those cases where the courts can eventually impose their own sense of constitutionality, however, legislatures and governments ought to exercise self-restraint and make a good-faith effort to determine what is required by the Constitution. Some departures from legality may never reach the courts; others may be sustained by the courts on the basis that, in a close case, respect for democratic process requires giving the benefit of the doubt to politically-responsible branches of government. In those cases where the potentially-groupist constitutional provision is nonjusticiable – i.e., not enforceable by the courts – it is absolutely essential that the legislature and executive exercise sound constitutional judgment. In almost all cases, legislatures and executives have major advantages over the courts in the flexibility they can bring to the solving of problems. Courts can only deal with the cases that happen to come before them, are generally limited in their remedial authority to ordering-about the actual litigants, and cannot implement policies that involve a number of public policy areas. Legislatures and governments, by contrast, can cope with potentially groupist provisions of the constitution by planning and implementing broad-ranging plans of action.

The strategy in this study will be applied primarily to constitutional reform by textual amendment. The decade of the 1980s will be remembered in Canadian history as a time of extraordinary activity on this front. Massive additions to the Canadian constitution are contained in the *Constitution Act, 1982*, and discussions over constitutional reform with respect to the aboriginal peoples of Canada have already produced results, and may produce more. There is already a massive (if pedestrian) literature on how amendments already promulgated (particularly those in the *Charter*) ought to be interpreted. Very little has been contributed by academics to the actual creation of these amendments. The federal government's rush to unilaterally "patriate" the constitution before opposition could be successfully mounted almost obliterated the possibility for independent comment. There was very little time for rumination on the substance of the federal proposals. Whatever time there was tended to be consumed in fulminations over the legitimacy of the federal process. The process of constitutional reform with respect to aboriginal peoples has discouraged academic and, even more seriously, public opportunity for informed comment. For eight or nine months prior to a First Ministers' Conference, various government officials, from bureaucrats to ministers, intermittently convene in secret to discuss positions and exchange proposals. Then there is a First Ministers' Conference. Suddenly a lengthy proposal is released publicly by several participants. Two days of public blather and backroom meetings ensue. At the end of them, the participants may reach a consensus on a constitutional amendment. Granted, personal experience leads me to accept that Canadians tend to be the sort of people who will sit quietly inside a publicly-owned airplane for two hours and never ask why it hasn't taken off yet. Still, it is an embarrassment to a democratic country that the fundamental law of the land can be changed on the basis of secret conclaves and two days of abstract public rhetoric.

The remaining assertion in this section concerns the special role of the courts in upholding the individualist conception of justice. A highly groupist theory of constitutional adjudication is expressed in John Hart Ely's recent work "Democracy and Distrust" (Ely 1980). Ely observes that any satisfactory theory of judicial review must accommodate the fundamental American commitment to popular democracy. Why should a branch of government immunized from political pressure be able to override democratically elected or accountable legislators and executive officials? A common answer is that majoritarian politics may result in tyranny for the minority. The People, in a moment of calm, constitutionally entrench certain constraints on later majoritarian action, and the judges simply enforce what the People earlier decided. The common answer, according to Ely, is not a satisfactory one. It is not democratic to favour the judgment of the dead over that of the living. Ely considers the more modest argument that when courts exercise judicial review, they are upholding the rule of objective law, or more precisely, rules of objective law. It is the specific, written sections of the Constitution that invalidate the actions of the other branches of the government not the will of the courts. All judges do in judicial review is determine whether a challenged action can be squared with this or that provision of the Constitution, interpreted according to the generally accepted canons of construction. Not necessarily so, according to Ely; indeed, necessarily not so. Certain sections of the Constitution are so open-ended that the application of legal techniques determines very little. No state can deny anyone the "privileges and immunities of citizens of the United States" (XIVth amendment); what *are* the privileges and immunities? What is the "due process of law" that the Fifth and Fourteenth Amendments guarantee to every person? What is the "equal protection of the laws" that states must extend to every person (XIVth Amendment)?

Ely proposes a method to interpret open-ended sections that he claims is consistent with a respect for democracy as the fundamental of American constitutionalism. The courts are to view themselves as the referees of democratic process. They do not second-guess outcomes. They merely ensure that the game is fairly played. In certain circumstances, judges should be especially suspicious that the game has not been played fairly. When a "discrete and insular minority" is expressly singled out for adverse treatment, or sustains the worst practical impact, then the courts should demand a justification for state behaviour.

Ely portrays his theory as agnostic among competing theories of substantive justice; the people must decide among them democratically. Ely admits that "positive law has its claims" and would allow the courts to uphold substantive values of liberal individualism when they are undeniably embodied in a particular constitutional amendment. His theory leaves some room for the substantive theory of liberalism to sneak in – and, if its interpreters are bold or disingenuous enough, barge in. The theory of democratic representation cannot mean that groups that constitute minorities of the population can never be treated less favourably than the rest, but it does:

> ... preclude a failure to *represent* them, the denial to minorities of what Professor Dworkin has called equal concern and respect in the design and administration of the political institutions that govern them (Ely 1980, 82).

A judge troubled by the substantive outcome of the democratic process could characterize his intervention as a corrective for the failure of democratic institutions to fairly *represent* the injured litigant. The outcome becomes compelling evidence for the breakdown of equal representation. A strong correlation can be found between outcomes that are unjust according to the substantive theory of liberal individualism and the breakdown of fair representation as defined by Ely. Both are concerned with equal respect and concern from the state. Granted, Ely expressly refers to groups as the beneficiaries of this regard by the state – but he does not deny that every *person* is entitled to equal respect. Indeed, Ely may (imaginatively) be construed as affirming that individuals are entitled to equal representation because Dworkin makes precisely that affirmation in the article Ely borrows from (see Dworkin 1978, 180). The substantive values of liberalism can also be incorporated in the scheme at the point when a judge has to decide whether there is a "compelling state objective" to justify a legislative or executive decision that seems highly suspicious.

While the games may be played to make Ely's world less alien to liberal individualism, the theory is, on the whole, objectionably indifferent to the political vulnerability of the groupless individual. The "discrete and insular minorities" that receive Ely's special sympathy are often, by virtue of their discreteness and insularity, *especially* capable of protecting themselves in the democratic process. (The point is forcefully and thoroughly made in Ackerman 1985; see also Schwartz 1983.) Discrete and insular minorities tend to have advantages in political mobilization such as an established and experienced leadership, a well-developed communications network, a strong sense of affiliation with the group and satisfaction from assisting it, and geographical areas which they are numerous enough to control. The politics of the drafting of the *Canadian Charter of Rights and Freedoms* was dominated by special interest groups, among the most effective of which were "discrete and insular minorities" such as aboriginal peoples, English-and French-language minorities and certain "ethnic" communities. "Discrete and insular minorities" were instrumental in securing a number of groupist amendments to the *Charter*, including s.15(2) (affirmative action for "historically disadvantaged" individuals *and* groups, s.25 (*Charter* to be construed so as to not derogate from rights of aboriginal peoples of Canada), s.18(2) (French an official language of New Brunswick) and s.27 (*Charter* to be construed so as to preserve and enhance the "multicultural heritage of Canada"). Some of these successes, such as 15(2), may prove seriously deleterious to individuals who do not happen to belong to constitutionally privileged groups.

When politics is dominated by special interest groups, a person whose concerns do not coincide with any of them is politically vulnerable. When many of those special interest groups make history-based groupist demands, disregard for individuality may become a matter of real or professed state philosophy and not simply a matter of electoral expediency. Even in a political world where groups have no political advantages over individuals, law makers are liable to pay insufficient attention to the special characteristics and aspirations of individuals. The social world is crowded and complex, and in order to "get a handle on it," law makers may tend to reflect and act on the basis of generalizations about various groupings of individuals.

The courts are peculiarly suited to protecting individuality. Indeed, one justification for judicial review is that courts have institutional advantages not enjoyed by other political branches when it comes to affirming the value of the individual. Courts are more immune than other branches from partisan politics, and hence the pressure of special interest groups, including those making groupist demands. While it is politically practicable for some officials to ignore the complaint of a solitary individual, the judicial system cannot. It *must* hear and decide the complaint of a single person that he is not receiving justice according to law. Senior appellate courts sometimes have discretion whether to hear appeals, but courts of first instance with jurisdiction over the subject matter of a complaint must hear it. They cannot simply tell the individual litigant that he or she is not important enough to warrant their valuable time and attention. Courts are allowed to turn away claims that are "frivolous and vexatious" on their legal merits, but as long as the contention of a person is marginally plausible, a court must give it honest and careful consideration. A court informed about the special circumstances and aspirations of a single person is in a highly advantageous position when it comes to ensuring that the law is sufficiently sensitive to individual differences. The court can then develop an interpretation of a rule that accommodates the individual, or find that a particular law is inconsistent with a higher level of law, up to and including the Constitution.

Canadian courts ought not to disregard the sections of the Constitution which are clearly history-based and groupist. Where the text leaves them a broad range of interpretive choice, however, courts ought to interpret them in a manner that is as consistent as possible with liberal individualism. Section 15(2) of the *Charter* provides that:

> . . . nothing [in the s.15(1) guarantee to every *individual* of equality before the law] precludes any law, program or activity that has as its object the amelioration of conditions of disadvantaged individuals or groups including those that are disadvantaged because of race, national or ethnic origin, colour, religion, sex, age or mental or physical disability.

The section can be construed as altogether preventing judicial review of any program that is aimed at improving the conditions of a group that is subjectively perceived as disadvantaged. It ought better to be construed as saying that s.15(1) does not *necessarily* invalidate reverse discrimination, or even that such programs should be given a sympathetic consideration by the courts. Courts might, nonetheless, review programs to determine whether the factual assumptions of the program are reasonable, and whether there is a plausible chance that the program will achieve its objectives. Courts might invalidate programs that give unfair advantages to one disadvantaged group over another, or whose objectives could be served in a way that is less injurious to individuals who do not belong to the beneficiary group.

Section 23(3) of the *Constitution Act, 1982*, entitles English- and French-language minorities where "numbers warrant" to have their children receive "instruction in minority language educational facilities provided out of public funds." The Ontario Court of Appeal has construed this section as entitling minority language communities to manage their own separate schools (*Reference Re Education Act of Ontario and Minority Language Education Rights* (1984), 10 D.L.R. (4th) 491).

The court held that section 23(3)(b) could not be construed as adding nothing to the requirements of s.23(3)(a). "No one questions," it said, "that paragraph (3)(b) at least means 'minority language educational facilities' separate from majority language education facilities, where numbers warrant" (10 D.L.R. (4th), 491, 527). The court might have had in mind a separate building, although perhaps it would allow a part of a building as long as the educational environment is of the minority language.

The Court found that s.23(3)(b) does more than guarantee a separate place in which there is a minority language educational environment. It noted that the French version of s.23(3)(b) speaks of "établissements d'enseignement de la minorité linguistique." In the court's opinion, the wording denoted that the facility must not only be of the minority language, but must belong to the linguistic minority; s.23(3)(b) imposes: "a duty on the Legislature to provide for educational facilities which, viewed objectively, can be said to be or appertain to the linguistic minority in that they can be regarded as part and parcel of the minority's social and cultural fabric" (10 D.L.R. (4th), 491, 533). The court found that one of the mischiefs that s.23 was aimed at was the situation where a school board dominated by anglophones failed to act to provide French-language instruction. Section 23 should therefore be construed as entitling s.23 parents to some measure of management over French-language facilities. The existing Ontario legislation failed in this regard. To be consistent with s.23 and with the policy already stated in a government white paper on French language education, the court concluded:

- the representation of the linguistic minority on local boards or other public authorities which administer minority language or instruction of facilities should be guaranteed;

- those representatives should be given exclusive authority to make decisions pertaining to the provision of minority language instruction and facilities within their jurisdiction, including the expenditure of the funds provided for such instruction and facilities, and the appointment and direction of those responsible for the administration of such instruction and facilities (10 D.L.R. (4th) 491, 533).

Notwithstanding its decision that a s.23 educational facility must belong to the linguistic minority, the court held that:

> . . . fundamental fairness impels the conclusion that those[non-section 23] parents whose children use

> minority language educational facilities should participate in managing and controlling them.
>
> Although some fears were expressed that this might pose a threat to the linguistic minority, nothing submitted to us indicates that the over-all protection of the minority will be prejudiced. If this should prove wrong in particular situations, s.24 of the *Charter* can be resorted to (10 D.L.R. (4th) 491, 532).

I would applaud the holding of the two paragraphs just quoted, but dispute the court's earlier reference to maintaining the "social and cultural fabric of the linguistic minority." Section 23 as a whole speaks of the rights of people who speak a particular language. It does not recognize rights of any particular ethnic groups.

The position of the French language and the French-language minority will be stronger in any province in which the people view the acquisition of the language as intrinsically desirable and its native speakers as a valuable asset – as a source of teachers of the language and producers of a living and accessible culture. It would promote the appreciation of the French-language speakers, for example, if their children were to help along their anglophone counterparts in immersing themselves in the French language.

It is not impossible to find speeches and articles in which a member of the traditional francophone community warns of the prospect of "assimilation" if its children are sent to schools with children whose first language is English. It is difficult to understand why anglophone children speaking in French to francophone children should cause the latter to abandon their native language and adopt English as their language of ordinary use. It may very well be that children from a French-language community will faithfully accept traditional cultural values if they are denied exposure to other cultures. Any culture of real value, however, should be able to sustain the loyalty of its children even if they are not isolated from other communities. Section 23 should not be construed as guaranteeing a minority *culture* the right to segregate itself, at public expense, from the rest of the public. Section 23 should be understood as a guarantee that certain speakers of a minority language can choose to have their children educated in that language. Generally speaking, as long as there is no significant interference with the linguistic atmosphere at a school, there should be no exclusion of other children from attending it, nor of their parents from participating in its management. The requirements of s.23(3)(b) are met, in my opinion, when there is an educational environment in which children of "s.23 parents" are immersed in the minority language, and the administrators of the school are able to communicate in the minority language.

It would be unfortunate if s.23 were construed in such a way as to preclude maximum co-operation and interchange among parents of different linguistic backgrounds. The Ontario court's ruling that "s.23 parents" are entitled not only to separate classes or facilities for their children, but also to their own administrative and political structures, might interfere with arrangements that produce better communication and understanding. There are grounds for questioning the Ontario court's reasoning. Its judgment banks heavily on the French word "établissement." The court points out that in the Larousse dictionary, "établissement public" is defined as an administrative agency in charge of a public service. It is illogical for the court to cite the administrative connotations of "établissement" when it is combined with the word "public" and ignore the fact that the same Larousse dictionary refers the reader to two, and only two, meanings of the combination "établissement d'enseignement"— namely, "college" and "école" (school). A broad understanding of "établissement" in s.23(3)(b) might encompass not only a building (or part of a building) in which the French language is used in the classroom or schoolyard, but one where the on-site administrators are able to operate in French. The definition need not extend to the level of political management. The court interprets "établissement" in light of the "mischief" it was "intended to remedy." The court notes that:

> Submissions were made that the statements by the Minister of Justice and others making presentations before the Special Joint Committee of the Senate and House of Commons on the Constitution of Canada indicate that management and control of minority language educational facilities were *not* intended to be included in s.23(3)(b). (10 D.L.R. (4th) 491, 529) (emphasis added)

The court immediately ignores this information by holding that: "However it does not appear that reliance should be placed upon specific statements made in Parliament or in committee as to what is contemplated, but rather in the historical context of the new provisions". The court cited three instances in which a local board resisted the creation of French-language schools. Even if we suppose that s.23(3)(b) was intended to "remedy" that sort of problem, would the section not be a sufficient and effective remedy if it created a binding legal requirement that separate facilities be established when numbers warrant?

The wording of the reference question and the court's affirmative conclusion seem to imply that parents have the right to management and control of French-language classes even if they are held in predominantly English-language facilities. The court seems to pay no heed to the fact that s.23(3)(a) contains not a hint that anything but language of instruction is being guaranteed.

Reformers of the provincial education system should create arrangements that ensure maximum co-operation among parents of different backgrounds and educational philosophies. They should aim beyond ensuring that minority language education rights are fully implemented. They should aim at providing to every child the opportunity to be immersed in the other official language. Separate political control for linguistic minorities may not always be sound policy, and, in my opinion, the courts should not construe s.23 as insisting on separate control as an independent right.

Further illustrations could be given, but it is time to reiterate the main point. Political pressure and practical convenience render nonjudicial branches of government susceptible to overlooking the special aspirations of individuals. The independence of the courts, and their case-by-case method of governing, makes them an especially suitable forum for the affirmation of individuality. Indeed, the special advantages of the courts in affirming individuality are a justification for judicial review of the activity of other branches of government. Courts ought to recognize and act upon the vital foundation for their most important powers.

Illustration of the Proposed Strategy in Another Context: The French Language Controversy in Manitoba in the Early 1980s

In 1982-1983, the people of Manitoba engaged in a bitter, divisive controversy over French-language rights in the province. Among ordinary citizens there was an extraordinary political mobilization, most of it vehemently against the government's French-language proposals, but some of it in support. The controversy over this issue illustrates, I would suggest, the philosophical and political advantages of the liberal individualist approach of this study over history-based groupism.

In 1870, when Manitoba was admitted as a province, the population was over 50 per cent French-speaking. Section 23 of the *Manitoba Act, 1870,* the basic constitutional text concerning the admission of the province:

> Either the English or the French language may be used by any person in the debates of the Houses of the Legislature, and both those languages shall be used in the respective Records and Journals of those Houses; and either of those languages may be used by any person, or in any Pleading or Process, in or issuing from any Court of Canada established under the British North America Act, 1867, or in or from all or any of the Courts of the Province. The Acts of the Legislature shall be printed and published in both those languages.

The section is essentially a copy of s.133 of the *Constitution Act, 1867,* which guarantees the same sort of linguistic equality in the federal level of government and the government of Quebec.

A post-admission flood of immigrants soon rendered French-speakers a small minority of the population. In 1890, the province of Manitoba enacted *The Official Language Act,* S.M. 1890, c.14, which purported to make English the exclusive official language of the legislature. Statutes were not translated into French, let alone enacted in that language. In 1892 and 1909, county courts in Manitoba ruled the 1890 statute unconstitutional (*Pellant* v. *Hebert,* 19 March 1892, reported in (1981) 12 R.G.D. 242 and *Bertrand* v. *Dussault,* 30 January 1909 St. B. Co. Ct. (unreported) reproduced in *Re Forest* (1977), 77 D.L.R. (3d) 445). Both rulings were either unknown or ignored by provincial governments.

Another legislative action of 1890 aroused a political and legal agitation of national dimensions. The dual Catholic-Protestant school system was abolished by *The Public Schools Act,* 1890, 53 Vict. c.38. Regardless of whether they sent their children to denominational school, both English- and French-speaking Catholics were required to pay the same taxes as everyone else to support the public school system.

The Supreme Court of Canada held that s.22(1) of the *Manitoba Act, 1870* had been contravened in that a right of Roman Catholics that existed at the time of Manitoba's admission had been denied (*Barrett* v. *The City of Winnipeg* (1891) 19 S.C.R. 374). The Privy Council, the British tribunal which at that time acted as Canada's court of last resort, reversed

([1892] A.C. 445). It noted in a later case, however, that under s.22(2) an appeal lay to the federal Cabinet for the denial of *any* Protestant or Catholic school right, regardless of whether it existed in 1870 (*Brophy* v. *A.G. for Manitoba*, [1895] A.C. 202). Under s.22(3), a remedial decision by the Cabinet could be implemented by Parliament. An appeal was brought to the federal Cabinet and a commission of inquiry was sent out. The Conservative government in Ottawa brought in a remedial bill that would have established a dual Catholic-Protestant school system, with a taxpayer's school contributions going to the institution his children attended. The Liberal party managed to block passage of the legislation and scored a massive election victory, largely on the basis of Quebec returns, based on its defence of "provincial rights" against federal interference. Finally, in 1897, the Liberal prime minister, Laurier, and Premier Greenway agreed on a compromise. In a public school where a high proportion of the students were Catholic, some teachers of that faith had to be employed. A half-hour religious studies period could be set aside every day, and children instructed in the religious class of their parents' choosing. When 10 students in a school spoke French or a language other than English, these children were entitled to instruction in "French, or such other language, and English, upon the bilingual system" (*The Public Schools Act*, S.M. 60, Vict., C.26; discussed in Morton 1957, 271).

The language provision of the compromise was abrogated in 1916 by *An Act to further amend the Public Schools Act* (1916 S.M. c.88). The teaching of many different languages (including French, German, Ukrainian, Polish) was considered to inhibit immigrant children from learning English and to promote social division. No recognition of a special position for the French language was recognized when the provincial legislature imposed a unilingually English system.

In 1976, a Mr. George Forest was convicted of a parking offence in a provincial court. He filed his appeal documents to the county court in French. When the attorney general maintained that there was no valid appeal because the documents were not in English, the county court judge held that *The Official Language Act* of 1890 contravened s.23 of the *Manitoba Act, 1870* (*Regina* v. *Forest* (1976), 74 D.L.R. (3d) 704). Forest was determined to have the constitutional ruling affirmed by a higher court. The attorney general resorted to a series of procedural manoeuvres and motions to prevent the language issue from being heard by a superior court on the merits. No one much cared about the five dollar fine (and costs) assessed against Mr. Forest on the original ticket. Eventually the Manitoba Court of Appeal heard an application for a declaration that *The Official Language Act* of 1890 was unconstitutional. The declaration was issued (98 D.L.R. (3d) 405). It was affirmed by the Supreme Court of Canada in a 1979 ruling (101 D.L.R. (3d) 385). Manitoba's constitutional authority under s.92(1) of the *British North America Act, 1867* to amend the "constitution of the province" did not, ruled the court, extend to s.23 of the *Manitoba Act*. Section 23 was part of the Constitution of Canada.

As the Supreme Court was asked only to answer a general legal question, rather than dispose of Forest's parking case, the implications of the unconstitutionality of *The Official Language Act* of 1890 did not have to be spelled out. One obvious possibility was that all the statutes and regulations of Manitoba enacted after 1890 were unconstitutional. Not only might there be no laws, but there might be no courts. The constitution of courts is a provincial subject matter, and the Manitoba statutes purporting to establish them might be void. There might also be no legislature capable of restoring judicial order by enacting bilingual laws; the would-be legislators had been elected under a unilingual elections act.

Insufficiently panicked by the *Forest* judgment, a Progressive Conservative government enacted a statute purporting to give interpretative supremacy to the English version of statutes (*An Act Respecting the Operation of Section 23 of The Manitoba Act in Regard to Statutes*, S.M. 1980, c.3). The statute also implied that the printing of a French translation of a statute satisfied the constitutional requirement of s.23 articulated in the companion case of *Forest – Attorney General of Quebec* v. *Blaikie* (1980), 101 D.L.R. (3d) 394 – that statutes be enacted in *both* languages. Most statutes continued, in 1980 and 1981, to be enacted, printed and published in English only.

The New Democratic government that won the provincial election in 1981 ensured that most of its new statutes were enacted in both English and French. Amendments to existing unilingual statutes, and some private acts, were published in English only. Ninety years of accumulated statutes, or attempted statutes, remained untranslated.

A 1980 speeding ticket to another Franco-Manitoban, Mr. Roger Bilodeau, advanced the judicial vindication of s.23 that the *Forest* case had begun. Bilodeau argued that the ticket was invalid because it was not in both languages, whereas s.23 allowed that any person "may use either French or English in the Courts". More importantly, he argued that the ticket was a nullity because *The Highway Traffic Act* which authorized it was enacted in English only. Section 23 provides that statutes "shall be printed and published" in English and French. The provincial court judge hearing the matter held that s.23 was "directory," rather than "mandatory," so the consequences of noncompliance were nil (*R.* v. *Bilodeau,* [1981] 1 W.W.R. 474).

In a split decision, the Manitoba Court of Appeal affirmed the lower court ruling that s.23 was "directory" only (*Bilodeau* v. *A.G. Man.*, [1981] 5 W.W.R. 393). The reasoning was consequentialist. The court of appeal did not first doctrinally determine the mandatory/directory distinction issue and then figure out the implications; it contemplated the chaotic implications of finding s.23 to be "mandatory," and accordingly it was not. Counsel for Bilodeau had proposed that the court follow a middle course: it should decree a timetable the legislature must follow in enacting a French version of the statutes. The English-only statutes would be valid in the meantime. Chief Justice Freedman tersely rejected the proposal as "inappropriate" for a Canadian court.

In a dissenting opinion, Mr. Justice Monnin held that "of necessity" he would find operative the statutes of Manitoba enacted prior to the decision of the Supreme Court of Canada in *Forest.* There was no excuse after December 13, 1979, however, for enacting English-only statutes, and all of them were invalid.

The government of Manitoba had little reason to feel secure as a result of the court of appeal's decision. The special position of the Supreme Court of Canada made it likely to be less forgiving of the province's default. A national institution, the Supreme Court of Canada, would be impressed by judgments coming out of another province, Quebec. According to these decisions, the wages of the sin of unilingual enactment is death. (For the statute, of course, not the legislators.) The Supreme Court of Canada would be expected to concern itself with the protection of the numerically and proportionately large English-language minority in Quebec, as well as the tiny French-language minority in Manitoba. The unique authority and prestige of the Supreme Court of Canada would encourage it to be more confident than the Manitoba Court of Appeal on the scope of its remedial powers. Perhaps the Manitoba Court of Appeal reasoned that a mild judgment would give the province some time to set its house in order through a vigorous translation effort or a constitutional amendment. The Manitoba court could count on the Supreme Court of Canada to more strongly vindicate the rule of constitutional law.

Under s.43 of the *Constitution Act, 1982*, s.23 of the *Manitoba Act* could be amended by the joint action of the

Manitoba legislature and the federal House of Commons and Senate. The provincial government thought that an amendment to s.23 might forestall a major constitutional crisis arising from a Supreme Court of Canada ruling in *Bilodeau*. It entered into negotiations with the federal government. Roger Bilodeau was involved. So was the non-official, cultural organization to which he belonged, the Société Franco-Manitobaine. Many members of the traditional francophone community were members of the organization, and its position on the *Bilodeau* matter was consistent with that of many, though far from all, nonmembers. Without much consultation with the public, a deal was reached. (The Official Opposition *was* informed of the substance of the deal that was about to be made and said nothing. Was the Opposition's silence motivated by a desire to see the government inadvertently provoke a backlash?)

Bilodeau would drop his appeal. In return, Manitobans would support a constitutional amendment to s.23 that would:

- declare English and French to be the official languages of Manitoba
- limit the translation of past statutes (about 4500) to the four-hundred-or-so statutes of most relevance to the Franco-Manitoban community
- move in stages to enact all new statutes in both languages
- give any member of the public the choice of English or French as the language of communication and service delivery with respect to:
  - (i) the head or central office of provincially-constituted agencies and departments of government, courts, and crown corporations;
  - (ii) the chief electoral officer
  - (iii) the office of the provincial ombudsman
  - (iv) any other office where there is significant demand for services in the language of choice, and the nature of the office makes it reasonable for it to communicate and provide services in that language (section 23.7, paraphrased, of the Draft Resolutions; the proposal was strongly analogous to section 20 of the *Canadian Charter of Rights and Freedoms*.

The government explained the proposals as a pragmatic solution to a serious legal threat. The proposals would direct governmental attention and money to operations that would offer practical benefit to the francophone community in Manitoba. The French-language service guarantees were the "quid pro quo" (in the language of the attorney general, Roland Penner; Hansard, 4 July 1983, 4061) for the elimination of the duty to translate and to re-enact almost a century of unilingual statutes. The only general benefit of the proposals that the government cited was that by helping a francophone community to thrive outside of Quebec, the proposals would contribute to "Canadian unity" (Hansard, 4 July 1983, 4066).

The Official Opposition Progressive Conservatives immediately expressed strong opposition to the proposal. Their leader, Sterling Lyon, claimed in the legislature that his party was not opposed to the expansion of French-language services by ordinary legislation. The entrenchment of broadly worded constitutional provisions, however, would transfer policy-making authority from the legislature to the courts. The constitutional package devised to settle one law suit, that of Roger Bilodeau, might result in constant, socially divisive litigation by "zealots." The implications of the package for the public service were unpredictable and partly beyond legislative control. The official languages policy of the federal government, contended Lyon, had resulted in linguistic hiring quotas and a subversion of the merit principle. There were no guarantees that a similar state of affairs would not develop in Manitoba. The amending formula established by the *Constitution Act, 1982* would require the consent of the federal Parliament before a Manitoba legislature could reverse, through constitutional amendment, unforeseen and onerous decisions of the courts.

The Opposition successfully insisted that there be extensive public hearings on the proposal, and on several occasions engaged in "bell-ringing" tactics. When a recorded vote is called in the legislature on any matter, including a motion to adjourn, the "division bells" (actually buzzers) are sounded in the legislative building to warn members of all parties that a vote is going to be held. According to some precedents, the bells cannot be turned off and the vote held until the whips of the government and Official Opposition parties agree. An opposition party can block a legislative program it opposes by letting the bells ring for extensive periods. The only checks on this obstructionist power of the Opposition are public disapproval and the authority of the speaker to terminate the bell-ringing. (After an extensive bell-ringing episode in the federal Parliament in 1982, the speaker (later governor general), Jeanne Sauve, established the precedent of adjourning the legislature and turning off the bells.)

A nominally non-partisan organization, Grassroots Manitoba, was formed. It organized a series of rallies at which a succession of speakers would condemn the government proposals to the cheers of an enthusiastically negative audience. A number of municipalities in the province, including the City of Winnipeg, exercised their authority under provincial municipal statutes (s.92 of *The Municipal Act*, S.M. 1970, c.100 and S.112.1 of *The City of Winnipeg Act*, S.M. 1971, c.105) and placed the language issue before the voters at the Oct. 26, 1983, round of municipal elections. The vote against the government's position (the issue was phrased differently by different municipalities) averaged about 75 per cent. The preponderant number of submissions and presentations to the legislative committee on the language bill were in opposition to the package. On December 15, 1983, the government house leader, Andy Anstett, introduced in the legislature major revisions in the language package. The most important was that the service delivery provisions were removed from the constitutional proposals and replaced by a draft piece of ordinary legislation. (The legislation was far more detailed than the constitutional provisions it had replaced.)

Opposition to the government plans did not relent. The more rational criticism concentrated on the reworded opening clause:

> 23.1 As English and French are the official languages of Manitoba, the freedom to use either official language enjoyed under the law of Manitoba in force at the time this section comes into force shall not be extinguished or restricted by or pursuant to any Act of the Legislature of Manitoba.

It was contended that the official language declaration, which the government defended as strictly symbolic, might be the inspiration or justification for excessive judicially-imposed extensions of bilingualism. There were also concerns that the constitutional protection of "rights in force" would encompass a highly indeterminate set of legally recognized practices—including, perhaps, those contained in the proposed legislative packages on services. Had the Opposition been more interested in developing a constructive solution to the impasse, and the government a little less battle-weary and a little more open to constructive suggestions, an alternate draft of s.23.1 could have been the keystone of a legislative solution that would have received support from both parties.

Although the mass opposition within Manitoba to the government's proposals continued, the government's proposals were strongly endorsed by editorial writers in Ontario and

Quebec. All three national political parties – the governing Liberals, the Official Opposition Progressive Conservatives, and the New Democratic party – agreed upon a resolution urging the prompt passage of the package.

The provincial Progressive Conservative party stepped up the frequency and length of its obstructionist tactics. On February 3, after the Official Opposition had held its fifth bell-ringing walk-out in seven sitting days, the minister of health, Larry Desjardins, said that he expected the speaker to put an end to the paralysis of the legislature. The speaker responded that his duty of impartiality and an earlier agreement between the House leaders limiting bell-ringing to two weeks (and implicitly legitimating episodes of up to two weeks) made it inappropriate for the speaker to intervene (see Winnipeg Free Press 7 and 13 March 1984, 7). A motion by the government to limit bell-ringing episodes was itself rung out of existence. Faced with mass public opposition, an 11 per cent approval rating in the opinion polls, and an inability to overcome the blockade in the legislature, the government prorogued the legislature. The language proposals automatically "died on the order paper." The Bilodeau case proceeded to a full hearing before the Supreme Court of Canada.

Concerned that the Bilodeau case might be disposed of by the Supreme Court on the basis of facts that would not be relevant to many other cases, or that the Supreme Court might rule on a narrow ground that would leave the general legal status of Manitoba laws uncertain, the federal government decided to refer four questions to the Court. The judicial response they would require was expected to provide guidance on the Manitoba language question that was explicit and general. The appeals were heard on June 11, 12 and 13, 1984, and judgment was rendered on the reference questions on June 13, 1985. The Court decided to hold off disposing of the Bilodeau action itself until a later date. Here are the questions and the Court's answers:

Question 1 - Are the requirements of s.133 of the *Constitution Act, 1867* and of s.23 of the *Manitoba Act, 1870*, respecting the use of both the English and French languages in

(a) the Records and Journals of the Houses of Parliament of Canada and of the Legislatures of Quebec and Manitoba, and

(b) the Acts of the Parliament of Canada and of the Legislatures of Quebec and Manitoba

mandatory?

Answer - Yes.

Question 2 - Are those statutes and regulations of the Province of Manitoba that were not printed and published in both the English and French languages invalid by reason of s.23 of the *Manitoba Act, 1870*?

Answer - Yes, but, for the reasons given by the Court, the invalid current Acts of the Legislature will be deemed temporarily valid for the minimum period of time necessary for their translation, re-enactment, printing and publication.

Question 3 - If the answer to question 2 is affirmative, do those enactments that were not printed and published in English and French have any legal force and effect, and if so, to what extent and under what conditions?

Answer - The Acts of the Legislature that were not enacted, printed and published in English and French have no legal force and effect because they are invalid, but, for the reasons given by the Court, the current Acts of the Legislature will be deemed to have temporary force and effect for the minimum period of time necessary for their translation, re-enactment, printing and publication.

Question 4 - Are any of the provisions of *An Act Respecting the Operation of section 23 of the Manitoba Act in Regard to Statutes*, enacted by S.M. 1980, Ch. 3, inconsistent with the provisions of s.23 of the *Manitoba Act, 1870*, and if so are such provisions, to the extent of such inconsistency, invalid and of no legal force and effect?

Answer - If *An Act Respecting the Operation of section 23 of the Manitoba Act in Regard to Statutes*, enacted by S.M. 1980, Ch. 3, was not enacted, printed and published in both official languages, then it is invalid and of no force and effect in its entirety.

If it was enacted, printed and published in both official languages, then ss. 1 to 5 are invalid and of no force and effect.

The short answers are justified in lengthy accompanying reasons. The mandatory/directory distinction is rejected because of "the harm that would be done to the supremacy of Canada's Constitution if such a vague and expedient principle were used to interpret it." The consequence of a government's failure to honour s.23 must be a judicial declaration of the invalidity of laws that do not comply with it. According to the joint opinion of the Court:

> The judiciary is the institution charged with the duty of ensuring that the government complies with the Constitution. We must protect those whose constitutional rights have been violated, whomever they may be, and whatever the reasons for the violation. . . .
>
> Since April 17, 1982, the mandate of the judiciary to protect the Constitution has been embodied in s.52 of the *Constitution Act, 1982*. This section reads:
>
> 52(1) The Constitution of Canada is the supreme law of Canada, and any law that is inconsistent with the provisions of the Constitution is, to the extent of the inconsistency, of no force or effect.

The Court found, however, that one aspect of the Rule of Law had a saving effect on the Manitoba legislation. On the one hand, according to the Court, the Rule of Law meant in part that the law is supreme over government as well as private individuals; s.52 of the *Constitution Act, 1982* embodied this aspect of the Rule of Law and required the Court to declare the Manitoba legislation to be invalid and of no force and effect. On the other hand, another aspect of the Rule of Law "requires the creation and maintenance of an actual order of positive laws which preserves and embodies the more general principle of normative order. Law and order are indispensable elements of civilized life." The Court noted the express recognition of the Rule of Law in the preamble to the *Canadian Charter of Rights and Freedoms* and its implicit recognition in the preamble of the *Constitution Act, 1867* (Canada is to have a "Constitution similar in Principle to that of the United Kingdom"). The Court went on to say that the Rule of Law must have been intended by the founders of Canada to be "one of the basic principles of nation building" and that "the Court may have regard to unwritten postulates which form the very foundation of the Constitution of Canada." The Court cited as authority for the latter assertion the dissenting opinions of Martland and Ritchie JJ. in the *Patriation Reference (Re Resolution to Amend the Constitution)* (1981), 125 D.L.R. (2d) 1), both of whom found the "federal principle" to be such an "unwritten postulate." Actually, Martland and Ritchie JJ. did not characterize the "federal principle" to be such an "unwritten postulate." They held that it was derivable from the written preamble and the written federal-provincial division of powers. Furthermore, most of the judges in the *Patriation Reference* (Dickson, Beetz, Estey, McIntyre, Lamer) had joined in an opinion that the federal principle did *not* as a matter of law (as opposed to judicially unenforceable, political convention) prevent the federal government from moving to unilaterally patriate the Constitution.

In any event, the Court concluded that the "normative order" aspect of the Rule of Law did not permit the Court to hold in such a way that would "deprive Manitoba of a legal order": "For the Court to allow such a situation to arise and fail to resolve it would be an abdication of its responsibility as protector and preserver of the Constitution". Accordingly, the Court ruled that from the day of its judgment, all laws in Manitoba must be enacted bilingually or be held invalid; past statutes were valid only for the "minimum time necessary" to translate and re-enact them in both languages. The record before the Court was not sufficient to permit it to determine what "minimum time" meant. The attorneys general of Canada or Manitoba were each authorized to come before the Court within 120 days of the judgment and ask the Court to set a special hearing at which the deadline would be further defined.

The Court rejected the several alternatives to placing the remedying of the constitutional default under judicial management. Counsel for the attorney general of Manitoba argued that the lieutenant governor could ensure that s.23 was suitably honoured by withholding assent from bills, or reserving them for the judgment of the governor general; see ss. 55, 57, 90 of the *Constitution Act, 1867*. The Court observed that these powers have not been exercised in recent years, and concluded:

> The fundamental difficulty with the Attorney General of Manitoba's suggestion is that it would make the executive branch of government, rather than the courts, the guarantor of constitutionally entrenched language rights. It should be noted that a decision of a provincial Lieutenant Governor as to whether to withhold assent or reserve a bill is not reviewable by the courts.

The Court rejected on similar grounds the suggestion by six intervenors that the federal power of disallowance (again, not exercised in recent years) could be brought to bear on an otherwise recalcitrant legislature.

The Court nowhere explains how, on a reference case – a request for a non-binding advisory opinion – the Supreme Court of Canada can declare that, from the date of its judgment forward, such-and-such is the new constitutional state of affairs. Nor does it adequately justify its repeated assertions of judicial supremacy. The *Constitution Act, 1867* expressly provides for control over the legislative process by the lieutenant governor and governor general. It also sets out federal and imperial powers of disallowance. It nowhere expressly provides for review of the constitutionality of legislation by the judiciary. The Judicial Committee of the Privy Council, which for eight decades acted as Canada's constitutional court of last resort, is nowhere mentioned in the *Constitution Act, 1867*. Section 101 authorizes Parliament to create a General Court of Appeal for Canada, but there is no mention of its having constitutional supremacy, or even the last judicial word. The Supreme Court of Canada is a creature of federal statute. Sections 41 and 42 of the *Constitution Act, 1982*, provide the formulae for amendments to the constitution with respect to the Supreme Court of Canada; but apart from s.101, it is not clear that at present there are any constitutional provisions that specifically relate to the Supreme Court.

The Supreme Court's judgment was the only wise and prudent alternative. My only criticism would be that the Court did not recognize with sufficient candour the textual difficulties with its claim to supremacy. The Court did not explain why the opinion of the courts should be the decisive one on a legal question charged with high constitutional policy.

The Court might have developed a justification for its assertion of authority on two fronts: it could have attacked the historical standing and intrinsic suitability of other methods of controlling constitutionality, and it could have emphasized the long Canadian history, reaffirmed and extended in 1982, of judicial control over constitutionality.

The attack on executive control of constitutionality could mention that the imperial power of disallowance over federal legislation was abolished by convention in 1930 and may well be legally obsolete because Canada is in no sense a colony anymore; see the *Canada Act 1982*, s.2. The courts thus remain the only apolitical arbiter of unconstitutionality. The possibility of executive control does not, in any event, relieve a court of its own duties to enforce the law of the constitution; what happens, for example, if a case gets to court before the two years available for federal disallowance has elapsed? Furthermore, executive authorities have traditionally left it to the courts to determine legal questions of constitutionality. Before it fell entirely into disuse, the federal government adopted the policy of leaving it to the courts to adjudicate the constitutionality of provincial legislation, as long as serious harm to the federal or public interest would not occur in the interim. When *The Official Language Act* was passed by the Manitoba legislature in 1890, the federal cabinet approved the following report by the minister of justice concerning possible federal disallowance:

> The power of the provincial legislature to amend or repeal this section of the Manitoba Act, so confirmed, admits of great doubt. The validity of the Act under consideration may be very easily tested by legal proceedings on the part of any person in Manitoba, who is disposed to insist on the use of the French language in the pleadings and process of the courts or in the journals and Acts of Assembly. As it is apparent that a large section of the people of the province desire that English alone shall be used in such matters, and that a very considerable section desire the provisions of the Manitoba Act upheld in this particular, there can be little doubt that a decision of the legal tribunals will be sought at an early date, as to the validity of the present legislation. A judicial determination of that question will be more permanent and satisfactory than a decision of it by the power of disallowance (Dept. of Justice 1896, 928).

The executive powers of reservation and disallowance are not suitable for the protection of individual or minority rights because they are, by convention, subject to political control. The lieutenant governor and governor general, by convention, act on the advice of the cabinet or first minister. Intruding on the determination of constitutionality may be such extraneous considerations as party politics, federal-provincial relations, and the government's policy position on related policy questions, as well as the one directly at stake.

The positive case for the role of the courts as constitutional guarantors would cite the long history in Canada of judicial review of the actions of other branches of government. It would be pointed out that in the last major round of constitutional reform, in 1982, legal constraints on legislative and executive action were massively increased by the entrenchment of the *Canadian Charter of Rights and Freedoms*, and the courts were expressly granted broad powers to fashion remedies for non-compliance; *Charter* s.24. (Included in the *Charter* are a number of minority language guarantees.) The Canadian tradition of judicial enforcement of the constitution was thus implicitly affirmed and expressly extended by the *Constitution Act, 1982*.

The Court's decision was, in effect, an invitation to the political parties to make a further effort at arriving at a constitutional deal. The Supreme Court of Canada acted much the same way in the *Patriation Reference* (1981), 125 D.L.R. (3d) 1. By holding that unilateral federal action was legally permissible but contrary to convention, the Court set the stage for the November, 1981 deal which resulted in the *Constitution Act, 1982*. It is a plausible guess that the Court would have been very relieved had a deal been made in the Manitoba context. Determining how fast the translation and re-enactments of Manitoba statutes must take place might have required the Court to immerse itself in complicated, time-consuming questions of fact. The Court might be left, moreover, with no choice but to make some prudential judgments on which it had no special expertise and which might undermine its earlier affirmation of principle. (If the Court says that it would be unduly expensive for a legislature to have to do all the translations in six months, is the Court not in a position of trading off money against principle?) Unfortunately, neither party was prepared to move. The provincial government immediately made it clear that there would be no initiatives on its part. It appears that the government concluded that any gesture on its part would revive anger among the public against the government and that the same sort of opposition, both reasonable and irrational, would arise with respect to any new proposal. The Official Opposition expressed no interest in a deal, perhaps because a reasonable settlement would defuse what it regarded as one of its best issues on which to bash the government at the next election.

The attorneys general of Canada and Manitoba and the Société Franco-Manitobaine did succeed in reaching agreement about the next step in the litigation. They all supported a timetable of translation submitted to the Supreme Court on November 4, 1985. It stipulated periods during which various classes of statutes and regulations would continue to be valid. The Court was not strictly bound to accept the agreement of the parties, but did so in a terse order on the same day.

An important caveat must be made here. It will be seen very shortly that there have been many proposals for "nonjusticiable" amendments to the constitution. These kinds of amendments are binding on the executive or legislative branches of government, but are not enforceable in the courts. The Supreme Court's claim in Bilodeau to be the "guarantor of the Constitution" could be construed as implying that nonjusticiable amendments are not possible. The Supreme Court was not called upon, however, to consider these kind of amendments, and the Court probably would not go so far as to dismiss such amendments as impermissible. It should not. The *Constitution Act, 1982* characterizes the constitution as supreme (and not any particular institution). If the constitution stipulates that another branch of government is to have the final say on the meaning of a constitutional provision, the courts ought not to impose their own judgment.

Does the condemnation of history-based groupism apply to the French-language controversy in Manitoba? Would the strategy recommended in this Introduction apply?

The government of Manitoba defended its proposals primarily as a practical solution to a serious threat, rather than on any lofty philosophical ground. In several respects, however, the government put a history-based groupist cast on the process. The proposals were first presented as a completed deal arising out of negotiations with Bilodeau, the Société Franco-Manitobaine, and the federal government. The impression was created that the proposals were a concession to one special interest group in the province, and that the status of the French language belonged to that one special interest group, rather than being a matter of general concern and benefit. The only intrinsically positive aspect of the deal cited by the government was that it contributed to Canadian unity—a suggestion which many Manitobans undoubtedly took as an invitation for them to sacrifice themselves for the greater good.

The federal minister responsible for funding Bilodeau's court challenge, Secretary of State Serge Joyal, was openly history-based and groupist in his rhetoric in a speech to the Société Franco-Manitobaine:

> I do not need to tell you, all of you have learned your history, as have all we Francophones, so we remember because we are rooted in history. And if there is one group that has built this country, if there is one group that has built this province, here in Manitoba, it is Francophones. As you are well aware. I do not need to recount the first 50 years of Manitoba's history to you.... we don't want to take anyone else's place, we want the place which is ours by right because we built this country. Our ancestors built it here. It was Francophones who were founders of Manitoba, along with the representatives of the native people at that time. It is easy enough to trace Manitoba's history in the Eighteenth and early Nineteenth Century. This is the Manitoba reality.

Joyal observed several times in his speech that it was in the general interest to maintain linguistic diversity in Canada; the only explanation he offered, however, was that diversity helped to maintain the Canadian identity. His appreciation of the political sensibilities of multiculturalism in Manitoba was confined to noting that:

> We have to learn to reconcile the equal status of the two languages in Canada with the needs of the other cultural communities that make up the country. That's important, paramount, and in this province and the western provinces in particular, it's a fundamental issue whose facets and implications we are going to have to discuss in the coming months. And it won't be easy, believe me.

The Joyal speech was quoted with gusto by vehement *opponents* of the government of Manitoba's proposal. The leader of the Opposition, Sterling Lyon, read from it extensively in the legislature in the course of his major speech on the language issue (Hansard, 12 July 1983, 4272-4274). The organizers of the massive Grassroots Manitoba rally held in Winnipeg went to the trouble and expense of copying and distributing copies of the speech to the audience.

Many Manitobans were offended by what appeared to be the granting of a special privilege to one, and only one, ethnic group in Manitoba. Their feelings were not in the least soothed by being told that the group had contributed more than any other to the building of the province. Even if the claim was true, why was it relevant? Some opponents of the language deal insisted that the demography of Manitoba changed radically after 1870 as a result of an influx of immigrants from Ontario and Eastern Europe. The operation of government in Manitoba, they argued, should reflect the reality of the province, not the situation in a distant past (Winnipeg Free Press, June 23, 1985, 7). Not that there was much inclination among opponents of the legislation to accept the validity of the historical claim. Many Manitobans undoubtedly regarded the claim that the francophones contributed more than any other group as untrue as well as irrelevant. On what basis was the labour of impoverished farmers and factory workers in the 20th century to be discounted related to the contribution of francophone and Métis trappers and traders in the 19th century? The more historically informed could well have questioned whether, even in the 19th century, the francophones contributed most to the development of the province. The British (mostly Scottish) officials who served with the Hudson's Bay Company contributed much to the development of the province. No less than the French-Canadians in western Canada, the British mixed with the Indian peoples, and half of the "half-breeds" in Manitoba in 1870 were English- rather than French-speaking. The Selkirk Settlers, mostly English-speaking, contributed greatly to the establishment of permanent urban settlements in Manitoba. Credit must also be given to the Indians of Manitoba, who were certainly in western Canada, including Manitoba, prior to the arrival of any French-speakers.

Some ethnic leaders expressed strong support for the French-language proposals. They argued that if the position of one ethnic community were advanced, there would be a precedent for assisting others (Globe and Mail, 27 July, 1983, 1). There can be no doubt, however, that a sense among ethnic Manitobans that one group was being singled out for especially favourable treatment was a major source of discontent with the legislation. There was a strong sense that not only were the other groups not equally benefitted, but that the need to learn French in order to work in the public service or government would work to the prejudice of the careers of the children of non-francophones.

The liberal, egalitarian, non-historical and individualist approach recommended in this Introduction would have suggested a far different constitutional package and marketing strategy to Manitoba politicians.

To begin with, the government would have been careful to portray itself as acting in the interests of all Manitobans. Public opinion would have been canvassed far more thoroughly before proposing any package. The "deal" with one special interest group, the Société Franco-Manitobaine, would not have been presented at first as an immutable deal. There would have been less emphasis on the "imaginary horrible" that might take place if no deal were reached. The possibility of the Supreme Court's plunging the province into legal chaos was very small, and by making that possibility the major ground for its proposals, the government appeared to be yielding to a extortionate threat. (In actual fact, Bilodeau and the Société Franco-Manitobaine both argued before the Supreme Court of Canada that the province should be allowed a certain period of grace in which they could, and would be required to, catch up on the translation and re-enactment of the statues.)

In proposing a package to deal with the language issue, the government would not have initially proposed that service delivery in French be constitutionally guaranteed, as opposed to embodied in ordinary legislation. The fears of pro-francophone discriminatory hiring in the public service, for example, would have been allayed if the people were assured that they could revise the service delivery provisions in the light of experience. While entrenchment may be reassuring to a political minority, it may be equally threatening to the political majority. The entrenchment aspect of the service delivery package might have raised anxieties among the public. If French-language service delivery was fair and reasonably economic, why would the public not be trusted to support it in the future?

The government should have attempted to sell the expansion of the language provisions as a project that would benefit Manitobans. No historical explanation was needed for giving a certain priority to French, rather than other heritage languages in Manitoba. The simple facts are that a limit on official languages is necessary in order to save on government expense. More importantly, as Canada is a political community, it is vital to its democratic vitality that people should be able to understand each other. The more official languages there are, the more people are encouraged to speak languages that many or most of their fellow citizens do not understand. In participation or evaluation of public life, it is highly valuable to be able to directly understand what others are saying. As Manitobans are also Canadians, they should be encouraged to learn the official languages of the larger political community in which they have a voice – and hopefully, an ear. If the number of official languages is to be limited, why English and French? Again no historical explanation is needed. You can just look around and see that French and English are, by far, the most widely-spoken languages in the country.

Quite apart from the considerations of convenience and democratic participation that argue in favour of supporting French-English bilingualism, the government could have cited the intellectual and cultural benefits of knowing more than one language. A person equally able to operate in two languages has a much wider world in which he or she can comfortably participate.

Instead of having a policy directed towards supporting the francophone community, the government should have had a policy of supporting the teaching and use of the French language. The francophone community could have been seen as a positive asset to everyone in the province – as a source of teachers of the language and as the promoters of cultural activities in which the language is used. The provision of governmental services in French would be justified as part of a policy of keeping alive a common resource for the province – a far more attractive idea for most Manitobans than that of granting special privileges to a small group because of a long-ago historical agreement.

Manitoba could have been the first province to announce a policy of entitling children to learn either English or French. As explained earlier in this chapter, constitutional language guarantees in the Canadian constitution are all minority-language rights. A French-speaker in Quebec, for example, has no right to learn English. Only the child of English-speaking parents does. There are in Manitoba tens of thousands of English-speaking children in French immersion programs, and many French-speaking children going to English schools. The government could have announced that it would, as soon as finances and available teachers permitted, ensure that every child who wished to could be educated in the other language. Doing so would have helped to allay the concerns of parents that their unilingual children would be discriminated against and would have emphasized that language policy in Manitoba was for the benefit of all Manitobans, not a privileged minority.

The government could have made a special reiterated commitment to providing, where finances permitted and numbers warranted, "heritage language schooling" – education in languages other than English and French. The priority given to English and French would not be to the exclusion of government support for other languages and cultures. In its final proposals, the government did attempt to give some acknowledgement to multiculturalism by adding s.23.9(2):

> This section shall be interpreted in a manner consistent with the preservation and enhancement of the multicultural heritage of Manitobans.

The government also actually attempted to reassure Manitobans on many of the points that follow, but might have been more persuasive had it issued a formal policy statement or embodied the reassurances in draft legislation. Among the reassurances that might have been formally stated:

- that there would be no hiring preferences on the basis of francophone ethnic origin, as opposed to linguistic ability

- that except for certain positions, such as translators, public service hiring would continue to be on the basis of merit, with merit assessed without regard to French language ability. A person hired or promoted to a position requiring French language skills would be given a publicly subsidized opportunity to learn French.

- that English would generally continue to be the internal working language of the public service of Manitoba, and no position would be declared bilingual unless French language ability is essential to the effective and efficient performance of the job (including communication with the public and members of the legislature). (Section 23 of the *Manitoba Act* probably does not require that French have equal status with English as the internal working language of the public service. The section may, however, entitle members of the legislature to French versions of any public service which they require for the performance of his official function.)

The decision of the Supreme Court of Canada in the Manitoba language reference has removed a gruesome hypothetical from deliberations on the position of the French language in Manitoba. The liberal individualist strategy recommended in this Introduction would suggest that the government of Manitoba now attempt to vigorously promote the teaching and use of the French language in Manitoba, not as a concession to one special interest group among many, but as creating opportunities for all. The French-language community might then be appreciated as an indispensable contributor to those opportunities.

Application to Constitutional Reform with Respect to the Aboriginal Peoples of Canada

What now follows is a legal and policy analysis of constitutional reform with respect to the aboriginal peoples of Canada, from patriation in 1982 to the 1984 First Ministers' Conference. There will be a critical account of the political negotiations leading up to each First Ministers' Conference and then a series of essays on various proposals and issues that were discussed during the year. Whenever possible, an attempt will be made not only to fairly present and evaluate the decisions and suggestions that have been made, but to present original and constructive recommendations.

Before proceeding, it may be useful to recap the basic features of the approach that will be taken to the analysis of police issues:

(i) The "liberal individualism" referred to above is not laissez-faire on economic issues, nor is it indifferent to the importance of association with others as an individual attempts to achieve his or her own ends in life. The study is based on social welfare forms of liberalism (of the kind in Rawls' *A Theory of Justice* and Ackerman's *Social Justice in the Liberal State*) and is sensitive to the value of free association and the desire of many individuals to participate in the preservation and enhancement of the culture of their traditional group.

(ii) In cases of irreconcilable conflict, liberal individualism is to be preferred by reformers over the accommodation of history-based groupism.

(iii) A gualification on (ii) is necessary. It is not recommended that constitutional reformers "roll back" existing constitutional rights that can only be characterized as groupist. Notwithstanding the theoretical weaknesses of history-based groupism, it can be unjust for a government to renege on previous promises or commitments to a group. A group unilaterally stripped of its entrenched rights (e.g., its treaty rights or traditional rights to the use of land) is not likely to cooperate in devising new arrangements that are practically beneficial and consistent with liberal principles as well as groupist ones. Existing constitutional group rights may appropriately be reduced, however, if necessary for the protection of the fundamental rights of individuals.

(iv) The merits of each substantive issue must be closely examined. Indeed, the assessments of various policy issues in this study can be understood and appreciated in their own right, independently of the identification of a more general approach. Among the factors that must be taken into account in evaluating a possible new arrangement are:

- does it at least take into account basic human rights and ensure that the individual has some protection against his or her own group?
- does it recognize that the member of a traditional group continues to have some rights and responsibilities in the wider community?
- does the arrangement have a reasonable basis of political support in the wider community and in the traditional group and is that support likely to continue? No reform arrangement is likely to function as agreed without the continuing cooperation of all parties;
- is the arrangement administratively feasible? The administrative structure of an arrangement should not be so complicated and costly that excessive resources and attention are diverted from the substantive goals the arrangement was designed to achieve;
- is the arrangement formulated in a way that is flexible enough to take account of the diversity of the different groups to which it applies and to allow some room for changing circumstances through time?
- at the same time, is the arrangement well enough defined that it does not entail high costs, prolonged delays, and bad feelings while the parties fight out too much unsettled business?
- is the arrangement too costly in terms of resources that might have been diverted to other, equally worthy, measures to promote individual rights and social justice?

The evaluations in this study on aboriginal self-government might be enumerated here to help illustrate the overall pattern:

- The movement towards enhancing the self-government of Indian reserves is endorsed. Local self-government is consistent with liberal individualist principles; at the present time, Indians on reserves have less control over their local affairs than do the residents of most municipalities. (Indian self-government will differ in some respects from other forms of local self-government, as Indians will want to retain their special land rights and special link to the federal government.) The *Penner Report*, which strongly endorses enhanced Indian self-government, is criticized somewhat for failing to recognize that aboriginal self-government must be limited by various liberal principles.
- The study supports the efforts of the Inuit to establish public governments in areas in which they form a majority. The "citizens" of these governments will have equal rights, regardless of ethnic origin. The aspirations of the Inuit to have local governments that understand and are responsive to their needs will be met. Yet no one will find himself a second-class citizen as a result. The Inuit approach is recommended for the Métis as well.
- The fiscal resourcing of aboriginal government is identified by the study as a key issue. Experience shows that local negotiations on aboriginal self-government will be severely complicated and delayed unless a larger framework of fiscal responsibility is established. It is believed that the appropriate level of support by the federal government can be justified by analogy to the liberal principles contained in the existing equalization provisions (s.36) of the *Constitution Act, 1982*. There is no need to rely on the theory that aboriginal peoples are "owed" by the general public for their past contributions. Just as it is argued that the residents of aboriginal communities are equally entitled to share in the nation's wealth, so it is maintained that the complete exemption of residents of reserves from taxation by the federal government ought not to be continued.
- It is maintained that the *Canadian Charter of Rights and Freedoms* ought to be applied to aboriginal governments; but that s.25 of the *Charter* should be construed by the courts as a signal to not apply *Charter*

norms mechanically, but rather to take into account the special circumstances of aboriginal communities.

The strategy of statecraft presented in this introductory chapter will be the framework for the analysis and prescriptions that will be presented in many different contexts.

Chapter II

The Preparatory Stage

The Lead Up

The November Accord of 1981 deleted from the federal constitutional package a section which "recognized and affirmed" the aboriginal and treaty rights of the "aboriginal peoples of Canada" (Sheppard and Valpy 1982, 293-294, 307-308; Zlotkin 1983, c.4; Romanow, Whyte, and Leeson 1984). Intense last-minute lobbying by aboriginal organizations led to its restoration – with one serious qualification. The word "existing" was added. No one could know exactly what effect the courts would give the word "existing," but then, nobody could know what the rest of the section meant in the first place. It is still unclear what "aboriginal rights" are; whether they include, for example, self-government as well as land use rights. The extent to which s.35 protects its contents from future legislative infringement is undetermined; "recognize and affirm" may mean anything from recognize at a merely symbolic level to guarantee in an indefeasible way. "Existing" may not have altered the meaning of the section, or it may have imported every qualification on aboriginal rights on April 17, 1982 – including legislative supremacy (Slattery 1982-83; McNeil 1982; Lysyk 1982). Sometimes the context of an ambiguous legal phrase helps to determine its meaning. In section 35, each individual ambiguity contributes to the excrescence of interpretive possibilities.

In acknowledgement of the vagueness of s.35 and the feeling of aboriginal groups that their rights should be more fully specified and more firmly secured, section 37 was added to the proposed *Constitution Act, 1982*. It required that within a year of the coming into force of the new Constitution, there would be a First Ministers' Conference, the agenda of which would include "an item respecting constitutional matters that directly affect the aboriginal peoples of Canada, including the identification and definition of the rights of those peoples to be included in the Constitution of Canada, and the Prime Minister of Canada shall invite representatives of those peoples to participate in the discussions on that item."

In preparation for the March '83 meeting, a series of officials and ministerial meetings were held to agree upon an agenda for First Ministers and possibly lay the groundwork for possible agreement by First Ministers. (The Constitutional authority to approve of constitutional amendments is vested in the House of Commons and Senate and provincial legislatures, so approval by First Ministers has, in itself, no legal effect; *Constitution Act, 1982*, s.28, 41.) In October, 1982, an officials' level meeting was held in Winnipeg to begin preparations. The Assembly of First Nations (AFN), the organization representing status Indians, boycotted the meeting, and all subsequent ones prior to January 1983, on the grounds that constitutional reform should result from bilateral, Indian-federal negotiations. It was the position of the AFN that the provinces have no legitimate role in Indian affairs; that bilateral Indian-federal talks could take place on the Constitution, with federal government duty bound to obtain provincial assent to any agreements reached; and that s.37 did not recognize the Indians as equal partners in constitutional reform, only as invitees of the other governments (Zlotkin 1983, 53). Eventually the AFN reversed itself and attended the meetings of spring 1983. The value of the meetings that were held in the absence of the AFN was diminished by the lack of input from this aboriginal organization, which has the largest membership and the most political influence. When the AFN finally did participate, it was necessary to return to many items that had already been discussed with the Inuit Committee on National Issues (ICNI) and the Native Council of Canada (NCC) (which then represented both non-status Indians and Métis).

Quebec representatives attended throughout in an ambiguous role; you might say that they began as interested observers and ended up as non-voting participants. After the patriation of the Constitution in 1982, without its consent, the government of Quebec took the position that it would not participate in federal-provincial meetings except for those concerned with economic matters. At the March First Ministers' Conference, Premier Levesque stated three conditions for Quebec recognition of the *Constitution Act, 1982*: that there be a constitutional guarantee of full compensation in all cases of a province's opting out of a constitutional amendment; that Quebec's powers over language and culture be fully restored (if they are impaired by s.23 of the *Canadian Charter of Rights and Freedoms* which guarantees minority language educational rights) and the recognition of not merely individual, but also collective rights in the constitution, including recognition of "l'existence, l'identité d'une autre nation tout aussi distincte que n'importe quelle autre et qui est concentrée au Québec" ('83 First Ministers' Conference [FMC] transcript, 48). According to Levesque, while individual rights are, to a certain point, fundamental, a collection of individuals has a distinct reality and character which must be recognized. Whether aboriginal and treaty rights are collective or individual and what is to be done when the interests of an individual conflict with those of his or her aboriginal collectivity are fundamental issues in the s.37 constitutional reform process.

The talks leading up to the March '83 Conference consisted of the aboriginal groups presenting various extensive proposals for constitutional reform, often in the form of a draft aboriginal charter of rights. The federal government and provinces generally reacted by asking for more information and clarification. Occasionally they hinted; infrequently, they plainly said that a particular proposal was acceptable. Rarely did a government have a positive suggestion of its own. It can be argued that the syntax of the meeting implied an understanding of the s.37 process as follows: the constitutional status quo is presumptively acceptable to governments; aboriginal organizations have the burden of explaining and justifying changes to it; governments pass judgment on whether an aboriginal proposal is acceptable; acceptance of a proposal is a concession to aboriginal peoples at the expense of society generally. For those governments interested in damage control, as opposed to long term social or constitutional reform, the game was an easy one to play. A government can stall indefinitely and never incur the political damage of having to say "no" to anything aboriginal peoples demand. It need merely ask, *ad infinitum*, for more clarification. While it never hurts governments to ask, there are political costs to aboriginal groups in answering. Doing so may require qualifications of the general rights they have claimed, thereby weakening its bargaining position; or it could require the contentious internal settling of an issue that was initially left ambiguous because of disagreement among different factions within the group.

The overall design of the '83-'84 process of meetings was that officials' level meetings would identify issues and options for ministerial meetings, which would in turn result in an agenda and a list of policy or drafting options for ministers. From the beginning of the s.37 process, however, a recurring set of problems has rendered officials' meetings of limited and sometimes no utility. Government bureaucrats are at times not authorized to express opinions, or claim that they are not in order to avoid taking any potentially embarrassing positions. Some aboriginal organizations are composed of disparate, often conflicting factions. At officials' level meetings, there is less incentive for the latter to work out a single, collective position. Representatives of various factions are often allowed to express themselves freely. At higher level meetings, by contrast, the political position a group takes may influence high level politicians on the other side, and whatever any delegation says cannot be easily disavowed in the future. Aboriginal organizations are therefore forced to determine and articulate with some precision what their positions actually are. Officials' level meetings often involve the exchange of mutable and minority positions from aboriginal organizations and no opinions at all from governments. To the limited extent that they are edified, government officials tend not to pass on their new found enlightenment to their political superiors. Even with the best efforts, an official might fail to distill from two or three days of rambling talks what is most informative or politically significant; and conveying that essence to a harried Minister is not easily accomplished. It is particularly difficult for an official to discern and convey the subtleties of emotion and attitude embodied at a meeting; yet these may be just as important as the formal policy positions.

It was not until February 1983 that some provinces and the federal government first disclosed that they were amenable to having a further series of constitutional conferences on aboriginal rights. During most of the preparatory process, the aboriginal organizations had no reason to be confident that the March '83 conference would not be the last one to which they would be invited. In the absence of any guarantee that there would be any further federal-provincial talks on aboriginal rights, it was impossible for participants to arrive at a limited and manageable agenda. All the aboriginal groups could do was insist that the agenda include everything. They did and it did.

The agenda for the First Ministers' Conference was that jointly proposed by the aboriginal groups at a ministerial conference in February '83, and it encompassed every issue of possible constitutional concern to aboriginal peoples. Some of the issues were even stated several ways. Aboriginal self-government, for example, could have been discussed under item 1 in the context of "preamble," "particular rights of the aboriginal peoples," "statement of principles," item 3 as "self-government," item 5 as "resourcing of aboriginal governments."

Some of the repetition was a result of the unwillingness of aboriginal groups to risk prejudice to their legal or political positions. The AFN consistently claimed that it was prepared to discuss self-government only in the context of "aboriginal rights." It did not want to discuss "self-government" as an independent item if that in any way suggested that there was not an inherent aboriginal right to self-government. The MNC, on the other hand, did not want its claims to self-government ignored by governments which tend to the view that the Métis have no aboriginal rights at all.

Redundancy in the agenda was also caused by uncertainty over drafting format. Some of the provinces had proposed that a statement of non-binding principles be temporarily placed in the Constitution to guide further discussions. The aboriginal groups had presented long lists of binding constitutional rights. The federal government had drafted proposals on a few specific issues, including sexual equality in the employment of aboriginal rights, the repeal of subsections 41(1)(e) and (f), and consultation with aboriginal organizations on amendments to certain parts of the Constitution. The aboriginal groups considered it appropriate for the agenda to include not only the whole range of issues, but also the whole range of drafting approaches.

It is possible that if governments had reached a consensus well before the March '83 conference to have further ones, a more focused agenda might have been developed for the benefit of First Ministers. There might have been more progress on substantive issues. Had governments agreed to further meetings early in the process, however, they would have denied themselves the favourable public relations effect of agreeing on further meetings at the March '83 First Ministers' Conference.

On March 7, 1983, the Métis organizations of the three Prairie provinces broke away from the NCC and formed the MNC. They brought an action in the Supreme Court of Ontario a few days later to enjoin the Prime Minister from convening the conference scheduled for March 15 and 16. The NCC no longer represented the Métis people of Canada, they claimed, so the prime minister would be in default of his duty under s.37 to invite "representatives of the aboriginal peoples of Canada" unless the MNC were invited. The NCC had, up until then, represented both the non-status Indians and Métis of Canada.

The distinction between the two groups is a contentious matter. It depends on how you define Métis. If a Métis is defined as a person of mixed Indian and non-Indian ancestry, then many non-status Indians across Canada qualify as Métis. Many Métis in Western Canada, however, adopt a nationalistic rather than a racial definition of Métis. They claim that the Métis were a distinct ethnic groups which became conscious of and fully realized its own identity in Western Canada in the 19th century. The Métis nation, they say, was centered around the Red River settlement in Manitoba. A person is not a Métis simply because of mixed ancestry; rather, he must identify himself as a Métis and be accepted as such by the successor community of the original Métis. The MNC adopted the nationalistic conception in its legal presentation to the Supreme Court of Ontario.

As the NCC, like all aboriginal organizations, was permitted two seats at the conference table, an obvious compromise would have been to permit one speaker to represent the Métis and non-status Indians in Canada generally and another to speak for the Prairie Métis. At one point there was such an agreement but it broke down because of strategic and personal differences (*AMNSIS* v. *Trudeau*).

In the end, the application for an injunction was dropped after the federal government agreed to invite the MNC to the table. In doing so, the federal government risked creating a precedent for factions of a national aboriginal group to demand separate representation. In such cases, the federal government might end up embroiled in an internal dispute within an aboriginal organization; and if, over the objections of the umbrella organization, it recognized further factions, it would be adding to the unwieldiness of the bargaining process. Despite the risk, the federal government had little choice but to allow both organizations seats at the table. It could not in good conscience permit tens of thousands, perhaps hundreds of thousands, of people who identify themselves as Métis to be unrepresented at the conference.

That the NCC still represented about a fifth of Canada's Métis by the MNC's own definition might not, in itself, have justified its continuing presence at the table. The non-status Indians of Canada, however, had to be represented at the table, and the AFN could not be relied upon to do so. Non-status Indians cannot vote in the elections of the band governments that make up the AFN and, to some extent, have conflicting interests with its members; the reinstatement and return to reserves of non-status Indians might be seen by some band members as a threat to their culture and material well-being. If a splinter group of the AFN ever tries to attain a separate seat at the table, the federal government can argue that the status/non-status distinction is a more important legal and political difference than that between, say, treaty and non-treaty status Indians.

One defect in political representation at the s.37 conference was never raised by any of the participants. There are tens of thousands of status Indians living in Canadian cities; the numbers will steadily increase. There are unresolved but fundamental issues about their participation in city life, such as whether the federal government is fiscally responsible for providing them with social services (predictably, the federal and provincial governments disagree) and whether they should be allowed special status of any sort, including the privilege of running their own educational or social welfare systems. If and when Indian First Nations governments are created, the scope of their jurisdiction over off-reserve Indians will have to be determined. Yet there is no assurance that any of the present participants in the s.37 process will adequately express the concerns of the urban status Indians. The AFN is composed of band governments. Urban Indians who wish to participate in band politics face not only practical difficulties but legal restrictions – such as residency requirements in band elections. Urban status Indians who would lobby the AFN or other s.37 participants can face serious organizational difficulties, including the dispersal of Indians in some cities, and meagre and episodic funding from provincial and federal governments.

Chapter III

The March '83 Conference

The March '83 conference began with a prayer by a member of the Assembly of First Nations (AFN). This practice had become established during the series of preparatory meetings. When the AFN again instituted a prayer ceremony at the beginning of the second day, Prime Minister Trudeau asked with obvious irritation, "Will you pray every morning in public?" (1983 First Ministers' Conference [FMC] transcript, 174). When Dr. Ahenakew, national chief of the AFN replied, "Yes, sir," Mr. Trudeau said, "Everyone should pray to his own God, and we will have a moment of meditation." After the Indian prayer was through, Prime Minister Trudeau recited in French the Lord's Prayer. The Prime Minister who allowed "the supremacy of God" to be inserted into the preamble of the *Canadian Charter of Rights and Freedoms* was in a compromised position from which to defend secularism at public meetings. (People who live in stained glass houses . . .). Nonetheless, there was some justification for the Prime Minister's attitude. The pragmatic objection to the ceremony was that it was time consuming. The principled one was that it put the religious belief of some Indians in a privileged position; no one else at the meeting asked everyone else to stop everything and listen to one of their religious invocations. (It may be assumed that Prime Minister Trudeau's mid-conference statement to an AFN leader, "Well, God bless you if you are going to deal with citizenship", was not meant in earnest.)

After the morning prayer of the first day, the AFN passed around a peace pipe. Photographs of the ceremony made front pages across the country. A (surely unintended) side-effect of the Indian ceremonies was that it encouraged public attention to focus on *Indian* issues, rather than on all three aboriginal peoples equally. The Inuit Committee on National Issues (ICNI) took a business-like approach at both '83 and '84 conferences; at the former, their opening speaker kept his remarks extremely brief in the interests of getting on with substantive discussions. The Métis National Council (MNC) did not make any attempt at ceremonial displays until the end of the '84 conference when it presented a sash to the prime minister. In one respect, the Indian ceremonies benefitted all of the aboriginal groups involved. They attracted media attention and helped engage the audience of the live television broadcasts. Drawing public attention to aboriginal issues is a vital use of s.37 conferences for aboriginal groups. One of the hardest obstacles to reform in any area is forcing a government to confront the issues. The public interest in aboriginal rights issues encourages governments to attend to them – and not only on the constitutional plane.

Most of the first day of the conference was consumed by the opening statements of the seventeen participants. As the prime minister read his, the federal proposals on constitutional amendments were circulated. As mentioned earlier, the federal and several other governments had submitted draft proposals on a number of issues in February. Delegations were thus technically prepared for many of the federal proposals and politically aware of how they might fare. Even before the conference began, it was generally believed that there was a good chance of constitutional progress on entrenching further meetings and on a few substantive issues. As will be seen in subsequent sections of this discussion, however, the federal proposal contained a number of significant novelties – including the "statement of principles" (known among some of the delegates from aboriginal organizations as the "bullets").

When open discussion began in the middle of the afternoon on the first day, it centered on the meaning of "aboriginal title," an issue on which the federal proposal said very little. The essential work of analyzing and refining the federal proposal took place that evening in a closed ministerial level meeting. The meeting was conducted under intense pressure – it began at 8:00 in the evening and concluded at 10:35. The minister of justice proposed that the parties reach a "conceptual agreement," and that federal drafters work through the night to prepare a legal draft reflecting that agreement. All decisions were subject to the approval of First Ministers. Had the latter vetoed substantial parts of the agreement of the evening, there probably would not have been sufficient time to construct a new one. Agreement was reached at the backroom meeting on some major points. One was that there would be not only a constitutional amendment guaranteeing further meetings, but also a political accord that would govern the period before the amendment could come into force. At the suggestion of some provincial governments, as well as aboriginal organizations, the preamble to the federal draft on the ongoing process was dropped. There was general, although not universal agreement, that there should be a clause guaranteeing sexual equality with respect to the rights of the aboriginal peoples. Several suggestions were made, but no consensus reached, on drafting changes. One of the aboriginal organizations, with the support of a provincial government that had been lobbied beforehand, suggested that the clause be added to s.35 of the *Constitution Act, 1982*, rather than s.25, and that the rights be "guaranteed equally" rather than "apply equally." There was discussion of the legal implications of the changes, and it is probable that few participants fully appreciated them. The transfer to s.35 was effected in the federal draft of the next morning, and the word "guaranteed" added after the ministerial drafting session of the next afternoon. The net effect of the changes may be to substantially bolster the legal protection given to *all* aboriginal rights and treaty rights by s.35(1).

The initial suggestion of the minister of justice that the federal officials work overnight to produce a legal draft based on the evening's discussion was carried out. It certainly facilitated progress that the single most powerful participant undertook to prepare a revised draft. Under the time constraints of the two-day conference, some expedient had to be used to crystallize the discussions. There were, on the other hand, serious risks implicit in the procedure. One was that the federal government would, in good faith, misperceive what had been agreed to. Another was that the drafting proposal would not benefit from the extensive and wide-awake reflection of many politicians and technicians, as opposed to that of a couple of federal lawyers who had already put in a very long day. One more was that it would be discovered that, on a particular point, nothing had been agreed to – leaving the federal government free to make up whatever solution suited its purposes. The possibility was also left open that the federal government would draft what had been agreed to "conceptually" and adopt legal phraseology that suited its own policy purposes but severely frustrated the aspirations of other participants. An apparently minor change in wording can have radical implications in terms of legal meaning, and ultimately a significant effect of the people's lives. Legal drafting can never be the faithful translation into an arcane language of what has been agreed to "conceptually." Instead, a dialectic process takes place. People have policy ideas. A legal expression of them is attempted. Out of a nebulous "conceptual agreement", there suddenly emerge disagreements that had not been perceived before, questions that had not been conceived before. Further discussions have to take place. Perhaps there will be concessions or novel alternatives developed at the policy level. Perhaps the disagreements or new concerns that have emerged will be ignored; others will be fogged over by making the language more vague. A new draft is attempted. And so it goes, until a stable solution is reached.

At the beginning of the First Ministers' session the next day, the federal draft accord and amendments were distributed to delegations. Mr. MacGuigan provided an oral commentary on them. One of the "bullets"–statements in the preamble to the initial federal draft on ongoing process that aboriginal organizations had found objectionable–reappeared unchanged in the preamble to the political accord. It referred to the education of aboriginal children in their own languages "as well as within one of the official languages of Canada, in order that their children may be equipped to live in the cultural milieu of their choice." As there had been general agreement to drop the statement of principles the previous evening, there was no justification for trying to slip in the philosophically portentous clause in the political accord. Mr. Watt of the ICNI (now a member of the Senate of Canada) objected to it almost immediately. Another aspect of the federal draft that might have been objected to on procedural grounds was its introduction of a clause on modern land claims agreement. Drafts of a clause had been submitted to preparatory conferences by the ICNI, and representatives of that organization had lobbied for it on a cross-Canada tour of governments they made just before the conference. It had not, however, appeared in the federal draft of the previous day. At the end of the ministerial meeting, Mr. Watt reminded the minister of justice about the ICNI's proposal on land claims agreement, and Mr. MacGuigan undertook to prepare a provision with respect to it. The provincial delegations had no comment on that undertaking one way or the other. The federal government can be faulted for not having distributed a modern land claims clause in its initial draft, but their last minute introduction was not without prior warning at the ministerial meeting. The federal proposal was, for the most part, tolerably drafted and a substantively fair attempt to build on the previous evening's discussions.

The attorney general of British Columbia, Mr. Williams, complained that on the previous evening, only amendments on sexual equality and ongoing process had been agreed to; "other than that nothing was agreed and I don't know where these words come from" (1983 FMC transcript, 197). The federal draft did, indeed, contain a number of deletions, additions, and alterations compared to the previous draft that the provincial delegations could not have fully anticipated. The novelty was largely unavoidable, however, in light of the vagueness of the previous evening's commitments. It had been agreed that there would be a political accord, but there had been little discussion of its details. Thus the seven-clause federal proposal was news to the provincial governments. There had been several suggestions that the sexual equality clause be moved from s.25 to s.35; it was, and the wording had been slightly altered in light of its new position. Some legal concerns had been expressed at the ministerial meeting about the clause in the initial federal draft requiring consultation with aboriginal groups before certain amendments to the Constitution were made; it had been suggested that the clause was, in effect, an amendment to the amending formula and as such required unanimous provincial consent. The government of Quebec had already made it clear it was not going to compromise its objections to the *Constitution Act, 1982* by enacting any amending resolutions. There had not been express agreement that the clause would be retained. Nonetheless, the clause was retained, and eventually was proclaimed into force by the Governor General.

Presented with a number of deletions, alterations, and additions to the previous federal draft that they could not have fully anticipated, a number of delegations – the ICNI, MNC, Canada, Alberta, Manitoba – responded to the prime minister's invitation for comments by proposing revisions of their own. other delegations debated whether the federal draft had properly reflected the previous evening's discussion. After about an hour of this, the suggestion was made (by Premier Bennett) and accepted that there be another backroom meeting to work out the remaining difficulties. While the First Ministers proceeded with the discussion of sexual equality, the ministers and bureaucrats went to work on the revised federal draft. Some radically important drafting changes took place with respect to the clause on sexual equality. The clause that emerged was:

> s.35(4) Notwithstanding other provisions of this Act, the aboriginal and treaty rights referred in subsection (1) are guaranteed equally to male and female persons.

The ambiguity in s.35(4) is whether "guaranteed" refers simply to equality between men and women, or whether it also implies that aboriginal and treaty rights of subsection (1) are guaranteed. The latter implication would substantially strengthen the constitutional protection afforded by s.35(1). The latter section "recognizes and affirms" aboriginal treaty rights. It is not clear whether that phraseology makes rights as secure from legislative encroachment as when those rights are "guaranteed." (The human rights identified in the *Canadian Charter of Rights and Freedoms* are characterized as being "guaranteed"; *Charter,* s.1.) I leave for Chapter XXIII a full account of the bizarre and largely underground battle over the draft s.35(4) continued at the March '83 Conference and the renewal of the struggle at the March '84 one. The draft amendment on modern land claims agreements was significantly reworded. There were substantial alterations to the political accord. The implications of these two changes will be analyzed in more detail shortly. It should be appreciated here, however, that a number of serious alterations were made to the package, elements of which could become part of the supreme law of the land, as a result of last-minute discussions which hardly anyone could have fully followed, understood and evaluated.

At a little before one o'clock, the prime minister said that documents were starting to emerge from the ministerial meeting and suggested the conference recess at the hour to permit delegations to examine them. Although they were reminded of the recess proposal by the prime minister, speakers from the aboriginal organizations continued their contributions to the afternoon discussion until 4:30. Some delegates recall an intense anxiety that the aboriginal organizations might have been talking themselves out of an agreement. The prolongation of the discussion might have provided some premiers with an excuse for not signing; they could say that they had not had sufficient opportunity to examine a document of such importance, and they had planes to catch. If the thought occurred to any of the premiers, they did not act on it. The recess took place; the meeting resumed at about five o'clock. The prime minister announced that there were only twenty minutes left to comment and sign the accord. It actually took almost three times that long, but at the end of the day, seven premiers, two attorneys general and one prime minister committed their governments to the political accord, including its undertaking to press for constitutional amendments. Under "with the participation of," the four leaders of the four aboriginal organizations added their signatures.

What everyone actually signed was the political accord absent the constitutional amendments. The federal government said that delays with the French translation made it impossible to prepare the annex in time for general circulation. The procedure had serious implications because the federal government slipped a new wording of the sexual equality clause into the constitutional amendment package. A member of one aboriginal organization tells me that the federal government did not even brief his leaders about the word change, let alone show them the revised text.

Despite the flaws in the process – the lack of technical preparation by many parties, the initial nonattendance of the AFN, Quebec's refusal to recognize the new amending formula, the gratuitously objectionable parts of the federal draft, the frenetic atmosphere of the backroom ministerial drafting sessions – the first year must be adjudged a considerable success. The amendment on modern land claims agreements was a significant step in defining and extending the scope of the constitutional protection given the rights of aboriginal peoples. The amendment on sexual equality did not resolve everyone's concern about discrimination against Indian women, but it did go a long way toward settling the issue. Had it not been enacted, even more time and attention might have been consumed by concerns over sexual equality the next year. An important and, by many participants, unintended effect of s.35(4) may turn out to be that it indirectly strengthens the constitutional protection given to all aboriginal and treaty rights by s.35(1); in the context of s.35(4), "recognize and affirm" may be construed as tantamount to "guaranteed." The constitutional guarantee of further meetings may result in some further progress on defining and securing the entrenched constitutional rights of aboriginal peoples. Its most valuable effect, however, may be in periodically attracting the attention of the public and their politicians to the concerns of aboriginal peoples. The resultant attention may encompass some highly consequential reform at the legislative level. In the end, the conditions of aboriginal people may be improved far more by ordinary legislation that develops in the light of the constitutional process than any alterations to the Constitution of Canada.

There were several respects in which the '83-'84 process was not as productive as it might have been. There was no agreement on a work plan for subsequent meetings. Ordinary citizens, politicians, and jurists were no better informed about the meaning of s.35(1) than they were when the process began; it was as unclear what interests were encompassed by "aboriginal and treaty rights," and how much protection they were offered by s.35(1). Better preparation by the participants and more forthrightness in stating their positions might have led to greater progress.

Chapter IV

Statements of Principles

The Federal Proposal

There was not enough technical preparation or political agreement at the March '83 First Ministers' Conference for many detailed constitutional amendments to emerge. A number of parties proposed that First Ministers agree on general principles to guide further negotiations. The format and legal effect of these proposals varied with the purposes of the proponent. What often looked like innocuous declarations of the incontrovertible actually had serious legal and political consequences.

The federal government proposed a long preamble for a section on further conferences. The least offensive part of a highly objectionable proposal was its presentation of aboriginal history. It is a minor slip to say that "*the* ancestors of the aboriginal peoples of Canada occupied it many centuries before the first settlers arrived on the Atlantic coast some four hundred years ago." Many of the ancestors of the Métis were European settlers, not indigenous people. Furthermore, many Indians have some European ancestry. Perhaps the use of "occupy" to refer to aboriginal people and "settlers" to refer to Europeans was understood as lacking in political significance. It may be ungenerous to suppose that the drafters of the preamble had in mind the idea that aboriginal title is confined to a right to use the land, as opposed to owning the surface and minerals below. The statement in the third preambular paragraph that "aboriginal peoples by their own courage and determination, have successfully lived until this day in their own cultures and communities ..." seems to deny that aboriginal people have suffered considerable hardship, much of it caused by the misguided, at times brutal policies of imperial and Canadian governments. It is possible the phrase is merely the result of a hasty mistranslation of the French version which says that the aboriginal peoples have succeeded in maintaining their own cultures. There are several other places in the preamble where the French version is factually, grammatically or rhetorically superior to the English one. (Perhaps the section was drafted in English, and as translators often do, the translators of this proposal omitted some of the dross).

Difficult to stomach is the theology of the third paragraph. It is not clear whether "the Creator of all things" is the Constitution's own characterization of the deity or the Constitution's description of what aboriginal peoples think of as the Supreme Being. If the former, why not use the less theologically contentious word God? That is what He's called in the preamble to the *Charter of Rights and Freedoms.* Many Christians would have trouble with the claim that God created all things. They would maintain that people made a lot of things, some good, some bad, in the exercise of the free will that God allows them. If the Constitution is describing the way aboriginal people view the Supreme Being, it overlooks that many of them were polytheists, and others have been or re mainstream Christians, some of whom would just as soon call God "God." All of these objections might seem rather quibbling. But it will only seem that way if the nature of the God is viewed as unimportant. If that is the case, there is no point mentioning Him in the Constitution. If His Nature does matter, then He should be spoken of with care and respect. He should not be slovenly described in secular documents in order to achieve partisan political aims.

Perhaps the drafters of the "Creator of all things" section were encouraged by a triumph of theological vulgarity only a year earlier. In April 1981, the House of Commons and Senate added to the *Charter of Rights and Freedoms* a preamble which recognized that "Canada is founded upon principles that recognize the supremacy of God and the rule of law." As a statement of constitutional history, this is hard to believe. About the closest the *Constitution Act, 1867* comes to recognizing the supremacy of God is that it requires governors general and lieutenant governors to take oaths of office. The preamble of the *Constitution Act, 1867* says that Canada is to have a Constitution "similar in principle to that of the United Kingdom." The cardinal doctrine of British constitutionalism was the supremacy of Parliament, not God. It is true that British constitutional law establishes the Queen as defender of the Anglican faith; there is nothing, however, to prevent Parliament from passing ordinary legislation to make the United Kingdom a strictly secular state. Furthermore, the Canadian constitution does not establish any religion as that of the state; s.93 of the Constitution protected the then existing school rights of all denominations, not merely those of High Church Protestants. What is more disturbing than its misstatement of the past, however, is the possibility that the "God clause" adversely affects the constitutional future. The Court might rely upon it when construing section 2(a) of the *Charter* which guarantees "freedom of conscience and religion"; they might hold that atheists and polytheists are entitled to less constitutional protection than those who believe in one Supreme Being. The historical and doctrinal infelicities of the "God clause" might be more forgivable if it had been authorized as an act of genuine faith – as opposed to an unprincipled concession by many of the Canadian politicians involved to a vocal faction of the electorate.

The "Creator of all things" clause in the federal preamble also claims that aboriginal peoples "held sacred their identity with the land, with the creatures that live upon it and in the rivers that traverse it, with the plant life that it supports, and with the seas that surround it." In his comprehensive ethnological study, *Indians of Canada*, Diamond Jenness wrote:

> Spiritual forces akin to those in his own being caused the sun to rise and set, the storms to gather in the sky, the cataract to leap among the rocks, and the trees to bud in springtime. A mentality similar in kind to his animated the bird, the animal and the fish. The same reason, the same emotions that actuated all his movements, actuated also all that moved on earth, in water and in sky. Reason and emotions were present, it is true, in varying degrees, and accompanied by different powers, some greater and some less. But ultimately (although few if any Indians consciously reached this generalization) all life was one in kind and all things, potentially at least, possessed life. . . . Thus the Objibwa of Lake Huron predicate a "soul" and a "shadow" even in rocks and stones (Jenness 1932, 168).

A little later he cautions: "Although this theory of the universe supported the whole fabric of his religious life, it is doubtful whether he ever formulated it clearly in his mind, or expressed it in words, any more than the ordinary European comprehends or expresses all the philosophical ideas implied in Christian rites and ceremonies" (Jenness 1932, 169).

It appears from Jenness that there is some validity to the federal description of Indian belief. It also appears that one should avoid summarizing in a couple of phrases the web of articulated belief and inchoate sense that made up the religious views of a disparate group of peoples. Jenness, it should be noted, compares and contrasts the original beliefs of Indians with Christianity. A great many Indians did adopt Christianity which, in almost all of its forms, maintains a sharp distinction between the essence of humankind and that of all other earthly entities. As the federal proposal refers to the way Indians "lived ... until this day" (presumably the authors meant "have lived" and did not contemplate that Indians would disappear with the promulgation of their amendment), the reference does little justice to an important part of religious development.

A preamble lacking in form might be partly redeemed by an exceptional grace of expression. The third paragraph of the federal draft is an execrable example of a failed attempt at eloquence. At the end of the paragraph, "it" stands for land and is used three times as the object of an active verb. "Their identity with the land, with the creatures that live upon it, and in the rivers that traverse it ... and the seas that surround it." Just before the end, however, "it" is used as the subject of "supports" ("with the plant life that it supports"), thereby destroying the rhythm and parallelism of the sentence. The French version, as usual, is less grating.

The most important aspect of the federal preamble, however, was not its misleading account of history, frivolous theology, or clumsy rhetoric. In the listing of points to be considered in the ongoing process were a number of implications that were adverse to the constitutional views that had been expressed by aboriginal persons. Having included in its preamble principles that had real legal substance, the federal government should have released a draft for delegations to study before the conference. It required some effort and care to discern the implications of the points in the first place, even more to assess their justice and legal merit.

The federal proposal identified four points for inclusion in an aboriginal charter of rights. The first was the identification of rights now recognized and affirmed in s.35, "and in particular, the rights of aboriginal peoples to the use and occupancy of land, and their rights to fish, hunt, trap and gather, based on traditional and continuing use and occupancy, and as recognized by treaty and land claims settlements." There are at least two significant implications to this paragraph. First, that aboriginal rights are confined to the use and occupancy of the land and do not extend to matters such as political autonomy. Second, that the aboriginal land use rights that do exist are limited to using the land for traditional purposes and do not include general ownership of land or the minerals below it. It could be argued that neither implication is really there because the paragraph says "includes," and so cannot be taken as an exhaustive definition of aboriginal rights. A court might, however, draw important inferences from the enumeration.

A second point that might be included in an aboriginal charter of rights, according to the federal draft, is the preservation and enhancement of traditional aboriginal cultures. The federal draft, however, insisted that aboriginal people must educate their children in French or English, as well as an aboriginal language, in order that the children "may be equipped to live in the cultural milieu of their choice." The larger implication is that aboriginal people and the political and cultural autonomy of aboriginal people is limited by their duty to give their children the education and freedom to enter mainstream society. As a matter of political philosophy, I basically agree with that proposition. Some aboriginal groups may not; according to the *Report of the Métis and Non-Status Indian Constitutional Review Commission*, "Native people feel that education should be a means toward an end, their social development as a collectivity rather than as individuals" (p. 12).

Whoever is right, the balance between collective political rights of aboriginal peoples and the individual freedom of aboriginal persons is a question of first importance. It ought to be raised forthrightly and discussed thoroughly. The federal draft on self-government refers to "the *institution* of various forms of aboriginal government." It can be argued that aboriginal peoples have the inherent constitutional right to self-government, that this is one of the rights recognized in s.35, and that their right has been to some extent exercised in practice – whether by continuing traditional forms of government or using the process sanctioned by provincial or federal law, such as Indian band governments. By mentioning self-government at a distance of a full paragraph from s.35 rights and by using the word "institution" (suggesting there had been no aboriginal self-government before), the federal draft would have seriously undermined some important legal positions that aboriginal people may wish to maintain.

Section 54(1) of the federal proposal signalled a renewed federal commitment to constitutional tidiness. It said that the entire amendment on holding additional conferences, including the preamble, would be repealed after the last mandatory First Ministers' Conference was held. Think of the possible consequences five or six years later. As the last First Ministers' Conference comes to a fruitless conclusion, the kind words about them in the constitution are by force of law torn from the constitution, never to reappear.

The Métis National Council Proposal

The Métis National Council submitted two major statements of Métis rights to the First Ministers' Conference. One of them, the "Revised Charter of Rights of the Métis People", was apparently intended to immediately create justiciable rights. Section 35.3 stated a number of "Collective Rights and Freedoms of the Métis Peoples of Canada," including "self government, which shall have jurisdiction over political, cultural, economic and social affairs and institutions deemed necessary to their survival and development as a distinct people. Section 35.4 said that the details of these rights should be spelled out in a schedule to the Constitution. What was to be done about the rights until they were spelled out through constitutional negotiations and amendments? Apparently, the details could be provided by "A Métis Peoples Court, a Court of Law and Equity which shall be the Court of final jurisdiction in regards to Métis Rights." Even if the final interpreter were to be the Supreme Court of Canada, the entrenchment of a justiciable set of principles would have been an enormous victory for the Métis.

Even if the courts adopted a very narrow construction of the principles, whatever the courts did allow, the Métis would be immune from legislative override. The Constitution is the Supreme Law of Canada, and a construction of it by the Supreme Court cannot be overridden by ordinary legislation. Given the threat of an expansive interpretation of the principles by the courts, moreover, governments would have some incentive to try to work them out through political negotiations. In *Unfinished Business* Professor Zlotkin argued that there are "serious problems" *from the point of view of aboriginal interests* in entrenching a statement of general principles (Zlotkin 1983, 59-60). First of all, Zlotkin contended, the courts have traditionally taken a "conservative approach" to native issues, so native people are better off trying to negotiate their rights. I would reply that even if Courts are "conservative" on native issues, they are much more likely to find in favour of aboriginal peoples if there is an entrenched statement of principles which endorses at a general level a broad range of native claims. Zlotkin also argued that a general statement of principles would be:

> . . . rather ineffective without further discussions between governments and aboriginal peoples on questions of identification and definition of rights. For example, the negotiation of land claim settlements will continue, but governments have not shown the same willingness to renegotiate treaties with the Indians of southern Canada to find a mutually acceptable interpretation based on modern conditions (Zlotkin 1983, 60).

Zlotkin's example undermines his point. A major reason why governments are anxious to negotiate land claims settlements is the risk of adverse Court decisions in the absence of an agreement; the case law on aboriginal rights is still very nebulous. Similarly, governments would have some incentive to negotiate the meaning of justiciable, but vague, constitutional statements of principle. Governments have little incentive to renegotiate the old treaties because it is fairly clear what rights they confer. Indians are not going to consent to having those rights diminished, so why should a government be eager to enter into a discussion on how much to revise them? It is not surprising that governments had expressed no interest in agreeing to a justiciable statement of principles at the March '83 Conference. The Native Council of Canada (NCC) did not misperceive its own interests when, at the March '84 Constitutional Conference, it proposed that a statement of principles be entrenched into the constitution, to be nonjusticiable for a period to allow negotiations, and justiciable after that ('84 First Ministers' Conference [FMC] transcript, 56).

The Métis National Council (MNC) also proposed, as an alternative to its Statement of Rights, a Statement of Principles which it probably understood as nonjusticiable. The draft uses the "committed in principle" formula that has often been understood (possibly wrongly) as an effective legal formula for making a section of the constitution judicially unenforceable. The Statement of Principles was intended to guide further negotiations. It was politically unacceptable to governments. Even the province of Manitoba would have had trouble accepting the principle that Métis are entitled to "self-government *as the*

Métis deem necessary for their survival and development as a distinct People."

The Manitoba Proposal

The government of Manitoba submitted two major documents as suitable guides for further discussion. One was a "framework agreement." It would have parties agree to turn Part II into an aboriginal rights section with a certain basic structure: *existing* would be removed from s.35(1) and *guaranteed* would be added after *affirmed*. There would be a definition of the term "Aboriginal Peoples," an "enforcement clause," a "clause relating to self-government," a "clause relating to fiscal responsibility" and so on. The framework agreement was generally agnostic on what the content of sections should be (the call for the removal of the word "existing" is an important exception) but did require that clauses be written.

It could be objected, with justification, that there is no point in agreeing to write a clause unless you have some idea of what policy it should embody; and that even if you do agree on policy, you might not be convinced that entrenchment, rather than ordinary legislation, is the best way to achieve it. More useful than a framework agreement along the lines proposed by Manitoba would have been a work plan, a detailed agreement by First Ministers on what should be discussed in the ongoing process and in what order. Because a final agreement on the ongoing process itself was reached only on the second day of the March '83 Conference, however, First Ministers had no time to develop a work plan, and the catch-all agenda of the March '83 Conference was extended into the future.

Manitoba also proposed that parties agree to a "Statement of Principles" to provide a basis upon which "specific items might be subsequently defined as rights for inclusion in the Constitution of Canada". The Manitoba statement (which was concurred in by its provincial Indian and Métis organizations) differed from statements proposed by the national aboriginal organizations in that it acknowledged the need for balance between aboriginal claims and those of the public generally. It said, for example, that aboriginal rights include "land entitlements . . . which are not subject to arbitrary interference of appropriation." Implied is that some justifiable interferences with aboriginal land rights may be constitutionally necessary.

Some authorities on international negotiations have maintained that the most productive way for parties to proceed is "deductive" – first agree upon a solution at a very general level, "a formula" – then work out details. "[The deductive approach] is desirable . . . because a formula or framework of principles helps give structure and coherence to an agreement on details, helps facilitate the search for solutions on component items, and helps create a positive, creative image of negotiation rather than an image of concession and compromise" (Zartman and Berman 1982, 93).

The opposite approach may be called "inductive." It involves working out agreements on small pieces of a problem and then assembling them into an overall accord. "If the two parties have irreconcileably different perceptions or conceptions of the problem and are unable to harmonize them, they may nevertheless be able to agree on certain details even though they attach different meanings to them" (Zartman and Berman 1982, 90).

After March '83, it might have appeared that the s.37 process was proceeding inductively. Agreement was reached on a small number of specific items, and provision made for further discussions. (Of course the points of agreement were immediately entrenched in the Constitution, rather than put on hold, pending the assembly of a comprehensive constitutional package). In fact, March '83 did not establish that substantial progress could be made one piece at a time. The items agreed to there were among the few easily agreeable ones. A couple of easy issues may have remained – a remedies clause for aboriginal peoples' rights, along the lines of s.24 of the *Charter of Rights and Freedoms* might be an example – but almost all of the outstanding issues after the March '83 First Ministers' Conference were far more intractable than ones already resolved.

Was there any merit in Manitoba's deductive proposal in the context of the aboriginal rights reform process? It would not have been helpful for the parties to try to agree on a comprehensive set of political principles at an early stage in the negotiations. Progress on more manageable issues would be stymied because of disagreement over the most intractable issues – disagreement that might continue indefinitely. As argued earlier, however, a realistic work plan for tackling the issues would have been useful. The Manitoba Statement of Principles did identify, comprehensively and with some precision, the major issues at stake and might have been of help in formulating a work plan. As particular points came up for discussion under the work plan, the Manitoba principles came up for discussion under the work plan, the Manitoba principles might have been a source of ideas for either a statement of principle on particular issues or a draft legal text.

A final point about the "deductive" approach in the context of constitutional negotiations. The definition of the approach given above distinguishes the principle state from the detail state. It would be a mistake to suppose that the two stages can be sharply distinguished when what is being prepared is a constitutional text. It is rarely a question of the politicians agreeing on "the principle" and the lawyers performing the mechanical task of translating their agreement into legalese and *jargon juridique*. The drafting and criticism of an actual legal text raises issues of policy, sometimes very subtle, sometimes fundamental, that may not have been recognized at an earlier state in the discussions.

Chapter V

The Constitutional Amendment with Respect to Ongoing Process

It is not easy to amend the Constitution of Canada. For most matters, the consent of the federal government and seven provinces with half the population is required (*Constitution Act, 1982*, S.38). If you do insert something in the Constitution, what you say will likely govern events you cannot foresee. The judgment you make now may count for more than the judgment of the people who are confronted with events beyond your anticipation. Yet it is they who must live with the consequences. Because of the insistence of some of the provinces, the *Constitution Act, 1982* provides several avenues of escape from its own prescriptions; s.33 allows legislatures to override many sections of the *Canadian Charter of Rights and Freedoms*; and s.38(3) allows provinces to opt-out of amendments sanctioned by the new amending formula.

Because of a constitution's permanence and pre-eminence, matters stated in it often assume great importance. Conversely, if a matter is not of some gravity in the first place, no one is likely to go to the trouble and risk of having it constitutionally entrenched. Ordinarily, therefore, you expect to see in a constitution general statements of fundamental principle. You don't expect to find a requirement that several discussions must take place over the next few years, especially when the discussions need not reach any particular conclusions.

A political agreement to have a specified number of additional conferences would not have given everyone sufficient assurance that they would take place. A political accord could not be enforced in the courts, and a new federal or provincial government could argue that it is not bound by the non-legal commitments of its predecessors. An agreement by all but one of the provincial premiers and the prime minister would, however, have had considerable moral force.

A number of factors account for the entrenchment of further meetings. From the point of view of aboriginal groups, political promises were suspect. Less than two years earlier, in the November 1981 settlement, a backroom deal among federal and provincial governments deleted the clause in the proposed package which recognized and affirmed aboriginal rights. Another factor, already mentioned is that the entrenchment of further meetings allowed everyone to claim that concrete constitutional progress had been made. A further influence was the massive amount of constitutional reform that had come into force less than a year earlier; a constitutional amendment did not seem as drastic a step as it ordinarily would have.

Public officials and special interest groups alike were rather accustomed to aiming at the constitutional entrenchment of their political programs. A few also seemed to think of the Constitution as an alternative to *Hansard*, constituency letters, and gothic archways as a suitable repository for expressions of noble sentiment. (Recall the "Statement of Principles" proposals at the March '83 conference, discussed in Chapter IV.) Finally, the March '83 meeting itself was constitutionally mandated. The entrenchment of meetings that followed March '83 might have been perceived as less solemn occasions if they too were not constitutionally entrenched.

The federal proposal tabled at the March '83 Conference proposed two options for the ongoing process. One proposal was for three meetings, the first no later than 17 April 1984, the others no more than two and four years after that. The alternative suggestion was for two entrenched meetings, the first no later than 17 April 1985, the other at most two years later. The technical difficulty with the first proposal was that under s.39(1) of the *Constitution Act, 1982*, a constitutional amendment can't take effect until at least a year after the first Canadian legislature (whether Parliament or provincial assembly) approves it. (The exception is if every provincial legislature expressly either approves it or dissents from it; but since the National Assembly of Quebec did not recognize the legitimacy of the new amending formula at all, it would have done neither.) Thus even if Parliament or a legislature had immediately passed a resolution approving the entrenchment of more meetings, it could not have come into force until late March 1984. Any constitutional meeting before then would lack a constitutional imprimatur. Yet it might have turned out that a meeting in, say, March 8-9, 1984 was convenient. (In fact it did.) A further difficulty with relying on a constitutional entrenchment to mandate a meeting in 1984 was that provincial legislatures or Parliament might not get around to considering a resolution for months; in the meantime, uncertainty would hamper attempts to prepare for a conference. The parties to the March '83 political accord therefore provided that there would be another conference within a year, but this was left as a political undertaking.

The parties agreed as well to the second federal alternative – to constitutionally entrench further meetings in 1985 and 1987. It is fortunate that they chose this option over the first. Most of the productive activity in a series of governmental negotiations usually occurs just before the deadline. In the meantime, governments devote their attention to matters which need immediate decision. They may also entertain the hope that the problem will expire before the deadline – or the fear that the government will. Furthermore, parties to a negotiation do not want to make concessions early in the game; the other party may only ask for more. The first federal alternative set the deadline too far away. It also left too much discretion to the federal government in setting the precise time of the meetings.

The wording of the constitutional amendment that the parties agreed to make in the March '83 Accord differed in several respects from the original federal draft. (The wording changes were the result of *in camera* (that is, off camera) meetings of ministers on the first evening and second morning of the First Ministers' Conference). *At least* was added to the new section 37.1 so that the meeting requirements stipulated there would be clearly understood as the minimum necessary. People have an unfortunate tendency to view compliance with what is constitutionally required as the most, rather than the least, that is to be expected of them. During the patriation debate, Prime Minister Trudeau complained in a television interview that he had promised to end his efforts to unilaterally patriate the Constitution if he lost the decision in the Supreme Court of Canada, but the provinces did not promise to stop their efforts to block patriation if they lost. The argument relied on a nonexistent symmetry. The judicial declaration that a course of political action is legally permissible does not mean that it is all right; the action might still be imprudent or, more seriously, it might be unjust. One of the dangers of entrenching a bill of rights is that the legislature and the electorate may start to view a Court's decision that something does not violate the *Charter* as meaning that it is not an affront to human rights. The wording of the *Canadian Charter of Rights and Freedoms* enhances this risk; the court may sustain governmental action that *prima facie* violates the *Charter* because that action is "demonstrably justified in a free and democratic society." But the court may merely be deferring to the judgment of a democratically elected legislature in a close case, rather than saying the legislature is right. To return to s.37, in the absence of the words "at least," it would have been almost certain that only two First Ministers' Conferences would be held on aboriginal rights. Their presence means that there is a significantly enhanced possibility that more than two will be held. Looking ahead, there is a real danger that when the new section 37 expires in 1987, participants will misunderstand its not being renewed as tantamount to saying that First Ministers are under no duty of any sort to discuss aboriginal rights any further. As a matter of political justice, however, they might still be.

The initial federal proposal would have kept the wording of the original s.37, which read "the conference convened . . . shall have included in its agenda an item respecting constitutional matters that directly affect the aboriginal peoples of Canada, including the identification and definition of the rights of [aboriginal] peoples to be included in the Constitution of Canada." The March '83 Accord contemplated a s.37 that merely said "each conference convened shall have included in its agenda constitutional matters that directly affect the aboriginal peoples of Canada." The extra wording was dropped partly because some aboriginal group leaders were concerned that it would be exploited by courts to deny the existence of rights under s.35. Courts might argue that the "identify and define" wording implied that rights under s.35 were not yet identified and defined, and so were not judicially recognizable or enforceable. The probability of the courts taking such a position was small; but inasmuch as the "identify and define" wording did not assure that any concrete results would emerge from First Ministerial discussions, it did no harm to drop it, and might have done some good.

Before the First Ministers' Conference another possible interpretation of s.37 had caused concern to some provincial legal advisors. In *Peters* v. *R. in Right of B.C. Minister of Lands, Parks and Housing, Dunsmore and Dunsmore* (1983), 42 B.C.L.R. 373 (B.C.S.C.), some Ohiat Indian Band members claimed that they had an aboriginal right to gather clams on a certain beach. A British Columbia minister of lands, parks and housing tentatively approved an application from the Dunsmores to use the beach for commercial clam production. The band members sought a judicial declaration that the minister could not do this prior to the s.37 Conference on Aboriginal Rights. They submitted "in effect, that the conference must reach a conclusion on aboriginal rights, and that such conclusion, once published, will, without more, entrench in the constitution those rights identified and defined by it" (42 B.C.L.R. 373, 380). The Dunsmores tried to have the band's application for a declaration struck out before it was heard on the merits, on the grounds that it did not disclose an arguable case. Mr. Justice Esson of the Supreme Court of British Columbia declined to do so. He held that the case raised untested questions of constitutional law, and the band members might alter their claim before trial to make it stronger; the claim was therefore not such an obviously unfounded one that it could be dismissed before it even came to trial. Some provincial legal advisors were concerned that if s.37 were renewed, acts of government would be challenged in the future on the same basis as the *Clam* case. But the risk was actually extremely small. Had the *Clam* case been heard on the merits, the band members would almost certainly have lost. Contrary to their claim, section 35 took effect on April 17, 1982, and courts were immediately bound to construe and enforce it, regardless of whether it would be amended as a result of further discussions pursuant to section 37. Furthermore, section 37 did not require First Ministers to agree on anything; any agreement they did reach had no direct legal effect. Resolutions of Parliament and seven provinces are required to amend the Constitution, not political agreement by First Ministers.

Lest it be lost to the annals of form versus substance, there will now be a brief account of the "vanishing amendment" argument. At a ministerial meeting in February 1983, when it was still uncertain that governments would agree on a formal political accord to ensure an ongoing process, the attorney general of Manitoba suggested another method of ensuring further talks. The proposal was that the prime minister might end the March '83 conference by finding it had not adequately discussed the issues and adjourn it to a future date, which might be weeks or months later. The prime minister might do this with the consent of participants or over the objection of a few. After all, s.37 mandated the prime minister to convene the conference, and he had some discretion over the timing and duration of the meeting. Some governments objected to the proposal of the attorney general of Manitoba on legal grounds. According to section 54 of the *Constitution Act, 1982*: "Part IV [which consists of s.37] is repealed on the day that is one year after this Part comes into force and this section may be repealed and this Act renumbered, consequentially upon the repeal of Part IV and this section, by proclamation issued by the Governor General under the Great Seal of Canada." Why repeal s.37 a year after the *Constitution Act, 1982* comes into force? Because by then the First Ministers' Conference that s.37 mandates must have started, and there is no point in permanently cluttering the Constitution with a section which has already done its job. The repeal of s.37 was merely a matter of constitutional aesthetics. (Notice that s.54 itself could be deleted after it had discharged its function.) Some governments argued, however, that once s.37 was repealed, any meeting convened under it was no longer a s.37 meeting. Therefore the Prime Minister could not adjourn the March '83 meeting to a date later than April 17, 1983.

Suppose this argument is correct; then if the '83 First Ministers' Conference had been scheduled for April 16-17, 1983, the first day of the meeting would have been constitutionally mandated by s.37, but the second day not. Yet s.37 only says when the prime minister must convene the meeting, not when he must end it. In my opinion, removal of s.37 from the Constitution as a matter of documentary tidiness did not mean it was immediately expunged from legal memory and denied any lingering legal effect. A valuable step in the constitutional advancement of aboriginal peoples in Canada might have been blocked by a misunderstanding of an earlier concern with constitutional cosmetics. Some governments which raised the s.54 objection were probably using it as a pretext; they opposed adjournment for other reasons such as their desire to make the constitutional entrenchment of further meetings look more necessary, and therefore more of an achievement.

Chapter VI

Consent to Constitutional Amendments

There was no provision in Part V of the *Constitution Act, 1982* (which deals with amendments) for participation by aboriginal peoples as such. The agreement of seven provincial legislatures and Parliament is sufficient to pass an amendment no matter how deleterious to aboriginal interest. On the other hand, the federal government can, by remaining passive, block any constitutional amendment which is favourable to aboriginal peoples' interests. Furthermore, a provincial government can "opt out" of the application of any constitutional amendment that "derogates from the legislative powers, the proprietary rights or any other rights or privileges of the legislature or government of a province" (*Constitution Act, 1982*, s.38(2)). It might be argued that because the federal government has exclusive jurisdiction over Indians under s.91(24) of the *Constitution Act, 1867*, a province's rights and powers are not impaired by a constitutional amendment that better protects the rights of those aboriginal peoples included in s.91(24). Several judgments of the Supreme Court of Canada, however, support the view that provincial laws of general application may apply of their own force, even to Indians on reserves (*Natural Parents* v. *Superintendent of Child Welfare* (1975), 60 D.L.R. (3d) 148; *Four B. Manufacturing* v. *Garment Workers of America* (1979), 102 D.L.R. (3d) 338). It would be possible for Parliament to use its s.91(24) power to expressly exclude the application of provincial laws to the extent that they violate rights of aboriginal peoples, and Parliament has in fact done so with respect to treaty rights; *Indian Act*, s.88.

From the point of view of aboriginal peoples, the amending formulae are rigged strongly in the favour of governments. The only say aboriginal groups were constitutionally assured in 1982 was that the prime minister would invite them to one First Ministers' Conference in 1983 at which their constitutional concerns would be discussed. There was no permanent guarantee of their even being consulted after that.

Several proposals were made by aboriginal organizations at the March '83 First Ministers' Conference on how their influence on constitutional amendment could be better protected. The most ambitious suggestions were those of the Assembly of First Nations (AFN). They submitted a draft section 42(3) of the Constitution which would have required that before governments approve any amendment affecting the rights of First Nations (including s.91(24) of the *Constitution Act, 1867*) the prime minister must first convene a constitutional conference to which the representatives of First Nations would be invited. No amendment could proceed without the consent of "the representative body of a First Nation." The phrase in quotes might refer to a national organization like the AFN if mandated to speak for a particular First Nation, but apparently the dissent of even one First Nation affected by an amendment would block its being approved. Under a proposed s.42(4) of the Constitution, a First Nation could also "opt out" of the application of any amendment prior to its coming into force. (A First Nation might go along with an amendment for the benefit of other First Nations, but still not want an amendment to apply to itself. A First Nation might also change its mind between the time of the conference at which the amendment is first assented to and the time legislatures consider them.)

Granting a veto to each and every First Nation could result in the obstruction of amendments that most First Nations, let alone governments, favoured. At the March '83 conference, the AFN did not have a mandate to even speak for a number of Indian bands. Furthermore, there is no generally accepted constitutional definition of a First Nation: is it a band or a group of bands sharing a common culture and history? (The *Penner Report* on Indian self-government proposed that the negotiations on self-government start off with individual bands establishing governments; these governments could then agree on amalgamating the bands into large units; *Penner Report*, 53-55.)

Allowing a single First Nation to "opt out" of, rather than to veto, a constitutional amendment does have some points in its favour. It avoids the problem of whether a national aboriginal organization should be able to disregard the objections of a member in collectively agreeing to an amendment. The different Indian Nations in Canada often have little more in common in terms of language, culture, and legal concerns than different countries in the European Common Market. "Opting out" is rhetorically more appealing than "veto." The former implies the nonobstructive withdrawal from the march of the majority; the latter implies standing in its way. If the "opting out" is sufficiently widespread, however, the distinction loses its validity. If many First Nations were to opt out of an amendment affecting aboriginal rights, the practical effect might be that the amendment would not have any effect. The aboriginal and treaty rights of different aboriginal peoples depends largely on their different histories, and it would be quite possible for an amendment to potentially affect only some Indian bands and no Inuit or Métis collectivities. If many of the affected bands opted out, the amendment would be rendered virtually ineffectual. In contrast, when a province "opts out" of a constitutional amendment, it will still be in force in at least seven other provinces, every one of which has very similar rights and privileges to the "opting out" province.

The fundamental question that must be addressed, whether in connection with a veto or with opting out, is the legitimacy of a minority group's blocking the constitutional will of the representatives of the preponderant majority of Canadians. It could be argued on behalf of aboriginal vetoes that according to international law the relative populations of sovereign states is irrelevant. A state cannot impose legal norms on another, no matter how tiny, without consent. The distinct cultural and political identity of different states prevents you from notionally lumping their populations into a single polity in which the majority rules. An adequate reply to the foregoing argument is that aboriginal collectivities in Canada are not in the same legal or moral position as sovereign states. Legally they are no more than subordinate entities to sovereign legislatures. It is morally significant that members of aboriginal collectivities are free to participate on the same basis as everyone else in the political life of the general political community.

The deletion of aboriginal rights in the November 1981 Constitutional Accord might be cited as proof that aboriginal rights cannot be adequately trusted to the discretion of federal and provincial leaders. What followed that incident, however, must not be forgotten. Leaders of aboriginal groups mounted an intense lobbying effort aimed at the reinsertion of the clause.

Their appeal won support from many Canadians convinced of its moral validity. Some politicians were also influenced by the voting strength of aboriginal people. On November 17, an New Democratic Party government was elected in Manitoba, partly because of the strong support from Indian and Métis votes. The new premier announced his support for the restoration of the aboriginal rights clause. On November 9 the premier of Saskatchewan, who also had both a genuine concern for aboriginal peoples in his heart and a large number of Indian and Métis voters in his electorate, announced that he would go along with strengthening the clause on sexual equality if other Premiers would accept the reinsertion of the aboriginal rights clause. "The next day, at the same time as Indians were addressing the provincial Social Credit convention, Premier Bennett announced British Columbia's support for the section. Alberta's Peter Lougheed, after negotiations with the province's Métis organizations, announced support for a modified section 34, limited to 'existing' rights" (Sanders 1983, 321). Even with the addition of *existing*, the aboriginal organizations scored a considerable political victory in obtaining the reinsertion of what is now section 35. Aboriginal groups have in recent times won battles on other constitutional fronts. Vehement opposition from Indian organizations forced the federal government to withdraw its 1969 White Paper on Indians, which proposed the abolition of special status for Indians and turning the reserves into municipalities. The natives of the Northwest Territories succeeded in persuading the federal government to accept in principle the division of the Northwest Territories into a largely Dene territory west of the tree line, and a largely Inuit territory on the east of it (Jull 1983, 59).

Because any change to the amending formula requires the consent of the federal government and all ten provinces, Quebec's nonrecognition of the *Constitution Act, 1982* was of itself sufficient to block the granting of a veto or opting out power to aboriginal groups. The only government to express its support in principle for an aboriginal peoples' veto was Manitoba; the others were not called upon to commit themselves, but they almost all would have expressed opposition. Individual Canadian provinces do not have vetoes over constitutional reform, and it is difficult imagining any of them agreeing to put aboriginal peoples in a better position than they themselves are.

Even Manitoba did not go beyond accepting an aboriginal peoples' veto as a general idea. The working out of the specifics would involve the resolution of some extremely difficult points of principle, not just technical details. Among them:

(i) Would the veto holder be a national organization or its constituent parts?

(ii) Could a single aboriginal group veto an amendment, or would the dissent of most or all of the aboriginal groups be required? The veto is often discussed in terms of a conflict between the interests of an aboriginal people and that of society at large. There are many cases, however, where the contest is between different aboriginal groups or between different factions of the same aboriginal group. An example that raises the former is the Métis demand that s.91(24) be amended to expressly refer to the Métis. Some Indian groups may be opposed because the inclusion of the Métis would result in the diversion of resources that otherwise would have gone to Indians.

An example of a conflict within a group is the controversy over the reinstatement of Indians who have lost or been denied status because of s.12(1)(b) of the *Indian Act*. The section says that an Indian woman who marries a white man loses her status; in contrast, a white woman who marries an Indian man automatically acquires Indian status. To some status Indians, justice requires the redress of this state-sponsored sexual discrimination. Other Indians, however, might object to the restoration of status – because of the influx of people who may be especially assimilated into mainstream culture, the exacerbation of overcrowding on reserves, and the diminution of royalty and treaty payments due to Indians who have retained status all along. Some Indians believe that those who intermarried knowing the consequences should have to live with them, just as Indians who refrained from intermarrying do (Cardinal 1977, 111; Sanders 1984).

The veto issue is often seen in terms of conflict between the interests of aboriginal peoples and those of society as a whole. A veto in the hands of an aboriginal organization might at times, however, prevent a Canadian government from intervening to protect a minority faction of an aboriginal group from the majority of that group. The government might wish to protect that minority faction because of a disinterested concern for justice; it would not necessarily be a case of advancing the interests of the majority of the electorate at the expense of aboriginal peoples. (It may still be argued, however, that proper respect for the political autonomy of aboriginal collectivities means letting them work out the balance of majority and minority themselves in all cases. This position will be discussed in some depth later in this study.)

(iii) What principles should guide the selection of leaders of veto-holding organizations? Should election standards be established, and polling supervised, by outside governmental organizations?

(iv) Precisely who are the constituents of the different aboriginal organizations? Is the AFN the sole legitimate representative of status Indians in Canadian cities, even though many of those Indians are not allowed to vote in band elections? The Métis National Council (MNC) claims that there are no Métis other than those who trace their origin to a distinct people that came into its own in Western Canada in the 19th century; the Native Council of Canada (NCC) says there have been and are Métis across Canada; who is right?

When aboriginal groups have a consultative, rather than a vetoing role at constitutional conferences, the foregoing kinds of questions can often be left unresolved. Prime Minister Trudeau did not have to decide the last question, for example, prior to the last First Ministers' Conference; he invited both the MNC and the NCC, and thereby gave a chance for both sides of the questions to be presented. If aboriginal organizations were to be given legally binding powers,however, precise answers to some tough questions would have to be given.

An objection might be made at the level of basic principle to a consultation clause for aboriginal peoples. Why should aboriginal people be guaranteed even a consultative role when others are not? The attack in principle can be blunted somewhat by pointing out that aboriginal peoples would not be entitled to a consultative role on all amendments, nor even on amendments that have an especially strong practical impact on them, but only on amendments to sections of the constitution that already recognize special rights for aboriginal peoples. That consultative role would be a rational way of dealing with the special privileges and liabilities of aboriginal peoples that are *already* ensconced in the constitution.

But the attack against a consultation clause for aboriginal peoples only might be renewed by pointing out that certain other groups can also point to sections of the Constitution that grant them special rights; e.g., Roman Catholics in Ontario could point to s.93 of the *Constitution Act, 1867* which protects the denominational school rights that existed in the four provinces that confederated in 1867. It is not much of an answer to say that the Roman Catholics of Ontario are not expressly named in s.93, whereas Indians and Aboriginal peoples are expressly named in certain sections of the Constitution. Whether a group is actually named in the constitution is too formalistic a basis for different treatment. Anyway, the distinction does not really hold up at even the formal level. "Indians" may be named in s.35 of the

Constitution Act, 1982, but the Nisgha Indians of British Columbia are not. Yet the Nisghas may have special rights, different from all other Indian groups, that are implicitly recognized and affirmed by section 35.

Some valid points of distinction *can* be made about the particular example of the school rights of Roman Catholics have in Ontario. Roman Catholics of Ontario are constitutionally entitled to complain to the federal Cabinet which may take remedial measures, if a provincial authority diminishes their special rights. Aboriginal peoples do not have this privilege. Furthermore, s.93(2) of the *Constitution Act, 1867* expressly extends to Protestants in Quebec the same rights as were enjoyed by Roman Catholics in Ontario in 1867. Almost everyone in Canada (especially in 1867) can see s.93 as protecting a minority with which he or she identifies. By contrast, only a small segment of the Canadian community would naturally identify with the minorities whose rights are protected by the aboriginal sections of the Canadian Constitution. It may well be that if the position of other groups in Canada were laboriously examined, a valid distinction could be drawn with respect to the claim of aboriginal peoples to a consultation clause.

To sum up, granting aboriginal peoples a consultative role on certain sections of the constitution is a reasonable way of proceeding with reform of the special privileges of aboriginal peoples that already exist in the constitution. Other groups with entrenched special rights have at most, a minimal complaint of unequal treatment in that they too are not guaranteed a consultative role. It may well be, however, that a thorough examination of the legal and political position of these other groups would justify rejecting altogether any charge of unequal benefit.

Chapter VII

Consultation on Constitutional Amendments with Respect to Aboriginal Rights Matters

The draft constitutional amendments that the prime minister released on the first day of the March '83 Constitutional Conference included a clause requiring that aboriginal groups be consulted before certain clauses of the Constitution are amended. The draft s.35.1 said that "the government of Canada and the provincial governments are committed to the principle" of having a type of First Ministers' Conference before amending s.91(24) of the *Constitution Act, 1867* or s.25 or Part IV of the *Constitution Act, 1982*. Why use the phrase "committed to the principle?" Because the drafters believed that the phrase might overcome the fact that unanimous consent of the provinces is needed before the amending formula is changed. The thinking was as follows: If you say that governments are "committed to the principle," the requirement will be understood as one merely binding in political morality, but not enforceable by an aggrieved aboriginal group in the ordinary Courts. If a requirement cannot be enforced in the Courts, it might not really count for the purposes of s.41(e) of the *Constitution Act, 1982*, the clause that requires unanimous consent to the amending formula; the consultation amendment could therefore succeed without the consent of Quebec or indeed two other provinces.

In my opinion, the federal proposal was misguided in two respects: first of all, as phrases, the amendment would have in fact been judicially enforceable; secondly, even if it were drafted so as to be nonjusticiable, the unanimous consent of the provinces would still have been required before it could become law. In order to explain my position, it will be necessary to look more generally at the theory and practice of nonjusticiability. The inquiry will be useful beyond the present context because proposals for nonjusticiable amendments to the constitution were frequent at the March '83 First Ministers' Conference, and a nonjusticiable proposal was the centrepiece of the federal government's March '84 First Ministers' Conference.

Because courts have the last word on the construction of written constitutions, people often think that a norm is only part of a constitutional law of a state if it can be enforced by a court. Courts are generally allowed the last word because of their impartiality; it is believed that it is better to have an impartial umpire of the federal-provincial division of powers under the *Constitution Act, 1867,* for example, than to let an interested party, such as the federal government, decide. Yet it is perfectly possible to allot the final power of adjudication over a constitutional norm to a body other than a court. The long course of judicial decisions on the division of powers can cause us to forget that the framers of the *Constitution Act, 1867* seemed to have provided for an alternative method of umpiring the division of powers. The federal executive was given (by s.90) the power to disallow provincial legislation and the imperial executive (by s.56) the power to disallow federal legislation.

The federal power of disallowance was in fact used early in Confederation to suppress provincial legislation that was perceived as unconstitutional, although in other cases the objection was merely that the legislation was unwise (Forsey 1974, 177-191; Hogg 1977, 39; LaForest 1965, 80-81). It may be that in some cases a non-judicial body is the best interpreter of a requirement of constitutional law because that body has more expertise in the area or has access to information that a court does not. In *R.* v. *Operation Dismantle* (1984), 3 D.L.R. (4d) 193, the plaintiffs argued that the government's decision to allow Cruise missile testing in Canada violated s.7 of the *Canadian Charter of Rights and Freedoms.* The section guarantees that: "Everyone has the right to life, liberty and security of the person and the right not to be deprived thereof except in accordance with the principles of fundamental justice". It was argued that because the defence decision was an exercise of the inherent power of the Crown (i.e. a royal prerogative power) it was immune from *Charter* review. Most judges of the Federal Court of Appeal rejected this contention. Most, however, also held that the plaintiffs had no arguable case on the merits of s.7. Ryan J. took an interesting middle position; he refrained from deciding the last point; instead, he held that whether Cruise testing would ultimately be to the benefit or detriment of the personal security of Canadians involved a complex of military, diplomatic, technical, psychological, and moral considerations – the evaluation of which was not manageable by a court of law. The judgment of Ryan J. left open the possibility that the norm in s.7 applied to the government of Canada which was bound to make a good faith effort to apply it, even if a court would not second-guess its decision.

The last statement may seem a bit fanciful because you would expect Canadian governments to attempt to avoid irresponsibly endangering the physical survival of the population even without being told by the Constitution to do so.

Perhaps a more persuasive demonstration of how norms can be legally binding, but judicially unenforceable, is found in s.36 of the *Constitution Act, 1982*. Section 36 says:

> 36(1) Without altering the legislative authority of Parliament or of the provincial legislatures, or rights of any of them with respect to the exercise of their legislative authority, Parliament and the legislatures, together with the government of Canada and the provincial governments, are committed to:
>
> (a) promoting equal opportunities for the well-being of Canadians;
>
> (b) furthering economic development to reduce disparity in opportunities; and
>
> (c) providing essential public services of reasonable quality to all Canadians.
>
> (2) Parliament and the government of Canada are committed to the principle of making equalization payments to ensure that provincial governments have sufficient revenues to provide reasonably comparable levels of public services at reasonably comparable levels of taxation.

The convoluted language of s.36(1) was probably intended to make the subsection nonjusticiable, i.e., not subject to binding judicial interpretation. It is not clear that the language chosen accomplishes that goal. A court might not accept that part of a document which describes itself as "the supreme law of Canada"

(*Constitution Act, 1982*, s.52) has no legal effect. If it does have a legal effect, the court might then reason, the ordinary principle that courts have the final say on what it means should apply. Nothing in the section expressly says that the final say in the matter lies with other branches of government. The court might then lend a narrow construction to the opening section, perhaps interpreting it as a signal that the federal-provincial division of powers is not altered. Some day, therefore, someone in a community which lacks safe drinking water may win a judicial declaration that the province has failed to meet its duty to supply him with "essential public services."

It is likely, however, that the courts will conclude that s.36(1) is nonjusticiable. The courts might support their interpretation of the language of s.36 with a number of jurisprudential considerations. American courts, in the last few decades exceptionally activist, have deliberately refrained from entering into matters of wealth distribution and public service delivery; to do so, they have reasoned, would result in an excessive interference with the workings of majoritarian democracy. Canadian courts might be impressed with the anti-democratic objection, or at least believe that the framers of s.36 were. It is well known that the word "property" was deleted from the usual "life, liberty and property" formula when s.7 of the *Charter* was drafted because of a fear that it would authorize the second-guessing of social welfare schemes engaged in by the U.S. Supreme Court in the beginning of the twentieth century (*R.* v. *Holman* (1982), 28 C.R. (3d) 378 (B.C. Prov. Ct.); Schwartz 1983, 36). Courts might also attribute to the framers of s.36(1) the belief that courts lack expertise in economic matters or that economic issues require systematic understanding and reform; whereas courts can only examine and respond to the narrow problems that particular lawsuits happen to raise. The nonjusticiability of s.36(1) does not mean that it is not legally binding, only that governments and legislatures must authorize interpreters rather than the courts. It might be argued once again, however, that s.36(1) is so vague and platitudinous that a government will always regard itself as complying with it.

Section 36(2), however, is not so bland that the federal government must perpetually be content to swallow it. Some federal government of the future may believe that it is better to encourage people to move to more prosperous regions of the country, rather than to subsidize their staying put; that the federal government should not obscure the effects of economic mismanagement by provincial governments; that the federal government should not incur the political costs of raising transfer payment money at the same time as provincial governments can improve their political standing by spending it; or that the federal spending power should be freely used to pressure provinces to comply with federal policies, even non-economic ones, such as encouraging official bilingualism; and that the power of the federal government is diminished if it is under a standing obligation to help out have-not provinces in any event. The federal government that has these beliefs will not be free to act upon them. Even if s.36(2) is not enforceable by court action, the government will be legally bound to comply with it.

It is likely that the framers of s.36(2) intended it to be nonjusticiable. As with s.36(1), however, it is not clear that the language serves any such intention. Indeed, the argument for justiciability is stronger with s.36(2) than s.36(1). The former, unlike the latter, does not contain the "without altering . . ." phrase, and that phrase does not grammatically extend into s.36(2). It could be argued that the jurisprudential reasons for making s.36(1) nonjusticiable apply with equal force to s.36(2); and therefore that the "without altering . . ." phrase should be assumed to extend to it; that it is excessively formalistic to let the period put an end to the effect of the "without altering . . ." phrase. A plausible reply to this, however, might point to several substantial differences between the subsections: subsection 36(2) is more narrow in its scope, so the anti-democratic object applies with less force; it is less platitudinous, so the possibility of its being breached is greater; it imposes a burden on one level of government for the benefit of others, rather than on a government for the benefit of its own electorate, so that the political costs of breaching it may be less. It could be argued that the word "principle" in subsection 36(2) implies that the norm is too vague and imprecise for judicial interpretation. To this it maybe replied that there are many sections of the constitution that are imprecise: what does section 91(2) of the *Constitution Act, 1867* mean when it gives the federal level of government power over "Trade and Commerce"? In the case of s.36(2), a court could accept that the federal government has a certain amount of discretion to interpret this principle, but could not the court also find in some egregious cases that the principle has clearly been unjustifiably violated?

I will now return to the starting point of this discussion—the federal proposal that governments commit themselves "in principle" to having a s.37 type of conference before amending certain sections of the constitution dealing with aboriginal peoples. The words "committed in principle" were probably intended by the federal drafters to establish the nonjusticiability of the proposed amendment. It may have been thought that the "committed to the principle" language of s.36(2) of the *Constitution Act, 1982* established a formula for making constitutional norms unenforceable. If s.36(2) is nonjusticiable, however, it may be partly because of its conjunction with s.36(1) which contains a somewhat clearer formula for nonjusticiability ("without altering the legislative authority of parliament or of the provincial legislatures . . ."). The federal proposal for an amendment on consultation does not appear in conjunction with any "without altering . . ." language. Furthermore, as has just been shown, s.36(2) itself may not be nonjusticiable. Looking at the federal proposal on consultation on its own terms, a court might view "in principle" as indicating that the prime minister is to be allowed a broad discretion on which aboriginal organizations to invite, when the conference should be, what the format for discussions should be, and so on. A court might still be prepared to adjudge the constitution as having been violated, however, in egregious cases. For example, could a court not refuse to recognize an amendment concerning aboriginal rights if no conference were held at all—or if no representatives of the Métis were invited? It would be surprising, indeed, if a court did otherwise. In my opinion, the federal proposal on the constitution was enforceable by court action. It therefore amounted to an amendment to the amending formula in s.38(2) of the *Constitution Act, 1982*, and as such clearly required unanimous provincial consent. Even if the federal proposed amendment had been nonjusticiable, however, it would still have imposed a legally binding restriction on the manner in which certain amendments to the constitution can be made. It would still have been an amendment to s.38(2) of the *Constitution Act, 1982* and would have required the unanimous consent of the provinces. Given that governments can be expected to comply with the law even if the courts do not reproach them for doing otherwise, a nonjusticiable amendment to the amending formula will have practically the same effect as a justiciable amendment and ought to require the same measure of governmental consent.

While no in-depth legal analyses were offered at the backroom ministerial meetings of the March '83 First Ministers' Conference, several delegations did express the view that the consultation clause would require unanimous consent, and these concerns were a major cause of the proposal's rejection. Before moving on, it is worth examining the difference between a nonjusticiable legal principle and a convention. The latter are norms created and interpreted by executive and legislative officials, rather than courts. That a government must resign when it loses a vote of confidence in the House of Commons is a convention, but the opposition could not bring an action to enforce the resignation if the government continued in power. The governor general might use his legal authority to ask another party to form a government, or to call an election, or he might leave it for the voters at the next election to determine the consequences of noncompliance with the convention. The distinction between conventions and legal norms was a central issue in the *Patriation reference (Reference Re Amendment of the Constitution of Canada* (1981), 125 D.L.R. (3d) 1). The Supreme Court of Canada in that case answered a number of reference questions (that is, requests for advisory opinions from federal or provincial governments) on whether a convention existed that required provincial consent before the federal government requested the British Parliament to amend the constitution of Canada on matters within provincial competence. The federal government halted its unilateral patriation plans and made one last try for a compromise agreement in light of a majority Supreme Court of Canada decision that substantial provincial consent was required by convention, though not by law. What difference did it make that the requirement was conventional, rather than legal? One difference was that the courts would not have recognized the new constitution had it been brought about by illegal action; whereas the courts would have respected the new legal state of affairs if it had been brought about by merely anti-conventional action. Another difference is that most observers regard it as a far more deplorable breach of political morality to break the law than to break a convention. Since political conventions are basically established by practice, they would be perpetually ensconced unless someone at some time contravened them. It is accepted that changed circumstances or ideas about political justice may require the development of new conventions. The federal government held open the possibility, even after the Supreme Court's ruling, that it might proceed unilaterally on patriation of the constitution. It is very doubtful whether it would have threatened unilateral action had it been declared illegal, and not merely anti-conventional.

The violation of a nonjusticiable rule of constitutional law should be seen as equivalent in political morality to violating a justiciable rule of law, as opposed to contravening a convention. The fact that there is no impartial adjudicator to enforce the rule makes it more likely that it will in practice be violated. Most political officials, however, can be expected to make a good faith effort to abide by the supreme law of the land.

I have spoken about nonjusticiable principles as those that are not subject to interpretation and enforcement by the courts. In the United States, this definition is unproblematic because American federal courts are constitutionally prohibited from giving advisory opinions; Article III, Constitution of the United States; see for example, *Valley Forge College* v. *Americans United*, 70 L.Ed. 2d 700 (1982). In Canada, however, reference cases are very common. The *Patriation Reference* established a precedent for the Supreme Court giving advisory opinions on a nonlegal matter—in that case, the content of a political convention. It is entirely possible that the Court will be prepared to give advisory opinions on the meaning of nonjusticiable sections of the constitution. The Court might, for example, answer a request from a province on whether a particular fiscal arrangement violated subsection 36(2) of the *Constitution Act, 1982*. (It will be assumed for present purposes that the subsection is in fact nonjusticiable.) Governments would not be bound to accept the Court's ruling on the meaning of a nonjusticiable section of the constitution, but would in practice find it politically difficult to maintain their own legal interpretation in light of a contrary opinion of the Supreme Court of Canada. Both the *de jure* and *de facto* differences between nonjusticiable and justiciable sections of the Canadian constitution may turn out to be minimal.

On 21 June, 1984, the governor general proclaimed into force s.35.1 of the *Constitution Act, 1982* as amended. It guarantees that First Ministers will meet with representatives of aboriginal organizations before there are any amendments to certain sections of the constitution that deal specially with the rights of aboriginal peoples: s.91(24) of the *Constitution Act, 1867* (federal jurisdiction over Indians and lands reserved for Indians), s.25 of the *Constitution Act, 1982* (the *Charter* should be construed as to not derogate from aboriginal and treaty rights) and Part II of the *Constitution Act, 1982* (which recognizes and affirms aboriginal and treaty rights). The preamble of the 21 June, 1984, proclamation of the amendment expressly cites the s.38 amending formula—the consent of the federal government and of at least two thirds of the provinces that have half of the population. Nine provinces had passed resolutions supporting the amendment. Quebec had not. According to the analysis in this chapter, s.35.1 was an amendment to the amending formula and really required unanimous provincial consent, as contemplated by s.42 of the *Constitution Act, 1982*. The mere fact that the resolution mistakenly assumes that the s.38 amending formula applies would not in itself make s.35 unconstitutional. If all 10 provinces had supported the amendment, the mistaken legal assumption probably would not matter. But now that the resolution has been proclaimed into force, it is probably too late for Quebec to "come on board." (The fact that the resolution has already been proclaimed is not the only technical problem with Quebec's now "coming on board." Another is that under the s.38 amending formula, a proclamation cannot take place more than three years after the first legislature has expressed its support for the amendment. It is not clear whether this three year rule would apply to a s.42 amendment – and even less clear whether it applies to what is really a s.42 amendment that has been mischaracterized as a s.38 amendment.) The best way to cure the constitutional infirmity of s.35.1 would not be for Quebec to now express its support and for the governor general to issue another proclamation. Rather, the whole amending process should start over. The House of Commons and Senate and all 10 provincial legislatures should pass resolutions supporting the amendment.

Section 35.1 will make little practical difference to anyone. Even if it did not exist, the precedent has already been established that First Ministers should meet with aboriginal organizations before amending the constitution on matters specially affecting aboriginal peoples. Both the precedents and the (mistakenly) perceived validity of s.35.1 will ensure that First Ministers will meet with aboriginal organizations whenever changes are contemplated in the constitutional rights of aboriginal peoples. The legal validity of s.35.1 may never be tested in the courts. It is disturbing, nonetheless, that the participants, the public, and the academics of Canada did not seriously consider whether on its very first use, the new amending formula has been misapplied.

Chapter VIII

Modern Land Claims Agreements

It was the Inuit Committee on National Issues (ICNI) that first proposed, during the series of preparatory meetings, an amendment that would expressly characterize modern land claims as "treaties" for the purposes of s.35(1) of the *Constitution Act, 1982*. Inuit were involved in massive land claim negotiations in the Yukon and Northwest Territories, and some Inuit were already operating in Northern Quebec under the terms of the James Bay Agreement of 1975. Many of the 19 sections of that agreement conclude with a statement that the section cannot be amended without the consent of the governments affected – including "the interested Native party." The agreement could not, of its own force, assure the Inuit or Cree subject to it that a legislature would not subsequently, in the exercise of its supremacy, violate or outright abrogate the agreement. There were some quasi-constitutional documents that might have protected the agreement to some extent. *The Canadian Bill of Rights*, Section 1(a) protects: "the right of the individual to life, liberty, security of the person and enjoyment of property, and the right not to be deprived thereof except by due process of law." There would be problems for a native group attempting to invalidate an infringement of the agreement on the basis of section 1(a). It refers to the rights of the individual, and so might not apply to the rights of a collectivity (Although I think protection of the former may require protection of the latter); violations of the agreement might not affect any interest enumerated in s.1(a); the clause may be essentially limited to requiring procedural fairness when rights are taken away, rather than prohibiting substantive unfairness. Even if a case could be made out, the *Canadian Bill of Rights* only applies to federal laws; and Parliament can override it by the simple expedient of stamping its legislation as "notwithstanding the Canadian Bill of Rights." There is a Quebec *Charter of Human Rights and Freedoms* (R.S.Q. 1977, c.12), but it is very doubtful that it would protect the James Bay Agreement. Section 6 is less than reassuring in its pronouncement of everyone's right "to the peaceful enjoyment and free disposition of property, except to the extent provided by law", and the legislature can override whatever protection the Quebec Charter does afford by the expedient of expressly saying that it is doing so. Aboriginal persons now enjoy, no less than everyone else, the guarantees of the *Canadian Charter of Rights and Freedoms*. Unlike the *Canadian Bill of Rights*, however, the Canadian *Charter* does not expressly guarantee property rights (although they may be implicit in the guarantee of "security of the person" in s.7 of the *Charter*; see *R.* v. *Fisherman's Wharf Ltd.* (1982), 40 N.B.R. (2d) 42).

While the *Charter* is entrenched, in the sense that it cannot be revoked or amended except through the s.38 amending process (House of Commons and Senate plus two thirds of the provinces with half the population), s.33 of the *Charter* permits Parliament or a provincial legislature to overcome many of its specific guarantees – by the traditional expedient of expressly admitting that it is doing so. Any particular override cannot have effect for more than five years, but there is nothing to keep Parliament or a legislature from reissuing the declaration over and over. The Canadian legal texts on universal human rights are too vague, too limited in scope, and too vulnerable to legislative override to ensure aboriginal groups that governments will duly honour the promises they make under land claims agreements.

Whether modern land claims agreements are constitutionally protected, therefore, depends primarily on the legal implications of s.35(1) of the *Constitution Act, 1982*. There were at least three causes for concern about whether it adequately protected the interests of aboriginal peoples:

(i) It was unclear whether "treaties" in s.35(1) included modern land claims agreements. Here's the argument for the negative: the older treaties were styled "treaties"; the modern land claims accords are almost always referred to as "settlements" or "agreements." The framers of s.35(1) chose a word associated with a particular period of aboriginal-Canadian relations. There are real differences in the nature of the old treaties and the modern land claims agreements. The former are fairly simple and concise; the latter tend to be massive documents containing all sorts of technical detail. The official publication of the James Bay Agreement by the Quebec Government (English version) is 455 pages long. It is a real question whether it is wise to preclude governments from ever unilaterally varying any part of such a complex agreement. Another significant difference between the old treaties and the modern land claims agreements is their subject matter. Only the latter contains guarantees with respect to local self-government. Whether that type of assurance should be constitutionally protected is debatable. The framers of s.35(1) would have had solid reasons for confining its scope to the simpler, more modest guarantees of the old treaties. The argument for the affirmative might go like this: although there are some differences in form and substance between the old and new treaties, their essential character is the same. An aboriginal group permanently surrenders its claim to a traditional land base in return for monetary, proprietary, or other types of compensation. Justice demands the enforcement of promises that have gained governments, and cost aboriginal groups, so much. Section 35(1) should be broadly construed to ensure that justice is done.

(ii) It was uncertain whether the "existing" treaty rights referred to in s.35(1) were only those surviving on April 17, 1982, or whether they also included treaty rights created from time to time thereafter. If the former interpretation was correct, then s.35(1) could protect the James Bay Agreement, but not the massive claims settlements that were being negotiated in the Yukon and Northwest Territories.

(iii) Even if (i) and (ii) were resolved in favour of aboriginal peoples, it would be unclear how much better off their legal position would be. Say that a particular land claims agreement is a s.35(1) "treaty"; what sort of constitutional protection does any treaty have under s.35(1)? Section 35(1) could have been understood as almost wholly ineffectual, as a strictly symbolic acknowledgement that certain rights exist; it could be understood as an unqualified guarantee that those rights will not be interfered with by legislatures; it could be understood as meaning something in between—perhaps that only justifiable interferences with the aboriginal and treaty rights are legally valid.

The constitutional amendment that emerged from the March '83 conference takes care of concerns (i) and (ii). It may have some effect on (iii): the prospect that contents of modern land claims agreements are s.35(1) treaties may worry some judges into adopting a more modest interpretation of the strength of the section in general. The amendment reads: "s.35(3) For greater certainty, in subsection (1), "treaty rights" includes rights that now exist by way of land claims agreements or may be so acquired." The original ICNI draft had read: "s.35(3) For the purposes of this Part, treaty includes any claims settlement entered into before or after the coming into force of this Act". The federal draft released on the morning of the second and final day of the March '83 First Ministers' Conference was worded a little differently: "s.35(3) For greater certainty, in subsection (1), 'treaty rights' include rights that have been or may be acquired by way of land claims settlements".

The insertion of the word "land" restricted the potential scope of the section, but otherwise the federal proposal probably had about the same effect as that of the ICNI. During the scramble at the ministerial drafting session on the last day, the federal proposal was altered. Most importantly, the reference to rights that "have been . . . acquired" was replaced by "rights that now exist." The former wording suggested that the protection of s.35(1) applied to rights under a treaty that governments originally agreed to. Section 35(3) must be read in conjunction with the "existing" reference in s.35(1), so it is unlikely that s.35(3) would be judicially construed as reviving land claims agreements rights that had been completely annihilated by legislative action prior to April 17, 1982. The former language of s.35(3) might, however, have helped to persuade a judge that a land claims agreement right that was *impaired* by legislative action on April 17, 1982, but not totally negated, would be protected in its original unrestricted form. The revised wording—"rights that now exist"—does not seem to colour the meaning of "existing" in s.35(1) one way or the other. It should be appreciated that the change in the drafting of s.35(3) has implications that extend well beyond modern land claims agreements. The "for greater certainty" and "includes" phraseology of s.35(3) appears to tell us that s.35(3) is elucidating what s.35(1) meant all along. Whatever s.35(3) says about modern land claims agreements, therefore, likely holds for treaties in general.

The final wording of s.35(3) replaces "settlements" with "agreements." The word "agreement" was my idea. It had for many years been an aspiration of mine to be able to point to a section of the constitution with some pride of authorship. I would like to think that "agreement" was a purely enlightened contribution to the protection of the rights of aboriginal peoples;

that I recommended the word because it would encompass a somewhat broader range of accords than would "settlement"; that it did not have the same negative connotation as "settlement" – of final renunciation by an aboriginal party. I would like to think all that, but I can't because it isn't true. If memory serves, rather than self-serves in this case, I did have some of those lofty considerations in mind in suggesting that the Manitoba delegation go along with the replacement of "settlement" by "agreement." But that alteration didn't happen in one step. It started off with one of the western delegations expressing the concern that the word "settlement" would encompass the scrip given to the Métis pursuant to the *Manitoba Act, 1870* and the *Dominion Lands Act, 1879*. The Manitoba delegation suggested that concern could be accommodated by changing the wording to "settlement agreement." It was an aboriginal organization that suggested dropping the word "settlement" altogether.

It was contended earlier in this chapter that what s.35(3) tells us about land claims agreements holds for treaties in general. An aspect of s.35(3) common to all three drafts was that it encompassed rights under future land claims agreements. It thus removed the doubt – or maybe established for the first time – that *in general*, treaties entered into after April 17, 1982, receive whatever protection s.35(1) affords to their contents. Question: is an agreement on self-government a "treaty"? I have no recollection of anyone discussing this possibility at the March '83 conference. In the fall of 1983 the *Penner Report* suggested that Indian First Nations governments be established by an agreement making process between the federal government and Indian governments. Could any of those agreements acquire the constitutional protection of s.35(3)? If the answer is yes, then by expanding the scope of s.35(1) to include post-April 17, 1982, agreements, s.35(3) may have provided a mechanism whereby Indian self-government in Canada can receive constitutional recognition and protection. Chapter XXI analyzes the legal position in some detail. For now, I will say only that the effect that s.35(3) may have on the constitutional position of aboriginal self-government may be one of the most important outcomes of the March '83 Conference – even if that effect did not occur to many, or even any, of the participants.

Chapter IX

The Creation of New Provinces

It was proposed by the Northwest Territories that s.42(1)(f) of the *Constitution Act, 1982* be repealed. The clause requires that the usual amending formula (consent of the House and Senate, and of at least two-thirds of the provinces containing at least 50 per cent of the population) apply where a new province is to be established. Until 1982, it was possible for Parliament by ordinary legislation to establish new provinces out of territories forming part of the Dominion. The provinces of Saskatchewan and Alberta were established in 1905 in this way. If the Yukon and Northwest Territories (or any part of them) are to become provinces, they will have to obtain the formal approval of seven provincial legislatures. The Yukon and Northwest Territories have large percentages of native people. In 1982, in accordance with a referendum approving the measure, the federal government agreed in principle to divide the Northwest Territories into two jurisdictions (Jull 1983). The southwest would be largely European, Indian, and Métis in ethnic composition. The northeastern part of the Northwest Territories would consist almost entirely of Inuit. It will be called Nunavut.

That section 42(1)(f) was inserted into the *Constitution Act, 1982*, at the request of some of the provinces gives the territorial governments some grounds for concern about whether they will be able to obtain the necessary consent when the time comes. Provinces would not have requested the inclusion of 42(1)(f) if they had not seen a possible threat to their own interests. One cause for concern on the part of provinces when the Territories seek provincial status might be the resultant diminution of the revenue base of the federal government. The federal government is constitutionally duty bound, under s.36 of the *Constitution Act, 1982,* to "the principle of making equalization payments to ensure that provincial governments have sufficient revenues to provide reasonably comparable levels of public services at reasonably comparable levels of taxation." At the present time, the Northwest Territories and Yukon cost the federal government at least as much to run as it takes back in taxes and royalties. But perhaps the day will come when they become profitable assets in the hands of the federal government. If this were to happen, provincial status for the Territories would not necessarily reduce the revenue base of the federal government that much because the federal government would retain its taxing power under s.91(3) of the *Constitution Act, 1867* – a power the government has used to ensure that the rest of Canada benefits from resource development in Alberta. On the other hand, it is possible that an Arctic province would exercise its power over non-renewable resources in section 92A of the *Constitution Act, 1867* to provide for slower resource development than the federal government would. A compromise that both Canada and the United States have used in connection with a resource rich but population poor territory is to allow it to become a province or state, but allow the federal government to retain property ownership over much of the land. It was not until 1930 that ownership of natural resources was transferred to the three Prairie provinces; *Constitution Act, 1930*.

Another concern on the part of some provinces might be the dilution of their ability to block unwanted constitutional change. Under s.38 of the *Constitution Act, 1982,* it takes the assent of two thirds of the provinces with half the population of Canada to authorize most constitutional changes. The approval of a new province might well authorize an amendment that would otherwise have failed. The Territories have very small populations, however, and any province created out of them would do little to contribute to the necessary "fifty percent of the population" figure. Furthermore, s.38(2) of the *Constitution Act, 1982* permits provinces to opt out of the application of unwanted constitutional change. Thus the admission of a new province would probably be seen as only a minor diminution of the constitutional voting power of existing provinces.

A related concern of the provinces might be that the addition of new provinces will reduce the power of existing provinces at nonconstitutional federal-provincial conferences.

Given Kennan's law – that the difficulty of negotiations varies with the square of the number of participants – it will be 39.7 per cent more difficult to obtain a consensus when there are twelve provinces rather than ten. This might enhance the federal ability to use lack of consensus as a justification for unilateral federal action. On the other hand, the federal government can always structure its proposals to ensure discord anyway. (It's a straightforward matter of combining a proposal of byzantine complexity with minimal opportunity for study.) Provinces are not likely to be impressed enough by the analogy with discipleship to prefer being one of twelve to being one of ten. Furthermore, the new provinces might be sufficiently dependent on federal subvention to generally behave as federal allies at conferences.

Should the Territories fear the reappearance of provincial dentism? (Dentism is to irredentism as patriation is to repatriation.) In 1968, Premier W.A.C. Bennett proposed the extension of provincial boundaries northward to encompass the entire Arctic. When asked whether he would allow a referendum for Northerners on the proposal, Premier Bennett replied that none was held when British Columbia was added to Confederation – and if there had been one, B.C. probably wouldn't have joined (*Globe & Mail*, December 14, 1968, p.1). Might the provinces one day reject an application by a northern Territory for provincehood, hoping that it will prefer annexation by a province to continued federal vassalage? Provinces realize that the people of the Territories would prefer limited autonomy under federal supervision to complete assimilation by a province. More importantly, the people of the Territories have made considerable progress in the last decade towards self-government, and it is now generally accepted that their wishes must be accorded some respect. Maybe not enough respect to oblige their desire for independent provincehood, but certainly enough to accept their distaste for annexation by an existing province.

It may have served a useful educational purpose for the Territories to remind the rest of Canada of the unusual obstacles they face to achieving provincehood. But there was no chance of success for the proposal to repeal s.42(1)(f) of the *Constitution Act, 1982* and return control of admission of new provinces to Parliament. The refusal of Quebec to recognize the new Constitution in itself would have blocked the repeal of s.42(1)(f) because amendments to Part V of the *Constitution Act, 1982* (which deals with amendments) require unanimous provincial consent. Furthermore, the provinces, which had earlier insisted on the inclusions of s.42(1)(f), did not exhibit any desire to reverse themselves. The proposal to repeal s.42(1)(f) would have required the provinces to give carte blanche to the federal government with respect to the admission of northern Territories. It is much more likely that seven of them will agree to a particular proposal when the time comes than that all 10 will agree to deny themselves any voice in the matter.

Chapter X

The 1983-84 Process and Conference

The Early Stages of the Preparatory Process

Seven months passed after the March '83 conference before another s.37 level meeting at an official level was held. It was not until a meeting on October 18, in Edmonton, which the federal invitation described as an "informal" meeting of officials, that the parties discussed an agenda for the '83-'84 First Ministers' Conference. In deference to the concerns of several delegations that the agenda be made more manageable than it had been the previous year, it was generally agreed that for '83-'84 "only" four items would be discussed:

1. aboriginal self-government
   - resourcing of self-government
   - language and culture
2. land base for the Métis
3. treaty rights and aboriginal title
4. equality rights

The headings actually allowed for the discussion of almost every one of the subitems left over from the '83 First Ministers' Conference. Wine had been poured out of a dozen old bottles into four new vats. There was room in the latter for some new concoctions to be added. Participants at the Edmonton meeting also discussed the combination of deputy ministerial and ministerial level meetings that should be used in the preparatory process. The matter was left for further consideration at a ministerial level meeting in Ottawa on November 2-3. The preparatory process might have been more productive if ministerial level meetings had dominated lower level ones-both numerically and in terms of guiding the discussions. From the 1982-1983 process, it could be expected that information and attitudes disclosed at officials level meetings would be inadequately transmitted up to higher echelons of government; that bureaucrats would cite their lack of authority to justify or rationalize their failure to substantively respond to aboriginal proposals; and that some aboriginal organizations would be slack about working out a corporate position and ensuring that their speakers espoused it, rather than that of their own faction. At a meeting in Ottawa on November 2-3, 1984, it was nonetheless agreed that there would be working groups of officials formed for each of the agenda items.

The agenda headings from Edmonton were reworded slightly. When the subitems they contained were agreed upon, it was obvious that the agenda was no more limited than it had been the previous year. The new list:

1. equality rights
2. aboriginal title and aboriginal rights, treaties and treaty rights
   (a) aboriginal title
   (b) aboriginal rights
   (c) treaties
   (d) treaty rights
   (e) removal of "existing"
   (f) First Nations' governments, including fiscal relations, jurisdiction, language, culture, education, and religions.
3. land and resources
   (a) Métis self-identification
   (b) Métis land base
   (c) Métis self-government on land bases (including economic development, education, training, language and culture, services, and resourcing of Métis government)
   (d) resources on and off existing and future Métis lands
   (e) existing Métis land base
   (f) implementation
4. aboriginal self-government
   Métis government outside Métis lands:
   (a) economic development
   (b) education and training
   (c) language and culture

(d) services
(e) resourcing of aboriginal governments
(f) implementation

There was an understanding between a couple of the aboriginal organizations that the working groups would not take their focus from subject matter, but rather from the identity of the aboriginal organization which would play the lead role. The Assembly of First Nations (AFN) concentrated their efforts on Working Group 2. Their representations were largely concerned with self-government, which they maintained was an aboriginal right. Working Group 3 was where the Métis National Council (MNC) presented most of their expositions and proposals. By default, the Inuit Committee on National Issues (ICNI) and the Native Council of Canada (NCC) were the most active aboriginal participants in Working Group 4.

Week-long sets of working group meetings were held in Winnipeg on November 14-18, 1983, and Ottawa, December 12-16. The chairman of each group (Ottawa bureaucrats except for the Northwest Territorial public servant who chaired Working Group 3) supervised the preparation of summary reports for the benefit of ministers. To finish off the discussions and assist the chairman in preparing his report, an extra meeting of Working Group 3 was held in Edmonton on January 11-12. The summaries, some of which were admirably thorough and impartial, may have helped ministers to appreciate the options outlined and proposals advanced at the officials level meeting. The upper limit of the usefulness of the summaries, of course, was defined by the productivity of the sessions on which they were based, and the latter were subject to the predictable drawbacks of conferences at the officials level.

The Penner Report

In the middle of October 1983, the *Penner Report* was released by the House Special Committee on Indian Self Government. It forcefully condemned the existing system of governing Indian communities. It cites and deplores the social, economic, educational, and health conditions in which many Canadian Indians must live. The words of Chief David Ahenakew are quoted: "Current federal policies and institutions are operating to reinforce Indian poverty and dependence, rather than to promote self-sufficiency" (*Penner Report*, 40). The powers of band governments under the *Indian Act* are characterized as excessively circumscribed. Condemned also is the failure of the *Indian Act* to make any concessions to the diversity of Indian communities. Reproduced is the view of the Department of Indian

Affairs and Northern Development (DIAND) that: "band governments are more like administrative arms of the Department of Indian Affairs than they are governments accountable to band members" (*Penner Report*, 17).

The *Penner Report* acknowledges that the federal government spent large amounts of money on service delivery to Indian communities and that in 1968 a decision was made to turn over administrative control to band governments. What actually happens, according to the *Penner Report*, is that band governments are required to devote inordinate amounts of time, money, and energy to obtain funding for particular items in their budget at one end and then justify the expenditures at the other. The effect is wasteful and demoralizing. There is a strongly held suspicion among Indians that the DIAND uses its control of funding to impose its own goals on Indian communities (*Penner Report*, 86). All this bureaucratic control is not only costly to Indian communities but also to the government itself; the accounting firm of Coopers & Lybrand concluded that one quarter of the funds that DIAND spent in 1981-1982 on its Indian and Inuit Affairs Program went to departmental administration (*Penner Report*, 86). The key elements of the *Penner Report*'s program for reform:

(i) Allow Indian bands to determine the constitutional structure of their own governments and form governments; each would decide whether to constitute a distinct Indian First Nation Government [IFNG] or amalgamate in some way with certain other bands (*Penner Report*, recommendation 8).

(ii) The federal government would formally recognize an IFNG as long as the latter satisfied certain criteria, including:

- demonstrated support for the governmental structure by a majority of the people;
- an adequate system of accountability by the government to the community;
- a system for deciding who can belong to the community that is consistent with international standards of human rights (recommendation 11).

(iii) The general principle that should apply is that "full legislative and policy-making powers on matters affecting Indian people, and full control over the territory and resources within the boundaries of Indian lands, should be among the powers of Indian First Nations governments" (recommendation 20).

(iv) Parliament should authorize the federal government to enter into bilateral agreements with IFNGs whereby the exact scope of their law making authority would be determined (recommendation 21).

(v) The economic base of IFNGs would be expanded and made more secure by granting Indian communities full legal control over their lands to fully share in the revenues from the development of natural resources; and by settling their outstanding land claims (recommendations 24, 39, 40, 43).

(vi) While the Committee "hopes and expects" that the measures in (v) and other long-term entrenched financial arrangements" would eventually provide IFNGs with adequate funding, the federal government should, in the interim, make transfer payments. These would be unconditional. Their quantum might be arrived at by having the federal government negotiate the subsidy the IFNGs would receive altogether. A formula based on population and need would determine what fraction of the total that any particular IFNG would be entitled to (recommendation 32).

The *Penner Report*'s critique of existing arrangements often hit on the mark, and there is much that is attractive in the alternative that it sketches. The report's usefulness as a program for reform is limited by its approach: it often reads more like an advocate's brief for Indian political autonomy than a balanced appraisal of how that goal can and should be reconciled with the interests of the larger Canadian community. The latter will be concerned about direct threats to its material welfare, such as pollution and wildlife depletion caused by activities on the reserve, yet the report onesidedly recommends that: "On their own lands, Indian First Nation governments would have the power to regulate traditional pursuits such as hunting, fishing and trapping without outside interference. On lands covered by treaties or aboriginal claims, such powers would be exercised jointly with other governments" (*Penner Report*, 66). The report does not acknowledge that federal and provincial governments must be concerned that the exemption of reserves from all sorts of regulatory schemes—fiscal, labour relations, and so on—might undermine their general effectiveness.

Because many members of Indian communities move to and remain in the cities of Canada, some Canadian governments might find that their self-interest urges them to impose certain educational standards on Indian First Nations governments. Other governments may pursue the same goal for principled, rather than self-regarding reasons; they might believe that the individual is primary and that he should be made aware of many possible ways of life and equipped with the knowledge to successfully travel many of them. The legitimacy of imposed schooling standards is not considered at all by the *Penner Report.* Nor is the appropriateness of insisting on other social standards of the larger Canadian community-such as universal access to free medical care or universal participation in the system of progressive income taxation. Should the *Canadian Charter of Rights and Freedoms*, binding on other public authorities in Canada, apply to Indian First Nations governments? The report does not say. It vaguely suggests that there be "some system of accountability by the government to the people concerned" (*Penner Report*, recommendation 11) which "might include . . . the protection of individual and collective rights" (*Penner Report*, 58).

The somewhat partial and advocatory nature of the report may well have made it more, rather than less, effective as a proposal for reform. As written, the report is easy to understand and hard to ignore. Had it been a more thorough judicious attempt to reconcile Indian political autonomy with the legitimate interests and concerns of the larger community, the main thrust of the report might have been obscured and its inspirational power diminished. The report points governments in a direction in which they ought to move; it imparts to their journey some impetus. There will be plenty of people with philosophical, ideological, or self-interested motivations for helping a government stop before it's gone too far.

If accommodation must be reached between Indian political autonomy and the interests of the larger community, how are its terms to be established? Almost a year after the *Penner Report*, the federal government introduced a draft "Act relating to self-government for Indian Nations" (Bill C-52, An Act relating to self-government for Indian nations, First Reading, June 29, 1984). It uses a variety of mechanisms. In some cases a substantive standard would be directly imposed by the legislation itself; section 28 requires that the laws of Indian nations conform to the *Canadian Charter of Rights and Freedoms* and international human rights covenants signed by the government of Canada. While some heads of legislative authority are granted by s.16 to all Indian First Nation governments, others enumerated in s.18 are left to bilateral negotiations between the Indian Nation and the federal government. Limitations may be attached to powers thereby granted. The federal government could, for example, insist on compliance with conservation laws as a condition of granting a First Nation legislative authority over the wildlife on its lands. Other limitations are left to the regulatory discretion of Cabinet; s.3(1)(a) contemplates the promulgation of rules concerning the recognition of Indian First Nations that would supplement the general criteria stated by s.6; the law of a First Nation could be disallowed at any time by the federal Cabinet (s.31). Section 6(vii) makes it a condition of the recognition of an IFNG that its constitution: "(vii) identify or provide for an independent system for reviewing executive decisions of the government of the Indian Nation on grounds that they are illegal, unreasonable or unfair".

It would be prudent to wait until negotiations with Indian First Nations governments begin before the federal government decides whether and in what areas limitations ought to be imposed. Hearing the ambitions and supporting arguments of Indian First Nations will give a government a better understanding of what issues about limitations must be addressed and how these issues should be resolved. Both participatory democracy and the interests of First Nations would be served in many cases, however, by a decision at some point to lay before Parliament limitations on First Nations government that the federal government considers just and expedient. The constraints could be enacted as directly binding on First Nations governments, framed instead as instructions to federal negotiations, or left in the form of a statement of government intentions. Any of these measures would facilitate public scrutiny and discussion. They would also assist First Nations. There can be no real doubt that the federal government will end up imposing, one way or another, certain limitations on Indian First Nations. In planning both its policy and political initiatives, it may assist a First Nation to learn from an authoritative pronouncement that a constraint on its political autonomy exists, rather than infer the constraint from a lengthy series of negotiations with the federal government or decisions by the federal Cabinet. Public disclosure may also be more fair to First Nations; it will help assure them that like cases are treated alike. It will also help ensure them ample opportunity to criticize unwarranted constraints and agitate for their modification or withdrawal.

Another forum that might be appropriate for developing guidelines on self-government agreements is the s.37 process. The principles might be embodied in a binding constitutional amendment; but a nonjusticiable amendment, or an altogether nonlegal political accord, is more likely to be the repository. Regular communication between bilateral negotiations (or trilateral-including the government of the province where the aboriginal community is situated) and the s.37 process might benefit both. Participants in the s.37 process could develop their understanding of the practical implications of self-government by learning how it is being implemented in particular communities. In return they might provide the negotiations with a formally expressed set of principles or suggestions, or at the very least, the odd bit of useful advice. Because the s.37 process involves First Ministers' meetings, its monitoring of the bilateral negotiations would bring to the latter public and media attention which might stimulate their progress. A countervailing risk that must be considered is that the infusion of opinion and criticism from the fourteen or fifteen s.37 participants who would ordinarily not be involved could impede or disrupt local negotiations. The timing and detail of the reporting relationship would have to be modulated to strike a balance between edification and deadification.

The 1984 Ministerial Meetings and First Ministers' Conference: Focus on Self-government

The release of the *Penner Report* helped to give the preparatory process – and ultimately the First Ministers' Conference – a central focus: aboriginal self-government. Pursuant to a standing rule of the House of Commons, the committee requested that the government issue a response to the report within 120 days of its release. The possibility was raised that the government would prepare draft legislation to implement the report some time after that. The *Penner Report* recommended immediate legislative changes to establish bilateral negotiations, but it also called – without much precision – for the right of Indian peoples to self-government to be "expressly stated and entrenched in the Constitution of Canada." There was widespread interest in how the federal government would respond on the constitutional plane. The concentration of attention on self-government was facilitated by working group meetings along organization, rather than subject, lines. The

AFN could speak to political autonomy in Working Group 2, the MNC in Working Group 3, the ICNI and the NCC in Groups 2, 3 and especially 4. It made a good deal of organizational sense to tackle self-government early in the s.37 process because any political authority granted to aboriginal groups could be used by them to secure or advance their other interests-cultural, economic, conservational, and so on.

Was it a drawback of the focus on self-government that attention was diverted from issues that required early resolution if they were to be settled by political negotiations rather than legal adjudication-issues such as the meaning of "existing" and "recognized and affirmed" in s.37 of the *Constitution Act, 1982*? On January 11, 1983, a Saskatchewan provincial court judge ruled in *R.* v. *Bear*, [1983] 2 C.N.L.R. 123 that s.35 did not restore to treaties their original force if they had been restricted by statute on April 17, 1982. A more detailed ruling to the same effect was delivered by the Saskatchewan Court of Queen's Bench on July 22, 1983. For all anyone knew in the fall of 1983 and spring of 1984 these cases were on the way to the Supreme Court of Canada where a definitive ruling on the general implications of "existing" would be made. It is highly unlikely that agreement would have been made on defining the structure and content of s.35 even if there had not been a primary emphasis on self-government. The AFN attempted to convey a broad, conceptual understanding of aboriginal title, leaving it for later, perhaps, to attempt to negotiate precise legal formulae. The federal government and most of the provinces made no effort to propose policy directions, let alone drafting suggestions, for the clarification of s.35. The concentration of attention on self-government did not divert water from a river that was rushing forward.

At the ministerial meeting in Yellowknife, the minister of justice said that the government was willing to consider two approaches to the constitutional implementation of self-government. One alternative would be for s.37 participants to agree on a statement of principles that would guide those charged with organizing institutions of self-government for aboriginal peoples. These principles would not be legally binding but would give direction to officials such as those involved in community based negotiations with respect to self-government agreements. The second alternative would be "accelerated negotiations." In between the 1984 and 1985 conferences, representative aboriginal communities would be chosen for intensive negotiations about and early implementation of self-government. The experience with these communities would be reported to the

1985 conference. Participants would then draw on what had been learned to determine what aspects of self-government should be entrenched in the Constitution.

The statement of principles proposal was not elaborated by the federal government at Yellowknife or at the subsequent preparatory meetings. The federal government did not release its reply to the *Penner Report* until March 5 – three days before the beginning of the First Ministers' Conference. If the act of publication did not lag far behind the completion of internal deliberations, the federal government was ill-positioned in late January (and even February) of 1984 to propose general guidelines on self-government with respect to all three aboriginal peoples. If the Yellowknife meeting was early in the federal government's process of reflection, it was late in the lead-up process to the First Ministers' Conference, very late for the purposes of working out an adequately well-understood set of substantial guidelines on self-government.

The considerable merit of establishing a process of communications between community based negotiations and the s.37 process has been discussed earlier in this chapter. If the federal Liberals had remained in power for the year after the March '84 conference; if the government had acted quickly after the Conference to select communities and establish ground rules for negotiations; if it had devoted a good deal of bureaucratic and political attention to them; if it had helped the communities obtain and pay for the necessary technical expertise; then, the "accelerated negotiations" proposal might have been a major contribution to the s.37 process and the development of aboriginal self-government in Canada. One year is not a long time for an experiment in self-government, but an intensive negotiating effort might have provided real edification to s.37 participants. The federal government, however, could not or did not supply the necessary assurances that all the above-cited "ifs" would become realities. It was generally (and correctly) believed that the governing party would not retain power after the next election. At preparatory meetings subsequent to Yellowknife, the federal government did not supply the sort of detail about the proposal to create any confidence that, even if it did remain in power, it would be able to implement its proposal with any promptness. "Accelerated negotiations" were seen by some aboriginal delegates as amounting to protracted delay; they wanted constitutional guarantees to emanate from the March '84 conference and did not want to see a failure to do so attributed to the need to await the results of an unpromising experiment.

An officials' level meeting was held in Toronto on February 11, 1984, to discuss the two options proposed by the federal government in Yellowknife. Two days later, again in Toronto, a final ministerial level meeting was held to discuss the subject matter of Working Groups 3 and 4. The federal government proposed that one more working group meeting be held, to clarify the range of options available to First Ministers. This last preparatory meeting, in Victoria, was marked by the strong rejection of the "accelerated negotiations" proposal by most of the aboriginal organizations and the inability of the federal government to satisfy requests from both the provinces and the aboriginal organizations that it specify what proposal it would lay before the First Ministers' Conference.

The centrepiece of the March '84 conference turned out to be the federal government's draft constitutional amendment on aboriginal self-government. Was what was put on the table a nutritious and mild offering rejected by a finicky company, or was it shiny waxed fruit? Chapter XVIII will attempt an answer. The discussion of the first day focussed on federal responsibility for the Métis, a subject that will be examined in Chapters XVI and XVII.

It was apparent on the first afternoon that the federal government's proposal on self-government would not be generally accepted. The federal government took no initiative in arranging backroom meetings of officials and ministers to work on draft amendments or an accord, but, at the end of the first afternoon, did go along with the suggestion of several delegations that they be held. There was some support among the provinces for proposals by Nova Scotia and Manitoba for a modest political accord, one that would principally serve to recognize the appropriateness of enhanced political authority for aboriginal peoples, and committing the parties to intensive study and negotiation on that issue over the coming year. Some provinces, however, objected to the proposal on the grounds that a political accord was unnecessary and that it might actually be deleterious to the process by prematurely narrowing the areas open for discussion. The aboriginal organizations were generally uninterested in a political accord that did not contain any constitutional amendments. They did not want to help give the conference the aura of success where it had failed to produce any constitutional reform.

There was actually an amendment that seemed innocuous enough to have been agreed upon. It was advanced at the conference by, among others, Manitoba, Nova Scotia and the ICNI. The Manitoba draft read:

> s.35(5) Any person or group whose rights, as guaranteed by this Part, have been infringed or denied, may apply to a court of competent jurisdiction to obtain such remedy as the court considers appropriate and just in the circumstances. Any application may be brought by a representative aboriginal organization or governmental entity.

All three drafts drew on the analogy of s.24(1) of the *Charter of Rights and Freedoms*: "Anyone whose rights or freedoms, as guaranteed by this *Charter* have been infringed or denied may apply to a court of competent jurisdiction to obtain such remedy as the court considers appropriate and just in the circumstances".

Even without a remedies clause, an aboriginal person or group should generally be able to litigate a perceived infringement on his or their aboriginal or treaty rights. An action for a judicial declaration of rights would be possible, for example, even without an express remedies clause. The inclusion of a clause would have confirmed that the substantive parts of s.35 are to be taken seriously by the courts; the existence of a remedies clause would discourage judges from viewing s.35 as merely symbolic. Most participants at the March '84 conference undoubtedly accepted that s.35 has at least some legal bite to it; had they considered a remedies clause on the merits, they would probably not have balked at its acceptance merely because the clause might have added a little to the legal credibility of s.35.

The last sentence of the Manitoba proposal—which is not contained in the Nova Scotia or ICNI drafts—might have troubled some delegations. It is not clear what a "representative aboriginal organization or governmental entity" means, although the courts might not have had too much difficulty applying the phrase to a concrete case. The last line of the Manitoba proposal might have been objectionable to some provinces because it acknowledges aboriginal political units. That proposition should actually not have been particularly alarming to anyone because there already are lots of aboriginal political units recognized in law—from band governments to the national organizations that are invited to s.37 conferences. In any event, if the participants could have agreed to the even more innocuous ICNI or Nova Scotia drafts, Manitoba would surely not have objected.

The main virtue of the agreement on the remedies clause, from the aboriginal peoples' point of view, would have been not legal but political. Had the March '84 conference generated even a minor constitutional amendment, there would have been a bolstering of the political and psychological expectations that when First Ministers meet, they bring about concrete constitutional reform. It may be that a desire to break those expectations had a role in the death (through apparent indifferences, rather than active opposition) of the remedies clause. The failure of the March '84 conference to produce any concrete constitutional results may have been a turning point in the whole process. It will make it easier for those who are so minded to take the approach that the aim of the process is now to discuss options that will be finally accepted or disposed of at the 1987 conference. The steady production of amendments along the way to the 1987 First Ministers' Conference might have ended up producing far greater constitutional gains than a final flurry of decisions.

Much of the second day of the conference was spent on the discussion of whether the sexual equality clause agreed to at the previous First Ministers' Conference should be amended or replaced. The concern of some aboriginal organizations and governments – most notably, New Brunswick – was the clause slapped together at the end of the previous First Ministers' Conference was not broad enough in scope; that it did not speak to sexual equality with respect to the statutory rights of aboriginal peoples, but was confined in its application to aboriginal and treaty rights. A backroom ministerial level meeting was called on the final afternoon to consider a revised clause. It may be recalled from Chapter III that s.35(4), the sexual equality clause agreed to at the March '83 First Ministers' Conference may have had the side-effect of strengthening s.35(1), the section that generally recognizes and affirms aboriginal and treaty rights. Section 35(4) may imply that not only sexual equality is guaranteed, but that also aboriginal and treaty rights are guaranteed. The federal government proposed at the final backroom meeting a clause that would have expanded the scope of s.35(4) but removed the possible implication that aboriginal and treaty rights, as opposed to sexual equality, are constitutionally guaranteed. There appeared to be a real chance that a clause based on the federal draft would be accepted at the end of the March '84 conference. There had been no outright dissents from the final version at the backroom meeting, and three of the four aboriginal organizations went along with it on the floor of the First Ministers' Session. Their acceptance of the amendment is attributable, among other things, to the limited opportunity for delegations to explore and explain to their membership the legal implications of the last minute proposal. The AFN, however, was alerted in time to the legal risks of the amendment and gave them as the basis for its rejection of the clause when its opinion was solicited. Prime Minister Trudeau accepted the AFN opposition to that particular draft as precluding its adoption. As mentioned in Chapter III, the little understood story of the drafting wars over s.35(4) warrants a much fuller treatment than can be provided here, and perhaps I shall attempt it another day.

The March '84 Conference thus ended without agreeing to an amendment that might have harmed the legal position of aboriginal peoples. It did not even come close to agreement on an amendment that might have enhanced their legal prospects. Nor was there any agreement on a work plan to facilitate concrete legal progress at future meetings.

Chapter XI

Federal-Provincial Problems and Aboriginal Peoples

In 1968, Maclean's Magazine ran a contest in which readers were invited to submit their candidates for the national Canadian joke. The winning entry, submitted by a dozen different readers from places as far apart as Princeton, British Columbia and Dartmouth, Nova Scotia, went like this: A professor asks an international group of students to write an essay on elephants. The American writes on the economic uses of the elephants; the French student on its amorous life; the German on its military potential; the Canadian on "Elephants: a federal or provincial responsibility?" (Maclean's, November, 1968, 111).

The federal-provincial division of powers and responsibilities is an issue that has arisen in many different contexts in the aboriginal rights process. The federal government's draft 1984 accord included a commitment that ". . . Canadian governments would collaborate in a review of all aspects of [program delivery] to the aboriginal peoples . . ." One of these objectives would be the "clarification of the federal and provincial responsibility for programs and services provided to the aboriginal peoples of Canada, having regard to the existing and potential roles of aboriginal governments." The Métis National Council (MTC) pressed at the March '84 conference the contention that the Métis should be expressly included under s.91(24) of the *Constitution Act, 1867* (which now gives the federal level of government jurisdiction over Indians and lands reserved for the Indians). In a strange departure from their usual jurisdictional acquisitiveness, the federal government opposed the expansion of its legislative authority, and some of the provinces were agreeable. Manitoba's statement of principles called for a recognition of federal *fiscal* responsibility for all aboriginal peoples including the Métis, thus distinguishing fiscal from legislative responsibility. A notable feature of the federal government's reply to the *Penner Report*, and its draft constitutional amendment on self-government at the March '84 First Ministers' Conference, is a rejection of the *Penner Report*'s suggestion that the federal government oust the application of provincial law to Indians on reserves and commence strictly bilateral negotiations with Indians. At first glance, it seems odd for a government led by Prime Minister Trudeau to be so solicitous of the role of the provinces in Confederation. Federal-provincial concerns have been prominent not only in the substantive proposals that have emerged from the s.37 discussions, but also in discussions over process. It will be recalled that the AFN initially refused to participate in preparatory meetings for the '83 conference on the grounds that it wanted to deal bilaterally with the federal government.

Because it comes up in so many different contexts, I believe it would be useful to devote several sections of this study to the federal-provincial division of authority and responsibilities with respect to Indians. In the course of doing so, the questions raised in the previous paragraph will be addressed, and some of the apparently eccentric behaviour of governments and aboriginal organizations explained.

In order to deal in an orderly fashion with the federal-provincial dimension of the section 37 process, it is helpful to distinguish among four different kinds of questions. First of all, there is legislative authority: can a government pass laws which regulate aboriginal peoples as such? That a government has jurisdiction over a subject matter does not oblige it to exercise that authority for the benefit of the group of people or, indeed, restrain it from doing them harm by passing repressive or destructive laws. Thus a second issue, distinct from legislative authority, is legislative *responsibility*. Indian organizations often argue that the federal government has a special "trust responsibility" towards Indians that obliges it to preserve and protect aboriginal lands and resources (Green 1976-77). In contemporary federalism, many programs established and financed under provincial law are financed in large part by the federal government. A longstanding controversy in Canadian constitutional law is the extent to which the federal authority's funding of programs, conditionally or with strings attached, exceeds federal authority to directly legislate. Thus the third and fourth questions concerning federal-provincial relations and aboriginal peoples are those of *fiscal authority* and *fiscal responsibility*.

Fiscal Authority

The question of fiscal authority can be disposed of straight away. The federal government often contributes financially with respect to activities that are not within its legislative jurisdiction. The constitutional question that has been much discussed by academics, but very little by courts, is whether there are any constitutional limits with respect to such grants. Some constitutional scholars have argued that there is no limit to the onerousness and detail of the conditions that the federal government may attach to its grant; that the federal government is free to give money to whomever it likes and on whatever terms it sees fit (Hogg 1977, 71). In his academic days, Pierre Trudeau attacked the legality and propriety of federal grants to universities; according to Trudeau, the practice undermined the principal of democratic responsibility (federal governments are elected to do federal things) and undercuts the ability of provinces to set their own policies (because the federal government has to raise taxes for its spending, thereby making it financially or politically impossible for the province to raise its own taxes) (Trudeau 1968, 79). The federal power to dispense money is supported by s.91(1A) of the *Constitution Act, 1967*, which gives Parliament authority over "The Public Debt and Property." One of the few cases commenting on the spending power, however, has insisted that that power be read against the heads of power allotted to the provinces; in the *Unemployment Insurance Case*, Lord Atkin said:

> That the Dominion may impose taxation for the purpose of creating a fund for special purposes, and may apply that fund for making contributions in the public interest to individuals, corporations or public authorities, could not as a general proposition be denied . . . [But] it by no means follows that any legislation which disposes of [a fund] is necessarily within Dominion competence. It may still be legislation affecting the classes of subjects enumerated in s.92, and, if so, would be *ultra vires*. In other words, Dominion legislation, even though it deals with Dominion property, may yet be so framed as to . . . encroach upon the classes of subjects which are

reserved to Provincial competence (*A.G. Can.* v. *A.G. Ont. (Unemployment Insurance)*, [1937] A.C. 355, 366 (P.C.)).

My own view is that the federal spending power, if uncabined, could be used to seriously disrupt the balance of federal and provincial authority, that federal governments are tempted to make excessive use of the power because special federal grants programs may maximize the gratitude governments receive and patronage they can dispense, and that the courts ought to develop doctrines limiting the use of the power. The task will require imagination and subtlety but is surely possible. Factors the courts could take into account in determining whether a use of the federal spending power is appropriate include the intrusiveness and detail of the conditions attached to the spending and the extent to which provincial governments participate in the policy making and administrative processes connected with the spending. One factor that should weigh in favour of federal authority to spend is that the grant is related to a national economic strategy. Another favourable consideration should be that the spending is related to a national scheme of distributive justice; the federal government is given the general power to tax under s.91(3) of the *Constitution Act, 1867*, and the federal government should be able to accomplish that end by varying what it pays out as well as what it takes in.

Even if the courts do constrain the federal spending power, however, it is very unlikely that they will do so in a way that would significantly hamper federal attempts to financially assist the economic and social development of aboriginal peoples. There are many levers of legislative authority that Parliament can use with respect to all aboriginal peoples, quite apart from the spending power – and most obviously and importantly s.91(24) of the *Constitution Act, 1867* ("Indians, and Lands Reserved for the Indians") – but also taxation, banks, interprovincial undertakings, agriculture, trade and commerce. The case that should warrant the most concern is that of the Métis, who may not be within federal jurisdiction under s.91(24). Even if they are not, other heads of federal power and the federal spending power (even if somewhat limited) permit the federal government to carry out almost all of its financially benevolent aims.

Federal and Provincial Legislative Authority

Section 91(24) of the *Constitution Act, 1867* gives the Parliament of Canada exclusive legislative authority over "Indians, and Lands reserved for the Indians." Parliament has used this authority to pass an *Indian Act* which defines, creates a registry for, and regulates the activities of status Indians—those who are registered or entitled to be registered under the *Indian Act.* There are people who are Indian by ancestry, culture, and self-conception but still do not have Indian status under federal law. Some people have lost their status by voluntary "enfranchisement" (see s.109 and 12(1)(a)(iii) of the *Indian Act*), others by operation of federal law; as has already been discussed, under s.12(1)(b) of the *Indian Act* an Indian woman who marries a non-status man automatically loses her own status. Conversely, it is possible to be non-Indian in almost every respect and still be a status Indian; for example, a white woman who marries a status Indian man automatically acquires status under s.11(1)(f) of the *Indian Act.* In some parts of Canada, almost all of the Indian bands are parties to treaties with the Crown; and the terms "status Indian" and "treaty Indians" are used by most people interchangeably. Not all status Indians, however, are treaty Indians; most of the bands in British Columbia, for example, have never entered into treaties with the Crown, and yet the members of these bands are registered under the *Indian Act.*

Under the *Indian Act* Parliament has not encompassed all the people that Parliament could specially regulate under s.91(24) of the *Constitution Act, 1867.* There is no doubt, for example, that Parliament could have always maintained the status of Indian women who married white men. It has also been held by the Supreme Court of Canada in a reference case, *Re Eskimo,* [1939] S.C.R. 104, that Inuit are subject to Parliament's authority under s.91(24). The MNC and NCC have both argued that Métis are, or at least should be, included under s.91(24) (see Chapters XVI and XVII).

The basic constitutional doctrine is that provincial laws of general application can apply to federal matters provided that they do not threaten to disrupt a federal activity and they do not conflict with any federal law in the area (*Multiple Access Ltd.* v. *McCutcheon,* (1982) 138 D.L.R. (3d) 1 (S.C.C.). (If the federal law is intended by Parliament to be exhaustive of the governmental regulation of the field the provincial law would be viewed as conflicting.) Both the courts and the academic commentators, however, should be skeptical of general constitutional doctrines that develop distinct approaches to different heads of federal power. Doctrines developed with respect to federal authority over "Banking, Incorporation of Banks, and the Issue of Paper Money" may have limited validity when applied to jurisdiction over "Indians, and Lands reserved for the Indians." This caution should be kept in mind when considering the many questions still unsettled about the application of provincial laws to Indians.

The Supreme Court of Canada has settled a number of issues in a series of decisions which began about a decade ago. Chief Justice Laskin, in his dissenting opinion, took the view in *Cardinal* v. *A.G. Alberta,* [1974] S.C.R. 695, that Indian reserves are "enclaves" with their own social, economic, and political structures, and as such, fall exclusively within federal legislative authority under s.91(24). The only way that the provincial laws may apply to them, he held, is by the operation of s.88 of the *Indian Act,* which says:

> Subject to the terms of any treaty or any other Act of the Parliament of Canada, all laws of general application from time to time in force in any province are applicable to and in respect of Indians in the province, except to the extent that such laws are inconsistent with this Act or any order, rule, regulation or by-law made thereunder, and except to the extent that such laws make provision for any matter for which provision is made by or under this Act.

According to Laskin J., s.88 "referentially incorporates" provincial laws, that is, a provincial law does not apply to Indians of its own force; rather, its terms become federal law and apply to Indians as such.

A number of Supreme Court of Canada judgments have contradicted the assertions of Mr. Justice Laskin. In *Cardinal* itself, Martland J. in his majority opinion rejected the enclave theory in terms; s.91(24) did not "define areas within a province within which the power of a Province to enact legislation, otherwise within its powers, is to be excluded" ([1974] S.C.R. 695, 703). According to him, "provincial legislation enacted under a heading of s.92 does not necessarily become invalid because it affects something which is subject to Federal legislation" ([1974] S.C.R. 695, 703). The test for Martland J. was whether the law was "in relation to" a s.92 subject matter ([1974] S.C.R. 703). Martland J. was able to dispose of the actual issue in the *Cardinal* case on the basis of s.12 of the *Natural Resources Transfer Agreement* (confirmed by the *Constitution Act, 1930*) that authorized the application of an Alberta provincial hunting law to the activities of an Indian on a reserve.

In *Natural Parents* v. *Superintendent of Child Welfare* (1975), 60 D.L.R. (3d) 148, the Supreme Court of Canada had to decide whether it was constitutionally valid for a court, pursuant to the *Adoption Act* of British Columbia, to authorize the adoption of an Indian child by non-Indian parents. The child had been apprehended under the *Protection of Children Act* after it arrived in a hospital at seven weeks of age so injured and neglected that it was near death. For seven years after that, the foster parents who now wished to adopt the child had taken care of it. Chief Justice Laskin held that a law which could result in the adoption of an Indian child against the wishes of his natural parents "would be to touch 'Indianness,' to strike at a relationship integral to a matter outside of provincial competence" (60 D.L.R. (3d) 148, 154). The adoption order was nonetheless valid, according to Laskin C.J.C., because the British Columbia Act was referentially incorporated under s.88 of the *Indian Act.* It did not conflict with any provision of the *Indian Act*; s.10(4a) of the British Columbia *Adoption Act* said that an adoption order did not affect the Indian status of a child, and in this it agreed with subparagraph 11(1)(d)(ii) of the *Indian Act,* which gave status to "the legitimate child" of a status Indian – regardless, held Laskin C.J.C., of whether the child was subsequently adopted.

Martland J. found that the provincial law applied of its own force. Section 88 did not referentially incorporate provincially made laws; it simply declared that they applied of their own force. Martland J. then took the same approach as Laskin C.J.C. to hold that in the case before him the terms of the *Adoption Act* did not conflict with or address a matter already provided for by the *Indian Act.* Three judges (including Ritchie J. in a separate judgment) agreed with Martland J. on the effect of s.88. Beetz J. did not find it necessary to split the four-four tie on the s.88 issue. He did not even find it necessary to determine whether the child maintained his status. Whether it did or didn't, held Beetz J., was determined by the *Indian Act*; if it did, it was because the *Indian Act* held the loss of status to be the consequence of adoption and not because of anything the provincial law said. Indeed, s.10(4a) of the *Adoption Act* was invalid, according to Beetz J., because the effect on status of adoption was not a matter for provincial law to determine one way or the other. Adoption was not a matter provided for by the *Indian Act,* and he held there was no possible conflict between the provincial law and the *Indian Act* because the latter determined the effect of adoption on status. He could "not be persuaded that laws general in their terms ought to be interpreted so as not to extend all their advantages to a child because he is an Indian" (60 D.L.R. (3d) 148, 173). Therefore, whatever view be taken of s.88, the adoption order was valid.

In *Four B Manufacturing Ltd.* v. *United Garment Workers of America* (1979), 102 D.L.R. (3d) 385, Beetz J. (concurred with by six other judges) upheld the application of provincial labour relations laws to the shoe manufacturing operation on an Indian reserve. The business was owned by a private corporation, the shareholders of which were Indians, and was heavily funded by the federal government. Nonetheless, held Beetz J., shoe manufacturing is not a federal type of activity, and so not subject to the federal *Labour Relations Act.* In response to the argument that not only did Indians, but Indians on a reserve, own the corporation, Beetz J. responded:

> . . . this submission is an attempt to revive the enclave theory of the reserves in a modified version: provincial laws would not apply to Indians on reserves although they might apply to others. The enclave theory has been rejected by this Court in *Cardinal* . . . and I see no reason to revive it even in a limited form. Section 91(24) of the *British North America Act,* 1867 assigns jurisdiction to Parliament over two distinct subject matters, Indians *and* lands reserved for the Indians, not Indians *on* lands reserved for the Indians. The power of Parliament to make laws in relation to Indians is the same whether Indians are on a reserve or off a reserve. It is not reinforced because it is exercised over Indians on a reserve any more than it is weakened because it is exercised over Indians off a reserve. . . . (102 D.L.R. (3d) 385, 398).

Once again Beetz J. refrained from deciding the precise implications of s.88; his judgment leaves no doubt, however, that the terms of provincial laws of general application could apply to Indians, reserves, and Indians on reserves, without the assistance of federal incorporation. (It is not a merely scholastic question whether a provincial law which could have operated of its own force has been transformed by s.88 into federal law. The *Canadians Bill of Rights* applies only to federal law. The authority of federal officials to prosecute may depend on whether a law is federal or provincial.) Laskin C.J.C. dissented. He was prepared to admit that there was authority in the cases for holding that provincial laws could apply to Indians off reserves and non-Indians on reserves, but not to the activities of Indians on reserves.

The phrase "provincial laws of general application" has occurred repeatedly in the foregoing discussion. Some bewildering problems arise when a province attempts to single out Indians for special—including especially favourable—treatment. A province might wish to give Indians preferred treatment when they apply for admission to law school; the University of Manitoba sets aside several places for native students who would not be admitted under the usual competitive standards. These places are set aside quite apart from those available under the "special consideration" program, whereby any person lacking in formal qualifications can ask to be admitted on the basis of his unusual experience or potential. A province might wish to set aside places for Indians, or natives generally, in its public service or legislatively require private employers to do so. In Manitoba, status Indians have requested that a special child welfare agency operated by status Indians be given jurisdiction over Indian children in the province but off reserves.

The case law in other areas suggests that a province can single out subjects of federal jurisdiction for special treatment, provided that its purpose in doing so is fundamentally rooted in provincial concerns. In *Bank of Toronto* v. *Lambe* (1887) 12 A.C. 575, for example, the Privy Council held that a Quebec statute could tax banks (over whom the federal government has jurisdiction under sections 91(15) and 91(16) of the *Constitution Act, 1867*). Other companies were taxed according to other criteria, which do not appear in any obvious way to have been any less onerous, but rather adapted to the different natures of the companies concerned. Railways were taxed on the basis of miles of railway worked, telegraph companies on the number of offices and so on. It could be fairly supposed that banks were singled out because of their special characteristics for provincial tax purposes and not because the province wanted to regulate banking activity, let alone interfere with it. The Privy Council found the legislation to be in relation to "Direct Taxation within the Province" (s.92(2) of the *Constitution Act, 1867*).

It is possible to argue that some passages in the series of cases mentioned imply that a province cannot single out Indians, whether for beneficial or detrimental purpose. In *Four B* Mr. Justice Beetz said a "similar reasoning [that provincial laws of general application apply to persons with respect to whom Parliament has exclusive legislative jurisdiction] must prevail with respect to the application of provincial laws to Indians, as long as such laws do not single out Indians nor purport to regulate them *qua* Indians" (102 D.L.R. (3d) 385, 398). Mr. Justice Beetz does not indicate that a province could single out Indians if it was doing so for their own benefit. The *Four B* case, however, did not involve "singling out," let alone singling out for special purposes; Mr. Justice Beetz's general statement, therefore, cannot be taken as authoritatively settling questions that never arose in the case itself, and which Mr. Justice Beetz may not have even considered. One commentator has flatly asserted that "a provincial law which is intended to benefit Indians (or more neutrally, does not have either the purpose or effect of impairing status) will be declared invalid if it purports to affect Indians specifically" (Hughes 1983). The only support offered for this generalization is "dicta" in the *Natural Parents* case. The latter does not adequately support the general proposition. An attempt by a province to determine whether a person remains an "Indian" for the purposes of federal law is an especially serious interference with federal Indian policy. It hardly follows that all attempts by a province to single out Indians for beneficial treatment are invalid. It should be noted that all the opinions in *Natural Parents* expressly observed that the provincial legislation extended rights to Indian children. A sensitivity to whether provincial legislation helps or hinders Indians may be a prominent feature of future Supreme Court rulings in the area under discussion.

It might be argued that whether legislation is good or bad for third parties should be irrelevant to the determination of whether it is within or outside provincial jurisdiction. As mentioned earlier, however, general constitutional doctrine with respect to federal undertakings, services, and businesses is that provincial laws must not threaten to interfere with or dismember them. An example of a provincial law that singled out Indians in a way that interfered with their activities was s.49 of the *Wildlife Act* of Manitoba (R.S.M. 1970, C.W. 140), which purported to characterize a number of areas as "occupied Crown lands to which Indians do not have a right of access." Its purpose was obviously to preclude Indians from relying on their constitutional right to hunt on "unoccupied Crown lands to which Indians have a right of access," under paragraph 13 of the *Manitoba Natural Resources Act.* Dickson J. found in *R.* v. *Sutherland* [1980] 2 S.C.R. 451, that section 49 had "effect only against Indians and its sole purpose is to limit or obliterate a right Indians would otherwise enjoy" ([1980] 2 S.C.R. 451, 455). He had "no doubt" that it was unconstitutional. (He went on, however, to quote Mr. Justice Beetz's more general dictum in *Four B* that provincial laws cannot single out or regulate Indians *qua* Indians). To say that a province cannot single out Indians for adverse treatment does not necessarily imply that it can single them out for favourable treatment. The courts may, however, take the view that s.91(24) cases should not be seen as more than simple, routine federal and provincial division of powers problems. They may find implicit in s.91(24) the constitutional value that Canada has some duty to protect and enhance the interests of Indian peoples, and that s.91(24) gives the federal government jurisdiction to permit the federal government to help them and prevent local governments from harming them. In *Re Eskimo* Duff C.J. quoted this passage from the *Senate Debates on the Constitution Act, 1867*:

> Resolved that upon the transference of the Territories in question to the Canadian Government, it will be the duty of the Government to make adequate provisions for the protection of the Indian Tribes, whose interest and well being are involved in the transfer ([1939] S.C.R. 104, 108).

With the foregoing in mind, Canadian courts may allow provinces considerable leeway to single out Indians for favourable treatment.

Now let us examine examples of provincial "singling out." One, mentioned earlier, is the University of Manitoba Law School's special admission program for native students. It would probably be constitutional for a university to include native students as one of a number of groups which receive special treatment. (Constitutional not only on a division of powers ground, but also on human rights grounds; the guarantee of equality in s.15(1) of the *Charter of Rights and Freedoms* does not "Preclude . . . any law, program or activity that has as its subject the amelioration of disadvantaged groups." I would hope that the courts will take "preclude" as meaning "does not *necessarily* prevent" and continue to exercise some scrutiny over affirmative action programs on human rights grounds and strike down those that are especially unfair to other individuals or groups. (The reference to "any law," however, may be taken by courts as a practically absolute prohibition on evaluating the justice of programs intended to benefit disadvantaged groups.) It is probably not "singling out" native Canadians as a group when a province includes them as one of a number of groups selected for special treatment. But what if native Canadians constitute the only group singled out for special treatment? In some cases, that might still be permissible. If native-police relations are worse than those involving any other group in a city, a decision to hire extra native police officers is probably within provincial jurisdiction as a matter of the "administration of justice" (s.92(14) of the *Constitution Act, 1867*); the law can be viewed primarily as a matter of police policy, rather than native policy.

The University of Manitoba special admissions program is rather problematic, however, in that its purpose is not to deal with the legal under-servicing of the native community, but to enhance the career prospects of native students regardless of what area of the law they will practice in. In essence, a decision has been made to give native students special treatment because of a special claim in political justice they are perceived as having by virtue of their aboriginality. It could be argued at this point that the faculty of law is dealing primarily with distributive justice to Indians as aboriginal peoples, rather than the native aspect of legal services. It may weigh in favour of the validity of the program that it is addressed to natives generally, not just Indians; Métis students are also eligible for special consideration. If Métis are not Indians for the purposes of s.91(24), then their inclusion in the group singled out for special treatment may be sufficient to meet the objection that a province is legislating with respect to a matter within exclusive federal jurisdiction.

Another problem mentioned earlier is that of granting a status Indian-operated child welfare service jurisdiction over status Indian children in the city. It can be argued with some merit that it could not be an infringement of exclusive jurisdiction over Indians to grant more autonomy to Indians; that provinces are prohibited from meddling in Indian affairs, not from leaving them to manage their own affairs. Against this it might be argued that the establishment and jurisdiction of Indian governments and agencies is a matter of Indian policy that should be left to Parliament alone. The case for federal jurisdiction is particularly strong where an Indian agency does not fit into a provincial scheme which accommodates other groups. On the general issue of the s.91-s.92 validity of provincial singling out, my view is that courts should take a permissive attitude. It would not be wise to insist that Parliament intervene whenever adjustments are required to provincial regimes because of the special circumstances of aboriginal peoples. It would not be practical, for one thing, to expect Parliament to consider and act with respect to programs operated by 10 different provincial governments. A blanket prohibition on provincial singling out could be used as an excuse for uninvited, as well as provincially requested, interventions by Parliament in programs better left to provincial management. It may not be desirable that a distant central government determine how the Regina police force adjusts to the social problems created by the influx of Indians off the reserves. One can imagine a scenario in which a federal government believes that Indians should be treated on a basis of strict equality with other Canadians and finds it objectionable that provincial governments run reverse discrimination programs for Indians. In such a scenario, provincial action would effectively be undermining an overall federal strategy towards Indians. If the federal policy were officially declared in some form, even short of legislation, the courts could rightly be less permissive with respect to the provincial singling out actions. Right now, however, the federal government is more enthusiastic than any of the provinces about giving special treatment to minority groups in general and has accepted the principle that Indians should be allowed some special status. This present attitude is in contrast with that manifested in the 1969 federal white paper on Indian policy, which was imbued with a sense that discrimination by governments only encourages invidious discrimination by other individuals and that Indians should not have special status (White Paper, 1969, 3).

Much of the discussion in this section has been about the extent to which provincial law can apply to Indians and lands reserved for the Indians. The obverse problem is the extent to which federal law which deals with Indians can intrude on provincial areas of jurisdiction. Suppose that the *federal* government required that law schools have special admissions programs for Indians; a province might then argue with some force that its jurisdiction over education was being invaded. (Is it possible that neither Parliament nor a provincial legislature could legislate on its own a certain measure with respect to Indians because each would be invading the other's jurisdiction? Actually, yes. Sometimes Parliament and a provincial legislature must enact dovetailing pieces of legislation in order to achieve a regulatory aim; *The King* v. *Eastern Terminal Elevator Co.*, [1925] S.C.R. 434.) In the last few decades, the Supreme Court of Canada has tended to find areas of activity to be within the reach of both federal and provincial governments, and many schemes intended for the benefit of First Nations may be found to be within the enacting power of both. A court might fortify its decision to follow this trend by observing that inasmuch as the federal government is able to and has established special status and living conditions for Indians, it should be construed as having ample jurisdiction to assist Indians in integrating into and succeeding in society at large. The limits of federal jurisdiction over Indians in areas of provincial jurisdiction is not likely to be much controverted, however, because federal action with respect to Indians on their traditional land bases will probably focus on providing special social welfare assistance or setting up autonomous Indian institutions, rather than directly intruding into provincial regulatory schemes or organizations.

Chapter XII

Federal Responsibility for Indians

A leading study of the constitutional position of Canadian Indians observes that there is great flexibility for a province to legislate with respect to Indians and Indian lands where Parliament has not acted and concludes with the assertion:

> Accepting that constitutional "responsibility" for Indians is the correlative of legislative authority, there is little justification for the reluctance not infrequently expressed by provincial governments to undertake the same responsibility for ameliorating the condition of Indians and Indian settlements that these governments would assume for non-Indians and non-Indian communities (Lysyk 1967, 553).

The passage is quoted because it provokes, without answering, just about all the relevant questions about federal and provincial responsibility for Indians. "Responsibility" is surrounded by scare quotes; does it refer to a merely political duty, a nonjusticiable legal one, or one enforceable in a court? Is it generally true that "responsibility" is the correlative of "legislative authority?" Is it true in the case of s.91(24)? Is it lawful for a federal or provincial government to provide a lower level of services for Indians and Indian communities than it provides to other people? Could it be argued that the failure to provide equal services is a violation of "equality before the law" contained in Canadian fundamental human rights documents, including the *Bill of Rights* and the *Charter of Rights and Freedoms*? Is it legitimate in any sense for a province to refrain from providing equal services to Indians or Indian communities on the basis that a province should not be bound to remedy a dereliction of federal duty? Can the dereliction of federal duty be used as a defence to charges that the province is denying Indians the equal protection or benefit of the law? There has been very little systematic study of these questions in the academic literature; discussion almost always focuses on the division of authority, rather than responsibility. (The essay about elephants by the Canadian student may have been entitled "Elephants – a federal or provincial responsibility", but it was probably about whether Parliament or provincial legislatures can exercise authority over elephants, and completely indifferent to whether either level of government was bound to promote the elephants' well-being.)

The first thing to be considered is whether under s.91(24) alone, Canadian governments and legislatures are under a legal obligation, justiciable or nonjusticiable, to use their heads of legislative authority to do good. With respect to their heads of legislative authority, courts have taken the view that the principle of legislative supremacy applies. According to that principle, inherited from Great Britain, legislatures are competent to do whatever they please about whatever issue they care to address. The wisdom or justice of legislative action or inaction is not to be second-guessed by courts. The latter are obliged to enforce the law as they find it. It was considered antidemocratic for nonelected courts to second-guess legislatures. The principles of legislative supremacy arose in the aftermath of the English Civil War and may be viewed as partly reflecting a sense that civil order requires that somebody be unequivocally in charge of things, as well as reflecting an enhanced respect for democracy. English political thought at the time of the emergence of Parliament's supremacy was more concerned with liberty than with social equality. Locke's *Two Treatises on Civil Government* argued that no man should be deprived of his life, liberty, or property; it did not insist that anyone should provide his brother with any of the above. The English *Bill of Rights* protected people from arbitrary governmental action; it did not assure them of any assistance. It is entirely consistent with the pattern just identified that English constitutional law was insistent on democratic control when taxes had to be raised; a principle of English constitutionalism, later adapted and inserted in Canada's own constitution, is that taxing bills must originate in the House of Commons rather than the Senate (*Constitution Act, 1867*, s.53). For a court to order a legislature to provide for someone's welfare would be more offensive to classic English juridical thought than a court's striking down legislation it considers unjust. The former action would be seen as more threatening to the democratic principle because the scope for antidemocratic action is far greater if a court can survey the social world and order things be set right than if the court is confined to gainsaying what a legislature has done wrong. To sum up, a head of legislative authority under the *Constitution Act, 1867* is, generally speaking, legal authorization to exercise power; it allows legislatures to do things *to* people, but does not require them to do anything *for* people.

There is really no arguable case that Parliament has under s.91(24) alone a special duty to promote the general welfare of Indians that is directly enforceable in the courts. Canadian courts held in a number of cases prior to the coming into force of s.35 of the *Constitution Act, 1982* that Parliament had the authority to pass laws which contravened treaties and interfered with aboriginal rights (*Hamlet of Baker Lake* v. *Minister of Indian Affairs and Northern Development*, [1980] 1 F.C. 518 (F.C.T.D.); *R.* v. *Derriksan* (1977), 71 D.L.R. (3d) 159 (S.C.C.)). Given that courts would have enforced federal laws that violated the rights of aboriginal peoples, the courts would certainly not have ordered Parliament to act to promote their social welfare. Parliament, and provincial legislatures as well, are now bound to respect aboriginal and treaty rights under s.35(1) of the *Constitution Act, 1982*; the diminution of their ability to violate positive rights of Indians, however, cannot be taken to imply the imposition of a court-enforceable duty to act for their welfare.

A fairly good case can be made that the federal government has a nonjusticiable constitutional duty under s.91(24) to protect the land and treaty rights of Indians, although the constitutional materials do not provide much support for the assertion that the federal government is bound to actively promote the social welfare of Indians through transfer payments and the delivery of programs and services. It is a fair surmise that the original purpose of allowing federal legislative jurisdiction over Indians was to facilitate the protection of their rights in the face of local pressures. An important feature of the history of settler-Indian relations in the Anglo-Canadian world is that central governments have been more inclined to protect Indian land and treaty rights than have local governments. The reasons are fairly obvious. Encroachment on Indian land and treaty rights may be highly advantageous to local settlers, who tend to be able to exert enormous pressure on local administrators. A central government may not even be politically responsible to local settlers (as in the case of England and the American colonies prior to 1776) or, if it is, may feel their political demands as only a relatively small pressure among many. It is thus insulated from the political pressures that would prevent it from doing justice to Indians. At times, the more beneficent policy of central government has not been based on the dictates of political conscience, but on a different perception of self-interest; the English government may have been especially solicitous of Indian land rights to the point of passing the Royal Proclamation of 1763 not only because of its sense of justice, but also because unfair and fraudulent land deals with Indians in North America were causing unrest among Indians that threatened British military security on the continent. Still, a genuine concern for fair play towards Indians to some extent accounted for the relatively decent behaviour that some central governments sometimes exhibited with respect to Indians.

It is consistent with the pattern just described that at the time of the American Revolution almost all of the Indian tribes allied with the Crown against the colonists. The Crown had increasingly acted as their protectors against encroachment by the colonists. After Independence, the new states agreed that the only way to prevent war with Indians caused by local land grabs was to give to Congress authority over commerce and treaty-making with Indians; U.S. Constitution Article I, s. 8, cl. 3, Article II, s. 2, cl. 2 (Canby 1981, 10). Given that historical pattern, it may be inferred that a major purpose in giving Parliament jurisdiction over Indians was to permit it to protect Indian land and treaty rights; MacDonald J.A. in his dissenting opinion in *R.* v. *Morley*, [1932] 2 W.W.R. 193, 218, stated that the "reservation of federal jurisdiction in respect to 'Indians and Lands reserved for the Indians' has a definite object in view, *viz.*, safeguarding the rights and privileges of the wards of the Dominion at all times." Should s.91(24) be understood as merely permitting Parliament to protect Indians' treaty rights and lands, or does it go so far as to imply a nonjusticiable duty that it do so? A respectable case can be made for the latter. It can be argued that in granting the Parliament of Canada the power to legislate with respect to Indians, the Parliament of the United Kingdom may be assumed to have intended that its delegate would honour existing obligations and continue the British policy, expressed in the Proclamation of 1763, of protecting Indian lands from private encroachment and having only the government acquire land, through agreements with Indian leaders and upon payment of substantial compensation.

Within six months of Confederation, in their formal request to Great Britain that it transfer Rupert's Land and the North-Western Territory to Canada, the House of Commons and Senate of Canada formally resolved that:

> And furthermore, that, upon the transference of the territories in question to the Canadian Government, the claims of the Indian tribes to compensation for lands required for purposes of settlement will be considered and settled in conformity with the equitable principles which have uniformly governed the British Crown in its dealings with the aborigines (Schedule A of Order of Her Majesty in Council admitting Rupert's Land and the North-Western Territory into the union, dated the 23rd day of June, 1870 [by the Schedule to *Constitution Act, 1982*, stated to be part of the Constitution of Canada and renamed the Rupert's Land and North-Western Territory Order.])

Two years later in a memorandum of agreement between the delegates of the Dominion of Canada and the Hudson's Bay Company concerning the transfer of Rupert's Land, the Speakers of the House of Commons and Senate of Canada undertook:

> That upon the transference of the territories in question to the Canadian Government, it will be our duty to make adequate provision for the protection of the Indian tribes whose interests and well-being are involved in the transfer, and we authorize and empower the Governor in Council to arrange any details that may be necessary to carry out the terms and conditions of the above agreement [Memorandum in Schedule B of the *Rupert's Land and North-Western Territory Order*].

The existence of these two undertakings so soon after Confederation bolsters the case for reading s.91(24) as positing a nonjusticiable duty in Parliament to protect Indian lands and treaty rights (see *Baker Lake* v. *Minister of Indian Affairs and Northern Development*, [1980] 1 F.C. 518, 566 with respect to s.14 of the *Rupert's Land and North-Western Territory Order*). The undertakings themselves, incidentally, may well create justiciable rights for Indians in a large part of Canada. They are contained in Schedules A and B respectively of the *Rupert's Land and Northwestern Territory Order*, which the *Constitution Act, 1982* has identified as part of the Constitution of Canada. The main text of the order includes a preamble which says the transfer of the territories is "upon the terms and conditions expressed in certain Resolutions . . . contained in the schedule to this Order annexed, marked B . . . and in the [1867] Address."

In 1871, Parliament was charged with the enforceable legal duty of taking proper care of Indian land interests in British Columbia; Article 13 of the British Columbia Terms of Union (also identified as part of the Constitution of Canada by the *Constitution Act, 1982*, s.52(2)), says:

> The charge of the Indians, and the trusteeship and management of the lands reserved for their use and benefit, shall be assumed by the Dominion Government, and a policy as liberal as that hitherto pursued by the British Columbia Government shall be continued by the Dominion Government after the Union.
>
> To carry out such policy, tracts of land of such extent as it has hitherto been the practice of the British Columbia Government to appropriate for that purpose shall from time to time be conveyed by the Local Government to the Dominion Government in trust for the use and benefit of the Indians on application of the Dominion Government; and in case of disagreement between the two Governments respecting the quantity of such tracts of land to be so granted, the matter shall be referred for the decision of the Secretary of State for the Colonies.

In *Jack* v. *The Queen* (1979), 100 D.L.R. (3d) 193, Chief Justice Laskin said the word "policy" in the first part of the article 13 had the same scope as it did in the second—and the context in the second paragraph showed that "policy" referred solely to the reservation of land and its subsequent management. In a dissenting judgment, Dickson J. was prepared to find that "policy" in the first paragraph extended to "broad general policy as affecting Indians and lands reserved for their use" (100 D.L.R. (3d) 193, 199), and it was therefore possible to find that a federal fishing law was invalid because it was less accommodating of Indian interests than had been the policy in British Columbia prior to its admittance into Confederation. Even if you adopt the approach of Mr. Justice Dickson, however, you cannot extract from Article 13 a duty on the part of Parliament to provide social services for Indians; very few were provided to Indians in British Columbia prior to 1871.

In the United States, the special link between the United States federal government and the Indian tribes is sometimes described by politicians and courts as a fiduciary or trust relationship. The idea is that while the United States has ultimate sovereignty over Indian lands, it should exercise this authority for the benefit of Indian peoples. The courts have held, however, that it will defer to Congress' judgment as to how this responsibility should be discharged; "plenary authority over the tribal relations of the Indians has been exercised by Congress from the beginning, and the power has always been deemed to be a political one, not subject to be controlled by the judicial department of the government"; *Lone Wolf* v. *Hitchcock*, 187 U.S. 553, 565 (1903). The passage just quoted is from a Supreme Court case in which Kiowa and Comanche Indians challenged the application of the federal "termination" policy to them. That policy (not unlike that of the Canadian White Paper on Indian Policy in 1969) was to end the special status of Indians and turn over tribal lands to individual Indians to maintain or alienate as they chose. The Supreme Court held that Congress could carry out this policy notwithstanding the principle that Indians are "wards of the nation" (*United States* v. *Kagama*, 118 U.S. 375 (1886)) and despite the express prohibition in treaties with the tribes in question against Congress' ceding the lands without tribal consent. The American courts have at times construed the statutory authority of the executive branch of the federal government in light of the trust relationship principle. A federal court of appeals found, for example, that the federal executive was by implication of the *Trade and Intercourse Act of 1790* a trustee of the land of the Passamoquoddy Indians of Maine and thus obliged in 1972 to bring an action to recover the lands from the state of Maine, which had purchased them without federal authorization in 1794; *Joint Tribal Council of Passamoquoddy Tribe* v. *Morton*, 528 F. 2d 370 (lst Cir. 1975). (The main action eventually succeeded, and Congress had to pass a statute substituting a massive monetary payment for the actual return of the land.)

The only legal effect the courts have given to the "trust relationship" is with respect to the executive management of Indian lands and assets:

> Arguments have also been offered, and occasional attempts have been made to enforce a broader trust responsibility, in recognition of a federal fiduciary duty to preserve tribal autonomy or to contribute to the welfare of the tribes and their members. As yet such attempts have not met with success in the courts, but it is likely that pressure toward enforcement of these broader responsibilities will continue (Canby 1981, 41).

To the extent that there is a trust responsibility towards Indians, it has been construed in recent times by American presidents as relating only to the management of Indian lands and assets, and not in terms of service delivery. In a message to Congress on July 8, 1970, President Nixon said that "The United States Government acts as a legal trustee for the land and water rights of American Indians" (Price 1973, 325). A policy statement by President Reagan on January 24, 1983, refers to the "federal trust responsibility for the physical and financial resources we hold in trust for the tribes and their members" (Statement of the President on Indian Policy, January 24, 1983, 3). The statement went on to cite as policy goals the enhancement of Indian self-government and economic self-sufficiency, the latter to be accomplished in part through the investment of capital from the private economy. The policy statement makes Indian governments eligible for the sort of block funding that American states receive, but does not acknowledge any special duty of the federal government to deliver services to Indians.

The trust responsibility of Parliament and the federal executive implied by the Canadian Constitution appears to be no more extensive in scope than is the American federal government's duties under the U.S. Constitution. It has already been argued that the nonjusticiable legal duties relating to Indians implied by s.91(24) of the *Constitution Act, 1867* relate principally to Indian lands and treaty obligations relating to those lands, as opposed to a more general duty to promote Indian welfare. (I do not doubt that Parliament has important responsibilities in this regard as a matter of political justice, but now I am addressing only the question of what s.91(24) can be taken to legally require.) The references to "trusteeship" in Canadian constitutional documents do not establish any broader duty. Section 109 of the *Constitution Act, 1867* says that Crown lands in the pre-Confederation colonies were to be owned by the new provinces "subject to any Trusts existing in respect thereof, and to any Interest other than that of the Province in the same." Even if the interests of Indians are considered as a s. 109 trust, it is difficult to infer a trust relationship from s. 109 that extends much beyond that relating to land management. In *St. Catherine's Milling and Lumber Company* v. *The Queen* (1889) 14 A.C. 46, Lord Watson referred to the proprietary interests of Indians as coming within "interest other than that of the Province" rather than a trust. In 1912, when Parliament in the exercise of its authority under s.3 of the *Constitution Act, 1871* extended the boundaries of Quebec, it said that "the trusteeship of the Indians in the said territory, and the management of any lands now or hereafter reserved for their use, shall remain in the Government of Canada subject to the control of Parliament" (*Quebec Boundaries Extension Act*, 1912, S.C. 1912, c.45, s.2). The initial trusteeship might be narrowly construed as relating only to the management of lands not yet expressly reserved to Indians. It is plausible, however, to take "trusteeship of Indians" as referring to duties to protect Indian people, as opposed to just their lands and assets. Even so, there is no indication that the responsibility extends to improving their social well-being. Indeed, the intent of the section was probably to preserve Parliamentary authority, rather than to acknowledge any affirmative duties on the part of Parliament.

Can the federal government of Canada be held liable in the courts for mishandling of Indian lands? While s.91(24) on its own does not generally appear to sustain such actions, the common law and statutes may provide the basis for court intervention. In *R.* v. *Guerin*, a band surrendered land to the federal government so that the latter could lease it out to a third party for the financial benefit of the band. The trial court found the federal government had not fulfilled its trust duty to obtain the consent of the band to the actual terms of the lease that was made; 10 E.T.R. 61 and 127 D.L.R. (3d) 170 (supplementary reasons). Ten million dollars in damages was assessed on the basis that the band would not have consented to the terms and would eventually have obtained a better deal. The Federal Court of Appeal reversed the trial decision, holding that the federal government's duty was a nonjusticiable "political" trust responsibility, not a "legal" one; 143 D.L.R. (3d) 416. On November 1, 1984, the Supreme Court of Canada restored the trial judgment. Chief Justice Dickson and Justice Wilson distinguished the "political trust" precedents on the basis, among others, that they involved legal responsibilities established by statute. The interest of aboriginal peoples in land is a right that pre-exists any statute. The federal government owed a legally enforceable fiduciary duty to the band, under a combination of common law and the relevant provisions of the *Indian Act*. *Guerin* is likely to be a very important step in the direction the American courts have gone – of holding the executive accountable to the courts for its management of Indian lands and assets.

Service Delivery and Equality Before the Law

It appears that s.91(24) does not of its own force legally require the federal government to deliver adequate services to Indians. The federal government has, however, undertaken responsibility for service delivery to Indians on their traditional land bases. Where it fails to deliver services of roughly equal quality to those it provides to other people under federal jurisdiction, it is open to Indians to argue that they have been denied the equal protection of the law under the *Canadian Bill of Rights*, s.1(b) or the new *Canadian Charter of Rights and Freedoms*, s.15(1). Cases involving Indians and equality before the law have been central to the development of *Canadian Bill of Rights* jurisprudence. In *Attorney General of Canada* v. *Lavell* (1973), 38 D.L.R. (3d) 481, a majority of the Supreme Court of Canada upheld s.12(1)(b) of the *Indian Act*, which removes the Indian status of an Indian woman who marries any man who is not a status Indian. To fortify his conclusion, Ritchie J. adopted an extremely narrow construction of the scope of the "equality before the law" guarantee of s. 1(b) of the *Canadian Bill of Rights* – that it did not have the "egalitarian concept" implied by the Fourteenth Amendment to the American Constitution" and merely meant "the equal subjection of all classes to the ordinary law of the land as administered by the ordinary courts" (38 D.L.R. (3d) 481, 495). In so holding, Ritchie J. contradicted his own reasoning in *R.* v. *Drybones* (1969), 9 D.L.R. (3d) 473, where he struck down a section of the *Indian Act* on the grounds that it was more extensive in its application and harsher in its penalties to Indians for intoxication than the counterpart *Northwest Territorial Ordinance* was with respect to non-Indians. After all, both the *Indian Act* and the relevant *Northwest Territory Ordinance* were enforced in ordinary courts; it is not as though the latter were adjudicated upon and enforced by a special, noncurial forum. Only three judges concurred in Ritchie J.'s reasons for judgment in *Lavell*; the pivotal judge in the case, Pigeon J., concurred in the result on the general ground that the *Canadian Bill of Rights* should not be construed as intending to effect a virtual suppression of federal legislation over Indians.

Laskin J.'s dissenting opinion was just as categorical as Ritchie J.'s, but in the opposite direction. He held as "marginally relevant" American jurisprudence under equal protection – whereby the reasonableness of a legislative classification is assessed in terms of the importance of the legislative purpose involved and the necessity of its use in terms of that purpose. According to Laskin J.:

> ... the Canadian Bill of Rights itself enumerates prohibited classifications which the judiciary is bound to respect; and, moreover, I doubt whether discrimination on account of sex, where as here it has no biological or physiological rationale, could be sustained as a reasonable classification even if the direction against it was not as explicit as it is in the Canadian Bill of Rights (38 D.L.R. (3d) 481, 510).

In *Attorney General of Canada and Rees* v. *Canard*, [1975] 3 W.W.R. 1, the widow of an Indian who died without leaving a will contended that s.43 of the *Indian Act* was contrary to s.1(b) of the *Canadian Bill of Rights*. The section empowered the minister of Indian affairs and northern development to appoint the administrator for an Indian who was ordinarily resident on a reserve or Crown land. Under it, the superintendent in charge of the local Indian district was appointed. A few months later, a provincial surrogate court in Manitoba, where the reserve was, purported to appoint Mrs. Canard as administratrix. The Manitoba Court of Appeal construed s.43 as not permitting the appointment of an Indian as administratrix, and so contrary to the *Canadian Bill of Rights*. Mr. Justice Beetz, in the majority judgment of the Supreme Court of Canada, held that an Indian could be appointed; that it was not a denial of equal protection of the law to provide Indians with a different legal regime than the provinces did. He found that the authority of the minister could be exercised in a judicial or quasi-judicial manner and would be subject to judicial review if discharged unlawfully. He continued:

> The sections of the federal statute we are concerned with relate to the administration of a private estate, a matter which, were it not for the fact that this estate is that of a deceased Indian, would normally fall under provincial jurisdiction. Accordingly, in a case such as the present one, in order to determine whether the principle of equality before the law has been complied with in the administration of federal law (or, in other

> words, whether an Indian is not deprived of a right generally recognized to other Canadians), some reference to the standards of provincial laws and practices may be unavoidable as there is no other basis for comparison except perhaps the ordinances of the Yukon and Northwest Territories, which, under the Canadian Bill of Rights, are laws of Canada.
>
> It could be argued that a reference to such a variety of standards might entail complications and variations in the administration of the Indian Act across Canada and, indeed, I do not wish to suggest that Parliament, in legislating on testamentary matters and causes with respect to Indians, or the Minister, in administering the Indian Act, are bound to follow all provincial enactments and practices over which they have no control in any event: this they might not be able to do, they might not find desirable to do and, in my view, they are not required to do in order to comply with the Canadian Bill of Rights. But there may well emerge from the variety of provincial laws on these matters a body of general rules common to all or to many provinces, which for want of other criteria and as a sort of just gentium [law of the peoples – i.e., a common ground among different legal principles] is susceptible to provide general minimum standards to which reference can be made for the purpose of deciding how the principle of equality can be safeguarded ([1975] 3 W.W.R. 1, 33).

The imaginative suggestion at the end of the passage – of determining a minimum standard of acceptability for federal law by comparing it with the general run of provincial laws – could prove useful in assessing the adequacy of federal service delivery to reserves. In making the comparisons, courts could look at the level of federal expenditure and quality of services. The courts would, of course, take into account any special logistical difficulties the federal government has in supplying services to Indian communities – e.g., the expense of shipping supplies and personnel to remote reserves.

The federal government should not be able to use defences against the charge of unequal treatment which rely on the special treaty entitlements of certain Indian bands. If a treaty guarantees (as does Treaty No. 3) that a school will be maintained on a reserve, that obligation should be in combination with s.15 – the school must be of roughly equal educational quality to that maintained for Canadians generally. To say that the treaty creates a special regime governing Indian-federal relations, and so saves the federal government from charges of inequality, would be to turn a treaty entitlement into a detriment. Thus if a treaty implicitly exempts Indian property from taxation – and Indian organizations have argued that some of them do – then the federal government should not be able to hold the lack of fiscal contribution by Indians themselves as a defence to its own failure to provide adequate educational services. Section 25 of the *Charter of Rights and Freedoms* provides that the *Charter* guarantees should be construed as not derogating from aboriginal, treaty, and other rights of aboriginal peoples of Canada.

The existence of treaty entitlements should never leave Indians in a worse position than Canadians generally. In some cases, however, it would be legitimate to, in effect, render irrelevant a treaty entitlement by putting Indians in the same position as other Canadians. If a clause in a treaty requires that the federal government maintain a "medicine chest" on a reserve, for example, it might be appropriate to put Indians in the same position, with respect to both benefits and burdens, as other Canadians under public health care schemes. The reasoning would be that a modern health care system offers far more extensive benefits, including access to highly trained physicians, than would the maintenance of a free supply of drugs. Therefore, the argument would go, it is fair to extract from Indians the same contributions as everyone else in the system; a very minor adjustment might be made in the premiums Indians pay to take into account their entitlement to free medicines. Or no adjustment at all might be made on the grounds that the overall package is better than the treaty's guarantee, and Indians should not legitimately complain that Canadians generally enjoy the same position that they do. The medicine chest clause would be viewed as primarily a recognition of a humanitarian duty by the government, rather than as part of the payment for land surrendered. On the other hand, governments must be careful to avoid what amounts to the unfair negation of treaty entitlements. If Indians receive treaty payments as a continuing payment for the land their ancestors surrendered to governments, a government cannot legitimately reduce its service delivery by the extent of these payments, on the argument that the total package of treaty payments and services is equivalent to what Canadians generally receive by way of government assistance. To do so would be like denying family allowance payments to a contractor because he is already getting paid for construction work he has done on a government building. The extent to which Indians may be treated equally under social welfare and public services schemes depends on the language and purpose of particular treaty provisions. It may be justifiable in certain cases for governments to insist that Indians make the same sort of contribution by way of taxes to their local education systems as Canadians do generally.

An American precedent brought to mind by the foregoing, and germane to the discussion as a whole, is *San Antonio Ind. School District* v. *Rodriguez*, 411 U.S. 1. The state of Texas ran a school financing system not unlike that typical in Canada; the state made standard grants to local school districts, and the latter had discretion to impose property taxes to raise further revenue. The plaintiffs contended that the system denied them the equal protection of the law. The Supreme Court of the United States decided 5-4 that it did not. The majority opinion argued that the system did not on its face or in its effect discriminate against a class of people who required special constitutional protection. The children of the poor were not necessarily found in areas with little taxable property. On the contrary, they were often clustered around commercial and industrial areas. The class discriminated against was simply people who happened to live in areas with low tax bases – and the benefit of allowing people local fiscal, and therefore, policy, control over their schools outweighed the discrimination against this class. Furthermore, the majority contended, the deprivation of educational opportunity was not absolute – and the connection between money spent and learning instilled was an "unsettled and disputed question." The majority found no precedent for the contention that education was a "fundamental right," making the unequal distribution of it subject to strict scrutiny by the courts. ("Scrutiny" in American jurisprudence involves examining two things: the importance of the state interest involved in a legislative classification or measure and the exactitude with which the classification or measure serves the purpose. American Courts apply "strict scrutiny" when legislation is aimed at, or has a disproportionate impact upon, certain types of groups – such as racial or religious ones – or interferes with "fundamental rights.") The court reiterated a policy it has followed ever since the New Deal of deferring to the democratically elected branches of government in matters of "social and economic legislation."

The dissenting opinion of Marshall J. argued that education is a matter of "fundamental importance." and its distribution entitled to "special judicial scrutiny" because of its close connection to the expressly guaranteed right to free speech under the First Amendment. The fact that the classification used was based on wealth also called for heightened judicial scrutiny. Local control over educational policy could be maintained using revenue raising techniques which did not impair the educational opportunities of "vast numbers of Texas school children."

The *San Antonio* case could be distinguished from inadequate delivery of educational services to reserves on the basis that the latter involves the singling out for adverse treatment of an enclave consisting almost entirely of a racial minority. Discrimination on the basis of race calls for the highest level of scrutiny by American Courts, and we may expect similarly stringent examination from Canadian Courts – s.1 of the *Canadian Bill of Rights* and s.15 of the *Charter of Rights and Freedoms* both identify race in their lists of expressly prohibited classifications. (Because of s.28 of the *Charter*, however, it can be argued that sexual discrimination is even more suspicious under the Canadian Constitution than is racial discrimination.)

One attitude expressed in *San Antonio* that Canadian courts might follow, however, might be the reluctance of the American courts to meddle in matters of economic and social policy. In *Morgentaler* v. *R.* (1975), 53 D.L.R. (3d) 161, Chief Justice Laskin (dissenting), who at that time was usually far more enthusiastic than his colleagues were about using the *Canadian Bill of Rights* against legislation, rejected a contention that Canadian abortion laws were invalid because, among other things, there was not equal access across Canada to hospitals with committees empowered to approve the procedure. In earlier parts of his judgment, he had emphasized that the *Canadian Bill of Rights* is merely a statutory, rather than a constitutional instrument, and that judicial review of the substantive content of legislation was foreign to Canadian constitutional tradition. He responded to the unequal access argument by saying that its acceptance:

> . . . would mean too that the Court would have to come to some conclusion on what distribution would satisfy equality before the law, and that the Court would have to decide how large or small an area must be within which an acceptable distribution of physicians and hospitals must be found. This is a reach for equality by judicially unmanageable standards . . . (53 D.L.R. (3d) 161, 175).

Laskin C.J.C.'s judgment does go on to observe that there was no denial of equality on the basis of a ground expressly prohibited by the *Canadian Bill of Rights*. This fact could, as with *San Antonio*, be used to limit the impact of *Morgentaler* on a case about service delivery to a reserve. Still, the judgment does indicate that even the most interventionist judges are liable to find that the *Canadian Bill of Rights* does not support their second-guessing legislatures in fairly complicated matters of social and economic policy. Service delivery to reserves might well be seen as falling within that category, and therefore outside of judicial interference.

The *Canadian Charter of Rights and Freedoms*, however, is a constitutional guarantee of equality. That legislatures have been allowed, with respect to s.15 of the *Charter* only, three years to clean up their acts before it comes into force shows that the section is intended to have some real force against discriminatory legislation. It surely cannot be construed as being merely directed against failures to subject everyone to the rule of law, the extravagantly inconsequential meaning Ritchie J. attributed to the equality guarantee in s.2(b) of the *Canadian Bill of Rights*. Section 15 also forbids such a constricting construction; it speaks of the equal protection and of the *equal benefit* of the law. The ability of legislatures, under s.33 of the *Charter*, to override judicial determinations of invalidity by stamping their legislation as "notwithstanding the Canadian *Charter of Rights and Freedoms*" should, if anything, encourage courts to intervene against injustice. They know if they err badly in their appreciation of the facts or norms, the legislatures can always intervene before the heavens fall.

In applying the *Charter* against an inequality of service delivery to reserves, a court could bolster its conclusion by referring to s.36 of the *Constitution Act, 1982*, the one which speaks about equal opportunity and transfer payments. A court might point out that Indians cannot have "equal opportunities for the well-being of Canadians," in the words of s.36(1)(a), if they do not have equal educational opportunities and that it would make sense that a federal government committed to the principle of making transfer payments to provinces so as to ensure "reasonably comparable levels of public services at reasonably comparable levels of taxation" should have to provide similar financial support for people under its own jurisdiction. The suggestion, in other words, is that the standards of justice in s.36 be used to colour the construction of s.15 of the *Charter of Rights*. A possibly reply would be that s.36 is itself nonjusticiable, and the reason it is nonjusticiable is that courts lack the expertise, tools, and a democratic mandate to interfere in matters of economic and social policy; and s.15 should be approached in the same spirit of restraint. I would agree that courts should be sensitive to the limitations inherent in their structure and respectful of the democratic process. It would be ironic, however, if s.36 which was intended to enhance the duties of Canadian governments to provide opportunity and reduce inequality were used to blunt the force of the equality guarantee.

It should not be forgotten, moreover, that s.36 may in fact be directly judicially enforceable (see Chapter VII); if so, it would provide additional legal support for Indians who perceive themselves as unfairly deprived of adequate social and public services.

Chapter XIII

Provincial Responsibility for Indians

It will be recalled that the provinces have no jurisdiction over Indians as such, but that laws primarily directed towards provincial subject matters may apply to Indians. In regulating a provincial subject matter, some special treatment for Indians may be permitted. Now, because of the express assignment of jurisdiction over Indians to the federal level of government by s.91(24) of the *Constitution Act, 1867*, it is generally agreed that whatever special "trust responsibility" there is for Indians is vested in the federal level of government. The fulfillment of treaty obligations is also, generally speaking, the obligation of the federal government. (Provinces may acquire some affirmative duties under certain modern land claims agreements, e.g. under the James Bay agreement.) Generally speaking, therefore, the legal duties of provinces to Indians must be found, if they exist at all, in the requirement of giving Indians the equal protection and benefit of provincial laws.

In *Director of Child Welfare for Manitoba* v. *B.*, [1979] 6 W.W.R. 229 (Man. Prov. Ct.), Provincial Court Judge Garson vigorously affirmed the provincial duty to supply equal services to Indians. The issue in that case was whether a permanent guardianship order should be granted to the Manitoba Director of Child Welfare with respect to two neglected Indian children living on a reserve. The order was granted over the objection of the mother. It was held on the evidence that she would not be able to look after them properly. The province was authorized to arrange a permanent adoption. In the course of giving judgment, Garson Prov. J. commented extensively on the federal-provincial battle over responsibility for child welfare services. A federal official had explained to him the federal view that child welfare was a provincial responsibility, while the province took the opposite view. Garson Prov. J. summarized the official's further testimony as follows:

> To confuse the matter even further, the federal government partially recognizes the provincial contentions by contracting in special cases with the provinces to provide health, social and child care services for a particular reserve, and the federal government will provide the funds. In short, the federal government purchases the expertise and staff of the provinces to supply these services. The contract is generally referred to as a 'tri-partite agreement' between the two senior governments and a particular Indian reserve or reserves. But these arrangements are made upon an ad hoc basis. Only certain reserves in Manitoba benefit from these types of agreements. There is no province-wide policy or agreement encompassing all Indian reserves. When questioned as to the likelihood of such an agreement or contract for services being instituted to cover the Little Grand Rapids Reserve, the witness replied: "And in April 1977 the tri-partite negotiations began in earnest. And it's like two years later and nothing has been resolved in discussions yet." The stark reality of the present situation at Little Grand Rapids is that the treaty Indian is caught in a political, financial and legal limbo, with both senior governments attempting to disclaim responsibility for the delivery of social and child welfare services, with the not unsurprising result that the treaty Indian fails to get the services except in life-threatening situations. As above stated, the treaty Indian in Little Grand Rapids is being denied those services that all other Manitobans receive or are entitled to receive as of right and as a matter of course. Such a denial of services, for whatever reasons, can only be termed discriminatory to the treaty Indian ([1979] 6 W.W.R. 229, 237).

The *Canadian Bill of Rights* did not (and still does not) apply to provincial governments; Manitoba did not have its own

Bill of Rights, and the *Charter of Rights and Freedoms* was still three years from coming into existence when Garson Prov. J. was considering the *Director of Child Welfare* case. He thus had to base his finding of illegality on common law doctrines of constitutional and administrative law. He found the applicable one to be that there is no power in the Crown (i.e. the executive branch of government) to dispense with or suspend the application of particular laws with respect to a particular group. Indeed, the Manitoba Court of Appeal had applied the principle *against* Indians the year before in *R.* v. *Catagas* (1978), 81 D.L.R. (3d) 396 when it held that government officials could not suspend without legislative authorization the application to Indians of the *Migratory Birds Convention Act.* It should be noticed that the principle Garson Prov. J. was relying upon is actually limited to discrimination by executive officials in their administration of laws of general application. The principle does not speak to the question of discrimination by legislatures in their passing of statutes. When s.15 of the *Charter of Rights and Freedoms* comes into force on April 17, 1985, it will apply to provinces. A powerful argument will thus be available that it is unconstitutional for legislatures to limit the availability of services to Indians at the statutory level. Could provinces defeat these arguments by citing federal responsibility?

When first presented with an equal protection case, a court might declare that it is the duty of the province and federal level of government to provide Indians with equal services whether they are on or off reserves. The court would refrain from sorting out responsibilities as between the two levels of government. By doing so, the court would avoid having to sort a tangle of economic, social, and historical considerations that would go into determining constitutional responsibility. There is a constitutional precedent for federal and provincial governments being constitutionally bound to come to an agreement for the benefit of Indians. When the Natural *Resources Transfer Agreement* transferred control of Crown land to the western provinces, Indians in those provinces still had entitlements under treaties for allotments of land as payment for their surrender of their old land. It was provided in s.10 of the Manitoba Agreement (affirmed by the *Constitution Act, 1930*) that the province would have to transfer back: "such further areas as the . . . Superintendent General of Indian Affairs may, *in agreement with the appropriate Minister* of the Province, select as necessary to enable Canada to fulfil its obligations under the treaties with the Indians of the province . . ." [emphasis added].

If forced to determine ultimate responsibility because of a failure of governments to agree, a court might take a number of different paths. It has been argued earlier that the "trust responsibility" legally implicit in s.91(24) of the *Constitution Act, 1867* is a narrow one, essentially confined to the proper management of Indian lands and assets and not extending to service delivery. A court might reason, however that inasmuch as paramount legislative authority over Indians is vested in the federal level of government, so must paramount responsibility. Or it might distinguish between ultimate responsibility for Indians on their traditional land bases and Indians in the rest of a province. The former, it might be argued, are ultimately federal responsibility because the federal government has chosen to establish for them special legal, political, and economic regimes. Where Parliament has established a special social system, the court might reason, it cannot pick and choose which parts of it the provinces must step in and handle. It is not fair to the provinces to require that they supply services when they have no control over the overall management of the areas. Without control, provinces have no ability to promote special and economic development on the reserve and thereby reduce the amount of external public support that is required. Nor can the province efficiently incorporate the reserves into its overall system of service delivery. The same court might hold, however, that Indians in urban centres should be considered a provincial responsibility on the grounds that, in the absence of Parliamentary intervention, responsibility over Indians should follow the division of powers apart from s.91(24). The court might fortify its conclusion by pointing to the relative efficiency of placing Indians into the ordinary scheme of social programs. There are many other routes a court could take and a number of justifications in every case for following such a path.

Whichever way a court went, it would be acting in a highly creative fashion; the text of the *Constitution Act, 1867* provides only limited guidance. It would be far better if the complex of social, economic, and political concerns connected with the provision of social services and assistance to Indians were solved by a simple, comprehensive agreement among federal and provincial governments and Indian organizations. The next section of this paper sketches a proposal in this regard.

Chapter XIV

Funding of Indian First Nation Governments

The Penner Report

The *Penner Report* on Indian self-government proposed that the federal government use its s.91(24) power to oust the application of provincial laws to reserves and then negotiate bilaterally with Indians on the form of local self government and the appropriate funding arrangements; *Penner Report*, recommendations 12, 33, 34, 35. In its chapter on the Trust Relationship between Indians and the federal government the *Penner Report* recommends:

> The Committee asserts that the special relationship between the federal government and Indian First Nations must be renewed and enhanced by recognizing the right of First Nations to self-government and providing the resources to make this goal realizable. This will require that the duties and responsibilities of the federal government to Indian First Nations be defined in the constitution and in legislation and that they be legally enforceable (*Penner Report*, recommendation 49).

Thus the primary onus for providing funding or services to Indian governments would, under the *Penner Report*, be vested in the federal government. The duty would be directly enforceable. The report is speaking, it should be remembered, to the relationship between Indians on traditional land bases and the federal government; neither here nor elsewhere does it have much to say about Indians living in the cities.

The *Penner Report* argues that the best way to ensure the economic self-sufficiency of Indian First Nation governments would be to expand and assert their revenue base by granting them more land, settling outstanding land claims, and guaranteeing them a greater share of revenues from resources connected with their lands. At least as an interim measure, however, federal grants to Indians would have to continue. The *Penner Report* vigorously and persuasively denounces the existing system. The federal government has nominally given Indians more responsibility under it for managing their own affairs. Programs are supposed to be run by Indian band governments, rather than the federal bureaucracy. In practice, band governments have to devote a demoralizing amount of time and money to lobbying the government for funding of these programs at one end and then accounting for how they have been operated at the other. According to the report:

> The result of the situation is unfortunate. Indian leadership feel that they have taken over a lot of administrative work and problems formerly borne by the Department without being properly compensated, without being given any discretion or control, and without resultant savings in departmental administrative costs (*Penner Report*, 87).

In expanding on the last point, the *Penner Report* cites a study by an accounting firm which found that in 1981-1982, one quarter of the $250 000 000 spent on the Indian and Inuit Affairs Program of the Department of Indian Affairs and Northern Development went to general department administration. The report recommends that the present system be replaced with one whereby the federal government makes unconditional grants to Indian First Nation governments. They would be accountable to their own people, rather than to the federal bureaucracy. In this way they would be able to exercise real control over policy, and an enormous waste of money and human energy inherent in the present system would be avoided. Indian governments would use their grant in any way they chose; they would determine, for example, how much is spend on health care, how much on education. According to the report:

> It can be assumed that Indian First Nation governments would provide many governmental

> services themselves. Alternatively, they could contract with a provincial government, a municipality, a private agency, a tribal council, or even the federal government. In the case of medical services, for example, Indian First Nation governments might find it more suitable to contract with an area medical facility. The essential principle is that each government would make its own decisions and agreements, applying its own values and standards, rather than having them imposed from the outside (*Penner Report*, 98).

Elsewhere in the *Penner Report*, it is proposed that Indian First Nation governments have the right to raise revenues for their own purposes; "some Indian First Nations might choose to exercise this power as an optional method to supplement its fiscal arrangements, to encourage and regulate development, and to ensure the economic well-being of the community" (*Penner Report*, 64).

The amount of federal funding, according to the *Penner Report*, should be determined by national-level negotiations between the federal government and designated representatives of First Nations. It would be extensive and time consuming for the federal government to try to negotiate separate fiscal arrangements with hundreds of different Indian First Nation governments. A formula should, however, be agreed upon which disperses money to Indian First Nation governments not only on the basis of their population, but also according to their need. A formula might be developed along the lines of the transfer payments formula for the provinces—which takes into account both number of persons in a province and a long list of revenue sources.

The *Penner Report* discusses two different lines of justifications for providing transfers to Indian First Nation governments. One is based on historical dealings. The report quotes Indian witnesses as saying:

> We ask you to consider the justice of our situation. In signing treaties, we have never surrendered our sovereignty or our resources. If we had controlled or even shared in the resource development of our area, we would not be in our present situation today.
>
> The First Nations have already made a one-time-only contribution of resources to Canada sufficient to

> capitalize a fund for current payments (*Penner Report*, 97).

The appeal to history is open to challenge. Some might argue that the treaties specified what payment Indians were to be given for surrendering their lands, and they cannot claim to be paid again. There is no doubt that Canadians would be far less prosperous had not federal and provincial governments obtained the full ownership of Indian lands. It would not be fair accounting, however, to ignore the contribution non-Indian technology and market demand has made to the present value of these lands. It is far from obvious what standards of justice you would use in determining the relative contribution of Indian and non-Indians to Canada's present wealth. Even if the accounting norms were established, applying them would involve an examination of a massive amount of historical data and unprovable guesses about "what might have been if". Again, there can be no doubt that Indians were not in a position to bargain freely with respect to the price they were paid for the lands they surrendered at the time of the treaties. They were not provided with independent legal advice, and in many cases they were made to know that if they did not agree upon a deal, the Canadian government would take their land anyway (Cumming and Mickenberg 1972, 122). The circumstances of the treaties raise the strong suspicion that Indians were not paid a fair price. But it is, again, extremely difficult to look back at transactions made almost a century ago and say what a fair price would have been – or figure out what would have happened economically to Indians and non-Indians if a fair price had been paid.

The *Penner Report* cites a second justification for funding Indian First Nation governments. It is more simple and more sellable than the historical one. It is that:

> Canada has a tradition of sharing the national wealth. For many years a system of federal equalization payments to those provinces whose revenues fall below the national average has been elaborated to permit poorer provincial governments to provide a minimum level of services. The principle of equalization payments has now been entrenched in the constitution (See section 36 to the *Constitution Act, 1982*, especially s.36(2)) (*Penner Report*, 97).

The appeal to a general Canadian principle of revenue sharing among governments involves no laborious appeal to history. It does not require that anyone acknowledge a debt to Indians over and above what is owed to everyone else. Instead, it calls for Canadians to give to Indian governments the same respect and concern as is shown other governments. Some might still argue that there should not be special Indian governments; but given that there are going to be some, providing them with proper resources to do the tasks of government seems only fair.

The approach of the *Penner Report* has much to recommend it. If the federal government ties enough strings to the funds it grants Indian First Nation governments, the present system will, in effect, continue. The nominal increase in the legal authority of Indian First Nation governments will make no real difference. Some limits must, however, be placed on the general principle of letting Indian First Nation governments determine their own spending priorities. The federal government should continue to be able to attach, by conditionality of grants or by regulation, certain minimal standards for the operation of programs. Indian communities will continue to be part of the Canadian polity, and some ability of the larger community to impose its basic standards of justice will have to be conceded. A refusal to do so would weaken the moral force of the appeal to the general Canadian principle of equalization. The principle is based on a concern for distributive justice among Canadians generally; Indian communities cannot bank on that concern to obtain funding and then expect Canadians to be indifferent to whether the funds are fairly spent among individuals within the Indian community. When the federal government provides provinces with funding for provincial health care schemes, it imposes the condition that everyone have equal access to health care, regardless of wealth. The federal government properly could, and probably will, extend that condition to health care schemes operated by Indian First Nation governments.

You might object that there is a leap of logic in the argument just presented. The argument, you might say, wrongly assumes that a federal concern for economic equality among communities legitimately extends to a concern for equality within communities. Section 36(2) of the *Constitution Act, 1982* talks about providing transfer payments to provinces, not to persons. My reply would be that the history of s.36, and a reading of its provisions as a whole, do not require that a sharp distinction be made between intercommunity and interpersonal sharing. At the time s.36(2) was agreed upon, Established Programs Financing, including the medicare fiscal system, was an accepted part of the federal-provincial payment arrangements (*Federal-Provincial Fiscal Arrangements and Established Programs*

Financing Act, 1977). This context suggests that "equalization payments" in s.36(2) should be construed as directing the federal government to fulfill its equalization duty only through unconditional transfers, as opposed to program grants with basic conditions. The phrase "reasonably comparable levels of service" in s.36(2), moreover, can be construed as referring to the distributive fairness of programs. Subsection 36(1) refers to the promotion of "equal opportunities for the well-being of Canadians" and providing "essential public service of reasonable quality to all Canadians." Parliament should be able to take these standards into account in discharging its duties to make transfer payments to provinces under subsection 36(2).

One of the standards of justice that the federal government should be able to impose is that everyone should have both the freedom and the education to choose his or her own path in life. I say this partly out of a preference for individual over collective self-determination, a preference that many people would, as an abstract matter, dispute. The empirical fact of the matter is, however, that many Indians will, because of economic pressure or personal choice, end up living in Canadian cities (Krotz 1980, 10). They should be equipped by their education to have a fair chance of achieving their goals in a highly competitive society. The federal government should, therefore, be able to impose basic education standards with respect to Indian communities as well. Detailed regulation should, of course, be avoided. Indians may have a much better idea of how to achieve stipulated educational goals than outside authorities. I should also hasten to say that it is very likely that most Indian governments would manage their programs in accordance with our general Canadian expectations even without a legal requirement that they do so.

Another point on which I would differ somewhat from the *Penner Report* concerns the role of internal taxation by Indian First Nation governments. The equalization payment formula in s.36 does refer to maintaining "reasonably comparable levels of public services at reasonably comparable levels of taxation." An appeal on behalf of Indian First Nation governments to the equalization principle must accept that with the benefit of the principle must come its implicit burdens. Indian First Nation governments will have to accept that unless a treaty justifies their exemption, they will be expected, like any other government, to raise a certain amount of their revenue by internal taxation. The *Penner Report* refers to the latter as an optional method whereby Indian governments can raise additional revenue; I would think it would have to be regarded as an integral part of any fiscal arrangements concerning Indian

First Nation governments. It must also be regarded as essential to ensuring adequate accountability by an Indian First Nation government to their own people. That a government's revenue must, to some extent, be raised by taxation is one way of ensuring that its citizens are aware of how much money is being spent and concerned with whether it is being well spent.

A fiscal issue related to that in the previous paragraph is whether Indians should be subject to federal income tax. Section 87 of the *Indian Act* provides that:

> Notwithstanding any other Act of the Parliament of Canada or any Act of the legislature of a province, but subject to s.83, the following property is exempt from taxation namely
> (a) the interest of an Indian or a band in reserve or surrendered lands; and
> (b) the personal property of an Indian or band situated on a reserve.

In *Nowegijick* v. *The Queen* (1983), 144 D.L.R. (3d) 193, however, the Supreme Court of Canada construed the exemption as extending to income earned on a reserve, even though it was obtained through an activity which did not centrally involve the possession or use of reserve property. The facts in the case were that a reserve based company conducted logging operations outside of the reserve. The minister of national revenue attempted to tax a resident of the reserve on the income he had earned as an employee of the company. The Supreme Court of Canada held that it could not. According to Dickson J. the *situs* of the salary was the Indian reserve. Furthermore, "a tax on income is in reality a tax on property itself." Therefore, the minister of revenue was wrongly attempting to tax an Indian in respect of personal property situated on a reserve.

There are some valid considerations in favour of exempting reserve lands from federal and provincial taxation. A great deal of reserve land was obtained by Indians in exchange for their surrender of other property to governments; the latter should not be able to have their cake and eat some of it too by taking a share of the property they have assigned to Indians. It may be convenient to generally exempt reserve land from taxation, rather than going into the circumstances whereby each reserve was created.

A justification that might be offered for a wider exemption, such as that provided by s.87, would be that if allowed to impose taxes, governments might impose especially harsh ones. That problem, however, could be precluded by allowing only non-discriminatory taxes of general application. The argument that provinces contribute very little to reserve service delivery and should therefore not be able to tax activities on them is sound—but can be met by an exemption from the part of the federally-administered income tax that goes to the province in which the reserve is situated. If and when the federal government ensures that Indian reserves are receiving essential public services roughly comparable to those enjoyed by other Canadians, however, there would appear to be no justification for completely exempting Indians from federal income taxation. If they are able to benefit equally from federal political and social rights, reserve residents should have to bear equal responsibilities. For many Indians the imposition of a federal income tax would not make that much financial difference. Some reserves, however, enjoy fairly high income levels; even on some of the poorer reserves, senior politicians and administrators are paid very well. It does not seem right that someone should be exempt from income tax for no other reason than his Indian status and reserve residence.

The federal government's reply to the *Penner Report* refused to accept some of its fundamentals with respect to fiscal responsibility. The government accepted the principle of establishing Indian First Nation governments with powers to be determined through negotiation. Point 10 of the *Federal Reply* said that "The Government acknowledges and accepts its special responsibilities for Indian people and Indian lands." Under the title "Improvements Under Existing Legislation", the federal government said that even without legislative changes it would be prepared, in accordance with the *Penner Report*, to "ease current administrative constraints in respect of program and service delivery." Under Point 10(ix), however, the federal government said that "to respect the need for diversity," it will leave funding arrangements to individual negotiations. The only principle it will acknowledge is one-time funding of Indian First Nation governments to negotiate their recognition and multi-year funding agreements. The *Federal Reply* thus acknowledges a general standard of fiscal responsibility and leaves open the possibility of burdensome conditions being attached to federal transfers. Furthermore, the *Federal Reply* leaves open the possibility that Indian First Nation governments, like band governments at the present, will have to engage in time-consuming and complicated trilateral negotiations with both the federal government and the provinces. Under "General Framework Legislation" the *Federal Reply* says cryptically "Any legislation must respect the provisions of the *Constitution Acts 1867-1982*, and thus, given current constitutional arrangements, not all powers envisioned by the Special Committee can be included in this framework legislation."

It is possible to imagine a number of constitutional concerns with respect to the *Penner Report*. The powers it would allow some Indian First Nation governments might be so extensive as to overstep the bounds of permissible delegation of authority from Parliament. The *Penner Report* suggests that the compliance of Indian First Nations with the *Charter of Rights and Freedoms* be left to negotiations; the *Federal Reply* may have regarded the application of some sections of the *Charter* as applicable to Indian First Nation governments, regardless of any federal attempt at waiver. But the most likely concern of the authors is the federal-provincial division of legislative authority. The *Penner Report* proposed that the federal government shield Indian First Nation governments from the application of provincial law. The *Federal Reply*, point 10(viii) stated:

> The Indian First Nation governments could, then, exercise a wide area of jurisdiction in accordance with the negotiated agreements, and some federal and provincial laws would likely not apply as a result. It is important to note, however, that federal legislation in areas of national concern would continue to apply. Furthermore, provincial legislation would continue to apply provided it was not inconsistent with the *Constitution Acts, 1867-1982*, the framework legislation and the Indian First Nation Government's internal constitution and exercise of powers under the framework legislation.

It is constitutional for the federal government to use its exclusive authority under s.91(24) to oust the application of provincial law. The respect for provincial jurisdiction probably did not arise out of a perceived legal compulsion. Nor did it likely spring from a federal respect for provincial authority above and beyond what the law perceivedly required – not where the government concerned was the same one that was prepared to radically change the Constitution of Canada over the objection of eight provinces. It is possible the federal government simply thought it sound policy for some provincial laws to apply: those regulating highway safety, for example, or those establishing occupational safety or school attendance standards. Another concern of the federal government, however, may have been to try to get the provinces to provide, and pay for, some programs and services on the reserve. A federal declaration that provincial laws generally do not apply to Indian communities would not exactly inspire provinces to take a more active role in providing for their social welfare. The *Federal Reply* does little to preclude a scenario in which Indian First Nation governments endlessly engage in negotiations with both the federal and provincial governments over what services and how much funding will be provided. In defence of the *Federal Reply*, it should be said that it invites the comments of provinces, and the federal government may not have wanted to commit itself clearly on the role of provinces prior to hearing from them. The federal government might not have wanted to commit itself to plenary responsibility for Indian communities until responsibility for Indians in the cities is sorted out, and that again would require extensive discussions with the provinces.

What Ought to be Done

If Indian First Nation governments are to succeed, they must be able to rely on a steady source of minimally conditional funding. The federal government ought to agree to the norm that Indian communities are entitled, at roughly comparable levels of taxation, to public services reasonably comparable to those available to other Canadians. "Public services" would include, among other things, social, health, and educational programs. Those Indian First Nation governments that are ready and willing to assume management of the programs themselves ought to receive sufficient funding to permit them to do so in a manner consistent with the equality of services norm. The equality principle might be embodied in the Constitution in the form of a s.36 variant. Regardless of whether or not it is embodied in the Constitution, the equality principle should be expressed in the framework legislation authorizing the establishment of Indian First Nation governments.

The *Penner Report*'s proposal that a standard formula be established, rather than leaving funding to be worked out in individual negotiations, should be followed. If the necessary accounting is possible, the formula should determine the overall package of direct service delivery or funding owing to every Indian community. The Indian First Nation government would be able to choose, without fear of cost to its people, the extent to which it will assume management of programs. It could use the funding to run the programs itself, or to pay private agencies or federal and provincial governments to run the programs. The waste and delay involved in trilateral negotiations would be avoided; with funding assured, Indian First Nation governments would be able to choose whether to allow federal or provincial service delivery according to the quality of the programs, rather than the willingness of levels of governments to provide them.

As part of a deal whereby the federal government assumes the equality of services norm and complete responsibility for financially supporting Indian governments, the provinces might make a number of concessions. They could agree to cooperate with Indian First Nation governments in working out agreements for the sale of provincial services to Indian communities. The provinces might also agree to accept the primary responsibility for Indians who have left their traditional communities. In some areas it may be appropriate for an Indian First Nation government, or an association of them, to operate services in the cities. An example would be an Indian child welfare agency. In such a case, the province would be responsible for funding since the Indian agency would be doing work that the province would otherwise have to do itself. The provinces might also agree that Indians in traditional communities should not be taken into account for the purposes of general equalization payments to the provinces. Since the provinces would not be fiscally responsible for the residents of those communities, they would not be able to receive equalization payments in respect of them. (A complaint that the federal government can make under the present system is that the provinces do, in effect, profit from the economic underdevelopment of Indian communities; their residents generally are below the Canadian average in generating sources of government revenue, and so raise the amount of money the province is entitled to receive under the equalization formula.)

The sharp distinction between fiscal responsibility for Indians in their own communities and Indians in the cities has the advantage of simplicity. Plenty of constitutional and policy arguments can be made for setting the boundaries elsewhere, and that is not so much an objection to the sharp distinction as a reason for having it. Political and legal disputes over the federal-provincial division of responsibility could go on with respect to program after program.

The provinces would not be giving up all that much by observing the distinction. Provincial complaints about the failure of the federal government to take responsibility for Indians who have left traditional communities are not likely to result in a substantial change of federal policy. The province of Manitoba has for years been sending the federal government bills for services it provides to Indians who have been off the reserve for less than a year. The federal government has never paid them.

The provinces might argue that the proposed distinction does nothing to discourage bad federal management of Indian communities and indeed encourages it. If the federal government is responsible for Indians who leave reserves, it has financial incentive to ensure that Indians are adequately equipped to succeed in the cities. On the other hand, the federal government is put in the position of financially benefitting from an exodus from Indian communities (a federal responsibility under my proposal) to the cities (a provincial responsibility). The force of these objections is blunted by the fact that my proposal would require the federal government to accept sole responsibility for adequately funding Indian communities. The highest standard of economic assistance by the federal government, the avoidance of trilateral bickering, and the advent of Indian self-government might all contribute to the improved quality of public services in Indian communities. That in turn might result in fewer people leaving them. Those who do, moreover, might be educated in a way that better equips them to adapt to urban life in the cities. Furthermore, the federal government would continue to be responsible, under s.36 of the *Constitution Act, 1982*, for providing provinces with funds sufficient to permit them to provide reasonably comparable levels of services to their citizens. Have-not provinces would be able to point to their responsibilities to urban Indians in negotiations over transfer payments formulae. It would also be expected that urban Indians would benefit from special programs for Indians in areas of federal legislative jurisdiction – e.g. the creation of a development bank for native peoples. They could continue to benefit as well under federal fiscal programs such as job creation grants and regional economic development.

Chapter XV

Fiscal Responsibility and the s.37 Process

As early as December, 1982, at a working group meeting in Montreal, Manitoba proposed that the Constitution extend the equalization principle to aboriginal peoples. Paragraph (4) of the Statement of Principles that the government of Manitoba submitted to the March '83 conference proposed recognition of a "special fiscal relationship" between aboriginal peoples and the federal government. Paragraph (5) again recommended that aboriginal governments be entitled to equalization payments so that they could provide services roughly comparable to those of other governments but adapted to the "special social, cultural, and economic needs" of aboriginal peoples. It is not clear from the Manitoba statement whether the federal government would be solely responsible for supplying the necessary financial support. One thing that is clear about the Manitoba statement is that the federal government would have at least some fiscal responsibility for urban Indians and the Métis. The federal government has not, in principle or practice, acknowledged a substantial fiscal duty towards either group.

Inspired in part by the Manitoba proposals, the Inuit Committee on National Issues (ICNI) included a transfer payments clause in the draft Aboriginal Charter of Rights it presented at a ministerial meeting in February '83. Unlike the Manitoba principles, however, the ICNI deleted the s.36 standard of reasonable comparability of services; Canadian governments are supposed to provide transfer payments sufficient to meet the economic, social, and cultural needs of aboriginal peoples. Period. Another distinction from the Manitoba proposal was that the transfer payments norm was expressly made applicable to both the federal and provincial levels of government. No attempt was made to solve the federal-provincial division of responsibility problem.

Fiscal arrangements did not receive much attention at the March '83 First Ministers' Conference. The package of constitutional reforms submitted by the Assembly of First Nations (AFN) included in the table of contents item 5.13, "Resourcing of First Nations Governments: Part III of the Constitution," but no proposed amendment was actually tabled. The draft Statement of Particular Rights of the First Nations included s.13, "the right to exemption from direct or indirect taxation by other levels of government," and s.15, "the right to fiscal relationships with other governments." It may in fact be that the only way to reach constitutional agreement on fiscal arrangements will be to find language that establishes some sort of equalization norm but dodges the federal-provincial issue.

The draft Statement of Rights of the Métis People submitted by the Métis National Council (MNC) included section 35.3(e), "fair and equitable compensation for Rights that have been infringed", and 35.3(f), "adequate fiscal arrangements to fulfill these Rights." The table of contents of the package of proposed amendments submitted by the AFN included the anticlimactic item "Resourcing of First Nations Governments: Part III of the Constitution (no amendment tabled)." Not much discussion of fiscal arrangements took place, however, during the March '83 conference. The federal government's four suggested guidelines for the ongoing process did not include any fiscal principles. On the morning of the second day of the conference, both Manitoba and the MNC suggested that a statement of fiscal principles be included in the political accord. There was essentially no follow-up discussion, however, either at the First Ministers' meeting or in the backroom ministers' meeting of that afternoon. A couple of provinces attempted to make fiscal arrangements a separate item of discussion at the beginning of the 1983-84 talks, but the proposal failed. Some governments were concerned that its inclusion would overload the agenda; others figured that the issue would come up under "self-government" anyway. In the position paper it submitted to the ministers' meeting at Yellowknife in January 1984, Manitoba proposed that a commitment to adequate funding be among the amendments to the Constitution establishing the basic structure of aboriginal self-government.

The federal draft amendment on self-government at the March '84 conference made no attempt to either establish a funding standard or to sort out federal-provincial responsibility. It spoke (paragraph 35.2.16) of the "right of aboriginal peoples to self-governing institutions that will meet the needs of their communities, subject to the nature, jurisdiction and powers of those institutions, *and to the financing arrangements relating thereto*, being identified and defined through negotiation with the government of Canada and provincial governments" (emphasis added). It is possible to argue that the norm of "meeting the needs of their communities" extends not only to the political structure of the communities, but to financing arrangements as well. The section as a whole, however, uses language that may establish its non-justiciability. The primary interpreters, in other words, would have been political officials. The draft amendment of the federal government, like the *Federal Reply* to the *Penner Report*, would do nothing to preclude aboriginal governments from being involved in continuing trilateral negotiations over the federal-provincial division of responsibility, the amount of support to be provided them, and the extent to which conditions may be attached to that support.

The federal government proposed that the political accord at the March '84 conference include a commitment by governments to participate in a comprehensive study of all aspects of social, cultural, and economic programs for, and services to, the aboriginal peoples of Canada. Among the objects of the review would be, paragraph 3:

> (a) clarification of federal and provincial responsibilities for programs and services provided to the aboriginal people of Canada, having regard to the existing and potential roles of aboriginal governments;
>
> (c) assessment of financial provisions, including consideration of existing arrangements between the government of Canada and the provincial governments;
>
> (e) examination of programs and services to the aboriginal peoples of Canada, including the degree to which they are comparable with services received by other Canadians residing in similar communities.

The definition of the objects of the review seems to raise all the right questions. The proposal itself, however, did not win much support. Some of the provinces saw no need for a formal accord to conduct a policy study. Aboriginal groups wanted to focus attention on constitutional reform; as presented by the federal government, the review study was a strictly political supplement to the federal government's constitutional proposal on self-government. It would be unfortunate if the federal proposal for a study were not in some form revived. In the aftermath of the rejection of its mealy-mouthed constitutional proposal, the federal government might be able to sell the proposal to aboriginal peoples as a step toward producing a satisfactory constitutional package. The provinces which object to constitutional reform might still be interested in the prospect of improving and rationalizing nonconstitutionalized service-delivery arrangements.

Chapter XVI

The Métis and Section 91(24): Policy Aspects

The March '84 Conference

The relationship between the Métis and the federal government was a principal subject of discussion on the first afternoon of the March '84 First Ministers' Conference. At the previous First Ministers' Conference, items of special interest to the Métis had received little attention. The agenda for March '84 included four headings, and it was under the third one, "Land and Resources," that Métis identification and Métis land base issues were raised. At the final working group meeting in late February in Victoria, concern was expressed by representatives of the Métis, and some provinces as well, that the special concerns of the Métis would lose out once again – to the serial priority of the first two agenda headings, "Equality Rights" and "Aboriginal Rights and Treaty Rights," and to the political priority of the last agenda item, "Aboriginal Self-Government."

The Métis are at several disadvantages in having their concerns addressed at s.37 conferences; they arguably have few or no aboriginal rights or treaty rights, and thus cannot take advantage of discussions of those; they are less numerous than the status Indians and so have less electoral strength; apart from the four thousand Métis who live in *Métis Betterment Act* settlements in Alberta, the Métis, unlike band Indians, cannot take advantage of the political structures established by law to assist in organizing themselves and obtaining funding. Unlike the Inuit and status Indians, the Métis do not have strong bilateral ties with the federal government, which chairs First Ministers' Conferences, and so cannot lobby as effectively as other aboriginal groups with respect to other meeting arrangements.

In his opening statement to the March '84 First Ministers' Conference, Prime Minister Trudeau expressly raised the issue of federal responsibility with respect to the Métis. He said that the federal view was that the Métis were not "Indians" under s.91(24), but that "the federal government accepts a measure of responsibility for them as disadvantaged peoples." He continued, "At this conference we must come to grips with the question of the complementarity and complementary responsibilities of the federal and provincial authorities and strive to resolve it in the interest of the Métis themselves" ('84 First Ministers' Conference [FMC] transcript, 19). The Prime Minister suggested that self-government for the Métis might be achieved by delegating legislation to the provinces, with any necessary complementary legislation then being passed by Parliament.

Later in the morning, by linking it to the "Equality of Rights" item, Mr. Bruyere of the Native Council of Canada (NCC) helped to ensure that s.91(24) would be discussed. In his opening statement, he said, "We want a commitment that there shall be equality of treatment of the aboriginal groups not only as between sexes but as between the three aboriginal groups themselves" ('84 FMC transcript, 48). He went on to say, "What we need now is for the federal government with the concurrence of the provinces to unequivocally accept that section 91(24) reference in the *Constitution Act, 1867*, embraces all aboriginal peoples, not simply those covered by the narrow and unjust definitions of the *Indian Act*" ('84 FMC transcript, 50). The Métis National Council (MNC) also protested the "unequal treatment of aboriginal peoples," in the sense that the federal government does not accept constitutional responsibility for the Métis.

That afternoon, after opening statements, Prime Minister Trudeau asked the conference to advise him on how to proceed with the agenda items. He mentioned "Equality of Rights" first, and here he referred to Mr. Bruyere's statement about equality among aboriginal peoples. The matter would have to be discussed, said Prime Minister Trudeau. That afternoon, it was.

The Inclusion of the Métis Under Section 91(24): Policy Considerations

In the next chapter, I will attempt a legal analysis of whether the Métis are "Indians" for the purposes of s.91(24). My conclusion is that the Red River Métis, the descendants of the distinct ethnic and political community that arose in western Canada in the 19th century, are not. Persons of mixed ancestry who identify themselves as Indians, and have strong cultural links with them, ought to be under federal jurisdiction pursuant to s.91(24). My evaluation is strongly based on my understanding of the historical and legal precedents. Like all legal assessments, however, it is also partly based on considerations of justice and policy. Federal legislative jurisdiction over the Red River Métis is not necessary to the attainment of their goals. It is liable, on the contrary, to impede them.

I will try to substantiate the last claim by examining the specific aims that the Métis organizations have expressed during the s.37 process.

One objective has been the economic development of the Métis people. The federal government, it might be argued, is more likely than provinces are to provide the necessary economic assistance. For one thing, it can raise money more conveniently than the provinces can. It is not limited to direct taxes, as the provinces are, and can raise revenues by a variety of means that are sufficiently subtle to escape taxpayer resentment. A Métis living in a have-not province might be more optimistic about federal assistance because the federal government can draw on the revenue sources of the most prosperous regions of the country. Premier Hatfield cited the limited revenue base of the have-not provinces including his own as a reason for placing all aboriginal peoples under federal responsibility ('84 FMC transcript, 172). it could also be argued that the federal government is more likely to have the will, and not simply the means, to assist. The argument might be elaborated as follows: If there are local sentiments against providing special assistance for aboriginal peoples, they will tend to be felt less acutely in Ottawa than by a provincial government. Furthermore, a central bureaucracy is more likely than a provincial one to actively promote programs for the benefit of aboriginal peoples. Bureaucracies in general are more likely to have a redistributive orientation than the general public because hard-minded, winner-take-all free enterprisers are more likely to choose private than public life. The federal bureaucracy is so massive that its operators tend to be more independent of political control than are their provincial counterparts. Aboriginal groups may therefore expect to find a relatively reliable source of assistance among the federal bureaucrats. Finally, given the extensive financial assistance it provides to status Indians, the federal government could not in good conscience refuse to assist the Métis if they too were under federal jurisdiction.

In reply to the foregoing arguments, it should first of all be pointed out that there is no necessary connection between legislative jurisdiction and legislative responsibility. The federal government undoubtedly has legislative jurisdiction over a great many aboriginal persons for whom it does next to nothing. The federal government has chosen to establish a special regime for status Indians on reserves, but it does not provide much assistance to status Indians off the reserves or to those Indians it has chosen to define as non-status. The federal government would not necessarily be shamed into providing Métis with a level of assistance equivalent to that it provides to status Indians. It could distinguish the case of status Indians on reserves by pointing to the special history of the federal relationship with them – including the establishment of a special regime under the *Indian Act* and the making of treaty commitments. The appeal to "equality among aboriginal peoples" must be received with caution. The individual rights in the *Charter of Rights and Freedoms* are largely based on the liberal belief in the political equality of individuals. Many of the rights of aboriginal peoples, by contrast, are based not on the intrinsic equality of individuals but on the special history of particular collectivities. Whether an Indian band has aboriginal rights or treaty rights depends on its particular history; a particular course of historical dealing may entitle a group to special treatment that others do not enjoy. Indeed, s.25 of the *Charter of Rights and Freedoms* shields the rights of aboriginal peoples from the application of the *Charter* – including s.15, the equality norm. The inclusion of the Métis in the definition of "aboriginal peoples" under s.35 of the *Constitution Act, 1982* did not necessarily establish them as having entitlements equal to those of the Inuit and Indians. All section 35 of the *Constitution Act, 1982* does is recognize and affirm the aboriginal and treaty rights of the aboriginal peoples of Canada; if, in light of their distinct history, the Red River Métis have no aboriginal or treaty rights, their inclusion in s.35(2) does not have that much legal significance. The inclusion of the Métis in s.91(24) might similarly prove inconsequential. It would definitely empower Parliament to do things *to* the Métis people. It would not require it to do anything *for* them.

On the other hand, the present constitutional arrangements (assuming the Red River Métis are not included in s.91(24)) do not significantly inhibit the federal government from assisting the Métis with economic development. In many cases, federal assistance is authorized by an express head of federal authority; the federal authority over banking and interest would sustain inclusion of Métis in development bank and mortgage loans programs specially designed for them or for native people in general. Similarly, federal authority over agriculture would justify direct delivery of federal programs to Métis farmers. As mentioned earlier, I would question the constitutionality of direct program delivery to the Métis which cannot be related to a head of federal jurisdiction for many of the same reasons that Professor Trudeau condemned direct grants to provincial universities (Trudeau 1968, 79). That is, I am generally concerned that directly delivered federal programs excessively blur the lines of democratic and fiscal responsibility that Canadians should be able to rely on in electing and assessing the performance of their governments, which should be more informed about, and responsive to, local needs. Nonetheless, most scholars have argued that the power of Ottawa to spend its money as it chooses is essentially unlimited; and the federal government has in some areas acted on this assumption for many years. The Department of Regional Industrial Economic Expansion, for example, provides hundreds of millions of dollars worth of grants, subsidies, and programs with respect to projects that are not of national importance.

The transfer of legislative authority to Parliament might be worse than futile for the Red River Métis. It might hurt them. The provinces might disclaim responsibility for economic assistance and service delivery for the Métis in the same way that provinces have excused themselves from helping Indian communities. The delay, confusion, and waste that has too often attended trilateral negotiations with respect to service delivery on reserves might extend to federal-provincial-Métis arrangements.

If enhanced federal economic assistance is the goal, it can be advanced by constitutional amendments that directly impose federal fiscal responsibility, rather than establishing federal legislative authority. One possibility would be a constitutional amendment that requires the federal government to make transfer payments to aboriginal (not Indian, but aboriginal) governments sufficient to permit them to maintain reasonably comparable level of services at reasonably comparable levels of taxation. Such an amendment would be of limited utility to the Red River Métis, however, inasmuch as only about four thousand of them, on Alberta *Métis Betterment Act* settlements, live on an exclusively Métis land base. It would be possible to frame an amendment that imposed direct federal fiscal responsibility to the non-ethnic regional governments of areas that have a predominantly Métis population. The federal government might, of course, view the implications of the last mentioned amendment as excessively costly; and some provincial governments might reject on principle the inclusion of non-aboriginal residents of a province in an almost exclusively federal fiscal regime.

Another possibility would be to put something in the Constitution like: "The federal government recognizes a special responsibility to assist provincial governments and Métis institutions in promoting the economic, social, and political development of the Métis people". Such a formulation would help to secure federal assistance for a broad range of programs, whether run by provincial institutions, including local governments, or by Métis governments or agencies. The word "assist" does imply that the federal responsibility is not exclusive. Provincial governments are not to use the amendment as an excuse for reducing their funding of programs that benefit the Métis. The formula proposed does not mention direct federal program delivery, and a reference to that might be added. It is not intended that the federal government exclude the Métis from general programs or special programs for native people, or refrain from designing programs specially for the Métis. A lot of confusion, duplication, and delay might be avoided, however, and the cause of Métis self-government advanced if the federal government channelled its economic assistance into programs run by provincial and Métis institutions.

The utility of such an amendment could be challenged with some force. It does not preclude trilateral disputes over who pays for what. It may also have very little practical effect. The Métis are concentrated in British Columbia, Ontario, Saskatchewan, Alberta, Manitoba, and the Northwest Territories. The last mentioned is a federal responsibility as it is. The first four are usually "have" or break-even provinces. Only Manitoba is habitually a beneficiary of the transfer payments system. One can contemplate the federal government, with justification, being less than munificent in its interpretation of the fiscal responsibility norm when it comes to applying it to the wealthier provinces. The have-not provinces are already indirectly assisted in providing programs for Métis in that the economic problems of the Métis are reflected in the general transfer payment formulae. The Métis in have-not provinces, moreover, may benefit from regional economic development and other federal programs.

Métis Land Base

The acquisition of land bases has been one of the primary demands of the MNC during the s.37 process. Land bases, it has been argued, are necessary for Métis economic development and the institution of Métis self-government. During the March 8 discussion, Mr. Munro, the federal minister of Indian affairs and northern development, said in the course of his vigorous intervention:

> In 1931 we transferred title to provincial Crown lands and we are still trying to negotiate with some provinces with respect to unfulfilled treaty land entitlements for treaty Indians under treaty. I suppose if we are going to start now to go down the road of inclusion of all the Métis people that are under federal jurisdiction, the first thing we will have to do is look to the provinces to see how generous they are in terms of land and resources for the Métis people and if it takes even one-tenth as long as it is still taking to resolve the Indian question we may be at this an awful long time ('84 FMC transcript, 189).

The next afternoon, true to form, Prime Minister Trudeau did not echo Mr. Munro's pessimism about whether protracted negotiations would result in the provinces turning over lands to the federal government for the benefit of the Métis; instead, he made the transfer of land an unconditional condition of any transfer of jurisdiction: "If I remain Prime Minister long enough we would be prepared to consider a constitutional amendment saying that the Métis come under Section 91(24), but they would come with their lands which is a message to you and to the other Premiers . . . " ('84 FMC transcript, 373). Prime Minister Trudeau justified his stance by arguing that when the "Fathers and Mothers of Confederation" provided for Crown lands to be owned by the provinces, "what was withheld from those provincial lands [was] . . . Indian lands." If the Métis are to be considered as Indians, "it is a matter of interpreting what of the Crown lands which went to the provinces in 1867 or since then really should not have come to the provinces because they should have stayed with the Indians" ('84 FMC transcript, 374).

The interpretive question stated by Prime Minister Trudeau is not as easy as he might have thought. The histories of Métis land and Indian land are radically different. There were practically no Red River Métis in the four-province Canada of 1867 (Census of Canada 1871). When the province of Manitoba was created by federal statute in 1870, the federal government retained ownership of Crown land (*Manitoba Act*, s.30). It provided for the recognition of existing individual land holdings by Manitoba residents, including the half-breeds. The federal government also allotted, "towards the extinguishment of the

Indian title to the lands in the Province," 1 400 000 acres of land to the children of the half-breed residents of the new province. The regulations governing this transfer of land to individuals were to be made by the governor-in-council – in effect, the federal Cabinet. The allotments, consistent with those demanded by Riel, were to individuals, not to the Métis nation as a collectivity. Before Alberta and Saskatchewan were admitted in 1905 – again without obtaining ownership of Crown lands – the federal government established a similar program of half-breed grants in the North-West Territories. By the time the Prairie provinces received ownership of half-breed land in 1930, Métis land claims were supposed to have been settled by federal legislation.

Métis political organizations have contended that through a series of unjust laws, and fraud and speculation by private citizens that was supported by governments, the Métis were unjustly denied the land they were supposed to have received (Sprague 1979-80; Sprague 1981; Sanders 1979). A Métis organization has brought an action against the government of Manitoba for its alleged complicity in the land swindles. Inasmuch as the jurisdiction of actual management of the half-breed land grant programs in Western Canada was federal, the federal government must be held primarily responsible for any abuses that occurred. If the Métis claim to a land base is based on historical legal injustice, it is, I would submit, primarily a federal responsibility to right that wrong. The federal government does not need general legislative authority over Métis to do so. It could simply subsidize the Métis purchase of Crown lands from the province. It could subsidize the purchase of lands under provincial jurisdiction by individual Métis or Métis organizations. The courts might well find that the continuing force of s.31 of the *Manitoba Act* gives the federal government the power to take other remedial measures, including the expropriation of provincial land in order to directly transfer it to individuals. Whether the federal government could expropriate provincial land in order to transfer it to Métis organizations is a more difficult question; it might be argued that the federal remedial power is limited to compensating individuals, as opposed to the Métis collectivity. The validity of that argument depends in part on whether the reference in s.31 of the *Manitoba Act* to the Indian title of the Métis refers to an aboriginal title they were recognized as having or, as Sir John A. Macdonald later contended, was political rhetoric lacking in legal accuracy. With respect to the Métis in Alberta and Saskatchewan, the courts might hold that the federal government has a continuing residual authority to remedy the wrongs it committed when it was still owner of the Crown lands there. To sum up, insofar as past legal injustice with respect to Red River Métis land grants supports their contemporary demands for a land base, the federal government ought to be held primarily responsible for providing them. It has considerable ability to do so even without having general legislative authority over the Métis under s.91(24) of the *Constitution Act, 1867*. If jurisdiction were transferred, the province would not be morally responsible for providing land on the basis of Prime Minister Trudeau's analogy to the history of Indian lands.

Métis representatives have often emphasized, during the s.37 process, the desirability of settling their demands through political discussion and accommodation, rather than legalistic debate or actual litigation. Their demand for land bases can be interpreted as a forward looking attempt to secure their economic and political development. A federal request that provincial land be delivered up onto the federal level along with jurisdiction over the Métis could be argued in terms of justice and convenience, rather than legal history. The federal argument could, for example, portray the surrender of land as payment for relief from their responsibility for social service delivery. Even if that principle were accepted, however, interpreting it in acreage would require more than a few stabs at a pocket calculator. Whether negotiations over the transfer of provincial land turned on legal or political principles, they would be, as Mr. Munro said, difficult and protracted.

Upon the transfer of legislative authority over Métis, the federal government might have the legal authority to short-circuit negotiations for expropriating the provincial lands needed for a Métis land base. Parliament almost always provides for compensation when it expropriates; in the case of provincial Crown land, however, it might well be constitutionally bound to do so (Hogg 1977, 397; LaForest 1969, 149-155, 173). The judicial precedents on the last point are not clear, but the prohibition against the taxation of provincial property in s.125 of the *Constitution Act, 1867* is a strong analogy for not permitting the expropriation of its property without compensation. It should be noted that Mr. Munro mentioned that the first thing to look at upon the transfer of legislative jurisdiction would be the generosity of the provinces in providing land. Paying for the land might be the last thing the federal government would look at. Without any transfer of legislative authority, however, any federal government willing to spend a lot of money could probably obtain a land base for the Métis simply by subsidizing the purchase of provincial lands.

My conclusion would be that the transfer of legislative authority to the federal government, which does not own the Crown land in Western Canada, would in general complicate and delay the efforts of the Métis to acquire further land bases.

A special concern must be the effect of a transfer of authority on the *Métis Betterment Act* settlements in Alberta. In his opening statement, Premier Lougheed mentioned that a joint committee of Métis and provincial representatives, chaired by Dr. Grant MacEwan, was studying revisions to the statute under which eight areas have been set aside for the exclusive use of Métis. Later in the afternoon, near the end of the open discussion on s.91(24), Premier Lougheed mused:

> I believe I was unequivocal a year ago in saying that I always presumed that we in the province of Alberta had the primary responsibility for the Métis people and we have been doing our best to do that. Now I am being informed that that wasn't our responsibility and that we shouldn't perhaps be looking at it that way. I then hear these arguments being presented, and I wonder if perhaps our *Métis Betterment Act* might be unconstitutional, so it has taken a very interesting twist and turn today I guess – I don't want to be abrupt about it, but it certainly has taken an unusual turn ('84 FMC transcript, 203).

The *MacEwan Report* was issued on July 12, 1984. It proposed to replace the *Métis Betterment Act* with as *Métis Settlements Act*. The latter would explicitly grant each community complete and collective ownership of the surface rights over its area. The powers of settlement governments would be roughly equal to those of a municipality. If these reforms are satisfactory to the Métis, it would be unfortunate if they were stalled or lost by a transfer of authority to the federal level of government.

Premier Lougheed's statement should also be pondered by those who would urge the courts to construe the Métis as coming within the existing wording of the *Constitution Act, 1867*. Suppose the courts did so. A necessary corollary might be that the *Métis Betterment Act* is unconstitutional. It is not impossible that the *Act* would still be sustained on the grounds that it is primarily a local economic relief measure, rather than an attempt to recognize any special political or legal claim the Métis have as an aboriginal people. It is well documented that the Alberta government so considered the *Act* when it enacted it in 1940. A court would, however, probably find the *Act ultra vires* on the basis that it singles out the Métis for eligibility in a comprehensive proprietary and political regime. It is not as though the province made special provision for the Métis as one limited aspect of its regulation of a provincial subject matter.

If the *Métis Betterment Act* were in fact ruled *ultra vires*, there might be a way for Parliament to come to a swift and effective rescue. It would ratify everything done and all rights acquired under the *Métis Betterment Act* since its would-be enactment by the province in 1940; then it would enact its terms as federal law, but substitute federal for provincial authorities at appropriate places. Serious complications might arise, however, with the course of action just sketched. Proprietary rights to land settlement and their revenues might be disputed among the province, federal government, and Métis. Subsurface rights are being litigated between the province and the Métis as it is. Parliament might find itself impaired in implementing the MacEwan proposals with respect to land rights, should ownership of the land remain with the provincial Crown. Serious delay by Parliament in making the rescue effort just sketched could result in the dismemberment of the settlement areas. For the settlement area Métis, a transitional period of legal chaos could lead to a new juridical era in which they are no better off than before; the prospect is not going to encourage judges to find the Métis generally included within s.91(24) of the *Constitution Act, 1867*.

Métis Self-government and Section 91(24)

Early in the preparatory meetings for the March '84 Conference, the MNC reserved the right to address Working Group 4 meetings on the subject of Métis self-government outside of Métis land bases. Its subsequent submissions, however, were confined to Working Group 3, land and resources, and tied to proposals that the Métis be granted exclusive homelands. Does the absence of federal legislative authority over the Métis impede travel towards political autonomy over their homelands?

Consider the roads that might be taken. One would be the delegation of legislative authority by provincial legislatures and Parliament. Most of the powers a Métis government would likely need – property and civil rights, education, local and private matters – are assigned to the provinces by sections 92 and 93 of the *Constitution Act, 1867*. The province could delegate them to Métis governments without even consulting the federal government. (There may be constitutional limits on the extent to which either a province or Parliament can delegate but these will be discussed in Chapter XX.) There may be a few types of jurisdiction suitable for a Métis government but outside the scope of a province. These could be directly delegated from Parliament to Métis governments. Provincially established agencies are often the recipients of adjudicatory, administrative, or policy-making authority from Parliament. (Examples: provincial Crown Attorneys are authorized to prosecute Criminal Code offences, *A.G. Canada* v. *Canadian National Transport Ltd.* (1983), 3 D.L.R. (4d) 15; provincial agricultural products marketing boards are empowered to regulate interprovincial and international trade, *P.E.I. Potato Marketing Board* v. *Willis*, [1952] 2 S.C.R. 392.)

A second route whereby the Métis could achieve self-government over their land bases is by entrenching their authority in a new section of the Constitution. The existing division of authority does not make that prospect any more difficult to achieve.

A third possibility would be for the Métis to enter into agreements on self-government which amounted to "treaties" within the meaning of s.35(1) of the *Constitution Act, 1982* (see Chapter XXI). Should the Métis be concerned that a province cannot enter treaties with an aboriginal group, that only the federal government can? The grounds for supporting this restriction would be that s.35 refers to "existing treaty and aboriginal rights," and what the framers had in mind in 1982 were treaties between the imperial and federal Crowns and Indians. There were no treaties between provinces and aboriginal people, and it was not intended that a mechanism for creating constitutionally protected rights be extended to provincial-aboriginal dealings. There are solid reasons to believe that s.35(3) of the *Constitution Act, 1982*, as amended, as a result of the March '83 Conference, makes treaty making by provinces possible if it was not before. Section 35(3) says, "For greater certainty, in subsection (1) "treaty rights" includes rights that now exist by way of land claims agreements or may be so acquired". The basic idea of section 35(3) was proposed by the Inuit Committee on National Issues (ICNI) in an effort to ensure that the James Bay Agreements would receive whatever constitutional protection section 35(1) afforded. The parties to that agreement are the federal government, James Bay aboriginal peoples, and the province of Quebec.

In conclusion, the status of the Red River Métis as provincial people would not impede their progress towards political autonomy or Métis land bases. The transfer of legislative authority to Parliament might in fact frustrate Métis efforts to obtain regional governments suited to their needs.

Once legislative jurisdiction over them was transferred, a province might be less inclined to take any special measures on behalf of the Métis.

There is another form of Métis self-government that should be considered with respect to the transfer of legislative authority over the Métis to Parliament. The form would be the empowering of Métis agencies to deal with particular subject matters. During the discussion of March 8, Mr. Chartier of the MNC expressed the concern that the Métis people not be fragmented by provincial legislation and gave Métis child welfare as an example of an area where national legislation establishing Métis control might be desirable ('84 FMC transcript, 188). It should not be forgotten, however, that the provinces will in any event retain control over child welfare for the general population. It would be necessary for the federal government to obtain the political and legal cooperation of all of the provinces concerned before it could establish a uniform regime of Métis control. On the other hand, if the political will were in fact there, and if the Métis remained a provincial responsibility, the western provinces could work with each other to coordinate their Métis child welfare schemes.

The Inuit in the James Bay area and north of 60° have chosen not to aim at securing ethnic governments over exclusive Inuit territories. Instead, they have worked towards the establishment of powerful local governments in which the Inuit are a majority, but in which everyone has full and equal rights to participate in public life. It may well be that the Inuit approach is the best one for the Métis to pursue. (It is the one they adopted in 1870, when they sought entry in Confederation as equal citizens of a predominantly Métis province.)

There are only about 4,000 Métis in settlement areas in Alberta. A much larger number live in mixed communities in rural or northern parts of Western Canada. To establish exclusively Métis homelands for these people would require their leaving their present areas or removing the non-Métis from them. Both possibilities entail not only sizeable governmental expenditures, whether in land or compensation money; they also involve the distasteful business of having the government pass binding judgments on the ethnic identity of people. They mean the disruption of communities in which people of all ethnic origins respect and cooperate. The special needs of the Métis might be met by gerrymandering regional government boundaries to produce areas with high concentrations of Métis; and if necessary, by granting the local government unusually extensive powers with respect to educational and cultural matters. The acceptability to the Métis of non-ethnic regional governments would depend in part on the perceived likelihood of a large influx of non-Métis into the regions. It did not take long after the admission of Manitoba into Confederation for immigration to make the Métis a small fraction of the total population. It may well be that the risk is relatively small that non-Métis would swamp the Métis populations in the area – usually rural, often northern – which could be drawn so as to make the Métis a preponderant majority.

My overall conclusion is that the economic and political development of the Métis would not be significantly advanced by including the Métis under s.91(24). In some ways, it might be impaired; provinces might become less willing to assist; trilateral jurisdictional and financial disputes might increase, and the special legislative programs already in place for the Métis in Alberta and elsewhere would be upset. The federal government does not lack the authority to extend greater economic assistance to the Métis. A constitutional amendment generally requiring the federal government to do so might prove useful to the Métis, but disputes over its interpretation and a slackening of provincial responsibility might diminish its effectiveness.

Chapter XVII

The Métis and Section 91(24): Legal History

This section will examine the arguments from legal history that the Métis already come within section 91(24) of the *Constitution Act, 1867*. Among the most important are that at the time of Confederation the term "Indian" was generally understood as applicable to the Métis and that a purpose of s.91(24) was to protect the land rights of Indians, and this same purpose applies to the land rights of the Métis. In the course of the afternoon of March 8 of the '84 First Ministers' Conference, Prime Minister Trudeau said that the federal opinion on the non-inclusion of the Métis in s.91(24) was based "on the judgments of the Supreme Court and the advice we received from our legal counsel as to what the Fathers of Confederation meant when they wrote in 1867 that the Indians were in section 91 of the British North America [BNA] Act" ('84 First Ministers' Conference [FMC] transcript, 149). Some comments here on the historical record should be useful because of the scarcity of academic studies in recent times on the historical side of the s.91(24) argument. The most extensive effort to make the case for inclusion of the Red River Métis is a student article by Clem Chartier in the 1978-1979 volume of the *Saskatchewan Law Review* (Chartier 1978-1979). (Mr. Chartier later acted at the First Ministers' Conference as one of the principal spokesmen for the Métis National Council [MNC].) His interpretation of the historical evidence is that "half-breeds" were understood as being included in the generic term "Indians." My own interpretation of both pre-

and post-Confederation history is that persons of mixed ancestry who identify as Indians have often been considered as Indians for legal purposes, but that the Red River Métis have been referred to, and legally treated, as distinct from the Indians.

The Supreme Court of Canada precedent of principal relevance is *Re Eskimo*, [1939] S.C.R. 104. The Court had been asked by the federal government to give an advisory opinion on whether the Inuit of Northern Quebec were included in the term "Indians" as used in s.91(24) of the *Constitution Act, 1867*. (At the time the people were called Eskimos and the document the *British North America Act*.) The Court unanimously answered in the affirmative. Three concurring judgments were delivered, by Chief Justice Duff and his colleagues Cannon and Crockett. All three opinions were based on an examination of the historical use of terms, including "Indian," "Esquimaux", and "Sauvage," during the period up to and immediately after Confederation.

A historical source that all three judges relied upon was the 1857 *Report of the Select Committee of the House of Commons*. That document contains the evidence before and recommendations by the British Committee studying the future of the enormous part of North America then under the administration of the Hudson's Bay Company. At the time, the company had rights under the Royal Charter to Rupert's Land – which included what is now Manitoba – the centre of the Métis people. Chief Justice Duff found: "It was quite clear from the material before us that this Report was the principal source of information as regards the aborigines in those territories until some years after Confederation" ([1939] S.C.R. 104, 109). The report contained a census and map which Chief Justice Duff describes as "evidence of the most authoritative character" on the use of the term "Indian." The "Aboriginal Map of North America denoting the Boundaries and Locations of Various Indian Tribes" includes the "Esquimaux" but makes no mention of half-breeds.

The summary of the census us as follows:

> The Indian races shown in detail in the foregoing census may be classified as follows:

Thickwood Indians on the East side of the Rocky Mountains	35 000
The Plain Tribes (Blackfeet & c.)	25 000
The Esquimaux	4 000
Indians settled in Canada	3 000

Indians in British Oregon and on the Northwest Coast	80 000
Total Indians	147 000
Whites and half-breeds in Hudson's Bay Territory	11 000
Souls	158 000

(attached to the report as Appendix, Number 2(c), Indian Population, at page 365)

The inclusion of the Esquimaux in the enumeration of "Indians" in the census and map was an important factor in the Court's conclusion that "Indian" in s.91(24) also encompassed the Inuit. The lumping together of half-breeds and whites must be given equal and opposite effect.

Chartier attempts to limit the significance of the census by contrasting it with oral evidence given to the British Committee (Chartier 1978-79, 44). With respect, it is my opinion that the transcript largely reinforces the evidence of the census that the half-breeds were understood as generally not coming under the term "Indian." Some examples. The testimony of Sir George Simpson (governor of the Hudson's Bay territories), according to Chartier, "appears to treat both the half-breeds and Indians as belonging to the same group of people or race" (Chartier 1978-79, 45). He quotes the following example:

> 1681. Mr. Roebuck.] In that census which you have given in, is there an account of the numbers of the half-breeds in the Red River Settlement. Yes; 8,000 is the whole population of Red River; that is the Indian and half-breed population.
>
> 1682. Can you give any notion of how many of those are half-breeds? - About 4,000 I think.

First of all, the exchange does distinguish between half-breeds and Indians and is immediately followed by a series of questions by Mr. Roebuck specifically on half-breed education. Mr. Roebuck then asks separate batches of questions about half-breed trading with the United States and then about Indian trading with the United States. Secondly, not much can be read into Governor Simpson's linking together half-breeds and Indians in his response to question 1681. At question 1462, he had been asked what the Red River population was and had answered, "The total population shown is 6,500; add the population of Portage la Prairie, Manitobah, and Pembina, making 1,500; making a total of 8,000". Now the census list identifies the figures for all six posts in the Red River Settlement as "including whites and half-breeds." What appears to have happened in exchange 1681, in other words, is that rather than answering the narrow question posed, Governor Simpson started off by recalling the entire population, *including whites*, of Red River. When pressed to be more precise about the half-breed population, he was able to make a separate estimate.

Another exchange in which the examiner (Mr. Gordon) and Governor Simpson use the terms "half-breed" and "Indian" to characterize different groups of people:

> 1054. The greater population of your European servants, I presume, come from England or Scotland; they are not born of white parents in the country? - The greater portion of our white servants are Orkney men; there are a few Highlanders, and a few few Shetlanders; a large proportion of our servants are half-breeds.
>
> 1055. With your Indian servants what sort of contract do you enter into; how long is their term of service? - Merely for the trip; merely for the summer. They are sometimes employed as express bearers going with letters, and they are frequently employed as boatmen, mixed with the Company's servants and with the half-breeds.

Chartier argues that the following set of exchanges (herein marked with an asterisk) show "there really was no need to differentiate between the two – half-breeds and Indians":

> * 1747. Mr. Grogan.] What privileges or rights do the native Indians possess strictly applicable to themselves? - They are perfectly at liberty to do what they please; we never restrain Indians.
>
> * 1748. Is there any difference between their position and that of the half-breeds? - None at all. They hunt and fish, and live as they please. They look at us for their supplies, and we study their comfort and convenience as much as possible; we assist each other.

1749. Lord Stanley.] You exercise no authority whatever over the Indian tribes? - None at all.

1750. If any tribe were pleased now to live as the tribes did live before the country was opened up to Europeans; that is to say, not using any article of European manufacture or trade, it would be in their power to do so? - Perfectly so; we exercise no control over them.

1751. Mr. Bell.] Do you mean that, possessing the right of soil over the whole of Rupert's Land, you do not consider that you possess any jurisdiction over the inhabitants of the soil? - No, I am not aware that we do. We exercise none, whatever rights we possess under our Charter.

* 1752. Then it is the case that you do not consider that the Indians are under your jurisdiction when any crimes are committed by the Indians upon the Whites? - They are under our jurisdiction when crimes are committed upon the Whites, but not when committed upon each other; we do not meddle with their wars.

With respect, questions 1747 and 1748 do not show that in general there was no need to differentiate half-breeds from Indians. They simply show that in one respect some half-breeds were in the same position as some Indians. The examiner, it should be noted, asked about the treatment of the two separately, using different terms. Compare the exchange with the following:

1050. Mr. Edward Ellice.] Is it not the fact that that is one of the districts into which spirits did not go at all? - No spiritous liquors have been sent northward of Cumberland to my knowledge since 1832.

1051. Either for the Company's servants or for the Indians? - Not for anybody; neither for officers, servants, nor Indians.

The equal treatment of company servants and Indians with respect to the distribution of liquor hardly establishes that in general there was no need to distinguish the groups.

The "no need to distinguish" argument is inconsistent with a vital and well founded claim of the MNC – that a distinct Métis people evolved in the Red River area in the 19th century. The development of distinctive behaviour and ethnic self-consciousness among the half-breeds would have been a matter of which a Hudson's Bay Governor would be well aware. A number of historians have attributed the origin of Métis nationalism to the struggle between the North West Company and the Hudson's Bay Company, particularly over the establishment by the latter of the Selkirk colony (Howard 1952, 36-37; Lussier 1978, 20; A.S. Morton 1978, 30; Stanley 1978, 74). That settlement was supposed to be an efficient source of labour and supplies for the Hudson's Bay Company's fur trading operation and was intended as well to bolster the company's claim to proprietorship of Rupert's Land. The Canadian-based North West Company attempted to destroy it by inciting the half-breeds in the area to regard it as a threat to their own land right. According to Dr. G.F.G. Stanley:

> At the door of the North-West Company must be laid the responsibility for rousing the racial consciousness of the Métis. The Nor'Westers carefully fostered the idea of half-breed territorial rights and informed the credulous Métis that the white settlers were interlopers who had come to steal the land from them (Stanley 1960, 11).

The North West Company's attempts to destroy the colony ultimately failed, and it merged with the Hudson's Bay Company. Métis nationalism, however, remained alive. Governor Simpson wrote in 1835: "The Brûlés are becoming clamorous about their rights and privileges as Natives of the soil and it required all our most skillful management to maintain the peace of the Colony during the Holidays while rum was in circulation" (A.S. Morton 1978, 31). An explanation that has been proposed for the use of the term "Bois Brûlés" to describe half-breeds is that the Ojibway Indians described them as "wissakodewinnii," meaning "half-burnt woodmen," because of their lighter complexions. "Bois brûlé" is an abridged French translation (Sealey 1978, 7).

In 1845, a group of Métis, describing themselves as "natives of this country, and half-breeds," submitted to the governor of Red River Settlement, Alexander Christie (a Hudson's Bay Company appointee), a series of 14 questions concerning the rights of half-breeds. The questions distinguished half-breeds from both Indians and other Europeans. Among the questions:

2. Has a native of this country (not an Indian) a right to hunt furs?

6. Can a half-breed receive any furs as a present from an Indian, a relative of his?

7. Can a half-breed hire any of his Indian relatives to hunt furs for him?

10. With regard to trading, or hunting furs, have the half-breeds, or natives of European origin, any rights or privileges over other Europeans? (Begg 1894-95, vol. 1, 261).

The reply was that as British subjects, the half-breeds had the same rights – no fewer, but no more – as residents of the country who had been born in the British Isles. Nonetheless the form of the questions indicates that the half-breeds had a strong sense of their distinct identify (Begg 1894-95, vol. 1, 263).

In 1849, the Hudson's Bay Company again faced a challenge from a distinctively Métis group. It had charged four half-breeds, including Pierre Guilleaum Sayer, with trading in violation of the company's monopoly. A large group of "Armed Half Breeds," to quote the trial transcript, surrounded the court-house; the leader of the group, James Sinclair, said they came as "Delegates of the people." Sayer was actually convicted by the jury. Sinclair argued, however, that Sayer's belief in the legality of his conduct justified the court in foregoing punishment. The prosecutor and the court agreed. The event was, in the end, interpreted by the Métis as a vindication of their right to trade notwithstanding the company's claim to a monopoly (Flanagan 1979, 4).

The distinction between Indians and half-breeds was reflected in the constitutional law of the Council of Assiniboia. First recall the reply by Governor Christie in 1845 that the half-breeds were British subjects like any others. Contrast it with the report of the Law Amendment Committee to the Council of Assiniboia in 1851:

> In addition to all the general restraints our local legislature lies under two special restrictions:
>
> *First.* The Indian tribes do not stand on the same footing as British subjects. Our local legislature, for instance, does not appear to be competent to regulate their right of cutting of hay for themselves. Mr.

> Governor Christie's proclamation as to the date of beginning to cut hay was understood not to extend to the members of Indian tribes (Oliver 1914, vol. 1, 371)

The 31 May 1849 Minutes of the Council of Assiniboia recalls the "unlawful assemblages of the people" in connection with the Guilleaum Sayer case and attributes the "excitement" to "a desire on the part of the Canadian and half-breed population to obtain, among other objectives, "the infusion into the Council of Assiniboia of a certain proportion of Canadian and half breed members" (Oliver 1914, vol. 1, 352. The council responded that it would bring the representation question to the attention of the Hudson's Bay Company. In 1857, three half breeds, Salomon Hamlin, Pascal Breland, and Francois Bruneau were appointed to the council.

To sum up, by 1857 the Métis had a distinct history of military, economic, legal, and political dealings with the Hudson's Bay Company. They had developed their identity in other ways including the institution of the buffalo hunt and their military victory over the Sioux at the Battle of Grand Coteau in 1851 (W.L. Morton 1978, 47). The distinctive cultures of the Métis and Indians were reflected in the different terminology used to describe them. There was, for many important purposes, a real need to distinguish between the two groups.

Chartier argues that exchange 1752, quoted above, "could be interpreted as saying that, as long as 'Indians,' which must include both the Indians and half-breeds, did not commit crimes upon the Whites the Hudson's Bay Company didn't interfere with their normal course of dealings" (Chartier 1978-1979, 46). The language of that exchange does permit that interpretation, but it far from compels it. Perhaps Governor Simpson was not thinking about the half breeds at all. Question 1749, which Chartier does not quote, expressly asks about "Indian Tribes," and that is whom Governor Simpson may have had in mind when asked just a little later about "Indians." Another possible interpretation of exchange 1752 is that the half-breeds were treated for legal purposes as whites. It has already been argued that that in fact was the case.

Several exchanges from the testimony of Reverend David Anderson, the Bishop of Rupert's Land, are cited by Chartier. The exchanges marked with an asterisk, he argues, show that half-breeds are referred to "as part of the aboriginal population" (Chartier 1978-79, 46):

4384. With regard to the half-caste population, will you have the kindness to tell the Committee your opinion in reference to that portion of the inhabitants of the Red River Settlement? My own impression is favourable; that we must look to the half-caste population as the strength of the settlement of the country. The number of those of pure blood, the Scotch population, is comparatively only small, so that dependence must be on the half-caste population in a great measure; and they are those more immediately connected with my own church.

4385. [Mr. Roebuck] Are you aware of any great settlement ever having been made by a half-caste population on the continent of America? - No, I have not.

4386. Are you at all aware of the fact the brown population dies out as the white population advances? Such is said to be the general statement; but still in our own case as regards the Indian Settlement parish, it is the other way, the population is increasing.

4387. How large is the population in that parish which you now speak of? - It is one of four churches on the Red River; the Indian Settlement parish has a population of 650.

4388. Indians or half-breeds? Indians.

4389. How many half-breeds are there? They come in the adjoining parish, higher up on the Red River

* 4390. How many half-breeds have you in your diocese? A very large number perhaps 1,500 or 2,000 on the Red River.

* 4391. So that taking them all together adding the 2,000 half-breeds to the 600 full-blooded Indians, you have 2,660 inhabitants with the Indian blood in them. - Yes.

There are a number of exchanges in Reverend Davidson's testimony in which half-breeds are included in a category with Indians. That does not show that they were considered to be Indians. On the contrary, throughout the testimony of Reverend Anderson there are many examples of the Indians being distinguished from the half-breeds; exchange 4388 is one of them. Another is:

> 4253. What are the number and character of the native agents? - I have two native ordained clergymen, that is to say native Indian clergymen and one who is a country-born clergyman, namely, born in the country, but not an Indian in the same sense as the other two.

Yet another is:

> 4423. Are there many who are clergymen of the Church of England? - Yes, there is the one whom I called a country-born clergyman, though not a native Indian clergyman.
>
> 4424. But has he Indian blood in his veins? He has.

On many occasions – exchange 4384, for example – distinct lines of inquiry are made about half-breed and Indian. Chartier notes one instance where the umbrella term used is "Indian":

> 4394. So that in fact, in all parts of the territory of America in which the white man has appeared, the brown man has disappeared? I am rather unwilling to believe it as regards one's own country because I think that more of effort [sic] is made for the Indians. I am sure that the Indian effort is more successful in our country than in the States or in Canada.
>
> 4395. You are speaking of the Indian effort applying to 2,600 persons? - To the much larger number of 8,000 Indians taking the whole territory.

It appears from exchange 4282 that Reverend Anderson's figure of 8,000 Indians refers to both Indians and half-breeds:

> 4282. Are you able to give the Committee any estimate of the total number of the members of the Church of England who you think are to be found in Rupert's Land: I mean among the Indian or half breed population? I think taking those acted upon by Christianity, they would be about 8,000.

Let's follow the testimony there because it actually includes another example, not cited by Charter, of the use of "Indian" as an umbrella term including the half-breeds:

> 4283. Do you mean including all denominations of Christians? - No even of our own Church.
>
> 4284. Taking all Christian sects into account, Roman-catholics and all, can you give the Committee any idea what, in your opinion, is the number of Christians altogether among the native population in Rupert's Land? - Perhaps about 6,000, added to the number which I have given.
>
> 4285. Do you mean of the native and half-breed population? Yes.
>
> 4286. Are you speaking of the Red River only, or of the whole of Rupert's Land? The whole of Rupert's Land. There are perhaps 8,000 of our own Church, and 6,000 besides, including Roman catholics and all others; that would make 14,000.
>
> 4287. Do you believe that there are only 14,000 persons of Indian origin in the whole of Rupert's Land who profess Christianity? - I do not think there are much more.
>
> 4288. Including the Red River Settlement? The number would not be much more; not more than 16,000, I think.
>
> 4289. I presume you mean to include in that answer the half-castes of the Red River, and in fact the whole of the Indian population, whether full blood or half-breed? I do.

The two related examples of the use of the term "Indian" to cover half breeds are exceptional. Usually other terms are used when both Indians and half-breeds are to be considered in an ensemble; in the passage just reproduced, "Indian or half-breed" (exchange 4282), "native" (exchange 4284), and "native and half-breed" (exchange 4285) all appear before "Indian population" is finally used. It is significant that these other terms not only outnumber "Indian population," but also precede it; the latter term is only used once it has been expressly established that it encompasses half-breeds. Reverend Anderson's initial exclusion of Roman Catholics from the flock of those "acted upon by Christianity" (exchange 4282) is an illustration that categorical terms can be employed in unusual ways.

From the testimony of Alexander Isbister, Chartier reproduces one instance in which "Indian" is applied to half-breeds; Isbister refers in exchange 2410 to his aim of improving the conditions of "the native and half-caste Indians in the Red River Settlement." Not reproduced is a latter reference to "extracts from a treaty between the United States government and the Indians and half-breeds occupying the upper part of the Red River valley" (exchange 2633). Nor are a number of questions and answers by various people in which the half-breeds are discussed as a distinct group. From the examination of John Ross, a member of the Parliament of Canada:

> 129. Mr. Gordon] Is it not practically found that a population consisting, as that of the Red River Settlement does, of a very great proportion of half-breeds and Indians is more difficult to govern than one consisting entirely of whites? I think so; all half-breeds are difficult to govern. I speak now particularly of the difficulty they created with the mining licenses.

Colonel John Crofton, who had been on duty at Red River was asked about his journey there: "3186. Were there many persons with you or were you a small party? A part of the way I proceeded with Indians in the canoe and two half-breeds." The discussion eventually turned to half-breed complaints about legal restrictions on trade. Some excerpts: "3232. Mr. Roebuck] When you were there, had you much communication with the half-breeds? A good deal." and "3246. Lord Stanley] You say the law forbids them to have any traffic with whom? With the Americans, or Indians in furs."

My respectful conclusion is that the testimony in the 1857 report generally supports, rather than contradicts, the usage of the census—that half-breeds are not comprehended by the term "Indian."

The appendices of the 1857 report contained the texts of a couple of Hudson's Bay regulations and resolutions. Chartier contends that they are significant in that "this material does not use the term half-breed" only the term "Indian," and that their correct interpretation is that the latter term applied to the former. The Regulation for Promoting Moral and Religious Improvement begins:

> Resolved, 1st. That for the moral and religious improvement of the servants, the more effectual civilization and the instruction of the families and Indians attached to the different establishments, the Sabbath be duly observed as a day of rest at all the Company's posts throughout the country, and Divine service be publicly read with becoming solemnity, at which all the servants and families resident be encouraged to attend, together any of the Indians who may be at hand, and whom it may be proper to invite.

As Chartier himself points out, many of the Hudson's Bay Company servants were half-breeds; thus many of them would have been covered by the reference to servants and families. It is possible, I would concede, that an independent half-breed in the vicinity of the post was supposed to be covered by the reference to "Indian." It is also possible that the drafters were less than exhaustive in their consideration of the possibilities. (Even if Chartier's suggestion is accepted, a non-native European or American happening at the post would be excluded from the literal scope of the regulation.) The drafters of an 1851 Hudson's Bay resolution on temperance, also cited by Chartier, seem to have been more meticulous: "Resolved, 42. . . . that from and after this date, no spirituous liquor be issued from the Moose depot either to the Company's officers or servants, to strangers or to Indians . . ."

Indians of Mixed Ancestry

The half-breeds referred to in the preceding analysis of the 1857 report are those who belonged to a group of people who developed a distinct culture, centered on the Red River Settlement area. Throughout this discussion, the term "Métis" will be reserved for that group of people and its successors. The conclusion just offered is that the 1857 report suggests that the Métis were not understood as included in the term "Indians." In a little while it will be argued that subsequent history supports the exclusion of the Métis from s.91(24). There were, however, many people, usually of mixed ancestry, who continued to closely associate with traditional Indian groups. Historical legal practice supports their inclusion within s.91(24). (Chartier's analysis does not observe the distinction just followed; many of its submissions–

some of which I respectfully concur in—actually apply to the latter category of people.)

An Act for the better protection of the Lands and Property of the Indians in Lower Canada, Statutes of Canada 1850, 13 and 14 Vict. C 42. provided in section 5:

> And for the purposes of determining any right of property, possession or occupation in or to any lands belonging or appropriated to any Tribe or Body of Indians in Lower Canada, Be it declared and enacted: That the following classes of persons are and shall be considered as Indians belonging to the Tribe or Body of Indians interested in such lands:
>
> *First*. All persons of Indian blood, reputed to belong to the particular Body or Tribe of Indians interested in such lands, and their descendants.
>
> *Secondly*. All persons intermarried with any such Indians and residing amongst them, and the descendants of all such persons.
>
> *Thirdly*. All persons residing among such Indians, whose parents on either side were or are Indians of such Body or Tribe, or entitled to be considered as such; And
>
> *Fourthly*. All persons adopted in infancy by any such Indians, and residing in the Village or upon the lands of such Tribe or Body of Indians, and their descendants.

An Act Respecting Civilization and Enfranchisement of Certain Indians, Consolidated Statutes of Canada 1859, 22 Vict. C.9, provides in section 1 that:

> In the following enactments, the term "Indian" means only Indians or persons of Indian blood or intermarried with Indians, acknowledged as members of Indian Tribes or Bands residing upon lands which have never been surrendered to the Crown . . .

An Act Respecting Indians and Indian Lands, Consolidated Statutes of Lower Canada 1860, 3 Vict. C.14 provided in s.11 that:

> For the purpose of determining what persons are entitled to hold, use or enjoy the lands and other immovable property belonging to or appropriated to the use of the various tribes or bodies of Indians in Lower Canada, the following persons and classes of persons, and one other, shall be considered as Indians belonging to the tribe or body of Indians interested in any such lands or immoveable property:
>
> *Firstly*. All persons of Indian blood, reputed to belong to the particular tribe or body of Indians interested in such lands or immoveable property, and their descendants;
>
> *Secondly*. All persons residing among such Indians, whose parents were or are, or either of them was or is, descended on either side from Indians, or an Indian reputed to belong to the particular tribe or body of Indians interested in such lands or immoveable property, and the descendants of all such persons; And
>
> *Thirdly*. All women lawfully married to any of the persons included in the several classes hereinbefore designated; the children or issue of such marriages, and their descendants.

For certain legislative purposes, then, persons of mixed or non-Indian ancestry who lived with a traditional Indian band were considered to be Indians. The term "Indian" was not, for legal purposes, strictly based on racial origin; it also depended on familial and cultural ties. The use of the word "Indian" in the *Constitution Act, 1867* should be understood in this context. The Parliament of 1868 certainly did; *An Act providing for the organization of the Department of the Secretary of State of Canada, and for the management of Indian and Ordinance Lands*, Statutes of Canada 1868, 31 Vict. C.42, (s.15) used essentially the same definition of "Indians" as the province of Canada had in its 1850 statute: that is, one which included persons of mixed ancestry living among an Indian group and women inter-married with one of its members.

Post-Confederation Practice

The conclusion from the preceding discussion is that under the ordinary and legal usages up to and including the time of Confederation, "Indian" did not include the Métis people. It might be countered, however that the framers of s.91(24) of the *Constitution Act, 1867* were not obliged to consider the Red River Métis, inasmuch as they were practically all living outside of the part of British North America that was about to be turned into a federation. Therefore, the argument would continue, subsequent history should be examined, and if practice and the underlying purposes of s.91(24) require, "Indian" should be given a broad construction so as to encompass the Métis. In reply, it will be shown that post-Confederation history in fact supports the exclusion of the Métis from s.91(24).

In 1868, the Hudson's Bay Company agreed to transfer Ruperts' Land to Canada. The inhabitants were not consulted. Louis Riel became a principal instigator and leader of the efforts by the people of the Red River area to determine and express their political demands in connection with the transfer. In early 1870, a Convention of Forty – half of them representing French-speaking Métis, half of them English-speaking Métis and white settlers – agreed on a List of Rights and approved the establishment of the Provisional Government. Riel was elected President, but (over his objections) the Convention chose to pursue territorial rather than provincial status. A few months later, the executive of the Provisional Government reversed that decision. The fourth and final List of Rights presented to the federal government requested provincial status. The final version of the list, like all previous versions, demanded that the local legislature have control over public lands. It did not say anything about Indian titles or half-breed land grants. When delegates of the Provisional Government negotiated the entry of Manitoba into Confederation, Sir John A. Macdonald insisted on federal control over Crown lands. I have not been able to discern whose inspiration it was to do so, but Prime Minister Macdonald did agree that, in addition to guarantees for existing individual land holdings, 1,400,000 acres of land go to the benefit of half-breeds. Section 31 of the *Manitoba Act 1870* reads

> And whereas, it is expedient towards the extinguishment of the Indian Title to the lands in the Province to appropriate a portion of such ungranted lands, to the extent of one million, four hundred thousand acres thereof, for the benefit of the families of the half-breed residents, it is hereby enacted, that, under regulations to be from time to time made by the Governor in Council, the Lieutenant-Governor shall select such lots or tracts in such parts of the Province as he may deem expedient, to the extent aforesaid, and

> then divide the same among the children of the half-breed heads of families residing in the Province at the time of the said transfer to Canada, and the same shall be granted to the said children respectively in such mode and on such conditions as to settlement and otherwise, as the Governor General in Council may from time to time determine.

The opening words of s.31, taken at face value, provide some support for the inclusion of the Métis within s.91(24). Having "Indian Title," however, is not necessarily the same thing as being an Indian. It is necessary to examine the purposes of assigning jurisdiction over "Indians" to the federal level of government. The same s.31 that refers to the "Indian title" of half-breeds also contemplates extinguishing it. That done, there would be no need for Parliament to retain jurisdiction over the Métis and Métis lands. By contrast, federal practice towards Indians in Manitoba was to reserve lands for the use of Indian collectivities, with both land and people subject to continuing federal regulation. If you believe that the Métis come under s.91(24) then you also have to believe that at the time Manitoba was admitted into Confederation, Parliament retained plenary legislative authority over 86 per cent of the population. I have found no evidence in the records of the internal deliberations or negotiating positions of the Provisional Government that the scope of s.91(24) was considered a threat to the local self-government it was struggling to establish (W.L. Morton 1965).

During the debates on the *Manitoba Act*, Mr. Wood expressed his concern about the care and guardianship of Indians and asked whether the Dominion government would retain in its own hands the power of dealing with Indians to whom annuities were owed. Prime Minister Macdonald answered that:

> . . . the reservation of 1,200,000 acres [sic] which it was proposed to place under the control of the Province, was not for the purpose of buying out the full blooded Indians and extinguishing their titles. There were very few such Indians remaining then in the Province, but such as there were they would be distinctly under the guardianship of the Dominion Government. The main representatives of the original tribes were their descendants, the half-breeds, and the best way of dealing with them was the same as United Empire loyalists had been dealt with, namely, giving small

> grants of land for them and their children (W.L. Morton 1965, 199).

Macdonald makes no mention of the Métis remaining under Dominion guardianship.

The legal accuracy of the opening words of s.31 should now be examined. Macdonald's answer compares their situation to that of the United Empire Loyalists, who had been given land grants in Canada after the War of Independence. (Macdonald also made his comparison in his speech introducing the legislation; W.L. Morton 1965, 168.) The United Empire Loyalists, of course, had no aboriginal claims. Sir Stafford Northcotte, observing the speech, called the reference to the United Empire Loyalists "very acceptable to the Ontario men." It seems that at that troubled time, Macdonald would characterize the grant in different ways depending on which political pressure group he wished to appeal to (W.L. Morton 1965, 99). His subsequent actions and conduct strongly suggest that he never took the "Indian Title" theory as an accurate statement of the legal state of affairs in 1870. In 1873, Parliament made a grant to the white Selkirk settlers very similar to that which had been made to the Métis. In 1885, Macdonald had this to say:

> In [the Manitoba Act] it is provided that in order to secure the extinguishment of the Indian title 1,400,000 acres of land should be settled upon the families of the half-breeds living within the limits of the then Province. Whether they had any right to those lands or not was not so much the question as it was a question of policy to make an arrangement with the inhabitants of that Province, in order in fact to make a Province at all. . . . That phrase [extinguishment of the Indian title] was an incorrect one, because the half-breeds did not allow themselves to be Indians (Flanagan 1983, 62).

The last sentence is supported by this excerpt from Alexander Mackenzie's speech to the House of Commons on the Manitoba Bill: "A certain portion [is] to be set aside to settle Indian claims and another portion to settle Indian claims that the half-breeds have. But these half-breeds were either Indians or not. They were not looked upon as Indians, some had been to Ottawa, and given evidence, and did not consider themselves Indians" (W.L. Morton 1965, 172).

Post-1870 legislative practice is consistent with the basic thesis offered here: that the Métis are not "Indians" for the purposes of s.91(24), but that persons of mixed or non-Indian ancestry who live among and as Indians are. It has already been mentioned that in 1868 Parliament adopted for the purposes of property ownership a definition of "Indian" that encompassed persons of part Indian descent who belonged to an Indian group and women who married Indians. The *Indian Act, 1876 (An Act to Amend and Consolidate the Laws Respecting Indians*, 1876, 39 Vict. c.18) defined "Indian," for the purposes of the act, as including men of Indian blood reputed to belong to a band, their wives, and children, and s.3(e) provided that: "No half-breed in Manitoba who has shared in the distribution of half-breed lands shall be accounted as Indian."

The Indian registration system of the 1951 *Indian Act* drew on previous definitions of Indian – which included persons of mixed or non-Indian ancestry – and excluded:

s.12(1)(a) a person who:

(i) has received or has been allotted half-breed lands or money scrip,
(ii) is a descendant of a person described in sub-paragraph (i).

The system used in Manitoba – granting individual land entitlements to half-breeds and reserves to Indian collectivities – was applied elsewhere. In 1879 the *Dominion Lands Act An Act to Amend and Consolidate the Several Acts Respecting the Public Lands of the Dominion*, 1879, 42 Vict. C.31 made provision for grants to half-breeds in the North-West Territories. Sometimes individuals were given the choice of whether to "take treaty" as Indians or scrip as half-breeds. The distinction between the Métis and persons of mixed ancestry who are Indians has never been precise. How a person is classified depends on the purpose of the classification; among the criteria used may be genealogy, cultural affiliation, political ties – and self-identification. That some people were allowed to determine whether they would be "Indians" or "half-breeds" for legal purposes does not undermine the basic distinction between the two groups for the purposes of s.91(24). There are ample grounds in history and legal practice to uphold its general validity.

The implications of the *Métis Betterment Act* enacted by the provincial legislature of Alberta in 1940 have been explored in a previous chapter. To recall the conclusion of that discussion, it is difficult to reconcile the existence of the act with federal jurisdiction over the Métis under s.91(24); judicial recognition of the latter would produce radical uncertainty about, and possibly serious harm to, the interests of settlement residents.

During the March 8 afternoon discussion at the '84 First Ministers' Conference, Mr. Chartier submitted that:

> The Supreme Court of Canada rendered a decision stating that the Eskimo people were in fact covered by the term [Indian] in a wide sense . . . They also stated in that case that the term "Indian" was meant to include all of the aboriginals within confederation and those aboriginees to enter into confederation. I would say that aboriginees and aboriginal people are the same people so that is the legal advice we have been given and that is the advice that has been put forward or taken by the native people or the Métis people over the past ten, fifteen, twenty years ('84 FMC transcript, 186-187).

The judgment of Cannon J. appears to be the one to which Mr. Chartier was alluding. The question the Court was asked was whether Eskimos were "Indians"; all of Cannon J.'s analysis is based on establishing that they were. He does not consider whether the Métis were "Indians." There is no evidence that his use of the umbrella term "aborigines" was intended to cover the Métis as well. There is some evidence to the contrary. He notes that the precursor of s.91(24) is the Quebec Resolutions of 1864 assigned to the federal government jurisdiction over "Indians and Lands Reserved for the Indians" (*Re Eskimo*, [1939] S.C.R. 104, 118). An official French translation was "Les *Sauvages* et les terres reservees pour les Sauvages." Cannon J. concludes that:

> The Upper and Lower Houses of Upper and Lower Canada petitioners to the Queen, understood that the English word "Indians" was equivalent to or equated with the French word "Sauvages" and included all the present and future aborigines native subjects of the proposed Confederation of British North America, which at the time was intended to include Newfoundland ([1939] S.C.R. 104, 118).

The use of "sauvages" to describe Indians was grossly unfair and insulting, especially if the term was understood as equivalent to the English term "savage" rather than "uncivilized", but attributable to the cultural differences between the Indians and Eskimos in traditional groups and the Europeans. It is difficult to imagine the epithet being applied to the half-breeds of the Red River area. They were Christian, partly European in ancestry, and spoke English or French, or both, often in addition to a native language. Many of them were no less literate or educated than the Europeans in Western Canada. Many of them worked as full time employees for the Hudson's Bay Company. They were governed by the same law as the Europeans; some of them served as magistrates, others as members of the Council of Assiniboia.

Late 19th and early 20th century definitions of "Indian" are examined in the judgment of Cannon J. He points out that many, albeit not all of them, include Eskimos. None of them mentions half-breeds or Métis. The characterization of Métis as aboriginal people is etymologically dubious. The Métis are certainly indigenous to North America – they came into being as a distinct people on this continent. But they are not aboriginal in the same sense as the Indian and Inuit; they were not here from the beginning, but instead they developed when a large number of Europeans came to Western Canada in connection with the fur trade.

Section 35(2) of the *Constitution Act, 1982* says that "the aboriginal peoples" referred to in the *Constitution Act, 1982* include "the Indian, Inuit, and Métis people of Canada." On its own, the section confers no rights on the Métis. It may turn out that the Métis have very few entitlements under the other sections of the Act which do speak to the rights of aboriginal peoples. Section 35(1) recognizes and affirms "the aboriginal and treaty rights" of the aboriginal peoples of Canada. It may be that on April 17, 1982, the Métis had no aboriginal or treaty rights. In any event, the survival of the constitutionally protected Métis rights does not require parliamentary, as opposed to judicial, authority. An expansive interpretation of s.91(24) is not justified by a necessity for Parliament to protect the newly assured rights of the Métis from local interference. The courts can do that. Nor is it legitimate to combine the judgment of Cannon J. "Indians are all aborigines" – with s.35(2) – "Métis are aboriginal peoples" – in order to conclude that Métis are s.91(24) Indians. As shown earlier, there is no evidence that Cannon J.'s definition of "aborigines" extended to the Métis, and some evidence that it did not.

Chapter XVIII

Entrenchment of Jurisdiction of Aboriginal Governments in the Constitution of Canada; the 1984 Federal Proposal

One way of constitutionally establishing aboriginal self-governments would be to specify their powers and immunities in a legally enforceable amendment to the Constitution of Canada. During the working group sessions, this approach received some attention and was often referred to as the "section 93" approach—after the section of the *Constitution Act, 1867* which defines the scope of, and constraints on, provincial powers over education. Some provincial delegations expressed the concern that the "section 93" approach would result in the creation of a third type of sovereign government in Canada, a state of affairs they considered unacceptable. The s.93 format, however, does not necessarily establish aboriginal governments as equal in authority to provinces. The section listing the powers of aboriginal governments might also include serious limitations. It might be provided that the federal government could disallow the legislation of aboriginal governments and that provincial legislatures and Parliament could continue to legislate in areas assigned to aboriginal governments, with conflicts being resolved, in some cases, in favour of the former types of government. The *formal*, s.93 approach of listing the powers of aboriginal governments does not necessarily produce the *substantive* result that they are equal in authority to provinces.

It is on the *formal* grounds alone, in fact, that the s.93 approach in its simple form, must be rejected as unworkable. A list of powers appropriate for Métis governments might be inapt for the Inuit or the Indians. Arrangements with respect to one

Indian collectivity, moreover, might be totally inappropriate with respect to another. There are more than 570 bands in Canada; even if they were amalgamated into larger units based on common language and culture, the remaining collectivities would have different economic, constitutional, and political histories and preferences. Furthermore, ethnic governments may not be desired by, or desirable for, many aboriginal groups; the Inuit have expressed a preference for public governments (regional, territorial, and, eventually in the Northwest Territories, provincial government) in areas defined to leave them as a majority of the population. A similar approach may be appropriate, in some cases, for the Métis. No definition of the nature and powers of aboriginal self-governments could possibly apply across the board.

The s.93 approach is open to objection on another ground, that of permanence. It may be premature to entrench the scope of authority that aboriginal governments should exercise, better to experiment for a while. It is impossible to foresee all the problems – or all the benefits – that would arise when aboriginal communities are permitted to exercise a large measure of self-government. Canadians in the future should have the ability to act on the wisdom they gain through experience. Look back to 1951 when Parliament granted Indian self-governments a minimal amount of legislative authority. At the time that must have seemed to a lot of people like a pretty good idea. Hardly anybody today thinks it is. Fortunately, s.81 of the *Indian Act* is not ensconced in the Constitution and can be replaced by the ordinary process of legislation. A quarter of a century from now, Canadians may look back on a lot of our ideas about aboriginal self-government as naive, unenlightened, or just plain stupid. If we are not cautious, they may be faced with extremely cumbersome obstacles to correcting our mistakes.

The diversity objection to the s.93 approach – that is, that one cloak of authority cannot properly fit all aboriginal groups – might be met by recharacterizing the list of powers as those which an aboriginal community can exercise if it wishes to do so. A group that perceived itself as unable or unwilling to assume the full ambit of powers could refrain from doing so. On the other hand, a group perceived by federal and provincial governments as incapable of exercising the maximum range of powers might choose to do so anyway. Provincial and federal governments looking at this "other hand" are likely to shake their heads at the whole arrangement. The next step in the recharacterization of the s.93 approach, then, would be to portray the list of powers as those an aboriginal group may exercise if it wishes *provided* federal and provincial governments consent. The consent would be irrevocable according to its terms. The legal mechanism just stated would not be much different from using the treaty making process to establish self-government. The list of powers would be no more than a compendium of things to be bargained about. As such, however, it might not be worth compiling. From the point of view of aboriginal peoples, the list of powers omitted from the list would be just as significant as those included. A court might well conclude that the former could not be exercised by aboriginal governments, regardless of whether other governments consented. Thus the compilation of the list would be viewed by aboriginal organizations as having serious negative implications. At the same time, it would not guarantee aboriginal governments any power—only create possibilities. The countervailing advantage of a list would be that it would prevent future federal and provincial governments from consenting to the devolution of powers that they ought always to reserve for themselves. The list would also simplify future bilateral negotiations by making certain demands legally out of bounds.

Legally Unenforceable Statement of Principles

The federal government's 1984 proposal on self-government was a brilliant public relations stroke. It was utterly vacuous; it contained no ideas on what self-government would look like in practice, no commitment to adequately fund them, no clarification of the federal-provincial division of powers and responsibilities in dealing with them. It was designed to be legally unenforceable. It might have prejudiced constitutional gains that aboriginal peoples had already made. It would almost certainly have impeded their progress towards substantive constitutional assurances on self-government. Yet the impression created for the public was that the federal government had unveiled a bold new picture of aboriginal self-government; that aboriginal peoples, while dubious about some of the detail work, were, on the whole, pleased with what they saw; and that it was the provinces, the philistine, reactionary provinces, who prevented it from finding a permanent place in the constitutional gallery. A sample of the newspaper stories: Jeff Sallot in the *Globe and Mail*, page 1, 10 March 1984, headline: "Natives fail to win a new political deal." Paragraphs two and three:

> Native leaders angrily denounced some provincial premiers as obstructionists with "red neck"

> views, warned that there would be growing militancy among their people, and urged the federal government to unilaterally recognize self-government rights in the Constitution. Federal officials said this was legally impossible.
>
> Instead, Prime Minister Pierre Trudeau, presiding at his last constitutional conference, tried to salvage what he could by telling native leaders to "continue to fight."

Patricia Poirer, *Le Droit*, page 1, 9 March 1984, headline: "Trudeau propose, les provinces s'oppossent." Opening paragraph: "La plupart des provinces ont accueilli froidement hier la proposition du premier ministre Pierre Trudeau d'enchasser dans la constitution le droit des autochones a des gouvernements autonomes."

Dan Smith, the *Toronto Star*, 9 March 1984, headline on page 1: "Natives must govern selves to end 'injustice' PM says." headline on inside continuation of the article: "Provinces quash bid for rights deal." Opening paragraph: "Prime Minister Pierre Trudeau has opened a constitutional conference with a bold plea for native self-government, but negotiators worked into the night to save even a symbolic gesture for native rights."

Mr. Sallot's story does go on to quote the Prime Minister to the effect that the new section would be nonjusticiable; Ms. Poirer reports that native leaders objected to the unenforceability of the section; and Mr. Smith cites the nonjusticiability of the proposal immediately *before* referring to provincial objections. There was enough information in the stories for an especially informed and careful reader to discern that the federal proposal was severely limited in effect. The impression left with the general public by the stories just cited, however, would be that the provinces blocked a bold proposal by the federal government to constitutionally promote aboriginal self-government.

Public Relations

Part of the success of the federal proposal is attributable to the timing of its disclosure. At each preparatory meeting leading up to the March '84 First Ministers' Conference, both provincial and aboriginal delegations became increasingly insistent that the federal government reveal what its proposal would be. The first preparatory meeting had been held in September; five more followed; yet the federal proposal was not released until the opening morning of the conference. The result was that there was little opportunity for its weaknesses to be understood by delegations and the media and explained in turn to the public. Another was that there was no adequate opportunity for the proposal to be improved through negotiations. Mr. Jim Sinclair of the Métis National Council (MNC) said at the end of the second day:

> I would suggest that before we come back next year that any constitutional amendments or any constitutional changes that will be brought to this table will not be brought to this table the day of the conference, but will be brought to this table at least three months before the conference so people have a chance to go over it and discuss it and then entrench it in the constitution if we feel it is necessary (1984 First Ministers' Conference [FMC] transcript, 368).

Premier Lougheed of Alberta picked up on the suggestion:

> Perhaps three months is impractical, but I really think that as we move towards another conference the ministers could agree on a cut-off date and make exceptions to that . . . there should be a real effort made to have a cut-off date in terms of something that is considered to be constitutional amendments (1984 FMC transcript, 370).

Prime Minister Trudeau made a number of attempts to deflect the implied criticism of the lateness of his government's proposal. He pointed out that if the three month rule had been in force, the federal response could not have taken into account the *Penner Report* (1984 FMC transcript, 368). To be sure, the need to study, discuss, and prepare a response to the *Penner Report* was a time-consuming process for the federal government and a legitimate reason for their delaying the preparation of a constitutional proposal. Nonetheless, the *Penner Report* was tabled in November 1983; the federal government had plenty of time to prepare its constitutional position in conjunction with its response. The formal response to the *Penner Report*, incidentally, was released on March 5 – a full three days before the conference was scheduled to begin. The federal government had its constitutional proposal ready in sufficient time to have it printed in large quantities. It might have at least distributed copies under embargo to provincial and aboriginal delegations a couple of days before the conference. (The embargo would have been to maintain in the public eye the dramatic effect of the opening statement.)

Mr. Trudeau also suggested that the federal government could not "force the pace" of the ongoing series of preparatory meetings, and that "we all hoped they would have moved faster and in different directions" (1984 FMC transcript, 369). The excuse is not convincing. The federal government was under no obligation to wait until the last proposal had been tabled before it submitted its own; it was not the chief constitutional reform judge, bound to entertain submissions before delivering its authoritative opinion. Progress in the preparatory meetings might have been quicker and far more satisfactory had the federal government contributed its own ideas.

The final defence of Mr. Trudeau was "let us not think that support for constitutional change is not forthcoming because somehow delegations only saw our final text yesterday morning" (1984 FMC transcript, 371). Some of the premiers had said that they would be debasing the Constitution by trying to amend it every year. The Prime Minister concluded:

> ... if it is just a matter of saying we don't have time to go out of here at 5:00 with a constitutional accord, but if we give you another 15 days we can get it, we will give you 15 days or three weeks or whatever is needed. I just want to make that clear because I am afraid there is going to be some attempt to say it would have all worked out better if all of us had brought in our texts several weeks ago (1984 FMC transcript, 372).

Presumably constitutional conferences are held because things do "work better" if the parties can discuss ideas and examine and revise texts together. With 17 delegations involved, the process of consultation and negotiation is impracticable without having joint discussions. At First Ministers' Conferences, the public attention encourages participants to work towards progress or at least commit themselves to a position. It is true that the premiers would not have agreed to the federal proposal on self-government even if they had had time to study it in advance. In a few cases, that would have been because of dislike for any aboriginal self-government. Other provinces, however, would have objected in good faith on the same basis that they expressed at the March 8 conference—that they are not yet sure what "self-government" means, and the federal proposal does nothing to enlighten them. Some provinces and aboriginal organizations, having seen the inadequacies of the federal proposal, might have tried to prepare a more acceptable one. At the very least, the participants would have been far more able to communicate to the public their understanding of, and objections to, the federal proposal.

Minor changes in the wording of a constitutional text can have drastically different legal implications. The federal proposal on self-government contained almost 200 words in each of the equally authoritative French and English versions. Granted, the proposal would probably have been unenforceable in the courts; still, it would have the moral force of a binding legal obligation on federal and provincial governments. Even if the federal proposal had been acceptable to him in principle, a provincial premier still would have been justified in declining to agree at the March '84 conference to recommend the adoption of its specific wording to his legislature. Words that will form part of the supreme law of Canada warrant sober and thorough examination.

The Substance of the Proposal

This discussion has not yet included a detailed examination of the words of the federal proposal, and it is time that it did so. First of all, the opening words should be considered: "35.2 Without altering the legislative authority of Parliament or of the provincial legislatures, or the rights of any of them with respect to the exercise of their legislative authority; (a) Parliament and the legislatures, together with the government of Canada and the provincial governments, are committed to . . ." They include the complete formula for nonjusticiability that is used in s.36(1) of the *Constitution Act, 1982* and part ("Parliament and the legislatures . . . are committed to") of the nonjusticiability formula of s.36(2). (See Chapter XVIII.) That unenforceability in the courts was the intention of the federal government could not have been made more explicit by the minister of justice, Mr. MacGuigan, in his intervention during the March 8 afternoon discussion. He said:

> The proposals that I was finding fault with in the earlier preparatory sessions had to do with large-scale changes which could have been judicially interpreted and the results would have been unknown and, therefore, we really would have been evading our responsibility by passing it over to the courts, but what we are proposing with our constitutional amendment here is something which I believe ingeniously gets around the problems that we had with earlier

> suggestions for constitutional amendments. What we do here as the Prime Minister has said is to constitutionalize the principle. We would entrench because we would put something in the constitution that could only be amended . . . by the minimum number of the federal government and the seven provinces, but what we would put in the constitution would not be judiciable. It would not be enforceable in a court against the governments and it would be the same kind of commitment that actually we made last year with respect to some of what we [the federal government] agreed to at that time, and perhaps an even better parallel is Part III of the Act of 1982, the equalization and regional disparity section of our constitution in which we made a political commitment, all us governments, to promote equal opportunities and a commitment respecting public services.
>
> In fact, Prime Minister, the introductory words of our present amendment are drawn exactly from the introduction to section 36(1) and the kind of recital is in exactly the same kind of form as in Section 36(1) . . . .
>
> I suppose that there may be those who would argue what use is it if it can't be enforced in the courts.
>
> Well, its use is a symbolic one. Its use is a commitment. It is a solemn political commitment on the part of the people . . . .
>
> So, therefore, I hope it will be appreciated in our overnight reflections that it is not going to be an albatross around the necks of the government, but on the other hand, it is a symbol of hope for the native peoples, and, therefore, we think we have suggested something that is acceptable to the governments within the parameters that we have heard them set out here today and previously and that it is also as the native peoples have suggested, something that is important from their point of view (1984 FMC transcript, 216).

The nonjusticiability of the self-government proposal was reinforced by the two subparagraphs on self-government. Subparagraph (b) proclaims: "The aboriginal peoples of Canada have the right to self-governing institutions that will meet the needs of their communities . . ." Forget the fact that the whole amendment is not enforceable in the courts. Overlook the clumsy drafting; the English version should say "institutions of self-government," not "self-governing institutions"—it doesn't do aboriginal peoples much good to have institutions which are free from outside interference but which have no authority over their communities. Disregard the difference in the French and English versions; the former speaks simply of "governmental institutions"—a better choice of words since it would encompass public governments rather than exclusively ethnic ones. Most importantly, stop reading at the word "communities." Do all of that, and you have a brave declaration. Now read on: ". . . subject to the nature, jurisdiction and powers of those institutions, and to the financing arrangements relating thereto, being identified and defined through negotiation with the government of Canada and the provincial governments." Not much of a "right" after all; its content is to be determined entirely by negotiations. Are the provinces and federal government bound to agree to anything? The next subparagraph makes it clear that they are not; their only duty is to participate in the negotiations and, if anything comes of them, implement the results through ordinary legislation. For all its grievous inadequacies, the federal proposal would have provided some encouragement to governments to seriously study, negotiate, and eventually implement aboriginal self-government. Mr. MacGuigan suggested a *Rime of the Ancient Mariner* metaphor for a justiciable amendment—an albatross around the necks of provincial governments; to use another maritime metaphor, the judicially unenforceable federal proposal might have been a light but persistent wind, slowly moving their ships of substate in the right direction.

In some respects, however, the federal proposal would have amounted to wind from the wrong direction. It would have threatened legal advances that aboriginal peoples had arguably already made. To begin with, the proposal would have made the aboriginal right to self-government entirely subject to the agreement of federal and provincial governments. The position of the Assembly of First Nations (AFN) has consistently been that the right to self-government is already an entrenched, judicially enforceable constitutional right—as one of the "aboriginal rights" that was "recognized and affirmed" by the *Constitution Act, 1982*. Perhaps, however, the position of the AFN had so little chance of vindication in the courts that it would have been wisely traded for the concrete (if nonjusticiable) recognition of self-government in the federal proposal.

There was another potentially retrogressive aspect of the federal proposal. It is arguable that without the proposed federal amendment, bilateral agreements on self-government would be "treaties" for the purposes of s.35(1) of the *Constitution Act, 1982*. As such, they would be "recognized and affirmed" in the Constitution – and so probably immune to some extent from subsection violation by governments and legislatures. The argument will be explored in more detail in Chapter XXI. In the meantime, it should be observed that the possibility is seriously threatened by the federal proposal. The agreements on self-government the federal proposal contemplates are to be implemented by ordinary legislation. There is no indication that this legislation would not be subject to modification or repeals by subsequent legislation. That is the ordinary state of affairs; subsequent statutes take priority over prior ones. If a government construed the federal proposal as allowing agreements to be breached by subsequent legislation, there might not be much that the innocent party to the agreement could do about it. The opening words of the federal proposal were intended by its authors to make the whole section nonjusticiable. A wronged aboriginal party might hope for an advisory opinion from a court in its favour. But faced with the nonjusticiability language of the federal proposal, a court might consider it improper to render even a non-binding interpretation of it. The court might not, however, even be given the opportunity to decline to provide an opinion. The power to ask for advisory opinions has been confined by legislation to governments; and it would be difficult for an aboriginal group to persuade a government to ask for an advisory opinion which might benefit the former to the embarrassment of the latter.

Another risk of the federal proposal was that after it pushed the constitutional development a certain distance, it would leave the voyagers becalmed. Attempts by aboriginal peoples to obtain a legally enforceable guarantee of self-government could be rejected by some governments on the basis that the matter had already been dealt with and that the Constitution should not be trivialized by overfrequent amendment.

The response to the federal proposal at the opening session of the First Ministers' Conference was subdued. An examination of the transcript does not disclose much direct criticism of it, either by aboriginal groups or by the premiers. Part of the explanation is procedural. Most of the first day was spent in delivering prepared opening statements. No participant had much of an opportunity, before delivering his own opener, to study and prepare a reply to the federal proposal. Some of the aboriginal groups have to negotiate a consensus among their internal factions on what position they will take and cannot rapidly declare their evaluation of a complicated proposal that speaks to their most fundamental concerns. Nonetheless, it was the aboriginal organizations who spoke immediately after the prime minister. The premiers had a little more time to prepare and, in some cases, a little more freedom of independent action than aboriginal leaders. Still, their objections to the federal proposal were mostly implied, deducible only from the general statements in their opening remarks. Premier Buchanan spoke of the lack of a "clear and agreed definition" of self-government and proposed a political accord whereby the parties to the s.37 process would work towards, among other things, increased authority and commensurate responsibility for aboriginal peoples with respect to their own affairs (1984 FMC transcript, 92). According to Premier Bennett "there was a good deal more preparatory work to be done in respect of most of the issues on the agenda before a decision can be made" to add provisions to the Constitution (1984 FMC transcript, 106).

About the only attempt at textual analysis by any premier was that of Premier Hatfield – who "on the whole" supported the federal amendment but took issue with some of its "caution words" (1984 FMC transcript, 96).

There were a couple of hours left for open discussion on March 8, after the conclusion of opening statements, but much of the time was spent on the inclusion of the Métis in s.91(24). Before the discussion moved to that subject, however, Dr. David Ahenakew of the AFN had a chance to respond to the substance of the federal proposal on self-government. He praised it as being "couched in terms that are more firm, more clear than we have ever heard before" (1984 FMC transcript, 150). He suggested, however, some improvements. Among them: the door should be left open for the recognition of a "distinct order of First Nations governments;" "it is necessary to talk about rights, not just needs;" there would have to be some talk about fiscal responsibility; and a stronger statement was necessary on "federal responsibility for implementation of treaties" (1984 FMC transcript, 152). At the end of the day, the discussion returned briefly to self-government. Mr. George Erasmus expressed a similar view to that of Dr. Ahenakew; Mr. Zebedee Nungak of the Inuit Committee on National Issues (ICNI) said that he was "heartened and uplifted by some of the things that have been said today, not only by the federal government, but by other governments." He suggested a working session that evening to distill from the various positions taken that day "some of the more agreeable aspects" (1984 FMC transcript, 218). The approach of two of the aboriginal organizations, then, was to welcome the federal proposal and express their reservations about it as constructive suggestions for improvement. It was wise diplomacy. They were able to make it look like the provinces, rather than the aboriginal groups, were the obstructionists. They avoided creating the impression that aboriginal organizations are unlikely to be satisfied with anything but the most extreme proposals. One side-effect of the tactic, however, was that the federal government's proposal looked much more acceptable to aboriginal organizations than it actually was.

Mr. Trudeau did not propose a ministerial level working group meeting that evening to work on draft amendments or a political accord. He did not detect "any wild enthusiasm" for doing so (1984 FMC transcript, 219). At the urging of several delegations, however, one was scheduled. In the course of that meeting, provincial delegations clearly demonstrated the ambiguity and ineffectuality of the federal proposal. The most thorough and forceful presentation was by the Nova Scotia delegation; that province had been instrumental in securing agreement to the political accord that had emerged the previous year and has always expressed a genuine interest in making constitutional progress. The closed door discussion did nothing to illuminate understanding of the issues among the general public. The next morning Mr. MacGuigan summarized the results of the working group meeting—only three provinces, Ontario, New Brunswick, and Manitoba, were in favour of the federal proposal. There was no summary of the reasons why the other provinces objected. Because of the preponderantly negative response of the provinces, there would be no detailed discussion of the federal proposal in the remainder of the conference. A lesson for the impresario in charge of an act of limited talent: insist on good production values, hope the audience likes the opening, and, if possible, pull it off the stage before the critics arrive.

Chapter XIX

Unilateral Federal Action to Amend the Constitution of Canada

On the morning of March 9, after Justice Minister MacGuigan's report that only three provinces favoured the federal proposal on self-government, Mr. Harold Cardinal of the Assembly of First Nations (AFN) made the following proposal:

> We have taken the position consistently throughout the year, Mr. Prime Minister, that we value the special relationship that we have with the federal government, that we have with the Crown, that we have as a result of the constitutional recognition of our rights both treaty and aboriginal. We feel that the time has come for us to exercise what we perceived to be our special position in the constitution which is simply one that would allow the federal government to move with our concurrence, with our agreement, to introduce a resolution before the House with the intent of amending the constitution in line with its jurisdiction, in line with its responsibilities and in line with the agreements that we have by treaty and through other relationships, with or without the concurrence of the provincial governments (1984 First Ministers' Conference [FMC] transcript, 231).

Later in the day, Mr. Edmund Morris, of Nova Scotia, expressed the belief of his government that the federal government cannot unilaterally amend the Constitution of Canada – except under s.44 of the *Constitution Act, 1982* "in respect of those matters that deal exclusively with its own house" (1984 FMC transcript, 274).

What does "its own house" mean? The federal Parliament has exclusive jurisdiction over Indians and Inuit under s.91(24) of the *Constitution Act, 1867*; could it use s.44 to amend the Constitution of Canada so as to establish Indian self-government for these peoples?

Section 44 of the *Constitution Act, 1982,* says, "Subject to sections 41 and 42, Parliament may exclusively make laws amending the Constitution of Canada in relation to the executive government of Canada or the Senate and House of Commons."

Section 52 of the *Constitution Act, 1982* provides a nonexhaustive definition of the Constitution of Canada. Included in the latter, according to s.52, is the long list of acts referred to in the schedule of the *Constitution Act, 1982* – among them, the *Constitution Act, 1867.* Why then, couldn't Parliament amend s.91(24) of the *Constitution Act, 1867* to read, say: Indians and the Lands Reserved for Indians; Parliament may, however, recognize the constitution of an Indian government; such constitutions shall be included in a schedule to this section.

The result would be that the constitution of an Indian Nation government would become explicit parts of the Constitution of Canada, hence, part of the supreme law of Canada (s.52 of the *Constitution Act, 1982*). No law inconsistent with these constitutions – including those enacted by Parliament itself – would be valid. Parliament could unilaterally amend its amendment to s.91(24) at any time, but until it did, the constitution of an Indian government would be solemnly recognized in the Constitution of Canada and be immune from ordinary political interference. Because of Parliament's paramount authority over Indians under s.91(24), the amendment to the federal Constitution would preclude any provincial legislation inconsistent with it. The mechanism would not be as effective as an amendment to s.35 of the *Constitution Act, 1982,* in that the latter could not be repealed by Parliament alone; seven provinces would have to go along. Still, it would give solemn, legal acknowledgement to the constitutions of Indian governments and require Parliament to take the extra formal step of amending the *Constitution Act, 1867* (as amended) before it could violate them.

It might be argued that the foregoing mechanism is of less utility than has just been portrayed; as long as Parliament expressly indicated its intention to amend the Constitution,

Parliament could override the amended s.91(24); that is, Parliament would not have to go to the trouble of changing the text. It can even be argued that Parliament would not have to bother signalling any "constitutional" intent; any legislation inconsistent with the amended s.91(24) would implicitly be a constitutional amendment. I will not explore these possibilities any further because there is a more basic objection to the unilateral federal amendment option. It is that Section 44 does not permit amendments to s.91(24) of the *Constitution Act, 1867*. It permits amendments to the way the House of Commons and Senate are organized but not to how they discharge their powers. Thus the sort of amendment to s.91(24) tossed off earlier in this discussion is not constitutionally possible.

First and foremost, let's look at the legal history of s.44. Its predecessor was ensconced in the Constitution of Canada by the *British North America (no. 2) Act, 1949* and unensconced by the *Constitution Act, 1982*. It was section 91(1) of the *British North America Act* (now called the *Constitution Act, 1867*) and gave the Queen-in-Parliament authority over:

> 1. The amendment from time to time of the Constitution of Canada, except as regards matters coming within the classes of subjects by this Act assigned exclusively to the Legislatures of the provinces, or as regards rights or privileges by this or any other Constitutional Act granted or secured to the Legislature or the Government of a province, or to any class of persons with respect to schools or as regards the use of the English or the French language or as regards the requirements that there shall be a session of the Parliament of Canada at least once each year, and that no House of Commons shall continue for more than five years from the day of the return of the Writs for choosing the House: provided, however, that a House of Commons may in time of real or apprehended war, invasion or insurrection be continued by the Parliament of Canada if such constitution is not opposed by the votes of more than one-third of the members of such House.

Section 91(1) was ambiguous in at least one important respect – whether "Canada" referred to the whole state, or merely the federal level of government. The *Upper House Reference (Reference Re Legislative Authority of Parliament to Alter or Replace the Senate* (1980), 102 D.L.R. (3d) 1), the last decided case on s.91(1), took the latter interpretation—and limited the application of the section even further. At issue was Parliament's authority to alter, or abolish outright, the method of appointing Senators. The Supreme Court of Canada observed that the amendments to the *British North America Act* passed under s.91(1) had all been of the "housekeeping" variety—on matters such as retirement age of Senators, the number of seats in the House of Commons, and the number of constituencies in the Northwest Territories. The Court concluded that:

> In our opinion, the power given to the federal Parliament by s.91(1) was not intended to enable it to alter in any way the provisions of ss.91 and 92 governing the exercise of legislative authority by the Parliament of Canada and the Legislatures of the Provinces. Section 91(1) is a particularization of the general legislative power of the Parliament of Canada. That power can be exercised only by the Queen, by and with the advice and consent of the Senate and House of Commons. Section 91(1) cannot be construed to confer power to supplant the whole of the rest of the section. It cannot be construed as permitting the transfer of the legislative powers enumerated in s.91 to some body or bodies other than those specifically designated in it ((1980), 102 D.L.R. (3d) 1, 13).

The first sentence may say more than was necessary to settle the question posed to the Court (in legal jargon, *obiter dictum*); therefore it is of limited authority. It was, nonetheless, the last case decided on s.91(1) before s.44 was framed, and it may be supposed that the drafters of the latter took it into account. The opinion of the Supreme Court, speaking as a collectivity, was that, despite the broad language of s.91(1), the section did not permit amendments to the other provisions of sections 91 and 92. The phrasing of s.44 is even narrower. The reference is to the executive government of Canada and the House of Commons and Senate. The phraseology is inconsistent with an intent to escape the limitations of the first sentence in the Supreme Court of Canada passage. It is consistent, however, with the only use to which s.91(1) had ever been put—to alter the internal organization of the institutions of the federal government.

You might try to support the historical argument with close textual analysis of the English version of s.44. Notice that it permits amendments to the "executive government of Canada *or* the Senate and House of Commons." Legislative power at the federal level, however, is vested by s.91 in the "Queen, by and with the Advice and Consent of the Senate and House of Commons"—that is, in the head of the executive government of Canada *and* the Senate and House of Commons. The contention, then, would be that s.44 contemplates alterations to either the executive branch or deliberative branch of the federal government but not to the manner of their joint operation. The "or" cannot really mean "and/or," the contention would continue, because the framers could not have intended "or" to mean the same thing as "and," and the "and" between "Senate" and "House of Commons" *does* mean "and/or." We know this because many provisions of the Constitution of Canada apply only to one deliberative chamber, and it must have been intended that Parliament could unilaterally change these. The predecessor of s.44—s.91(1)—was always used with respect to either the House of Commons or Senate, never both simultaneously. In my opinion, the foregoing line of reasoning establishes nothing. It is the sort of argument lawyers and judges use to justify conclusions they have reached on other grounds. It is entirely possible that the framers of s.44 never thought very hard about their chosen conjunctions. That they did not is strongly suggested by the equally authoritative French version of the section. It says, "Sous réserve des articles 41 et 42, le Parlement a compétence exclusive pour modifier les dispositions de la Constitution du Canada relatives au pouvoir executif fédéral, au Senat ou à la Chambre des communes."

The literal translation would be "in relation to the federal executive power, to the Senate or to the House of Commons." The grammatical structure is different from the English version; there is no indication whether "or" means "and/or." It could be that the English version was written first, and the translator had to change the grammatical structure in order to accommodate the fact that the proper noun for Senate is masculine (hence "au Senat") whereas the proper noun for House of Commons is feminine ("à la Chambre des communes").

Another argument that will only be persuasive to the already persuaded is that in s.44 "executive government of Canada" means the Governor General on down, and hence does not mean the Queen; thus s.44 cannot be used to amend the Constitution in relation to the federal legislative process, which is vested in the Queen with the advice and consent of the House of Commons and Senate. A downright silly argument would be that s.44 cannot apply to the legislative process because that involves the Queen, and s.41(a) requires the consent of the House of Commons, Senate, and all 10 provincial legislatures to amend the

Constitution in relation to "the office of the Queen . . .". If this contention were correct, no amendments to section 91 or 92 could be made by the ordinary amending formula – House of Commons, Senate, and two-thirds of the provinces with half the population. What then would be the purpose of s.38(3), which allows provinces to "opt out" of amendments which derogate from their "legislative powers"?

The "housekeeping" theory does have strong support in the following consideration. It was generally understood in 1982 that the *Charter of Rights and Freedoms* was entrenched – that it could only be altered (except for the language rights provision) by the s.38 amending process. If s.44 is broadly construed, it would permit Parliament to unilaterally amend the *Charter* in relation to Parliament to repeal, for example, section 32(1)(a):

> This *Charter* applies
>
> (a) to the Parliament and government of Canada in respect of all matters within the authority of Parliament including all matters relating to the Yukon Territory and Northwest Territories . . .

Could not such an amendment be considered "in relation to the executive government of Canada or the Senate and House of Commons"? Not on the "housekeeping theory." I grant that the argument just made does not absolutely preclude a broad construction of s.44. A theory of s.44 could be developed whereby Parliament can *restrict* its powers (and amend s.91 to do so) but not *expand* them (by altering the *Charter*). Notice, however, that the framers of s.44 did not bother to expressly exclude the *Charter* from the operation of the section. They *did* take the trouble to make s.44 subject to sections 41 and 42 – both of which require elaborate amending processes for a list of matters which essentially involve the organization and institutions of government. That is, s.44 is expressly excluded from operating with respect to certain "housekeeping matters"; the powerful implication is that it was only intended to deal with such matters in the first place.

It might be maintained that, despite its history and related provisions, s.44 should be given a broad construction because doing so allows for a very useful legal mechanism. Useful, in that it would permit Parliament to constrain its successors; ordinarily, later statutes have priority over earlier ones. The s.44 mechanism would enable one Parliament to require its successors to take an extra formal step before violating an important legal norm. Useful also in that it provides a form whereby the solemnity and importance of a legal principle can be signalled.

In response to the first assertion of utility, I would point out that there are other mechanisms whereby Parliament can limit the actions of its successors. The *Canadians Bill of Rights*, enacted by Parliament in 1960, established a human rights code for the federal level. Section 3 requires the Minister of Justice to examine every bill or proposed regulation to determine whether it is inconsistent with the purposes and provisions of the *Canadian Bill of Rights*. Section 2 provides that legislation must be construed and applied so as to be consistent with all of the rights, unless the legislation is expressly declared to operate notwithstanding that statute. In *R.* v. *Drybones*, [1970] S.C.R. 282, the Supreme Court of Canada held inoperative a section of the *Indian Act* on the basis that it was repugnant to the equality provision of the *Canadian Bill of Rights*. If a parliament wishes to ensure that agreements on self-government are treated with respect by law makers and appliers in the future, it can use "manner and form" requirements similar to those employed for the *Canadian Bill of Rights*. It could require that the minister of Indian affairs and northern development or a minister of Indian First Nations relations examine legislation to determine whether it will derogate from rights under Indian-government agreements. It could prescribe that Parliament expressly state its intention of contravening agreements on self-government as a condition of doing so.

The second assertion of utility is answerable in a similar way. There are ways of expressing the special solemnity of a legal norm besides changing the text of the Constitution of Canada. The *Penner Report* recommends that Indian self-government be entrenched in the Constitution of Canada, but also suggests that "The Governor General should establish a register of Indian First Nation governments and that a formal ceremony mark the registration of each government" (*Penner Report*, 61). The foregoing analysis demonstrates that a broad construction of s.44 would not make available to Parliament a legal mechanism that is indispensable. The risks of creating that legal mechanism ought also to be considered.

Amendments under s.44 are repealable by the unilateral action of Parliament, and so are far less entrenched than amendments under the s.38 (House of Commons and Senate plus supermajority of provinces) mechanism; yet in a consolidated edition of the Constitution, they will look just the same. If the s.44 mechanism can be used for a broad variety of purposes, and in fact is, the public is apt to be left with a confused impression of what the Constitution is and what it means to amend it. (There is room here for flights of typographical and elocutional fancy. Editions of the Constitution are issued in which sections amendable by s.41 appear in thick black type; those amendable by s.38 in ordinary grey lettering; and those supremely vulnerable sections of the Constitution, amendable by unilateral federal action under s.44, in hollow characters sketched in thin and wavering lines of palest blue. In reading from the Constitution, its exponents could modulate the degree of assurance in their voices to reflect the relative permanences of the provision being voiced. Unfortunately, some provisions of the Constitution have aspects which can be amended in different ways, and no single typeface or voicing could do justice to them.)

The danger exists that the credibility of the Constitution as a whole would be undermined by excessively frequent amendments to it under a broadly read s.44. Political pressure groups and electoral parties are liable to see their principles at any given time as the most sacred and immutable. If there is an easy road to amendment – by Parliament's amending s.91 – a lot of norms may be placed in the Constitution. When social circumstances, perceptions of justice, or political power shifts, these norms will have to be displaced. Universality of social welfare programs, once a sacred principle of Canadian politics, is now under question; perhaps scarce resources should not be diverted to those who are not in need of them. Nondiscrimination in public employment is under attack from those who favour mandatory affirmative action, or even quotas, based on ethnic affiliation or gender. Perhaps the risk just outlined is actually very small. Federal institutions – the Senate, boards and commissions, the federal courts – have often been misused, however, for partisan political purposes. (For example, by using openings on them to reward the party faithful, rather than appointing the most qualified persons available.) The possible misuse of a constitutional mechanism is a factor that must be at least considered in deciding whether it should be created or recognized.

Apart from the exchange quoted at the beginning of this section, there has been practically no discussion in the s.37 process of unilateral federal amendment to the Constitution of Canada. If the legal analysis just offered is correct, nothing has been lost by this silence. I would hope, however, that other legal commentators will consider and report their views on whether the legal avenue exists. It should not remain untravelled merely because it was left off of everyone's map by oversight or mistake.

Chapter XX

Ordinary Legislation

Legal Impediments to the Establishment of Aboriginal Self-government

Some of the provinces have expressed the view during the s.37 process that it would be unwise, or at least premature, to establish self-government by amending the Constitution; that the process of ordinary legislation can reflect more subtly the diversity of aboriginal communities and embody more quickly new insights gained through experience. The tenants of this position ought, however, to consider the possibility that it does not necessarily lead to total quietism. It may be that some legislative measures to establish aboriginal self-government are not permitted by the existing law of the Constitution and that constitutional reform is necessary to carry on certain kinds of non-constitutional reform.

One legal obstacle that might exist is the equality guarantee in s.15 of the *Constitution Act, 1982*. It came into force on April 17, 1985. Any constraints it may impose can be overcome by using the legislative override section of the *Charter*, section 33. It gives effect to a legislative decision to expressly characterize a statute as operating notwithstanding the *Charter*. It is to be hoped, however, that legislatures will adopt the general policy of using the override sparingly. Thus it is necessary to look more closely at whether they would ever have to. The text of s.15(1): "Every individual is equal before and under the law and has the right to the equal protection and equal benefit of the law without discrimination and, in particular, without discrimination based on race, national or ethnic origin, colour, religion, sex, age, or mental or physical disability".

It is not clear what the opening phrase – "every individual is equal before and under the law" – adds to the rest of the paragraph. The French version – "La loi ne fait acception de personne et s'applique egalement à tous" – suggests that the opening phrase embodies the old principle of English constitutional law expounded by Dicey in the 19th century – that no person is above the law, that everyone is subject to the rules and jurisdiction of the ordinary courts (Dicey 1965). The rest of the paragraph, by contrast, is intended to exclude legislation that adversely discriminates against certain social groups. It may be that whatever the original intent, the language of the rest of the paragraph takes care of the concern of the opening phrase. Be that as it may, let us assume that the paragraph as a whole does address two different sorts of problems. On the basis of the opening phrase, it could be argued that legislation on self-government is not permissible if it goes too far in establishing a special system of rules and courts for an aboriginal group. It could be argued on the basis of the rest of the paragraph that aboriginal self-government legislation would give to those belonging to an aboriginal community privileges which are denied to other people. The latter would thus be denied the equal benefit of the law. The converse argument could also be made: aboriginal self-government subjects members of aboriginal communities to burdensome rules no one else must abide by, and so denies them the equal protection of the law.

One response that could be made to both arguments is that s.25 shields legislation on aboriginal self-government from the application of s.15. Section 25 says:

> The guarantee in this *Charter* of certain rights and freedoms shall not be construed so as to abrogate or derogate from any aboriginal, treaty or other rights or freedoms that pertain to the aboriginal peoples of Canada including
> (a) any rights or freedoms that have been recognized by the Royal Proclamation of October 7, 1763; and
> (b) any rights or freedoms that may be acquired by the aboriginal peoples of Canada by way of land claims settlement.

A lot of things about s.25 are obscure. Does it speak only to rights that existed on April 17, 1982, when it came into force or also to rights that come into being from time to time—including those created by legislation on self-government? Even if the former view is taken, it could be argued that one of the rights of Indians on April 17, 1982, was to special legislative treatment—otherwise s.91(24) of The *Constitution Act, 1867* would have been of no force or effect. It could also be maintained that unless barred by a provincial human rights act, the Métis had the right to special governmental regimes—and some of the Métis in Alberta in fact had one. Another uncertainty about s.25 is the scope to be given "construed"; unlike the *Canadian Bill of Rights*, it does not say "construed and applied"; the implication may be that in the case of a conflict that cannot be resolved by modifying the interpretations of the norms, the *Charter* prevails over the right of an aboriginal group. The legalistic analysis of s.25 could be pursued at excruciating length; anyone who has followed it this far has suffered enough. A general assertion that can be made with some confidence is that s.25 will strongly discourage any court from applying the egalitarian and individualistic norms of the *Charter of Rights and Freedoms* against self-government legislation.

The shielding effect of s.25 is only necessary if a valid attack can be mustered to begin with from the rest of the *Charter of Rights and Freedoms*. It may be that the courts will construe s.15 as not raising even a *prima facie* case against regimes of aboriginal self-government. The Diceyan objection might be rejected in an appropriate case on the basis that the citizens and officials of a self-governing community continue to be subject to a substantial body of general law—including the *Criminal Code* and the *Charter of Rights and Freedoms*—or that the court system of the aboriginal community continues to be subject to appeal or review by ordinary Canadian courts. The social equality objection might be met by holding that different governmental arrangements for different groups do not necessarily mean that anyone has been denied the equal protection or benefit of the law. Equal respect for different special groups, it could be argued, does not necessarily mean equal treatment. It might entail varying the law to meet the varying requirements of different groups. You might try to support this construction by reference to s.15(2): "Subsection (1) does not preclude any law, program or activity that has as its object the amelioration of conditions of disadvantaged individuals or groups including those that are disadvantaged because of race, national or ethnic origin, colour, religion, sex, age or mental or physical disability."

Section 15(2) is not, in itself, a satisfactory defence for all aboriginal self-government legislation. Some of it will be based, at least in part, on the acceptance of the claim that regardless of whether or not they are "disadvantaged," aboriginal communities have a claim in political justice to maintain some measure of governmental and cultural autonomy. At the March '84 First Ministers' Conference, Mr. Jim Sinclair of the Métis National Council (MNC) took exception to Prime Minister Trudeau's characterization of the Métis as a "disadvantaged people." According to Mr. Sinclair, the Métis were recognized in the Constitution as an aboriginal people – a people with a special political claim apart from any based on social disadvantage – not as a disadvantaged people (1984 First Ministers' Conference [FMC] transcript, 157). You might use s.15(2) as evidence that s.15(1) does not require equal treatment, only equal respect, so that favourable legal treatment for aboriginal peoples should not be seen as discriminatory. My own view is that while the conclusion may be correct, s.15(2) does little to establish it. Section 15(2) merely says that formal legal equality should not stand in the way of rectifying inequality of actual conditions. It does not challenge the liberal *ideal* of a society in which everyone starts off with a fair stake and freely competes and associates with everyone else on the basis of equality. Aboriginal self-government does challenge that ideal.

Even if a *prima facie* case can be made under s.15, it might be defeated by the application of s.1 of the *Charter*, which provides: "The *Canadian Charter of Rights and Freedoms* guarantees the rights and freedoms set out in it subject only to such reasonable limits prescribed by law as can be demonstrably justified in a free and democratic society." Thus even if aboriginal self-government legislation is discriminatory under s.15, it might be upheld as constitutionally valid because it is a just and necessary form of discrimination. If American equal protection jurisprudence is any guide, the courts will determine whether there are valid purposes behind the discrimination, and then, if there are any, the courts will explore whether the purpose could be achieved by less discriminatory measures (Gunther 1972).

The second line of inquiry might lead to judicial requirements for the refinement of a self-government scheme. So long as it had the support of the aboriginal group affected as well as that of a democratically elected legislature, however, a court would be reluctant to take it upon itself to impugn the basic aims of an enactment of self-government.

To summarize, section 15 does present some cause for concern about whether aboriginal self-government can be achieved through ordinary legislation. The likelihood, however, is that the courts would not find it to be a serious constraint. The uncertainty could be diminished by amending the Constitution – say by amending s.25 to expressly shield legislation on aboriginal self-government – but doing so should not be considered a priority of the s.37 agenda.

Another possible constraint on the legislative establishment of aboriginal self-government may be a limit on the extent to which Parliament and provincial legislatures can delegate law making authority to other entities. It was established in *Hodge* v. *The Queen* (1883), 9 A.C. 117 that the legal maxim *delegatus non potest delegare* – a delegate has no power to (further) delegate – has no application to Parliament or a legislature; they were not delegates of the imperial Parliament, but rather sovereign authorities over the matters assigned to them by the *Constitution Act, 1867*. In *Hodge*, the Privy Council upheld the authority of a provincial board to make liquor licensing regulations. A key passage is:

> It is obvious that such an authority is ancillary to legislation, and without it an attempt to provide for varying details and machinery to carry them out might become oppressive, or absolutely fail. . . . It was argued at the bar that a legislature committing important regulations to agents or delegates effaces itself. That is not so. It retains its powers intact, and can, whenever it pleases, destroy the agency it has created and set up another, or take the matter directly into his own hands. How far it shall seek the aid of subordinate agencies, and how long it shall continue them, are matters for each legislature, and not for Courts of Law, to decide ((1883), 9 A.C. 117, 132).

It should be noticed that the opinion cites the continuing power to undo what has been wrought. The point is important because that power may not exist when aboriginal self-government is established by treaty that is constitutionally protected under s.35(1) of the *Constitution Act, 1982*. This problem will be further explored in the next chapter.

A wholesale delegation of legislative authority by Parliament to the governor-in-council (that is, the governor general acting with the advice and consent of the federal cabinet) under the *War Measures Act* was upheld by the Supreme Court of

Canada in *Re George Edwin Gray* (1918), 57 S.C.R. 150. Anglin J. held that short of "abdication," Parliament could delegate its powers as it saw fit. Chief Justice Fitzpatrick was more cautious, holding that Parliament could delegate its authority to the executive "within reasonable limits"; (1918), 57 S.C.R. 150, 157. He noted that the powers could be revoked by Parliament at any time. Duff J. made the same observation in his judgment and added that the authority devolved upon the governor-in-council was "strictly conditioned" in two respects: it was exercisable only during wartime and only included measures deemed advisable by reason of war ((1918), 57 S.C.R. 150, 170). Idington J. outright dissented on the ground that "its entire powers [of Parliament] cannot be by a single stroke of the pen surrendered or transferred to anybody" ((1918), 57 S.C.R. 150, 165). The precedential effect of *Gray* is arguably limited by the fact that the delegation there was to the governor-in-council, a body which is, for practical purposes, directly responsible to Parliament. Perhaps Parliament has less freedom to delegate powers to a subordinate body not answerable to it. It should also be noted that *Gray* was decided during a wartime emergency. It is well settled that Parliament can invade areas of provincial jurisdiction during such times of crisis; its authority to delegate may also be greater.

The *Initiative and Referendum Act* of Manitoba permitted laws to be made or repealed by a direct vote of the people. The Privy Council found the alternative legislative process to be unconstitutional because it bypassed the lieutenant-governor's veto power. The court added, however, this observation:

> No doubt a body, with a power of legislation on the subjects entrusted to it so ample as that enjoyed by a Provincial Legislature in Canada, could, while preserving its own capacity intact, seek the assistance of subordinate agencies, as had been done in *Hodge* v. *The Queen* . . .; but it does not follow that it can create and endow with its own capacity a new legislative power not created by the Act to which it owes its own existence. Their Lordships do no more than draw attention to the gravity of the constitutional questions which thus arise (*In Re The Initiative and Referendum Act*,[1919] A.C. 935, 945).

The judges of the Manitoba Court of Appeal had been less restrained and expressly found that the *British North America Act* did not permit the establishment of an alternate process equal in authority to the legislature and capable of negating the legislature's efforts or even destroying it; (1918) 27 Man. R. 1.

The legal possibility that the creation might destroy the creator would not exist with respect to self-government legislation. Furthermore, any delegation of authority to an aboriginal government would be confined to certain communities and areas and would involve less than the whole catalogue of federal powers. The most informative precedents would be those dealing with far more limited delegations of authority than the one at issue in the Manitoba case.

One possible analogy would be to Parliament's creation of institutions of self-government for the Yukon and Northwest Territories. Duff J. made much of the analogy in the *Gray* reference:

> Our own Canadian constitutional history affords a striking instance of the "delegation" so called of legislative authority with which the devolution effected by the "War Measures Act" may usefully be contrasted. The North West Territories were, for many years, governed by a council exercising powers of legislation almost equal in extent to those enjoyed by the provinces.
>
> The statute by which this was authorized, by which the machinery of responsible government, and what in substance was parliamentary government, was set up and maintained in that part of Canadian territory, was passed by the Parliament of Canada; and it was never doubted that this legislation was valid and effectual for these purposes under the authority conferred upon parliament by the Imperial Act of 1871:
>
>> to make provision for the administration, peace, order and good government in any territory not for the time being included in any province.
>
> That, of course, involved a degree of devolution far beyond anything attempted by the 'War Measures Act.' In the former case, while the legal authority remained unimpaired in parliament to legislate regarding the subjects over which jurisdiction had been granted, it was not intended that it should continue to be, and in fact it never was, exercised in the ordinary course; and the powers were conferred upon an elected body over

> which parliament was not intended to have, and never attempted to exercise, any sort of direct control. *It was in a word strictly a grant (within limits) of local self government.* In the case of the 'War Measures Act' there was not only no abandonment of legal authority, but no indication of any intention to abandon control and no actual abandonment of control in fact, and the council on whom was to rest responsibility for exercising the powers given was the Ministry responsible directly to Parliament and dependent upon the will of Parliament for the continuation of its official existence [emphasis added] ((1918), 57 S.C.R. 150, 170).

The analogy between aboriginal self-government and territorial self-government is somewhat problematic in that the *Constitution Act, 1871* provides special support for Parliament's authority to establish the former. Section 2 of the statute (now inoperative by virtue of s.42(f) of the *Constitution Act, 1982*) said that Parliament could admit new provinces into Confederation and provide for the provincial constitutions. Section 4, quoted by Duff in the passage just reproduced, expressly allows Parliament to make provision for the "administration, peace, order and good government of any territory not for the time being included in any province." The formula for the general exercise of Parliament's authority in s.91 of the *Constitution Act, 1867* des not include the word "administration." Its mention in Section 4 shows that the framers contemplated that Parliament could establish special governmental structures for a territory; the fact that under s.2 Parliament could create sovereign provinces strongly suggests that Parliament was entirely free under s.4 to grant a large measure of self-government to territories not yet ready for provincehood. There is no constitutional text expressly authorizing Parliament to establish self-government for Indian reserves.

In *A.G. Nova Scotia* v. *A.G. Canada* (Nova Scotia Interdelegation),[1951] S.C.R. 31, the Supreme Court of Canada struck down an attempt by the Nova Scotia legislature to authorize Parliament to pass laws with respect to certain types of Nova Scotia enterprises that come under provincial jurisdiction pursuant to s.92 of the *Constitution Act, 1867*. The case is once again of limited applicability to the self-government issue. A number of plausible objections to federal-provincial interdelegation have no application to aboriginal self-government. Among them: that interdelegation blurs the jurisdictional boundaries the *Constitution Act, 1867* attempted to fix; that it confuses the accountability of federal and provincial governments to their electorates; it risks putting one sovereign legislature in a position of subordination to the delegating legislature; and it poses a conflict of interest for the federal government, which cannot always do justice to both the national interest and that of a province which has entrusted it with authority over a local matter. There is a dictum of Rand J. in the *Interdelegation* case that at first glance seems relevant to aboriginal self-government:

> Notwithstanding the plenary nature of the jurisdiction enjoyed by them, it was conceded that neither Parliament nor Legislature can either transfer its constitutional authority to the other or *create a new legislative organ in a relation to it similar to that between either of these bodies and the Imperial Parliament* [emphasis added] ([1951] S.C.R. 31, 47).

Rand J. apparently relied on this passage in the Privy Council's decision, in *The Queen* v. *Burah*, about the power of the colonial Indian legislature to delegate its authority: "Their Lordships agree that the [Indian legislature] could not, by any form of enactment, create in *India*, and arm with general legislative authority, a new legislative power, not created or authorized by the [Act establishing the Indian legislature]"; (1877) 3 A.C. 889, 905. Two years after its decision in the *Nova Scotia Interdelegation* case, the Supreme Court held that Parliament and provincial legislatures could delegate powers over products marketing to one and the same provincially-constituted marketing board; *Potato Marketing Board* v. *Willis*, [1952] 2 S.C.R. 392. This precedent reduces the possibility that the courts will attack delegations by both Parliament and a province to one aboriginal government.

My overall conclusion from the preceding survey is that the case law is inconclusive. My prediction and prescription would be that the courts should allow governments almost unlimited scope to vest legislative authority in aboriginal governments by means of ordinary legislation. The continuing authority of Parliament and provincial legislatures to legislatively override a decision of an aboriginal government, or to modify or withdraw the delegation of authority, would be a strong factor in holding that there had not been a disruption in the basic scheme of authority and responsibility contemplated by the *Constitution Act, 1867*. (Some constitutional changes will obviously go beyond the scope of what is authorized by sections 44 and 45 of the *Constitution Act, 1982*; their predecessors were given a narrow reading in the *Senate Reference* (1980), 102 D.L.R. (3d) 1). It is possible that such a disruption would be found in the very unlikely case that an aboriginal community was authorized to cut itself almost entirely free from the criminal, regulatory, and social welfare laws applicable to the rest of the country. Like the "impediment" to self-government posed by s.15 of the *Charter of Rights and Freedoms*, the case law on the delegation of authority is unlikely in practice to interfere with the establishment of self-government by ordinary legislation. A constitutional amendment expressly stating the extent to which Parliament and provincial legislatures can delegate their authority to aboriginal governments would relieve some uncertainty; it is doubtful, though, whether it is worth attempting to draft and concur upon one at the s.37 process. The diversion of attention from other issues might be a cost disproportionate to any gain.

Chapter XXI

The Treaty Making Process

In the afternoon, March 9 discussion at the '84 First Ministers' Conference, three of the four aboriginal organizations jointly submitted a proposal for a political accord. (The Métis National Council [MNC] was apparently in agreement with the proposal but reluctant to co-sign a document with the Native Council of Canada [NCC].) A crucial aspect of the joint submission was that First Ministers agree to submit to their legislatures the following constitutional amendment:

> 35.2(1) The government of Canada and the provincial governments, to the extent that each has jurisdiction, are committed to negotiating and concluding treaties with the aboriginal peoples for the specific implementation in the various regions of Canada of the rights of the aboriginal peoples, including self-government.
>
> (2) Such treaties shall be treaties within the meaning of section 35(1).
>
> (3) Subsections (1) and (2) shall apply to First Nations with Treaties, only to the extent so elected by them.

The key difference from the federal proposal was the characterization of the bilateral agreements on self-government as s.35(1) treaties. The goal was to secure for agreements on self-government whatever constitutional protection s.35(1) offers to its contents. By contrast, the federal proposal attempted to make sure that agreements on self-government do not enjoy judicially enforceable constitutional safeguards.

In assessing the proposal of the aboriginal organizations, the first order of business is to determine whether it was really necessary to their aims. It may be that s.35(1) of the *Constitution Act, 1982*, "clarified" by s.35(3) in 1984, *already* gives constitutional protection to agreements on self-government. To recall the relevant texts:

> s.35(1) The existing aboriginal and treaty rights of the aboriginal peoples of Canada are hereby recognized and affirmed.
>
> s.35(3) For greater certainty, in subsection (1) "treaty rights" include rights that now exist by way of land claims agreements or may be so acquired.

A strong case can be made even without further constitutional amendment that Parliament and aboriginal governments can enter into constitutionally protected treaties on self-government. It would go something like this:

> Section 35(3) establishes that "existing" in section 35(1) means such rights as existed on April 17, 1982, and rights that are created thereafter. Surely it is not only land claims agreements after April 17, 1982, that are protected. Notice that 35(3) refers to "land claims *agreements*"; some bilateral accords that are not expressly labelled as "treaties" obviously count as s.35(1) treaties. Some sort of test will have to be developed for what agreements on self-government count as "treaties"; perhaps the intention of both sides to create constitutionally binding obligations will be one of them. In any event, it makes no sense to say that *all* land claims agreements receive constitutional protection but *no* agreements on self-government do. The most important land claims agreement at the time s.35(3) was enacted was the James Bay agreement; and it included a number of promises by governments to attempt to secure passage of legislation on regional self-government (as requested by the Inuit) and ethnic local self-government (as requested by the Cree). It is

beyond doubt that land claims agreements which come under s.35(3) receive some constitutional protection from s.35(1). Are we to say that agreements on self-government can only be constitutionally protected if they are part of a larger deal that involves land claims? If that is the case, it makes all the difference in the constitutional world whether an aboriginal group manages to toss a provision about one square centimetre of disputed territory into its self-government deal. If it does, the agreement can be constitutionally recognized and affirmed by s.35(1); if it doesn't, the agreement is just an ordinary contract which is vulnerable to legislative override. The example establishes the irrationality of attempting to make a categorical distinction between land claims agreements and agreements on self-government. The correct view is that both types of agreement can count as s.35(1) treaties. Remember that to hold otherwise is to deprive both aboriginal peoples *and* governments of a constitutional mechanism they might wish to employ. To hold otherwise is to say that even if the federal government *wants* to enter into a constitutionally protected treaty on self-government alone, it cannot do so. The only way that the agreement on self-government alone could be constitutionally protected would be by going through the cumbersome process of s.38(1) entrenchment. As there may be hundreds of agreements on self-government, and scores of these which the parties would want constitutionally protected, the s.38(1) route would obviously be unworkable. To sum up, holding that agreements on self-government cannot count as s.35(1) treaties requires an artificial yet crucial distinction between agreements that involve some dispute over land and those that don't; and it deprives both aboriginal peoples and public governments of a constitutional mechanism they might both find very useful.

A strong case can be made to the contrary, that agreements on self-government *cannot* be considered s.35(1) treaties. It would go something like this:

The "treaties" mentioned in s.35(1) were primarily intended to be the old self-styled treaties whereby

Indians surrendered their land rights in return for reserve land entitlements and other social welfare benefits. They did not guarantee self-government. Contemporary agreements on self-government would be categorically different from these old treaties. To begin with, their subject matter is essentially different from that of the old treaties. Unlike the old treaties, modern agreements on self-government would deal with the subject of political autonomy. They would do more than create rights for Indians against non-Indian governments. They would create rights for Indians as a collectivity against individual members of the collectivity; an agreement on self-government would authorize an Indian group to exercise a certain measure of control over individuals within that group.

What are the consequences of saying that agreements on self-government are s.35(1) treaties? In effect, they are that an agreement between the federal government and an Indian group will be immune from derogation by a subsequent legislature. Unless there are substantial limitations on the constitutional protection given by s.35(1), recognizing an agreement on self-government as a s.35(1) treaty is not substantially different from entrenching it in the Constitution. The only way to undo what has been done is to obtain the consent of the aboriginal group—which is not a significant difference because almost all constitutional rights can be waived—or go through the cumbersome s.38 amending process. You end up with the remarkable result that a federal government could unilaterally set up an aboriginal group with powers exceeding even those of a province, and there would be no way to undo the result against an unwilling beneficiary except to obtain the consent of the House of Commons, Senate, and two thirds of the provinces. The sound and generally applicable principle of the Canadian Constitution is that it is equally hard to enact a constitutional provision on the one hand and to repeal or alter it on the other. This principle should apply to a matter as important as the governmental arrangements under which a community will live.

There is a second major difference between the old treaties and agreements on self-government. The former were *bargains*; the aboriginal group permanently surrendered entitlements vital to their existence in return for the promises under the treaties. There would be no such cost with respect to agreements on self-government. They would not involve the surrender of entitlements aboriginal groups already have. The justification for permanently protecting the benefits of the agreement is far weaker where there is no permanent cost.

Now consider the effect s.35(3) has on s.35(1). The second major distinction between treaties and agreements on self-government still applies; under modern land claims agreements, aboriginal groups permanently surrender claims of fundamental importance in return for what is promised. Thus, even if the distinction in subject-matter between the old treaties and modern treaties does not hold – because modern land claims agreements do include some provisions on self-government – there is still in the element of exchange a solid basis for excluding agreements on self-government from the scope of s.35(1).

As for the argument that the exclusion of agreements on self-government from s.35(1) is artificial because it could be overcome by tossing a minimal dispute over land into an accord that generally deals with self-government – the premise of the argument is wrong. The courts would look at the substance of the agreement to see whether it involves a substantial and plausible dispute over land.

It may be argued that section 35(3) destroys the distinction in subject matter between treaties and agreements on self-government. The James Bay agreement shows that some arrangements on political autonomy may be part of a treaty that is protected by s.35(1). On a close examination of the James Bay treaty, however, it appears that only limited self-government is guaranteed. Both the regional public government promised the Inuit and local ethnic government promised the Cree have powers that do not

> much exceed that of an ordinary municipality; the citizens of both continue to be subject to ordinary federal and provincial law; and many important decisions of both types of government are subject to disallowance by either the government of Quebec or Canada. The James Bay precedent should not be taken as establishing the ability of governments to enter into constitutionally binding treaties on any degree of aboriginal self-government. If section 35(3) does so expand s.35(1), then section 35(3) itself is—because it has the practical effect of creating an alternate route to major constitutional amendment—an amendment to the amending formulae. Changes to the amending formulae in the Constitution require the consent of all the provinces; and Quebec did not agree to s.35(3). There is no need, however, to go so far as declaring s.35(3) void. It can be read as allowing agreements on limited local self-government to receive the protection of s.35(3) as part of an agreement that has land claims as a principal subject.

In rebuttal to the case just made for limiting s.35(3), the following might be said:

> It has been argued that giving constitutional protection to agreements on self-government would allow, in effect, the unilateral entrenchment of self-government agreements. This is said to be contrary to the general principle that it is equally hard to entrench and unentrench. That principle does not, however, always hold in the Canadian Constitution; under s.38(3), a province can unilaterally opt out of a new constitutional amendment; but if at any point it ever does opt in, it can never again escape the amendment without obtaining the usual s.38 consent—the House of Commons, Senate, and two thirds of the provinces with a majority of the population. There is good reason for allowing a lack of symmetry in the way that aboriginal rights are protected and derogated from. Aboriginal peoples are a small political minority of the population. It can be expected that governments answerable to the general public will not give away those parts of the shop that it ought to keep. By contrast, any time the governments of Canada and seven provinces (with half the population) find

inconvenient a constitutional safeguard previously granted an aboriginal group, they can abolish it—despite the objections of the group affected. When there is no symmetry with respect to political power, it is illogical to insist on symmetry in the process of constitutionalization.

One of the factors complicating the choice between the two positions is the uncertainty over what sort of constitutional protection s.35(1) actually gives. The more vulnerable s.35(1) treaties are to legislative override, the less persuasive is the argument that the treaty making process is a back-door route to constitutional amendment. Another complicating factor is the uncertainty over the contents of s.35(1). Another complicating factor is the uncertainty over the contents of s.35(1). Suppose, contrary to what has been assumed above, that among the "aboriginal rights" s.35(1) mentions is self-government. An agreement on self-government might then be viewed as involving the permanent exchange of that inherent right for the rights expressly provided for in the agreement. The benefit of permanent exchange would be a strong ground for considering the agreements on self-government to be morally analogous to the old treaties, hence a "treaty" for the purposes of s.35(1).

Which of the two positions is stronger, I am not at all sure, although I tend towards the former. It may be a long time before the courts have to decide. Governments may build enough "safety valves"—limits on the exercise of power by aboriginal governments in the form of standards and independent review mechanisms—into self-government agreements that no subsequent government finds it necessary to tamper with them. It would be helpful to clarify the issue now, however, because the parties to agreements on self-government will want to know what they are getting themselves into. If there is the possibility that the agreement will be unalterable without the consent of the aboriginal group, the federal government may try to put a lot of "safety valves" (or, if you prefer, "weasel tunnels") that they would otherwise forego. Their attempt to do so may complicate negotiations. If the intent to enter a constitutionally protected treaty is a key element in determining whether it is one, then the federal side may attempt to have the agreement disclaim that intention while the aboriginal group tries to have it expressly recognized.

There are some respectable positions between the two poles defined earlier. You might adopt the first position but insist on some strict conditions before an agreement on self-government can be validly considered a s.35(1) treaty. One condition you might stipulate is that since constitutionalizing an agreement has serious consequences, the parties should enter into it with full knowledge and consent; an agreement on self-government should not be recognized as a s.35(1) treaty unless the parties expressly or impliedly acknowledge it as such. Another condition would be that the aboriginal government cannot be given authority tantamount to that enjoyed by a province. If it were, the net effect of the transfer of authority and the constitutional protection provided by s.35(1) would be a substantial constitutional amendment. The amendment itself, you might say, might be a just and prudent one, but it ought not to be effected by Parliament alone. It would be odd, you could say, if the new Constitution required the s.38 amending process to be used for the admission of new provinces into Confederation – but permitted the federal level of government to establish on its own an equivalent order of government for a reserve. You could cite some of the case law on the excessive delegation of authority – the Manitoba *Initiative and Referendum Act Reference,* [1919] A.C. 935; *The Nova Scotia Interdelegation* case, [1918] S.C.R. 31; *The Senate Reference* (1980), 102 D.L.R. (3d) 1 – to support your contention that the Constitution contemplates that legislative authority should be vested in Parliament, and it cannot irrevocably devolve a substantial part of that authority to another order of government except by constitutional amendment.

An aspect of the controversy that must be considered is the federal-provincial relations one. It is well settled that under s.91(24) of the *Constitution Act, 1867,* the federal government became solely responsible for the obligations under the old treaties; see *R.* v. *Secretary of State for Foreign and Commonwealth Affairs, ex parte Indian Association of Alta.,* [1982] Q.B. 892. Thus if s.35(1) stood alone, a powerful case could be made that provinces were not contemplated as eligible parties to s.35(1) agreements. With the addition of s.35(3), the more persuasive case at first glance is that provinces are indeed eligible. The reason? The province of Quebec was a party to the James Bay agreement, and it was the outstanding precedent for a modern lands claim agreement when s.35(3) was framed. A complication that immediately arises, however, is that a province might enter into a bilateral agreement with an aboriginal group over a matter within concurrent federal and provincial jurisdiction – say, education on a reserve. If the agreement counts as a s.35(1) treaty and if s.35(1) constitutionally protects its contents, then Parliament cannot undo what the province has done. In other words, Parliament's authority has been ousted without its consent. One way of avoiding this difficulty would be to say that provinces can enter into s.35(1) agreements with aboriginal groups only if the federal government is also a party to the treaty.

The preceding analysis suggests the opposite question. What happens if the federal government enters into a s.35(1) treaty, and the results are offensive, or at least inconvenient, to the existing or a successor provincial government? "Tough cookies," might be your initial response; the federal government always has paramount authority over the provinces when it comes to Indians. Yes, but ordinarily a provincial government or the unhappy federal electorate of a province can, with some hope of success, urge a federal government to adjust its policies to accommodate provincial concerns. Once the moving pen hath signed a s.35 treaty, not all the piety nor wit of a provincial government can lure it back, nor all its tears wipe out a word of it – unless the aboriginal group and the federal government are moved to revise the text, or six other provinces and the federal government conspire to erase it. Provincial governments will have a number of concerns about the agreements. Most will have a genuine altruistic concern about the future of aboriginal peoples; they will also be concerned about the indirect effects of aboriginal self-government, in that many people educated and trained under it will eventually move to the cities; and they will want to ensure that their environmental interests are not adversely affected by reserve activities. The bilateral treaty making process may give them an inadequate opportunity to protect or at least communicate their interests.

The involvement in self-government negotiations of the province in which the community is located will often be essential to the success of the venture. The close co-operation of provincial governments – including a willingness to enter into contracts to provide services and expertise – will be less likely if they are not adequately involved in constitutional arrangements concerning the aboriginal community. My suggestion would be that the s.37 process consider clarifying agreements on self-government by way of constitutional amendment.

The position that no constitutional mechanism should be recognized can be argued with some plausibility. It could be said that the mechanism is basically unnecessary; that governments can be expected to generally honour their agreements with aboriginal governments, just as they generally honour agreements on fundamental matters such as oil-pricing and fiscal transfers. Occasionally circumstances may require a government to alter an agreement over the objection of the aboriginal group concerned, but it is just as well to trust the fairness of a government than to try in advance to stipulate the constitutional conditions under which an agreement may be abrogated. The latter option will require prolonged negotiations and, at best, result in a formula that is open to widely differing interpretations. The existence of the mechanism (that is, entering into constitutionally protected treaties on self-government) will consistently complicate and delay negotiations between governments and aboriginal groups. There will be disputes about whether the agreement ought to be self-styled as a treaty; the inescapability of the obligations will cause governments to insist on all sorts of "safety valves" they might ordinarily forego. The most important thing right now is to get on with the practical business of negotiating and implementing self-government for aboriginal peoples.

The contrary position could cite some advantages to creating the mechanism. It would enable aboriginal groups to enter into medium and long term agreements which give security and certainty to their planning; they will not have to worry that an unsympathetic future government will disrupt or destroy the political and fiscal arrangements they have with an existing government. The mechanism, in fact, could be seen as a one-way ratchet; it would permit progress on self-government to be made under governments receptive to aboriginal concerns and prevent hostile or indifferent governments from moving backwards. The constitutionalization of agreements would add an extra element of solemnity and dignity to them. It would enhance the confidence and pride aboriginal groups would have in the agreements that would, in effect, be their constitutions.

A prudent course of action might be to tie together the first round of bilateral negotiations on self-government and s.37 negotiations on whether they should be constitutionally protected. The federal provincial and aboriginal governments involved in a particular negotiation or agreement could report to s.37 meetings (whether officials, ministers, or even First Ministers), and thereby give all the s.37 participants a better appreciation of the practical problems of aboriginal self-government and the nature of the agreements that can be expected to emerge. At a s.37 First Ministers' meeting no later than 1987 (the last one required by the 1984 amendment to the Constitution) an attempt could be made to determine whether the agreements ought to be constitutionally protected and, if so, by what mechanism.

One of the simplest constitutional amendments worth considering would stipulate that agreements on self-government are to be considered as s.35(1) treaties. It could be expressly added that provinces may enter into constitutionally protected agreements; the qualification might be made that an agreement cannot limit the purposes of Parliament unless the federal government is also a party. To require the consent of the province before an agreement would be constitutionally protected would probably be unacceptable to aboriginal organizations. They would justifiably be concerned about some of the most unsympathetic provinces blocking an agreement that was acceptable to both the federal government and an aboriginal group. A suggestion worth considering, however, is that before an agreement receives constitutional protection as a treaty, it must first have been submitted for discussion to a s.37-style First Ministers' Conference. There are several advantages to this proposal. It would ensure that agreements received adequate public scrutiny and discussion before they became largely immune from alteration. On the other hand, the proposal would not enable a province or group of provinces to veto the agreement's inclusion under s.35(1). Section 37(1) participants not directly involved in the agreement might derive from the discussion some ideas they could implement themselves. The prime minister would be implicitly (or expressly) obliged to convene s.37-style conferences from time to time to consider the agreements – with the result that aboriginal issues would be sure of attracting the periodic attention of governments, the media, and the public. Against the proposal just made, it would have to be considered whether the number and complexity of agreements would prevent their being intelligently considered by First Ministers.

It will be worthwhile to consider substantive as well as procedural constraints on the constitutionalizing of self-government agreements. It would be possible, for example, to stipulate that the agreements can only transfer authority over a specified range of subject matters; that they can have a maximum duration of only a certain number of years; that they must provide for independent review of the group's fiscal affairs; or that they must provide for independent review of decisions on grounds of illegality or unreasonableness.

Whether or not self-government agreements are constitutionalized, it does seem highly desirable that they be an essential aspect of establishing a new type of political order for aboriginal communities. They will help to ensure that the superior understanding of aboriginal communities of their own circumstances and aspirations will be adequately reflected in the legal order that emerges. The agreement making process will also help to overcome some of the disputes over symbolism that would otherwise stall progress for many groups. One of the longest debates in the history of the Canadian Parliament was over the replacement of the Red Ensign flag by the Maple Leaf. Whether an aboriginal group is characterized as a protected independent state, a domestic dependent nation, a band, or a municipality may not actually make a bit of difference in the distribution of power over it. But it may be a matter charged with significance for both the members of the community and the general Canadian public. The agreement making process is useful because it does not necessarily require either side to surrender their symbolism or accept the other's. An aboriginal group can, if it wishes, regard an agreement as an international treaty between two sovereign states. No Canadian court will ever agree with it, but the group itself remains free to maintain its interpretation of the significance of the transaction. By contrast, if self-government is established by legislation alone, the exercise of authority by aboriginal governments may inescapably look like their acceptance of delegated authority from a superior power. There may be ways of drafting the legislation so as to some extent avoid this implication—for example, using the word "recognition" wherever possible, rather than "delegation"—but the process would not be as subject to diverse characterizations as would one that includes bilateral agreements. The agreement making mechanism might allow each party to say that the other has a bad theory—that works in practice.

Chapter XXII

The April '85 Process and Conference

Swan Song

On June 27, 1984, the minister of Indian affairs and northern development, John Munro, introduced into the House Bill C-52, "An Act relating to self-government for Indian Nations." It was two days before the adjournment of the Second Session of the Thirty-Second Parliament. The government almost certainly did not intend that the legislation would be processed through the committee, third reading in the House, and Senate passage stages in a couple of days. The political motivation for introducing the legislation might have been to signal the attitude towards self-government of the minister or the government (with a view to the next general election). In any event, Bill C-52 does provide a model approach to implementing self-government, and policy-makers might benefit, whether through emulation or avoidance, from a study of its main ideas.

The bill contemplates the creation of a Recognition Panel that would determine whether an Indian collectivity should be recognized as an Indian Nation. The panel would be appointed, in effect, by the federal cabinet. Three of its seven members must be Indians. To be recognized by the panel, an Indian group would have to submit a written constitution (approved in an internal referendum) that satisfied certain conditions, including (in the words of Bill C-52):

- the accountability of the government of the Indian Nation to the members of the Indian Nation (s.6(iii));
- the protection of individual and collective rights (s.6(vi));
- an independent system for reviewing executive decisions of the government of the Indian Nation on grounds that they are illegal, unreasonable, or unfair (s.6(vii));
- a system of financial accountability of the government of the Indian Nation to its members, including audit arrangements and the publication of financial reports (s.6(viii)).

These provisions probably strike an appropriate balance between Indian autonomy and the protection of individual rights. Indian Nations seem to have considerable discretion to devise their own systems of political and fiscal accountability to their own people under such a scheme.

Section 28 of Bill C-52 would make the *Charter* applicable to Indian Nations. The measure is consistent with what Chapter XXIII of this study would have recommended. Unnecessarily burdensome is another aspect of s.28 of Bill C-52, which would have made invalid any Indian Nation law that was inconsistent with "any international covenant relating to human rights" signed by the government of Canada. If you include those sponsored by the International Labor Organization, Canada has signed (and in most cases, ratified) dozens of international human rights conventions. The terms of many of these conventions are vague, and sometimes one convention conflicts with another. It is unnecessary to impose on Indian Nations this loss of political discretion, as well as the confusion and expense that would be involved in attempting to comply with all the international human rights covenants that Canada has signed. It is not as though other levels of government are themselves bound. Federal and provincial law is generally not altered by the mere fact that Canada has signed and ratified a treaty; implementing legislation is needed. So far, Canadian courts have generally held that Parliament and provincial legislatures are free to legislate in ways that are inconsistent with Canada's international treaty obligations.

Section 63 of Bill C-52 would allow a federal cabinet to determine the eligibility criteria that the Recognition Panel is supposed to apply. As recognition is the prerequisite to the acquisition of substantial governmental powers by an Indian Nation, the criteria for eligibility ought to be stated plainly in the bill. The federal cabinet should not be able to frustrate the development of Indian self-government by imposing restrictive or paternalistic criteria for eligibility.

Once an Indian Nation has been recognized, its executive and legislature would automatically acquire the range of powers set out in sections 16 and 17 of the bill. Among the subject matters within the legislative authority of all Indian Nations would be taxation for local purposes and primary and secondary education. Bill C-52 does not provide any guidelines on what sort of minimal standards must be met with respect to curricula and teaching qualifications. It would be better for these to be specified in the legislation, or at least in follow-up regulations, than to leave it to the federal executive to insist on certain basics by making them the condition of funding or by disallowing Indian legislation. The more that is spelled out in advance, the more opportunity there is for public debate and criticism, and the less justification there is for imposition of values by the federal executive later on.

By section 19 of the bill, an Indian Nation government can acquire, by agreement with a province or the federal government, authority over an item in a long list of governmental powers. Some of the items are of high importance and responsibility – for example, 19(d), the environment within the boundaries of the lands of the Indian nation, or 19(j), the administration of justice. The exercise of authority with respect to an acquired power would be subject to any limitations specified in the agreement with the province or the federal government. An effort should be made, if there is another attempt at legislation like Bill C-52, to specify in the legislation or in a formal policy statement some of the principles that should guide the federal executive in its negotiations.

Sections 40 and 41 of the bill provide, in essence, that federal and provincial laws of general application can apply to Indian Nations, except to the extent that they are inconsistent with the bill itself. Fair enough. The agreements an Indian Nation made with a province or the federal government pursuant to the bill might provide for extensive areas in which provincial or federal laws would not operate, and in which Indian Nations would have the final say.

The financial provisions of the bill are not satisfactory. They do nothing to diminish the prospect of continuing and wasteful federal-provincial-Indian Nation fights over who-pays-for-what or to diminish the ability of the federal government to impose its policy preferences by conditioning its grants. Section 55 of the bill allows an Indian Nation and the minister responsible for Indian Nations to enter into funding agreements.

There is no acceptance of federal fiscal responsibility, no distributive principle that must be observed (such as that "contained in s.36 of the *Constitution Act, 1982* with respect to federal-provincial equalization payments), and no limits on the number or tautness of strings that may be attached to federal grants.

By s.31 of the bill, any law of a recognized Indian Nation may be disallowed by the federal cabinet at any time. A provision that allows for review by elected officials cannot be condemned out of hand. The reassurance that the general public and citizens of an Indian government would have a means of redressing exceptionally unwise or unfair laws may encourage federal and provincial governments to confer broader powers on an Indian Nations government. The preferable course of action, though, would generally be to specify the constraints on Indian Nation governments by statute or agreement and let the courts or other independent agencies enforce the rules. In this way, Indian Nations have the opportunity to participate in the formulation of the limitations on their powers, and the way is not opened for arbitrary, paternalistic, or self-interested interventions by the federal government. If a review power is to be allowed, it should certainly not be the completely open-ended authority contemplated by s.31. The standards of review ought to be spelled out, and provisions should be made for the Indian Nation concerned to have a fair hearing before a decision is made and the benefit of reasons for any disallowance that ensues. It might be better to confer any disallowance power on a single minister, rather than on the cabinet, as it is much more difficult to persuade Parliament and the courts to constrain the way cabinet does its business.

The minister responsible for Indian Nations is authorized by s.26 of the bill to appoint an administrator to take over the operation of government where an Indian Nations government has "abused its powers, is in serious financial difficulty or is unable to perform its functions." The circumstances that justify this extraordinary intervention are phrased in much too general a manner, and there is no appeal provided to an independent agency to ensure that the minister is justified in his actions.

Bill C-52 was condemned by some analysts with Indian organizations as falling far short of the recommendations of the *Penner Report*. In defence of Bill C-52, a responsible federal government must necessarily take a somewhat more balanced and cautious approach to self-government than the *Penner Report*. Bill C-52 does contain a number of interesting ideas. On the whole, though, it confers too lavish and too unstructured an authority over Indian self-government on the federal government.

The Search for Harmony

One of the themes of the election campaign of Brian Mulroney was national reconciliation. During the Trudeau years, there had been political tensions between Quebec and the rest of Canada over political autonomy, between western Canada and central Canada over energy policy, and between eight of the provinces and the federal government over patriation of the constitution. When Prime Minister Trudeau left office, there was not a Liberal government left in power in any of the provincial legislatures and not a Liberal member of Parliament from the three westernmost provinces. A separatist government in Quebec continued to refuse to endorse the package of constitutional reforms that nine provinces and the federal government had finally agreed upon in 1982. According to some political analysts, Brian Mulroney considered himself to be similar in political philosophy to Prime Minister Trudeau, but equipped by personality and training to bring about the greater spirit of co-operation that was needed among Canadians. He had worked as a labour lawyer, and so could claim experience at finding common ground where interests conflict.

The Progressive Conservatives won an overwhelming majority of the seats in the House of Commons in the 1984 federal election. Progressive Conservative governments were in power in seven provinces. An eighth province, British Columbia, was governed by the Social Credit party, many of whose supporters vote for the Progressive Conservative party at the federal level. The circumstances seemed more amenable than usual to producing intergovernmental co-operation. If there was solidarity among Progressive Conservative governments, the numbers were available to produce constitutional amendments under the general amending formula.

In the first few months, Prime Minister Mulroney presided over a federal-provincial conference on the economy. It was choreographed well in advance so as to present the television audience with a good picture of good will and dedication to common goals. The communiqué, prepared well ahead of time, contained nothing of substance, but everyone involved seemed to agree that everyone had been agreeable. Prime Minister Mulroney also conducted a televised conference in which representatives of interest groups from across the country discussed the economic future of Canada. Not surprisingly, there was no consensus on a bold plan of action, but the process was supposed to be at least as much consultative as deliberative. The economic summit came and went without results, but without rancour.

The April '85 First Ministers' Conference was seen as an important test of Mulroney's skills as a conciliator. The government was, from the beginning, eager that a deal be reached.

The national level preparatory process leading up to the '85 First Ministers' Conference began with a ministerial level meeting in Ottawa on December 17 and 18, 1984. A few weeks earlier, at an attornies' general meeting in Toronto, the federal government had informed the provinces of some of the key elements of its strategy for the coming year: no last-minute surprises, a removal of certain nonconstitutional issues from the s.37 process, and an effort to develop an orderly and productive process for the talks after the 1985 conference leading to the last constitutionally-mandated conference in 1987. Some participants at the meeting expressed the view that there was unlikely to be an accord prior to 1987.

Accord Progression

December 17-18, Ottawa, Meeting at Ministerial Level

Aboriginal organizations were in attendance. Some of the provinces attempted to define the goal of April 1985 as a political accord not involving any constitutional amendments. The accord would include a workplan of preparations for the 1987 conference. The workplan would contain a schedule for continued national-level discussions but would also mandate regional discussions which would include the subject of self-government. At the 1987 conference, the parties would agree on what sort of constitutional protection should be afforded the results of regional negotiations.

Aboriginal organizations insisted that the goals of the April '85 conference include constitutional amendments.

The federal government reviewed the basic constitutional options:

1. Entrenchment of rights in general, indeterminate terms.
2. Entrenchment of rights in general terms, with the definition and realization of the rights entirely subject to regional negotiations and follow-up legislation. Of this character was the late, unlamented federal proposal at the March '84 conference (Discussed in Chapter XVIII).

3. A nonjusticiable statement of principles of rights (Chapters VII and XVIII).
4. A commitment in some form by governments to negotiate regional agreements to define rights of the aboriginal peoples. The results of the agreements would be constitutionally protected in the same way that treaties and modern land claims agreements already are (s.35(1) and 35(3) of the *Constitution Act, 1982*, as amended).
5. Same as (1), only the rights would not come into force until several years had passed, during which the parties would try to agree on definitions (Chapter IV).

Then the federal government announced that the most promising approach was a combination of a general statement of rights and option no. 4. The constitutional protection of the results of regional negotiations was a basic element of the joint proposal of aboriginal groups at the March '84 First Ministers' Conference. As there would be no constitutional protection for self-government rights unless there were first a regional agreement, the federal proposal should seem relatively unthreatening to provincial governments.

The federal proposal was an auspicious start. Zebedee Nungak of the Inuit Committee on National Issues (ICNI) proclaimed that the efforts of the minister of justice warranted ordering the pedestal of a statue with the minister's name on it.

On two issues which eventually emerged as pivotal, the federal proposals were indeterminate. Would the commitment by governments to negotiate regional agreements be justiciable? Could the federal government and an aboriginal community agree upon and "constitutionalize" a regional agreement without the consent of the province in which the community is situated?

February 21-22, Winnipeg, Officials' Level Meeting

Aboriginal organizations declined to attend. The federal government circulated a not very elaborate "elaboration" of its December ideas. One crucial point was made. The regional negotiations contemplated would not be confined to consideration of an ethnically-exclusive government on a land base belonging to an aboriginal collectivity. The Inuit had already expressed a preference for public governments in areas in which they constituted a majority. The same sort of approach might be appropriate for Métis and for Indians living in mixed communities. Some of the provinces expressed their concern that the phrase "self-government" might raise expectations among landless aboriginal peoples that they had a real chance to acquire a territory of their own. Certain provinces reiterated their objection to placing undefined phrases and commitments in the constitution and their preference for a strictly political accord at the April '85 First Ministers' Conference.

February 28, Toronto, Officials' Level Meeting

The first draft text was distributed by the federal government. The federal government had been reluctant to comply with the requests from some provinces that it draft a strictly political accord rather than take the lead on a constitutional accord only. The expedient it adopted at the February 28 meeting and at most subsequent meetings might be called the "push me-pull you" document. It would contain the material for both types of accord. There were many common elements to the two approaches, and many paragraphs would serve double-duty. When the approaches differed, two different versions of the same-numbered paragraph would be presented one after the other; or words appropriate to one approach only would appear in bracketed inserts to a paragraph; or there would be an annex whose survival depended on the ultimate choice of First Ministers. At the March 21 officials' level meeting, the federal government distributed a draft constitutional accord only but, at the insistence of certain provinces, reverted to push me-pull youism at the final officials' level meeting and the First Ministers' Conference.

The preamble of the federal draft of February 28 was, for the genre, refreshingly bland. It contained almost no implications that were subversive of aboriginal legal and political claims. A sharp lawyer might have noticed that among the sources of aboriginal rights referred to were "special rights flowing from their status as aboriginal peoples, from historical treaties, and from land claims settlements"—there was no mention of historical use and occupation of land. (The omission was never criticized and survived right through to the final federal drafts at the April '85 First Ministers' Conference.) The draft constitutional amendment began with: "35.2(1) The aboriginal peoples of Canada have the right to institutions of self-government within the context of the Canadian federation, defined by agreements or parts of agreements that are within the meaning of the expression "treaty rights" in subsection 35(1)".

A number of interpretations could be, and at various times were, offered for the phrase "within the context of the Canadian federation." It could mean that aboriginal governments are not a "third order of government," whatever that means (see Chapter

XVIII). "[W]ithin the context . . ." could mean that basic elements of Canadian constitutionalism, including the *Canadian Charter of Rights and Freedoms*, are binding on aboriginal governments. It could mean simply that aboriginal governments are not independent in the international sense. The end of the draft paragraph established that agreements on self-government would have the same constitutional protection as is provided by s.35(1) for treaties and land claims agreements. (What protection is that? No one knew. See Chapters XXI and XXIV.) The opening phrase attempts to accommodate aboriginal demands that there be general recognition of the "right to self-government." In this form, the recognition is more optical than legal. The right is made entirely dependent for its realization on federal and provincial governments coming to regional agreements with aboriginal communities. The next federal draft amendment did provide for some constitutional pressure on federal and provincial governments to negotiate and conclude agreements. It read:

> 35.2(2) Without altering the legislative authority of Parliament or of the provincial legislatures, or the rights of any of them with respect to the exercise of their legislative authority, the Government of Canada and the provincial governments are committed to:
>
> (a) participating in negotiations directed towards entering into agreements relating to institutions of self-government with representatives of communities all or a majority of the members of which are from among the aboriginal peoples of Canada and have expressed their desire to enter into those agreements; and
>
> (b) discussing with representatives of the aboriginal peoples of Canada from each province and from the Yukon Territory and Northwest Territories the timing and nature of the negotiations referred to in (a).

The opening phrase is the usual legal chemist's formula for nonjusticiability. (For earlier denunciations please see Chapters VII and XVIII. Is there any context in which the phrase would not be deplorable? Maybe the first line of a limerick.) Leaving aside its intrinsic lack of merit, the formula was inapt. The drafters of s.35.2(2) surely intended that only the commitment to negotiate would be nonjusticiable, but a court might have inferred that the agreements that resulted from the negotiations were also supposed to be nonjusticiable. Yet the major selling point of the federal proposal was its creation of a mechanism whereby certain agreements would be judicially protected from legislative interference.

On the other hand, the draft did not necessarily accomplish its authors' intention of making nonjusticiable the commitment to negotiate. The draft contained several potential encouragements for courts to intervene in a regional negotiation. The recognition of the right to self-government in s.35.2(1) might be given some force. The phrase "directed towards" in s.35.2(2) might be construed as requiring governments to go beyond discussing self-government with aboriginal communities; they might be required to advance reasonably forthcoming positions. A requirement of "good faith" might be read into the duty to negotiate, and "good faith" might, again, mean that federal and provincial governments have to make some real concessions to aboriginal autonomy. Never seriously discussed was the option of flatly stating that the commitment to negotiate was not justiciable. Perhaps participants were concerned that if they were plain-spoken, aboriginal organizations would condemn the amendment as having no more value than a strictly political commitment.

According to s.35.3 of the draft, agreements on self-government would be deemed to be "treaties" within the meaning of s.35(1) of the *Constitution Act, 1982* only "where the agreement includes a declaration to the effect that the agreement or part thereof as the case may be, is to be within the meaning of the expression 'treaty rights' in subsection 35(1) and the agreement is approved by an Act of Parliament and Acts of the legislatures of any provinces the governments of which are parties to the agreement". The parties would have to expressly concur that the government should count as a s.35(1) treaty, and there would have to be ratification by the legislature of a governmental party to the agreement. As argued in Chapter XXI, it makes sense to give parties the choice whether their agreements will be constitutionally protected. Many useful agreements might not be consummated due to fears of a governmental party about judicial interpretations that a government could not override or to changed circumstances that would require derogation from the original agreement. The requirement of legislative ratification was consistent with democratic principles. Irreversible changes to public ordering should not be made by executive decisions alone. There should be the opportunity for public criticism that is provided by a legislative debate. It should be observed that ratification is required only from "parties to the agreement." Apparently, it is not necessary from the provinces in which an aboriginal group is situated, unless the province is a party to the agreement.

The federal document that contained the constitutional drafts also contained the material for a strictly political accord similar in its requirements – including regional negotiations on self-government. A concluding section common to both accords committed the federal and provincial governments to entering into discussions to determine their respective responsibilities to aboriginal peoples. A few of the provinces proposed that the federal-provincial division of responsibilities be discussed on its merits at the April '85 First Ministers' Conference. It has been argued earlier in this study (Chapters XIV and XV) that regional negotiations on self-government would be greatly expedited if there was a simple and clear understanding among all parties of the lines of fiscal responsibility.

At the February 28 meeting, federal officials, as usual, resisted the proposal to come to grips with the fiscal responsibility issues. It is a good bet that the federal government did not want to have to shoot down suggestions that federal fiscal responsibility be extended and constitutionally formalized. It is a fair guess that the federal government, on the contrary, saw trilateral, federal-provincial-aboriginal, negotiations as an opportunity to reduce its fiscal commitments. Through the trilateral process, provincial governments would become increasingly enmeshed in the provision of programs and fiscal support for Indian communities.

March 11-12, Toronto, Meeting at Ministerial Level

Now that they finally had the attendance of senior political officials, aboriginal organizations returned to the table. The federal government had made a number of changes, a few of them major, to its document. The opening amendment on self-government now read: "35.01(1) The rights of the aboriginal peoples of Canada to institutions of self-government within the context of the Canadian federation, *when* defined by agreements or parts of agreements in accordance with s.35.02, are hereby recognized and affirmed" (emphasis added). The addition of the word "when" was intended to make it clear that until there is a self-government agreement, s.35.01(1) does not recognize and affirm rights to self-government.

Section 35.01(1) now served no positive purpose. Two clauses only were needed: one to state that governments had a duty to enter into regional negotiations on self-government, the other to state that certain agreements would be considered constitutionally recognized treaties. The original purpose of s.35.01(1), which was to legally suggest that there is some inherent right of aboriginal peoples to self-government, had by this time been thoroughly subverted by the drafting changes. Section 35.01 was now delusory. Worse still, it contained a subtle threat to the legal position of aboriginal peoples. A court might deduce that aboriginal groups had a constitutionally-protected right to self-government *only* if it was a party to a regional agreement. The word "hereby" in s.35.01 would only contribute to the impression that s.35.01 is where aboriginal rights to self-government are recognized—and not s.35(1) of the *Constitution Act, 1982*, where "aboriginal and treaty rights" are "recognized and affirmed."

Premier Hatfield of New Brunswick tossed in an alternative draft which aboriginal organizations found more appealing as a basis for further negotiations than the federal effort:

> 35.01.(1) The aboriginal peoples have the right to self-government within the Canadian federation as provided in this Part.
>
> (2) The government of Canada and where appropriate the provincial governments are committed to negotiate agreements to give effect to the right of the aboriginal peoples to self-government.
>
> (3) When an agreement concluded pursuant to subsection (2) is ratified by Parliament and by the legislature of a province which is party to the agreement, the agreement shall thereby be constitutionally recognized and affirmed.
>
> (4) Nothing in this Part alters the legislative authority of Parliament or provincial legislatures or the right of any of them to exercise its legislative authority.

The reference to "in this Part" in s.35.01(1) fudged the issue of whether s.35(1) of the *Constitution Act, 1982* recognizes the right of aboriginal peoples to self-government. Subsections (1) and (2) were otherwise far more simple and forthright than their equivalents in the federal draft. The affirmation of the right to self-government was certainly stronger. The only major problem with the New Brunswick draft, as the aboriginal organizations saw it, was subsection (4) – which had the effect of almost completely undermining all the good work that had come before. If "[n]othing in this Part alters the legislative authority of Parliament . . ." then what good is it? Isn't the purpose of Part II of the *Constitution Act, 1982* supposed to be that it protects the rights of aboriginal peoples from governmental interference?

Nova Scotia distributed a proposal that was weaker than the federal proposal, but which did contain constitutional elements. Under this proposal, the commitment to negotiate would be strictly political, but any agreements reached would be constitutionally protected. The accord used, instead of the term "self-government," the phrase "significant increased authority, and commensurate responsibility, of the Aboriginal Peoples for the government of their own affairs . . ." The government of Nova Scotia took the position that the term "self-government" was insufficiently understood to be included in a political commitment or a constitutional amendment. It might be interpreted as implying the authority to regulate a subject matter without any participation by another level of government. The basic elements of the Nova Scotia proposal were a political commitment to develop political autonomy for aboriginal peoples through negotiated agreements and a constitutional amendment to provide that the self-government agreements would be considered "treaties" for the purposes of s.35(1) of the *Constitution Act, 1982*. As will soon be seen, these basic elements of the Nova Scotia proposal would define the essence of the final negotiating text at the April '85 First Ministers' Conference.

A new element in the federal draft was a political commitment by governments on "Statistical Data Respecting Aboriginal Peoples." It recognized that federal and provincial governments needed "an improved socio-economic data base with respect to aboriginal peoples" and proposed federal-provincial co-operation and cost-sharing to obtain needed data in the course of the 1986 census. Under s.91(6) of the *Constitution Act, 1867*, "[t]he Census and Statistics" is a matter assigned to the exclusive authority of the federal level of government. I do not think, though, that the federal government has to pick up the entire tab for extra information that is compiled in order to assist provinces with their responsibilities (e.g. towards the Métis). The data-gathering proposal remained a part of the political and constitutional draft accords right through to the end of the April '85 First Ministers' Conference.

The original impulse behind the data-gathering proposal was the far more questionable plan the Métis National Council

(MNC) had advanced during the 1983-84 process for establishing a Métis registry system. A core community of Métis would be identified by reference to their descent from the individuals who were entitled to half-breed scrip under the *Manitoba Act* and *Dominion Lands Act*. Other Métis would be identified by the criteria of aboriginal ancestry and community acceptance. Appeal panels consisting of Métis, federal, and provincial appointees would decide contested cases. It is easy to sympathize with the desire of the Métis to reassure themselves and governments about the identity of their membership. The Métis had also been told by some governments that identifying their membership would be a necessary first step to giving them special rights. Yet there are serious considerations against establishing a Métis registry. It would be expensive. It would create hard feelings among those excluded. It would involve governments in the distasteful business of stamping people with an imprimatur of ethnic identity. And it would not be necessary. It may seem undeniable that you have to systematically establish the membership of a group in order to satisfy its legal and political demands. Like many utterly undeniable propositions, this one is false. The first response to "who is a Métis" should be "for what purpose do we need to know?" If you want to respond to Métis political aspirations by enhancing the authority of regional governments in which the Métis happen to be majority, you don't have to identify particular Métis. You only have to know approximately how many of them are in an area, and the number on a census might be entirely satisfactory. If you want to give the Métis representation on a governmental board, you can appoint a member of one of the provincial Métis organizations; there is no need for an official registry. For many programs, the identification of the Métis by individual self-identification or by the membership criteria established by a private organization may be entirely sufficient. A Canada-wide, all-purpose, official Métis registry is probably not necessary or desirable.

By the end of the March 11-12 meeting, there was considerable optimism among individuals involved in the process that there would be a limited constitutional deal in April. Several factors had contributed to the progress towards an agreement. The federal government had made its position known early. The new Conservative government wanted a concrete demonstration that it could bring about reconciliation and co-operation among Canadian power groups. The aboriginal organizations had stuck to a strategy of pushing for constitutional amendments and of remaining profoundly uninterested in a strictly political accord. The New Brunswick and Nova Scotia proposals had stimulated the drafting process. Insiders considered it unlikely that there would be a consensus on constitutionally entrenching a commitment to negotiate, but the chances seemed good that the parties would agree upon the mechanism whereby the results of negotiations could be constitutionally protected.

March 21, Ottawa, Officials' Level Meeting

Aboriginal organizations considered that sufficient progress had finally been made on the political front to justify their attendance at an officials' level meeting. They reiterated their preference for the plain-spoken New Brunswick proposals but, in the face of opposition to them by a number of provinces, participated in a detailed discussion of possible improvements to the latest federal draft. Some crucial legal and policy points were identified and squarely contested. The aboriginal organizations and a few provinces proposed that there be added to the federal draft a "non-derogation clause" with respect to the scope of s.35(1). They were concerned that the federal draft implied that self-government rights for aboriginal peoples would exist only if regional self-government agreements are achieved. Aboriginal groups claim that certain aboriginal and treaty rights to self-government were already recognized under s.35(1) of the *Constitution Act, 1982*. Why not supplement the regional agreement amendment with a clause to say that it is without prejudice to the scope of s.35(1)? There are at least half-a-dozen clauses in the *Constitution Act, 1982* that stipulate what another clause does not do. Example: s.26 of the *Charter of Rights*, "The guarantee in this *Charter* of certain rights and freedoms shall not be construed as denying the existence of any other rights or freedoms that exist in Canada".

The federal government resisted the inclusion of a non-derogation clause on the grounds that it would not be neutral. If you say the regional self-government agreement clause does not diminish the effect of s.35(1), aren't you implying that s.35(1) does in fact deal with self-government? I suggested that if you simply said "this clause does not affect" s.35(1), the obvious interpretation would be that s.35(1) would not be affected. This argument made no headway at all, nor did the more one-sided, non-derogation (as opposed to non-enhancement) drafting suggestions put forward by aboriginal groups at this and other meetings – until the first evening of the First Ministers' Conference when, in an effort to secure a deal, the federal government suggested its own wording of a non-derogation clause.

Another of my suggestions that did not meet with federal favour was that the range of legitimate possible outcomes of self-government negotiations be included in the package of constitutional amendments. The concerns of some provinces that "self-government" necessarily implies ethnic exclusivity, a land base, and quasi-provincial powers might be alleviated if the term were expressly defined as encompassing a broad variety of arrangements. Among them could be public regional governments in areas where aboriginal peoples form a majority, participation in governmental operations which specially affect aboriginal peoples, and support for aboriginal social and educational agencies. The final package advocated by the federal government did set out the range of options for self-government, but in its political commitments part, not in the constitutional amendments themselves. Writing the definition of self-government directly into the amendments might assuage the concerns of some governments and ought to be considered in the preparatory process leading up to the '87 First Ministers' Conference.

One of the provinces proposed that it be expressly stated that the province in which an aboriginal group is situated might agree before a regional self-government agreement can be constitutionally protected. The federal draft, like its December discussion paper, stated that the consent of all parties *to the agreement* was necessary. What if an affected province was not a party? The federal government said that it understood its text as allowing for constitutionalization only of tripartite agreements. There could be bilateral—federal-aboriginal or provincial-aboriginal—agreements on self-government, but they would not be eligible for constitutional protection. The federal interpretation of its own text was probably mistaken.

March 27, Ottawa, Officials' Level Meeting

One last officials' meeting was held. The draft federal amendments now began: "35.01(1) The rights of the aboriginal peoples of Canada to self-government, within the context of the Canadian federation, *that are* defined by agreements in accordance with s.35.02 are hereby recognized and affirmed" (emphasis added). The replacement of "when defined" with "that are" made the draft slightly more neutral about whether any self-government rights are contained in the "existing aboriginal and treaty rights" already "recognized and affirmed" in s.35(1) of the *Constitution Act, 1982*. Aboriginal organizations continued to press for an express non-derogation clause. As a result of other wording changes in the federal draft, it now hinted that provincial consent was a prerequisite to the constitutional protection of a self-government agreement. There were urgings that the role of the provinces be made explicit. The concern of the provinces over their role would be fully satisfied by s.35.02(6) of the opening federal proposal at the April '85 conference; and the concerns of aboriginal peoples over a non-derogation clause would not be. I suspect that the strategists at the federal government left the non-derogation clause out not for technical reasons, but in order to keep in reserve something of value to aboriginal organizations (but of no real cost to the governments). The non-derogation clause could then be "conceded" as part of a final round of negotiations. The concession that might have to be made to the provinces would be the softening or deletion of the commitment to negotiate.

The "without altering" incantation did not appear in the March 27 draft. No one seemed to miss it.

April 2-3, Ottawa, First Ministers' Conference

The proposal that the federal government would table at the '85 First Ministers' Conference was released the day before. Its key sections were the following:

> Rights to self-government
>
> 35.01(1) The rights of the aboriginal peoples of Canada to self-government, within the context of the Canadian federation, that are set out in agreements in accordance with section 35.02, are hereby recognized and affirmed.
>
> Commitment relating to negotiations for self-government
>
> (2) The government of Canada and the provincial governments are committed, to the extent that each has authority, to
>
> (a) participating in negotiations directed towards concluding, with representatives of aboriginal peoples living in particular communities or regions, agreements relating to self-government that are appropriate to the particular circumstances of those people; and

(b) discussing with representatives of aboriginal peoples from each province and from the Yukon Territory and Northwest Territories the timing, nature and scope of the negotiations referred to in paragraph (a).

(3) The government of Canada may invite the government of the Yukon Territory or the Northwest Territories to participate in negotiations referred to in paragraph 2(a) where the negotiations relate to communities or regions within the Yukon Territory or the Northwest Territories, as the case may be.

Application of 35.01(1)

35.02. The rights of the aboriginal peoples of Canada to self-government may, for the purpose of subsection 35.01(1), be set out in agreements concluded pursuant to paragraph 35.01(2)(a) with representative of aboriginal peoples that

(a) include a declaration to the effect that subsection 35.01(1) applies to those rights;

and

(b) are approved by an Act of Parliament and Acts of the legislatures of any provinces in which those aboriginal people live.

The April '85 First Ministers' Conference did not begin without a prayer. For the first time, it was in Inuktutuk. The elder who led the ceremony concluded it by presenting Prime Minister Mulroney with a wood-carved gavel. In another elegant but functional move on the symbolic front, the Inuit had convinced the leaders of aboriginal organizations to show up at the opening session wearing Nova Scotia tartan ties. Nova Scotia was understood to be a "swing" province, and the ties were the continuation of diplomacy by other means (Clausewitz 1976). Premier Buchanan had no choice but to send his officials out for some tartan ties, a quest that was successful in time for the premier's opening statement. He even had an extra for the prime minister.

In his opening statement, the prime minister spoke of his "determination to breath new life [into] and restore harmony to federal/provincial relations" (1985 FMC transcript, 3). Yet

> . . . I want to say that with the imperfections of any government, including the federal government, that we nonetheless will demonstrate our new approach at this Conference by not surprising you with initiatives for which you are not prepared nor adopting pressure tactics to try to move into the system with which you are not agreed. We are going to be up front and open (1985 First Ministers' Conference [FMC] transcript, 3).

The philosophical part of the speech was, on the surface at least, uncontentious. The prime minister used somewhat groupist language but did not present any particularly controversial vision of Canada. He attempted to portray aboriginal self-government as consistent with basic principles which almost all Canadian would agree upon: self-reliance, regional self-government, and respect for cultural diversity.

According to the prime minister, the solution to the social problem of aboriginal people was not "more welfare, more social workers, more programs . . . clearly history has shown that [this] is the way to dependency and misery. As George Manuel, the Indian leader whose work has contributed greatly to our being here, said, 'Indians are not seeking the best welfare system in the world' " (1985 FMC transcript, 8). Rather, "[t]he key to change is self-government for aboriginal peoples within the Canadian federation. . . . It is through self-government that a people can maintain its sense of pride and self-worth, and only through that that a people can maintain its sense of pride and self-worth which is necessary for happy and productive lives" (1985 FMC transcript, 10).

The prime minister portrayed aboriginal self-government as the continuation of Canadian tradition, "the creativity that Canadians have always shown in developing their own democratic institutions" (1985 FMC transcript, 10). He also said:

> Different forms of self-government already exist in Canada and most Canadians take them for granted. Apart from electing their federal and provincial governments, Canadians run their own school boards, village and town councils, and you name it. Canadians have also created regional governments when urban centres become too complex to be administered by a single council (1985 FMC transcript, 9).

According to the Prime Minister:

> In Canada, if you want to get a real good argument going, all flags flying in this country – including some people around this table – in Canada, we assume that our cultural and our linguistic backgrounds and traditions will be respected, even cherished and enhanced. Let somebody put a finger on them and see what happens. But Indian, Inuit and Métis people do not have this assurance, . . . nor the power to determine their own cultural development. In fact, there were times when aspects of their cultures were subject to legal sanctions and suppression (1985 FMC transcript, 10).

In the round of opening statements that followed, five provinces expressed their willingness to sign on to the federal proposal. They were Ontario, New Brunswick, Prince Edward Island, Manitoba, and Newfoundland. Two provinces seemed to be probable "no's": premiers Lougheed of Alberta and Bennett of British Columbia both maintained that they had been taking practical measures to improve the social life and governmental arrangements of aboriginal communities but that the federal draft amendments raised too many questions it could not answer. Quebec, as usual, could be counted on to express its sympathy for the aspirations of aboriginal peoples but to refuse to sign any political accord involving a constitutional amendment – and thereby lend the appearance of legitimacy to the patriation package that had gone forward to Great Britain in 1982 without Quebec's consent. Premier Levesque found it ironic that governments were interested now in recognizing the collective rights of aboriginal peoples; the rest of Canada had refused to admit the existence of a distinct nation in Canada whose homeland was Quebec. Individual rights are fundamental at some point, but a person belongs to a human community. The people of Quebec had been treated as a collection of individuals, whereas in reality "le Québec français possède un caractère indiscutablement national" – French Canada has, incontrovertibly, the character of a nation (1985 FMC transcript, 44).

Seven provinces are needed to amend the constitution. At the end of the opening round, there appeared to be five "yeahs", two probable "no's", one abstention – and two maybes. The provinces that might come around were Nova Scotia and Saskatchewan. After donning his Nova Scotia tie and passing on one to the prime minister, Premier Buchanan expressed his support for the development of enhanced political authority for aboriginal groups. His government was, however, "reluctant to use the words self-government until there is a much greater measure of shared understanding of the words for inclusion in the supreme law of Canada and within the context of the Canadian federation" (1985 FMC transcript, 57-58). Nova Scotia and Nova Scotians have, however, "long been known for our fairness, equality, a sense of justice and rightness, and our understanding. And ... those qualities will not be missing for myself and the members of our delegation over the next two days" (1985 FMC transcript, 59).

Saskatchewan was concerned about the nature of the commitments in the federal proposal and the possibility of judicial intervention to define and enforce them. Premier Devine was not, however:

> ... a man who seeks confrontation. I cannot think of anybody else in Canada who I would rather co-operate with than the Chairman. I prefer a hug to confrontation – give me a hug. See, it works every time.
>
> In previous negotiations, Mr. Prime Minister, there have been serious and honest differences in discussion, but in my view, common sense has prevailed (1985 FMC transcript, 72).

While aboriginal organizations do not have a "vote" that is recognized by the amending formulae in the Canadian constitution, the support of at least some of them is a political prerequisite for any amendments on aboriginal self-government. The rejection of the package by most aboriginal organizations would relieve the moral and political pressure on wavering provinces and indeed make it illegitimate for governments to proceed.

The opening statement of the Assembly of First Nations (AFN) did not expressly reject the federal proposal. It did, however, insist that "any relationship with Canada must begin with the basic unqualified constitutional recognition" of the inherent right of Indian Nations to self-government (1985 FMC transcript, 23).

The Native Council of Canada's (NCC) opening statement found that the federal proposals "[fell] significantly short of meeting the needs of [its] constituents" (1985 FMC transcript, 28). Still, "[it] is a proposal from which we can start, on which we can build" (1985 FMC transcript, 28, comma added). There ought to be a clear recognition of the right of aboriginal groups to self-government. The NCC would not press the issue of federal responsibility for all aboriginal peoples under s.91(24) of the *Constitution Act, 1867* but considered "equality for all Aboriginal Peoples" a "critical issue" that would have to be dealt with in the ongoing process. The opening statement of the MNC on the federal proposal was noncommittal. The objectives of the MNC at the conference were defined as seeking the constitutional entrenchment of the recognition of the right of the Métis to self-government and to secure a land base.

The Inuit Committee on National Issues (ICNI) had the most upbeat opening statement; it stressed that "this document [the federal draft] represents the closest the Constitutional process has come to producing a workable amendment on self-government. . . . we cannot afford to allow the remaining obstacles to stand in our way" (1985 FMC transcript, 26).

One other aboriginal organization should be mentioned. A faction within the AFN, the Prairie Treaty Nations Alliance (PTNA), had asked for a separate seat at the April '85 conference. They had cited the precedent of the agreement at the March '83 conference whereby the MNC, which had split from the NCC, had been allowed its own seat. Although the AFN had supported the request of the PTNA, the prime minister had rejected it the day before the conference (1985 FMC transcript, 110).

The highlight of the afternoon was the candid but spirited defence of the federal proposal by the minister of justice, John Crosbie. He attempted to calm the anxieties of the premier of Saskatchewan, Grant Devine, that the meaning of "self-government" was not understood and that the prospect of special political rights for Indians in urban centres was troubling. Crosbie contended that:

- if there are no regional agreements, there are no rights;

- given all the possible varieties of self-government, there is no way to define them in advance;

- the only commitment that governments would be making would be to negotiate; no particular results are guaranteed;

- special political rights for Indians in a place like Regina are probably not appropriate, and probably would not be agreed to;

- the proposed federal amendment is "pretty well nonjusticiable"; the most the courts could do would be to remind politicians "that they were breaking their word and not carrying on in good faith" (1985 FMC transcript, 138);

- "we have to have an act of faith here ... I remember Mr. Chairman – if I might get parochial – it was 36 years ago on Sunday past that Newfoundland joined Confederation. That was a leap in the dark. I am not going to say how it ended up. The Atlantic Accord brought some light, I do not mind saying that.... If Newfoundland had waited for it all to be defined and then signed, we would not be part of Canada. We would have all the oil and gas and all the fish. We would not have to share them with the Prime Minister. As a matter of fact, Mr. Chairman, they voted in Newfoundland to confederate, and then they negotiated the terms of the union. Now, how is that for an act of faith?" (1985 FMC transcript, 139-140).

At the end of the afternoon, Prime Minister Mulroney proposed that there be a backroom meeting at the ministerial level, commencing at 8:00 that evening, to try to reach common ground. The attorney general of Manitoba, Mr. Roland Penner, asked, "A point of clarification, if I may, Mr. Chairman. You suggested a rather limited list [of officials for the meeting] and I presume Ministers like myself who do not know much about the law can bring at least our legal advisors. I would not dare enter a room with John Crosbie without my legal advisor close by" (1985 FMC transcript, 183). Although this remark was broadcast live on network television, no one asked for my autograph, or even free legal advice, as I walked over to the meeting rooms.

After about half-an-hour of discussion, there appeared among the "maybe" and "probably not" provinces no greater amenability to the federal package. The chairman asked whether it was time to give up. The Nova Scotia delegation had a question for the aboriginal organizations. In order to reach a deal, would they agree to move the commitment to negotiate regional self-government agreements out of the constitutional amendments and into the political part of the federal draft? The advantage of the proposal for reluctant provinces is that it would relieve their anxieties about being hauled into court over the way they conducted their negotiations. Some of the aboriginal organizations seemed willing to discuss a softening of the commitments clause. Shortly thereafter, in response to a note from a person who was "not his wife," the minister of justice recessed the meeting.

It is known that the prime minister met Premier Devine that evening, and it is reported that it was a mixture of hugging and mugging. When the meeting reconvened, the Saskatchewan delegation proposed a compromise set of constitutional amendments. The commitment to negotiate would be political only, but otherwise, the amendments were essentially the same as the federal ones. The federal government did not definitely accept the Saskatchewan proposal but did immediately propose to add a non-derogation clause. The version it included in the next day's draft read: "Nothing in this section abrogates or derogates from any rights to self-government, or any other rights, of the aboriginal peoples of Canada".

The elements of the final deal were now in place. The chairman proposed that the First Ministers reconvene early the next morning. Just before they did, the British Columbia delegation introduced a last-minute recipe for turning a soft agreement into mush. Instructions: replace the phrase "within the context of the Canadian federation" with a phrase like "within the context of the sovereign authority of Canada and the provinces." The only remaining selling point of the federal package for aboriginal peoples was that it constitutionally allowed the regional agreements on self-government to be constitutionally "recognized and affirmed." The value to aboriginal peoples of having agreements "recognized and affirmed" by the Constitution would be that the agreements would, at least to some extent, be protected from the exercise of the sovereign authority of Parliament and the provincial legislatures. Aboriginal organizations rejected the British Columbia proposal outright at the final backroom ministerial meeting, and Prime Minister Mulroney characterized it as "eviscerating" when Premier Bennett unveiled it the next day.

The morning session of the First Ministers was delayed for more than two hours while a backroom meeting failed to agree on any substantial alteration to the previous night's deal. Some of the aboriginal organizations pressed unsuccessfully for the removal of the "provincial veto" over the constitutional protection of a regional self-government agreement. Provinces maintained, among other things, that they should be able to protect their interests and that there would be greater popular support for aboriginal self-government that was discussed and ratified by provincial legislatures. The meeting adjourned with the understanding that federal officials would draft a final proposal.

The morning session of the second day of the First Ministers' Conference began and was largely occupied, for the third straight time, by a discussion of sexual equality. It was generally agreed that even if the matter was already adequately covered, a fourth sexual equality clause ought to be added to the constitution; the remaining anxieties of aboriginal women would be quelled, and the matter would finally be removed from the s.37 process. The prime minister proposed a backroom meeting of legal advisors to draft some sort of generally tolerable wording. He then recessed the meeting for a "short coffee break." The federal government had decided to endorse the deal of the previous evening—making the commitment to negotiate a political promise only and adding a non-derogation clause. Prime Minister Mulroney summoned senior aboriginal leaders, one organization at a time, to persuade them to accept.

Hours later, when the meeting reconvened, Prime Minister Mulroney formally circulated the final draft and asked for the reaction of the provincial premiers. The two "maybe" provinces, Nova Scotia and Saskatchewan, were now on board. The five "yes" provinces were then consulted. They were prepared to accept the final package, although several of them—including Ontario and Manitoba—would not give a definitive answer until they had heard from the aboriginal organizations. There were now enough provinces to produce a constitutional amendment. Prime Minister Mulroney had ignored the request of the "no" provinces to speak, apparently wishing to have the maximum pressure on them build up. British Columbia was prepared to accept the deal if its "sovereign authority" mushifier was inserted. Alberta would seek legal advice about the effects of the final deal but remained disinclined to entrench. Naturally, Prime Minister Mulroney started with aboriginal delegations which he knew would sign: the NCC and the MNC. Before recognizing Mr. Harry Daniels of the MNC, Prime Minister Mulroney had "a word that [he] ought to have made yesterday." He promised to convene and chair a conference specifically devoted to the problems of the Métis and non-status Indians. Mr. Daniels asked for a short break to consult with the president of the MNC. The deal had been worked out beforehand, but Mr. Daniels wanted to make sure about one aspect of it. A minute or two later, he asked the prime minister whether the agenda of the promised conference would include the need for a land base for the Métis. "Yes", said the prime minister. "You have our support," concluded Mr. Daniels.

The ICNI was known by the federal government to be a reluctant "no." It did not want to block the agreement but it was distressed by the implications for the Inuit of Northern Quebec and Labrador of the "provincial veto" over the constitutional protection of self-government agreements and, to a lesser extent, by the de-constitutionalization of the commitment to negotiate. Several provinces had accepted the final federal proposal. Prime Minister Mulroney had just established that two of the aboriginal organizations were ready to go along. The force of the probable rejection of the package by the AFN had been diminished when the prime minister publicly announced (while Mr. Daniels consulted his president) that the PTNA, a very large breakaway faction of the AFN, supported the package. The ICNI would have to bear much of the responsibility for a failure to produce an accord.

Zebedee Nungak spoke on behalf of the ICNI, and his conclusion was:

> I have great respect for what has been accomplished here this afternoon, but, unfortunately, because of the conditions and concerns that I have expressed to you, and because we feel that our people in the various far flung communities of the North deserve a chance to examine and take part in a decision that we, as leaders here, would be forced to make, leaves us no recourse other than to say, no, but with the condition that we have a very solid hope that if further meetings could take place within the next year, solutions that we are seeking and the concerns that we have will be addressed in a substantial way (1985 FMC transcript, 272).

Prime Minister Mulroney seized on the references to further consultation among the Inuit:

> Just before you do, I will try and see if we can begin the process of transforming a reluctant no into an embryonic yes . . . I think the Premiers could, I hope, keep their consent on hold for a period of time, say, six weeks or two months, during which you could consult with your people back home. If that were acceptable, and if the results were positive, you could convey them to me (1985 FMC transcript, 273).

It is not clear what Prime Minister Mulroney had in mind. Was he proposing that the parties tentatively agree on the final package, with the understanding that the deal would be off if the

Inuit later decided against it? The possibility had been suggested to the Inuit by federal officials. It would not have been a pleasant one for the Inuit. Dissolving an agreement already in place is even more stressful than preventing the agreement from happening in the first place.

The Inuit representatives, Zebedee Nungak and John Amagoalik, responded favourably but seem to have understood the prime minister's proposal as a delay in going ahead, rather than going ahead with an option on the part of the Inuit to pull everyone back. Prime Minister Mulroney responded:

> My intention is not to adjourn the meeting. My intention is to proceed and to hear a final presentation from the AFN but to give you ample time to hold the matter in abeyance pending your checking with your people up North and letting us know. In other words, we would not proceed – I think we could probably hold things up until we heard from you. . . . . We will, hopefully, have an agreement, with a suspensive condition on your part we could agree to but nothing that would take place that would prejudice your rights, give you ample time to consult with people back home and let us know (1985 FMC transcript, 275).

The last sentence is rather confusing but seems to imply that there would be an agreement by the end of the day, with some provision to allow the Inuit to consider and then (it is not clear) decide that they would not be affected by the agreement. The earlier part of the quote seems to say that the entire agreement would not go ahead unless and until the Inuit agreed. Perhaps Prime Minister Mulroney was mulling over the different options. After Mary Simon of the ICNI elaborated on the organization's concern, Prime Minister Mulroney stated:

> As agreed, Zebedee [sic], we will readily acknowledge on behalf of our colleagues that it would be fair that you have the opportunity of going back and consulting with your principals and your colleagues. I would think that a two-month delay would not be abusive at all in the circumstances. If that is okay, we will work that out in the mechanisms of consultation here (1985 FMC transcript, 278).

Was he still mulling?

The AFN was finally given its turn. Mr. George Erasmus briefly explained its objections. Like the ICNI, the AFN objected to the "provincial veto" and the deconstitutionalization of the duty to negotiate. Unlike the ICNI, the AFN insisted that there should be a clear recognition of the inherent right of aboriginal peoples to self-government. When Mr. Erasmus said his colleague wanted to make a few statements, Prime Minister Mulroney attempted to staunch the flow of negativity: "I think we have agreed, Colleagues, in fairness, that there would be one spokesman. I don't mean to cut anyone off, but there should be one spokesman per group. I think we have had that privilege, and I thank you all for it" (1985 FMC transcript, 282). Had the prime minister really forgotten that he had just recognized three speakers from the ICNI?

He almost immediately relented. After sizable speeches from leaders of the AFN, Prime Minister Mulroney summarized. The final federal draft accord had the support in principle of seven provinces, two of the four aboriginal groups at the table, and of the PTNA. A few delegations – Alberta and the ICNI – wanted more time to study the proposal. Could the prime minister have pushed ahead? The three provinces definitely outside of the accord would have had almost 50 per cent of the Canadian population; the two westernmost provinces would be imposed upon by a government that was supposed to end western alienation; the ICNI had not agreed, and its delegation was highly respected for its technical understanding and accommodating attitude. The AFN was still the only representative of status Indians, and its rejection of the proposal was firm. It might have tarnished the conciliatory image of the new government to push ahead with the amendment despite the dissenters.

On the other hand, British Columbia and Alberta could have "opted out" of the amendment insofar as it affected the rights and privileges of their legislatures and governments, *Constitution Act, 1982*, s.38(3). The "non-derogation" clause of the draft amendments would have preserved the legal claim of the AFN that Indian groups had an inherent right to self-government. If any band in the AFN did not take advantage of the provision allowing it to constitutionalize self-government no one would force it to. The only prejudice to aboriginal peoples of the deal was relative to a better deal that might be made in 1987.

Prime Minister Mulroney concluded that he did not have to decide immediately. He proposed that the parties reconvene a few months later, at the ministerial level. By then, the ICNI and the Alberta government would have had an opportunity to complete their reflections and consultations. He did not pursue the option of pushing for a tentative agreement immediately, with the Inuit having the option of scuttling it later on. The pressure on the Inuit might have been irresistible. Perhaps the Prime Minister figured that it was dangerous to push for even a tentative agreement. Provinces deferential to the dissenting opinions of sister provinces or the AFN might have balked. By delaying the day of decision, the federal government would have extra time to press the ICNI. The conference would end without definitely having failed.

June 6-7, Toronto, Meeting at Ministerial Level

There was no breakthrough at the follow-up meeting. The ICNI and the government of Alberta had not changed their minds. A backroom officials' level meeting was held to try to draft a sexual equality clause. The prime minister had proposed such a meeting on the second day of the conference, but it was more or less forgotten in all the excitement over the self-government deal. It is difficult to devise a sensible solution to a legal problem that does not exist, and the effort failed.

The Maestro Conducts a Meeting

The format of the s.37 process makes backroom manoeuvering and conference technique far more important than it ought to be. Constitutional reform ought to take place under public scrutiny and with the benefit of public discussion. What happens instead is that there is a series of closed-door officials' and ministerial meetings; negotiating texts are publicly disclosed the opening day of the First Ministers' Conference; and agreement, if any, is reached on the basis of the decision of First Ministers about texts that are finally settled at meetings of officials and ministers over a two-day period.

Prime Minister Mulroney used a number of clever negotiating techniques at the April '85 Conference. Among them may have been:

- holding in reserve something that cost his government very little to give up, and then "conceding it" when the crunch comes (hence the non-derogation clause);
- recognizing at the conference table speakers known to be favourable to his position first, and only then allowing potential dissenters to speak – by which time they may not be able to resist the momentum;
- trying to limit the number of speakers from a delegation that is speaking against his position (e.g. the final speaker of the AFN);

- pre-arranging conversations that will take place at a larger gathering (e.g., the Mulroney-Daniels swap);
- preparing in advance not only the opening statement of the prime minister, but many of the interventions and those of other federal ministers, during open discussions (I have no hard proof on this score. It is my impression based on the content and delivery of a number of federal speeches, quips, and "spontaneous" outbursts. For example, at the backroom ministerial level meeting on the first day, a senior federal minister said that he hadn't been planning to say anything but felt compelled to by the course of the discussion. He then delivered a detailed, well-crafted, politically pointed address of some length.);
- pressuring potential dissenters at one-on-one backroom meetings;
- multiplying, dividing, and conquering potential dissenters; e.g., reading out the letter from the PTNA in order to undermine the probable opposition from the AFN. (As the NCC is likely to again support federal initiatives, it can be expected that the prime minister will continue to invite them to the '87 conference, even though a great many non-status Indians (the NCC's main constituency) will have been reinstated by the operation of a statute enacted in 1985. The prime minister did not allow the PTNA its request for a separate seat at the April '85 First Ministers' Conference, but the PTNA's support for his position has surely enhanced their chances in 1987.

In a little political fable that appeared a few years ago in the Toronto Globe and Mail, the novelist Margaret Atwood named the Mulroney character "King Stroke." Much of the prime minister's performance at the First Ministers' Conference might be described as utterly fabulous.

Here are some of the personal compliments of the prime minister to the premiers in response to their opening addresses:

Premier Miller, Ontario	"Thank you, Mr. Premier, for a very thoughtful statement of national leadership by the Government of Ontario" (1985 FMC transcript, 41).
Premier Levesque, Quebec	"Merci, Monsieur Levesque, I would be personally hard pressed to improve upon a statement of accomplishment

	and intention that powerful and compelling and I thank Premier Levesque for his intervention" (1985 FMC transcript, 53).
Premier Buchanan, Nova Scotia	"May we turn to the distinguished Premier of Nova Scotia." And after his speech, "As a former member for Central Nova with great pride I listened to your remarks and I thank you, sir, for them" (1985 FMC transcript, 56, 59).
Premier Hatfield, New Brunswick	Prime Minister Mulroney saved his praise for the next day. ". . . [P]remier Hatfield who has over many, many years taken an eloquent position in this regard (1985 FMC transcript, 188)."
Premier Lee, P.E.I.	"May I turn to the Chairman of the Conference of Premiers, whose, may I say, leadership and good work has certainly facilitated our initiatives, not only in this, but in the Regional First Ministers' Conference and in other areas, and I thank you for that Jim, and I invite you to please proceed" (1985 FMC transcript, 61).
Premier Devine, Saskatchewan	"I now welcome Premier Devine, who welcomed us with such warmth in Saskatchewan in January." And at the end of his speech, "Thank you for your thoughtful remarks. In the spirit of Mr. Levesque, we will invoke the words of Isaiah and

> we will reason together" (1985 FMC transcript, 66, 72).

Premier Peckford of Newfoundland had to stay home for election day, and so was not available for the dispensation of verbal sunshine. Premiers Lougheed of Alberta and Bennett of British Columbia were opposed to the federal proposal and not likely to change and, accordingly, went unpraised. Premier Pawley of Manitoba was a member of the New Democratic Party and a strong supporter of the federal initiative. It was thus neither desirable nor necessary to say anything but: "May I turn please to Premier Pawley of Manitoba." And after his speech, "Thank you, Mr. Premier" (1985 FMC transcript, 53, 56).

Program Notes

The participants in the s.37 process were not far from agreement in April 1985. The final federal proposal will be the basis for the national level preparatory discussions leading up to the '87 First Ministers' Conference, the last one that is constitutionally mandated.

It should not be expected that further discussions will take place at the national, multiparty, s.37 level only. A number of provinces will probably begin discussions on self-government with selected aboriginal communities or organizations. The federal government will likely proceed with administrative changes that will result in enhanced autonomy—though not necessarily enhanced funding—for Indian governments. There will be continued efforts to develop the authority of the government of the Northwest Territories and to consider the division of the Territories in order to create a predominantly Inuit political unit. The participants at the '87 First Ministers' Conference should have a little better appreciation of the meaning and practical problems of self-government.

It is worth considering how the final federal proposal of April 1985 might be improved, or how it might be changed in order to bring about more widespread agreement. The two types of alteration, unfortunately, are not necessarily identical.

It does not seem likely that many governments are going to agree to acknowledge that aboriginal groups have a "right to self-government." The highly convoluted form of the federal amendments might be viewed as an attempt at the old, hidden-absence-of-ball trick. Most participants were not fooled. The amendments could be simplified and condensed without doing any real harm to the legal position of aboriginal organizations.

The range of meanings for "self-government" might be included in a constitutional amendment. If it were stipulated that self-government does not necessarily mean ethnically-exclusive government on a land base, some provinces might be more comfortable about entrenching a commitment to negotiate regional self-government agreements. If the commitment to negotiate is restored to the draft constitutional amendments, it should be placed in a time frame. Governments ought not to be able to delay negotiations indefinitely. Aboriginal organizations, on the other hand, should be encouraged to press their demands indefinitely. Sometimes governments will be justified, after negotiations, in completely or partly rejecting the proposals of an aboriginal community. The s.37 participants might consider something like a fifteen-year period in which the constitutional duty to negotiate would be operative. There could be a commitment to hold First Ministers' Conferences at five-year intervals to monitor progress and exchange the lessons of experience.

The "provincial veto" over giving constitutional protection to the results of self-government agreements is a legitimate cause of concern for aboriginal groups. It allows a party that may not have contributed constructively to discussions to interfere in the relations of parties who have actually reached agreement. On the other hand, the provincial veto does not preclude bilateral, federal-aboriginal agreements—it only prevents them from receiving constitutional recognition. The provincial veto does contribute to the procedure for democratic review of processes that may seriously and irreversibly change the way Canada is governed. I tend to think the democratic argument outweighs the concern about gratuitous meddling. In Chapter XXI, I suggested a possible compromise—provinces would not be given a "veto," but rather a bilateral self-government agreement would not be constitutionally protected unless and until it had been tabled at a First Ministers' Conference. The process of democratic scrutiny would be enhanced, and there would be a built-in necessity for First Ministers to meet once in awhile to focus their attention on aboriginal issues.

The final federal proposal of April 1985 contained no constitutional amendments relating to fiscal responsibility. The political part of the accord contained no principles or commitments, other than an undertaking by governments to discuss among themselves and with aboriginal organizations the federal-provincial division of powers and responsibilities. As fiscal disputes are likely to delay or even frustrate negotiations on self-government, it is essential that parties finally come to grips with the issue.

At the April '85 conference almost everyone agreed that a mechanism should be created whereby the results of regional negotiations on self-government would be "constitutionally recognized and affirmed." It is about time that the participants attempt to figure out what sort of constitutional protection would be consequent.

Cadenza: Some Talk About the Absence of Talk about the Talks about Agreeing to Talk about Agreeing

In 1982, the First Ministers made a constitutional commitment to hold a First Ministers' Conference the next year to attempt to identify and define the rights of the aboriginal peoples of Canada.

In 1983, they met and constitutionally entrenched a commitment to hold at least two more First Ministers' Conferences.

In 1985, they came close to agreeing to a political commitment to enter into discussions with aboriginal communities on self-government.

Some community-level discussions will take place prior to 1987, despite the failure of the First Ministers to agree on a general commitment to hold them. Such a commitment may very well be made in 1987, in which case there will be many such negotiations. Some changes for the better – and maybe some for the worse – may then result.

Although the focus of the process thus far has been on talk, the level of discussion that has taken place by participants in the process has not been inspiring. At the preparatory stages, there has been an almost total failure to engage in serious discussions of the legal and policy details associated with self-government. There have been some interesting philosophical presentations by aboriginal organizations (as well as some counter-productive rhetoric) but not many substantive responses by provincial officials. Some of the First Ministers have been more frank and thoughtful than others in their contributions to discussions at the conferences, but time is severely limited at the meetings, and many First Ministers confine themselves to the usual inoffensive, vague, political speeches.

Almost entirely left out of the whole process has been the public. It is true that participants at preparatory meetings may be a little more relaxed and a little more candid because they know that the proceedings are confidential. There is no adequate justification, however, for governments not releasing their position papers and draft proposals as the process moves along. It is entirely unacceptable for a democratic country to change its fundamental law without enabling the general public to inform themselves of the options and make their opinions known to the decision makers. We accept it, but it is unacceptable.

I should add that not only is the general public not informed about what is going on, it is pretty well kept in the dark about what went on. Is there any reason for the transcripts of preparatory meetings to be kept confidential indefinitely? They ought to be made available to the press, to scholars, and to the public immediately after the relevant First Ministers' Conference.

I am trying not to be naive about the other barriers to informed public discussion of constitutional reform concerning aboriginal peoples. The press and media do not always do a very good job of getting the facts straight, let alone explaining their implications. Maclean's, which styles itself as Canada's "weekly newsmagazine," concluded its reporting on the Yellowknife constitutional meeting with an account of an agreement supposedly reached there. In fact, the agreement referred to was the product of almost entirely unrelated land claims negotiations that were taking place at the same time. If not hampered by the secrecy associated with the s.37 process, however, the media would undoubtedly do a better job of informing and stimulating public debate.

Another barrier to informed public discussion is the political and practical pressures on the persons who could lead the debate, the politicians. Politicians have to severely ration the time they give to actually thinking about substantive issues, and many of them are not well-informed or reflective about aboriginal rights issues. Some of those who do have ideas are guarded about sharing them with the public. No politician wants to appear reactionary: sincere and sometimes reasonable concerns about enhancing the various rights of aboriginal peoples tend to be left unvoiced. Instead, the politicians with doubts stall, delay, mumble – or agree to more talks. Progress for aboriginal groups might actually be accelerated if the discussions were more candid. Unfounded objections by governments to aboriginal aspirations might be abandoned in the light of informed criticism, while legitimate concerns might be accepted by aboriginal groups and some sort of accommodation reached.

There is a group in society that is supposed to have the independence and the ability to frankly explore the development of public policy with respect to aboriginal peoples. The group is the academics. Unfortunately, we have not always supplied the searching and balanced criticism that might be hoped for. In February 1985, the Queen's Institute of Intergovernmental Relations sponsored a meeting on aboriginal self-government. It invited academics, governmental officials and representatives of aboriginal organizations. The plan was to have a forum in which people could candidly express their real concerns and aspirations. They could drop the usual posturing, speak as individuals, and maybe enhance their understanding or contribute to that of others. The public and the press were excluded in order to reduce inhibitions. Perhaps the discussion was still not as frank in all respects as it could have been. Toward the end of the conference, one of the Indian representatives mentioned that Canadian academics are sometimes criticized for "cheerleading" on behalf of aboriginal political claims. And then he asked, "what's wrong with that?" If another group in society, the academics, helps to persuade the Canadian public as a whole to satisfy the demands of aboriginal peoples, that could only be to the good.

But it isn't. I do not believe that political justice necessarily lies half-way between competing positions. It may not even lie in between. Sometimes, there is justice on the side of one group of claimants and fear, hatred, stupidity, and self-interest on the other. I do believe that constitutional reform with respect to aboriginal peoples is an area where there is a need to develop structures and principles that will accommodate the just concerns of many different groups. There are enough skilled politicians, technical employees, and consultants available that academics are not needed to act as servants and mouthpieces for the competing interests. Their function ought to be to supply independent criticism and creative suggestions. The principal function of academics, and the reason for their special privileges—including tenure, small teaching loads, academic freedom, unstructured work weeks—is to honestly, if necessary, courageously seek out and disseminate knowledge. In political and legal matters, individual conscience is as important as rationality. There is wide room for academics of integrity to disagree. A position that is extreme may be correct or at least responsible. It may be legitimate for an academic to conclude that absolutely everything an aboriginal group or a government wants is just and workable. That belief must be based, however, on an attempt to assess the merits of opposing views and without regard to what is popular with the general public, the academic community, or the marketplace.

One of the constraints on the contribution to the debate by Canadian academics may be a certain scarcity of workers in the area. There are not that many political science, public policy, native studies, and public law academics in the country, and most of them are busy with other things besides institutional reform with respect to aboriginal peoples. The inaccessibility of much of the transcripts and documents discussed at the preparatory stages may discourage academic commentators who might otherwise have valuable contributions to make. Among those academics who do attempt to make scholarly criticism of the process, there are two factors that sometimes distort the perspective. One factor is the existence or prospect of a professional association with one of the political organizations involved in the reform process. Many academics acquire their knowledge of the process from first-hand participation in aboriginal matters as paid consultants to aboriginal organizations or governments. When writing or speaking in the academic mode, we do not always succeed in detaching ourselves from the self-persuasion or political sympathy that arises from an advocacy role. The desire to remain popular with current or potential clients may also colour attempts at independent and forthright criticism.

The second tendency is zealotry. An academic may be so sincerely outraged by the injustice that has been done to aboriginal groups that he or she loses the ability to rationally and fairly assess the merits of differing evaluations of the past or proposals for the future. Again, it is not necessarily true that justice lies somewhere in between; it is the duty of a scholar to assess with intellectual rigour, as well as humane concern, whether it does.

If we're going to talk, let's talk.

Chapter XXIII

The Amendments on Sexual Equality

The aim of this section is to bring to light the underground war that has taken place in the s.37 process with respect to the drafting of a constitutional amendment on sexual equality. It has been a weird series of battles of which the public had practically no knowledge, and even some of the senior participants in the s.37 process had very little. The 1982-83 campaign ended with the substantial strengthening of the legal position of all aboriginal and treaty rights. These gains were almost annihilated at the end of the 1983-84 campaign—but emerged intact.

The Necessity of an Amendment on Sexual Equality

Any account of why an amendment on sexual equality was strongly lobbied for at the March '83 conference would have to begin with mention of s.12(1)(b) of the *Indian Act*. (On the history of s.12(1)(b), see Jamieson 1978.) Under s.11(1)(f) of the *Indian Act*, when a status Indian man married a non-Indian woman, the latter was entitled to registration as an Indian. In contrast, s.12(1)(b) revoked the Indian status of an Indian woman who married a non-Indian man. In *Attorney General of Canada* v. *Lavell* (1973), 38 D.L.R. (3d) 481, the Supreme Court of Canada held that the section did not violate the guarantee of "equality before the law" in s.1(b) of the *Canadian Bill of Rights*. The challenge had been brought by two Indian women who had lost their status by the operation of s.12(1)(b). Their action was supported by the Native Council of Canada (NCC), the organization then representing non-status Indians and Métis, but was opposed by a number of Indian organizations, including the National Indian Brotherhood (NIB), the forerunner of the Assembly of First Nations (AFN). Among the concerns of the Indian groups who filed interventions were that the Court would find the whole *Indian Act* invalid as a form of racial discrimination, that some bands might face an unmanageable influx of persons to whom status was restored or provided by the Court's decision, and that the general ability of governments and bands to establish membership criteria would be seriously impaired.

The majority judgment of Ritchie J. in *Lavell* is difficult to follow, but it seems to be based primarily on the proposition that it was not the intention of Parliament in enacting the *Canadian Bill of Rights* to repeal the *Indian Act* or to abandon its constitutional authority over Indians. That proposition is essentially valid, but it does not preclude the conclusion that particular sections of a federal statute on Indians discriminate in ways that are not warranted by the goals of legitimate federal Indian policy. Ritchie J. himself had written the majority opinion in *The Queen* v. *Drybones* (1969), 9 D.L.R. (3d) 473, a case that held s.95(b), formerly s.94(b) of the *Indian Act* inoperative because it ran contrary to the guarantee of racial equality in the *Canadians Bill of Rights*. (The section made it an offence for an Indian to be intoxicated off a reserve.) There is no close examination in *Lavell* of whether s.12(1)(b) served any legislative ends or whether those ends could have been accomplished in a sexually non-discriminatory way. Commenting on *Lavell* in his judgment in *A.G. Canada* v. *Canard*, [1975] 3 W.W.R. 1, Beetz J. said:

> A very real issue also in *Lavell* was not only whether a fundamental change in Indian status could be done for one or two individuals, on an ad hoc basis and without risk of social disruption, but whether, as a matter of principle, it should be done on a possibly large scale, in one stroke (since the courts are without much power to insure transitory stages for any reform that they be called to bring about), regardless of local wishes, desires or preparation ([1975] 3 W.W.R. 1, 30).

The *Optional Protocol to the International Covenant on Civil and Political Rights* authorizes individuals to complain to a

Human Rights Committee about alleged violations of the *Covenant* by their own states. The *Protocol* came into force against Canada on 19 August 1976. Several years earlier, Sandra Lovelace, a Maliseet Indian from the Tobique reserve of New Brunswick, had lost her Indian status through the operation of s.12(1)(b) of the *Indian Act*. After the break-up of the marriage, she returned to the reserve and lived with her parents. Section 28 of the *Indian Act* makes void any agreement by a band member purporting to permit a non-member to reside on the reserve. The Band Council made no move to expel her but denied her application to obtain a new house on the reserve on the basis that priority ought to be given to status Indians. On 29 December 1977, Mrs. Lovelace filed a letter with the Human Rights Committee charging Canada with a violation of article 23 of the *Covenant* (protection of the family unit, equal rights as between spouses), article 26 (equality before the law), and article 27, which reads: "In those States in which ethnic, religious or linguistic minorities exist, persons belonging to such minorities shall not be denied the right, in community with the other members of their group, to enjoy their own culture, to profess and practise their own religion, or to use their own language." The committee gave its decision on the merits on 30 July 1981 (Human Rights L.J. Vol. 2, No. 1-2, 158 (1981)). It denied its own competence to evaluate an alleged violation of *Covenant* rights that took place before Canada was subject to the *Covenant* and *Protocol*. It did hold itself authorized to evaluate the post-entry effects of a pre-entry event.

The majority opinion of the Committee recognizes that membership limitations may be necessary to preserve the resources and identity of the people on a reserve. These limitations must, however, "have both a reasonable and objective justification." The Committee concluded that "[w]hatever may be the merits of the *Indian Act* in other respects," its operation in Mrs. Lovelace's case was neither reasonable nor necessary. It unjustifiably denied her rights under article 27 of the *Covenant*, read in the context of other provisions of the *Covenant* (Human Rights L.J., Vol. 2, No. 1-2, 158, 166).

The decision in *Lovelace* arguably did not imply that all sexual discrimination with respect to band membership is invalid. The situation in *Lovelace* itself was that an Indian woman was attempting to return to the reserve after the break-up of a marriage – a type of situation that does not, it may be safe to assume, seriously threaten Indian bands with overpopulation or cultural assimilation. *Lovelace* did, however, encourage the federal government to announce a policy of suspending the operation of the section to individual bands upon their request (Bayefsky 1982, 260, citing press release, minister of Indian affairs and northern development, John Munro, July 24, 1980).

The strongly-worded equality guarantee of the *Charter of Rights and Freedoms* came into force on April 17, 1985. If a section is challenged under s.15 of the *Charter of Rights and Freedoms*, the first line of defence would be to attempt to define the equality guarantees in section 15 in such a way that a prima facie case of unconstitutionality cannot be made out. The second line would be to show that even though there is discrimination within the meaning of s.15, it serves important ends that cannot be accomplished at a reasonable cost in a less discriminatory way. The odds are that the Court would hold that a rule like s.12(1)(b) of the *Indian Act* does violate s.15(1) of the *Charter* and that it is not saved by section 1. The Court might give only prospective effect to its decision to avoid massive social disruption. The Court would likely find that the preservation of the cultural identity of bands is a legitimate legislative purpose, as is control of band size, but that these aims could be accomplished by legislation that does not discriminate on the basis of sex.

The application of sections 15 and 1 would not exhaust the legal examination of legislation under the *Constitution Act, 1982* as it came into force on April 17, 1982. The implications of s.25 of the *Charter of Rights and Freedoms* must be considered. The section reads:

> 25. The guarantee in this *Charter* of certain rights and freedoms shall not be construed so as to abrogate or derogate from any aboriginal, treaty or other rights and freedoms that pertain to the aboriginal peoples of Canada including
>
> (a) any rights or freedoms that have been recognized by the Royal Proclamation of October 7, 1763; and
>
> (b) any rights or freedoms that may be acquired by the aboriginal peoples of Canada by way of land claims settlement.

(To maintain consistency with s.35(3) of the *Constitution Act, 1982* the amendment on modern land claims agreements that was agreed to at the March '83 First Ministers' Conference, paragraph (b), was redrafted as:

(b) any rights or freedoms that now exist by way of land claims agreements or may be so acquired.)

Section 25 does not create any rights, nor, as a general matter, does it protect them from legislative interference. All that it does is shield rights of aboriginal peoples from the effects of the rest of the *Charter of Rights and Freedoms*. The precursor of s.25 was part of the original constitutional proposal brought forth by the federal government in October 1980. It was not until the end of January 1981 that the Special Joint Committee on the Constitution accepted the insertion of the forerunner of s.35, which positively recognizes and affirms aboriginal and treaty rights. How strong of a shield is s.25? Perhaps one that deflects attacks from an angle but yields to blows that are dead on. The section speaks of how the rest of the *Charter* shall be "construed." It does not say "construed and applied." The *Canadian Bill of Rights*, by contrast, says that every law of Canada shall be "construed and applied" so as not to derogate from the human rights and freedoms that the *Bill* recognizes and declares.

It was over the dissenting opinion of Chief Justice Cartwright that a majority of the Supreme Court of Canada held, in *The Queen* v. *Drybones* (1969), 9 D.L.R. (3d) 473, that "construed and applied" rendered inoperative a statute of Canada that on *any* reasonable construction was contrary to the *Canadian Bill of Rights*. Cartwright C.J.C. would have held that the courts should try to find an interpretation of a statute that reconciles it with the *Canadian Bill of Rights*; if they cannot do so, it is the challenged statute that prevails. Because of the absence of the words "and applied," the courts may very well use an approach like Cartwright's with respect to s.25 of the *Charter*. They may attribute to *Charter* guarantees a certain amount of permissiveness when it comes to aboriginal peoples matters but strike down laws that are plainly contrary to the letter and spirit of *Charter* guarantees.

Even harder to understand than the shielding effect of s.25 on s.15 is the added force, if any, that s.28 *adds* to s.15. Section 28 was introduced in the constitutional package as a response to a well-organized and vigorous lobbying effort by feminists (Kome 1983). It says: "Notwithstanding anything in this *Charter*, the rights and freedoms referred to in it are guaranteed equally to male and female persons." Is this an absolute guarantee of equality that overrides everything, including the reasonable limitations clause, s.1, and the shielding clause, s.25? To begin with, s.28 of its own force guarantees nothing at all. The section tells you how to understand the other rights and freedoms referred to in the *Charter*. Indeed, a possible interpretation of s.28 is that it means practically nothing. First, you read the rest of the *Charter*, and whatever rights that emerge both men and women have. If a man has the free expression right under s.2(b) of the *Charter* to spend as much as he wants on an election campaign, so does a woman. The logical problem with this approach comes when you try to apply it to s.15. If a construction of s.15 leaves men and women in a different legal position, how can you say that the equality rights of the *Charter* are "guaranteed equally" to male and female persons? Does it make sense to say that the situation of inequality between the men and women is, by s.28, guaranteed equally to men and women?

It is textually difficult and philosophically untenable to hold that s.28 tells you to construe s.15 so that it *never* permits discrimination between men and women. Section 15(2) expressly contemplates affirmative action on the basis of sex. Furthermore, some types of sexual discrimination both are, and are perceived as, legitimate. Almost no one would object to Canada's subsidizing Olympic sports teams, even though the competition is almost entirely segregated along sexual lines. A philosophical problem is that sexual equality is not a more morally-compelling norm than racial or religious equality, yet reading sections 15(1) and 15(2) of the *Charter* together, you don't have absolute guarantees of equality on the basis of race or religion—criteria that are even less likely than sex to be a legitimate basis of legal discrimination.

Although it may not be possible to produce a strictly logical account of the textual implications of sections 1, 15, and 28, the courts might try to make some sense of the lot by saying that a heavy burden of justification inheres in an attempt by a legislature to discriminate on the basis of sex—no less, but no more, than when it discriminates on the basis of race or religion. The exception will be that affirmative action programs will be entirely exempt from, or subject to a lesser degree of, judicial scrutiny.

The next question is how a court would deal with a s.15 case where both section 25 and section 28 were invoked. As section 28 says "notwithstanding anything in this *Charter*," its solicitude for sexual equality might predominate over the protection of the rights of aboriginal peoples provided by s.25. In their account of the making of the *Constitution Act, 1982* Romanow, Whyte, and Leeson (all of whom were intimately involved in the process as officials of the government of Saskatchewan) write:

> The other purpose behind section 28 was to counter the inclusion in the *Charter* of the guarantee that the rights and freedoms would not be construed to derogate from rights pertaining to the aboriginal peoples of Canada. Women's rights groups, including organizations of Indian women, feared that the exception to the application of the charter's provisions would permit the continuation of Indian membership rules which discriminate against women. It was sought to trump this exception to the provisions of the charter with a section which would not allow aboriginal rights to be more important than sexual equality. The opening phrase in section 28, "notwithstanding anything in this *Charter*," is meant precisely to indicate that the exemption in favour of the rights of aboriginal people is to be subordinate to it (Romanow, Whyte, and Leeson 1984, 255-256).

There are textual and historical grounds for supposing that s.28 would invalidate most legislative attempts at discrimination against women in aboriginal peoples matters, including a rule like s.12(1)(b) of the *Indian Act*. Courts may not be impressed, however, by historical arguments in general, or by the record with respect to s.28 in particular; and when faced with the ambiguities, incoherencies, and apparent contradictions of the *Charter*, it would be neither astonishing nor plainly irrational for a judge to uphold, despite a s.15 challenge, sexually discriminatory aspects of some statutes addressed to aboriginal peoples matters.

The legal analysis so far has all been based on the assumption that the sexual inequality under attack was established by Parliament, a provincial legislature, or a body deriving its authority from one or the other. If aboriginal self-government derives its legal authorization entirely from the delegation of authority from a superior legislature, then that aboriginal government is almost certainly subject to the same *Charter* restrictions as the ultimate source of authority. In the United States, however, it has been held by the Supreme Court that Indian nations have an inherent right to self-government (*Cherokee Nation* v. *Georgia*, 30 U.S. 1 (1831); *Worcester* v. *Georgia*, 31 U.S. 515 (1832)). Since the American *Bill of Rights* applies only to federal and state governments and their delegates, it does not apply of its own force to Indian governments; *Talton* v. *Mayes*, 163 U.S. 376 (1896). (In order to make a modified form of the American *Bill of Rights* applicable to

Indian governments, Congress, in the exercise of its legislative supremacy in Indian matters, enacted the *Indian Civil Rights Act* in 1968.)

Section 32 of the *Canadian Charter of Rights and Freedoms* states:

> 32(1) This *Charter* applies
>
> (a) to the Parliament and government of Canada in respect of all matters within the authority of Parliament including all matters relating to the Yukon Territory and Northwest Territories; and
>
> (b) to the legislature and government of each province in respect of all matters within the authority of the legislature of each province.

Assume that section 32 exhaustively maps out the realm in which the *Charter* applies of its own force; then, to the extent that self-government is an inherent aboriginal right, aboriginal governments are potentially able to operate free of its constraints. (Whether Parliament can legislatively foist the *Charter* on aboriginal governments would depend on the extent to which s.35 protects aboriginal rights from legislative override – a highly uncertain matter.) It is probable that the courts will find that there is no inherent right of aboriginal peoples to self-government or that the right is very restricted in the matters that it applies to and in its immunity from legislative interferences. That aboriginal governments might have been legally able to sexually discriminate in the discharge of their inherent powers of self-government may have been a small risk, but it was not altogether negligible. It was thus another plausible ground for viewing as necessary in March 1983 an amendment to the constitution of Canada. (For an in-depth analysis of the *Charter* and aboriginal government, see Chapter XXV.)

At the March '83 conference, the federal government and the provinces were generally not averse to amending the constitution to ensure sexual equality in aboriginal matters. They perceived the issue as a fairly narrow (and manageable) one, not involving the complicated and potentially costly demands of aboriginal peoples with respect to land, resources, and self-government. Producing a constitutional amendment on it would help to create the impression that real progress was made at the conference, and it would please people concerned about women's rights, a possibly larger group than those with a sympathetic interest in aboriginal peoples' affairs.

Of the four aboriginal groups present, only the AFN did not support the amendment. The AFN had concerns about impairing the political autonomy of First Nations governments; in particular, their authority to determine membership criteria in light of their own perceptions of the traditions and needs of Indian people. The AFN speakers did not dwell on their objections. The organization had to be careful not to be perceived, even if unfairly so, as defending unjust sexual discrimination. Had it decided to oppose the amendment on the second day of the conference, the AFN would have risked scuttling the entire constitutional package. On the final afternoon, a short statement of the Assembly was read – a sexual equality clause was accepted on the condition that the "issue of citizenship be left for further discussions" (1983 First Ministers' Conference [FMC] transcript, 243-244).

Guaranteed vs. Recognized and Affirmed

A preliminary legal point that must be appreciated is the possible legal difference between "guaranteeing" rights and "recognizing and affirming" them. Section 1 of the *Canadian Charter of Rights and Freedoms* states that "[T]he *Canadian Charter of Rights and Freedoms guarantees* the rights and freedoms set out in it subject only to such reasonable limits prescribed by law as can be demonstrably justified in a free and democratic society" [emphasis added]. The word "guarantee" carries a strong implication of security against legislative interference. Section 24 of the *Charter* establishes that a person whose rights have been infringed may apply to a court "to obtain such remedy as the court considers appropriate and just." Section 32 expressly provides that the *Charter* applies to Parliament and provincial legislatures. That section 33 allows these entities to override certain sections of the *Charter* by expressly stating their intention to do so is a backhanded acknowledgement that the guarantees are serious obstacles to legislative action.

Section 35 of the *Constitution Act, 1982* is not in the *Charter of Rights and Freedoms* but rather in *Part II, Rights of the Aboriginal Peoples of Canada*. It reads: "35.(1) The existing aboriginal and treaty rights of the aboriginal peoples of Canada are hereby *recognized and affirmed*" [emphasis added]. Notice that the operative word is *not* "guaranteed." "Recognized and affirmed" sounds less safe than "guaranteed." A court might rely on the difference to justify or rationalize its taking a permissive attitude towards interferences with aboriginal and treaty rights by Parliament and provincial legislatures. The court might find support in its approach from the absence, in connection with s.35, of any "reasonable limits" clause or override provision. Surely, the court would reason, it was not the intention of the framers to make aboriginal and treaty rights the only absolute rights in the constitution; even the "fundamental" rights and freedoms of the *Charter* are generally subject to reasonable limits and legislative override. The court would have to confront the following argument.

Section 52 of the *Constitution Act, 1982* says:

> The Constitution of Canada is the supreme law of Canada, and any law that is inconsistent with the provisions of the Constitution is, to the extent of the inconsistency, of no force or effect.
>
> Section 35 "recognizes and affirms" existing aboriginal and treaty rights. Ordinary legislation that infringes on those rights is inconsistent with the constitution. "Recognize and affirm" is therefore just as strong as "guarantee."

The court might overcome the preceding contentions by pointing out that legislative powers are granted to Parliament and provincial legislatures by sections 91 and 92, respectively, of the *Constitution Act, 1867*. In particular, section 91(24) of the *Constitution Act, 1867* gives Parliament exclusive legislative authority with respect to Indians. The venerable sections 91 and 92 are no less a part of the constitution of Canada than the arriviste s.35. An acknowledgement of rights in a constitution, the court would reason, must be read in conjunction with grants of legislative authority. Where the former is a robust "guarantee," it generally prevails over the latter; where the former is an anemic "recognition and affirmation," it generally yields to the latter.

It is possible to construct a position contrary to that just sketched. It might include the following points:

- unless the "recognize and affirm" language protects rights from legislative override, it does nothing. There is no textual basis on which a court can find a middle position between making "recognize and affirm" just as strong as "guarantee" on the one hand and relegating it to strictly symbolic (un)importance on the other. The latter possibility is unjust on the merits, and attributes insufficiently noble intentions to the framers.

- the absence of reasonable limits and override clauses may be attributed to many considerations that do not imply the weakness of the legal protection of s.35; these considerations include:
  - "existing" imports sufficient limitations;
  - aboriginal and treaty rights are based on historical practice and are not as open-ended as many *Charter* rights;
  - an override clause would allow a majoritarian political process to negate the rights of a permanent political minority.

As the immediately preceding position has no certainty of judicial acceptance, the legal prospects of aboriginal peoples would have been significantly enhanced by a drafting change to s.35 that made it clear that "recognized and affirmed" operated to "guarantee" rights. (The next chapter will explore the legal structure of s.35 in more detail.)

The Drafting Wars of March '83

The political and legal context established, it is time to look at the weird machinations with respect to drafting. The federal government's draft constitutional package released on the morning of the first day of the March '83 FMC read: "s.25(2) Notwithstanding any other provision of this Act, the aboriginal, treaty and other rights and freedoms that pertain to the aboriginal peoples of Canada apply equally to male and female persons." Note the following features of this draft:

location: section 25 of the *Canadian Charter of Rights and Freedoms*, Part I of the *Constitution Act, 1982*

scope: aboriginal, treaty, and other rights and freedoms of the aboriginal peoples of Canada

legal effect: forbid sexual discrimination.

The Inuit Committee on National Issues (ICNI) included a clause on sexual equality in the draft *Charter of Rights* it had circulated a month earlier, and which it (1983 FMC transcript, 191) and the Native Council of Canada (NCC) pushed for at the March '83 First Ministers' Conference. The wording: "s.35(10)

Notwithstanding anything in this Part, the rights of the aboriginal peoples of Canada are guaranteed equally to male and female persons." This clause is marked by:

> location: s.35 of Part II of the *Constitution Act, 1982, Rights of the Aboriginal Peoples of Canada*
>
> scope: aboriginal, treaty, and other rights of the aboriginal peoples of Canada
>
> legal effect: forbid sexual discrimination, and perhaps establish that all the rights of the aboriginal peoples of Canada are constitutionally guaranteed.

The last possibility is startling. It needs a little explanation. Section 35(10) contains a basic ambiguity. When it says that "rights . . . are guaranteed equally" does it merely guarantee (sexual) equality, or does it mean that men and women have the equal right to enjoy the rights of the aboriginal peoples of Canada and that those rights are guaranteed? Consider this rough analogy. If Diogenes says, "Loyd and Flloyd are equally stupid," the ordinary listener would understand that Loyd and Flloyd rank equally on the scale of intellect. The statement has a *comparative* implication. It is not impossible that Diogenes considers that Loyd and Flloyd are actually both brilliant; if two people are brilliant in the same degree it would not, in the comparative sense, be wrong to say that they are equally stupid (i.e., both are not very stupid at all). It would sound rather peculiar to say that, however, because statements like Diogenes' can also have an aspect of *common descriptions*. The ordinary listener would understand Diogenes' statement as meaning that *both* Flloyd *and* Loyd are stupid. Section 35(10) of the ICNI draft contains an ambiguity of the same general sort. Section 35(10) surely implies that the rights of aboriginal peoples are shared in equal measure by men and women, but it may also imply that those rights have the quality of being guaranteed.

Within the organization that pushed for a s.35(10) type of clause, there were technicians who were aware of its potential for strengthening s.35(1). It is doubtful that all of their political superiors were fully aware of the possibility. The same state of divided awareness was likely widespread among the governments that were persuaded by aboriginal groups to press for the inclusion of "guaranteed" in s.35(10) or at least assent to its inclusion. One minister's acceptance of its inclusion at the meeting on the final afternoon was delivered against a background of bureaucrats shaking their heads and with his express acknowledgement that he was acting contrary to their advice.

A number of delegations pressed for a s.35(10) type of clause at a ministerial level drafting session on the evening of the first day of the March '83 First Ministers' Conference. The federal government's draft of the next day responded in part; the sexual equality clause was moved out of s.25 of the *Charter of Rights and Freedoms* and into s.35 of Part II of the *Constitution Act, 1982*. It read: "s.35(4) Notwithstanding any other provision of this Act, the aboriginal and treaty rights referred to in subsection (1) apply equally to male and female persons." To fill in our chart:

location: s.35 of Part II of the *Constitution Act, 1982*

scope: aboriginal and treaty rights

legal effect: forbid sexual discrimination.

The last entry is explained by the use of "apply" rather than "guarantee" in the federal draft. Why is the scope limited to "aboriginal and treaty rights," rather than all rights? Perhaps the federal drafters had no particular political or legal aims in mind; they simply figured that if the sexual equality clause was going to be in s.35, it would make more sense, in terms of the logic and aesthetics of legal drafting, for the clause to address the substantive rights acknowledged by s.35. It is possible that the federal framers wanted to buy a little time for the government before sexual discrimination would be forbidden in *Indian Act* matters. When the sexual equality clause was in s.25, it operated in conjunction with s.15 of the *Charter of Rights*. The latter was not scheduled to come into force until April 17, 1985. By contrast, an amendment to s.35 could have come into force within a year of the March '83 conference. Whatever the rationale on the federal side, several other delegations found the revised version inadequate. One ground of concern was that the word "guaranteed" was omitted. The other was that the scope was too narrow; discrimination against women with respect to the statutory rights of Indians, for example, would not be covered. The notorious s.12(1)(b) of the *Indian Act* would not fall within the prohibitive ambit of the draft s.35(4).

At the open, First Ministers' level meeting on the second morning of the March '83 conference, both the Inuit Committee on National Issues (ICNI) and the NCC reiterated their preference for a s.35(10) type of clause (1983 FMC transcript, 191,

192). Their advocacy of such an equality clause was resumed in the backroom ministerial level meeting charged with the refinement of the revised federal draft. (After the Conference, some aboriginal organizations publicly claimed that the federal minister of justice had agreed to insert the word "guarantee" *and* to expand the scope of the section to include *all* aboriginal and treaty rights. Like many delegates, I have no recollection of the latter commitment being made. It is possible that some brief remark was made by the minister about his intentions and that it was misunderstood by the delegates, who took it as a commitment. The remarks might have been at the tail-end of the session when many delegates were not paying attention because they thought the meeting was essentially over, were ruminating on the changes that had just been agreed to, or were just plain tired. What happened at the meeting became a matter of hot dispute. The Canadian Intergovernmental Conference Secretariat has released transcripts of every other ministerial backroom meeting at the March '83 and March '84 conferences – except the crucial one now under discussion. Some people find this fact suspicious. I leave it to Canadian Woodwards and Bernsteins to determine, if they wish, whether there was misadventure or foul play. One delegate recalls having seen a tape recorder operating and speculates that Rosemary Woods, the transcriber of the famous Watergate tape from which eighteen minutes were deleted, must have been called in on the case.)

In any event, the draft that the federal government released to the First Ministers' Conference – too late for adequate scrutiny – and that is now a part of the Constitution of Canada is as follows: "35(4) Notwithstanding any other provision of this Act, the aboriginal and treaty rights referred to in subsection (1) are guaranteed equally to male and female persons." This time the chart reads:

location: s.35 of Part II of the *Constitution Act, 1982*

scope: aboriginal and treaty rights

legal effect: forbid sexual discrimination and possibly establish that the aboriginal and treaty rights of the aboriginal peoples of Canada are constitutionally guaranteed.

The last entry reflects the "Loyd and Flloyd are equally stupid" ambiguity of the final draft; that is, the uncertainty over whether the draft s.35(4) contemplates that only sexual equality is guaranteed or that aboriginal and treaty rights are guaranteed as well. Both s.35(1) of the *Constitution Act, 1982* ("aboriginal and treaty rights ... are hereby recognized and affirmed") and the final draft of s.35(4) refer to "aboriginal and treaty rights." The identical subject matter of the two clauses makes it plausible to read them together and conclude that s.35(4) confirms that the aboriginal and treaty rights are "guaranteed" by s.35(1). To put it another way, s.35(4) can be read as confirming that the "recognize and affirm" language of s.35(1) has the same effect as the forceful "guarantee" language of the *Charter*.

(If the sexual equality clause that finally emerged had been worded along the lines of s.35(10) of the ICNI draft, the result would have been less favourable to the general legal position of aboriginal peoples. The ICNI's draft would have "guaranteed equally" aboriginal and treaty *and* other rights of the aboriginal peoples of Canada. No judge is going to conclude that *all* the rights of aboriginal peoples of Canada are constitutionally guaranteed. On the contrary, referring to all rights of aboriginal peoples would have made it obvious that the clause only referred to sexual equality.)

Aboriginal organizations might have been wise to accept their good fortune and to avoid any attempt to disturb the form of s.35(4). It is true that its scope was limited, but it did bolster the legal position of all aboriginal and treaty rights, and the possibility was small that a judge would disregard all the sexual equality guarantees in the constitution and uphold an invidious form of sexual discrimination in an aboriginal peoples matter. Section 35(4) does not address statutory rights of aboriginal peoples, but it does provide an additional powerful signal to the courts that sexual equality is to be valued highly in aboriginal peoples matters.

After the conference was over, the ICNI, the NCC and the Native Women's Association of Canada alleged that the federal government had unilaterally changed the wording of the sexual equality clause at the last minute (Globe & Mail, March 23, 1983 p. 8). They contended that the federal government had, without dissent, accepted that the scope of the clause should include all rights of the aboriginal peoples of Canada. The minister of justice said in the House of Commons that:

> We took soundings across the country from the Attorneys General . . . to see, first of all, whether or not the communiqué we believed was exact was in fact exact, and the answer was, yes it is; secondly, whether

> or not it would be possible to have an agreement to a further variation or a new variation which would now be agreed. A very large number of the Provinces were against that . . .
>
> [Hansard, March 21, 1983, 1st Session, 32nd Parliament, p. 23962]

In the end, the dissatisfied aboriginal organizations agreed to go along with the clause rather than continue a dispute that might have lead to the unravelling of the whole March '83 accord. They looked to the next year's conference to agree on a refinement of s.35(4) or a superior replacement.

The sexual equality clause that the federal government distributed at the opening of the March '84 First Ministers' Conference was neutral with respect to the "Loyd-Flloyd" controversy over section 35. It would have amended s.25 of the *Constitution Act, 1982* to ensure that the full force of the sexual equality guarantee in the *Charter* would extend to aboriginal peoples. The relevant sections would have read (only s.25(2) would be new):

> s.15(1) Every individual is equal before and under the law and has the right to the equal protection and equal benefit of the law without discrimination and, in particular, without discrimination based on race, national or ethnic origin, colour, religion, *sex*, age or mental or physical disability (emphasis added).
>
> (2) Subsection (1) does not preclude any law, program or activity that has as its object the amelioration of conditions of disadvantaged individuals or groups including those that are disadvantaged because of race, national or ethnic origin, colour, religion, sex, age or mental or physical disability.
>
> s.25(1) The guarantee in this *Charter* of certain rights and freedoms shall not be construed so as to abrogate or derogate from any aboriginal, treaty or other rights or freedoms that pertain to the aboriginal peoples of Canada . . .

(2) *Nothing in this section abrogates or derogates from the guarantees of equality with respect to male or female persons under s.28 of this Charter.*

s.28 Notwithstanding anything in this *Charter*, the rights and freedoms referred to in it are guaranteed equally to male and female persons.

The amendment would not necessarily have closed off all the not-impossible loopholes through which sexually unequal measures might pass. While the "full force" of the *Charter* would have applied to aboriginal peoples, it was not certain that the *Charter* would apply to aboriginal governments. Another loophole might have been s.15(2) of the *Charter*, which might permit sexually discriminatory laws to be sustained as part of an affirmative action program in favour of aboriginal groups. These considerations might have been involved in the response of some of the aboriginal groups – requesting that the amendment be to s.35 rather than to s.25 – at the backroom ministerial meeting that evening. Another factor was the desire of some aboriginal tacticians to focus attention on s.35, and thereby produce some improvements to it – perhaps the addition of the word "guaranteed" to s.35(1) or at least a remedies clause.

A number of provinces agreed that an amendment to s.35 was preferable. Some provincial delegations simply wanted to be helpful to aboriginal groups; at least one figured that the ss.15, 25, and 28 route was too circuitous.

The wish of some of the aboriginal groups to move the draft amendment to s.35 was eventually granted – in a "Twilight Zone" sort of way. (In the "Twilight Zone" television series, if a character asked for, say, "a moment to myself," mysterious forces would permanently suspend him in time at, say, 2:54 a.m., February 29, 1960.)

The federal government was initially opposed to moving the amendment to s.35. It figured that s.35(4), the previous year's amendment, had taken care of sexual equality with respect to aboriginal treaty rights. They considered the amendment unnecessary. Some were concerned that gratuitous amendments would diminish respect for the constitution, others that any amendment on any issue would build expectations that every s.37 First Ministers' Conference must end with constitutional changes.

"Equality" was the agenda item discussed on the morning of the second day. Most of the talk was not about sexual equality, though; it was about equality among aboriginal groups and whether the Métis ought to be, like Indians and the Inuit, a federal responsibility under s.91(24) of the *Constitution Act, 1867.*

That afternoon, the prime minister led off by promising to steer the conversation to the sexual aspect of equality.

After two of his Indian women constituents, including Mrs. Sandra Lovelace, had spoken in favour of a constitutional amendment on sexual equality, Premier Hatfield delivered a fervent plea of his own: "the legitimate fears" that had been raised must be allayed. On the principal issue of the conference, self-government, he stated:

> I came out in favour of self-government. I don't know what it means. I want to make it very clear I don't know what it means. I didn't intend to know what it means because I have listened to what the aboriginal people have said and what they have said is that they have rights and I believe they do. They have convinced me. Are we going to act on it or aren't we? (1984 FMC transcript, 325).

He called for aboriginal peoples to "keep fighting, and settle for nothing less" than constitutional amendment (1984 FMC transcript, 328).

Premier Hatfield insisted that "what the constitution is about is not a legal opinion" (1984 FMC transcript, 331). It would be possible to get a legal opinion to state that s.28 of the *Constitution Act, 1982* was not necessary, but "it wasn't good enough for the women of Canada . . . they insisted on it being there and they got it there" (1984 FMC transcript, 331). The reason for bringing up another amendment on sexual equality was that "native women . . . are concerned, worried, afraid, and that is what a constitution is about I think" (1984 FMC transcript, 331).

Prime Minister Trudeau responded that no one was against sexual equality: many Premiers simply considered that it had been adequately ensured by the previous year's constitutional amendment. The federal government agreed, although it was prepared to consider a further amendment to produce greater certainty.

The minister of justice was asked by the prime minister to comment on whether a further amendment on sexual equality was legally necessary. It wasn't, said Mr. MacGuigan, but to clarify the matter and accommodate the desire of a number of participants to put the amendment in s.35, he proposed that s.35(4) be supplemented as follows:

> s.35(4) Notwithstanding any other provision of this Act, the aboriginal and treaty rights referred to in subsection (1) are guaranteed equally to male and female persons.
>
> s.35(5) The guarantee of equality under subsection (4) applies in respect of all rights of the aboriginal peoples.

The proposed amendment would have tended to undermine the argument that s.35(1) rights are guaranteed. Section 35(5) would have helped persuade a court that s.35(4) is a "guarantee" of sexual equality only and was not intended to speak to the general status of aboriginal and treaty rights. No court would accept that all the rights of aboriginal peoples are constitutionally guaranteed.

The attorney general of Manitoba, Roland Penner, suggested a backroom meeting at the ministerial level to work out the wording if agreement could not be reached on the floor. Officials should be able to come back "in half an hour" with a text (1984 FMC transcript, 341, 342). Premier Bennett of British Columbia was fed up: "I guess what happens to us is what frustrates most people in this country most of the time, trying to get what they want done through the legal mumbo-jumbo of lawyers and I must say being one of the very few people that isn't a lawyer in this room that I share that frustration" (1984 FMC transcript, 344). He had been advised that the equality problem had been taken care of by last year's amendment. If a problem arose, he would participate in an emergency meeting to strengthen the constitution. He was offended that a government might be accused of sexism merely because it thought that last year's amendment was sufficient. But "[i]f you want to send the lawyers out again I would be quite willing to send as many as I can find. In fact I will do the public a favour. We will get all the lawyers in this country and put them in a room and perhaps we could get down to business" (1984 FMC transcript, 345).

Premier Lougheed would not send a delegate to a last-minute drafting session. That would just open the way to a repetition of the previous year's events, the results of which were now under criticism. He promised, like Premier Bennett, to participate in an emergency meeting to strengthen the constitution if sexual equality for Indian women were successfully challenged.

The attorney general of Manitoba stated that:

> . . . the notion that I heard from the Premier of British Columbia that we should leave it up to the lawyers is an abdication of political responsibility, a constitution is a political document. What have we heard from one of the major constituencies in this country, the women, they are not satisfied with what we did (sic). Why don't we go and produce something that they will be satisfied with and never mind the lawyers (1984 FMC transcript, 355, 356).

The backroom meeting began at 4:10 that afternoon. It was, as Karl Marx never quite put it, a case of history repeating itself twice: the first time as farce, the second time as farce. A couple of the technical advisors to aboriginal organizations realized that the amendment would undermine the status of s.35; but their organizations had favoured in principle a further amendment on sexual equality, and that the amendment be to s.35. In an attempt to escape both political and legal embarrassment, these technical advisors attempted to "run out the clock" at the backroom meeting. They adduced quibble after quibble, hoping that the First Ministers' Conference would end before agreement could be reached.

The attorney general of Manitoba did attempt to explain to the meeting that the ambiguity of s.35(4) might be reduced in a way that was detrimental to the general, long-term legal position of aboriginal organizations. The subtlety of the "Loyd-Flloyd" issue, the suddenness with which the federal draft had emerged, the intense time pressure, and the farrago of drafting suggestions, all helped to ensure that, once again, many of the participants did not fully appreciate what was going on. Some of them did not know that a fillibuster was being attempted, let alone why.

After about an hour of whatever it was that was happening, the following draft emerged: "s.35(4) Notwithstanding any other provision of this Act, the aboriginal and treaty rights referred to in subsection (1) are guaranteed equally to male and female persons, and this guarantee of equality applies in respect of all other rights and all freedoms of the aboriginal peoples of Canada."

The phrase "this guarantee of equality" would have come close to eliminating the "Loyd-Flloyd" ambiguity. It would be pretty well established that the word "guaranteed" in s.35(4) referred only to sexual equality. There were no dissents from the draft when the backroom meeting adjourned.

To their credit, the minister of justice at the backroom meeting and the prime minister at the conference table both allowed that any objection by an aboriginal organization at the table would be the end of the amendment. When polled by the prime minister, the Métis National Council (MNC), NCC and the ICNI agreed to the amendment. Meanwhile, some officials of the AFN had become aware of the Loyd-Flloyd ambiguity. At the last minute, they obtained a written explanation of it from a lawyer with one of the governments and passed it on to their leadership. Dr. Ahenakew responded to the prime minister's poll by asking for more time to consider the amendment. He was anxious about the effects of the amendment on the rights of First Nations to determine their own citizenship. Chief Sol Sanderson added:

> Mr. Prime Minister, we just want to read for the record our concern on the clause. Section 35(4) . . . in its present form arguably implies that Section 35(1) rights are guaranteed, not just recognized and affirmed. The proposed draft makes it clear that only equality of men and women before the law is guaranteed, not aboriginal and treaty rights themselves. The new Section 35(1) (sic) may therefore seriously weaken the impact of Section 35 in its present form. To repeat, [under] Section 35(1) and Section 35(4) together, rights may well be guaranteed, the new Section 35(4) in no way suggests 35(1) rights are guaranteed (1984 FMC transcript, 436, 437).

The prime minister decided to let the matter rest pending further consultation. A few weeks after the conference, the AFN gave a definitive "no" to the federal amendment.

On June 18, 1984, the minister of Indian affairs and northern development introduced legislation to repeal s.12(1)(b) of the *Indian Act*. It would have restored status to women who had lost it by direct operation of the *Act* and to certain of their descendants. Indian bands and native women's organizations jointly contended that the legislation should be improved by giving bands control over whether a reinstated Indian could take up residence on a reserve (Sanders 1984). The government managed to rush the legislation through the committee stage and have it passed by the House of Commons. With the end of the

Thirty-second Parliament days away, the legislation would pass only if the members attending the Senate deliberations unanimously agreed that it should be voted on without debate. Senator Watt, a former co-chairperson of the ICNI, voiced his opposition. He felt that more deliberation was necessary (Winnipeg Free Press, June 30, 1984, 18).

In the 1984-85 process, the aboriginal organizations and native women's groups displayed unprecedented tepidness in their support for a further sexual equality amendment. Their members were more aware of the legal side-effects. There was a strong and justified expectation that the federal government would try to enact legislation to eliminate s.12(1)(b) of the *Indian Act* prior to April 17, 1985 – the date the equality section of the *Charter* would come into force. The aboriginal organizations also did not want attention diverted from the primary issue of aboriginal self-government. At the ministerial level meeting in Toronto on March 11 and 12, 1985, several aboriginal organizations took the line that consideration of the sexual equality issue should be postponed until the 1987 First Ministers' Conference. Premier Hatfield successfully insisted that the item remain on the agenda for 1985.

The day before the opening of the April '85 Conference, the four national aboriginal organizations sent a letter to the prime minister with their proposal on sexual equality. It read: "s.25(2) Notwithstanding anything in this *Charter*, all rights and all freedoms of the aboriginal peoples of Canada are guaranteed equally to male and female aboriginal persons". The clause was considered objectionable by federal officials. There were concerns that it would open up a whole new area of operation for the Loyd-Flloyd ambiguity; that a court might read s.25(2) and conclude that *all* the rights and *all* the freedoms of the aboriginal peoples of Canada were constitutionally guaranteed.

The federal government did not include a sexual equality amendment in the draft accords it circulated at the April '85 First Ministers' Conference. The agenda item for the morning of the final day of the conference was equality. The prime minister circulated and read out a "lead statement". His government wanted the fears and confusion on sexual equality settled at the April '85 conference. His government would support an amendment that clarified the matter, *provided* that the amendment did not either "directly or indirectly" serve any other purpose.

A consensus emerged fairly quickly among the provincial governments that an amendment on sexual equality was probably not legally necessary but that it would be a good thing to allay the remaining anxieties. Prime Minister Mulroney proposed that technical officials meet in a backroom at lunch and try to work out an amendment. A little later in the morning, however, a possible deal on self-government emerged, and in all the excitement, the sexual equality issue was forgotten.

At the follow-up meeting of ministers in Toronto on June 5, 6, officials finally met to draft a sexual equality amendment. After a couple of hours of haggling, they agreed that they did not agree.

On June 12, 1985, the House of Commons passed Bill C-31. It repealed s.12(1)(b) of the *Indian Act* and made many persons eligible for "reinstatement." Despite the misleading features of the *Act*, it was not easy to be misled. It was hard to follow it anywhere. It was a concoction of technical words, many of them redundant, piled into long phrases that were often stitched together by semicolons to form huge sentences. Puzzling through a continuous mangle of words is frequently not sufficient; you run into a cross-reference and face a whole new challenge. The "misleading" aspect of the *Act* is that it is chock full of sections that tell you various ways to get yourself onto a "band list." The practical value of these sections is seriously undercut by a little phrase tucked away in section 15. It adds to the subject matters on which a band council can make by-laws; "the residence of band members and other persons on the reserve."

A band council is thus authorized to control the influx onto the reserve of persons who have exercised their rights under Bill C-31 and had themselves placed on the band list. Despite the form of the legislation, the federal government was not attempting to sneak anything through. Authorizing bands to control influx had been urged by not only Indian bands and national organizations, but also by native women's organizations. While Bill C-31 spells out no constraints on the exercise of exclusionary powers by bands, an individual might successfully attack certain arbitrary decisions. He or she might attack an arbitrary decision as contrary to administrative law concerning the exercise of delegated powers, to the *Canadian Bill of Rights*, or to the *Charter of Rights and Freedoms*.

Bill C-31 might alleviate some of the remaining anxieties about the equal treatment of native women, and thus there may be less pressure in the future to add yet another amendment to the constitution on sexual equality.

A special amendment is not legally necessary and attempts to produce one threaten to undermine the general legal position of aboriginal groups. The constitution should not be cluttered with unnecessary additions. Appealing to the powerful women's rights lobby is not an adequate excuse for doing so. Those concerned about individual rights, including sexual equality, ought to focus their attention on constitutionally ensuring that the *Charter* applies to aboriginal self-governments. The fact that two sections of the *Charter*, 15 and 28, guarantee sexual equality should virtually eliminate anxieties about the scope of the constitutional protection of the rights of native women.

Chapter XXIV

Unstarted Business: Two Approaches to Defining s.35 – "What's in the Box?" and "What Kind of Box?"

The "s.37 process" of national-level discussion on constitutional reform with respect to aboriginal peoples has failed almost entirely to better define, or even discuss in any depth, the legal implications of s.35 of the *Constitution Act, 1982* – which reads: "35(1). The existing aboriginal and treaty rights of the aboriginal peoples of Canada are hereby recognized and affirmed".

One kind of question the participants might have discussed in detail was "what's in the box?" In other words, what are the legal characteristics of the aboriginal and treaty rights that do or should receive some sort of constitutional recognition? The only amendment thus far to better define the contents of s.35(1) was agreed upon at the March '83 First Ministers' Conference: "35(3). For greater certainty, in subsection (1), "treaty rights" includes rights that now exist by way of land claims agreements or may be so acquired" (*Constitution Act, 1982* as amended).

The acquisition of ultimate political authority and ultimate title to the land by European powers did not immediately annihilate under their own law any and all rights an aboriginal group might have to continue to use the land, develop its culture, and govern its own internal affairs. Canadian courts had recognized prior to 1982 that aboriginal groups in Canada could have surviving aboriginal rights. The cases were, however, few in number; their subject matter was basically limited to interests in land and their definitions of aboriginal title vague.

In 1888, the Judicial Committee of the Privy Council had characterized Indian title as: "a personal and usufructuary right, dependent on the goodwill of the sovereign" (*St. Catherine Milling and Lbr. Co.* v. *The Queen* (1888), 14 A.C. 46).

Almost nine decades later, in response to a claim by the Nishga Indians that they had aboriginal title to an area of British Columbia, Judson J. of the Supreme Court of Canada held that:

> . . . the fact is that when the settlers came, the Indians were there, organized in societies and occupying the land as their forefathers had done for centuries. This is what Indian title means, and it does not help one in the solution of this problem to call it a "personal or usufructuary right." What they are asserting in this action is that they had a right to continue to live on their lands as their forefathers had lived, and that this right has never been lawfully extinguished. There can be no question that this right was "dependent on the goodwill of the sovereign" (*Calder* v. *A.-G. for B.C.* (1973), 34 D.L.R. (3d) 145, 156).

Judson J. did not expressly rule for or against the submission that the Nishgas ever had aboriginal title. He concluded that if they did, it had been extinguished by the actions of colonial, British, and Canadian authorities.

Might not unilateral interference by a government with Indian property interests at least give rise to a right, perhaps an "aboriginal right," to just compensation? Judson J. does not squarely confront these issues but does cite, with apparent approval, the decision of the United States Supreme Court in *Tee-Hit-Ton Indians* v. *The United States* (1955), 348 U.S. 272, 279 that: "[Indian title] is not a property right, but amounts to a right of occupancy which the sovereign grants and protects against intrusion by third parties but which right of occupancy may be terminated and such lands fully disposed of by the sovereign itself without any legally enforceable obligation to compensate Indians".

Hall J., by contrast, was prepared to recognize that the Nishgas did have aboriginal title. It was not necessary to precisely define the legal nature of that interest:

> [It] is not a claim to title in *fee* [that is, complete ownership of the surface of the land, minerals below and sky above, subject only to the overriding title of the Crown,] but is in the nature of an equitable title or

> interest . . . a usufructuary right and a right to occupy the lands and to enjoy the fruits of the soil, the forest and of the rivers and streams which does not in any way deny the Crown's paramount title as it is recognized by the law of nations (34 D.L.R. (3d) 145, 173).

In case the title was expropriated in the future, held Hall J., there would be a presumption by the common law of a right to just compensation from the Crown. The Nishgas actually lost the *Calder* case. Two judges agreed with Hall J., two with Judson J., and a seventh judge, Pigeon J., found that the Nishgas had not complied with the necessary procedures for suing the Crown, so there was no case properly before the Court. The opinions of the Supreme Court did, nonetheless, spur the federal government to adopt a general policy of negotiating agreements with aboriginal groups to settle outstanding claims of aboriginal title (see Chapter I).

Are aboriginal rights confined to land use rights, or do they include the right to self-government? The question was not seriously analyzed by pre-1982 cases more on this in the next chapter. Nor was the scope of the land use rights themselves. It was not determined whether there was a cut-off date for determining the land uses that are protected. In one of the very few Canadian rulings on point, *Baker Lake* v. *Minister of Indian Affairs and Northern Development* [1980] 1 F.C. 518, a federal court judge found that aboriginal title is confined to "incidents" of the "enjoyment of land" that were "given effect to" by the aboriginal society prior to the assertion of sovereignty over the area by England; "The aboriginal title asserted here encompasses only the right to hunt and fish as their [the Caribou Indians'] ancestors did"; ([1980] 1 F.C. 518, 559; See also *A.G. Ontario* v. *Bear Island,* (1985), 49 O.R. (2d) 353. There are alternatives to confining aboriginal land use rights to the continuance of practices that antedated European domination. It could be held that any resource exploited prior to European sovereignty may continue to be exploited. If an Indian band caught fish using spears, it may now operate a commercial fishery. It would be possible to hold that use and occupation of land gives rise to ownership no less extensive than that of an owner at common law of the fee simple in a piece of land. If an individual acquires ownership by occupation of land, he is not confined under the common law to using the land in the same way that he first acquired it. If prescriptive title is acquired by building a wood shanty and cultivating cucumbers on a certain plot of land, the owner may thereafter (subject to zoning and other regulatory laws) replace the shanty with an office tower and the cucumbers with rubber plants. American courts have held that for the purposes of determining compensation for expropriation of Indian land interests, aboriginal rights to use and occupancy of land are no less valuable than the fee simple and include mineral rights. "The value of land held by Indian title is . . . not the value to its primitive occupants relying upon it for subsistence." (*Tlingit and Haida Indians of Alaska* v. *United States*, 389 F. 2d. 778, 782 (1968).

Can aboriginal title over water be established by walking on it? The Inuit have on occasion maintained that they should be recognized as having established rights over bodies of water by occupying them while they were frozen.

The national level process might have addressed and answered a number of basic questions of legal principle concerning aboriginal title. It would be, on the whole, counterproductive for participants to attempt to redress their past inaction. The legal position of most aboriginal groups is based primarily on a treaty or land claims agreement, rather than aboriginal title, and it may be expected that a number of the remaining outstanding aboriginal title claims will be settled through agreement in the decade-or-so to come. The issues of general principle addressed at the national level would be of drastically different interest and importance to different aboriginal communities, and negotiations about aboriginal title at the community level might be far more efficient and focussed.

There is another aspect of s.35(1) that warrants close attention as a result of the shift in focus to aboriginal self-government. A crucial aspect of many proposals, including the one that gained broad support at the '85 First Ministers' Conference, is to amend s.35(1) so that agreements on self-government receive the same measure of constitutional protection as are afforded aboriginal and treaty rights by s.35(1). But what constitutional protection does s.35(1) afford its contents? What kind of box is it? Cast iron? Wet cardboard? It is not necessarily optimal or prudent that the same "recognize and affirm formula" be used for agreements on self-government. It is worth considering establishing a special formula for the constitutional protection afforded to treaties in general or agreements on self-government in particular. Options with respect to the last-mentioned have been discussed in Chapter XXI. The last part of this chapter will attempt to bring to the reader a basic appreciation of the range of possible conclusions about the present s.35(1).

A Note on Limitation Periods

An issue which has been largely overlooked by theorists, but which will be of intense interest to litigation lawyers, is the extent to which s.35(1) gives legal enforceability to rights whose vindication would ordinarily be barred by statutes of limitations or by the doctrine of equity ("laches") that law suits must be brought without undue delay. (In *Bear Island,* Steel J. found against the Indian plaintiffs on these bases, among others). The theoretical status of most limitations statutes is that they bar legal actions to enforce the substantive rights – but that they do not annihilate the right itself. If s.35(1) "hereby recognizes and affirms" "existing" aboriginal and treaty rights, might it not have the effect of overriding the pre-1982 operation of time-limitation rules? It could be maintained that, at the very least, limitation periods should not start to run until April 17, 1982. The theory might be that one of the purposes of s.35(1) is to solemnly commit Canadian governmental agencies to a recognition of a class of rights whose importance they had not adequately appreciated in the past. It might be conceded that some aboriginal groups may not have been sufficiently familiar with the Canadian legal system or financially able to retain legal advisors to press their rights in court. It would not be fair to aboriginal peoples or the lofty purposes of s.35, the argument might go, to hold that limitation rules seriously curtail the scope of the rights that s.35(1) protects. Would the operation of pre-1982 limitation rules not effectively render the constitutional recognition by s.35(1) of aboriginal rights next to meaningless? Advocates of the foregoing might concede that limitation periods may validly begin to operate on April 17, 1982.

The General Nature of the Legal Procedures Afforded by s.35

(i) Section 35 as worthless symbolism

Section 35 nihilists have several lines of argument at their disposal. They might begin by comparing the performative language of the *Charter* – which "guarantees" its contents – with that of s.35(1) which merely "recognizes and affirms" them. "Guarantee" sounds stronger than "recognize and affirm." Section 35(1) must be construed, the argument would continue, as merely giving solemn acknowledgement that the rights included exist – but it does not protect them from legislative override. In reply, it might be maintained that the difference in performative language is explicable in terms of the different nature of the *Charter* and s.35(1) rights, as opposed to a difference in the level of legal protection. The framers of the *Charter* did not want to commit themselves to any view of Canada's legal past. The framers of the *Canadian Bill of Rights* had declared that certain rights "have existed and continue to exist" in Canada, and a number of judges have concluded that the safeguards it provides were more or less defined by the standards of civil liberty and legal equality that existed in Canada when the *Canadian Bill of Rights* came in to force in 1960 (see *Robertson and Rosetanni* v. *R.* (1964), 41 D.L.R. (2d) 485). "The "1960 freeze" approach was later rejected by a majority of the Supreme Court of Canada in *R.* v. *Drybones* (1969), 9 D.L.R. (2d) 473). If the framers of the *Charter* wished to avoid freezing the extent of certain rights by reference to history, the framers of s.35(1) obviously wished to do the opposite. Aboriginal and treaty rights are both the consequences of historical processes and transactions, and by inserting the word "existing", the framers emphasized that s.35(1) only protected rights that legal history had already produced. Hence the language of "recognize and affirm." The word "affirm" ensures that s.35(1) rights are protected to at least some extent from legislative infringement. Section 52 of the *Constitution Act, 1982* stipulates that: "52(1) The Constitution of Canada is the supreme law of Canada, and any law that is inconsistent with the provisions of the Constitution is, to the extent of the inconsistency, of no force or effect". Ordinary legislation that would interfere with rights "recognized and affirmed" by s.35(1) would therefore be invalid.

A second line of nihilist argument would play up the word "existing." The case law prior to 1982 had established that aboriginal rights were subject to federal and provincial regulation; *Kruger and Manuel* v. *The Queen* (1978), 75 D.L.R. (3d) 434. No compensation was payable for regulatory restrictions; *ibid.* The *St. Catherine's* case had established that aboriginal title existed "at the pleasure of the Crown," and so could be freely extinguished—and the judgment of Judson J. in *Calder* had suggested that there was no common law presumption of a right to just compensation. The pre-1982 case law also made it clear that Parliamentary authority was not impaired by Indian treaties; see *Kruger* and *Manuel.* Section 88 of the federal *Indian Act* did protect treaty rights from provincial legislation. Even that safeguard for Indian rights, it might be argued, was a statutory right, rather than an aboriginal or treaty right, and thus not ensconced by s.35(1). Conclusion: even if s.35(1) rights are absolutely guaranteed, they are so intrinsically weak that s.35(1) has no real value. Critics of this argument might protest that a section of the Constitution should not be construed in a way that renders it downright delusive (McNeil

1982, 25). The critics might ask why participants at the '83 First Ministers' Conference would have bothered to give land claims agreements the same protections as treaties if the latter are completely vulnerable to legislative infringement. The word "affirm" must be given some effect, and it cannot be that aboriginal and treaty rights are just as open to governmental attack after April 17, 1982, as they were before.

A third line of nihilist argument would present the nihilist interpretation of s.35(1) as the more reasonable alternative to an absolutist interpretation. Section 1 of the *Charter of Rights,* it would be pointed out, makes all of its contents subject to "such reasonable limits prescribed by law as can be demonstrably justified in a free and democratic society." Many of the sections contain internal limitations, such as s.8, which protects everyone from "*unreasonable* search or seizure" only; many of the sections, including "equality" (s.15) and the right to "life, liberty and security of the person" (s.7) are subject to override by any legislature that expressly declares that it is doing so (s.33 of the *Charter*). What limitations exist on s.35(1)? Can we really believe that aboriginal and treaty rights are absolutely guaranteed and cannot be infringed upon—even if the cause is compelling or even if just compensation is paid? It would be wrong to suppose that s.35(1) does more than symbolically acknowledge that certain rights existed, the argument would conclude, because it is unacceptable that the rights would be absolutely guaranteed. There are no "safety valves" in the text of s.35(1) which would permit an intermediate position.

There are a number of possible replies to the "nothing is better than everything" contention. One response might be "everything is better than nothing." "Everything" is not all that much. The treaties generally contain internal limitations that would permit most necessary governmental limitations on the activities of aboriginal peoples; e.g. Treaty No. 3 makes Indian hunting and fishing rights "subject to regulation" and authorizes the government to appropriate Indian land. Aboriginal land use rights should not pose much of a threat to the general interest. Aboriginal peoples rely heavily on the renewable resources of the land and will not abuse them. When the general interest requires compromise, aboriginal peoples can be relied upon to negotiate a fair one. Indeed, most aboriginal groups with outstanding aboriginal land claims have been eager to negotiate agreements to settle them. Another possible reply to "nothing is better than everything" is that the word "existing" imports serious limitations on the exercise of aboriginal and treaty rights. The regulatory restrictions that existed on April 17, 1982—and maybe even new ones of the same kind—would continue to operate.

(ii) Section 35(1) makes aboriginal and treaty rights subject only to regulatory restrictions that existed on April 17, 1982

It might be conceded that s.35(1) restricts the general operation of legislative supremacy. Laws that restrict rights recognized and affirmed by s.35(1) are, generally speaking, invalid. The word "existing," however, must be given full effect. If a treaty right to hunt was restricted by the *Migratory Birds Act,* then that act can continue to be enforced. The merit of this approach is that it gives some effect to s.35(1) while allowing some room for the protection of the general interest. The disadvantage is that restrictions on rights depend entirely on the state of affairs on April 17, 1982, regardless of whether that state of affairs was just and prudent. There is no opportunity for a court to say that a particular regulatory restriction that existed on April 17, 1982, was not required for legitimate public purposes such as conservation, health and safety. On the other hand, there is no opportunity for legislatures to introduce new restrictions on aboriginal and treaty rights as necessary.

(iii) Section 35(1) leaves aboriginal and treaty rights subject only to restrictions that existed on April 17, 1982 and new restrictions of the same kind.

This line of interpretation removes some of the inflexibility of (iv). Its disadvantage is that it may leave too much scope for legislatures to introduce new restrictions on aboriginal and treaty rights that are not sufficiently sensitive to the interests of aboriginal people.

(iv) Section 35(1) protects aboriginal and treaty rights in their unimpaired form.

Under this theory, as long as a right was not altogether extinguished prior to April 17, 1982, it was thenceforth protected in its original and unimpaired form. If an aboriginal or treaty right has been impaired by regulations, then the right re-emerges in its unrestricted form and dominates over the usual supremacy of legislatures. If a treaty right to hunt, for example, was impaired by the *Migratory Birds Act,* the treaty right must now be respected according to its original terms. Complicated questions will arise about whether a right had been extirpated by April 17, 1982, or merely paralyzed or left staggering. There will be no resurrection of the dead, but there will be complete cures for the wounded. Apart from the messiness of the extinguished/ impaired distinction, the drawback of this approach is that it does not allow legislatures much scope to regulate the exercise of aboriginal and treaty rights.

(v) Same as (iv) – s.35(1) protects aboriginal and treaty rights in their unrestricted form – but the degree of protection is left entirely to be determined by reference to other guarantees in the Charter.

The courts might hold that "recognize and affirm" means that aboriginal and treaty rights must be given the same protection as analogous rights of the general public. Aboriginal land use rights would receive the same degree of constitutional protection as ordinary property rights, and treaty rights the same sort of protection as contractual rights against the government. A drawback of this approach is that property and contractual rights of ordinary citizens may not be very well protected by the *Charter* – or other human rights texts. The need to resort to other *Charter* sections may lead to an inadequate analysis of the unique legal concerns connected with aboriginal and treaty rights.

(vi) Same as (iv) – rights are protected in their unrestricted form – only the rights that are protected in the unrestricted form are subject to legislative restrictions that are found by the courts to be justified on their merits.

It would be possible for the courts to read into the unqualified language of s.35(1) the limitation that legislatures may impair aboriginal and treaty rights if and only if there is a strong justification. Gone would be the history-based test of whether a restriction existed on April 17, 1982, or is like a restriction that existed on April 17, 1982. Instead, the courts would assess each restriction on its merits. Is there a strong reason of public policy behind the impairment of an aboriginal or treaty right? Is there a way of achieving the public policy goal in a way that is less injurious to the interests of the aboriginal group? The courts might also determine in some cases that even though the restriction on the rights of aboriginal peoples is necessary, compensation ought to be paid. If an aboriginal right to fish must be restricted for conservation reasons, the court might find that Indians ought to be compensated to the extent of their economic loss. The court might examine whether the restriction on fishing rights has been necessitated primarily by overfishing or pollution by outsiders, or whether some natural disaster of overfishing by the Indians themselves has contributed to the conservation problem.

The merit of this approach is that it permits a fresh assessment of the underlying necessity and legal refinement of a restrictive measure.

Section 35 obviously is devoid of any language that authorizes a court to assess the legitimacy of a restriction on an aboriginal or treaty right. The First Amendment to the Constitution of the United States is also couched in absolute terms – "Congress shall make no law . . . abridging the freedom of speech" – but that has not stopped (merely discouraged) the courts from finding that some limitations on free speech are constitutional. To help justify approach (vi), a court might point out that while s.35 "recognizes and affirms" aboriginal and treaty rights, nothing in the *Constitution Act, 1982* expressly repeals the sections of the *Constitution Act, 1867* that authorize the exercise of legislative authority over aboriginal peoples by Parliament and the legislatures. Still "on the books" is s.91(24) of the *Constitution Act, 1867* which expressly authorizes Parliament to make laws with respect to Indians. Section 35 and the power-granting sections of the Constitution must be read together, and the best way to do so, a court might reason, would be to permit only impairments of aboriginal and treaty rights that are strictly necessary.

Approach (vi) would, in my opinion, have been the most rational basis for a constitutional reformulation of s.35. An illustration of the sort of amendments that might have been explored;

> s.35(1) The aboriginal and treaty rights of the aboriginal peoples of Canada that existed on April 17, 1982, and those rights created thereafter, are hereby recognized and guaranteed.
>
> (2) Same as present.
>
> (3) Same as present.
>
> (4) The rights that are guaranteed by subsection (1) shall not be considered to be:
>
> (i) subject to the general doctrine of legislative supremacy
> (ii) existing at the pleasure of the Crown

(iii) subject to regulatory restrictions that existed on April 17, 1982, unless they are justified under (5).

(5) The rights guaranteed by subsection (1) are subject only to limits prescribed by law that have a compelling objective and achieve it with as little interference as possible to aboriginal and treaty rights.

(6) Where a government action permitted by (5) impairs or suspends a right guaranteed by subsection (1) to the substantial detriment of an aboriginal person or group, just compensation shall be promptly paid.

As mentioned earlier, it is not necessarily wise to define the constitutional protection afforded to aboriginal rights, treaty rights, and agreements on self-government. Now that the focus of the national level constitutional process has settled on the self-government agreements, participants ought to reflect on the level of protection that is appropriate. There will, unfortunately, be the usual barriers to an in-depth discussion of legal meaning: some participants will continue to be strictly reactive; others will confine their initiatives to those that cannot possibly give offence; and others will insist that discussions be kept at the "political" rather than technical level. Thus far, the legal meaning of s.35's protection has been less the subject of discussion than an unrecognized source of confusion and machinations. The subterranean battle over the drafting of the sexual equality clause has been largely based on the implications of the clause of the broader legal meaning of s.35(1). Considerable confusion was reflected in the proposal of the government of British Columbia at the April '85 First Ministers' Conference that the constitutional commitment to negotiate self-government agreements contain a reference to the "sovereign authority" of Parliament and the legislatures. If agreements on self-government are supposed to be constitutionally recognized and affirmed, and if that means they are to some extent protected from legislative override, has there not been a diminution of the sovereign authority of Parliament and the legislatures? And if there hasn't been, why bother acknowledging self-government agreements in the constitution?

The cases on s.35(1) so far have consistently upheld the continuing supremacy of regulations that existed on April 17, 1982, over Indian treaty rights (*R.* v. *Eninew* (1984), 1 D.L.R. (4th) 595 (Sask. Q.B.) affd. on other grounds at (1985), 10 D.L.R.

(4th) 137 (Sask. C.A.), *Steinhauer* v. *R.*, [1985] 3 C.N.L.R. 187 (Alta. Q.B.), *R.* v. *Hare and Debassige*, [1985] 3 C.N.L.R. 139 (Ont. C.A.), *R.* v. *Riley et al.*, [1984] 2 C.N.L.R. 154 (Ont. Prov. Off. Ct.)). (The courts have suggested that a treaty right is protected by s.35(1) only in the impaired form in which it existed on April 17, 1982. They have not had to deal head-on with a case of a regulatory restriction that is no more severe than one existing on April 17, 1982, but their reasoning suggests that these regulations could be valid.)

Chapter XXV

The Application of the Canadian Charter of Rights and Freedoms to Aboriginal Governments

At a ministerial meeting on February 13-14, 1984, the attorney general of Manitoba tabled a position paper on self-government. It called for a political accord which would commit the parties to recognize the right of aboriginal peoples to self-government and provide those governments with adequate fiscal support. The political accord would also provide for "the applicability of the *Charter of Rights and Freedoms* to aboriginal governments with such modifications as may be necessary to ensure the preservation and development of distinctive aboriginal traditions, cultures, languages and institutions". The general issue raised by the Manitoba paper has received very little attention during the s.37 conferences. The application to aboriginal governments of the particular principle of sexual equality was reinforced by a constitutional amendment agreed to at the March '83 First Ministers' Conference. Dissatisfaction in some quarters with the scope of that amendment was a contributing factor to the obscure and farcical struggle at the March '84 First Ministers' Conference to agree upon a further amendment. At the April '85 First Ministers' Conference, there was broad agreement among the First Ministers that further express recognition of sexual equality was a good thing, but the consensus on an essentially unnecessary amendment was forgotten when the parties could not agree on amendments dealing with the fundamental issue of the conference – aboriginal self-government. The injustice wreaked by the sexually discriminatory s.12(1)(b) of the *Indian*

Act, finally repealed in 1985, caused serious and legitimate concern about sexual equality in aboriginal communities. (The section withdrew Indian status from Indian women who married non-status men, but bestowed Indian status on the non-Indian wife of an Indian man.) Politicians have been eager to agree upon amendments that looked ideologically correct, appealed to supporters of women's rights, and did not cost governments anything substantial in the way of power or money. Meanwhile, the abstract and electorally irrelevant issue of the applicability of the *Charter* to Indian governments has gone basically unnoticed. If aboriginal governments grow in autonomy and authority, however, it is of first importance to consider how they will treat their own people.

The American Experience

A useful preliminary to diagnosis and prescription of the equivalent problem in Canada may be a study of how American constitutional law has dealt with the applicability of the *Bill of Rights* and the Fourteenth Amendment ("equal protection of the laws") to Indian government.

Talton v. *Mayes*, 163 U.S. 376 (1896) is the leading case on the applicability of the *Bill of Rights* to Indian government. The case began in the federal courts as a writ of habeas corpus filed in a district court by a prisoner sentenced to death by a Cherokee court. The victim was a Cherokee, and the crime took place in Cherokee territory. The claim for federal relief maintained, among other things, that the indictment was issued by a Cherokee grand jury of only five members, which body was not a valid grand jury as contemplated by the Fifth Amendment to the American Constitution. The federal judge discharged the writ. The prisoner appealed to the United States Supreme Court. The Supreme Court ruled against him. The Fifth Amendment, it said, applied to only the federal level of government. Indian governments did not derive their authority from the federal government; as semi-independent political communities, they had inherent authority to regulate their internal affairs.

The official report records a dissent by Mr. Justice Harlan but no reasons. It seems to me that there were very strong grounds for disagreement with the Court's reasoning. Article 5 of the 1835 treaty with the Cherokee (1835, 7 Stat. 478, 481) provided that the Cherokee could make and enforce their own laws ". . . provided always that *they shall not be inconsistent with the Constitution of the United States* and such acts of Congress as have been or may be passed regulating trade and intercourse with the Indians . . ." (emphasis added).

Section 31 of *An Act to provide a temporary government for the Territory of Oklahoma, to enlarge the jurisdiction of the United States court in the Indian Territory, and for other purposes* (approved May 2, 1890, c.182, 26 Stat. 81) provided that:

> *The Constitution of the United States* and all general laws of the United States which prohibit crimes and misdemeanors in any place within the sole and exclusive jurisdiction of the United States, except the District of Columbia, and all laws relating to national banking associations, *shall have the same force and effect in the Indian Territory as elsewhere in the United States; but nothing in this act shall be so construed as to deprive any of the courts of the civilized nations of exclusive jurisdiction* over all cases arising wherein members of said nations, whether by treaty, blood or adoption, are the sole parties, *nor so as to interfere with the rights and powers of said civilized nations to punish said members for violation of the statutes and laws enacted by their national councils where such are not contrary to the treaties and laws of the United States* (emphasis added).

The Court could have held that a Cherokee law was inconsistent with the Constitution if it violated a basic principle of the *Bill of Rights*. The Court could have adopted the sort of approach that some of its members would later apply to state governments: not all the detailed provisions of the *Bill of Rights* apply to Indian governments, only those rights which are among "the fundamental principles of liberty and justice which lie at the base of all our civil and political institutions" (*Herbert* v. *Louisiana*, 272 U.S. 312, 316 (1926)); in the context of civil and criminal proceedings, "a fundamental right, essential to a fair trial" (*Gideon* v. *Wainwright*, 372 U.S. 335 (1963)). The Court would then embark upon the difficult and somewhat subjective task of determining which aspects of the individual guarantees in the American Constitution are essential. The inquiry would be conducted with respect for the traditions and inherent autonomy of Indian nations. In *Talton*, for example, it might have been held that the defendant was not seriously prejudiced by the mere fact that Cherokee law provided for a grand jury smaller than the usual Anglo-American one. (On the facts of the *Talton* case, the approach I am suggesting would have required the Court to go on and examine whether Cherokee law on grand jury indictments was in fact honoured and whether the trial itself was sufficiently fair to be consistent with the Fifth Amendment.) It should be remembered that in deciding *Talton*, the Court relied on its own precedents that the Fifth Amendment did not apply to American states—a view it would later abandon (see Gunther 1980, 478). While the change in practice with respect to states would have justified a re-examination of the validity of *Talton*, the Supreme Court has never done so.

An even later development that might have been applied to Indian governments was the Supreme Court's decision in *Marsh* v. *Alabama*, 326 U.S. 501 (1946). A Jehovah's Witness was convicted under state trespass law for distributing pamphlets in a company town against the wishes of the owner. The Supreme Court reversed the conviction on the grounds that it violated the First Amendment's guarantee of religious freedom. The Court did not rely principally on the involvement of the state of Alabama in enforcing the private owner's illiberality. Rather, the Court found that the town "in its community aspects did not differ from other towns" and that its private managers were exercising what was essentially a "public function."

> *The managers appointed by the corporation* cannot curtail the liberty of press and religion of these people consistently with the purposes of the Constitutional guarantees, and a state statute, as the one here involved, which enforces such action by criminally punishing those who attempt to distribute religious literature clearly violates the First and Fourteenth Amendments to the Constitution (326 U.S. 501, 508 (1946)) (emphasis added).

The Court might have extended *Marsh* and the applicability of the *Bill of Rights* to other communities governed by non-state, non-federal authorities—including Indian tribes. It could, again, have applied the guarantees of the federal Constitution with sensitivity to the constitutionally recognized autonomy of Indian bands. It must be conceded, however, that various rights guarantees of the Constitution expressly refer to state and federal authorities but nowhere to other kinds of governments. The *Marsh* precedent concerned an entity which, unlike an Indian tribe, had no inherent authority to make laws and enforce them. The texts of the Constitution and interpretive precedents would not have provided strong support for a judicial extension of individual rights guarantees to persons under the jurisdiction of Indian tribal governments.

The analysis just provided of *Talton* suggests that a particular treaty and statute could have been relied upon by the court wishing to apply the *basic* individual rights constraints of the federal Constitution to the Cherokee nation. A strictly constitutional route was available to reach the same result. The Court could have held that adherence to the basic principles of constitutional fairness are implicit limitations on the inherent sovereignty of Indian nations. In *Oliphant* v. *The Squamish Indian Tribe,* 435 U.S. 191 (1978), for example, the United States Supreme Court held that one implicit limitation was that Indian courts could not try non-Indians. "Upon incorporation into the territory of the United States, the Indian tribes thereby come under the territorial sovereignty of the United States and their exercise of separate power is constrained so as not to conflict with the interests of this overriding sovereignty" (435 U.S. 191, 209). Minimal fairness to Indians from their own governmental agencies, no less than the protection of non-Indians from an alien legal system, could have been held to be a fundamental interest of the ultimately sovereign federal level of government.

A resource available to interventionist federal courts in the general run of cases would have been the federal role in the constitution and operation of Indian governmental agencies. In two cases involving different tribes, federal courts actually held that federal involvement in the establishment of constitutions and funding of tribal Courts warranted considering them "in part, at least, arms of the federal government" (see *Colliflower* v. *Garland,* 342 F. 2d 369, 379 (1965); *Settler* v. *Yakima Tribal Court* 419 F. 2d 486 (1968)). The courts concluded that a writ of habeas corpus to the federal courts was available to challenge the constitutional propriety of a person detained by a tribal court. The "in part" language might have been later developed to prevent courts from imposing the entire corpus of federal constitutional safeguards on the bands and instead apply only those most essential to maintaining basic fairness. The reasoning would be that tribal courts are also "in part" Indian courts, and due regard must be paid to Indian autonomy. A larger number of federal cases, however, focussed on Indian institutions other than courts and followed *Talton*. This line of cases was affirmed and applied in connection with a Navajo Tribal Court in the 1978 United States Supreme Court case *United States* v. *Wheeler*, 435 U.S. 313. The Court unanimously held that federal statutes and executive decisions which authorized or approved the operation of the Navajo Court did not turn it into an arm of the federal government. According to Justice Stewart:

> But none of these lawyers *created* the Indians' power to govern themselves and their right to punish crimes committed by tribal offenders. . . . That Congress has in certain ways regulated the manner and extent of the tribal power of self-government does not mean that Congress is the source of that power.
>
> In sum, the power to punish offenses against tribal law committed by Tribe members, which was part of the Navajos' primeval sovereignty, has never been taken away from them, either explicitly or implicitly, and is attributable in no way to any delegation to them of federal authority. It follows that when the Navajo Tribe exercises this power, it does so as part of its retained sovereignty and not as an arm of the Federal Government (435 U.S. 313, 328).

Wheeler had been convicted of contributing to the delinquency of a minor by a Navajo Tribal Court. When indicted in federal court for rape on account of the same incident, he pleaded the Fifth Amendment's guarantee against double jeopardy. The Supreme Court ruled that the federal trial could proceed; double jeopardy only applied to a second trial by the same sovereign authority. The Navajo Tribal Court in *Wheeler* had been established by the Navajo Tribal Council in 1958; the Supreme Court expressly (footnote 25 of its judgment) left undecided whether certain courts established by federal regulations ought to be considered arms of the federal government.

Indian Civil Rights Act

The balance between Indian autonomy and the individual safeguards of the Constitution was finally struck not by the courts but by Congress, in the 1968 *Indian Civil Rights Act*. Among the motivating factors at play in Congress were:

- a philosophical commitment of the lead legislator, Senator Sam Ervin of North Carolina, to the extension of constitutional protections to Indians (Burnett 1971-72, 557, 575)
- perceived defects in the Indian Court system, including in various cases:
  - the right of refusal to allow lawyers to represent litigants in the court
  - no right against self-incrimination
  - small juries, often allowed to decide by majority, or in some areas, no right to a jury trial at all

- inadequate appeal provisions, such as *ad hoc* appellate panels which included laymen (Burnett 1971-72, 557, 577-81).

- oppressive legislation by some tribal councils; for example, a Navajo ban on the use of peyote which is the central sacrament of the Native American Church (see *Toledo* v. *Pueblo de Jemez*, 119 F. Supp. 429 (D.N.M. 1954); cf. *People* v. *Woody*, 40 Cal. Rptr. 69, in which the state supreme court held that a California law that prohibited peyote use could not constitutionally be applied against its ceremonial use by the Native American Church.)

The act balanced its limitation on the power of band governments with a number of provisions protecting their sovereignty. Of particular importance is §25 U.S.C.A. 1321-1322 (Supplement 1969), which provided that states could not apply their civil and criminal law to an area of Indian country without the consent of the band expressed through a special election. Title II is the major limitation on band authority. It applies to bands many of the guarantees of the federal Constitution. Here is the text, along with some comments on the source of each provision in the federal Constitution, and the reasons for any modifications:

Text:	§1302. No Indian Tribe in exercising powers of self-government shall – (1) make or enforce any law prohibiting the free exercise of religion, or abridging the freedom of speech or of the press, or the right of the people peaceably to assemble and to petition for a redress of grievances;
Source and Modification:	First Amendment. The ban on the establishment of religion is removed in order to protect the theocratic constitutions of some tribes.
Text:	(2) violate the right of the people to be secure in their persons, houses, papers and effects against unreasonable search and seizures, nor issue warrants, but upon probable cause, supported by oath or affirmation, and particularly describing the place to be searched and the person or thing to be seized;

Source and Modification: Fourth Amendment. The Second Amendment (right to maintain state militia, bear arms) and Third Amendment (right to refuse to quarter soldiers) were omitted on the theory that tribes are not authorized to maintain armies (Burnett 1971-72, 590).

Text: (3) subject any person for the same offense to be twice put in jeopardy;

Source and Modification: Fifth Amendment, only not confined to cases involving "life and limb." No Indian cases would involve either, and American Courts have, by interpretation, extended double jeopardy to all serious offences; *Ex parte Lange* 85 U.S. (18 Wall) 163 (1873).

Text: (4) compel any person in any criminal case to be a witness against himself

(5) take any property for a public use without just compensation

(6) deny to any person in a criminal proceeding the right to a speedy and public trial, to be informed of the nature and cause of the accusation, to be confronted with the witnesses against him, to have compulsory process for obtaining witnesses in his favor, and at his own expense to have the assistance of counsel for his defense;

Source and Modification: Sixth Amendment. The venue rules are deleted. The right to trial by jury is provided in limited form by subsection (10). The requirement of a Grand Jury indictment in serious criminal cases (Fifth Amendment) and the right to a jury in common law actions where twenty dollars or more are at stake (Seventh Amendment) were considered to be too expensive a burden for tribes and of doubtful value in any event (Burnett 1971-72, 590). Expressly denied, for fiscal reasons also, is the duty of the government to pay the counsel fees of an indigent accused; in

	Gideon v. *Wainwright*, 372 U.S. 335 (1953) the Supreme Court found such a duty to be implicit in the Fifth Amendment.
Text:	(7) require excessive bail, impose excessive fines, inflict cruel and unusual punishments, and in no event impose for conviction of any one offense any penalty or punishment greater than imprisonment for a term of six months or a fine of $500, or both;
Source and Modification:	Eighth Amendment. The $500/6 months limitation is an addition. The federal "Seven Major Crimes Act" (*Indian Appropriations Act,* 23 stat. 385) of 1885, vests in federal courts exclusive jurisdiction over the most serious types of crime on Indian reserves (Burnett 1971-72, 562). Aggravated assault was added to the list by another section of the *Indian Civil Rights Act* (s.501).
Text:	(8) deny any person within its jurisdiction the equal protection of its laws or deprive any person of liberty or property without due process of law.
Source and Modification:	Fourteenth Amendment. The prohibition on denying any person the "privileges and immunities" of an American citizen is deleted, for reasons I have not yet determined – possibly the obscurity of meaning.
Text:	(9) pass any bill of attainder or ex post facto law; or
Source and Modification:	Article I, Section 9
Text:	(10) deny to any person accused of an offense punishable by imprisonment the right, upon request, to a trial by jury of not less than six persons.

Source and Modification: Sixth Amendment, but applicable only to offenses punishable by imprisonment, rather than "all criminal cases." The Sixth Amendment does not expressly speak to jury size but was held in 1970 to allow six-member juries; *Williams* v. *Florida*, 399 U.S. 78 (1970).

Text: §1303 *Habeas Corpus*
The privilege of the writ of habeas corpus shall be available to any person, in a court of the United States, to test the legality of his detention by order of an Indian tribe.

Source and Modification: Article I, Section 9, which prohibits the suspension of habeas corpus except during emergencies.

A 1969 note in the Harvard Law Review (82 Harv. L.R., 1343 (1969)) considered what turned out to be a crucial ambiguity in the *Indian Civil Rights Act*—whether §1303, which guaranteed habeas corpus to federal courts, was the only remedy contemplated by Congress or merely an especially important one among many:

> The Senate committee expressed no intention to limit remedies to habeas corpus. Rather, provision of the writ resulted from the special concern that there be means of assuring that the statute's procedural rights were effectively guaranteed to criminal defendants.
>
> Also the Senate committee, in its report listing habeas corpus amidst the other guarantees, seems to have regarded habeas corpus not simply as a remedy but also as a right. For these two reasons, the provision for habeas corpus should not be taken as implying that other remedies were intended not to be available.
>
> If no remedy other than habeas corpus were available, a large portion of the rights guaranteed by the statutes—all those which might be infringed without "detention by order of an Indian tribe"—would be unprotected and therefore ineffectual (82 Harv. L.R. 1343, 1371 (1969)).

The last sentence should have been qualified a little. Many Indian institutions could be expected to make a good faith effort to constrain their own conduct in accordance with federal law. Enforcement by the federal courts, however, would obviously ensure more widespread, invariant and strict compliance. It seems very unlikely that a Congress that was itself subject to federal judicial review, in the same era in which it was passing many new statutes providing for the federal judicial enforcement of civil rights, intended Indian institutions to be immune from such scrutiny.

Most of the federal courts faced with Indian Civil Rights Act (ICRA) suits held that they did indeed have jurisdiction, citing 28 U.S.C.§1343 (4) which gives a federal district court jurisdiction over:

> any civil action authorized by law to be commenced by any person:
>
> (4) To recover damages or to secure equitable or other relief under any Act of Congress providing for the protection of Civil rights, including the right to vote.
>
> (see for example: *Dry Creek Lodge Inc.* v. *United States*, 515 F. 2d 926 (10th. Cir. 1975); *Crowe* v. *Eastern Band of Cherokee Indians Inc.*, 506 F. 2d 316 (4th Cir. 1974). Cf. *Yellow Bird* v. *Oglala Sioux Tribe of South Dakota*, 380 F. Supp. 438 (D.S. Dak. 1974)).

Tribal governments have been held to have the same common law immunity from law suits as other "sovereigns;" *Turner* v. *The United States*, 248 U.S. 354, 358 (1919); *Puyallup Tribe* v. *Department of Game of Washington*, 433 U.S. 165, 172-173 (1977). The federal courts held that this immunity was implicitly abrogated by the *Indian Civil Rights Act* to the extent necessary to enforce it; *Daly* v. *The United States*, 483 F. 2d. 700, 705 (1973).

The federal courts began to develop a line of interpretation that was sensitive to both the liberal individualist safeguards of ICRA and the statute's general reaffirmation of tribal political autonomy. In *Daly* v. *The United States*, for example, a federal court of appeal held that the precedents on the equality guarantee of the Fourteenth Amendment should not always be strictly applied to the interpretation of the ICRA. Although the Fourteenth Amendment case law makes racially-based legislative classifications highly suspect, the Court upheld a provision in the constitution of the Crow Creek Sioux Tribe that members of the government be of at least one-half Indian ancestry. The tribe had a sufficient "cultural interest" to sustain the discrimination. On the other hand, the Court found "intolerable" a voting district plan (ordered by a lower court) that would have grossly deviated from the one person one vote standard that the Supreme Court has applied to state legislatures. (While I have cited *Daly* as an example of an attempt to produce a balanced interpretation of the ICRA, the Court might have been more searching in its examination of the blood quantum requirement.)

The efforts of the federal courts to develop a sophisticated approach to the interpretation of the ICRA were abruptly squelched by the decision of the Supreme Court of the United States *in Santa Clara Pueblo* v. *Martinez*, 436 U.S. 49 (1978). The federal courts were informed that they generally lacked jurisdiction to hear ICRA cases.

The council of the Santa Clara Pueblo adopted, in 1939, an ordinance that stipulated the following rules on tribal membership:

1. When two Santa Clarans marry each other, the children are Santa Clarans.
2. If a male Santa Claran marries an outsider, the children are Santa Clarans.
3. If a female Santa Claran marries an outsider, the children are not members of Santa Clara.
4. No one can be naturalized as a member of Santa Clara under any circumstances.

By virtue of rule (3), the eight living children of Mrs. Martinez were not eligible for membership in the Pueblo. As a result, they did not have full political rights, did not have equal land use rights, and were not guaranteed that they would be able to stay in the Pueblo after their mother's death. Mrs. Martinez brought a class action suit on behalf of the female members who had intermarried and their children, challenging the Pueblo ordinance as a sexually discriminatory contravention of the equal protection clause of the ICRA.

The district court held that it had jurisdiction to hear the case but ruled against the plaintiffs "on the merits." The scare quotes are used because Justice Mechem declined to adjudicate the necessity and effectiveness of the discriminatory measures. The plaintiffs had argued that it was irrational to exclude from membership people like the children of Mrs. Martinez, who lived on the reserve and spoke its language, whereas the totally assimilated, off-reserve offspring of a male Santa Claran would be entitled to membership. Replied Justice Mechem:

> Even assuming plaintiffs are correct, the equal protection guarantee of the Indian Civil Rights Act should not be construed in a manner which would require or authorize this Court to determine which traditional values will promote cultural survival and therefore should be preserved and which of them are inimical to cultural survival and should therefore be abrogated . . .
>
> Much has been written about tribal sovereignty. If those words have any meaning at all, they must mean that a tribe can make and enforce its decisions without regard to whether an external authority considers those decisions wise. To abrogate tribal decisions, particularly in the delicate area of membership, for whatever "good" reasons, is to destroy cultural identity under the guise of saving it. Congress has not indicated that it intended the Indian Civil Rights Act to be interpreted in such a manner (402 F. Supp. 1, 18-19 (1975)).

What then was the point of passing the *Indian Civil Rights Act*? It rather obviously was intended to establish for Indian governments a set of external standards and external enforcement. The difficulty of construing the act should not have led the district court to balk at making the attempt.

The Federal Court of Appeal confronted the issues directly. It held that "the interest of the Tribe in maintaining its integrity and in retaining its tribal culture is entitled due consideration" (540 F. 2d 1039, 1046 (1976)). The Fourteenth Amendment standards did not "apply with full force" but did "serve as a persuasive guide to the decision" (540 F. 2d 1039, 1047 (1976)). The court found that the tribe had no compelling interest in maintaining its sexually discriminatory membership test. If the problem was ensuring that membership in the Pueblo was not extended to persons who were insufficiently educated in its traditions, solutions were available that were not sexually discriminatory. Prior to the passage of the ordinance in 1939, the status of mixed-marriage children was decided on a case-by-case basis. If the ordinance was directed towards keeping population growth on the Pueblo within manageable bounds, all the children of mixed marriages could have been excluded from membership. There would seem to have been other non-sexist alternatives besides the case-by-case determination or total exclusion options suggested by the court. The band might have extended membership only to any mixed-marriage child who was raised on the reserve or any such child fluent in the native language. The sexist aspect of the ordinance does indeed seem to have been unwarranted by any strong consideration of cultural integrity or even administrative convenience.

The Supreme Court of the United States held that the federal courts had no jurisdiction in the matter (436 U.S. 49 (1978)). Apart from allowing habeas corpus proceedings, the ICRA did not limit the sovereign immunity from suit of Indian tribal governments. Apart from habeas corpus proceedings, no private remedy was express or implied in the ICRA, so 28 USC §1343(4) was not available to give the federal courts jurisdiction over an action for declaratory and injunctive relief. Marshall J., who wrote the majority opinion, cited the legal tradition of Indian tribal sovereignty and the provisions of the ICRA that affirmed Indian political autonomy. A construction of the ICRA should not be adopted that gives too much weight to the civil rights objectives of the act at the expense of its other goal of strengthening tribal sovereignty. If the federal courts allowed private actions, apart from habeas corpus, the authority of tribal courts would be undermined, and serious financial burdens would be imposed on "financially disadvantaged" tribes; 436 U.S. 49, 64 (1978). The civil rights concerns of Congress would be sufficiently protected by tribal courts, which were obliged to apply the substantive provisions of the ICRA; "Tribal Courts have repeatedly been recognized as appropriate forums for the exclusive adjudication of disputes affecting important personal and property interests of both Indians and non-Indians" (436 U.S. 49, 65 (1978)). The legislative history of the ICRA is cited by Justice Marshall as supporting the view that habeas corpus by prisoners was the federal remedy available to band members aggrieved by non-compliance with the act. Yet no statement by any legislator involved that habeas corpus was the sole remedy is adduced by Marshall J. The best he can do is show that Congress was concerned with balancing tribal sovereignty against individual rights, that Congress rejected proposals for full federal review of *all* convictions in tribal courts, and that it rejected another proposal authorizing the federal attorney general to investigate and launch criminal or civil proceedings in connection with complaints by a band member concerning a violation of statutory or constitutional rights.

In the sole dissenting opinion, Justice White held that: "To suggest that this tribal body is the 'appropriate' forum for the adjudication of alleged violations of the ICRA is to ignore both reality and Congress' desire to provide a means of redress to

Indians aggrieved by their tribal leaders" (436 U.S. 49, 82 (1978)).

It may be that the Supreme Court thought it was avoiding a difficult value question by exercising one of the "passive virtues" – in this case, declining jurisdiction (Bickel 1962). Whatever the reasoning behind the reasoning, the result of the Supreme Court's ruling is that federal remedies are altogether unavailable to an Indian whose ICRA rights have been violated – unless he or she is fortunate enough to be placed in involuntary confinement.

The Canadian Charter of Rights and Freedoms and Indian Government in Canada: Does the Charter apply only to federal, provincial and territorial governments?

The American doctrine that the individual rights guarantees of the federal Constitution do not of their own force apply to Indian bands is founded on two premises:

(i) the guarantees in the federal Constitution generally apply only to the federal level of government and, through the operation of the Fourteenth Amendment, the states; they have never applied of their own force against persons in the private sphere. (Involvement by federal and state authorities – funding, encouragement, authorization – may constitute sufficient state involvement to turn the conduct of a private individual into "state action" (see generally, Tribe 1978, 1149; Swinton 1982; Gibson 1983).)

(ii) Indian bands have inherent self-governing authority and are not delegates of the federal government or the states.

Does the first premise hold for Canada? The answer may vary among different sections of the *Charter* according to their nature and language. A provision that might be of overriding force is s.32:

32(1) This *Charter* applies

(a) to the Parliament and government of Canada in respect of all matters within the authority of Parliament including all matters relating to the Yukon Territory and Northwest Territories; and

(b) to the legislature and government of each province in respect of all matters within the authority of the legislature of each province.

The drafting history speaks strongly, though not irresistibly, against the application of the *Charter* to the private sector. The first version of s.32 used the phrase "and to" in place of the present "in respect of." The earlier version was thus far more favourable to the position that the *Charter* is supposed to apply to both the government and private sector. Senior officials at the Department of Justice testified even in the face of the earlier version that it was the department's or the government's understanding that the *Charter* did not apply to private transactions (H.C. and Senate, 23rd, 1st Sess., Sp. Jt. Com. on Constitution of Canada, Minutes Nos. 35-47 and Nos. 48-57 (1980-81); see for example, Tasse 15 January 1931, 50; Jordan 29 January 1981, 33; Jordan 30 January 1981, 47 ([during a discussion of the earlier version of s.32])).

Usually, the opinion of federal officials at the time of the drafting of the *Charter* should not be given much weight (see Gibson 1982). According to the Supreme Court of Canada in the *Patriation Reference* ((1981), 125 D.L.R. (3d) 1), the legal sovereign over the Canadian constitution in 1981 was the Parliament of Great Britain. Its members by and large expressed no opinion on the meaning of merits of the *Charter*, and their silence was justified by the principle of Canadian political independence. Furthermore, the common law rule in the United Kingdom continues to be that Parliamentary debates cannot be cited in court. If interpreters are to look instead to the intentions of Canadians who were politically responsible for bringing about the *Charter*, they must look well beyond the opinions of senior federal bureaucrats. Even if they represent the understanding of the justice minister of the government at the time, they may not represent the views of the prime minister, the rest of the Cabinet, or the ordinary members of the Parliament who voted for the package. The opinion of provincial officials must also be considered; according to the Supreme Court of Canada, a "substantial measure" of provincial support was a constitutional (although strictly conventional) prerequisite to the federal government requesting the British Parliament to enact the patriation package; *Patriation Reference* (1981), 125 D.L.R. (3d) 1. Often, the unascertainability of divergence of opinions would leave an interpreter considerable justification for giving little or no weight to "original intentions."

In the case of s.32, however, the legislative history provides somewhat more guidance than usual. The general understanding of its drafters that the *Charter* did not apply to the private sector is on the record. Mr. Robinson of the New Democratic Party proposed to the Special Joint Committee on the Constitution that s.15 be amended so that discrimination in employment and accommodation would be proscribed. Senior Counsel Fred Jordan of the Department of Justice stated in the presence of his minister that the government's view was that the *Charter* generally ought not to apply to the private sector and that private discrimination ought to be dealt with by human rights legislation (H.C. and Senate, 33rd., 1st Sess., Sp. Jt. Com. on Constitution of Canada, Minutes Nos. 48-57 (1980-81); Jordan 29 January 1981, 29)). The amendment was defeated by a vote of 21 to 2. When section 32 was substantially amended so as to be much less amenable to the interpretation that the private sector was covered by the *Charter*, there was, it appears, little or no Parliamentary, provincial, or public protest.

Whatever the subjective intentions behind it, the textual fact remain that s.32 expressly states that the *Charter* applies to governments. It nowhere states that the *Charter* applies to private activity. The actual provisions of the *Charter* are replete with express and implied limitations on the powers of governments and legislatures. In the absence of any reference to the scope of the *Charter*, it would have been obvious that it applies to governmental activity. If the *Charter* is, for interpretive purposes, supposed to be the product of an imaginary "skilful framer," it would seem that a primary function of s.32 is to establish that the *Charter* generally applies *only* to governmental activities. A skilful framer who wanted the *Charter* to apply to the private sector would not have inserted section 32. The risk would have been too high. The tradition in Canadian and American constitutional law is that constitutional safeguards in favour of individuals and minorities operate only against the state. By stipulating that the *Charter* applies to governmental activity and failing to indicate that it applies to the private sector, s.32 provides powerful ammunition for those who would maintain that the usual constitutional practice is being followed. The countervailing benefits would have appeared minimal to any well-informed framer, as will now be shown.

Professor Gibson has suggested that the framers of s.32 could have wished to avoid three possibilities:

- that courts would honour the common law presumption that statutes do not limit the powers of the Crown
- that courts would continue the Canadian tradition of deference to legislative bodies and hold that the *Charter* does not apply to the latter
- that courts would hold that the *Charter*, like the *Canadian Bill of Rights*, applies only to the federal level of government (Gibson 1982).

The language of Professor Gibson's article is unclear on whether it is talking about what the framers of s.32 *actually did* intend as opposed to what a hypothetical framer might have intended. The concerns mentioned should not have loomed large to any skilful framer, real or hypothetical. The presumption against restrictions on Crown powers, as Professor Gibson acknowledges, yields to necessary implications to the contrary. Some sections of the *Charter* are expressly applicable to the executive institutions (e.g., ss. 16 and 20). Many others are implicitly applicable to Crown agents (e.g., s.8, guarantee against unreasonable search and seizure). Similarly, there are sections of the *Charter* (e.g. sections 3, 4, 5, 16, 17, 18, 19, 20) that are expressly applicable to legislative bodies, and many others (e.g. s.23, minority language educational rights; s.15, equality before the law) that implicitly limit or mandate legislative activity. Section 33 of the *Charter* (which allows legislation to override certain sections of the *Charter* if the legislation says it does) would be useless if the *Charter* did not bind legislatures in the first place. The applicability of the *Charter* to provincial legislatures, rather than simply Parliament, is made apparent by sections that expressly encompass legislatures (ss. 3, 4, 5) and others that deal with areas of exclusive provincial jurisdiction (s.23).

It has been argued that the complexities of working out a doctrine of what constitutes "state action" as opposed to "private activity" should encourage the courts to hold that the *Charter* applies to all activity (Gibson 1983). I would agree that the American case law is inconsistent and confused. It will be difficult for the Canadian courts to articulate principles that provide genuine guidance for future cases. But these difficulties will not be averted by holding that the *Charter* applies to both public and private activity. The difficulties will re-emerge when the merits of a *Charter* case must be assessed. Even if the *Charter* applies to a private person, the fact that it is not a government agency will be of first importance in assessing whether its activity passes muster under the *Charter*. A court might hold that the freedom of religion and association guaranteed by s.2 of the *Charter* would justify a private religious school in hiring only teachers of its faith. These defences would surely not be available to a provincial government that discriminated in its hiring practices for public schools. A court would be justified in holding that the government is not a beneficiary of s.2; from the point of view of the state, section 2 rights are only constraints. According to the political theory of liberal individualism, the role of the state is to impartially and fairly assist its citizens in pursuing the ends they each have freely chosen. The state is not allowed to impose its own ideas of the good life. This basic idea should and will be reflected, in some form, in the deliberations of judges about how the substantive guarantees of the *Charter* ought to be understood. The public/private distinction is not neat, but it is inevitable and necessary.

It must be acknowledged that powerful philosophical arguments can be made in favour of construing the *Charter* as applicable to the private sphere. Liberal theories of justice from John Locke's *The Second Treatise of Government* to Bruce Ackerman's *Social Justice in the Liberal State* have started with the premise that individuals have rights against all other individuals. The state is conceived of as an instrument for protecting rights. My own views are consistent with this line of theories. Private individuals may exert no less power over your life than public institutions and may be no less ruthless in their tyranny. We should not unreflectively follow the American doctrine that the Constitution applies only to governments. The American *Bill of Rights* was inserted in the federal Constitution as a safeguard against abuses by a federal authority whose power was being greatly enhanced. The federal Constitution was itself enacted in the aftermath of a revolutionary war against the tyranny of a central government.

If the *Charter* is construed as not applying to the private sector, then it is inevitable that in some cases a person will have no legal remedy when he is grievously injured by the injustice of another person. The risk should not, however, be overestimated. Ordinary civil litigation, the pursuit of administrative remedies (for example the intervention of provincial Human Rights Commissions), and the application of the *Criminal Code* will generally provide at least some relief for a person seriously wronged by another. Indeed, a legitimate objection to construing the *Charter* as applicable universally is that it is unwise to constitutionalize a number of social areas that are presently regulated by other legal regimes.

Section 24(1) of the *Charter* states that: "Anyone whose rights or freedoms, as guaranteed by this *Charter*, have been infringed or denied may apply to a court of competent jurisdiction to obtain such remedy as the court considers appropriate and just in the circumstances". The availability of a judicial remedy to anyone wronged by another individual contrary to the guarantees of the *Charter* may seriously undermine alternate dispute settlement schemes. Provincial human rights acts, for example, provide a specialized body of rules and remedies for discrimination in the private sector. These regimes may be more expeditious, inexpensive, and conciliatory than the court battles contemplated by section 24(1) of the *Charter*. The substantive rules may strike a better balance between equality and liberty than the Supreme Court will in its interpretation of s.15 of the *Charter* (every individual is equal before and under the law). If the *Charter* applies to the private sector, and if the courts give a broad construction to the substance of s.15 – if most human activity is considered as being "before and under the law" – then individuals with equality complaints could ignore the provincial rules and remedies for discrimination.

In the end, it may make very little difference to the "won-lost column" of lawsuits how the courts construe s.32. The courts might hold that the *Charter* only applies to governments but turn around and adopt a very encompassing definition of "state action" and of the scope of the substantive provisions of the *Charter*. One recommendation I would make to the courts would be that they not lose sight of the distinction in principle between public and private activity while they struggle through a thicket of more legalistic issues – e.g. whether the internal corporate by-laws of a private school that discriminate against non-members of the faith are "law," and thus subject to the "equality before the law" guarantee of s.15 of the *Charter* (see generally Slattery 1985).

From the foregoing analysis, it appears likely that the courts will hold that the *Charter* only applies to the activities of federal and provincial governments and not to the private sector. To determine whether the activities of an Indian government are constrained by the *Charter*, it would be necessary to examine the level of federal and provincial involvement in the activities of the Indian government. The next section will examine the principles that would be involved.

It might be suggested that, regardless of federal or provincial involvement in its activities, a private entity should be viewed as constrained by the *Charter* whenever it is acting like a government (see Gibson 1983). It may be recalled that in *Marsh* v. *Alabama*, 326 U.S. 501 (1946), the United States Supreme Court held that a company in a town wholly-owned by the company and occupied by company employees was governed by the American *Bill of Rights*. It might be urged, with *Marsh* serving as an analogy, that an Indian government in Canada should be held to be subject to the *Charter* if it exercises government-like power over the lives of the residents of the community. (Policy arguments in favour of applying the *Charter* to Indian governments will be advanced a little later in this discussion.) If an aboriginal government were held to have inherent powers over a broad range of internal issues, including the right to use force to carry out its collective judgments, then there would be much appeal to following the *Marsh* analogy.

There are weighty textual arguments, however, against applying the reasoning in *Marsh* to Canadian Indian governments. Section 30 establishes that references in the *Charter* to provincial governments and legislatures apply to their counterparts in the Yukon and Northwest Territories. Nowhere is there any suggestion that Indian governments are bound by the *Charter*. It is possible that the framers of the *Charter* did not seriously consider the possibility that Indian bands might have an inherent constitutional right to self-government.

Do Aboriginal Governments Have Inherent Authority?

The American doctrine that the *Bill of Rights* does not of its own force apply to Indian governments is based on their constitutional status as "domestic dependent nations"; *Cherokee Nation* v. *Georgia*, 3 U.S. (5 Pet.) 2 (1831), per Marshall C.J. Indians have long been recognized as having the inherent right to govern themselves, free from the unauthorized interference of American states and subject only to the supreme authority of the federal level of government. It may be recalled that in *United States* v. *Wheeler*, 435 U.S. 313 (1978) 1, the Supreme Court held that when the federal government authorizes or approves a tribe's adoption of a constitution or law code, it merely regulates, rather than creates, tribal authority. The latter does not become an arm of the federal government. If aboriginal governments in Canada have inherent authority, rather than that delegated by Parliament or the provincial legislatures, they may be exempt from the direct application of the *Canadian Charter of Rights and Freedoms*.

Generally speaking, a *government* established by Parliament or a provincial legislature must be regarded as constrained by the same *Charter of Rights* guarantees as the delegating authority. The reasoning would be that constraints on the most powerful and politically accountable branches of government ought, *a fortiori*, to constrain authorities granted some of the higher authority's power. It might be argued that *any* entity that exercises authority from the legislature is bound by the *Charter*. Would it not be a violation of the *Charter* by a legislature if it granted legal authority to an entity which the entity could use to act in a way contrary to the *Charter*? At first glance the argument may seem persuasive, but it is, in my opinion, simplistic. Suppose a province grants a corporate charter to a religious organization. The latter ought, in my opinion, to be generally as free as it was prior to its incorporation to practice its beliefs. It ought to be able, as it was prior to incorporation, to continue to discriminate in some respects even where a government would have to be strictly neutral about religious affiliation. Even if incorporated, a religious organization remains a private body which should be allowed some of its discriminatory preferences.

It is entirely possible that the Canadian courts will hold that the legal history of Canada has resulted in its aboriginal peoples having no surviving aboriginal and treaty rights to self-government and that the authority derived by aboriginal governments is delegated. Of the Métis, it might be observed that they generally participated as legal and political equals in the quasi-public government of the Red River area, the Council of Assiniboia. While some Métis did voluntarily participate in the para-military structure of a buffalo hunt, they were not recognized as being exempt from the application of the general law of the land. Some such exemption is necessary if an aboriginal people is to lawfully exercise self-governing powers; the seizure of property or infliction of punishment that is sometimes necessary to enforce collective decisions involves a governmental authority in actions that would ordinarily be a violation of a person's political and civil rights. The Métis of the Red River area agreed in 1870 to seek the creation of a new province, eventually called Manitoba, in which they would participate as political equals. They were successful. Only limited advisory powers were granted to the councils of Métis Settlement Areas in Alberta by the *Métis Betterment Act* of 1938. The settlements were established as an economic relief program and not as recognition of any special aboriginal rights believed to inhere in the Métis of Alberta. (These matters are discussed in some detail in Chapter XVII, above.)

The constitutional claim of the Inuit would be more difficult to assess but it may not be worth the intellectual bother to do so. The Inuit themselves have chosen to seek an adequate control over their own lives by seeking to establish public governments in regions and territories in which they form a majority. They have not so far shown any interest in establishing self-government by litigation, as opposed to land-claims agreements, self-government agreements, or constitutional amendment. Prior to European arrival the Inuit did not have centralized structures of government, and thus they do not have useful historical precedents and traditions to draw on if they were suddenly asked to establish in court that they have the right to govern themselves. A liberal and democratic spirit among the Inuit also discourages them from seeking ethnically-based forms of political organization, which are the only sort they could establish as a matter of right. (It should be noted that if the Inuit were to press a claim, it could be replied that Canadian governments have almost never granted the Inuit any exemption from the general application of Canadian statutory and common law.)

The case against there being in Canada a surviving right of Indians to self-government might begin by modestly noting that there have been no court decisions recognizing such a right. The only decisions recognizing aboriginal title have involved land use rights. The *Constitution Act, 1867* does not acknowledge any self-governing authority for Indians. On the contrary, it makes them the subject of the lawmaking authority of Parliament under s.91(24). The argument might then be developed by contrasting the comprehensive regulation of Indian life by federal and provincial governments with the more laissez-faire practices in the United States. The right to self-government necessarily involves some exemption for the governing authority from the ordinary laws of the land. The enforcement of collective decisions on dissenting individuals sometimes involves measures such as the seizure of property or imprisonment, that a private person cannot lawfully carry out. While federal law for many years exempted Indians from certain political rights and responsibilities – including the opportunity to vote and the liability to be conscripted – it generally did not allow Indians any exemptions from the application of federal criminal and regulatory law. The only governing authority expressly allowed Indians by the *Indian Act* was the power to make by-laws – in a small number of regulatory areas, within the limits allowed by federal legislation and regulations, and subject to the veto power of the minister of Indian affairs and northern development; *Indian Act*, s.81. The constitution of Indian band councils is established by the *Indian Act*. Its whole framework for Indian law-making authority, it could be argued, appears to be a delegation of authority from Parliament, not an implementation of pre-existing powers. Whereas Indian tribes in the United

States have been held to be immune from the unauthorized interference of state governments, s.88 of the *Indian Act* expressly recognizes the applicability of provincial laws of general application to Indian reserves.

The case against there being an inherent right of aboriginal peoples to self-government might point out that where treaties were entered into with Indian bands, they generally involved a commitment by Indians to obey the sovereign. Whatever recognition of Indian political authority was implicit in the treaty-making process itself, no continuing right to self-government is mentioned in any of them.

The case in favour of there being an inherent aboriginal right to self-government might begin by observing that Indian nations in Canada were fully autonomous political units prior to European arrival. Even after, in many parts of what is now Canada, they were, in practice, left entirely free to manage their internal affairs and unmolested by government regulation. Many Indian bands have never entered into treaties with governments, or otherwise formally accepted any loss of political autonomy. Most Indian bands are parties to treaties, it is true, and most of these treaties contain clauses pledging obedience to the Queen. The treaties must be construed, however, in the context of the understanding of them by the Indian peoples who entered into them. A publication by the Federation of Saskatchewan Indians claims that:

> There is unanimity among the elders that Indian people retained the right to govern themselves. Elders state that white men have usurped this authority and that the Indian Act is purely a white instrument for the purposes of governing Indians and usurping the treaties (Opekokew 1980, 13).

and also that:

> The Indian nations retained sovereignty over their people, lands, and resources, both on and off the reserves, subject to some shared jurisdiction with the appropriate government bodies on the lands known as unoccupied Crown lands. This is the foundation of Indian government (Opekokew 1980, 11).

The publication does not grapple with the meaning of the "obedience to the Queen" clauses in the treaties. An advocate for inherent Indian political autonomy might concede that treaty

Indians accepted the federal government as having supreme authority in some spheres (international relations, criminal law) or even, on the American model whenever it chooses expressly to exercise that authority. The *ultimate* supremacy of the federal level of government in some, or even all, areas is not inconsistent with Indians having a persistent right to self-government. An analogy: The Crown has ultimate title to all lands in the realm, but that does not prevent there being a subordinate legal interest of great importance, such as aboriginal title. (The recognition and affirmation of aboriginal and treaty rights by s.35 of the *Constitution Act, 1982* may mean that the ultimate authority of the federal level of government is now subject to judicially enforceable limits that did not previously exist.)

Those advocating the existence of an aboriginal or treaty right to Indian self-government have available a long line of United States Supreme Court cases that recognize such a right. Canadian courts have almost never been expressly presented with the issue. In *A.G. for Ontario* v. *Bear Island Foundation et al.* (1984), 49 O.R. (2d) 353, the claim of inherent authority was tersely rejected. The definition of aboriginal title given by Judson, J. in *Calder* v. *A.G. of British Columbia* (1973), 34 D.L.R. (3d) 145 is capable of being construed as encompassing the whole traditional way of Indian life, including its political organization, and not merely land use rights:

> Although I think it is clear that Indian title in British Columbia cannot owe its origin to the Proclamation of 1763, the fact is that when the settlers came, the Indians were there, organized in societies and occupying the land as their forefathers had done for centuries. This is what Indian title means and it does not help one in the solution of this problem to call it a "personal or usufructuary right." What they are asserting in this action is that they had a right to continue to live on their lands as their forefathers had lived and that this right has never been lawfully extinguished. There can be no question that this right was "dependent on the goodwill of the sovereign" (34 D.L.R. (3d) 145, 156).

It might also be noted that Canadian courts have expressly recognized the existence of aboriginal land use rights (see *Hamlet of Baker Lake v. Minister of Indian Affairs and Northern Development,* [1980] 1 F.C. 518) and that these rights belong to the aboriginal *collectivity*. If the collectivity has rights, it must have the right as a collectivity to determine how it will exercise and dispose of those rights. To that extent at least, there must be an inherent right to self-government.

The *Indian Act* provisions on Indian government might be characterized by an Indian rights advocate as amounting to a (deplorably) limited recognition and implementation of the inherent right of bands to govern themselves.

The foregoing presentation of the arguments on both sides is intended to be suggestive of only some of the principal contentions. A very thorough historical-legal analysis of the position of each individual community would be necessary to complete a scholarly investigation.

If there is an aboriginal or treaty right of an Indian band to self-government the next question would be the extent to which it is protected from legislative interference. Section 35(1) of the *Constitution Act, 1982* states that the "existing aboriginal and treaty rights of the aboriginal peoples of Canada are hereby recognized and affirmed." Some possibilities for what s.35 means for Indian self-government:

> s.35 only symbolically acknowledges aboriginal and treaty rights. The right to self-government is thus fully subject to legislative override; or
>
> s.35 protects aboriginal and treaty rights only from interference that the court deems unjustified. Furthermore, the word "existing" implies that any *kind* of restriction on the right to Indian self-government that existed on April 17, 1982 remains forever permissible; or
>
> s.35 renders its contents, including the right to Indian self-government, completely immune from any legislative restriction.

There are many other possibilities (see Chapter XXII). Those in the middle range are most likely to be consistent with the approach the courts will eventually adopt with respect to the general nature of s.35. Even if a court found that Indians had some residual rights to self-government on April 17, 1982, it would probably not go on to conclude that the right was constitutionally guaranteed in its fully unrestricted form. The order of authority exercised by Indian band councils on April 17, 1982, is probably the upper limit of self-government that Indians can possibly achieve through litigation.

Advice to Policy-Makers

What are the results of the analysis so far on applicability of the *Charter* to aboriginal governments? Most likely, the courts will not find that aboriginal groups have an inherent right to self-government. They will therefore construe steps by Parliament and provincial legislatures that recognize enhanced authority for aboriginal governments as delegating legislation. Accordingly, aboriginal governments will usually be held to be bound by the *Charter*. Parliament and the provincial legislatures are allowed by s.33 of the *Charter* to exempt themselves from the application of certain sections of the *Charter*. If they wanted to, they could similarly exempt the aboriginal governments they establish. For reasons that will be discussed in the last section of this chapter, it would not be a good statecraft for them to do so.

If aboriginal groups do have an inherent right to self-government, the *Charter* may not apply to them of its own force. Federal and provincial legislation that sets out the authority of an aboriginal government might be construed by the courts as merely implementing a pre-existing right. The *Charter* could not then be held applicable on the basis that a recipient of delegated governmental authority is bound by the same constraints as the source. (But federal and provincial governments might be able, notwithstanding s.35 of the *Charter*, to enact statutes—like the ICRA—that make the *Charter* applicable to aboriginal governments.)

One more possibility must be considered. Constitutional discussions in 1984-85 focussed on the creation of a constitutional commitment by federal and provincial governments to negotiate and conclude self-government agreements with aboriginal communities. The draft amendments in this regard did not speak of delegating authority to aboriginal communities. You could argue that an aboriginal government whose powers are defined by such an agreement is not receiving delegated authority. Rather it has "negotiated authority." Even if aboriginal groups do not have the inherent right to govern themselves, you could argue, they could acquire authority through an act of collaborative definition that did not involve delegation. Aboriginal governments would therefore be free of *Charter* constraints. According to ss.30 and 32 of the *Charter*, it only applies to federal, provincial, and territorial governments (and implicitly, their delegates).

I would disagree. Even though the draft amendments on self-government agreements scrupulously avoided the language of "delegation," the fact of the matter is that aboriginal governments would acquire authority only through the agreement of the levels of government that now have it. (Assuming, of course, that aboriginal groups do not have an inherent right to self-government.) The substance of the transaction would be the delegation of authority. To parties to the negotiation and implementation of enhanced aboriginal self-government, this basic advice is offered:

- parties should be aware that there is a small possibility that the *Charter* will not of its own force constrain aboriginal governments. A court might hold that an aboriginal group had an inherent right to govern itself and that a self-government agreement and follow-up legislation only implemented that right. The *Charter*, the court might conclude, applies only to federal, provincial, and territorial governments and their delegates. A court might reach the same result a different way. It could hold that an aboriginal group has no inherent right to self-government—but that the acquisition of authority through constitutionally mandated negotiations does not amount to a delegation of authority.
- parties should agree and, if necessary, federal and provincial governments should insist that aboriginal governments be governed by either
  (i) the terms of the *Charter*

or

  (ii) a modified version of the *Charter*, on the analogy of the American *Indian Civil Rights Act*.

Option (i) would probably be adequate. Section 25 of the *Charter* provides the necessary instruction to the courts that they should construe the *Charter* with sensitivity to the special legal position and cultural needs of aboriginal groups. The actual text is:

> The guarantee in this *Charter* of certain rights and freedoms shall not be construed so as to abrogate or derogate from any aboriginal, treaty or other rights or freedoms that pertain to the aboriginal peoples of Canada including
> (a) any rights or freedoms that have been recognized by the Royal Proclamation of October 7, 1763; and
> (b) any rights or freedoms that now exist by way of land claims agreements or may be so acquired.

The word "construed" means that the *Charter* should be interpreted in a way that is sensitive to the special legal and political position of aboriginal people. The courts may still find that a particular right of an aboriginal group is inconsistent with the *Charter*, and thus invalid, where it would betray the letter and spirit of the *Charter* to do otherwise. The "construed" language of s.25 should be compared with the language of s.2 of the *Canadian Bill of Rights*, which provides that "[e]very law of Canada shall . . . be so construed *and applied* as not to abrogate, abridge or infringe . . . the rights or freedoms herein recognized . . ." (emphasis added). The phrase "construed and applied" has been interpreted by the courts as meaning that where there is an irreconcilable conflict between a federal law and the *Canadian Bill of Rights*, the *latter* prevails. It is a fair assumption that the drafters of s.25 deliberately chose *not* to include "and applied." If the foregoing interpretive moves are in fact played by the Canadian courts, they would be able to use s.25 to develop the same sort of balanced jurisprudence that American federal courts were developing with respect to Indian governments and the *Indian Civil Rights Act.*

The alternative, option (ii), would force Canadian legislatures to pass the same sort of legislation as the ICRA. They could use their override authority under s.33 of the *Charter* to render many of its sections inapplicable to aboriginal governments and replace them with statutory constraints similar to those norms in the *Charter*, but subtly reworded to reflect the special circumstances of aboriginal peoples. There would be certain advantages to such a procedure. Aboriginal peoples would have political input into the drafting of the section. Studying the emergent statute would give everyone a clearer idea of the limitations on the powers of an aboriginal government than would be available through speculating on the outcome of law suits involving section 25 of the *Charter*. The costs of developing an ICRA-style statute might, however, be unwarranted. Much time, money and intellectual exertion might be spent on the legal and philosophical intricacies of drafting the statute—and even then, the statute itself would be subject to varying interpretations. The marginal advantage of an ICRA-style statute compared to option (i) might not justify the diversion of resources and attention from other aspects of self-government.

Policy Considerations in Favour of Applying the Charter to Aboriginal Governments

The legal scene has now been surveyed, and a basic suggestion about landscaping offered. Obviously, my proposal to have the *Charter* apply in some form to aboriginal governments is based on the general philosophical commitment to liberal individualism argued in the Theoretical Introduction. What follows is an analysis of the special features of aboriginal governments that reinforce the argument from abstract principle.

The analysis might begin with a few modest observations about the links between aboriginal governments and "outsiders." If ethnically-based aboriginal governments are established, they will inevitably find themselves exercising power over visitors and residents who are not members of the community. These people will not have either the formal political voice or informal political influence to protect themselves from unwarranted discrimination or mistreatment. The application of the *Charter* to aboriginal governments would ensure some protection for "outsiders." It should also be recognized that aboriginal governments will participate in many programs run with the financial, bureaucratic, or regulatory co-operation of federal and provincial governments. These levels of government are constrained by the *Charter* in their dealings with all of their citizens – including those who are "citizens" of aboriginal political units. These governments ought not to be put in the position of lending assistance to aboriginal governments that do not apply basic individual rights standards.

It should not be forgotten that there will be within an aboriginal community many "insiders" who cannot adequately protect themselves by political activity. The alternative option of protecting oneself by emigrating is simply not available to some members such as children. Others may be capable of adapting to life outside the community but would find doing so highly undesirable. Not only must familiar geography be abandoned, but often the irreplaceable home of a language and culture. Contemporary law and policy is that an Indian who leaves the reserve remains entitled to his usual share of treaty payments and natural resource royalties (telephone conversation with Mr. LeKuke, D.I.A.N.D., 1985). The costs of exiting may become considerably higher if and when aboriginal governments acquire a greater say in their fiscal affairs including the benefits paid to "emigrants."

Attention should be paid to the risks involved in the process of creating self-government. Those aboriginal officials who negotiate enhanced political authority for aboriginal communities are very likely to be among the first power-holders in the newly-created office. People likely to hold power may not be especially sensitive to the risk that it will be abused. Once in power, people are even less inclined to insist upon checks and balances. Federal and provincial governments ought to be aware, in the transition stages to aboriginal self-government, that internal aboriginal processes cannot necessarily be relied upon to ensure that all members of the community are sufficiently protected.

The most important considerations in favour of the applicability of the *Charter* lie in the political structure of aboriginal communities.

(1) Aboriginal communities have small populations. As a result, it is relatively easy for one faction, or coalition of factions, to dominate the rest. In the most famous of the *Federalist Papers*, No. 51, Publius (the pseudonym of either James Madison, a principal architect of the American Constitution, or Alexander Hamilton) argued that the size and diversity of the American population would have to ensure that the United States remained a just republic;

> It can be little doubted that if the State of Rhode Island was separated from the Confederacy and left to itself, the insecurity of rights under the popular form of government within such narrow limits would be displayed by such reiterated oppressions of factious majorities that some power altogether independent of the people would soon be called for by the voice of the very factions whose misrule had proved the necessity of it. In the extended republic of the United States, and among the great variety of interests, parties, and sects which it embraces, a coalition of a majority of the whole society could seldom take place on any other principles than those of justice and the general good . . . (Madison et al, 1952).

In a large and diverse community, the political clout of any one faction is diluted, and it is difficult for it to form enough coalitions to establish a dominant majority.

A related problem with a small political community is that many or most of the people will have a personal relationship of kinship, friendship, or enmity with many of the office-holders and that these relationships will seriously influence the distribution of government benefits.

(2) In aboriginal communities economic and political life is likely to be tightly intertwined. The power of an aboriginal government may thus be especially extensive and intrusive. The poverty of many aboriginal communities will mean that aboriginal governments will be responsible for funnelling large amounts of social welfare grants to members of the community. As the natural resources of a community are likely to be

collectively owned, the distribution of these revenues is likely to be determined by the government. The small population and economic underdevelopment in many communities encourages economic development projects to be conducted by the community government, in co-operation with federal and provincial agencies. There is only a small pool of persons from which to draw entrepreneurs. Would-be businessmen are likely to lack the capital to start an independent venture. Alternative sources of employment to a person disaffected with the government are thus limited, and the independent business community is not likely to arise as a countervailing power to the government. (The theoretical danger cited here should be compared with a painstaking empirical study of the political dynamics of one particular Indian community, Yngve Georg Lithman's *A Community Apart* (1984). It differs from an earlier examination of the same community (Hawthorn 1967) which had claimed that the community was divided into an "in" majority of Catholic, French-surnamed Indians and an "out" minority of Protestant, English-surnamed Indians. According to Lithman, the most significant division is into a group of about twenty-five small cliques, each of which is concerned that none of the others "gets too much." Any coalition of cliques that would threaten the rest is resisted by them and a balance of power and benefits is maintained.)

(3) The subsidization of the aboriginal governments by other levels of government (which one would expect and hope would occur) may diminish the value of an important control mechanism on government—the necessity a government usually has to raise taxes from its citizens to pay for its expenditures.

(4) In an ethnically homogeneous community whose members have a strong sense of political grievance against white society, there is the possibility of a charismatic leader acquiring power and exceptionally emotional support. Dissidents within the community may find it difficult to protest and impossible to adequately protect their interests.

The foregoing analysis of the features of aboriginal political communities is not intended as an objection to establishing aboriginal governments with broad authority. It is not suggested that aboriginal peoples have any less respect for democracy and fair play than anyone else; nor that, in general, their governments would be unusually oppressive or discriminatory. The contention is simply that certain features of aboriginal communities create risks of unfair treatment to individuals under the jurisdiction of aboriginal governments and that the *Charter* should, in some form, be applied to limit those risks. A measure of assurance that the basic individual rights will be respected by aboriginal governments can only enhance the philosophical appeal and political palatability of legal and financial support for enhanced aboriginal self-government.

References

Notes to Chapter I

Bruce Ackerman, *Social Justice in the Liberal State.*

Ackerman, "Canada at the Constitutional Crossroads."

Ackerman, "Beyond Carolene Products."

Edwin R. Black, *Divided Loyalties.*

Bork, "Neutral Principles and Some First Amendment Problems."

B. Young U.L. Rev., "Tribal Sovereignty and the Supreme Court 1977-78 Term."

Hugh Brody, *The People's Land.*

Canada. D.I.A.N.D., *Citizens Plus, Red Paper on Indian Affairs.*

Canada. D.I.A.N.D., *In All Fairness; A Native Claims Policy.*

Canada. D.I.A.N.D., *Outstanding Business; A Native Claims Policy.*

Canada. Dept. of Justice, *Dominion and Provincial Legislation, 1867-1895.*

Canada. Government of Canada, *Statement of the Government of Canada on Indian Policy.*

William Canby, *American Indian Law.*

Peter Cumming and Neil Mickenberg, eds. *Native Rights in Canada.*

John H. Ely, *Democracy and Distrust.*

Thomas Flanagan. *Riel and the Rebellion.*

James Frideres, ed., *Native People in Canada.*

Garet, "Communality and Existence: The Rights of Groups."

Gibson, "The Charter of Rights and the Private Sector."

Gibson, "Distinguishing the Governors from the Governed."

Gerald Gunther, *Constitutional Law; Cases and Materials.*

Peter Hogg, *Canada Act 1982: Annotated.* (Toronto: Carswell, 1982).

Jennings, "Constitutional Interpretation: The Experience of Canada."

Leckow, "The Protection of Minorities."

William L. Morton, *Manitoba: A History.*

A. Olmsted, "The Mixed Bloods in Western Canada."

Rene Prefontaine, "Métis Speech."

John Rawls, *A Theory of Justice.*

Schwartz, "General National Agreement."

Schwartz, "The Charter and Due Process."

Schwartz and Whyte, "The Patriation References and the Idea of Canada."

Francis R. Scott, *Essays on the Constitution.*

Slattery, "Override Clauses under Section 33."

Pierre E. Trudeau, *Federalism and the French Canadians.*

Gerald S. Vano, *Neo-Feudalism: The Canadian Dilemma.*

Sally M. Weaver, *Making Canadian Indian Policy.*

Notes to Chapter II

Lysyk, "The Rights and Freedoms of the Aboriginal Peoples of Canada."

McNeil, "The Constitutional Rights of the Aboriginal Peoples of Canada."

Robert Sheppard and Michael Valpy, *The National Deal.*

Roy Romanow et al, *Canada Notwithstanding.*

Norman K. Zlotkin, *Unfinished Business: Aboriginal Peoples and the 1983 Constitutional Conference.*

Association of Métis and Nonstatus Indians of Saskatchewan et al v. *Trudeau.* (unreported), cross-examination of John Weinstein.

Notes to Chapter IV

Diamond Jenness, *Indians of Canada.*

Métis and Non-Status Indian Constitutional Review Commission, *Native People and the Constitution of Canada* (Henry W. Daniels, Commissioner). (Ottawa: The Commission, 1981).

I. William Zartman and Maureen R. Berman, *The Practical Negotiator.*

Zlotkin, *Unfinished Business.*

Notes to Chapter VI

Canada. House of Commons, *Indian Self-Government in Canada.*

Harold Cardinal, *The Rebirth of Canada's Indians.*

Peter Jull, *Nunavut.*

Sanders, "Indian Status: A Women's Issue or an Indian Issue?"

Notes to Chapter VII

Eugene Forsey, *Freedom and Order.*

Peter Hogg, *Constitutional Law of Canada.*

Gerard V. La Forest, *Disallowance and Reservation of Provincial Legislation.*

Schwartz, "The Charter and Due Process."

Notes to Chapter VIII

Canada. House of Commons, *Indian Self-Government in Canada.*

Notes to Chapter IX

Jull, *Nunavut.*

Notes to Chapter XI

Canada. Government of Canada, *Statement on Indian Policy.*

Canada. Government of Canada, *Response of the Government to the Report of the Special Committee on Indian Self-Government.*

Green, "Trusteeship and Canada's Indians."

Hogg, *Constitutional Law of Canada.*

Hughes, "Indians and Lands Reserved for the Indians: Off-Limits to the Provinces?" (1983) 21 Osgoode Hall L.J. 82.

Pierre E. Trudeau, "Federal Grants to Universities," in Trudeau, *Federalism and the French Canadians.*

Update Note

On 31 October, 1985, Beetz J., in *R.* v. *Dick* (1985), 62 N.R. 1 (S.C.C.), speaking for a unanimous five member panel of the Supreme Court of Canada, addressed several unresolved issues concerning the effect of s.88 of the *Indian Act.* He distinguished between:

(i) Provincial laws of general application that do not "touch on Indianness" (e.g., traffic laws). These laws apply of their own force.

(ii) Provincial laws of general application that touch on "Indianness." These laws would ordinarily be invalid, because they would invade the exclusive federal jurisdiction over "Indians and the land reserved for Indians" under s.91(24) of the *Constitution Act, 1867.* Section 88 of the *Indian Act* transforms or "referentially incorporates" these provincial laws; that is, s.88 makes the terms of the provincial laws apply to Indians as federal law.

What about a provincial law that "singles out" Indians? Section 88 does not seem to speak to such laws at all. The text of Chapter XI argues that such laws may be valid if they are attempts to address the Indian aspect of provincial subject matter. In *Dick,* Beetz J. refers to federal laws that "single out" Indians for special treatment as "prima facie suspicious," a phrase that allows that some such laws may, on close examination, turn out to be valid.

On the facts of *Dick,* Beetz J. found it unnecessary to determine whether the application of a provincial hunting law to the defendant would touch on his "Indianness." It made no difference to his culpability whether the terms of the law applied as provincial law or as federal law.

Notes to Chapter XII

Canada. Government of Canada, *Statement of the Government on Indian Policy.*

Canby, *American Indian Law.*

Lysyk, "The Unique Constitutional Position of the Canadian Indian."

Monroe E. Price, *Law and the American Indian.*

Statement by the President, *Indian Policy.*

Notes to Chapter XIV

Canada. House of Commons, *Indian Self-Government in Canada.*

Cumming and Mickenberg, *Native Rights in Canada.*

Larry Krotz, *Urban Indians.*

Notes to Chapter XV

Canada. Government of Canada, *Response of the Government to the Report of the Special Committee on Indian Self-Government.*

Notes to Chapter XVI

Alberta. Municipal Affairs, *Foundation for the Future of Alberta's Métis Settlements.*

Hogg, *Constitutional Law of Canada.*

Gerard V. La Forest, *Natural Resources and Public Property under the Canadian Constitution* (Toronto: University of Toronto, 1969).

Douglas Sanders, "Métis Claims in Western Canada."

Sprague, "Government Lawlessness in the Administration of Manitoba Land Claims, 1870-1887."

D.N. Sprague, "Métis Land Claims."

Trudeau, *Federalism and the French Canadians.*

Notes to Chapter XVII

Alexander Begg, *History of the North-West*, vol. 1.

Britain. House of Commons, *Report from the Select Committee on the Hudson's Bay Company*.

Chartier, "'Indian': An Analysis of the Term as used in Section 91(24) of the British North America Act, 1867."

Thomas Flanagan, *Louis 'David' Riel*.

Thomas Flanagan, *Riel and the Rebellion*.

Joseph Howard, *Strange Empire*.

Antoine Lussier, "The Métis."

A.S. Morton, "The New Nation, The Métis."

William L. Morton, ed. *Manitoba: The Birth of a Province*.

William L. Morton, "The Battle at Grand Coteau."

Edmund Henry Oliver, *The Canadian Northwest, Its Early Development and Legislative Records*, vol. 1.

D. Bruce Sealey, "One Plus One Equals One."

George F.G. Stanley, "Confederation 1870 – A Métis Achievement."

Notes to Chapter XVIII

Canada. House of Commons, *Indian Self-Government in Canada*.

Notes to Chapter XIX

Canada. House of Commons, *Indian Self-Government in Canada*.

Notes to Chapter XX

Albert Venn Dicey, *The Law of the Constitution.*

Gunther, "A Model for a Newer Equal Protection."

Update Note

Chapter XX raises the possibility that a constitutional amendment to constitutionally protect self-government agreements would be tantamount to an amendment to the amending formula, and would thus require the support of the federal government and all ten provinces. The general amending formula requires concurring resolutions by the federal government and two thirds of the provinces with half of the population; *Constitution Act, 1982*, s.38(1). Section 41(e) of Part V of the *Constitution Act, 1982* (which is titled "Procedure for Amending the Constitution of Canada") requires the unanimous consent of the provinces for "amendments to this part." The contention that constitutionally protected self-government agreements would amount to amendments to the constitution has strong intuitive appeal. If the contention cannot be refuted, it may not be possible to come to any constitutionally valid agreements at the 1987 First Ministers' Conference. The dissent or even non-participation, of even one province would preclude the constitutional recognition of self-government agreements. Although Chapter XX of the present study was included in a discussion paper released in the spring of 1985, the "unanimity contention" was not mentioned at a "s.37" (national level constitutional) meeting until an officials' level meeting in Halifax on May 22, 1986.

The importance of the issue may warrant an attempt here to summarize some of the points that might be made on both sides of the issue.

The argument against the unanimity requirement might include the following points:

(i) A constitutional amendment to protect new agreements on aboriginal self-government would not change the text of Part V (amending formula). *Formally*, then, it is not an amendment to the amending formula.

(ii) An amendment to protect the results of self-government agreements would merely establish a new class of rights that are constitutionally protected. Adding a new class of rights to those already constitutionally protected does not require the consent of all of the provinces; it is clear that the *Canadian Charter of Rights and Freedoms*, for example, can be amended with the consent of only seven provinces with half of the population.

(iii) Section 35 of the *Constitution Act, 1982* allows for the constitutional protection of treaty rights. Self-government agreements are just a particular type of treaty right. An amendment to recognize self-government agreements is just an extension, or perhaps merely a clarification, of s.35 of the *Constitution Act, 1982*. Amendments to s.35 are *not* among those that are on the list in s.41 of amendments that require unanimous consent. Yet the framers of the amending formula in Part V of the Constitution knew that Part IV of the Constitution would require that there be a further First Ministers' Conference in 1983 for the specific purpose of considering constitutional amendments to better identify and define the rights of the aboriginal peoples of Canada.

(iv) The point in (iii) is bolstered by a consideration of s.35(3) of the *Constitution Act, 1982*, as amended pursuant to the March '83 First Ministers' Conference. Section 35(3) reads:

> For greater certainty, 'aboriginal and treaty rights' in section 35(3) includes rights that now exist by way of land claims agreements or may be so acquired.

The phrase "for greater certainty" tells us that the framers of s.35(3) thought that they were merely clarifying what was already implicit in s.35(1). Now, s.35(3) was the inspiration of the Inuit Committee on National Issues, which was largely concerned with ensuring that the James Bay Agreement of 1975 would be constitutionally protected. But the James Bay Agreement included arrangements for Inuit and Cree self-government. So, the framers of s.35(3) must have thought that self-government arrangements could be protected by at least some "treaties." Furthermore, the phrase "rights . . . that may be so acquired" shows that the framers of s.35(3) thought that s.35(1) had originally implied that modern land claims agreements would be an ongoing mechanism for protecting certain kinds of self-government arrangements. Conclusion: If the framers of s.35(3) knew what they were doing and meant what they said, then the use of the agreement-making process to establish self-government was already established, at least to some extent, in 1982. An amendment to protect self-government agreements in general (that is, regardless of whether they are tied to land claims agreements) would only clarify or extend what section 35(1) has always said. An amendment on self-government agreements, therefore, would *in substance* be an amendment to s.35 of the *Constitution Act, 1982*. It would not be a new kind of constitutional mechanism that is "really" an amendment to the amending formula.

(v) The point in (iii) would be especially compelling if s.35(1) *already* allows for the constitutional protection of self-government agreements.

Those advocating the unanimity requirement might attempt the following arguments by way of rebuttal:

- Point (i) relies on form. We should look instead at substance. An amendment to protect aboriginal self-government agreements would establish a mechanism whereby new structures for the discharge of state authority would be established. These structures could not be altered by the unilateral action of either Parliament or a provincial legislature. Permanent alterations to the governmental structure of Canada are by their very nature "constitutional." A constitutional amendment to make these alterations possible is, therefore, an amendment to the amending formula.
- Point (ii) is not persuasive because it overlooks the difference between amendments that create rights against existing governments and amendments that create new governments.
- Point (iii) disregards the difference between self-government agreements and the "treaties" contemplated by the framers of the *Constitution Act, 1982*. The framers had in mind transactions that involved the exchange of land for other rights and that did not involve guarantees of self-government. Furthermore, the framers of the *Constitution Act, 1982* inserted the word "existing" before the phrase "aboriginal and treaty rights"; they meant rights that existed prior to April 17, 1982, when the new Constitution came into force. Self-government

agreements would *not* be merely another kind of s.35 "treaty."

- Point (iv) mistakenly assumes that the framers of s.35(3) properly understood the meaning of s.35(1). Chapters III and VIII of this study show how little attention was given in the s.37 process to the technical implications of s.35(3).
- To the extent that s.35(3) implies that *any* post-1982 agreement on aboriginal self-government is constitutionally protected, s.35(3) is itself invalid because it would be an amendment to the amending formula. (Only nine provinces passed resolutions in support of s.35(3); Quebec failed to do so as part of its protest against the patriation of the Constitution without its consent in 1982.
- If the last rebuttal argument goes too far, then at least this is true: future self-government agreements will only be constitutionally protected by s.35(1) if they are part of land claims settlements and if they involve the limited kinds of self-government allowed by the James Bay Agreement of 1975. An amendment that would *generally* allow self-government agreements to be constitutionally protected would go well beyond s.35. It would not be an amendment to that section; it would, in substance, be an amendment to the amending formula.

Advocates of both positions will have to be wary of tactics that lead to Pyrrhic victories. An advocate of the "anti-unanimity" side might unwisely claim that an amendment on self-government agreements does not amount to an amendment to the constitution because Parliament and the provincial legislatures would retain considerable authority to override these agreements (see Chapter XXIV). If the Supreme Court agrees, the amendment would be valid, but also, to a large extent, useless.

Suppose that the federal level of government and seven or more provinces do pass resolutions in support of an amendment to constitutionally protect aboriginal self-government agreements. Suppose that a few provinces do not go along. Is the Supreme Court likely to hold the amendment invalid? Probably not. The Court would not be eager to stand in the way of a deal that had such widespread support among democratically elected legislatures and among aboriginal peoples themselves. Those provinces opposed to the amendment could probably "opt-out" of it, as authorized by s.38(3) of the *Constitution Act, 1982*.

Notes to Chapter XXII

Karl von Clausewitz, *On War*.

Notes to Chapter XXIII

Bayefsky, "The Human Rights Committee and the Case of Sandra Lovelace."

Canada. House of Commons, *Indian Self-Government in Canada.*

Kathleen Jamieson, *Indian Women and the Law in Canada.*

Penney Kome, *The Taking of Twenty-Eight.*

Romanow et al., *Canada Notwithstanding.*

Sanders, "Indian Status: A Women's Issue or an Indian Issue?"

Notes to Chapter XXIV

McNeil, "The Constitutional Rights of the Aboriginal Peoples of Canada."

Notes to Chapter XXV

Ackerman, *Social Justice in the Liberal State.*

Alexander M. Bickel, *The Least Dangerous Branch.*

Burnett, "An Historical Analysis of the 1968 Indian Civil Rights Act."

Gibson, "The Charter of Rights and the Private Sector."

Gibson, "Distinguishing the Governors from the Governed."

Gerald Gunther, *Constitutional Law.*

Harvard Law Review, "The Indian Bill of Rights and the Constitutional Status of Tribal Governments."

Yngve Lithman, *The Community Apart.*

John Locke, *The Second Treatise of Government.*

Madison et al., "The Federalist."

Delia Opekokew, *The First Nations.*

Slattery, "Charter of Rights and Freedoms – Does it Bind Private Persons?"

Katherine Swinton, "Application of the Canadian Charter of Rights and Freedoms (ss. 30, 31, 32)."

Laurence H. Tribe, *American Constitutional Law.*

Transcripts

1983 FMC Transcript
1984 FMC Transcript
1985 FMC Transcript

Bibliography

Ackerman, Bruce. *Social Justice in the Liberal State.* New Haven: Yale University, 1980.

________. "Canada at the Constitutional Crossroads," (1984), 34 U. of T.L.J. 117.

________. "Beyond Carolene Products," (1985), 98 Harv. L. Rev. 713.

Alberta Municipal Affairs. *Foundations for the Future of Alberta's Métis Settlements*, (Report of the MacEwan Joint Committee to Review the Métis Betterment Act and Regulations). Edmonton, 1984.

Asch, Michael. *Home and Native Land: Aboriginal Rights and the Canadian Constitution.* Toronto: Methuen, 1984.

Backeland, Lucille and James S. Frideres. "Franco-Manitobans and Cultural Loss: A Fourth Generation," Prairie Forum, 2, 1 (May 1977).

Badcock, William T. *Who Owns Canada: Aboriginal Title and Canadian Courts*. Ottawa: Canadian Association in Support of the Native Peoples, 1976.

Barkwell, Peter A. "The Medicine Chest Clause in Treaty No. 6," [1981] 4 C.N.L.R. 1.

Barsh, Russell L. "Indigenous North America and Contemporary International Law," (1983) 62 Or. L. Rev. 73.

Bartlett, Richard H. "The Indian Act of Canada," (1978) 27 Buff. L. Rev. 581.

________. "Making Land Available for Native Land Claims in Australia: An Example for Canada," (1983) 13 Man. L.J. 73.

Bayefsky, Anne F. "The Human Rights Committee and the Case of Sandra Lovelace," (1982) 20 Can. Yearbook of Int'l. Law 244.

Beatty, Donald R. *History of the Legal Status of the American Indian with Particular Reference to California.* San Francisco: R and E Research Associates, 1974.

Begg, Alexander. *History of the North-West*, Vol. 1. Toronto: Hunter, Ross, 1894-95.

Bennett, Gordon I. "Aboriginal Title in the Common Law: A Stoney Path Through Feudal Doctrine," (1978) 27 Buff. L. Rev. 617.

________. *Aboriginal Rights in International Law.* London: Anthropological Institute [for] Survival International, 1978.

Berger, Thomas R. *Fragile Freedoms: human rights and dissent in Canada.* Toronto: Clarke, Irwin, 1981.

Berman, Howard R. "The Concept of Aboriginal Rights in the Early History of the United States," (1978) 27 Buff. L. Rev. 637.

Bickel, Alexander M. *The Least Dangerous Branch; the Supreme Court at the Bar of Politics.* Indianapolis: Bobbs-Merrill, 1962.

Bickenbach, Jerome E. "The Baker Case: A Partial Recognition of Inuit Aboriginal Title," (1980) 38 U.T. Fac. L. Rev. 232.

Black, Edwin R. *Divided Loyalties: Canadian Concepts of Federalism*. Montreal: McGill-Queen's University, 1975.

Boldt, Menno and J. Anthony Long, eds. *The Quest for Justice: Aboriginal Peoples and Aboriginal Rights*. Toronto: University of Toronto, 1985.

Bork, Robert H. "Neutral Principles and Some First Amendment Problems," (1971-72) 47 Ind. L.J. 1.

Brigham Young University Law Review, "Tribal Sovereignty and the Supreme Court 1977-78 Term," (1978) B. Young U.L. Rev. 911.

Britain. House of Commons. *Report from the Select Committee on the Hudson's Bay Company*. British Parliamentary Papers, Session 1857, Colonies Canada, Vol. 3.

Brody, Hugh. *The People's Land: Eskimos and Whites in the Eastern Arctic*. Harmondsworth: Penguin, 1975.

Burnett, Donald L. "An Historical Analysis of the 1968 Indian Civil Rights Act," (1971-72) Harv. J. Legis. 557.

Burrell, Gordon, et al., eds., *Indian Treaties and the Law*. Edmonton: Indian Association of Alberta, 1975.

Canada. Advisory Council on the Status of Women. *Indian Women and the Indian Act*. Ottawa, 1976.

_______. *Women, Human Rights and the Constitution*, (submission to the Special Joint Committee on the Constitution). Ottawa, 1980.

Canada. Department of Indian Affairs and Northern Development. *Citizens Plus, Red Paper on Indian Affairs*, (submission by the Indian Chiefs of Alberta). Ottawa, 1970.

_______. *In All Fairness: A Native Claims Policy*. Ottawa, 1981.

_______. *Outstanding Business: A Native Claims Policy*. Ottawa, 1981.

Canada. Department of Justice. *Dominion and Provincial Legislation, 1867-1895*. Ottawa, 1896.

Canada. Government of Canada. *Statement of the Government of Canada on Indian Policy*, (White Paper). Ottawa, 1969.

________. *Response of the Government to the Report of the Special Committee on Indian Self-Government*, (Reply to the Penner Report). Ottawa, 1984.

Canada. House of Commons. *Indian Self-Government in Canada: Report of the Special Committee*, (Keith Penner, Chairman). Ottawa, 1983.

Canada. Indian and Northern Affairs Canada. *The Elimination of Sex Discrimination from the Indian Act*. Ottawa, 1982.

Canadian Association of Social Workers. *The Métis in Manitoba*. Winnipeg: Provincial Council of Women, 1954.

Canby, William. *American Indian Law*. St. Paul: West Publishing, 1981.

Cantlie, R.B. "The Extinguishment of Aboriginal Title," (1982) 60 Can. Bar Rev. 819.

Cardinal, Harold. *The Rebirth of Canada's Indians*. Edmonton: Hurtig, 1977.

Challies, George Swan. *The Law of Expropriation*, 2nd ed. Montreal: Wilson and Lafleur, 1963.

Chambers, Reid Peyton. "Judicial Enforcement of the Federal Trust Responsibility to Indians," (1975) 27 Stan. L. Rev. 1213.

Chartier, Clem. "'Indian': An Analysis of the Term as used in Section 91(24) of the British North America Act, 1867," (1978-79) 43 Sask. L. Rev. 37.

Cheffins, Ronald I. "The Constitution Act, 1982, and the Amending Formula: Political and Legal Implications," (1982) 4 Supreme Court L. Rev. 43.

Cherukapalle, Nirmala devi. *Indian Reserves as Municipalities: Problems and Prospects*. Vancouver: Centre for Continuing Education, University of British Columbia, 1972.

Ciaccia, John. "The Settlement of Native Claims," (1977) 15 Alta. L. Rev. 556.

Clausewitz, Karl von. *On War*. Princeton: Princeton University Press, 1976.

Clinebell, John Howard and Jim Thomson, "Sovereignty and Self-Determination: The Rights of Native Americans under International Law," (1977-78) 27 Buffalo L. Rev. 669.

Clinton, Robert N. "Isolated in Their Own Country: A Defense of Federal Protection of Indian Autonomy and Self-Government," (1981) 33 Stan. L. Rev. 979.

Cohen, Felix S. "Original Indian Title," (1947) 32 Minn. L. Rev. 28.

_______. "The Spanish Origins of Indian Rights in the Law of the United States," (1942) 31 Geo. L.J. 1.

Colvin, Eric. *Legal Process and the Resolution of Indian Claims*. Saskatoon: University of Saskatchewan Native Law Centre, 1981.

Cover, Robert M. "The Supreme Court 1982 Term; Forward, Nomos and Narrative," (1983) 97 Harv. L. Rev. 4.

Crawford, James. *The Creation of States in International Law*. Oxford: Clarendon, 1979.

Cumming, Peter and Neil Mickenberg, eds. *Native Rights in Canada*. Toronto: Indian-Eskimo Association of Canada in assoc. with General Publishing, 1972.

Danforth, Sandra C. "Repaying Historical Debts: The Indian Claims Commission," (1973) 49 N.D.L. Rev. 359.

Daniels, Harry, ed. *The Forgotten People: Métis and Non-Status Indian Land Claims*. Ottawa: Native Council of Canada, 1979.

Dicey, Albert Venn. *The Law of the Constitution*, 10th ed. London: Macmillan, 1965.

Dinstein, Yoram. "Collective Human Rights of Peoples and Minorities," (1976) 25 Int'l. & Comp. L.Q. 102.

Doerr, Audrey and Micheline Carrier, eds. *Women and the Constitution in Canada*. Ottawa: Canadian Advisory Council on the Status of Women, 1981.

Driedger, E.A. "The Canadian Bill of Rights and The Lavell Case: A Possible Solution," (1974) 6 Ottawa L. Rev. 620.

Ely, John H. *Democracy and Distrust: A Theory of Judicial Review*. Cambridge: Harvard University, 1980.

Ericson, Robert and D. Rebecca Snow. "The Indian Battle for Self-Determination," (1970) 58 Calif. L. Rev. 445.

Favreau, Guy. *The Amendment of the Constitution of Canada*. Ottawa: Queen's Printer, 1965.

Fillmore, W.P. "Half-Breed Scrip," Man. Bar News, 39, 2 (August 1973).

Fingers, Wallace M. "Aboriginal Peoples and the Constitution," (1981) 19 Alta. L. Rev. 428.

Fingland, F.B. "Administrative and Constitutional Changes in Arctic Territories: Canada," In *The Arctic Frontier*. Edited by Ronald St. J. MacDonald. Toronto: University of Toronto, 1965.

Fiss, Owen M. "Groups and The Equal Protection Clause," (1975) 5 Phil. & Public Affairs 107.

Flanagan, Thomas. *Louis 'David' Riel: Prophet of the New World*. Toronto: University of Toronto, 1979.

________. *Riel and the Rebellion: 1885 Reconsidered*. Saskatoon: Western Producer Prairie Books, 1983.

Forsey, Eugene. *Freedom and Order*. Toronto: McLelland & Stewart, 1974.

Foster, J.E. "The Origins of the Mixed Bloods in the Canadian West." In *Essays on Western History*. Edited by Lewis H. Thomas. Edmonton: University of Alberta, 1976.

_______. "The Métis: The People, the Term." Prairie Forum, 3, 1 (Spring, 1978).

Frideres, James, ed. *Native People in Canada: Contemporary Conflicts*. Scarborough: Prentice-Hall, 1983.

Frum, David. "Equal Opportunity." Saturday Night, 99, 1 (January 1984).

Fulford, Robert. "By the Book." Saturday Night, 99, 4 (April 1984).

Gagne, Jocelyn. "The Content of Aboriginal Title at Common Law," (1983) 47 Sask. L. Rev. 309.

Garet, Ronald R. "Communality and Existence: The Rights of Groups," (1983) 56 South Cal. L. Rev. 1001.

Gibson, Dale. "The Charter of Rights and the Private Sector," (1982-83) 12 Man. L.J. 213.

_______. "Distinguishing the Governors from the Governed: The Meaning of 'Government' Under Section 32(1) of the Charter," (1983) 13 Man. L.J. 505.

Giraud, Marcel. Métis Settlement in the Northwest Territories," Saskatchewan History, 7, 1 (Winter, 1954).

Green, L.C. "Canada's Indians: Federal Policy, International and Constitutional Law," (1970) 4 Ottawa L. Rev. 101.

_______. "Legal Significance of Treaties Affecting Canada's Indians," (1972) 1 Anglo-American L. Rev. 119.

_______. "The Canadian Bill of Rights, Indian Rights, and the United Nations," (1974) 22 Chitty's L.J. 22.

_______. "Trusteeship and Canadian Indians," (1976) 3 Dal. L.J. 104.

________. "Aboriginal Peoples, International Law and the Canadian Charter of Rights and Freedoms," (1983) 61 Can. Bar Rev. 339.

Gunther, Gerald. "A Model for a New Equal Protection," (1972) 86 Harv. L. Rev. 1.

________. *Constitutional Law; Cases and Materials*. 10th ed. Mineola: Foundation Press, 1980.

Harvard Law Review. "The Indian Bill of Rights and the Constitutional Status of Tribal Governments," (1969) 82 Harv. L. Rev. 1343.

Harvard Law Review. "In Defence of Tribal Sovereign Immunity," (1982) 95 Harv. L. Rev. 1058.

Hatt, Fred K. "The Canadian Métis: Recent Interpretations," Canadian Ethnic Studies, 3, 1 (June 1971).

Hawkes, David C. *Negotiating Aboriginal Self-Government: Developments Surrounding the 1985 First Ministers' Conference*. Kingston: Institute of Intergovernmental Relations, Queen's University, 1985.

Hawthorn, Harry B., ed. *A Survey of the Contemporary Indians of Canada*, 2 vols. Ottawa: Indian Affairs Branch, 1967.

Henderson, William B. "Canada's Indian Reserves: The Usufruct in our Constitution," (1980) 12 Ottawa L. Rev. 167.

Hogg, Peter W. "Equality Before the Law – A.G. Can. v. Lavell," (1974) 52 Can. Bar Rev. 263.

________. *Constitutional Law of Canada*. Toronto: Carswell, 1977.

Hosek, Chaviva. "Women and the Constitutional Process" in *And No One Cheered*. Edited by Keith Banting and Richard Simeon. Toronto: Methuen, 1983.

Howard, Joseph. *Strange Empire*. Toronto: James Lewis & Samuel, 1952.

Hughes, Patricia. "Indians and Lands Reserved For the Indians: Off-Limits to the Provinces?" (1983) 21 Osgoode Hall L.J. 82.

Hutchinson, Allan C. and Patrick J. Monahan. "Law, Politics, and the Critical Legal Scholars: The Unfolding Drama of American Legal Thought," (1983-84) 36 Stan. L. Rev. 199.

Iowa Law Review. "Systemic Discrimination in the Indian Claims Commission," (1972) 57 Ia. L. Rev. 1300.

Jamieson, Kathleen. *Indian Women and the Law in Canada: Citizens Minus*. Ottawa: Minister of Supply and Services, 1978.

Jenness, Diamond. *Indians of Canada*. Ottawa: National Museums of Canada, 1932.

Jennings, W. Ivor. "Constitutional Interpretation: The Experience of Canada," (1937) 51 Harv. L. Rev. 1.

Jull, Peter. *Nunavut*. Ottawa: Nunavut Constitutional Forum, 1983.

Katz, Leslie. "The Indian Act and Equality Before The Law," (1973) 6 Ottawa L. Rev. 277.

Kelly, Ian F. "The Bill of Rights, The Indian Act, and Equality Before the Law; The Need for, and the Development of a 'Reasonableness' Test," (1974) 2 Queen's L.J. 151.

Kelly, James M. "Extent of the 'Fair and Honorable Dealings' Section of the Indian Claims Commission Act," (1971) 15 St. Louis U.L.J. 491.

Kome, Penney. *The Taking of Twenty-Eight: Women Challenge the Constitution*. Toronto: Women's Press, 1983.

________. "Anatomy of a Lobby." Saturday Night, 98, 1 (January 1983).

Krotz, Larry. *Urban Indians, the Strangers in Canada's Cities*. Edmonton: Hurtig, 1980.

La Forest, Gerard V. *Disallowance and Reservation of Provincial Legislation.* Ottawa: Queen's Printer, 1965.

Leckow, Ross. "The Protection of Minorities: Educational Rights for Minorities in International and Canadian Constitutional Law," Unpublished paper, 1983.

Lederman, W.R. "The Process of Constitutional Amendment for Canada," (1966-67) 12 McGill L.J. 371.

Lithman, Yngve. *The Community Apart: A Case Study of a Canadian Indian Reserve Community.* Winnipeg: University of Manitoba, 1984.

Locke, John. *Second Treatise of Government.* Indianapolis: Bobbs-Merrill, 1952.

Long, J. Anthony, et al. "Federal Indian Policy and Indian Self-Government in Canada: An Analysis of a Current Proposal," (1982) 8 Can. Pub. Pol. 189.

Lussier, Antoine. "The Métis," In *The Other Natives: The Métis,* Vol. 1. Edited by Antoine Lussier and D. Bruce Sealey. Winnipeg: Manitoba Métis Federation, 1978.

Lysyk, Kenneth. "The Unique Constitutional Position of the Canadian Indian," (1967) 45 Can. Bar Rev. 513.

________. "The Indian Title Question in Canada: An Appraisal in the Light of Calder," (1973) 53 Can. Bar Rev. 450.

________. "Constitutional Developments Relating to the Indians and Indian Lands: An Overview," (1978) L.S.U.C. Lectures 201.

________. "The Rights and Freedoms of the Aboriginal Peoples of Canada (ss. 25, 35 and 37)," (1982) Can. Charter 467.

Madison, et al. "The Federalist." *Great Books of the Western World,* Vol. 43. Edited by Robert Maynard Hutchins. Chicago: Encyclopedia Britannica, 1952.

Malone, Marc. *Financing Aboriginal Self-Government in Canada.* 1986. Kingston: Institute of Intergovernmental Relations, Queen's University, 1986.

Matas, David. "Indian Women's Rights," (1974) 6 Man. L.J. 195.

McConnell, William H. *Commentary on the British North America Act.* Toronto: Macmillan, 1977.

McCoy, Robert G. "The Doctrine of Tribal Sovereignty: Accommodating Tribal, State, and Federal Interests," (1978) 13 Harv. Civil Rights L. Rev. 357.

McCullum, Hugh. *This Land is Not for Sale.* Toronto: Anglican Book Centre, 1975.

McDonald, Patrick N. "Equality Before the Law and the Indian Act: In Defence of the Supreme Court," (1977) 3 Dal. L.J. 726.

M'Gonigle, R. Michael. "The Bill of Rights and the Indian Act: Either? Or?," (1977) 15 Alta. L. Rev. 292.

McNeil, Kent. "The Constitutional Rights of the Aboriginal Peoples of Canada," (1982) 4 Supreme Court L. Rev. 255.

Meekison, J. Peter. "The Amending Formula," (1983) 8 Queen's L.J. 99.

Morse, Bradford. *Indian Tribal Courts in the United States: A Model for Canada?* Saskatoon: Native Law Centre, Univ. of Saskatchewan, 1980.

Morton, A.S. "The New Nation, The Métis." In *The Other Natives: The Métis*, Vol. 1. Edited by Antoine Lussier and D. Bruce Sealey. Winnipeg: Manitoba Métis Federation, 1978.

Morton, William L. *Manitoba: A History.* Toronto: University of Toronto, 1957.

________, ed. *Manitoba: The Birth of a Province*, Vol. 1. Winnipeg: Manitoba Record Society, 1965.

________. "The Battle at Grand Coteau, July 13 and 14, 1851." In *The Other Natives: The Métis*, Vol. 1. Edited by Antoine Lussier and D. Bruce Sealey. Winnipeg: Manitoba Métis Federation, 1978.

New Brunswick. Human Rights Commission. *Selected Documents in the Matter of Lovelace v. Canada Pursuant to the International Covenant on Civil and Political Rights*. Fredericton, 1981.

Niedermeier, Lynn. "The Content of Aboriginal Rights: Definition or Denial," [1981] 1 C.N.L.R. 1.

Oliver, Edmund Henry. *The Canadian Northwest, Its Early Development and Legislative Records*, Vol. 1. Ottawa: Government Printing Bureau, 1914-15.

Olmsted, Dr. A. "The Mixed Bloods in Western Canada: An Ecological Approach." In *Native People in Canada: Contemporary Conflicts*. Edited by James Frideres. Scarborough: Prentice-Hall, 1983.

Opekokew, Delia. *The First Nations: Indian Government and the Canadian Confederation*. Saskatoon: Federation of Saskatchewan Indians, 1980.

Oregon Law Review. "Symposium on Indian Law," (1983) 62 Or. L. Rev. 3.

Paquette, Jerald E. *Aboriginal Self-Government and Education in Canada*. Kingston: Institute of Intergovernmental Relations, Queen's University, 1986.

Pelletier, Emile. *A Social History of the Manitoba Métis*. Winnipeg: Manitoba Métis Federation, 1974.

Pannekoek, F. "A Probe into the Demographic Structure of the Nineteenth Century Red River," In *Essays on Western History*. Edited by Lewis H. Thomas. Edmonton: University of Alberta, 1976.

Pomerance, Michla. *Self-Determination in Law and Practice: the new doctrine in the United Nations*. The Hague: Nijhoff, 1982.

Prefontaine, Rene. "Métis Speech," In *The Other Natives: The Métis*, Vol. 3. Edited by Antoine Lussier and D. Bruce Sealey. Winnipeg: Manitoba Métis Federation, 1980.

Price, Monroe E. *Law and the American Indian, Readings, Notes and Cases*. Indianapolis: Bobbs-Merrill, 1973.

Pugh, Robert D.J. "Are Northern Lands Reserved for the Indians?" (1982) 60 Can. Bar. Rev. 36.

Rawls, John. *A Theory of Justice*. Cambridge: Belknap, 1971.

Romanow, Roy et al. *Canada Notwithstanding: The Making of the Constitution, 1976-1982*. Toronto: Methuen, 1984.

Sanders, Douglas. "The Bill of Rights and Indian Status," (1972) 7 U.B.C.L. Rev. 81.

_______. "Indian Act, Status of Indian Women on Marriage to a Person Without Indian Status," (1972) 38 Sask. L. Rev. 243.

_______. "The Indian Act and the Bill of Rights," (1974) 6 Ottawa L. Rev. 397.

_______. "Indian Women: A Brief History of Their Roles and Rights," (1975) 21 McGill L.J. 656.

_______. "Métis Claims in Western Canada," In *The Forgotten People: Métis and Non-Status Indian Land Claims*. Edited by Harry Daniels. Ottawa: Native Council of Canada, 1979.

_______. "Métis Rights in the Prairie Provinces and the N.W.T.: A Legal Interpretation," in *The Forgotten People*. Edited by Harry Daniels. Ottawa: Native Council of Canada, 1979.

_______. "Aboriginal Peoples and the Constitution," (1981) 19 Alta. L. Rev. 410.

_______. "The Indian Lobby," in *And No One Cheered*. Edited by Keith Banting and Richard Simeon. Toronto: Methuen, 1983.

_______. "Prior Claims: An Aboriginal People in the Constitution of Canada," In *Canada and The New Constitution, The Unfinished Agenda*. Edited by Stanley M. Beck and Yvan Bernier. Montreal: Institute for Research on Public Policy, 1983.

________. "The Rights of the Aboriginal Peoples of Canada," (1983) 61 Can. Bar Rev. 314.

________. "Indian Status: A Women's Issue or an Indian Issue?" [1984] 3 C.N.L.R. 30.

Sawatzky, H.L. "Viability of Ethnic Group Settlement, with Reference to Mennonites in Manitoba," Canadian Ethnic Studies, 2, 2 (December 1970).

Sawchuk, Joe. *The Métis of Manitoba: reformulation of an ethnic identity.* Toronto: P. Martin Associates, 1978.

Schwartz, Bryan. "General National Agreement: The Legal Sanction for Constitutional Reform in Canada," (1981) 6 Queen's L.J. 513.

________. "The Charter and Due Process, (panel discussion)" in *1983 Pitblado Lectures.* Winnipeg: Law Society of Manitoba, 1983.

Schwartz, Bryan and John D. Whyte, "The Patriation References and the Idea of Canada," (1982-83) 8 Queen's L.J. 158.

Schwarzenberger, Georg. *The Frontiers of International Law.* London: Stevens, 1962.

Scott, Francis R. "The British North America Act (No. 2) 1949," (1949) 8 U. of T. L.J. 201.

________. *Essays on the Constitution.* Toronto: University of Toronto, 1977.

Scott, Stephen A. "Pussycat, Pussycat or Patriation and the New Constitutional Amendment Process," (1982) 20 U.W.O.L. Rev. 247.

Sealey, D. Bruce and Antoine Lussier. *The Métis: Canada's Forgotten People.* Winnipeg: Pemmican, 1975.

Sealey, D. Bruce. "One Plus One Equals One," in *The Other Natives: The Métis*, vol. 1. Edited by Antoine Lussier and D. Bruce Sealey. Winnipeg: Manitoba Métis Federation, 1978.

Sheppard, Robert and Michael Valpy. *The National Deal: The Fight for a Canadian Constitution.* Toronto: Fleet, 1982.

Slattery, Brian. *The Land Rights of Indigenous Canadian Peoples.* Saskatoon: College of Law, University of Saskatchewan, 1979.

_______. "The Constitutional Guarantee of Aboriginal and Treaty Rights," (1983) 8 Queen's L.J. 232.

_______. "Override Clauses under Section 33 – Whether Subject to Judicial Review under Section 1?" (1983) 61 Can. Bar Rev. 391.

_______. "Charter of Rights and Freedoms – Does it Bind Private Persons?" (1985) 63 Can. Bar Rev. 148.

Slobodin, Richard. *Métis of the MacKenzie District.* Ottawa: Canadian Research Centre for Anthropology, 1966.

Smitheram, Henry Arthur. *Brief on the Non-Status Indians of B.C.* Toronto: Indian-Eskimo Association of Canada, 1971.

Snow, Alpheus H. *The Question of Aborigines in the Law and Practice of Nations.* Arlington Heights: Metro, 1972.

Sowell, Thomas. *Ethnic America: a history.* New York: Basic Books, 1981.

_______. "The Uses of Government for Racial Equality," National Review, 33, 17 (September 1981).

Sprague, D.N. "Government Lawlessness in the Administration of Manitoba Land Claims, 1870-1887," (1980) 10 Man. L.J. 415.

_______. "Métis Land Claims," In *Native People and the Constitution of Canada: the Report of the Métis and Non-Status Indian Constitutional Review Commission.* (Harry W. Daniels, Commissioner). Ottawa: The Commission, 1981.

Stanford Law Review. "Indian Tribes and Civil Rights," (1955) 7 Stan. L. Rev. 285.

Stanley, George F.G. *The Birth of Western Canada: a history of the Riel Rebellions*, 2nd ed. Toronto: University of Toronto, 1960.

_______. "Confederation 1870 – A Métis Achievement" In *The Other Natives: The Métis*, vol. 1. Edited by Antoine Lussier and D. Bruce Sealey. Winnipeg: Manitoba Métis Federation, 1978.

Statement by the President, *Indian Policy*. The White House, Office of the Press Secretary, January 24, 1983.

Swinton, Katherine E. "Application of the Canadian Charter of Rights and Freedoms (ss. 30, 31, 32)," in *The Canadian Charter of Rights and Freedoms*. Edited by Walter S. Tarnopolsky and Gerald-A. Beaudoin. Toronto: Carswell, 1982.

Tarnopolsky, Walter S. "The Canadian Bill of Rights and the Supreme Court Decisions in Lavell and Burnshine: A Retreat from Drybones to Dicey?" (1975) 7 Ottawa L. Rev. 1.

The Métis and Non-Status Indian Constitutional Review Commission (Harry W. Daniels, Commissioner). *Native People and the Constitution of Canada*. Ottawa: The Commission, 1981.

Thomas, Lewis H., ed. *Essays on Western History*. Edmonton: University of Alberta, 1976.

Todd, Eric C. *The Law of Expropriation and Compensation in Canada*. Toronto: Carswell, 1976.

Tribe, Laurence H. *American Constitutional Law*. Mineola: Foundation, 1978.

Trudeau, Pierre E. *Federalism and the French Canadians*. Toronto: Macmillan, 1968.

Tulsa Law Journal. "Self-determination through Effective Management of Natural Resources," (1982) 17 Tulsa L.J. 507.

Tyler, Kenneth J. "A Modest Proposal for Legislative Reforms to Facilitate the Settlement of Specific Indian Claims," [1981] 3 C.N.L.R. 1.

Umozurike, Oji. *Self-Determination in International Law.* Hamden: Archon, 1972.

Utah Law Review. "Rights of Tribal Self-Government and Jurisdiction of Indian Affairs," (1970) Utah L. Rev. 291.

Vance, John. "Indian Claims: The U.S. Experience," (1974) 38 Sask. L. Rev. 1.

Vano, Gerald S. *Neo-Feudalism: The Canadian Dilemma.* Toronto: Anansi, 1981.

Warren, John S. "An Analysis of the Indian Bill of Rights," (1973) 33 Mont. L. Rev. 255.

Watkins, Mel, ed. *Dene Nation: The Colony Within.* Toronto: University of Toronto, 1979.

Weaver, Sally M. *Making Canadian Indian Policy: The Hidden Agenda, 1968-70.* Toronto: University of Toronto, 1981.

Weinstein, John. *Aboriginal Self-Determination Off a Land Base.* Kingston: Institute of Intergovernmental Relations, Queen's University, 1986.

Werhan, Keith M. "Sovereignty of Indian Tribes: A Reaffirmation and Strengthening in the 1970's," (1978) 54 Notre Dame Lawyer 5.

Williams, Robert A. Jr. "The Medieval and Renaissance Origin of the Status of the American Indian in Western Legal Thought," (1983) 57 S. Cal. L. Rev. 1.

Young, "Aborigines and the Constitutions of Australia, Canada and the United States," (1977) 35 U. of T. Fac. L. Rev. 87.

Zartman, I. William and Maureen R. Berman, *The Practical Negotiator.* New Haven: Yale University, 1982.

Zlotkin, Norman K. *Unfinished Business: Aboriginal Peoples and the 1983 Constitutional Conference.* Kingston:

Institute of Intergovernmental Relations, Queen's University, 1983.

________. "The 1983 and 1984 Constitutional Conferences: Only the Beginning," [1984] 3 C.N.L.R. 3.

Synopsis

Overview

The Overview attempts to state the basic aims and structure of the study. It attempts to briefly define the basic approach advocated by the study for handling conflicts between advocates of two competing conceptions of Canada. Some hold that Canada is a community of free and equal individuals; others emphasize that certain groups have special rights based on their special histories. The "strategy of statecraft" that is proposed favours the liberal individualist conception, but advocates that vigorous and imaginative attempts be made to devise solutions that are, both in form and in substance, acceptable to those who favour the "history-based groupist" philosophy. The Overview attempts to show how this accommodationist approach, this "strategy of statecraft," is applied to the wide range of policy issues arising out of the constitutional reform process with respect to aboriginal peoples.

Chapter I: Individuals, Groups, and Canadian Statecraft

Chapter I attempts to present the theoretical and practical foundations for the "strategy of statecraft" and then to show how it applies in several non-aboriginal contexts.

Chapters II and III: The March '83 Preparatory Process and Conference

On April 17, 1982, there came into force the *Constitution Act, 1982*, including s.35 ("the existing aboriginal and treaty rights of the aboriginal peoples of Canada are hereby recognized and affirmed"). Section 37 mandated a First Ministers' Conference to be held within a year to clarify the meaning of s.35.

A series of officials' level and ministerial level meetings were held to prepare for the March '83 meeting. Without any guarantee that there would be further First Ministers' meetings, aboriginal organizations insisted on putting every possible issue on the agenda. No in-depth discussion took place on the legal and policy implications of any substantive issues; governments took a non-committal, "tell-me-more" approach. The precedent was set for holding the meetings behind closed doors and for not releasing the transcripts. There was no invitation for, and no real opportunity for, public and academic participation.

Representing the Inuit at the meetings was the Inuit Committee on National Issues (ICNI). The status Indians were represented by the Assembly of First Nations (AFN). At first, the Native Council of Canada (NCC) represented both the Métis people (descendants of the distinct Anglo- and Franco-Indian people that developed in western Canada in the 19th century) and non-status Indians (persons of Indian ancestry who identify themselves as Indians, but who are not on the official register of Indians). On March 7, the Métis of the three Prairie provinces (Alberta, Saskatchewan, Manitoba) formed their own organization, the Métis National Council (MNC). After initiating litigation against the prime minister, the Métis National Council obtained its own seat for the First Ministers' Conference.

In March, a two-day First Ministers' Conference was held. The federal government released some draft amendments. As expected, the federal government proposed, and the parties eventually agreed with, constitutionally mandating at least two further First Ministers' Conferences (viz Chapter VI).

The parties rejected a veto for aboriginal groups over constitutional amendments specially affecting them (viz Chapter VI).

First Ministers accepted an amendment requiring that aboriginal peoples be consulted on amendments specially affecting them (Chapter VII). There was no real discussion or recognition of the probable unconstitutionality of the amendment. It is, in reality, an amendment to the amending formula and required the consent of all the provinces. (Quebec attended the Conference, but refused to sign any accord.)

First Ministers agreed to an amendment that gave modern "land claims agreements" the same constitutional protection as "treaties" (Chapter VIII). There was no apparent recognition that they may have inadvertently created a mechanism whereby agreements on self-government can be constitutionally protected.

First Ministers agreed to an amendment to further assure sexual equality in the enjoyment of aboriginal and treaty rights (Chapter XXIII). The wording of the amendment was debated in the frenzied backroom meetings of the final day, and the final text was not even available to First Ministers when they signed the accord on the last afternoon. The amendment was probably unnecessary, but helped to create the appearance of progress at the meeting, and to score political points with those concerned with women's rights. The amendment also had the possible unintended side-effect of substantially strengthening the legal protection afforded to *all* aboriginal and treaty rights.

While several substantial amendments did emerge from the March meeting, they were inadequately debated and understood. The secretive nature of the process and the last minute release and discussion of federal drafts resulted in a process that was insufficiently democratic, informed,and deliberate. Some of the most important effects of the meeting may well be the unanticipated side-effects of the land claims and sexual equality amendments.

Chapter IV: Statements of Principle

The approach to constitutional reform recommended by this study urges that participants agree upon concrete solutions that are carefully shaped to be acceptable to parties with differing ultimate philosophies.

To help foster the impression of progress, the federal government included in its draft package a preamble containing "basic principles." These principles, if properly understood, would necessarily have offended the philosophical and theological sensibilities of many participants. On the other hand, they would not have helped to solve the practical problems of aboriginal peoples. The "principles" approach was exactly the opposite of what is recommended by this study. Chapter III does a close analysis of the implications of the federal "principles," something the participants themselves had very little time to do.

The Métis National Council's proposal to constitutionally entrench a statement of principle is assessed. A list of constitutionally entrenched principles would not stimulate further discussions; it would have ended them. Once their general aims were constitutionally endorsed in unqualified terms, there would have been little reason for aboriginal groups to negotiate precise and more limited statements of their rights.

The government of Manitoba proposed that the parties agree on a strictly political statement of principles. While some experts on political negotiations recommend early agreement on the basic principles, it is doubted that the approach would have worked in the s.37 process. An attempt to achieve a comprehensive framework on all the disparate issues would not have succeeded. The best approach would have been to concentrate on a few key issues. This study generally recommends proceeding by a dialectic process; legal drafts should be produced at a fairly early stage; the policy issues that are brought to light and sharpened by the draft should be discussed; new drafts should be produced, and so on.

Chapter V: The Constitutional Amendment with Respect to Ongoing Process

The constitutional amendment to mandate further First Ministers' Conferences is assessed. Had this amendment been agreed upon earlier (as it easily could have been), parties could have selected a smaller number of issues to focus on prior to, and at, the First Ministers' Conference. By leaving doubt about the continuation of the s.37 process and coming to agreement at the March '83 meeting, the parties helped to create the impression that the meeting was a success.

Chapter VI: Consent to Constitutional Amendments

Aboriginal organizations sought a veto over constitutional amendments that specially affected them. The liberal individualist approach of this study is brought to bear. The veto is rejected as excessively inegalitarian. It would allow a small segment of society, by virtue only of its special history, to block the constitutional judgment of an overwhelming majority of Canadians. Furthermore, the veto would prevent the larger community from settling disputes among and within aboriginal groups. For example, it might prevent the larger community from amending the constitution in order to ensure that the various norms of the *Charter of Rights and Freedoms* apply to aboriginal communities. Chapter V also points out the extremely difficult technical problems that would arise with trying to constitutionally state how the aboriginal peoples' veto would be expressed.

Chapter VII; Consultation on Constitutional Amendments with respect to Aboriginal Rights Matters

The basic normative approach of this study is to favour liberal individualism over history-based groupism but to seek accommodation whenever possible. It is believed that recent history justifies confidence that a constitutional right of aboriginal peoples to consultation when their rights are affected would go a very long way to protecting them from unjust amendments. Granting aboriginal peoples a consultative role on certain sections of the constitution is a reasonable way of proceeding with reform with respect to the special privileges of aboriginal peoples that already exist in the constitution. Other groups with entrenched special rights have, at most, a minimal complaint of unequal treatment, in that they too are not guaranteed a consultative role. It may well be, however, that a thorough examination of the legal and political position of these other groups would justify rejecting altogether any charge of unequal treatment.

The amendment on consultation strongly substantiates this study's critique of the s.37 process. In the last-minute rush, there was no adequate opportunity for the participants to discuss the possibility that the amendment is invalid; that as an amendment formula, it requires the unanimous consent of the provinces. This study presents the only scholarly analysis to date of this question and concludes that the amendment is in fact inoperative. The amendment's being nonjusticiable would not alter its essential character: a legally binding statement of how parties should proceed when amending the constitution.

Chapter VIII: Modern Land Claims Agreements

Although it has barely been discussed in the preparatory process, the federal government included in its draft constitutional package an amendment on modern land claims agreements. These are modern-day deals whereby an aboriginal collectivity surrenders its aboriginal land title (i.e. the rights the group has under the common law to its traditional land base) in return for money, real property rights, and, sometimes, guarantees of local self-government. The old (late nineteenth, early twentieth century) treaties between the Indians and the federal government generally involved the exchange of land in return for cash and the establishment of reserves. The amendment on modern land claims agreements was largely the product of the lobbying of the Inuit Committee on National Issues, which was interested in securing constitutional protection for the deal it had made with Quebec and Canada over its traditional land base in the James Bay area.

The amendment stated that the rights that aboriginal groups have or *will* acquire under modern land claims agreements will be considered "treaty" rights for the purposes of s.35(1) of the *Constitution Act, 1867* ("the existing aboriginal and treaty rights of the aboriginal peoples of Canada are hereby recognized and affirmed"). It was not clear prior to the modern land claims amendment whether s.35(1) would protect treaty rights acquired after April 17, 1982, the day the *Constitution Act, 1982* came into force. The modern land claims amendment thus had the (little understood) consequence of making the treaty-making process a living mechanism for constitutionally protecting rights. Furthermore (and there was absolutely no discussion of this point), modern land claims agreements have included guarantees of rights to self-government. It is thus entirely possible that the parties inadvertently created a mechanism whereby modern agreements on self-government can be constitutionally protected, regardless of whether they involve the surrender of land rights (see Chapter XXI). At the very least, aboriginal groups with outstanding land claims can obtain, as part of the package deal, constitutional protection for certain rights to self-government. After the March '83 conference, the focus of the process became aboriginal self-government, and, in particular, the establishment of constitutional mechanisms whereby agreements on self-government can be constitutionally protected. Surprisingly, there has been essentially no discussion of the possibility that the mechanism has already been established and no discussion of the legal interaction of the amendment on modern land claims agreements and a possible further amendment on self-government agreements.

Chapter IX: The Creation of New Provinces

The Yukon Territory has a large aboriginal population, and the Northwest Territories has an aboriginal majority. These territories may eventually become Canadian provinces. Another possibility is that the Northwest Territories will be divided into a northeastern governmental region (which will be predominantly Inuit and called Nunavut) and a largely Dene Indian southwestern governmental region. These regions might eventually seek provincial status.

Whereas the federal level of government was, prior to the *Constitution Act, 1982* authorized to unilaterally create new provinces out of the northern territories, section 42(f) of the *Constitution Act, 1982* made the establishment of new provinces a matter to be disposed of in accordance with the s.38 amending formula – consent of the federal level of government and of at least two thirds of the provinces that have at least half of the population of Canada. The Northwest Territorial government pushed for the repeal of s.42(f). To repeal s.42(f) would have been an amendment of the amending formulae, and so would have required the unanimous consent of the provinces. Quebec was not disposed to participate in any use of the new amending formulae, and several of the provinces expressed the continued desire to have a voice in the creation of new provinces. As a result, section 42(f) was not altered.

Both under the James Bay Agreement and in their Nunavut proposal, the Inuit have sought to secure adequate control over their own political destiny by establishing public governments in areas in which they are a majority. No one is made a second-class citizen; rather, everyone in the community is equally able to participate in public life. The public government approach is entirely consistent with the basic philosophical and practical approach of this study. Chapter XVI suggests that the public government approach might be appropriate for some of the Métis in Western Canada.

Chapter X: The March '84 Process and Conference

Early in the preparatory process (which began with an officials' level meeting in October 1983), the participants agreed to limit the agenda to "only" four items. These items actually encompassed almost every sub-item left over from the March '83 First Ministers' Conference.

Officials' level working groups were set up to discuss each of these four items. There was no sufficient political direction to make these meetings satisfactorily productive.

In the middle of October, the *Penner Report* on self-government was released. It called for the federal government to negotiate with Indian communities on the establishment of self-government. Chapter XX agrees with much of the *Penner Report* but criticizes it for paying insufficient attention to the limits that must exist on Indian self-government and the mechanisms whereby these limits will be established. Indian self-government must be limited by the interests of other Canadians; just as importantly, it must also be limited by the continuing status of an individual within an Indian community as a free and equal member of the wider political community.

The *Penner Report* helped to give the discussions a focus they had previously lacked: aboriginal self-government.

The federal government failed to release draft amendments until the morning of the First Ministers' Conference. A purported nonjusticiable amendment was introduced that would commit federal and provincial governments to negotiating self-government agreements. There were no provisions for the resulting agreements to be constitutionally protected. The federal amendments were a public relations success but, on close analysis (Chapter XVIII), were unimpressive and potentially even subversive of the legal position of aboriginal peoples. Many provincial governments considered that "self-government" was insufficiently well-understood and defined to be the subject of even a nonjusticiable amendment, and the federal proposal fell short of the minimum support necessary for an amendment.

The federal government included in its package a further amendment on sexual equality in the enjoyment of aboriginal rights. When the last-minute drafting scramble was over, a draft emerged that would have undermined the legal position of all aboriginal and treaty rights under s.35 (see Chapter XXIII). The Assembly of First Nations, alerted to the legal difficulties at the last second, expressed its concern, and despite widespread support for the amendment, the federal government dropped it.

Chapter XI: Federal-Provincial Problems and Aboriginal Peoples

An appreciation of the federal-provincial division of powers and responsibilities is a prerequisite to a satisfactory understanding of most issues concerning aboriginal peoples. Chapter X distinguishes among the different issues – including the division of duties towards aboriginal peoples, as opposed to authorities over aboriginal peoples – and clarifies the division of legislative responsibility.

Chapter XII: Federal Responsibility for Indians; and Chapter XIV: Funding of Indian First Nation Governments

Indian self-government will not work if, in the guise of promoting Indian self-reliance, federal and provincial governments cut back on the support they presently provide to Indian peoples. Indeed, present levels of fiscal support do not ensure that Indians on reserves are able to enjoy the same level of essential public services as most other Canadians.

Do Indian groups have rights, based on history, to federal support for public service and social welfare programs? A detailed analysis of various constitutional texts and the "trust responsibility" concept concludes that Indians do not have a court-enforceable right to such federal support. The "trust responsibility" of the federal parliament, if any exists, is not enforceable by the courts; furthermore, it is confined to protecting land use rights, as opposed to promoting Indian social welfare. (The federal executive, under various statutes and the common law, may in some cases be liable for the mismanagement of Indian assets.)

On the other hand, the social welfare variants of liberal individualism do provide a constitutional basis for a claim against the federal level of government if it fails to provide adequate social services for Indian communities. It is believed that a plausible case can be made under s.15 of the *Charter* that the federal level of government must ensure that members of Indian communities obtain roughly the same level of essential public services (including education) as other Canadians.

In Chapter XIV, another aspect of the issue of fiscal support will be examined. It will be considered whether the constitution ought to be amended so that the Indian governments are expressly entitled to federal equalization payments, in the same way as provincial governments are by s.36 of the *Constitution Act, 1982*. Once again, the history-based groupist approach will be contrasted with a liberal individualist approach. It will be argued that the latter provides a more intellectually satisfactory and politically appealing basis for making a version of s.36 applicable to Indian governments.

Chapter XIV also explores the issue of the taxation of Indian peoples. It is argued that Indian governments ought to be empowered to raise revenues through internal taxation and that, notwithstanding the *Penner Report*, Indian governments ought to be expected to do so. That a government's revenues must, to some extent, be raised by taxation is one way of ensuring that its citizens are aware of how much money is being spent and concerned that it is well spent. Furthermore, if and when the federal government ensures that Indian reserves are receiving essential public services roughly comparable to those enjoyed by other Canadians, there would appear to be no justification for completely exempting them from federal income taxation. If they are able to benefit equally from federal political and social rights, reserve residents should have to bear equal responsibilities.

Chapter XIV also considers whether the federal government ought to be able to attach "strings" to the payments it makes to Indian communities. The conclusion is reached that it is consistent with the treatment accorded provinces that transfer payments may be tied to the observance of certain principles of distributive justice. Indian communities will continue to be part of the Canadian policy, and some ability of the larger community to impose its basic standards of justice must be conceded.

Chapter XIII: Provincial Responsibility for Indians

The responsibility of a province for Indians must be based on the constitutional principle that every individual is entitled to the equal protection and benefit of the law. There is a discussion of the extent to which a province can shield itself from its responsibilities by pointing to federal responsibility for Indians under s.91(24) of the *Constitution Act, 1867*. Chapter XIII maintains that federal-provincial-Indian disputes over who is fiscally responsible for what have seriously hampered efforts to improve economic and social conditions in Indian communities. It is strongly urged that self-government negotiations are liable to be bogged down in these trilateral squabbles unless a framework is established that clearly and simply determines the extent and division of fiscal responsibility for aboriginal self-government. One possibility would be for the federal government to assume fiscal responsibility for on-reserve Indians, and the provinces the responsibility for off-reserve Indians.

Chapter XV: Fiscal Responsibility and the s.37 Process

One of the main conclusions of Chapters XI through XIV is that a framework of fiscal responsibility would greatly facilitate community legal negotiations on self-government. Several delegations have formally proposed the constitutional entrenchment of an equalization payments principle for Indian governments. A serious failure of the s.37 process, however, has been that almost no serious discussion has taken place on these issues. The federal government has expressed no interest in assuming exclusive responsibility in certain areas or in constitutionally establishing a certain level of fiscal support. The March '84 political accord submitted by the federal government did propose that governments participate in a study of the division of responsibilities, including fiscal issues, but the package as a whole was rejected. Chapter XXII shows that the 1984-85 process also made no headway on the fundamental issue of fiscal responsibility.

Chapter XVI: The Métis and Section 91(24): Policy Aspects

Section 91(24) of the *Constitution Act, 1867* assigns to the federal government exclusive constitutional authority over "Indians and

Lands reserved for Indians." A 1939 declaration of the Supreme Court of Canada determined that the Inuit (then called "Eskimos") were "Indians" for the purpose of s.91(24). At the March '84 First Ministers' Conference, the Métis National Council urged that the federal government and provinces recognize that Métis also come within the terms of s.91(24).

The general approach of this study is to resist claims to special status based on group history, but nonetheless to accommodate the aspirations of various groups. Chapter XVI argues that almost any aspiration of the Métis (groupist or otherwise) can be accomplished without their having special federal status:

- The lack of general authority over the Métis would not preclude the federal government from making redress for its alleged maladministration of the Métis land grant provisions of the *Manitoba Act, 1870*.
- Métis communities can acquire self-government by the transfer of powers from provincial legislatures as well as the federal level of government.
- The federal government has ample authority to extend economic assistance to the Métis, regardless of whether it has exclusive legislative authority over the Métis.

Rather than helping the Métis, the acquisition of exclusive authority over them by the federal level of government might actually be deleterious to their interests. Rights of the Métis under existing provincial legislation might be undermined. Provincial governments might attempt to shift greater responsibility for assisting the Métis to the federal government, which might resist assuming it; federal authority over the Métis would not necessarily guarantee enhanced federal assistance to the Métis.

At the end of Chapter XVI, it is suggested that the public government option favoured by the Inuit (see Chapter IX) might be appropriate for the Métis.

Chapter XVII: The Métis and Section 91(24): Legal History

There are only a few cases and one major article on whether legal history supports the view that the Métis are already included under s.91(24) of the *Constitution Act, 1867*. In deciding the *Re Eskimo* case of 1939, the Supreme Court of Canada used historical usage of the term "Indian" to determine whether the Inuit were supposed to be included as "Indians" for the purpose of s.91(24). The Supreme Court relied heavily on the "Eskimos" under the term "Indians" in the 1867 *Report of the Select*

Committee of the House of Commons. Chapter XVII argues that prior to 1867 the Métis had already acquired a distinct ethnic identity and that they were *not* commonly understood as being "Indians." A close study of the 1867 *Report* supports this assertion. Chapter XVII also points out that the Métis were considered to be the legal equals of European residents of Western Canada and actively participated in the "public" government of the Red River area.

The post-1870 constitutional practice is also studied. The Métis supported the admission of Manitoba into Confederation as a province, like the others, in which the Métis were equal citizens. It does not seem to have occurred to anyone that the federal government would, under s.91(24) of the *Constitution Act, 1867,* retain comprehensive authority over 86 per cent of the population of the new province.

The federal government established reserves for Indians but gave individual land allotments to the Métis. The federal *Indian Act* expressly excluded from Indian status those who receive such an allotment. A few Métis groups did adhere to Indian treaties, but the assimilation of a few such communities into the federal Indian regime does not undermine the general validity of the Indian/Métis distinction. The reference in the *Manitoba Act* to the "Indian title" of the Métis seems to have been a matter of political expediency, rather than serious constitutional reflection.

A number of exclusively Métis land bases were established by the Alberta Legislature's *Métis Betterment Act.* While these settlements were established as an economic relief measure, rather than as settlement for "aboriginal title," it is difficult to understand how the *Act* could have been constitutionally valid if the Métis were under federal legislative authority. The conclusion is thus reached that history does not compel a court to conclude that the Métis already have special status under s.91(24) of the *Constitution Act, 1867.*

Chapters XVIII to XXI canvass the various constitutional mechanisms that might be used to establish aboriginal self-government.

Chapters XVIII: Entrenchment of Jurisdiction of Aboriginal Governments in the Constitution of Canada; the March '84 Federal Proposal

Chapter XVIII analyzes two possibilities for constitutionally establishing aboriginal self-government. One would be the "s.93" approach – to entrench in the Constitution a list of the powers that may be exercised by aboriginal governments. This approach was opposed partly on philosophical grounds—that constitutionally listing the powers of aboriginal governments would imply that they were sovereign authorities like provinces. A number of provinces said they would not support a move towards creating a "third order of government." The "section 93" approach was also perceived as too rigid. Different aboriginal governments might be transferred to different kind of powers. Chapter XXII of this study suggests, in sharp contrast to the s.93 approach, that the constitution set out the broad variety of arrangements that can qualify as "self-government," depending on the outcome of local negotiations.

Chapter XVIII also analyzes the federal proposal at the March '83 Conference. It demonstrates that despite its success as a public relations coup, the last-minute federal proposal was an extremely weak gesture in the direction of aboriginal self-government. Both the commitment to negotiate local arrangements on self-government and the agreements themselves were intended to be non-justiciable. The federal proposal might have even been a step backwards for some aboriginal groups. It would have undermined the claim the aboriginal peoples already have on enforceable rights to self-government under section 35 of the *Constitution Act, 1982*.

The federal proposal at the March '85 Constitutional Conference made much more headway for several reasons. Among them: a mechanism was created whereby the results of local negotiations on aboriginal self-government could be constitutionally protected; and a "non-derogation" clause was proposed, that is, a constitutional assurance that a new amendment on aboriginal self-government would not always subvert any existing rights of aboriginal peoples to self-government.

Chapter XIX: Unilateral Federal Action to Amend the Constitution of Canada

At the March '84 First Ministers' Conference, the Assembly of First Nations proposed that the federal government move unilaterally to amend the constitution to better protect the rights of Indian peoples. The Nova Scotia delegation responded that the federal level of government's authority to amend the constitution was confined to "matters that deal exclusively with its own house." Chapter XIX explores in some depth the possibilities created by the new amending formulae in the *Constitution Act, 1982*; its conclusion is the same as that of the Nova Scotia delegation. It is not open to the federal government to unilaterally alter the text of, say, s.91(24) of the *Constitution Act,*

1867 in order to formally recognize certain rights of Indian peoples.

Apart from the single Assembly of First Nations-Nova Scotia exchange, there has been practically no discussion in the s.37 process of unilateral federal amendment to the Constitution of Canada. If the legal analysis of Chapter XIX is correct, nothing has been lost by this silence. It is hoped, however, that other legal commentators will consider and report their views on whether the option exists.

Chapter XX: Ordinary Legislation

Is constitutional amendment indispensable to establish aboriginal self-government? Chapter XX discusses two possible legal impediments under the existing constitution. One possible obstacle is the guarantee of individual equality under s.15(1) of the *Charter of Rights and Freedoms*. It is concluded that there are strong legal defences to the application of the equality norm against the establishment of special governmental regimes for aboriginal peoples.

Another possible obstacle which has gone almost entirely without notice, is that there may be constitutional limitations on the extent to which the federal Parliament and the provincial legislatures can delegate their powers. The case law is unclear. Chapter XX predicts and prescribes that the courts should allow governments almost unlimited scope to vest legislative authority in aboriginal governments by means of ordinary legislation. The continuing authority of Parliament and provincial legislatures to override a decision of an aboriginal government or to modify or withdraw the delegation of authority would be a strong factor in holding that there had not been a disruption in the basic scheme of authority and responsibility contemplated by the *Constitution Act, 1867*.

Chapter XXI: The Treaty Making Process

Chapter XXI discusses whether s.35 can and should be amended to allow the results of local negotiations on self-government to be constitutionally protected. (As will be seen in Chapter XXI, an amendment to s.35 along these lines was the main focus of the March '85 First Ministers' Conference.) The astonishing fact is that the constitution may *already* allow for the constitutional protection of local agreements on self-government. The 1983 amendment on modern land claims agreements may have had the unanticipated side-effect of making the treaty-making process a method for constitutionally protecting self-government agreements – *regardless* of whether land claims are at issue. The arguments on both sides of this issue are presented.

(A disturbing legal possibility raised by Chapter XXI is that an amendment to the constitution on self-government agreements might be, in effect, an amendment to the amending formulae. The creation of a mechanism whereby new basic structures of government may be irrevocably established may be tantamount to amending the amending formulae – a move that requires the consent of all 10 provinces.)

Chapter XXI goes on to study the policy advantages and disadvantages of using the treaty-making process to establish aboriginal government. The general philosophical and practical strategy of this study recommends the use of the agreement-making process. It is useful because it does not necessarily require either side to surrender their symbolism or adopt the other's. An aboriginal group can, if it wishes, regard an agreement as an international treaty between two quasi-sovereign entities. Governments, by contrast, can regard the agreement as one between a sovereign entity and a subordinate group. "The agreement-making mechanism might allow each party to say that the other has a bad theory – that works in practice."

Chapter XXII: The April '85 Process and Conference

Chapter XXII begins by evaluating the initiatives of the dying days of the Liberal government. Bill C-52, "An Act relating to self-government for Indian Nations," is assessed as containing some interesting items but being insufficiently precise about the principles and mechanisms that will constrain Indian self-government.

The rest of Chapter XXII describes the remarkable story of how the new Progressive Conservative government of Brian Mulroney almost managed to bring together a deal at the April '85 conference.

A laudable move on the part of the new government was to reveal at the outset of the preparatory process what its basic position was. The prime minister would support the creation of a mechanism whereby the results of local negotiations on self-government could be constitutionally protected. The drafting stage was reached early enough that participants had some opportunity to appreciate some of the finer legal and policy implications. Left unexplored, however, were many issues concerning the framework of aboriginal self-government, including:

- the nature of the legal protection that self-government agreements would have;
- the interplay between the amendment on modern land claims agreements and the more general amendment on aboriginal self-government;
- fiscal arrangements for aboriginal self-government;
- whether the *Charter of Rights* applies to aboriginal self-government.

In a public and deliberate constitutional reform process, the political dynamics of a two-day First Ministers' Conference would not be of fundamental importance. Unfortunately, in the s.37 process, large differences in the outcome may depend on the conferencemanship of some of the key players. Chapter XXII identifies some of the subtle and varied manoeuvres of Prime Minister Mulroney—a successful veteran of backroom politics and labour negotiations—at the April '85 First Ministers' Conference.

The key move at the conference was to delete from the constitutional amendment package a commitment on the part of governments to participate in local negotiations on aboriginal self-government. Appearances to the contrary, there was no guarantee in the April '85 package of any inherent right of aboriginal peoples to self-government. All that was really left of the constitutional package, therefore, was a mechanism whereby the results of local negotiations on self-government could be constitutionally protected. A local agreement would not be constitutionally protected unless the parties to the agreement expressly stipulated as much. Furthermore, an agreement would not be constitutionally protected unless the province in which the community is situated agreed that it should be protected—regardless of whether that province was a party to the self-government agreement.

Although the final deal was weak from the point of view of aboriginal groups, last-minute negotiations with two aboriginal organizations resulted in their supporting it. Seven provinces, the minimum necessary for constitutional amendment, stated their willingness to support the amendment. British Columbia and Alberta, however, remained opposed, as did the Assembly of First Nations (status Indians) and the Inuit Committee on National Issues. The Prime Minister refrained from pressing the deal at the April meeting, and no further progress was made at a follow-up meeting of ministers in June.

Chapter XXIII: The Amendments on Sexual Equality

The aim of Chapter XXIII is to bring to light the underground war that took place in the s.37 process with respect to the drafting of a constitutional amendment on sexual equality. It has been a weird series of battles of which the public has had practically no knowledge. Even some of the senior participants in the process have not had much appreciation of what has been happening.

Chapter XXIII argues that the existing provisions of the *Constitution Act, 1982* were probably sufficient to prevent any sexually discriminatory governmental activity (federal, provincial, or aboriginal). The cause of sexual equality for Indian women had not, however, fared well in the Canadian courts prior to the *Constitution Act, 1982*; and in light of the sexually discriminatory section 12(1)(b) of the *Indian Act*, some concern over sexual equality might have been justified. The constitutional amendment that emerged from the last-minute backroom confusion at the March '83 First Ministers' Conference had very significant and unanticipated consequences. The way the clause was drafted suggested that *all* aboriginal and treaty rights were constitutionally *guaranteed*, not just sexual equality. (Rights that are "guaranteed" may be more strongly protected than rights that are merely "recognized and affirmed".)

The March '83 amendment on sexual equality added a third guarantee of sexual equality to the constitution of Canada. It would have taken an extraordinarily sexist or stupid judge to uphold a sexually discriminatory provision with respect to aboriginal women. Some aboriginal women, however, were led to believe that the March '83 amendment still left some room for sexual inequality. Many governments were prepared to support the addition of a fourth sexual equality clause to the constitution. (It never hurts a Canadian politician to appear to be in favour of equal rights for women.) The March '84 First Ministers' Conference once again featured a last-second drafting frenzy. The emergent draft would have destroyed the support the March '83 amendment tended to give to *all* aboriginal and treaty rights. This side-effect of the March '84 draft was, again, less than fully appreciated by all of the participants. As the conference closed, the Assembly of First Nations was alerted to the legal risks of the amendment and, for perhaps other reasons as well, opposed the amendment. Prime Minister Trudeau allowed this opposition to end the matter for the time being.

The sexual equality issue was once again on the agenda at the April '85 Conference. Premier Hatfield of New Brunswick had strongly insisted on its importance. In all the excitement over aboriginal self-government at the April meeting, the sexual equality issue was temporarily forgotten. It was discussed at an officials' level meeting in June, but no agreement was reached. The whole series of episodes is a remarkable illustration of the extent to which participants in the constitutional process can concentrate on political appearances at the expense of legal consequences.

Chapter XXIV: Unstarted Business: Two Approaches to Defining s.35 – "What's in the Box?" and "What Kind of Box?"

The s.37 process has failed almost entirely to better define or even discuss the legal implications of s.35 of the *Constitution Act, 1982*.

(Section 35, it may be recalled, states that the "existing aboriginal and treaty rights of the aboriginal peoples of Canada are hereby recognized and affirmed".)

One avenue that might have been travelled would have been to better determine what kind of rights are included in the umbrella phrase "aboriginal and treaty rights." Apart from the March '83 amendment that made it clear that "treaty rights" includes modern land claims agreements, no progress has been made in listing and defining "what's in the s.35 box."

Another possible line of inquiry would have been to explore the nature of the legal protection that s.35 affords to its contents. "What kind of box" is s.35? Does it absolutely guarantee its contents from legislative override? Does it merely give its contents symbolic affirmation?

It is very likely that the outcome of the '87 First Ministers' Conference will be that agreements, like "existing aboriginal and treaty rights," will be "recognized and affirmed." In other words, agreements on self-government will be given the same measure of legal protection as is provided by s.35 to its contents; yet there has been no in-depth study of what that protection is.

Chapter XXIV focusses on the "what kind of box" question. It sets out a variety of different theories on the strength or weakness of the legal protection afforded by s.35. It then suggests a possible approach to reforming s.35. The language of s.35 and the case law that has emerged so far tend to take a predominantly historical view of the limits of s.35 protection: those limits that existed as a matter of positive law on April 17, 1982, forever define the extent to which a particular aboriginal or treaty right is constitutionally protected. Consistent with the general normative approach of this study, it is proposed that the historical test might be replaced with an evaluation of the actual merits of a contemporary restriction on an aboriginal or treaty right. The interests and principles of the wider community would be weighed against the concerns of the aboriginal group. Only a compelling justification would sustain an incursion on the rights of the aboriginal group; and even then, just compensation would have to be paid.

Chapter XXV: The Application of the Canadian Charter of Rights and Freedoms to Aboriginal Governments

Although the Manitoba delegation has raised the issue of whether the *Canadian Charter of Rights and Freedoms* ought to apply to aboriginal governments, no serious discussion has yet taken place. From start to finish, Chapter XXV exemplifies the overall normative approach of this study. It insists that the basic liberal individual principles of the *Canadian Charter of Rights and Freedoms* ought to apply to aboriginal governments. At the same time, Chapter XXV throughout considers ways by which to accommodate the special needs and circumstances of aboriginal communities.

Chapter XXV begins with a comparative analysis of the American doctrine concerning Indian government and the American *Bill of Rights*. The Supreme Court of the United States held in *Talten* v. *Mayes* (1896) that the American Bill of Rights did *not* of its own force apply to Indian governments. Chapter XXV critically evaluates the American case law prior to 1968 and makes a number of novel suggestions on how the courts could have developed a more balanced doctrine. In 1968, Congress enacted the *Indian Civil Rights Act* (ICRA) which made a statutory version of the American Bill of Rights binding on Indian governments. Chapter XXV concisely explains the political origins of ICRA and explains precisely what variations were made with respect to the American *Bill of Rights* and why. The analysis of the American situation is completed by assessing the jurisprudence under ICRA. It is suggested that the federal courts were well on their way to developing an interpretation of ICRA which was true to its liberal individualist intentions, but at the same time adequately sensitive to the special social and political conditions of Indian communities. In 1978, *Santa Clara Pueblo* v. *Martinez*, the United States Supreme Court greatly diminished the effectiveness of ICRA by holding that it could only be enforced by a writ of *habeas corpus*. Chapter XXV criticizes the procedural holding of *Santa Clara* and suggests how it ought to have been decided on the merits.

The American doctrine that the *Bill of Rights* does not of its own force apply to Indian government is based on two premises:

1) the *Bill of Rights* applies only to the federal and state governments and their delegates;
2) Indian governments rule by inherent right, rather than by authority delegated by federal or state governments.

Do these premises hold, mutatis mutandis, in Canada?

Chapter XXV explores the very difficult and important issue of whether the *Canadian Charter of Rights and Freedoms* applies of its own force to the private sector. The conclusion is reached that it does not.

Then Chapter XXV asks whether aboriginal communities in Canada have the inherent right to govern themselves.

To parties to the negotiation and implementation of enhanced aboriginal self-government, this basic advice is offered:

- parties should be aware that there is a small possibility that the *Charter* will not of its own force constrain aboriginal governments. A court might hold that an aboriginal group had an inherent right to govern itself and that a self-government agreement and follow-up legislation only implemented that right. The *Charter*, the court might conclude, applies only to federal, provincial, and territorial governments and their delegates. A court might reach the same result a different way. It could hold that an aboriginal group has no inherent right to self-government—but that the acquisition of authority through constitutionally mandated negotiations does amount to a delegation of authority.
- parties should agree, and if necessary, federal and provincial governments should insist that aboriginal governments be governed by either
  (i) the terms of the *Charter*
  or
  (ii) a modified version of the *Charter*, on the analogy of the American *Indian Civil Rights Act*.

Option (i) would probably be adequate. Section 25 of the *Charter* provides the necessary instruction to the courts that they should construe the *Charter* with sensitivity to the special legal position and cultural needs of aboriginal groups.

The policy advice offered by Chapter XXV follows very directly from the general normative approach of this study. The advice is backed up, however, by an examination of the special political conditions of small aboriginal communities. Among the causes for concern are the liability of small polities to domination by one faction (Madison's famous observation in the Federalist); and the fact that the likely integration of the political and economic sectors of small aboriginal communities will limit the extent to which there are countervailing or at least alternative sources of power in the community. These theoretical concerns derive some support from the sociological studies that have been done of the political dynamics on aboriginal communities.

Documents

Proposed Resolution – Government of Canada

1983 Constitutional Accord on Aboriginal Rights – Final Draft Adopted by the Conference – Government of Canada

Proposed 1984 Constitutional Accord on the rights of the Aboriginal Peoples of Canada – Government of Canada

Proposed 1985 Constitutional Accord Relating to the Aboriginal Peoples of Canada – Government of Canada (Initial)

Proposed 1985 Constitutional Accord Relating to the Aboriginal Peoples of Canada – Government of Canada (Final)

Proposed Resolution to authorize His Excellency the Governor General to issue a proclamation respecting amendments to the Constitution of Canada

Projet de résolution autorisant Son Excellence le gouverneur général à prendre une proclamation portant modification de la Constitution du Canada

THE PRIME MINISTER

LE PREMIER MINISTRE

25827–15-3-83

Motion for a Resolution to authorize His Excellency the Governor General to issue a proclamation respecting amendments to the Constitution of Canada

Whereas the *Constitution Act, 1982* provides that an amendment to the Constitution of Canada may be made by proclamation issued by the Governor General under the Great Seal of Canada where so authorized by resolutions of the Senate and House of Commons and resolutions of the legislative assemblies as provided for in sections 38 and 41 thereof;

And Whereas the Constitution of Canada, reflecting the country and Canadian society, continues to develop and strengthen the rights and freedoms that it guarantees;

And Whereas, after a gradual transition of Canada from colonial status to the status of an independent and sovereign state, Canadians have, as of April 17, 1982, full authority to amend their Constitution in Canada;

And Whereas historically and equitably it is fitting that the first exercise of that full authority should relate to the rights and freedoms of the first inhabitants of Canada, the aboriginal peoples;

Now Therefore the Senate and the House of Commons resolve that His Excellency the Governor General be authorized to issue a proclamation under the Great Seal of Canada amending the Constitution of Canada as follows:

PROCLAMATION AMENDING THE CONSTITUTION OF CANADA

1. (1) Section 25 of the *Constitution Act, 1982* is renumbered as subsection 25(1).

Motion de résolution autorisant Son Excellence le gouverneur général à prendre une proclamation portant modification de la Constitution du Canada

Considérant :

que la *Loi constitutionnelle de 1982* prévoit que la Constitution du Canada peut être modifiée par proclamation du gouverneur général sous le grand sceau du Canada, autorisée par des résolutions du Sénat et de la Chambre des communes et par des résolutions des assemblées législatives dans les conditions prévues aux articles 38 et 41;

que la Constitution du Canada, à l'image du pays et de la société canadienne, est en perpétuel devenir dans l'affermissement des droits et libertés qu'elle garantit;

que les Canadiens, après la longue évolution de leur pays de simple colonie à État indépendant et souverain, ont, depuis le 17 avril 1982, tout pouvoir pour modifier leur Constitution au Canada;

que l'histoire et l'équité demandent que la première manifestation de ce pouvoir porte sur les droits et libertés des peuples autochtones du Canada, premiers habitants du pays,

le Sénat et la Chambre des communes ont résolu d'autoriser Son Excellence le gouverneur général à prendre, sous le grand sceau du Canada, une proclamation modifiant la Constitution du Canada comme il suit :

PROCLAMATION MODIFIANT LA CONSTITUTION DU CANADA

1. (1) Le numéro d'article 25 de la *Loi constitutionnelle de 1982* est remplacé par le numéro de paragraphe 25(1).

(2) Section 25 of the said Act is further amended by adding thereto the following subsection:

Aboriginal rights apply equally to both sexes

"(2) Notwithstanding any other provision of this Act, the aboriginal, treaty and other rights and freedoms that pertain to the aboriginal peoples of Canada apply equally to male and female persons."

(The following clause is an alternative to clause 5.)

[2. The said Act is further amended by adding thereto, immediately after section 35 thereof, the following section:

Commitment to constitutional conference

"35.1 The government of Canada and the provincial governments are committed to the principle that, before any amendment is made to Class 24 of section 91 of the *Constitution Act, 1867*, to section 25 of this Act or to this Part,

(*a*) a constitutional conference that includes in its agenda an item relating to the proposed amendment, composed of the Prime Minister of Canada and the first ministers of the provinces, will be convened by the Prime Minister of Canada; and

(*b*) the Prime Minister of Canada will invite representatives of the aboriginal peoples of Canada to participate in the discussions on that item."]

3. The said Act is further amended by adding thereto, immediately after section 37 thereof, the following Part:

"PART IV.1

CONSTITUTIONAL CONFERENCES

Whereas the ancestors of the aboriginal peoples of Canada occupied the forests, plains, arctic ice, mountains and seacoasts of the vast territories now known as Canada for many centuries before the first settlers arrived on the Atlantic coast some four hundred years ago;

(2) L'article 25 de la même loi est modifié par adjonction de ce qui suit :

Égalité d'exercice des droits par les deux sexes

«(2) Indépendamment de toute autre disposition de la présente loi, les droits et libertés — ancestraux, issus de traités ou autres — des peuples autochtones du Canada peuvent être exercés également par les personnes des deux sexes.»

(L'article qui suit est une variante de l'article 5.)

[2. La même loi est modifiée par insertion, après l'article 35, de ce qui suit :

Engagement relatif à la tenue d'une conférence constitutionnelle

«35.1 Les gouvernements fédéral et provinciaux sont liés par l'engagement de principe selon lequel le premier ministre du Canada, avant toute modification de la catégorie 24 de l'article 91 de la *Loi constitutionnelle de 1867*, de l'article 25 de la présente loi ou de la présente partie :

a) convoquera une conférence constitutionnelle réunissant les premiers ministres provinciaux et lui-même et comportant à son ordre du jour la question du projet de modification;

b) invitera les représentants des peuples autochtones du Canada à participer aux travaux relatifs à cette question.»]

3. La même loi est modifiée par insertion, après l'article 37, de ce qui suit :

«PARTIE IV.1

CONFÉRENCES CONSTITUTIONNELLES

Attendu :

que les ancêtres des peuples autochtones du Canada, lors de l'arrivée des premiers colons sur la côte atlantique voici quelque quatre cents ans, occupaient depuis bien des siècles les forêts, les plaines, les glaces

And whereas the aboriginal peoples, over the decades in which the settlers moved across the continent, shared with those settlers their knowledge of the land and of the skills needed to survive and flourish upon it;

And whereas the aboriginal peoples by their own courage and determination have successfully lived until this day in their own cultures and communities, cherishing their own customs and ways, under the Creator of all things, continuing to hold sacred their identity with the land, with the creatures that live upon it and in the rivers that traverse it, with the plant life that it supports and with the seas that surround it;

And whereas the aboriginal peoples, as Canadians, are entitled to the rights and freedoms guaranteed to all Canadians by the *Canadian Charter of Rights and Freedoms*;

And whereas the aboriginal peoples continue, each in a unique manner, to make a contribution to Canadian society;

And whereas it is fitting, in the process of constitutional renewal, to identify the distinct place that the aboriginal peoples occupy in Canadian society, having regard to the cultural differences between those peoples, and to define their rights as aboriginal peoples for entrenchment in the Constitution as a charter of rights of the aboriginal peoples;

And whereas it is fitting for the conferences provided for in this Part to consider the following for inclusion in that charter of rights of the aboriginal peoples:

- the identification of the rights now recognized and affirmed in section 35 of the *Constitution Act, 1982*, and in particular the rights of the aboriginal peoples to the use and occupancy of land and their rights to fish, hunt, trap and gather, based on traditional and continuing use and occupancy and as recognized by treaties and land claim settlements,
- the preservation and enhancement of the use by the aboriginal peoples of their own cultures, customs, traditions, religions and languages including the education of their children within their own languages, as well as within one of

polaires, les montagnes et le littoral des vastes territoires qui constituent le Canada d'aujourd'hui;

que ces peuples, tout au long des décennies au cours desquelles les nouveaux arrivants se sont établis dans le continent, ont partagé avec eux leur connaissance du pays et de l'art d'y survivre et de s'y épanouir;

que ces peuples, grâce à leur courage et à leur détermination, ont réussi jusqu'à ce jour à maintenir leur civilisation au sein de leurs collectivités, dans l'attachement à leurs coutumes et à leurs usages et avec la foi dans le Créateur de toutes choses, en conservant leur lien sacré avec la terre, les fleuves, les rivières et les océans, ainsi qu'avec les animaux et les plantes qui y vivent;

que les hommes et les femmes de ces peuples sont des Canadiens et qu'à ce titre ils bénéficient des droits et libertés garantis à tous les Canadiens par la *Charte canadienne des droits et libertés*;

que ces peuples continuent, chacun à sa manière, à apporter leur contribution à la société canadienne;

qu'il s'impose, dans le cadre du renouvellement constitutionnel, de déterminer dans la Constitution la place qui est la leur dans la société canadienne, eu égard aux différences culturelles existant entre eux, et de définir leurs droits de peuples autochtones en vue de les inscrire dans la Constitution sous la forme d'une charte des droits des peuples autochtones;

qu'il s'impose lors des conférences prévues par la présente partie, d'examiner les points suivants pour inscription dans cette charte des droits des peuples autochtones :

- la détermination des droits actuellement reconnus et confirmés à l'article 35 de la *Loi constitutionnelle de 1982*, notamment ceux qui portent sur l'usage et l'occupation des terres et sur la pêche, la chasse, le piégeage et la cueillette, dans la mesure où ils s'appuient sur la tradition et la continuité et où ils sont reconnus par les traités et les textes portant règlement de revendications territoriales, the official languages of Canada, in order that their children may be equipped to live in the cultural milieu of their choice,

- the institution of various forms of aboriginal government within the Constitution of Canada and under the laws of Canada to meet the respective needs of their communities and aggregations of communities, and
- the definition of whatever additional rights may be identified and agreed upon at such conferences;

And whereas it is fitting that a charter of rights of the aboriginal peoples provide for the enforcement of the rights contained within it:

- le maintien et la valorisation de l'usage de leurs cultures, de leurs coutumes, de leurs traditions, de leurs religions et de leurs langues, y compris l'instruction de leurs enfants dans celles-ci, ainsi que dans l'une des langues officielles du Canada, afin que ceux-ci puissent disposer des moyens nécessaires pour vivre dans le milieu culturel de leur choix,
- l'établissement, dans le cadre de la Constitution et des lois du Canada, de différentes formes de gouvernement autochtone adaptées aux besoins propres de leurs collectivités ou groupes de collectivités,
- la définition de tous autres droits susceptibles d'être déterminés et convenus;

qu'il s'impose dans une charte des droits des peuples autochtones de prévoir des dispositions propres à assurer le respect des droits qui y seront inscrits :

(First alternative — three conferences)

Constitutional conferences

[37.1 (1) In addition to the conference convened in March, 1983, three constitutional conferences composed of the Prime Minister of Canada and the first ministers of the provinces shall be convened by the Prime Minister of Canada, the first within two years after April 17, 1982, the second within three years after that date and the third within four years after that date.

Participation of aboriginal peoples

(2) Each conference convened under subsection (1) shall have included in its agenda an item respecting constitutional matters that directly affect the aboriginal peoples of Canada, including the identification and definition of the rights of those peoples to be included in the Constitution of Canada, and the Prime Minister of Canada shall invite representatives of those peoples to participate in the discussions on that item.

Participation of territories

(3) The Prime Minister of Canada shall invite elected representatives of the governments of the Yukon Territory and the Northwest Territories to participate in the discussions on any item on the agenda of a

(Première de deux variantes : trois conférences)

Conférences constitutionnelles

[37.1 (1) En sus de la conférence convoquée en mars 1983, le premier ministre du Canada convoque trois conférences constitutionnelles réunissant les premiers ministres provinciaux et lui-même, la première dans les deux ans, la deuxième dans les trois ans et la troisième dans les quatre ans suivant le 17 avril 1982.

Participation des peuples autochtones

(2) Sont placées à l'ordre du jour de chacune des conférences visées au paragraphe (1) les questions constitutionnelles qui intéressent directement les peuples autochtones du Canada, notamment la détermination et la définition des droits de ces peuples à inscrire dans la Constitution du Canada. Le premier ministre du Canada invite leurs représentants à participer aux travaux relatifs à ces questions.

Participation des territoires

(3) Le premier ministre du Canada invite des représentants élus des gouvernements du territoire du Yukon et des territoires du Nord-Ouest à participer aux travaux relatifs à toute question placée à l'ordre du jour des

conference convened under subsection (1) that, in the opinion of the Prime Minister, directly affects the Yukon Territory and the Northwest Territories."]

conférences visées au paragraphe (1) et qui, selon lui, intéresse directement le territoire du Yukon et les territoires du Nord-Ouest.»]

(*Second alternative — two conferences*)

(*Seconde variante : deux conférences*)

Constitutional conferences

[**37.1** (1) In addition to the conference convened in March 1983, two constitutional conferences composed of the Prime Minister of Canada and the first ministers of the provinces shall be convened by the Prime Minister of Canada, the first within three years after April 17, 1982 and the second within five years after that date.

Conférences constitutionnelles

[**37.1** (1) En sus de la conférence convoquée en mars 1983, le premier ministre du Canada convoque deux conférences constitutionnelles réunissant les premiers ministres provinciaux et lui-même, la première dans les trois ans et la seconde dans les cinq ans suivant le 17 avril 1982.

Participation of aboriginal peoples

(2) Each conference convened under subsection (1) shall have included in its agenda an item respecting constitutional matters that directly affect the aboriginal peoples of Canada, including the identification and definition of the rights of those peoples to be included in the Constitution of Canada, and the Prime Minister of Canada shall invite representatives of those peoples to participate in the discussions on that item.

Participation des peuples autochtones

(2) Sont placées à l'ordre du jour de chacune des conférences visées au paragraphe (1) les questions constitutionnelles qui intéressent directement les peuples autochtones du Canada, notamment la détermination et la définition des droits de ces peuples à inscrire dans la Constitution du Canada. Le premier ministre du Canada invite leurs représentants à participer aux travaux relatifs à ces questions.

Participation of territories

(3) The Prime Minister of Canada shall invite elected representatives of the governments of the Yukon Territory and the Northwest Territories to participate in the discussions on any item on the agenda of a conference convened under subsection (1) that, in the opinion of the Prime Minister, directly affects the Yukon Territory and the Northwest Territories."]

Participation des territoires

(3) Le premier ministre du Canada invite des représentants élus des gouvernements du territoire du Yukon et des territoires du Nord-Ouest à participer aux travaux relatifs à toute question placée à l'ordre du jour des conférences visées au paragraphe (1) et qui, selon lui, intéresse directement le territoire du Yukon et les territoires du Nord-Ouest.»]

4. (1) Paragraph 42(1)(*e*) of the said Act is repealed.

(2) Paragraph 42(1)(*f*) of the said Act is repealed.

4. (1) L'alinéa 42(1)*e*) de la même loi est abrogé.

(2) L'alinéa 42(1)*f*) de la même loi est abrogé.

(*The following clause is an alternative to clause 2*)

(*L'article qui suit est une variante de l'article 2.*)

[**5.** The said Act is further amended by adding thereto, immediately after section 48 thereof, the following section:

[**5.** La même loi est modifiée par insertion, après l'article 48, de ce qui suit :

Constitutional conference respecting certain amendments

"**48.1** Before any amendment is made to Class 24 of section 91 of the *Constitution Act, 1867*, to section 25 or 35 of this Act or to this section,

Conférences constitutionnelles concernant certaines modifications

«**48.1** Avant toute modification de la catégorie 24 de l'article 91 de la *Loi constitutionnelle de 1867*, de l'article 25 ou 35 de la présente loi ou du présent article, le premier ministre du Canada :

(*a*) a constitutional conference that includes in its agenda an item relating to the proposed amendment, composed of the Prime Minister of Canada and the first ministers of the provinces, shall be convened by the Prime Minister of Canada; and

(*b*) the Prime Minister of Canada shall invite representatives of the aboriginal peoples of Canada to participate in the discussions on that item."]

6. The said Act is further amended by adding thereto, immediately after section 54 thereof, the following section:

Repeal of Part IV.1 and this section

"**54.1** Part IV.1 and this section are repealed on April 18, [1986] [1987]." (*The date depends on which alternative is chosen in Clause 3.*)

7. The said Act is further amended by adding thereto the following section:

References

"**61.** A reference to the *Constitution Acts, 1867 to 1982* shall be deemed to include a reference to the *Constitution Amendment Proclamation, 1983*."

Citation

8. This Proclamation may be cited as the *Constitution Amendment Proclamation, 1983*.

a) convoque une conférence constitutionnelle réunissant les premiers ministres provinciaux et lui-même et comportant à son ordre du jour la question du projet de modification;

b) invite les représentants des peuples autochtones du Canada à participer aux travaux relatifs à cette question.»]

6. La même loi est modifiée par insertion, après l'article 54, de ce qui suit :

Abrogation de la partie IV.1 et du présent article

«**54.1** La partie IV.1 et le présent article sont abrogés le 18 avril [1986] [1987].» (*La date dépend de la variante de l'article 3 qui sera retenue.*)

7. La même loi est modifiée par adjonction de ce qui suit :

Mentions

«**61.** Toute mention des *Lois constitutionnelles de 1867 à 1982* est réputée constituer également une mention de la *Proclamation de 1983 modifiant la Constitution*.»

Titre

8. Titre de la présente proclamation : *Proclamation de 1983 modifiant la Constitution*.

DOCUMENT: 800-17/041

FINAL - FINAL

FIRST MINISTERS' CONFERENCE ON ABORIGINAL CONSTITUTIONAL MATTERS

CONFÉRENCE DES PREMIERS MINISTRES SUR LES QUESTIONS CONSTITUTIONNELLES INTÉRESSANT LES AUTOCHTONES

1983 CONSTITUTIONAL ACCORD ON ABORIGINAL RIGHTS

ACCORD CONSTITUTIONNEL DE 1983 SUR LES DROITS DES AUTOCHTONES

FEDERAL
FÉDÉRAL

Ottawa
March 15-16, 1983

Ottawa
15 et 16 mars 1983

1983 CONSTITUTIONAL ACCORD ON ABORIGINAL RIGHTS

Whereas pursuant to section 37 of the Constitution Act, 1982, a constitutional conference composed of the Prime Minister of Canada and the first ministers of the provinces was held on March 15 and 16, 1983, to which representatives of the aboriginal peoples of Canada and elected representatives of the governments of the Yukon Territory and the Northwest Territories were invited;

And whereas it was agreed at that conference that certain amendments to the Constitution Act, 1982 would be sought in accordance with section 38 of that Act;

And whereas that conference had included in its agenda the following matters that directly affect the aboriginal peoples of Canada:

AGENDA

1. Charter of Rights of the Aboriginal Peoples (Expanded Part II) Including:

   -- Preamble

   -- Removal of "Existing", and Expansion of Section 35 to Include Recognition of Modern Treaties, Treaties signed Outside Canada and Before Confederation, and Specific Mention of "Aboriginal Title" Including the Rights of Aboriginal Peoples of Canada to a Land and Water Base (including Land base for the Metis)

   -- Statement of the Particular Rights of Aboriginal Peoples

   -- Statement of Principles

   -- Equality

   -- Enforcement

   -- Interpretation

2. Amending Formula Revisions, Including:

   -- Amendments on Aboriginal Matters not to be Subject to Provincial Opting Out (Section 42)

   -- Consent Clause

3. Self-Government

4. Repeal of Section 42(1)(e) and (f)

5. Amendments to Part III, Including:

-- Equalization)	Resourcing of Aboriginal Governments
-- Cost-Sharing)	
-- Service Delivery)	

6. Ongoing Process, Including Further First Ministers Conferences and the Entrenchment of Necessary Mechanisms to Implement Rights

And whereas that conference was unable to complete its full consideration of all the agenda items;

And whereas it was agreed at that conference that future conferences be held at which those agenda items and other constitutional matters that directly affect the aboriginal peoples of Canada will be discussed;

NOW THEREFORE the Government of Canada and the provincial governments hereby agree as follows:

1. A constitutional conference composed of the Prime Minister of Canada and the first ministers of the provinces will be convened by the Prime Minister of Canada within one year after the completion of the constitutional conference held on March 15 and 16, 1983.

2. The conference convened under subsection (1) shall have included in its agenda those items that were not fully considered at the conference held on March 15 and 16, 1983, and the Prime Minister of Canada shall invite representatives of the aboriginal peoples of Canada to participate in the discussions on those items.

3. The Prime Minister of Canada shall invite elected representatives of the governments of the Yukon Territory and the Northwest Territories to participate in the discussions on any item on the agenda of the conference convened under subsection (1) that, in the opinion of the Prime Minister, directly affects the Yukon Territory and the Northwest Territories.

4. The Prime Minister of Canada will lay or cause to be laid before the Senate and House of Commons, and the first ministers of the provinces will lay or cause to be laid before their legislative assemblies, prior to December 31, 1983, a resolution in the form set out in the Schedule to authorize a proclamation to be issued by the Governor General under the Great Seal of Canada to amend the Constitution Act, 1982.

5. In preparation for the constitutional conferences contemplated by this Accord, meetings composed of ministers of the governments of Canada and the provinces, together with representatives of the aboriginal peoples of Canada and elected representative the governments of the Yukon Territory and the Northwest Territories, shall be convened at least annually by the government of Canada.

6. Nothing in this Accord is intended to preclude, or substitute for, any bilateral or other discussions or agreements between governments and the various aboriginal peoples and, in particular, having regard to the authority of Parliament under Class 24 of section 91 of the Constitution Act, 1867, and to the special relationship that has existed and continues to exist between the Parliament and government of Canada and the peoples referred to in that Class, this Accord is made without prejudice to any bilateral process that has been or may be established between the government of Canada and those peoples.

7. Nothing in this Accord shall be construed so as to affect the interpretation of the Constitution of Canada.

Signed at Ottawa this 16th day of March, 1983 by the Government of Canada and the provincial governments:

Fait à Ottawa le 16 mars 1983, par le gouvernement du Canada et les gouvernements provinciaux:

Canada

Ontario

British Columbia
Colombie-Britannique

Québec

Prince Edward Island
Île-du-Prince-Édouard

Nova Scotia
Nouvelle-Écosse

Saskatchewan

New Brunswick
Nouveau-Brunswick

Alberta

Manitoba

Newfoundland
Terre-Neuve

AND WITH THE PARTICIPATION OF:

ET AVEC LA PARTICIPATION DE:

Assembly of First Nations
Assemblée des Premières Nations

Inuit Committee on National Issues
Comité inuit sur les Affaires nationales

Métis National Council
Ralliement national des Métis

Native Council of Canada
Conseil des Autochtones du Canada

Yukon Territory
Territoire du Yukon

Northwest Territories
Territoires du Nord-Ouest

Proposed Resolution to authorize His Excellency the Governor General to issue a proclamation respecting amendments to the Constitution of Canada

Projet de résolution autorisant Son Excellence le gouverneur général à prendre une proclamation portant modification de la Constitution du Canada

THE PRIME MINISTER

LE PREMIER MINISTRE

25827—6-4-83

Motion for a Resolution to authorize His Excellency the Governor General to issue a proclamation respecting amendments to the Constitution of Canada

Whereas the *Constitution Act, 1982* provides that an amendment to the Constitution of Canada may be made by proclamation issued by the Governor General under the Great Seal of Canada where so authorized by resolutions of the Senate and House of Commons and resolutions of the legislative assemblies as provided for in section 38 thereof;

And Whereas the Constitution of Canada, reflecting the country and Canadian society, continues to develop and strengthen the rights and freedoms that it guarantees;

And Whereas, after a gradual transition of Canada from colonial status to the status of an independent and sovereign state, Canadians have, as of April 17, 1982, full authority to amend their Constitution in Canada;

And Whereas historically and equitably it is fitting that the early exercise of that full authority should relate to the rights and freedoms of the first inhabitants of Canada, the aboriginal peoples;

Now Therefore the House of Commons resolves that His Excellency the Governor General be authorized to issue a proclamation under the Great Seal of Canada amending the Constitution of Canada as follows:

PROCLAMATION AMENDING THE CONSTITUTION OF CANADA

1. Paragraph 25(*b*) of the *Constitution Act, 1982* is repealed and the following substituted therefor:

"(*b*) any rights or freedoms that now exist by way of land claims agreements or may be so acquired."

Motion de résolution autorisant Son Excellence le gouverneur général à prendre une proclamation portant modification de la Constitution du Canada

Considérant :

que la *Loi constitutionnelle de 1982* prévoit que la Constitution du Canada peut être modifiée par proclamation du gouverneur général sous le grand sceau du Canada, autorisée par des résolutions du Sénat et de la Chambre des communes et par des résolutions des assemblées législatives dans les conditions prévues à l'article 38;

que la Constitution du Canada, à l'image du pays et de la société canadienne, est en perpétuel devenir dans l'affermissement des droits et libertés qu'elle garantit;

que les Canadiens, après la longue évolution de leur pays de simple colonie à État indépendant et souverain, ont, depuis le 17 avril 1982, tout pouvoir pour modifier leur Constitution au Canada;

que l'histoire et l'équité demandent que l'une des premières manifestations de ce pouvoir porte sur les droits et libertés des peuples autochtones du Canada, premiers habitants du pays,

la Chambre des communes a résolu d'autoriser Son Excellence le gouverneur général à prendre, sous le grand sceau du Canada, une proclamation modifiant la Constitution du Canada comme il suit :

PROCLAMATION MODIFIANT LA CONSTITUTION DU CANADA

1. L'alinéa 25*b*) de la *Loi constitutionnelle de 1982* est abrogé et remplacé par ce qui suit :

«*b*) aux droits ou libertés existants issus d'accords sur des revendications territoriales ou ceux susceptibles d'être ainsi acquis.»

2. Section 35 of the *Constitution Act, 1982* is amended by adding thereto the following subsections:

Land claims agreements

"(3) For greater certainty, in subsection (1) "treaty rights" includes rights that now exist by way of land claims agreements or may be so acquired.

Aboriginal and treaty rights are guaranteed equally to both sexes

(4) Notwithstanding any other provision of this Act, the aboriginal and treaty rights referred to in subsection (1) are guaranteed equally to male and female persons."

3. The said Act is further amended by adding thereto, immediately after section 35 thereof, the following section:

Commitment to participation in constitutional conference

"35.1 The government of Canada and the provincial governments are committed to the principle that, before any amendment is made to Class 24 of section 91 of the *Constitution Act, 1867*, to section 25 of this Act or to this Part,

(*a*) a constitutional conference that includes in its agenda an item relating to the proposed amendment, composed of the Prime Minister of Canada and the first ministers of the provinces, will be convened by the Prime Minister of Canada; and

(*b*) the Prime Minister of Canada will invite representatives of the aboriginal peoples of Canada to participate in the discussions on that item."

4. The said Act is further amended by adding thereto, immediately after section 37 thereof, the following Part:

"PART IV.1

CONSTITUTIONAL CONFERENCES

Constitutional conferences

37.1 (1) In addition to the conference convened in March 1983, at least two constitutional conferences composed of the Prime Minister of Canada and the first ministers of the provinces shall be con-

2. L'article 35 de la *Loi constitutionnelle de 1982* est modifié par adjonction de ce qui suit :

Accords sur des revendications territoriales

«(3) Il est entendu que sont compris parmi les droits issus de traités, dont il est fait mention au paragraphe (1), les droits existants issus d'accords sur des revendications territoriales ou ceux susceptibles d'être ainsi acquis.

Égalité de garantie des droits pour les deux sexes

(4) Indépendamment de toute autre disposition de la présente loi, les droits — ancestraux ou issus de traités — visés au paragraphe (1) sont garantis également aux personnes des deux sexes.»

3. La même loi est modifiée par insertion, après l'article 35, de ce qui suit :

Engagement relatif à la participation à une conférence constitutionnelle

«35.1 Les gouvernements fédéral et provinciaux sont liés par l'engagement de principe selon lequel le premier ministre du Canada, avant toute modification de la catégorie 24 de l'article 91 de la *Loi constitutionnelle de 1867*, de l'article 25 de la présente loi ou de la présente partie :

a) convoquera une conférence constitutionnelle réunissant les premiers ministres provinciaux et lui-même et comportant à son ordre du jour la question du projet de modification;

b) invitera les représentants des peuples autochtones du Canada à participer aux travaux relatifs à cette question.»

4. La même loi est modifiée par insertion, après l'article 37, de ce qui suit :

«PARTIE IV.1

CONFÉRENCES CONSTITUTIONNELLES

Conférences constitutionnelles

37.1 (1) En sus de la conférence convoquée en mars 1983, le premier ministre du Canada convoque au moins deux conférences constitutionnelles réunissant les premiers ministres provinciaux et lui-même, vened by the Prime Minister of Canada, the first within three years after April 17, 1982 and the second within five years after that date.

Participation of aboriginal peoples

(2) Each conference convened under subsection (1) shall have included in its agenda constitutional matters that directly affect the aboriginal peoples of Canada, and the Prime Minister of Canada shall invite representatives of those peoples to participate in the discussions on those matters.

Participation of territories

(3) The Prime Minister of Canada shall invite elected representatives of the governments of the Yukon Territory and the Northwest Territories to participate in the discussions on any item on the agenda of a conference convened under subsection (1) that, in the opinion of the Prime Minister, directly affects the Yukon Territory and the Northwest Territories.

Subsection 35(1) not affected

(4) Nothing in this section shall be construed so as to derogate from subsection 35(1)."

5. The said Act is further amended by adding thereto, immediately after section 54 thereof, the following section:

Repeal of Part IV.1 and this section

"54.1 Part IV.1 and this section are repealed on April 18, 1987.

6. The said Act is further amended by adding thereto the following section:

References

"61. A reference to the *Constitution Acts, 1867 to 1982* shall be deemed to include a reference to the *Constitution Amendment Proclamation, 1983.*"

Citation

7. This Proclamation may be cited as the *Constitution Amendment Proclamation, 1983.*

la première dans les trois ans et la seconde dans les cinq ans suivant le 17 avril 1982.

Participation des peuples autochtones

(2) Sont placées à l'ordre du jour de chacune des conférences visées au paragraphe (1) les questions constitutionnelles qui intéressent directement les peuples autochtones du Canada. Le premier ministre du Canada invite leurs représentants à participer aux travaux relatifs à ces questions.

Participation des territoires

(3) Le premier ministre du Canada invite des représentants élus des gouvernements du territoire du Yukon et des territoires du Nord-Ouest à participer aux travaux relatifs à toute question placée à l'ordre du jour des conférences visées au paragraphe (1) et qui, selon lui, intéresse directement le territoire du Yukon et les territoires du Nord-Ouest.

Non-dérogation au paragraphe 35(1)

(4) Le présent article n'a pas pour effet de déroger au paragraphe 35(1).»

5. La même loi est modifiée par insertion, après l'article 54, de ce qui suit :

Abrogation de la partie IV.1 et du présent article

«54.1 La partie IV.1 et le présent article sont abrogés le 18 avril 1987.»

6. La même loi est modifiée par adjonction de ce qui suit :

Mentions

«61. Toute mention des *Lois constitutionnelles de 1867 à 1982* est réputée constituer également une mention de la *Proclamation de 1983 modifiant la Constitution*.»

Titre

7. Titre de la présente proclamation : *Proclamation de 1983 modifiant la Constitution.*

Ministers Conference
Ottawa, March 8-9, 1984

des premiers ministres
Ottawa, 8-9 mars 1984

PROPOSED 1984 CONSTITUTIONAL ACCORD ON THE RIGHTS OF THE ABORIGINAL PEOPLES OF CANADA

PROJET D'ACCORD CONSTITUTIONNEL DE 1984 SUR LES DROITS DES PEUPLES AUTOCHTONES DU CANADA

Tabled by the Prime Minister of Canada

Déposé par le Premier Ministre du Canada

Canada

Proposed 1984 Constitutional Accord on the rights of the Aboriginal peoples of Canada

Projet d'Accord constitutionnel de 1984 sur les droits des peuples autochtones du Canada

THE PRIME MINISTER OF CANADA

LE PREMIER MINISTRE DU CANADA

PROPOSED 1984 CONSTITUTIONAL ACCORD ON THE RIGHTS OF THE ABORIGINAL PEOPLES OF CANADA

WHEREAS pursuant to the 1983 Constitutional Accord on Aboriginal Rights a constitutional conference composed of the Prime Minister of Canada and the first ministers of the provinces was held on March 8 and 9, 1984, to which representatives of the aboriginal peoples of Canada and elected representatives of the governments of the Yukon Territory and the Northwest Territories were invited;

AND WHEREAS it was agreed at that conference that certain amendments to the *Constitution Act, 1982* would be sought in accordance with section 38 of that Act;

AND WHEREAS that conference had included in its agenda the following matters that directly affect the aboriginal peoples of Canada:

— Equality Rights

— Aboriginal Title, Aboriginal Rights, Treaties and Treaty Rights

— Land and Resources

— Aboriginal or Self Government

AND WHEREAS it was agreed in the 1983 Constitutional Accord on Aboriginal Rights that future conferences be held at which constitutional matters that directly affect the aboriginal peoples of Canada will be discussed;

AND WHEREAS the Senate and House of Commons of Canada and the legislatures of nine provinces that have, in the aggregate, more than fifty per cent of the population of all the provinces have passed resolutions supporting changes to the Constitution of Canada that were the subject of the 1983 Constitutional Accord on Aboriginal Rights;

NOW THEREFORE the government of Canada and the provincial governments hereby agree as follows:

1. The Prime Minister of Canada will lay or cause to be laid before the Senate and House of Commons, and the first ministers of the provinces will lay or cause to be laid before their legislative assemblies, prior to December 31, 1984, a resolution in the form set out in the Schedule to authorize a proclamation to be issued by the Governor General under the Great Seal of Canada to amend the *Constitution Act, 1982*.

2. The government of Canada and the provincial governments are committed to negotiating with representatives of the aboriginal peoples of Canada to identify and define the nature, jurisdiction and powers of self-governing institutions that will meet the needs of their communities, as well as the financing arrangements relating to those institutions, and to presenting to Parliament and the provincial legislatures legislation to give effect to the agreements resulting from the negotiations.

3. The government of Canada and the provincial governments, in consultation with representatives of the aboriginal peoples of Canada and representatives of the governments of the Yukon Territory and the Northwest Territories, shall review all aspects of social, cultural and economic programs for and services to the aboriginal peoples of Canada, with the following objectives:

(*a*) clarification of federal and provincial responsibilities for programs and services provided to the aboriginal peoples of Canada, having regard to the existing and potential roles of aboriginal governments;

PROJET D'ACCORD CONSTITUTIONNEL DE 1984 SUR LES DROITS DES PEUPLES AUTOCHTONES DU CANADA

Attendu :

qu'une conférence constitutionnelle réunissant le premier ministre du Canada et les premiers ministres provinciaux, à laquelle avaient été invités les représentants des peuples autochtones du Canada et des représentants élus du territoire du Yukon et des territoires du Nord-Ouest, a eu lieu les 8 et 9 mars 1984 en application de l'Accord constitutionnel de 1983 sur les droits des autochtones;

qu'il a été convenu, à cette conférence, que la *Loi constitutionnelle de 1982* ferait l'objet d'une procédure de modification dans les conditions prévues à son article 38;

que les questions suivantes qui intéressent directement les peuples autochtones du Canada avaient été placées à l'ordre du jour de cette conférence :

— droits à l'égalité,

— titre autochtone, droits ancestraux, traités et droits issus de traités,

— terres et ressources,

— gouvernement autochtone;

qu'il a été convenu, dans l'Accord constitutionnel de 1983 sur les droits des autochtones, d'examiner à des conférences ultérieures les questions constitutionnelles qui intéressent directement les peuples autochtones du Canada;

que le Sénat et la Chambre des communes du Canada et les législatures de neuf provinces dont la population confondue représente plus de cinquante pour cent de la population de toutes les provinces ont adopté des résolutions en vue d'apporter à la Constitution du Canada les modifications qui avaient fait l'objet de l'Accord constitutionnel de 1983 sur les droits des autochtones,

le gouvernement du Canada et les gouvernements provinciaux sont convenus de ce qui suit :

1. Le premier ministre du Canada et les premiers ministres provinciaux déposeront ou feront déposer avant le 31 décembre 1984, devant le Sénat et la Chambre des communes et devant les assemblées législatives respectivement, une résolution, établie en la forme de celle qui figure à l'annexe, autorisant le gouverneur général à prendre sous le grand sceau du Canada une proclamation portant modification de la *Loi constitutionnelle de 1982*.

2. Le gouvernement du Canada et les gouvernements provinciaux s'engagent à négocier avec les représentants des peuples autochtones du Canada en vue de déterminer et de définir la nature, le champ de compétence et les pouvoirs d'institutions gouvernementales adaptées aux besoins de leurs collectivités, de même que les arrangements financiers afférents, et à présenter au Parlement et aux législatures les mesures législatives propres à donner effet aux accords issus de ces négociations.

3. Le gouvernement du Canada et les gouvernements provinciaux, en consultation avec les représentants des peuples autochtones du Canada, ainsi qu'avec ceux des gouvernements du territoire du Yukon et des territoires du Nord-Ouest, étudieront tous les aspects des programmes et services sociaux, culturels et économiques destinés à ces peuples, avec les objectifs suivants :

a) clarification des responsabilités fédérales et provinciales en matière de programmes et services destinés aux peuples autochtones du Canada, eu égard au rôle présent et éventuel des gouvernements autochtones;

(*b*) enhanced participation of the aboriginal peoples of Canada in the area of programs and services, including their increased involvement in the design and delivery of programs and services, taking into account the special social, cultural and economic needs of the aboriginal peoples of Canada;

(*c*) assessment of financial provisions, including consideration of existing arrangements between the government of Canada and the provincial governments;

(*d*) examination of eligibility requirements of programs and services for the aboriginal peoples of Canada, including residency requirements; and

(*e*) examination of programs and services to the aboriginal peoples of Canada, including the degree to which they are comparable with services received by other Canadians residing in similar communities.

4. The government of Canada and the provincial governments shall report on the findings of the review referred to in article 3 to the first constitutional conference held pursuant to the proposed section 37.1 of the *Constitution Act, 1982*, as agreed to in the 1983 Constitutional Accord on Aboriginal Rights.

5. In preparation for the constitutional conferences contemplated by the changes to the Constitution of Canada that were the subject of the 1983 Constitutional Accord on Aboriginal Rights, meetings composed of ministers of the government of Canada and the provincial governments, together with representatives of the aboriginal peoples of Canada and representatives of the governments of the Yukon Territory and the Northwest Territories, shall be convened at least annually by the government of Canada.

6. Nothing in this Accord is intended to preclude, or substitute for, any bilateral or other discussions or agreements between governments and the various aboriginal peoples and, in particular, having regard to the authority of Parliament under Class 24 of section 91 of the *Constitution Act, 1867*, and to the special relationship that has existed and continues to exist between the Parliament and government of Canada and the peoples referred to in that Class, this Accord is made without prejudice to any bilateral process that has been or may be established between the government of Canada and those peoples.

7. Nothing in this Accord shall be construed so as to affect the interpretation of the Constitution of Canada.

b) participation accrue des peuples autochtones du Canada aux programmes et services, notamment à l'élaboration et à la mise en oeuvre de ceux-ci, compte tenu des besoins sociaux, culturels et économiques particuliers de ces peuples;

c) évaluation des dispositions financières, notamment des ententes en vigueur entre le gouvernement du Canada et les gouvernements provinciaux;

d) examen des conditions, notamment de résidence, à remplir pour bénéficier des programmes et services destinés aux peuples autochtones du Canada;

e) examen des programmes et services destinés aux peuples autochtones du Canada, notamment de la mesure dans laquelle ils se comparent aux services reçus par les autres Canadiens résidant dans des zones semblables.

4. Le gouvernement du Canada et les gouvernements provinciaux feront rapport des résultats de l'étude mentionnée à l'article 3 pour la première conférence constitutionnelle à tenir, suivant le projet, dans sa version conforme à l'Accord constitutionnel de 1983 sur les droits des autochtones, d'article 37.1 de la *Loi constitutionnelle de 1982*.

5. En vue de la préparation des conférences constitutionnelles prévues par les modifications de la Constitution du Canada qui avaient fait l'objet de l'Accord constitutionnel de 1983 sur les droits des autochtones, des réunions, convoquées au moins une fois par an par le gouvernement du Canada, seront tenues regroupant des ministres fédéraux et provinciaux, ainsi que les représentants des peuples autochtones du Canada et ceux des gouvernements du territoire du Yukon et des territoires du Nord-Ouest.

6. Le présent accord n'a pas pour effet d'empêcher ou de remplacer les discussions, bilatérales ou autres, ou la conclusion d'accords, entre gouvernements et les divers peuples autochtones. Plus particulièrement, eu égard à la compétence dévolue au Parlement en vertu de la catégorie 24 de l'article 91 de la *Loi constitutionnelle de 1867* et aux relations particulières qui ont existé et continuent à exister entre le Parlement et le gouvernement du Canada et les peuples mentionnés dans cette catégorie, la conclusion du présent accord n'a pas pour effet de porter atteinte aux actions bilatérales menées, ou susceptibles de l'être, entre le gouvernement du Canada et ces peuples.

7. Le présent accord n'a pas pour effet de déroger à l'interprétation de la Constitution du Canada.

SCHEDULE

Motion for a Resolution to authorize His Excellency the Governor General to issue a proclamation respecting amendments to the Constitution of Canada

WHEREAS the *Constitution Act, 1982* provides that an amendment to the Constitution of Canada may be made by proclamation issued by the Governor General under the Great Seal of Canada where so authorized by resolutions of the Senate and House of Commons and resolutions of the legislative assemblies as provided for in section 38 thereof;

AND WHEREAS the Constitution of Canada, reflecting the country and Canadian society, continues to develop and strengthen the rights and freedoms that it guarantees;

AND WHEREAS it is fitting that the government of Canada and the provincial governments work with the representatives of the aboriginal peoples of Canada to develop their special place in Canadian society through the strengthening of self-governing institutions and the preservation of their cultural heritage.

NOW THEREFORE the [Senate] [House of Commons] [legislative assembly] resolves that His Excellency the Governor General be authorized to issue a proclamation under the Great Seal of Canada amending the Constitution of Canada as follows:

PROCLAMATION AMENDING THE CONSTITUTION OF CANADA

1. (1) Section 25 of the *Constitution Act, 1982* is renumbered as subsection 25(1).

(2) Section 25 of the said Act is further amended by adding thereto the following subsection:

Rights of equality of both sexes

"(2) Nothing in this section abrogates or derogates from the guarantees of equality with respect to male and female persons under section 28 of this Charter."

ANNEXE

Motion de résolution autorisant Son Excellence le gouverneur général à prendre une proclamation portant modification de la Constitution du Canada

Considérant :

que la *Loi constitutionnelle de 1982* prévoit que la Constitution du Canada peut être modifiée par proclamation du gouverneur général sous le grand sceau du Canada, autorisée par des résolutions du Sénat et de la Chambre des communes et par des résolutions des assemblées législatives dans les conditions prévues à l'article 38;

que la Constitution du Canada, à l'image du pays et de la société canadienne, est en perpétuel devenir dans l'affermissement des droits et libertés qu'elle garantit;

qu'il convient que le gouvernement du Canada et les gouvernements provinciaux collaborent avec les peuples autochtones du Canada en vue de leur assurer la place qui leur revient tout particulièrement, grâce à la consolidation d'institutions gouvernementales et au maintien de leur patrimoine culturel,

[le Sénat] [la Chambre des communes] [l'assemblée législative] a résolu d'autoriser Son Excellence le gouverneur général à prendre, sous le grand sceau du Canada, une proclamation modifiant la Constitution du Canada comme il suit :

PROCLAMATION MODIFIANT LA CONSTITUTION DU CANADA

1. (1) Le numéro d'article 25 de la *Loi constitutionnelle de 1982* est remplacé par le numéro de paragraphe 25(1).

(2) L'article 25 de la même loi est modifié par adjonction de ce qui suit :

Égalité des droits pour les deux sexes

«(2) Le présent article n'a pas pour effet de porter atteinte aux garanties d'égalité prévues pour les personnes des deux sexes par l'article 28 de la présente charte.»

2. The said Act is further amended by adding thereto, immediately after Part II thereof, the following Part:

"PART II.1

COMMITMENTS RELATING TO ABORIGINAL PEOPLES OF CANADA

Commitments relating to cultural heritage and self-government

35.2 Without altering the legislative authority of Parliament or of the provincial legislatures, or the rights of any of them with respect to the exercise of their legislative authority,

(*a*) Parliament and the legislatures, together with the government of Canada and the provincial governments, are committed to

(i) preserving and enhancing the cultural heritage of the aboriginal peoples of Canada, and

(ii) respecting the freedom of the aboriginal peoples of Canada to live within their heritage and to educate their children in their own languages, as well as in either or both of the official languages of Canada;

(*b*) the aboriginal peoples of Canada have the right to self-governing institutions that will meet the needs of their communities, subject to the nature, jurisdiction and powers of those institutions, and to the financing arrangements relating thereto, being identified and defined through negotiation with the government of Canada and the provincial governments; and

(*c*) the government of Canada and the provincial governments are committed to participating in the negotiations referred to in paragraph (*b*) and to presenting to Parliament and the provincial legislatures legislation to give effect to the agreements resulting from the negotiations."

2. La même loi est modifiée par insertion, après la partie II, de ce qui suit :

«PARTIE II.1

ENGAGEMENTS RELATIFS AUX PEUPLES AUTOCHTONES DU CANADA

Engagements relatifs au patrimoine culturel et aux gouvernements autochtones

35.2 Sous réserve des compétences législatives du Parlement et des législatures et de leur droit de les exercer :

a) le Parlement et les législatures, ainsi que les gouvernements fédéral et provinciaux, s'engagent à :

(i) maintenir et valoriser le patrimoine culturel des peuples autochtones du Canada,

(ii) respecter la liberté de ces peuples de vivre dans leur milieu culturel et d'instruire leurs enfants dans leurs langues ainsi que dans les deux langues officielles du Canada ou l'une de celles-ci;

b) les peuples autochtones du Canada ont droit à des institutions gouvernementales adaptées aux besoins de leurs collectivités, la nature, le champ de compétence et les pouvoirs de ces institutions, de même que les arrangements financiers afférents, étant à déterminer et à définir par négociations avec les gouvernements fédéral et provinciaux;

c) les gouvernements fédéral et provinciaux s'engagent à participer aux négociations visées à l'alinéa *b*) et à présenter au Parlement et aux législatures les mesures législatives propres à donner effet aux accords issus de ces négociations.»

First Ministers Conference

The Rights of Aboriginal Peoples

Conférence des premiers ministres

Les droits des autochtones

Ottawa, April 2-3, 1985

Ottawa, les 2 et 3 avril 1985

PROPOSED 1985 ACCORD
RELATING TO THE
ABORIGINAL PEOPLES OF CANADA

PROJET D'ACCORD DE 1985
CONCERNANT LES
PEUPLES AUTOCHTONES DU CANADA

THE PRIME MINISTER OF CANADA

LE PREMIER MINISTRE DU CANADA

Canada

PROPOSED 1985 ACCORD
RELATING TO THE
ABORIGINAL PEOPLES OF CANADA

PROJET D'ACCORD DE 1985
CONCERNANT LES
PEUPLES AUTOCHTONES DU CANADA

April 1, 1985

PROPOSED 1985 ACCORD
RELATING TO THE ABORIGINAL PEOPLES OF CANADA

[The portions of the Accord highlighted in square brackets relate to the constitutional amendment proposal]

WHEREAS the aboriginal peoples of Canada, being descendants of the first inhabitants of Canada, are unique peoples in Canada enjoying the rights that flow from their status as aboriginal peoples, from treaties and from land claims agreements, as well as rights flowing from Canadian citizenship, and it is fitting that

[(a) there be protection of rights of aboriginal peoples in the Constitution of Canada,]

(b) they have the opportunity to have self-government arrangements to meet their special circumstances as well as the opportunity to exercise their full rights as citizens of Canada and residents of the provinces and territories, and

(c) they have the freedom to live in accordance with their own cultural heritage and to use and maintain their distinct languages;

AND WHEREAS, pursuant to section 37.1 of the Constitution Act, 1982, a constitutional conference composed of the Prime Minister of Canada and the first ministers of the provinces was held on April 2 and 3, 1985, to which representatives of the aboriginal peoples of Canada and elected representatives of the governments of the Yukon Territory and the Northwest Territories were invited;

AND WHEREAS it was agreed by the government of Canada and the provincial governments, with the support of representatives of the aboriginal peoples of Canada and elected representatives of the governments of the Yukon Territory and the Northwest Territories, that

[(a) the Constitution of Canada should be amended

(i) to recognize and affirm the rights of the aboriginal peoples of Canada to self-government within the Canadian federation, where those rights are set out in negotiated agreements, and

[(ii) to commit the government of Canada and the provincial governments to participate in negotiations directed toward concluding agreements with aboriginal people relating to self-government that are appropriate to the particular circumstances of those people,]

[(b) the Constitution of Canada should be further amended to clarify the provisions relating to equality rights for aboriginal men and women,]

(c) direction should be provided for the continuing discussions leading up to the second constitutional conference required by section 37.1 of the Constitution Act, 1982,

(d) governments and aboriginal peoples would benefit from a greater degree of federal-provincial-territorial cooperation with respect to matters affecting the aboriginal peoples of Canada, including programs and services provided to them, and

(e) governments and the aboriginal peoples of Canada would benefit from better statistical information relating to the circumstances of aboriginal peoples, which could be achieved most efficiently by means of the proposed 1986 Census of Canada;

NOW THEREFORE the government of Canada and the provincial governments hereby agree as follows:

PART I

SELF-GOVERNMENT [AND EQUALITY RIGHTS]

[1. The Prime Minister of Canada will lay or cause to be laid before the Senate and House of Commons, and the first ministers of the provinces will lay or cause to be laid before their legislative assemblies, prior to December 31, 1985, a resolution in the form set out in Schedule I to authorize an amendment to the Constitution of Canada to be made by proclamation issued by Her Excellency the Governor General under the Great Seal of Canada.]

2. The objectives of agreements negotiated pursuant to [the proposed paragraph 35.01 (2)(a) of the Constitution Act, 1982 set out in Schedule I] shall be, where appropriate,

(a) to allow aboriginal people increased authority over and responsibility for lands that have been or may be reserved or set aside for their use;

(b) to ensure increased participation of the aboriginal peoples of Canada in government decision-making that directly affects them;

(c) to maintain and enhance the distinct culture and heritage of the aboriginal peoples of Canada; and

(d) to recognize the unique position of the aboriginal peoples of Canada.

3. The negotiations referred to in [the proposed paragraph 35.01 (2)(a) of the Constitution Act, 1982 set out in Schedule I] may have regard to the following factors:

(a) that agreements relating to self-government for aboriginal people may encompass a variety of arrangements based on the particular needs and circumstances of those people, including ethnic-based government, public government, modifications to existing governmental structures to accommodate the unique circumstances of the aboriginal peoples of Canada and management of, and involvement in, the delivery of programs and services;

(b) the existence of an identifiable land base for the aboriginal people concerned;

(c) aboriginal and treaty rights, or other rights and freedoms, of the aboriginal people concerned;

(d) the rights and freedoms of the non-aboriginal people in the communities or regions where the aboriginal people live; and

(e) any relationship between the matters being negotiated and land claims agreements that have been, are being or may be negotiated with the aboriginal people concerned.

4. The negotiations referred to in [the proposed paragraph 35.01 (2)(a) of the Constitution Act, 1982 set out in Schedule I] may address any appropriate matter relating to self-government including, among other matters,

(a) membership in the group of aboriginal people concerned;

(b) the nature and powers of the institutions of self-government;

(c) responsibilities of, and programs and services to be provided by, the institutions of self-government;

(d) the definition of the geographic areas over which the institutions of self-government will have jurisdiction;

(e) resources to which the institutions of self-government will have access;

(f) fiscal arrangements and other bases of economic support for the institutions of self-government; and

(g) distinct rights for the aboriginal people concerned.

[5. During the period between the date this Accord is signed and the date the constitutional amendment set out in Schedule I comes into force, the government of Canada and the provincial governments, in consultation with representatives of aboriginal people, shall take such measures as are necessary to commence the negotiations contemplated by that amendment.]

6. Periodic reports on the progress of negotiations contemplated by [the constitutional amendment set out in Schedule I] shall be made to the ministerial meetings referred to in article 8 of this Accord.

PART II

PREPARATIONS FOR CONSTITUTIONAL CONFERENCE

7. In preparation for the second constitutional conference required by section 37.1 of the <u>Constitution Act, 1982</u>, the government of Canada and the provincial governments shall, with the participation of representatives of the aboriginal peoples of Canada and representatives of the governments of the Yukon Territory and the Northwest Territories, conduct such meetings as are necessary to deal with the items included in the agenda of the constitutional conference held on March 15 and 16, 1983 and listed in the 1983 Constitutional Accord on Aboriginal Rights and to deal with the constitutional proposals of the representatives of the aboriginal peoples of Canada.

8. Ministerial meetings, composed of designated ministers of the government of Canada and the provincial governments, representatives of the aboriginal peoples of Canada and elected representatives of the governments of the Yukon Territory and the Northwest Territories, under the chairmanship of a designated minister of the government of Canada, shall be convened at least twice in the twelve month period immediately following the date this Accord is signed, and at least twice in the period between the end of that twelve month period and the date on which the second constitutional conference required by section 37.1 of the <u>Constitutional Act, 1982</u> is held.

9. The ministerial meetings referred to in article 8 of this Accord shall

(a) issue directions as to work to be undertaken by technical or other working groups and review and assess that work on a periodic basis;

(b) seek to reach agreement or consensus on issues to be laid before first ministers at the second constitutional conference required by section 37.1 of the <u>Constitution Act, 1982</u>; and

(c) receive periodic reports, in accordance with article 6 of this Accord, on the progress of negotiations referred to in that article.

PART III

FURTHER UNDERTAKINGS RELATING TO THE ABORIGINAL PEOPLES OF CANADA

10. The government of Canada and the provincial governments, with the participation of the aboriginal peoples of Canada and elected representatives of the governments of the Yukon Territory and the Northwest Territories, further agree on the matters affecting the aboriginal peoples of Canada set out in Schedules II and III.

PART IV

GENERAL

11. Nothing in this Accord is intended to preclude, or substitute for, any bilateral or other discussions or agreements between governments and the various aboriginal peoples of Canada.

Signed at Ottawa this 3rd day of April, 1985 by the government of Canada and the provincial governments:

Fait à Ottawa le 3 avril 1985, par le gouvernement du Canada et les gouvernements provinciaux:

Canada

Ontario

British Columbia
Colombie-Britannique

Québec

Prince Edward Island
Île-du-Prince-Édouard

Nova Scotia
Nouvelle-Écosse

Saskatchewan

New Brunswick
Nouveau-Brunswick

Alberta

Manitoba

Newfoundland
Terre-Neuve

WITH THE PARTICIPATION OF:

AVEC LA PARTICIPATION DES:

Assembly of First Nations
Assemblée des premières nations

Inuit Committee on National Issues
Comité inuit sur les affaires nationales

Métis National Council
Ralliement national des Métis

Native Council of Canada
Conseil des autochtones du Canada

Yukon Territory
Territoire du Yukon

Northwest Territories
Territoires du Nord-Ouest

SCHEDULE I

RESOLUTION

Motion for a Resolution to authorize an amendment to the Constitution of Canada

WHEREAS the Constitution Act, 1982 provides that an amendment to the Constitution of Canada may be made by proclamation issued by the Governor General under the Great Seal of Canada where so authorized by resolutions of the Senate and House of Commons and resolutions of the legislative assemblies as provided for in section 38 thereof;

NOW THEREFORE the (Senate) (House of Commons) (legislative assembly) resolves that an amendment to the Constitution of Canada be authorized to be made by proclamation issued by Her Excellency the Governor General under the Great Seal of Canada in accordance with the schedule hereto.

SCHEDULE

AMENDMENT TO THE CONSTITUTION OF CANADA

[Possible Equality Rights Amendment]

1. The Constitution Act, 1982 is amended by adding thereto, immediately after section 35 thereof, the following sections:

Rights to self-government

"35.01(1) The rights of the aboriginal peoples of Canada to self-government, within the context of the Canadian federation, that are set out in agreements in accordance with section 35.02 are hereby recognized and affirmed.

Commitment relating to negotiations for self-government

(2) The government of Canada and the provincial governments are committed, to the extent that each has authority, to

(a) participating in negotiations directed toward concluding, with representatives of aboriginal people living in particular communities or regions, agreements relating to self-government that are appropriate to the particular circumstances of those people; and

(b) discussing with representatives of aboriginal people from each province and from the Yukon Territory and Northwest Territories the timing, nature and scope of the negotiations referred to in paragraph (a).

Participation of territories

(3) The government of Canada may invite the government of the Yukon Territory or the Northwest Territories to participate in negotiations referred to in paragraph (2)(a) where the negotiations relate to communities or regions within the Yukon Territory or the Northwest Territories, as the case may be.

Application of section 35.01(1)

35.02 The rights of the aboriginal peoples of Canada to self-government may, for the purposes of subsection 35.01(1), be set out in agreements concluded pursuant to paragraph 35.01(2)(a) with representatives of aboriginal people that

(a) include a declaration to the effect that subsection 35.01(1) applies to those rights; and

(b) are approved by an Act of Parliament and Acts of the legislatures of any provinces in which those aboriginal people live."

2. Section 61 of the said Act is repealed and the following substituted therefor:

References

"61. A reference to the Constitution Act, 1982, or a reference to the Constitution Acts 1867 to 1982, shall be deemed to include a reference to any amendments thereto."

3. This Amendment may be cited as the Constitution Amendment, year of proclamation (Aboriginal peoples of Canada).

SCHEDULE II

FEDERAL-PROVINCIAL-TERRITORIAL COOPERATION ON MATTERS AFFECTING THE ABORIGINAL PEOPLES OF CANADA

1. The government of Canada and the provincial and territorial governments are committed to improving the socio-economic conditions of the aboriginal peoples of Canada and to coordinating federal, provincial and territorial programs and services for them.

2. In order to achieve the objectives set out in article 1 of this Schedule, the government of Canada and the provincial and territorial governments shall, with the participation of representatives of the aboriginal peoples of Canada, enter into regular discussions, on a bilateral or multilateral basis as appropriate, which shall have the following additional objectives:

   (a) the determination of the respective roles and responsibilities of the government of Canada and the provincial and territorial governments toward the aboriginal peoples of Canada;

   (b) the improvement of federal-provincial-territorial cooperation with respect to the provision of programs and services, as well as other government initiatives, to the aboriginal peoples of Canada so as to maximize their effectiveness; and

   (c) the transfer to institutions of self-government for the aboriginal peoples of Canada, where appropriate, of responsibility for the design and administration of government programs and services.

SCHEDULE III

STATISTICAL DATA RESPECTING THE ABORIGINAL PEOPLES OF CANADA

1. It is recognized that the government of Canada, the provincial and territorial governments and representatives of the aboriginal peoples of Canada are in need of improved data relating to the socio-economic situation of the aboriginal peoples of Canada, including the numbers and geographic concentrations of those peoples, so as to facilitate the structuring of initiatives to better meet their social, economic and cultural needs.

2. In order to obtain data referred to in article 1 of this Schedule, the government of Canada and the provincial governments, with the participation of representatives of the aboriginal peoples of Canada and representatives of the governments of the Yukon Territory and the Northwest Territories, shall forthwith establish a technical working group for the purpose of developing a proposal to use the 1986 Census of Canada and, if considered necessary, to supplement information taken therefrom, which group shall present its recommendations to the participants no later than the end of May, 1985.

3. The proposal referred to in article 2 of this Schedule shall include recommendations for use of and access to the data obtained and for cost-sharing with respect to the implementation of measures to obtain data that are to be taken in addition to measures taken within the existing structure of the 1986 Census of Canada.

DOCUMENT: 800-20/041

FIRST MINISTERS' CONFERENCE
ON
ABORIGINAL CONSTITUTIONAL MATTERS

PROPOSED 1985 ACCORD
RELATING TO THE
ABORIGINAL PEOPLES OF CANADA

Federal

OTTAWA, Ontario
April 2 and 3, 1985

April 3, 1985

PROPOSED 1985 ACCORD
RELATING TO THE ABORIGINAL PEOPLES OF CANADA

WHEREAS the aboriginal peoples of Canada, being descendants of the first inhabitants of Canada, are unique peoples in Canada enjoying the rights that flow from their status as aboriginal peoples, from treaties and from land claims agreements, as well as rights flowing from Canadian citizenship, and it is fitting that

(a) there be protection of rights of aboriginal peoples in the Constitution of Canada,

(b) they have the opportunity to have self-government arrangements to meet their special circumstances as well as the opportunity to exercise their full rights as citizens of Canada and residents of the provinces and territories, and

(c) they have the freedom to live in accordance with their own cultural heritage and to use and maintain their distinct languages;

AND WHEREAS, pursuant to section 37.1 of the Constitution Act, 1982, a constitutional conference composed of the Prime Minister of Canada and the first ministers of the provinces was held on April 2 and 3, 1985, to which representatives of the aboriginal peoples of Canada and elected representatives of the governments of the Yukon Territory and the Northwest Territories were invited;

AND WHEREAS it was agreed by the government of Canada and the provincial governments, with the support of representatives of the aboriginal peoples of Canada and elected representatives of the governments of the Yukon Territory and the Northwest Territories, that

(a) the Constitution of Canada should be amended to recognize and affirm the rights of the aboriginal peoples of Canada to self-government within the Canadian federation, where those rights are set out in negotiated agreements,

(b) the Constitution of Canada should be further amended to clarify the provisions relating to equality rights for aboriginal men and women,

(c) direction should be provided for the continuing discussions leading up to the second constitutional conference required by section 37.1 of the Constitution Act, 1982,

(d) governments and aboriginal peoples would benefit from a greater degree of federal-provincial-territorial cooperation with respect to matters affecting the aboriginal peoples of Canada, including programs and services provided to them, and

(e) governments and the aboriginal peoples of Canada would benefit from better statistical information relating to the circumstances of aboriginal peoples, which could be achieved most efficiently by means of the proposed 1986 Census of Canada;

NOW THEREFORE the government of Canada and the provincial governments hereby agree as follows:

PART I

SELF-GOVERNMENT [AND EQUALITY RIGHTS]

1. The Prime Minister of Canada will lay or cause to be laid before the Senate and House of Commons, and the first ministers of the provinces will lay or cause to be laid before their legislative assemblies, prior to December 31, 1985, a resolution in the form set out in Schedule I to authorize an amendment to the Constitution of Canada to be made by proclamation issued by Her Excellency the Governor General under the Great Seal of Canada.

2. The government of Canada and the provincial governments are committed, to the extent that each has authority, to

   (a) participating in negotiations directed toward concluding, with representatives of aboriginal people living in particular communities or regions, agreements relating to self-government that are appropriate to the particular circumstances of those people; and

   (b) discussing with representatives of aboriginal people from each province the timing, nature and scope of the negotiations referred to in paragraph (a).

3. The government of Canada and the governments of the Yukon Territory and the Northwest Territories are committed to participating in negotiations directed toward concluding, with representatives of aboriginal people living in particular communities or regions, agreements relating to self-government that are appropriate to the particular circumstances of those people, and the minister of the government of Canada responsible for the negotiations shall invite elected representatives of the government of the Yukon Territory or the Northwest Territories to participate in those negotiations where, after consultation with representatives of the aboriginal peoples of Canada from the Yukon Territory or the Northwest Territories, as the case may be, the minister is of the opinion that those negotiations directly affect the Yukon Territory or the Northwest Territories, as the case may be.

4. The objectives of agreements negotiated pursuant to article 2 of this Accord shall be, where appropriate,

(a) to allow aboriginal people increased authority over and responsibility for lands that have been or may be reserved or set aside for their use;

(b) to ensure increased participation of the aboriginal peoples of Canada in government decision-making that directly affects them;

(c) to maintain and enhance the distinct culture and heritage of the aboriginal peoples of Canada; and

(d) to recognize the unique position of the aboriginal peoples of Canada.

5. The negotiations referred to in article 2 of this Accord may have regard to the following factors:

(a) that agreements relating to self-government for aboriginal people may encompass a variety of arrangements based on the particular needs and circumstances of those people, including ethnic-based government, public government, modifications to existing governmental structures to accommodate the unique circumstances of the aboriginal peoples of Canada and management of, and involvement in, the delivery of programs and services;

(b) the existence of an identifiable land base for the aboriginal people concerned;

(c) aboriginal and treaty rights, or other rights and freedoms, of the aboriginal people concerned;

(d) the rights and freedoms of the non-aboriginal people in the communities or regions where the aboriginal people live; and

(e) any relationship between the matters being negotiated and land claims agreements that have been, are being or may be negotiated with the aboriginal people concerned.

6. The negotiations referred to in article 2 of this Accord may address any appropriate matter relating to self-government including, among other matters,

(a) membership in the group of aboriginal people concerned;

(b) the nature and powers of the institutions of self-government;

(c) responsibilities of, and programs and services to be provided by, the institutions of self-government;

(d) the definition of the geographic areas over which the institutions of self-government will have jurisdiction;

(e) resources to which the institutions of self-government will have access;

(f) fiscal arrangements and other bases of economic support for the institutions of self-government; and

(g) distinct rights for the aboriginal people concerned.

7. During the period between the date this Accord is signed and the date the constitutional amendment set out in Schedule I comes into force, the government of Canada and the provincial governments, in consultation with representatives of aboriginal people, shall take such measures as may be appropriate to commence the negotiations contemplated in article 2 of this Accord.

8. Periodic reports on the negotiations referred to in article 2 of this Accord shall be made to the ministerial meetings referred to in article 10 of this Accord.

PART II

PREPARATIONS FOR CONSTITUTIONAL CONFERENCE

9. In preparation for the second constitutional conference required by section 37.1 of the Constitution Act, 1982, the government of Canada and the provincial governments shall, with the participation of representatives of the aboriginal peoples of Canada and representatives of the governments of the Yukon Territory and the Northwest Territories, conduct such meetings as are necessary to deal with the items included in the agenda of the constitutional conference held

on March 15 and 16, 1983 and listed in the 1983 Constitutional Accord on Aboriginal Rights and to deal with the constitutional proposals of the representatives of the aboriginal peoples of Canada.

10. Ministerial meetings, composed of designated ministers of the government of Canada and the provincial governments, representatives of the aboriginal peoples of Canada and elected representatives of the governments of the Yukon Territory and the Northwest Territories, under the chairmanship of a designated minister of the government of Canada, shall be convened at least twice in the twelve month period immediately following the date this Accord is signed, and at least twice in the period between the end of that twelve month period and the date on which the second constitutional conference required by section 37.1 of the Constitutional Act, 1982 is held.

11. The ministerial meetings referred to in article 10 of this Accord shall

(a) issue directions as to work to be undertaken by technical or other working groups and review and assess that work on a periodic basis;

(b) receive periodic reports, in accordance with article 8 of this Accord, on the negotiations referred to in that article and consider further constitutional amendments relating to self-government; and

(c) seek to reach agreement or consensus on issues to be laid before first ministers at the second constitutional conference required by section 37.1 of the Constitution Act, 1982.

PART III

SECOND CONSTITUTIONAL CONFERENCE REQUIRED BY SECTION 37.1 OF THE CONSTITUTION ACT, 1982

12. The second constitutional conference required by section 37.1 of the Constitution Act, 1982 shall have included in its agenda an item relating to self-government for the aboriginal peoples of Canada.

PART IV

FURTHER UNDERTAKINGS RELATING TO THE ABORIGINAL PEOPLES OF CANADA

13. The government of Canada and the provincial governments, with the participation of the aboriginal peoples of Canada and elected representatives of the governments of the Yukon Territory and the Northwest Territories, further agree on the matters affecting the aboriginal peoples of Canada set out in Schedules II and III.

PART V

GENERAL

14. Nothing in this Accord is intended to preclude, or substitute for, any bilateral or other discussions or agreements between governments and the various aboriginal peoples of Canada.

Signed at Ottawa this 3rd day of April, 1985 by the government of Canada and the provincial governments:

Fait à Ottawa le 3 avril 1985, par le gouvernement du Canada et les gouvernements provinciaux:

Canada

Ontario

British Columbia
Colombie-Britannique

Québec

Prince Edward Island
Île-du-Prince-Édouard

Nova Scotia
Nouvelle-Écosse

Saskatchewan

New Brunswick
Nouveau-Brunswick

Alberta

Manitoba

Newfoundland
Terre-Neuve

WITH THE PARTICIPATION OF:

AVEC LA PARTICIPATION DES:

Assembly of First Nations
Assemblée des premières nations

Inuit Committee on National Issues
Comité inuit sur les affaires nationales

Métis National Council
Ralliement national des Métis

Native Council of Canada
Conseil des autochtones du Canada

Yukon Territory
Territoire du Yukon

Northwest Territories
Territoires du Nord-Ouest

SCHEDULE I

RESOLUTION

Motion for a Resolution to authorize an amendment to the Constitution of Canada

WHEREAS the Constitution Act, 1982 provides that an amendment to the Constitution of Canada may be made by proclamation issued by the Governor General under the Great Seal of Canada where so authorized by resolutions of the Senate and House of Commons and resolutions of the legislative assemblies as provided for in section 38 thereof;

NOW THEREFORE the (Senate) (House of Commons) (legislative assembly) resolves that an amendment to the Constitution of Canada be authorized to be made by proclamation issued by Her Excellency the Governor General under the Great Seal of Canada in accordance with the schedule hereto.

SCHEDULE

AMENDMENT TO THE CONSTITUTION OF CANADA

[Possible Equality Rights Amendment]

1. The Constitution Act, 1982 is amended by adding thereto, immediately after section 35 thereof, the following section:

Rights to self-government

"35.01 (1) The rights of the aboriginal peoples of Canada to self-government, within the context of the Canadian federation, that are set out in agreements referred to in subsection (2) are hereby recognized and affirmed.

Agreements

(2) Subsection (1) applies in respect of any agreement with representatives of aboriginal people that sets out rights of self-government and that

(a) includes a declaration that subsection (1) applies; and

(b) is approved by an Act of Parliament and Acts of the legislatures of any provinces in which those aboriginal people live.

Rights not affected

(3) Nothing in this section abrogates or derogates from any rights to self-government, or any other rights, of the aboriginal peoples of Canada.

2. Section 61 of the said Act is repealed and the following substituted therefor:

References

"61. A reference to the Constitution Act, 1982, or a reference to the Constitution Acts 1867 to 1982, shall be deemed to include a reference to any amendments thereto."

3. This Amendment may be cited as the Constitution Amendment, year of proclamation (Aboriginal peoples of Canada).

SCHEDULE II

FEDERAL-PROVINCIAL-TERRITORIAL COOPERATION ON MATTERS AFFECTING THE ABORIGINAL PEOPLES OF CANADA

1. The government of Canada and the provincial and territorial governments are committed to improving the socio-economic conditions of the aboriginal peoples of Canada and to coordinating federal, provincial and territorial programs and services for them.

2. In order to achieve the objectives set out in article 1 of this Schedule, the government of Canada and the provincial and territorial governments shall, with the participation of representatives of the aboriginal peoples of Canada, enter into regular discussions, on a bilateral or multilateral basis as appropriate, which shall have the following additional objectives:

   (a) the determination of the respective roles and responsibilities of the government of Canada and the provincial and territorial governments toward the aboriginal peoples of Canada;

   (b) the improvement of federal-provincial-territorial cooperation with respect to the provision of programs and services, as well as other government initiatives, to the aboriginal peoples of Canada so as to maximize their effectiveness; and

   (c) the transfer to institutions of self-government for the aboriginal peoples of Canada, where appropriate, of responsibility for the design and administration of government programs and services.

SCHEDULE III

STATISTICAL DATA RESPECTING THE ABORIGINAL PEOPLES OF CANADA

1. It is recognized that the government of Canada, the provincial and territorial governments and representatives of the aboriginal peoples of Canada are in need of improved data relating to the socio-economic situation of the aboriginal peoples of Canada, including the numbers and geographic concentrations of those peoples, so as to facilitate the structuring of initiatives to better meet their social, economic and cultural needs.

2. In order to obtain data referred to in article 1 of this Schedule, the government of Canada and the provincial governments, with the participation of representatives of the aboriginal peoples of Canada and representatives of the governments of the Yukon Territory and the Northwest Territories, shall forthwith establish a technical working group for the purpose of developing a proposal to use the 1986 Census of Canada and, if considered necessary, to supplement information taken therefrom, which group shall present its recommendations to the participants no later than the end of May, 1985.

3. The proposal referred to in article 2 of this Schedule shall include recommendations for use of and access to the data obtained and for cost-sharing with respect to the implementation of measures to obtain data that are to be taken in addition to measures taken within the existing structure of the 1986 Census of Canada.

Members of the Institute

Board of Directors

The Honourable John B. Aird, O.C.,Q.C. (Honorary Chairman)
Aird & Berlis
Toronto

The Honourable Robert L. Stanfield, P.C., Q.C., (Chairman)
Ottawa

Roger Charbonneau (Vice-Chairman)
Président du conseil d'administration
Banque Nationale de Paris (Canada)
Montréal

Dr. Robert Bandeen
President and Chief Executive Officer
Cluny Corporation
Toronto

Larry I. Bell
Chief Executive Officer
Vancouver City Savings Credit Union

Nan-Bowles de Gaspé Beaubien
Vice-présidente, ressources humaines
Télémédia Inc.
Montréal

Louis A. Desrochers, Q.C.
McCuaig, Desrochers
Edmonton

Peter C. Dobell
Director, Parliamentary Centre for Foreign Affairs and Foreign Trade
Ottawa

Dr. Rod Dobell
President, The Institute for Research on Public Policy
Victoria

Dr. Regis Duffy
President
Diagnostic Chemicals Ltd.
Charlottetown

Dr. James D. Fleck
Faculty of Management Studies
University of Toronto

Peter C. Godsoe
Vice Chairman of the Board
The Bank of Nova Scotia
Toronto

Dianne I. Hall
Senior Vice-President,
NOVA, AN ALBERTA CORPORATION
Calgary

David Hennigar
Atlantic Regional Director
Burns Fry Limited
Halifax

Roland J. Lutes, C.A.
Clarkson Gordon
Montreal

Dr. Tom Pepper
Pepper Consultants Ltd.
Saskatoon

Terrence Mactaggart
Managing Director
Sound Linked Data Inc.
Mississauga
Claude Morin
École nationale d'administration publique
Québec
Milan Nastich
Canadian General Investments Limited
Toronto
Professor William A. W. Neilson
Dean, Faculty of Law
University of Victoria
Roderick C. Nolan, P.Eng.
Executive Vice-President
Neill & Gunter Limited
Fredericton
Robert J. Olivero
United Nations Secretariat
New York
Gordon F. Osbaldeston
Senior Fellow, School of Business Administration, University of Western Ontario
London
Garnet T. Page, O.C.
Calgary
Dr. K. George Pedersen
President
University of Western Ontario
London
Professor Marilyn L. Pilkington
Osgoode Hall Law School
Toronto
Dr. Stuart L. Smith
Chairman
Science Council of Canada
Ottawa
Eldon D. Thompson
President, Telesat
Vanier
Dr. Israel Unger
Department of Chemistry
University of New Brunswick
Fredericton
Philip Vineberg, O.C., Q.C.
Phillips & Vineberg
Montreal
Dr. Norman Wagner
President and Vice-Chancellor
University of Calgary
Ida Wasacase, C.M.
Winnipeg
Mr. Ronald L. Watts
Department of Political Studies
Queen's University
Kingston
Dr. R. Sherman Weaver
Director
Alberta Environmental Centre
Vegreville
Dr. Blossom Wigdor
Director, Program in Gerontology
University of Toronto

Government Representatives

Roger Burke, Prince Edward Island
Herb Clarke, Newfoundland
Joseph H. Clarke, Nova Scotia
Christian Dufour, Québec
Hershell Ezrin, Ontario
George Ford, Manitoba
Barry Mellon, Alberta
John H. Parker, Northwest Territories
Norman Riddell, Saskatchewan
Eloise Spitzer, Yukon
Barry Toole, New Brunswick

Institute Management

Rod Dobell	President
Peter Dobell	Vice-President and Secretary-Treasurer
Yvon Gasse	Director, Small & Medium-Sized Business Program
Barbara L. Hodgins	Director, Western Resources Program
John Langford	Director, Governability Research Program
Barry Lesser	Director, Information Society Studies Program
Shirley Seward	Director, Studies in Social Policy
Frank Stone	Director, International Economics Program
Parker Staples	Director, Financial Services
Donald Wilson	Director, Communications
Louis Vagianos	Director, Publishing Services
Tom Kent	Editor, *Policy Options Politiques*

Fellows- and Scholars-in-Residence:

Edgar Gallant	Fellow-in-Residence
Tom Kent	Fellow-in-Residence
Eric Kierans	Fellow-in-Residence
Jean-Luc Pepin	Fellow-in-Residence
Gordon Robertson	Fellow-in-Residence
David Burgess	Scholar-in-Residence
Barry Cooper	Scholar-in-Residence

Publications Available —January 1987

Order Address

The Institute for Research on Public Policy
P.O. Box 3670 South
Halifax, Nova Scotia
B3J 3K6

Leroy O. Stone & Claude Marceau	*Canadian Population Trends and Public Policy Through the 1980s.* 1977 $4.00
Raymond Breton	*The Canadian Condition: A Guide to Research in Public Policy.* 1977 $2.95
J.W. Rowley & W.T. Stanbury (eds.)	*Competition Policy in Canada: Stage II, Bill C-13.* 1978 $12.95
C.F. Smart & W.T. Stanbury (eds.)	*Studies on Crisis Management.* 1978 $9.95
W.T. Stanbury (ed.)	*Studies on Regulation in Canada.* 1978 $9.95
Michael Hudson	*Canada in the New Monetary Order: Borrow? Devalue? Restructure!* 1978 $6.95
David K. Foot (ed.)	*Public Employment and Compensation in Canada: Myths and Realities.* 1978 $10.95
Raymond Breton & Gail Grant Akian	*Urban Institutions and People of Indian Ancestry: Suggestions for Research.* 1979 $3.00
Thomas H. Atkinson	*Trends in Life Satisfaction Among Canadians, 1968-1977.* 1979 $3.00

W.E. Cundiff & Mado Reid (eds.)	*Issues in Canadian/U.S. Transborder Computer Data Flows.* 1979 $6.50
Meyer W. Bucovetsky (ed.)	*Studies in Public Employment and Compensation in Canada.* 1979 $14.95
Richard French & André Béliveau	*The RCMP and the Management of National Security.* 1979 $6.95
G. Bruce Doern & Allan M. Maslove (eds.)	*The Public Evaluation of Government Spending.* 1979 $10.95
Leroy O. Stone & Michael J. MacLean	*Future Income Prospects for Canada's Senior Citizens.* 1979 $7.95
Richard M. Bird	*The Growth of Public Employment in Canada.* 1979 $12.95
Richard J. Schultz	*Federalism and the Regulatory Process.* 1979 $1.50
Richard J. Schultz	*Le fédéralisme et le processus de réglementation.* 1979 $1.50
Elliot J. Feldman & Neil Nevitte (eds.)	*The Future of North America: Canada, the United States, and Quebec Nationalism.* 1979 $7.95
David R. Protheroe	*Imports and Politics: Trade Decision Making in Canada, 1968-1979.* 1980 $8.95
G. Bruce Doern	*Government Intervention in the Canadian Nuclear Industry.* 1980 $8.95
G. Bruce Doern & Robert W. Morrison (eds.)	*Canadian Nuclear Policies.* 1980 $14.95
Allan M. Maslove & Gene Swimmer	*Wage Controls in Canada: 1975-78: A Study of Public Decision Making.* 1980 $11.95
T. Gregory Kane	*Consumers and the Regulators: Intervention in the Federal Regulatory Process.* 1980 $10.95
Réjean Lachapelle & Jacques Henripin	*La situation démolinguistique au Canada: évolution passée et prospective.* 1980 $24.95
Albert Breton & Anthony Scott	*The Design of Federations.* 1980 $6.95
A.R. Bailey & D.G. Hull	*The Way Out: A More Revenue-Dependent Public Sector and How It Might Revitalize the Process of Governing.* 1980 $6.95
David R. Harvey	*Christmas Turkey or Prairie Vulture? An Economic Analysis of the Crow's Nest Pass Grain Rates.* 1980 $10.95
Donald G. Cartwright	*Official Language Populations in Canada: Patterns and Contacts.* 1980 $4.95
Richard M. Bird	*Taxing Corporations.* 1980 $6.95

Leroy O. Stone & Susan Fletcher	*A Profile of Canada's Older Population.* 1980 $7.95
Peter N. Nemetz (ed.)	*Resource Policy: International Perspectives.* 1980 $18.95
Keith A.J. Hay (ed.)	*Canadian Perspectives on Economic Relations With Japan.* 1980 $18.95
Dhiru Patel	*Dealing With Interracial Conflict: Policy Alternatives.* 1980 $5.95
Raymond Breton & Gail Grant	*La langue de travail au Québec : synthèse de la recherche sur la rencontre de deux langues.* 1981 $10.95
David M. Cameron (ed.)	*Regionalism and Supranationalism: Challenges and Alternatives to the Nation-State in Canada and Europe.* 1981 $9.95
Heather Menzies	*Women and the Chip: Case Studies of the Effects of Information on Employment in Canada.* 1981 $8.95
H.V. Kroeker (ed.)	*Sovereign People or Sovereign Governments.* 1981 $12.95
Peter Aucoin (ed.)	*The Politics and Management of Restraint in Government.* 1981 $17.95
Nicole S. Morgan	*Nowhere to Go? Possible Consequences of the Demographic Imbalance in Decision-Making Groups of the Federal Public Service.* 1981 $8.95
Nicole S. Morgan	*Où aller? Les conséquences prévisibles des déséquilibres démographiques chez les groupes de décision de la fonction publique fédérale.* 1981 $8.95
Raymond Breton, Jeffrey G. Reitz & Victor F. Valentine	*Les frontières culturelles et la cohésion du Canada.* 1981 $18.95
Peter N. Nemetz (ed.)	*Energy Crisis: Policy Response.* 1981 $10.95
James Gillies	*Where Business Fails.* 1981 $9.95
Allan Tupper & G. Bruce Doern (eds.)	*Public Corporations and Public Policy in Canada.* 1981 $16.95
Réjean Lachapelle & Jacques Henripin	*The Demolinguistic Situation in Canada: Past Trends and Future Prospects.* 1982 $24.95
Irving Brecher	*Canada's Competition Policy Revisited: Some New Thoughts on an Old Story.* 1982 $3.00
Ian McAllister	*Regional Development and the European Community: A Canadian Perspective.* 1982 $13.95
Donald J. Daly	*Canada in an Uncertain World Economic Environment.* 1982 $3.00

W.T. Stanbury & Fred Thompson	*Regulatory Reform in Canada.* 1982 $7.95
Robert J. Buchan, C. Christopher Johnston, T. Gregory Kane, Barry Lesser, Richard J. Schultz & W.T. Stanbury	*Telecommunications Regulation and the Constitution.* 1982 $18.95
Rodney de C. Grey	*United States Trade Policy Legislation: A Canadian View.* 1982 $7.95
John Quinn & Philip Slayton (eds.)	*Non-Tariff Barriers After the Tokyo Round.* 1982 $17.95
Stanley M. Beck & Ivan Bernier (eds.)	*Canada and the New Constitution: The Unfinished Agenda.* 2 vols. 1983 $10.95 (set)
R. Brian Woodrow & Kenneth B. Woodside (eds.)	*The Introduction of Pay-TV in Canada: Issues and Implications.* 1983 $14.95
E.P. Weeks & L. Mazany	*The Future of the Atlantic Fisheries.* 1983 $5.00
Douglas D. Purvis (ed.), assisted by Frances Chambers	*The Canadian Balance of Payments: Perspectives and Policy Issues.* 1983 $24.95
Roy A. Matthews	*Canada and the "Little Dragons": An Analysis of Economic Developments in Hong Kong, Taiwan, and South Korea and the Challenge/Opportunity They Present for Canadian Interests in the 1980s.* 1983 $11.95
Charles Pearson & Gerry Salembier	*Trade, Employment, and Adjustment.* 1983 $5.00
Steven Globerman	*Cultural Regulation in Canada.* 1983 $11.95
F.R. Flatters & R.G. Lipsey	*Common Ground for the Canadian Common Market.* 1983 $5.00
Frank Bunn, assisted by U. Domb, D. Huntley, H. Mills, H. Silverstein	*Oceans from Space: Towards the Management of Our Coastal Zones.* 1983 $5.00
C.D. Shearing & P.C. Stenning	*Private Security and Private Justice: The Challenge of the 80s.* 1983 $5.00
Jacob Finkelman & Shirley B. Goldenberg	*Collective Bargaining in the Public Service: The Federal Experience in Canada.* 2 vols. 1983 $29.95 (set)
Gail Grant	*The Concrete Reserve: Corporate Programs for Indians in the Urban Work Place.* 1983 $5.00
Owen Adams & Russell Wilkins	*Healthfulness of Life.* 1983 $8.00
Yoshi Tsurumi with Rebecca R. Tsurumi	*Sogoshosha: Engines of Export-Based Growth.* (Revised Edition). 1984 $10.95

Raymond Breton & Gail Grant (eds.)	*The Dynamics of Government Programs for Urban Indians in the Prairie Provinces.* 1984 $19.95
Frank Stone	*Canada, The GATT and the International Trade System.* 1984 $15.00
Pierre Sauvé	*Private Bank Lending and Developing-Country Debt.* 1984 $10.00
Mark Thompson & Gene Swimmer	*Conflict or Compromise: The Future of Public Sector Industrial Relations.* 1984 $15.00
Samuel Wex	*Instead of FIRA: Autonomy for Canadian Subsidiaries?* 1984 $8.00
R.J. Wonnacott	*Selected New Developments in International Trade Theory.* 1984 $7.00
R.J. Wonnacott	*Aggressive US Reciprocity Evaluated with a New Analytical Approach to Trade Conflicts.* 1984 $8.00
Richard W. Wright	*Japanese Business in Canada: The Elusive Alliance.* 1984 $12.00
Paul K. Gorecki & W.T. Stanbury	*The Objectives of Canadian Competition Policy, 1888-1983.* 1984 $15.00
Michael Hart	*Some Thoughts on Canada-United States Sectoral Free Trade.* 1985 $7.00
J. Peter Meekison Roy J. Romanow & William D. Moull	*Origins and Meaning of Section 92A: The 1982 Constitutional Amendment on Resources.* 1985 $10.00
Conference Papers	*Canada and International Trade. Volume One: Major Issues of Canadian Trade Policy. Volume Two: Canada and the Pacific Rim.* 1985 $25.00 (set)
A.E. Safarian	*Foreign Direct Investment: A Survey of Canadian Research.* 1985 $8.00
Joseph R. D'Cruz & James D. Fleck	*Canada Can Compete! Strategic Management of the Canadian Industrial Portfolio.* 1985 $18.00
Barry Lesser & Louis Vagianos	*Computer Communications and the Mass Market in Canada.* 1985 $10.00
W.R. Hines	*Trade Policy Making in Canada: Are We Doing it Right?* 1985 $10.00
Bertrand Nadeau	*Britain's Entry into the European Economic Community and its Effect on Canada's Agricultural Exports.* 1985 $10.00
Paul B. Huber	*Promoting Timber Cropping: Policies Toward Non-Industrial Forest Owners in New Brunswick.* 1985 $10.00

Gordon Robertson	*Northern Provinces: A Mistaken Goal. 1985* $8.00
Petr Hanel	*La technologie et les exportations canadiennes du matériel pour la filière bois-papier.* 1985 $20.00
Russel M. Wills, Steven Globerman & Peter J. Booth	*Software Policies for Growth and Export.* 1986 $15.00
Marc Malone	*Une place pour le Québec au Canada.* 1986 $20.00
A. R. Dobell & S. H. Mansbridge	*The Social Policy Process in Canada.* 1986 $8.00
William D. Shipman (ed.)	*Trade and Investment Across the Northeast Boundary: Quebec, the Atlantic Provinces, and New England.* 1986 $20.00
Nicole Morgan	*Implosion: An Analysis of the Growth of the Federal Public Service in Canada (1945-1985).* 1986 $20.00
Nicole Morgan	*Implosion: analyse de la croissance de la Fonction publique fédérale canadienne (1945-1985).* 1986 $20.00
William A.W. Neilson & Chad Gaffield (eds.)	*Universities in Crisis: A Mediaeval Institution in the Twenty-first Century.* 1986 $20.00
Fred Wien	*Rebuilding the Economic Base of Indian Communities: The Micmac in Nova Scotia.* 1986 $20.00
D.M. Daly & D.C. MacCharles	*Canadian Manufactured Exports: Constraints and Opportunities.* 1986 $20.00
Gerald d'Amboise, Yvon Gasse & Rob Dainow	*The Smaller, Independent Manufacturer: 12 Quebec Case Studies.* 1986 $20.00
David J. Roy & Maurice A.M. de Wachter	*The Life Technologies and Public Policy.* 1986 $20.00
David Feeny, Gordon Guyatt & Peter Tugwell (eds.)	*Health Care Technology: Effectiveness, Efficiency, and Public Policy.* 1986 $20.00
International Symposium	*Les répercussions de l'informatisation en milieu de travail / The Impact of New Information Technologies on the Workplace.* 1986 $20.00
N.G. Papadopoulos	*Canada and the European Community: An Uncomfortable Partnership?* 1986 $15.00
W.T. Stanbury (ed.)	*Telecommunications Policy and Regulation: The Impact of Competition and Technological Change.* 1986 $22.00

James Gillies	*Facing Reality: Consultation, Consensus and Making Economic Policy for the 21st Century.* 1986 $15.95
International Seminar	*The Management of Water Resources – Proceedings / La gestion des ressources en eau – Actes.* 1986 $20.00
William J. Coffey & Mario Polèse (eds.)	*Still Living Together: Recent Trends and Future Directions in Canadian Regional Development.* 1987 $25.00
Bryan Schwartz	*First Principles, Second Thoughts: Aboriginal Peoples, Constitutional Reform and Canadian Statecraft.* 1987 $25.00